THE THEATRE

Three Thousand Years
of
Drama · Acting
and Stagecraft

WILLIAM SHAKESPEARE

[From the Droeshout portrait in the Shakespeare Memorial Gallery at
Stratford-on-Avon.]

THE
THEATRE

THREE THOUSAND YEARS
of DRAMA, ACTING and STAGECRAFT

BY

SHELDON CHENEY

WITH 204 ILLUSTRATIONS

TUDOR PUBLISHING COMPANY

NEW YORK

CHENEY
THE THEATRE

TUDOR PUBLISHING CO., 1941, 1943.

CONTENTS

DIONYSUS

DIONYSUS came down from the wild mountains of Thrace into Hellas, already worshipped as a god of the groves and the fields and of fertility; and with the very special power of lifting mortals to a share in divine ecstasy. The people of Greece took him for their own, the common people. They were filled with his spirit and honored him (and themselves) in joyous festival and ritual and wild revels; until he was so celebrated that he could be excluded no longer from the company of true Olympians. And so, with elements of the earth and of wildness clinging to him, and trailing an uncommon sympathy with humankind, he became the youngest of the gods.

As was the way in those times, the guardians of orthodox religion made a myth to account for his coming. The All-father Zeus had loved the beautiful princess Semele, daughter of Cadmus. Misled by the jealous Juno, this mortal asked that her Heavenly lover appear before her once in all his glory. In the flaming splendor of his presence Semele was utterly and ecstatically consumed. But her child Dionysus, delivered before his time, was saved from the flames by the great God, his father, who sewed up the babe in his own flesh. Hidden thus from the prying eyes of Juno, Dionysus came to maturity, and in a second birth was miraculously delivered into the world, a true god, son of Zeus, mystic wanderer.

But to the people he remained first of all the god of nature and of wild things, and of all human-divine wild impulses. It was seen that earlier deities of the earth and the fields, of the groves and the vineyards, had simply awaited his coming; and he was known now as Dionysus and Bacchus, as Bromius and Nysæus.

At once god of the joy-giving vine and of mystical inspiration, he brought to his celebrants a spiritual intoxication. He entered into their being, they became gods in his name: Bacchants and Bacchantes. Theirs was the Dionysian experience. He exacted neither adoration nor worship from them; rather he accorded them a share in his ecstasy, they celebrated, god-like, joyed in " doing," danced, marched, sang.

Drama grew directly out of the Dionysian celebrations, out of the rites, the dances, the songs that were sung, the parades with cymbals and torches and masks, in honor of Dionysus; and the consecrated place of the revels was called a " theatre." Some of the celebrants became priests, and these later were called " actors "; and others, who had led in the singing, who could even invent new songs, became poets, and by a final extension of grace, dramatists; and still others became the audience, those who asked no more than participation in the spirit, the emotional exaltation of Dionysian celebration.

And what has been finest in the theatre, down through the ages, is the Dionysian intoxication, the exaltation out of emotional-spiritual participation, the transcending dramatic experience. No other god has so discovered divinity to the god-in-man; no other art has so contacted the mystic creativeness of its artists with the receptiveness in the spec-

tator's soul, has so immersed its audiences in the glow of
the spirit.

Dionysus has lived twenty-five hundred years. Today
a world that had almost learned to scorn him turns back,
with the old hunger of the soul, the old impulse toward
divine living, with not a little of the old wildness. For
we later mortals, as we view about us the decay of moralistic religions, the chaos of conquest-mad civilizations and
the spiritual bankruptcy of the prosperous-scientific life,
we seek again the roads to emotional-spiritual inundation,
to ecstasy, to the experience of God.

We turn confidently back. For Dionysus is immortal
and the theatre lives alway.

THE THEATRE

*Three Thousand Years
of
Drama · Acting
and Stagecraft*

THE THEATRE

THREE THOUSAND YEARS
of DRAMA, ACTING *and* STAGECRAFT

CHAPTER I

The Theatre, Human and Divine

WHEREVER and whenever humans have progressed beyond the mere struggle for physical existence, to gods and recreation and self-expression, there has been theatre in some sense: an inevitable place for acting, dancing, dialogue, drama, in the ordered scheme of life.

The resultant world drama, the collective theatre, from primitive dance to modern journalistic play, from divine ritual to profane representation, from Greek tragedy to " the pictures," escapes, in its confusingly various aspects, all recorded definitions of " theatre " and of " drama." If one could spread out a picture of the world's stages, if the entire pageant of their activities could be momentarily fixed on a magic canvas, the spectator would know at once that no definition ever can be broad enough, elastic enough, to snare in words the elements and the modes of the art, the facets and the directions of theatric-dramatic life.

The diversity and the confusion arise no less from the mixed form and the composite method — this being the art where all arts meet — than from the dual nature of the impulse underlying dramatic expression; call it divine and human, or religious and social, or spiritual and convivial. There are other significant parallels and contrasts; for gaiety and glow are of the very essence of theatre, while " dramatic " suggests the event that cuts directly and vividly into life, having to do with the deepest currents of man's being, with personal crises and the intensest moments of experience. But most notably, theatre is the art where spiritual light illuminates human living.

In the absence of definitions, each man will form his own mental one — first of all from what he has seen in theatres, but filling out the impression, the outline, from such parts of the world-picture as may have come to his notice.

Let us suppose for a moment that such a picture, of the theatre in all ages and all places, in all its varieties, is spread before us, on a gigantic and crowded canvas. Immediately one beholder sees " the drama " as the main motive, and is off tracing its development; another sees the actor as all-important, and the story of acting as the key to the composition; and still another sees the form of the stage and the elements of stagecraft, the ways and means of bringing drama to the audiences, as a predominant interest. But the man who wishes to bring the whole picture into focus, who hopes to have the view complete, finds it necessary to see beyond all these to a deeper design that binds the picture together, to a thing that is " theatre " in the largest sense.

It is one of the pleasant facts about theatre-study today, that in regarding a single play performance the student or artist has learned that no one element constitutes the chief or essential matter; recognizes, rather, that the several " means " of the production contribute to a total effect that is the all-important thing, a complete theatrical action accomplished. Actors, lights, movement, dialogue, noises, silences, color, scenery, stage, he marks for what they are, merely the resources of the art made expressive when combined in a procession or flow. Over and above the seen-and-heard elements, he is attentive to a rhythmic wave of performance that registers beyond the conscious minds of the spectators, like a tide to the soul.

Just so, in regarding the larger composition of the world theatre, the student or interested playgoer — or reader — must vision a similar binding force, a theatrical unity, a deeper all-pervading essence; for it is this that lends design to the actor in relation to the drama, the physical theatre and the craft of staging. And it is this that I shall try to keep forward throughout my story of " the theatre art." The sensuous glow and the deep emotion arise alike out of elements deeper than colored lights and enchanting setting, beyond the actors' performances, beyond drama.

If, however, one holds in mind this broader effectiveness, one may profitably disengage the drama or the actor briefly from the

Forgetting the nineteenth century " picture " scene, the reader should visualize the actor in continually changing relationship to his background. This is a simple platform stage for classic revivals, of the early Renaissance. [From a drawing by Warren D. Cheney, after a model based on old prints.]

larger design; and as introduction to the related history that begins in the next chapter, I wish to pause with the reader for the briefest " over-look " at three component elements — hoping that this may help us to orientate ourselves, to find the best beginning point for a trip through the mazes of the world-picture.

The actor, the human medium by which the drama speaks to us — it is he who lends vividness, intensity, and humanity to the art beyond any possible in mere paint, stone, or sound — the actor has a history that spans the whole gulf between priesthood and bawdry. Actors have been the servants of gods, and mentors of manners, but again they have been panderers to men's grossest appetites. In Greece long after the Dionysian rites and revels gave way to composed plays, they were privileged and honored members of society; but in Rome they fell to sad depths of disgrace. Thereafter they were honored by governments and entertained by kings and queens — nay, commanded and pled with to attach themselves to courts; and other governments branded them as vagabonds, and other kings banished them and persecuted them as undesirables, rogues, and idlers. The Church called them into its service, but again excommunicated them, and through many centuries refused them Christian burial. Today kings knight them, but within our own lifetimes we have heard bishops crying out that no good ever has come from the theatre, or ever will come, because for a person to go on the stage is in itself a besmirchment of character. (Yet announce that a well-known actor will be at Mrs. Smyth's at tea on Tuesday, and your invitations won't half go round those who want to come.)

The story of what these actors do, of acting in the narrower sense, illustrates in little a truth pertinent to the whole theatre art: that from Greek times to twentieth century, there has been a wider and wider deviation from *conventional* methods toward *naturalism*. (This is a thread we shall follow, from earliest chapter almost to latest.) In Greece a fine stateliness of gesture and movement, together with beauty of diction, constituted the art of acting; the very conditions of the actor's appearance made for slow and broad declamation: the immense bowl-like theatre, the mask hiding facial display, the stuffed-out costumes and cothurnus-boots. In each succeeding age thereafter, in Rome, in Renaissance Italy, in France, England, Germany, down to " the era of great acting" in the eighteenth century, there is the recurrent report: " acting now became more human, more real, more life-like than ever before." Finally, with the coming of electric lights, characterization arrived at a perfection of outward naturalism. From being a convention, it had progressed through all the stages of part-artificial-part-imitational portrayal until it arrived at photographic representation of familiar men and women.

A Renaissance stage, with a typical " picture " scene behind a proscenium frame. In contrast with the theatre designed to emphasize the actor, this is an example of the theatre of emphasized scenic display — and the beginning point of the courtly staging that persisted from about 1600 to 1900. [From a painting ascribed to Ferdinando Bibbiena, in the National Gallery, London.]

SOCIAL ROOMS ETC. | AUDITORIUM | STAGE | DRESSING ETC.

Ancient and recent European theatres contrasted. Above, a reconstruction of the theatre at Priene, as seen from the outside, showing the large open auditorium and the small stage building. Below, a sectional view of the Paris Opera House, illustrating the immensity and the elaboration of the stage, with eight floors of machinery above and below, and the extensiveness of the social rooms, as compared with the "place for seeing" which is the first essential in any theatre. [The drawing above from A. von Gerkan's *Das Theater von Priene*. The section by Karl Fichot and Henri Meyer, from a reproduction in *Illustrirte Zeitung*.]

The path is not so straight along which we may trace the changes in the physical playhouse; but the difference at the two extremes is no less marked. Barring a few very modern houses, the theatre has run down from openness and nobility to a form that is cramped and trivially fussed-up. From the dancing-circle as stage, perhaps in some sacred grove, at the foot of a hillside hollow, through the beautifully proportioned wooden, then marble playhouses of the Greeks, and on to the magnificently

The theatre a part of the temple group. A reconstruction by A. von Gerkan of the Greek-Roman theatre at Priene. (This is the interior of the upper theatre shown on the page opposite.)

showy theatres of the Romans, was logical progress. Thereafter the forms change, waver. But through it all the theatre building follows the curve of so-called civilization: rises as a reflection of aspirations, spiritual flowerings and service to gods: stands beside temples and cathedral altars when man is most spiritual, has its appointed place in palaces when courts are most royal, most magnificent; but again falls to rude makeshift in dark centuries, or becomes a tawdrily ornamented show-box in materialistic ones — and so to the pinched peep-hole proscenium-frame affair of today.

And so too, the story of the drama. There is the same gulf between the Greek play, with its inexhaustible depths of emotion and its beautiful poetry, and our contemporary, pinched, realistic, peep-hole plays. Again the progression has not been direct: rather the history of dramatic literature has been dotted with glorious periods. Shakespeare came twenty centuries after Sophocles, and it is hardly more than a hundred years since Goethe and Schiller worked something of the same splendid magic. Since then the poetry as well as the ecstasy and the fervor has weakened, almost disappeared.

There are those — count me not among them — who say that the curve has been downward only in obedience to the law of *audiences:* that spectators, from being splendid-minded and spiritual, have become sentimental, trivial, and prying, and that the theatre inevitably comes down to please them. But it is probable that there are good audiences everywhere, if the political, economic, and spiritual conditions are ripe for good drama, good theatres, and acting and staging. And indeed there are some hopeful ones — count me among *them* — who refuse to be long depressed by the obvious cheapness of most of the dramatic output of today, by the trivially over-ornamented playhouses, the journalistic plays, the uncreative acting. For we see in a mighty activity — the *livest* stages of all time — the beginnings of a new upward curve: a physical theatre going back to a new simplicity (not primitive, but simple as the automobile is simple: why not a theatre as clean-walled, sheer of line, tranquilly comfortable as your car, and equally bright, warm, pleasurable?); drama that escapes the photographic-reportorial mold, that weds a new daring to a new human intensity of life; acting that is less imitation than revealment.

But most of all we see a new spirit emerging in the Western theatre. And really it is the intangible spirit of an institution or a race or a nation that carries it triumphantly down the ages. Certainly it is the flaming eternal spirit of the stage that has driven the course of dramatic art through the great and the decadent, the glorious and the terrible periods of mankind's history. It has sustained the theatre when the foundations of living and of liberty seemed breaking up, and it has persisted through the wrecking of empires and the waging of devastating wars and the coming of science. And now again it begins to push through the barriers set up by generations trained in timidity and selfishness and right-by-might.

We may indeed have our pessimistic days, when we gain a perspective on the immediate theatre of today, down in the market-places, its activities being pursued as energetically as those of food-selling, baseball, or stock-brokering. In spite of seeing that an extraordinary amount of material wealth is flowing into the playhouses, that an amazing number of shows will be seen in our town this year, that the institution is simply bursting with hustle, enthusiasm, effort — in spite of this typically tumultuous outpouring of effort, we recognize a separation from the deeper springs of life. Perhaps never, we think, has the stage been farther from the divinity with which it was marked in other eras. It has dug down into human experience not in a way that uncovers divinity, but in a way that shows humanity its weaker face, that lays bare deformities and perversities and flea-bites. It has become a narrow, prying, gossipy-minded theatre, with the bigness and the fineness gone out of it. Only once in a hundred visits do we glimpse rapture or high nobility or sheer purging beauty.

And yet each one of us, in his collective experience, has known that other divine theatre. In the playhouses of our time we have been stirred by the old expectant excitement, have revelled in being part of a gay responsive crowd, have felt our nearness to the gods in the hushed auditorium, when everything on the stage and in the world fell into a unison, stilling the conscious mind; have been miraculously purged by tragedy, have been healed with the tonic of laughter at comedy, have felt pleasantly sinful, have been revolted, have been lifted again to the realm of beauty, wisdom, and perfect understanding.

This is how it is — on that hundredth attendance:

Here we are in the mercifully darkened auditorium, whole banks of us facing the glow of the stage. We are a little too hot this summer night. For an hour we have watched people acting in and out of a perfectly ordinary plot, with flashes of humor here and there, a pretty intrigue posed, youth drawing toward beauty. But we have not quite been able to forget the heat. The appealing story, the facile acting, the color and light manipulated now with such virtuosity: everything is *pleasant* — that is just the word. But the actors are obviously working, this show of color and light and designed movement remains an accompaniment, the story is a diversion not too moving to be seen dispassionately, from the outside, from the hot auditorium.

Then in a sentence one of the actors makes us catch our breath. The story, the accompaniment, the night are forgotten. Everything drops into place, quietly, the house becomes doubly hushed, a thousand souls strain forward toward one little group there on the dais in the centre. Our bodies are motionless, our throats contracted, strange emotions press in, we feel the hot tears welled behind our eyes. A " moment " has come. Before the silence proves unbearable, this actress, this woman standing there before us, must speak, must move. We wait, suspended. In this hush the slightest thing she does or says may precipitate the thousand watchers into tears and grief, into perfect understanding, into gentle laughter. The sudden quivering of her lips — what is that to make a thousand men and women draw their breath in a stifled sob? Her shudder seems echoed in something that is crawling down our spines. Her half-articulated " yes " tears us like a knife plunged into our own flesh.

For a few moments we have known a cessation of the outward life of the world. We have known an intensification of the life of the spirit. Everything has been so clarified that a gesture, a poetically right phrase, a sob, seemed to resolve all that has puzzled us in living, seemed to lift us up, to glorify us.

This is the moment toward which all drama tends. This is the inundation of the spirit, in beauty and clarity, toward which the art of the theatre gropes. And this, in a world from which divinity and mystery have been unsparingly shorn, this is as near as we are likely to come to the divine and the spiritual. It is the Dionysian experience, our ecstatic participation in the divine life. Unless you have known that moment, you have not really penetrated into the theatre. It is, of course, the thing that escapes all definitions of theatre or drama.

And whatever may be the direction of the next great change in the stage art — and epoch-making changes are pending — we

An eighteenth century French theatre that retained the picture setting but made the actor predominant by bringing him down into the midst of the audience. Note also the aristocratic boxes combined with a large pit for standees. [Redrawing by the author after fugitive sketches by P. A. Wille, 1767.]

may be sure that the artists of the theatre will be working around somehow to this revealing moment, this transcending of surface life, will aim to afford us, the spectators, that clarity, that absolute of spiritual participation.

For we are humans, and during some moments the actors have made us gods.

Mask for primitive dramatic dance. [This and the drawings of masks in Chapter II are by Warren D. Cheney.]

CHAPTER II

Where the Theatre Came From, and When

MAN DANCES. After the activities that secure to primitive peoples the material necessities, food and shelter, the dance comes first. It is the earliest outlet for emotion, and the beginning of the arts. Civilized man of today, despite ingrained inhibitions and cultivated reserve, instinctively expresses emotional joy by action; primitive man, poor in means of expression, with only the rudimentary beginnings of spoken language, universally expressed his deeper feelings through measured movement. Nature about him moved rhythmically, in the wave motion of the waters and in the wind-blown fields; the sun and moon rose and fell; his own heart-beats were rhythmic. It was natural, then, that he should create rhythmic movement to externalize any felt joy.

He danced for pleasure and as ritual. He spoke in dance to his gods, he prayed in dance and gave thanks in dance. By no means all this activity was dramatic or theatric; but in his designed movement was the germ of drama and of theatre. The dance exists even today, separately, for all the purposes to which primitive peoples put it; but somewhere in its history it gave rise to this other more inclusive art. In Cambodia the very name for theatre means " dance-house." Records of the dancing figure, in painting, sculpture, and written account, go back almost as far as the existence of those arts. In addition to these historic records there is the analogy of scores of " backward " peoples still living in the darker spots of the world today: the African jungles, the South Sea Islands, the United States, etc. Wherever " primitive " peoples are found and their customs studied, there is ritual and usually dramatic dance.

Not only did drama as such — the art in which *action* is a pivotal material — arise out of primitive dance; in its later marriage with poetry it took to itself another element born of dance-gesture: poetry. The modern European drama traces its ancestry to Greece, and the common assumption is that it became important as an art-form when the ritual dances were combined with elements out of dithyrambic poetry. But recited poetry had been a second child of the dance, in this manner: the noises man made, as he rhythmically moved, took on the measure of the swaying body and the tapping feet, gradually became war-song or prayer, developed into traditional tribal chant, ultimately led to conscious poetry. (It is no chance that the unit-measure of verse is called the " foot," or that the words " ballad " and " ballet " are so alike.) Music, too, which can hardly be dissociated from the theatre's beginnings, traces its ancestry to the sounds made to accentuate the primitive dance rhythm, the stamping of feet and clapping of hands, the shaking of rattles, the beating of drums and sticks.

Dance, then, is the great mother of the arts. It is impossible to say when or where it developed first. It came to mankind in a thousand places and at a thousand times, wherever an isolated group came to expressiveness. It antedated all the recording processes of mankind. Nor is it easier to determine when drama emerged, when dance-and-poetry-with-music took on story or plot-action to complete the dramatic form. We can only construct a composite picture out of bits of evidence, analogy, inference, always against that known background of universal occurrence of dance, and man's impulse to mimic and retell.

Where dance is approaching drama, and in the field where a reciter of an incident approaches acting (this seems to most anthropologists to come later), one may inquire by way of test, does the performer assume a character? and does " the thing done " have plot-action, not merely the action of physical movement? If Ug or Kar dances " simply instinctively" to his totem or in celebration of a fight won, he is not yet of the theatre. But if he dances out his victory in the fight, showing how he stole up, saw his enemy, clashed, fought hand to hand, parried, killed, beheaded, he is very near to true drama.

Beyond the mere joy of rhythmic movement, the " actor " has

been impelled to express, in mimetic action, something experienced or imagined, and he has taken on the character of himself in another time, or of an ancestor or an animal or a god. In acting over a period of time, he has fulfilled the first requirement of " drama ": for the word comes from the Greek word δράω, " I do." Primarily it implies " a thing done."

In Australia one of the primitive tribes has a Canoe Dance. Men and women take up positions in lines. They are armed

A religious-dramatic ceremony of the Amer-inds: the Bull Dance of the Mandan tribe, as depicted by an eye witness, George Catlin.
[By courtesy of the Smithsonian Institution.]

with sticks, symbolizing paddles. As the bodies begin to move, the sticks are rhythmically swung with the paddle-motion. When the whole company has swayed into full movement, there is no mistaking the pleasure they are deriving from the retelling and the reliving of earlier canoeing on the water. This is, of course, a merely social activity; unlike most early dancing, it is without ritualistic significance or practical end. It is primarily for the pleasure of remembering, merely an emotional discharge. There is a considerable range of similar social dances, from what may be termed instinctive dancing " merely for the joy of living," to mimetic dancing for the pleasure of remembering, and so to the field of comic and erotic exhibition.

We cannot know what comedy-dances the prehistoric tribes may have had (though gorillas are said to have a lively sense of humor); but the type is not wholly unknown among primitive peoples studied in modern times. Hunting or battle scenes may be burlesqued, and quite often there is the clown character: the man who hits hard but always misses or strikes somebody or something other than the object intended. Imitations of the motions of animals or birds may also be made richly humorous.

Most of the examples, when examined, however, will be found to come within the range of religious or initiatory dance. The love-pantomimes range from idyllic duets to what seems in the European mind obscene representation. The action usually concerns itself with that still favorite theme, the man who admires, desires, parades, sues, and the woman who is coy, teases, holds back, finally yields. But even in many of these amatory examples the significance is religious: related to fertility rites or phallic symbolism.

The savage's world is almost universally peopled with all-powerful gods or spirits. These are associated with the forces controlling nature, with " causes," or perhaps with the souls of dead ancestors, or with fabulous animals or trees or stars. At any rate, man's welfare depends upon the gods being on his side. He must do what will be pleasing to them, he must indicate to them what he wants, he must never omit to show them his appreciation of favors. The primitive seldom worships in our later sense. The Amer-indian of our arid West does not vaguely pray for rain; he does something: he dances a Rain Dance to his gods. Other tribes do Sun Dances. A tribe facing starvation does an Antelope Dance.

Dance is so essentially the primitive method of showing attention and devotion to the spirits that almost everywhere the place for dancing precedes the temple. Here the chief representative of the gods, medicine man or priest or witch doctor, devises dances for such different purposes as appeasing a spirit who has withheld the rain or the sunshine, or driving out the evil spirit in the body of a sick member of the tribe. or securing luck to the new wine.

Three of the religious dances mentioned may be considered as of a special sort known as food ceremonies. The tribe wants rain to make the crops grow, in order to have more food. Its first recourse is to the gods who can send all blessings. They must be shown rain, and so the Rain Dance is performed: clouds gathering, lightning flashing, thunder roaring, finally rain falling — tableau, happiness. With some of the Southwestern Indians, the

The Buffalo Dance of the Mandan Indians.
[By courtesy of the Smithsonian Institution.]

priest or medicine man is first of all " Rain-maker," for the heavens can provide no other gift so precious as water.

This sort of ceremony, for the increase of plant food, developed, as the importance of agriculture grew, until finally there emerged those seasonal festivals, particularly of the Springtime and the Harvest, which persist over practically all the world today, not seldom with mimetic and symbolic dance. The planting, the harvesting, the first tasting of the new wine — these all suggest special forms of ceremonial and revel. Earth-gods and wine-gods here entered into man's pantheon.

Even before the plant ceremonies, probably, there were the animal-food dances. In that stage of savagery where hunting was the chief occupation in life, threatened starvation must be met by direct measures to replenish the game supply. The Mandan Indians of northern Missouri used to stage a " Buffalo Come " dance when meat became scarce. And if the gods were slow in answering, the dancers continued the ceremony in relays for days; indeed, until scouts sent in word from the country round that herds of buffaloes had been sighted. In New Britain a love dance of the birds is held, to suggest that the game-birds might well have greater fertility, and consequently the natives a more abundant food supply.

Fear-inspiring masks.

The known initiation ceremonies are chiefly rituals performed when a boy comes to puberty, when he is to be initiated into man's estate in the tribe; and this is often an initiation into a secret society at the same time, so that complete evidence of the nature of the dances has seldom been taken. The boy's education, beyond such elementals as hunting and fishing, may have been entirely neglected up to this time. Now he must know the tribal history and the tribal rules and customs. So the maturer tribesmen act out for him the myths and legends of the totem, graphically, through pantomimic dance. Many of the most interesting known animal dances originate from this totemic teaching, and hero-ancestors are common figures. There are some tribes that shape the initiation ceremony primarily to place the boys and young men in fear of the elders of the tribe, so that the latter may keep control of communal affairs; and here the dances strive toward awe and terror — which explains the fearsome aspect of many primitive masks.

War dances occur among practically all primitive tribes. They seem at first to have two objects: to get the gods on the side of the performer in the fight to come, and to stir the warriors themselves to a " concert pitch " of bravery and daring. In the building up of war-frenzy by dance, is an instance of those types of performance in which the elements of drama, religion, and practical purpose are inextricably mixed. Loomis Havemeyer[1] describes a war dance of the Naga tribes of Northeast India as follows:

It commences with a review of the warriors who later advance and retreat, parrying blows, and throwing spears as though in a real fight. They creep along in battle array, keeping as near the ground as possible so that nothing shows but a line of shields. When they are near enough to the imaginary enemy they spring up and attack. After they have killed the opposing party they grab tufts of grass, which represent the heads, and these they sever with their battle axes. Returning home they carry the clods over their shoulders as they would the heads of real men. At the village they are met by the women who join in a triumphant song and dance.

Another war ceremony may serve to carry us over from a review of general primitive dance to the field where drama is recognizably emerging as a separate and complete entity. Henry Ling Roth reports a Dyak native play as follows:

One warrior is engaged in picking a thorn out of his foot, but is ever on the alert for the lurking enemy, with his arms ready at hand. This enemy is at length suddenly discovered, and after some rapid attack and defence, a sudden plunge is made at him and he is dead upon the ground. The taking of his head follows in pantomine . . . The story then concludes with the startling discovery that the slain man is not an enemy at all but the brother of the warrior who has slain him. At this point the dance gives way to what was perhaps the least pleasing part of the per-

---

[1] *The Drama of Savage Peoples,* by Loomis Havemeyer (New Haven, 1916). This is a standard and easily read summary of the subject of primitive dance and drama. The great monumental work is *The Golden Bough: A Study in Magic and Religion,* by J. G. Fraser (3d ed., in 12 vols., London, 1911-15), a fascinating collection which no student should overlook. For a brief introduction, very understandingly written, read *Ancient Art and Ritual,* by Jane Harrison (London and New York, 1913). Very difficult to read, but important to advanced students, is *The Dramas and Dramatic Dances of Non-European Races,* by William Ridgeway (Cambridge, 1915). See also the chapters on dance and poetry in *The Beginnings of Art,* by Ernst Grosse (New York, 1907).

formance — a man in a fit, writhing in frightful convulsions, being charmed into life and sanity by a necromantic physician.[2]

A surprise element of a different sort is found in a play reported by Professor Ernst Grosse, with a " plot " akin to a legend found in the folklore of many peoples. An Aleut pursues a bird, and finally brings it down with an arrow. The hunter then laments, and the dead bird rises up and turns to a beautiful woman, who falls into his arms. Here, and in the Dyak example, are elements of a consciously compositional sort. The discovery of the slain man's identity as brother, and the metamorphosis of the bird-woman, are clearly steps beyond mere narrative war and hunt dances, adding emotional complication and dramatic complexity.

How this added dramatic element is strengthened, until finally drama becomes more important than dance, perhaps stripping off all dance elements, is particularly illustrated in the religious rituals. Gradually a priesthood evolves: ordinary man cannot take too much time from his hunting and warfare to keep in touch with the gods. The priests, once appointed and looked up to, strive constantly to make stronger their position. They must prove that they are in touch with the spirits, that they even sway the decisions of the gods. Rituals become more complex, everything that increases the element of mystery is played up. A clan of priest-actors emerges. It is especially trained for dance and pantomime. Ultimately a body of dramatic works, not incomparable to the later Christian " Mystery Plays," comes into being. At this time, of course, there is no written dramatic literature.

The fraternity of the Areoi in Polynesia, originally a secret society with religious duties and privileges, exhibits the whole range from ritual dance to comparatively complex play, in the " repertoire " which its members take to the tribes on different islands of the Polynesian group. The strictly religious dances and pantomimes, we are told, are there followed by lengthy historical sketches, amorous pantomimes, and comedy-pieces. The Duk-Duk Society of New Pomerania, also descended from a religious priesthood, takes its expanded plays from village to village.

Now obviously I have not been writing *history* here; though in

[2] Quoted from *The Natives of Sarawak and British North Borneo*, by Henry Ling Roth (London, 1896).

this chapter I am beginning my account of the historic theatre. I have taken evidence from modern primitives, from sources as widely separated as the South Sea Islands and the American plainland, as the Aleutian Islands and Australia, as Borneo and Central Africa.   It has seemed to anthropologists that modern man might justly infer from the occurrence of dramatic dance in these separated localities an almost universal dance activity, and that this is safely comparable to the pre-Greeks and others from whom the known European and Asiatic theatres inherited.   In short, knowing how the undeveloped, even savage, races of today dance, we may picture our hairier ancestors as similarly dancing, on the occasions of births, deaths, matings, hunts, wars, seasonal changes, initiations, sacrifices to the gods, etc.   Knowing how their ritual dance became dramatic, we may picture an almost world-wide theatre activity that existed before (and long after) what is usually regarded as the birth of Western drama in Greece in the sixth century B.C.   We shall do better not to try to detail the picture too exactly: there must have been a multitude of types of dance.   And often the elements of rhythmic movement, lyric and narrative, are mixed; and æsthetic impulse is by no means to be disentangled from religious impulse and practical purpose.   But now we are sure that just as there were long ages of " prehistoric man," there were almost equally long ages of prehistoric dance and rudimentary drama.

Of the theatres we know next to nothing, and can infer but little.   There is one outward dance custom, however, that is notably widespread, and it can be ascribed to ancient as well as modern primitives with the greater certainty because it emerged at the earliest dawn of historic drama: the use of the mask.   In the great ethnographic museums there is no object more outstanding than the colorful ritual masks, none on which primitive artists everywhere have expended more care and more devotion. We need not inquire here whether the purpose of the mask was wholly characterization and heightening of dramatic effect.   We know that with tribe after tribe the mask was worn in dance and dramatic sketch.   Sometimes it is recognizably a " disguise," a known animal or type of man or perhaps the spirit of a departed ancestor.   More often it is a conventionalization, a symbol, or itself the god. Occasionally it seems to be that thing so sought after by a few contemporary mask-makers, an abstraction of an emotion, fear or grief or jealousy. If it is sometimes explained as the outward sign of membership in a secret society or cult, we may remember that these societies were little more than groups of actor-priests. They knew well that the wearer took on mysteriously and mystically the spirit of the totemic animal or god or ancestor to whom the mask was, so to speak, erected.

A highly conventionalized mask, with more than one face.

We shall come to masks again, and here we need note only the prevalence of this aid to dramatic effect, among primitive peoples, and the elaborateness, picturesqueness, and jewel-like intricacy — not to say beauty — of many examples. The animal which gave the mask its reason for being was a common bear or buffalo, or perhaps a hawk or a horn-bill. But the mask itself is a work of art, precious, expressively molded, enriched, worthy of a god. The simpler forms are made of light carved wood, painted or stained. But there are more elaborate ones incorporating almost every material light enough to be worn: stiffened cloth, hides, shell, precious metals, beads, feathers, cork. Some ancient examples are formed over the front portions of human skulls. The awe-inspiring masks are a special and particularly interesting class. I have tried in choosing my illustrations to show the range graphically, in subject matter, in degree of elaboration, and territorially. The least "artistic" of the masks are the real animal heads, like those worn in the "Buffalo Come" dance of the Mandans, as shown a few pages back; the more elaborate ones may be as different as the abstract or awesome or humorous examples shown here, and on pages 16 and 21.

While Greek, Hindu, Japanese, and other early racial theatres can be traced back to known dance origins, it would be dangerous to presume that drama never emerged as mimetic action, unaccompanied by rhythmic movement. There are authorities who believe that the hunting dance, based on an actual episode or exploit, grew out of the retelling of the story around a camp-fire. Robert Edmond Jones has given a hypothetical account of such a spontaneous emergence of drama-story, with so much of under-

African and Asiatic masks.

standing of the theatrical impulse, and with such vividness, that I reprint it here. From it the reader may feel a more direct sense of the inevitableness of drama than from all that has been said about dance and ritual; and it will serve to emphasize — or perhaps bring back into proportionate importance — that other main-root of the stage art, the sheer impulse to reproduce, to image, to retell the heroic episode in vivid action.

Let us imagine ourselves back in the Stone Age, in the days of the cave man and the mammoth and the Altamira frescoes. It is night. We are all sitting together around a fire — Ook and Pow and Pung and Glup and little Zowie and all the rest of us. Over on that side of the fire the leaders of the tribe are sitting together — the strongest men, the men who can run fastest and fight hardest and endure longest. They have killed a lion today. We are excited about this thrilling event. We are all talking about it. . .

The lion's skin lies close by, near the fire. Suddenly the leader jumps to his feet. "I killed the lion! I did it! I followed him! He sprang at me!

I struck him with my spear! He fell down! He lay still!" He is telling us. We listen. But all at once an idea comes to his dim brain. "I know a better way to tell you. See! It was like this! *Let me show you!*"

In that instant drama is born.

The leader goes on. "Sit around me in a circle — you, and you, and you — right here, where I can reach out and touch you all. . .

"You, Ook, over there — you stand up and be the lion. Here is the lion's skin. You put it on and be the lion and I'll kill you and we'll show them how it was." Ook gets up. He hangs the skin over his shoulders. He drops on his hands and knees and growls. How terrible he is! Of course he isn't the real lion. We know that. The real lion is dead. We killed him today. Of course Ook isn't a lion. Of course not. He doesn't even look like a lion. "You needn't try to scare us, Ook. We know you. We aren't afraid of you!"

And yet in some mysterious way, Ook *is* the lion. He isn't like the rest of us any longer. He is Ook all right, but he is a lion too.

And now these two men — the world's first actors — begin to show us what the hunt was like. They do not tell us. They *show* us. They *act* it for us. The hunter lies in ambush. The lion growls. The hunter poises his spear. The lion leaps. We all join in with yells and howls of excitement and terror — the first community chorus! The spear is thrown. The lion falls and lies still.

The drama is finished.[3]

If mimicry, growing out of the imitating, reproductive impulse, came first, before dance and the other elements of composite theatre, we may well say, "that, then, was the way it was." In any case, noting how much of human nature and of theatre understanding there is here, we may be sure that this is one way in which drama occurred in many places and at many times — before the known birth of the theatre in Greece. We may say still that it is very rudimentary drama: two characters; a story with only a bare beginning of plot, as compared with later design and complexity; produced spontaneously, without rehearsal. But when the actor has thus repeated his story often, it crystallizes, takes on design, becomes perhaps a ritual-drama of all hunting instead of the recounting of one actual hunt — leads inevitably to a story-music-dance theatre as the race advances culturally.

In closing this brief survey of the beginnings of drama among primitive peoples, I must add that I don't take a great deal of

[3] From a lecture delivered at the University of California, as printed in *Theatre Arts Monthly,* September 1927.

stock in talk about " backward " peoples in this connection. Certainly their drama meant more to the tribesmen than theatre does to " civilized " mankind at the beginning of the twentieth century. According to our material and scientific standards, their civilization was crude; but dramatically and religiously they felt more deeply, expressed more intensively, lived their productions more emotionally than the " advanced " peoples of today. Their dance-dramas lacked plot-complexity; but technical intricacy went with absolute precision in performance.

In dances lasting hours, even days, with constantly varying steps and figures, a mis-step was considered a crime against the tribe and an offence to the gods. In some cases among primitives to-day, if the slightest mistake is made the dance is stopped, and the whole ceremony must be repeated. Among the Maoris if even a single word is dropped or incorrectly spoken in certain rituals, the mistake is believed to presage the death of the performer. In other cases a mistake is actually punishable by death. (A note of this might profitably be posted on the call-boards of our opera houses and little theatres!) Nor does this precision pertain only where solo or small-group dancing is practised. Among the Australians several tribes would sometimes join together for the *corroborry* dances — four hundred participants have been counted at once — and yet the accounts agree that a remarkable precision obtained. Incidentally an official director of the dance was leader and called the directions, another step toward complex theatre.

As THE curtain of obscurity lifts, then, historic man emerges already possessed of a certain degree of culture and civilized custom. As he first comes into the light, he brings dance and dramatic ritual with him. There are such gaps in our knowledge, however, that we need pause only over two later ancient nations before the Greeks. Let us inquire what were the dramatic features of the famous Egyptian religious ceremonials, and what were the dramatic elements in Hebrew literature and life. Of the other pre-Greek civilizations we have practically no theatre knowledge. We know very little about the forms of ancient Egyptian dance, so far as that goes: little beyond the fact of its existence and wide prevalence. But there is contemporary evidence about one form of religious drama.

Osiris, the chief Egyptian god, legendary king-divinity, was the central figure of a "Passion Play" bearing notable resemblances to those still performed in the twentieth century. In a document estimated to date from 2000 B.C., we have an outline description of the ceremony and drama as then executed. The purpose was exactly that of the famous Ober-Ammergau and Tyrolean Passion Plays of today, and of the Persian Passion Play of Hussein; that is, they all served or serve to keep vivid in the memories of the faithful the sufferings and triumph of a god. The historical background of the Egyptian play is this: Osiris after ruling wisely was treacherously murdered, and his body was cut in pieces which were scattered to a great distance. But his wife Isis and her son avenged the murder, gathered the pieces for pilgrimage relics, won back the throne, and established the cult of Osiris-worship. The Passion Play, recounting the sufferings of Osiris, and emphasizing his resurrection, became an annual event.

The evidence that is available outlines only the ceremony at Abydos, but other Passion Plays were performed yearly at Busiris, Heliopolis, and elsewhere. Very little is included about the "theatre" or surroundings. The incidents, indeed, are described as progressive, moving from place to place, and very different in kind, ranging from pure mimetic drama to processionals and even sham battles. (Drama is here still very much entangled with practical life, for those who were taken prisoners in the "sham" battles are supposed then to have acted the least desirable rôles in an actual ceremony of human sacrifice.)

What we know is that King Usertsen III sent a man named I-kher-nefert to Abydos to build a new shrine to Osiris; he regulated the ceremonies and festivals for the gods, and built certain of the "properties" used in the Passion Play, such as the sacred boat duplicating that in which Osiris had set forth on his expedition against his enemies. This is recorded on a stele [4] now pre-

---

[4] Known as the Stele of I-kher-nefert. The date is of the XIIth Dynasty, about 2000 B.C. My excerpts are taken from the chapter on "Shrines, Miracle Play and Mysteries" in E. A. Wallis Budge's *Osiris and the Egyptian Resurrection* (London and New York, 1911).

served in a Berlin museum; and from the second portion of this
" document " we learn that I-kher-nefert himself played important parts in the drama that year:

" I performed the coming forth of Ap-uat when he set out to
defend his father . . . I drove back the enemy from the Neshmet Boat, I overthrew the enemies of Osiris . . . I performed
the ' Great Coming-forth,' I followed the god in his footsteps . . .
I made the boat of the god to move . . ." And so on to the
great climax: " I caused him [Osiris] to set out in the Boat, which
bore his Beauty. I made the hearts of the dwellers in the East to
expand with joy, and I caused gladness to be in the dwellers in
the West, when they saw the Beauty as it landed at Abydos, bringing Osiris Khenti-Amenti, the Lord of Abydos, to his palace."
From which we may visualize the Passion Play as something like
this (relying on the learned Egyptologists for certain collateral
bits of evidence):

A great pageant-procession of priests, attendants, and worshippers, including warriors, sets out from the " palace," our actor-
recorder going first, personifying Ap-uat. A float representing
the sacred boat of Osiris is the central feature of the procession,
and is guarded as it moves by groups of attendants. At a given
point on the line of march, actors representing the enemies of
Osiris attack the boat. The forces of Ap-uat drive them off. The
procession then continues to the temple. At this point a purely
dramatic scene is enacted, in the " Coming Forth " of Osiris from
the temple. It ends with the departure of his body for the
tomb, to the accompaniment of sacramental ceremonies and
mass-laments. Along the procession route again there is a battle,
and here, we are told — by later Greek historians — many actor-
warriors died of their wounds. After this there seems to have
been a recess for the audience; for the " following of the god in
his footsteps " is interpreted to mean that the actors searched for
the lost body of Osiris — for three days, it is said (this is primarily
a devotional play, remember); and on each day another sham
battle is fought.

When the body has been found the procession forms again, the
body is placed in state on the rich float, and the whole company
resumes the interrupted march to the tomb — actually a mile and

a half from the Temple of Osiris. Another great battle is fought, probably at dawn, and Ap-uat's forces win a decisive and final victory, symbolizing the defeat of the murderers of Osiris and the rout of his enemies at the hands of his avengers. The procession returns to the palace whence it originally started; and there is staged the final glorious scene in which Osiris reappears as a living God, in the sacred Neshmet Boat, bringing joy to the people as a symbol of their coming resurrection. And so the pageant and drama blend again into worship and ritual.

Naturally I-kher-nefert mentions only the parts he played, for at that time it would be taken for granted that everyone would know all the details about the drama itself; and this leaves us with only a scrappy conception of the play, four thousand years later. But it is the world's earliest report of a dramatic production. The actor-reporter was of the XIIth Dynasty, and there are occasional records from the XIIIth to the XXVIth Dynasty, in comparatively recent times. But this was still six or seven centuries before Christ, and well before the emergence of Greek drama as such.

THE BIBLE contains many references to the dance, ranging from Miriam and the Hebrew women going out " with timbrels and with dances " after the drowning of Pharaoh, and the exhortation in the Psalms to " praise his name in the dance," to the performance of Salome before Herod — often re-enacted and often abused. But it would be hazardous to try to reconstruct on this evidence any certain picture of a type of dancing. That the dance persisted in later Christian worship, re-enforced with non-Hebrew elements, is certain: a decree of the year 744 was necessary to abolish " dancing-places " in and about the churches, and there was another in the twelfth century.

As a matter of fact, a group of boys called *Seises* — because originally six in number — still dance in costume, to music, before the high altar in the Cathedral of Seville, at several church festivals each year. There is a legend to the effect that when a Pope some centuries ago again determined to ban all dances in churches, he was asked particularly to exempt the *Seises*. His bull stipulated that they could continue until such time as their

costumes were worn out. The authorities therefore never provided new costumes without sewing on patches off the old, by
which they technically conform to the decree, and so still enjoy
the indulgence of His Holiness. Other isolated examples of Christian ritual dance can still be found in Catholic countries.

But for us it will be more fruitful to inquire into the *literary-
dramatic* parts of the Bible. The *Book of Job* and the *Song of
Solomon* are actually cast in dialogue form. Both may be described as long dramatic poems rather than as poetic drama; and
since we know nothing of any ancient performances of them with
action, we shall do better to consider them for their dramatic-
poetic merit rather than as stage pieces (not forgetting, however,
that both have been "adapted" in modern times for occasional
production).

The Song of Songs is an idyll in dramatic form. The action,
insofar as it is indicated or implied, seems processional rather than
designed for a set stage. It may be that the composition is made
up of grouped chants or songs, thus possibly allying it with the
older rituals and progressive dance-dramas; or it may have been
designed for recitative purposes rather than for combined speak-
ing-and-acting. Its sheer artistic value as poetic dialogue is such,
however, that one cannot omit it from consideration: in the accepted English translation it stands forth as one of the most beautiful things in all dramatic literature.

Professor Richard G. Moulton, in the *Modern Reader's Bible,*
has arranged the various books in the forms they originally had.
Since there is still some controversy over the matter, the following
lines may be quoted as indicating definitely the dialogue origin;
the words "among the daughters" and "among the sons" seeming final proof of *two* speakers. (The early texts of the Bible
are written without separation even of the words, like this:
IAMAROSEOFSHARONALILYOFTHEVALLEYS.)

THE BRIDE

I am a rose of Sharon,
A lily of the valleys.

THE BRIDEGROOM

As a lily among thorns,
So is my beloved among the daughters.

THE BRIDE

As the apple tree among the trees of the wood,
So is my beloved among the sons.

The entire scene wherein this passage occurs is exquisite poetic dialogue. But as an example of the more sustained lyrical-emotional speeches, one cannot do better than quote:

THE BRIDE

The voice of my beloved! Behold, he cometh,
Leaping upon the mountains,
Skipping upon the hills.
My beloved is like a roe or a young hart:
Behold, he standeth behind our wall,
He looketh in at the windows,
He showeth himself through the lattice.
My beloved spake and said unto me:
" Rise up, my love, my fair one,
And come away.

" For lo, the winter is past,
The rain is over and gone;
The flowers appear on the earth;
The time of the singing of birds is come,
And the voice of the turtle is heard in our land . . .
Arise, my love, my fair one,
And come away."

We shall go far before we come again to poetic dialogue so finely lyrical as this. If as drama it is as slow-moving, as " reminiscent," as the pre-Æschylean dithyrambs, it has none the less a continuous action of thought, even movement toward a foreshadowed end. We wonder whether the ancient world knew other works by the unnamed Hebrew author. If a theatre, a place for productions of which this is the only remaining, the literary part, existed in those times, we may mark it as rich even in comparison with those of Fifth Century Greece or of Elizabeth's time in England.

Job, chosen more often than any other book out of the Bible group as a world masterpiece of literature, is more definitely dramatic in structure than is *Solomon's Song.* Job is presented, a main actor going through a series of events, in a drama that may seem in our energetic times to lack direct theatric action; but which has a well-stressed action of spiritual thought, even of emotion.

After the short explanatory prologue, it begins with (shall we say, the curtain goes up on?) Job's soliloquy:

> Let the day perish wherein I was born;
> And the night which said, There is a man child conceived!
>   Let that day be darkness;
>   Let not God regard it from above,
>   Neither let the light shine upon it!
>   Let darkness and the shadow of death claim it for their own . . .
> Because it shut not up the doors of my mother's womb,
> Nor hid trouble from mine eyes!

From this beginning it passes through five distinct acts in dialogue, until Job's final summarizing words to the Lord:

> I had heard of thee by the hearing of the ear;
> But now my eyes see-eth thee:
> Wherefor I abhor myself, and repent
> In dust and ashes.

The drama of Job's soul is over. The Bible author adds the conventional happy ending in a brief few paragraphs of narrative at the end, as epilogue. In the body of the work he has written down what remains in translation one of the finest literary dramas of all time.

YET — much as I may enjoy these beautiful things, there is something lacking out of my fullness of satisfaction at this point: precisely because I cannot talk definitely about theatre as well as drama, about stages and actors and movement as well as about texts. Gathering together all the fragments treated in this chapter, these texts and these Passion Play outlines and these reconstructions of primitive dance, we may return to the solid fact that the first complete theatre that we know about, the first surviving drama coupled with a constructed theatre and a method of presentation, is the Greek. We have discovered where the theatre came from — fragmentarily — and approximately when; but we have yet to get any full view of it as a rounded-out living human institution.

CHAPTER III

Tragedy: The Noble Greeks

IN GREECE, in the sixth and fifth centuries before Christ, there was a flowering of beautiful living and of the arts such as mankind never had known before; and Tragedy then was born. In the progress of humankind in the Western world during twenty-four centuries since, there has been no rival to Greek civilization. No other state has ever reached the standard set by the Hellenes in those accomplishments esteemed by men to be most high, most desirable, most beautiful. Other races and other countries, even single cities, have had their brief periods of creativeness, have carried conquest farther, have won miraculous victories over material obstacles to progress. But the proudest boast a nation can make is that of being successor to the ancient Greeks. In short, there is world recognition that for a considerable period the people of Hellas solved better than any other the problem how to live their lives reasonably and finely.

Not only in those too stressed accomplishments of winning wars with courage and daring, thus protecting and expanding their civilization, and in feats of strength and physical perfection, but more especially in the fields of artistic and intellectual accomplishment, they came to a surpassing achievement. Perhaps most important, they adjusted art and life to a perfect balance; philosophy and living sustained each other. They made their buildings lovely, they learned to adorn beautifully rather than lavishly, they were wise in their pleasures, cultivating those of the emotions, the mind, and the æsthetic senses, those that may be enjoyed with least danger of satiation, headache, or boredom. Even today, their architecture, their poetry, their sculpture — and their drama — spread before us glories almost unmatched.

In this present period of revaluation, at the end of the first quarter of the twentieth century, when sophisticated commentators are taking cynical delight in demolishing old human and racial idols, pointing out the flaws in everything that mankind has esteemed, there is little attempt to pull down Greece. Even the Modernists in art, instead of depriving the Greeks of a place in the new hierarchy, are content with a shift of emphasis from the late, less vigorous Greek works to the early strong ones. There is, indeed, no other development in human life to match this one.

If we inquire into the reasons why later civilizations have failed to surpass that of Greece, we may find ourselves compelled to blame ideals and institutions that we have been taught to reverence, that perhaps we hold most dear: Christianity, Hebraism, ideals of conquest, Roman law, compulsory education, unquestioning patriotism, even our most esteemed kings, prophets, and sages. The pursuit of that inquiry should form little part in a story of one of the arts; but in studying the theatre, we cannot avoid some consideration of *religion* as an element in Greek life, and as a thing comparatively lacking in the life of today. The drama in Greece was inextricably bound up with religious feeling and religious observance.

Religion — not an exacting one, but truly spiritual, felt, ever-present — is not easy for us to understand today, so different is it from the usual church-formed conception of it. A lived and companionable religion, inspirational but seldom rule-making, was at the base of Greek life. It was a religion not of conformance but of celebration. It left man free to create, himself god-like. Necessarily man and his activities must be beautiful. Exercise of the artist's creativeness, in architecture and sculpture, in the service of the gods; dramatic ritual, dancing and full theatre production; games, and processions: all these rose from spiritual and devotional sources in the hearts of the people. The drama from its beginnings to the days of late comedy was intertwined with religion, a part of sacred ceremonial.

Bands of Greek revellers met to celebrate when the time of vintage had come. They went swinging through the town streets and the country groves in processions, or danced and sang in improvised " dancing rings." They drank the wine, as was doubly appropriate when the new grapes were in, and they sang of, and to, Dionysus, the wine-god. They had begun by making sacrifice to him, by pledging their allegiance, their devotion. But as his spirit entered into them, it transformed them, too, into gods. The glow of man-made revels, of marching shoulder to shoulder, of shouting and singing and laughing, changed to a divine ecstasy. The god-in-man became alive, radiant, social, inspired.

In such a time only the arts could satisfy: the dance and poetry and music. Not that the many listened silently and reverently, in those early days, while a few recited or danced or played sweet melodies. Where every youth or maid was in some measure a god, all joined in — though the most god-like might improvise

Performers in a Greek Comus. [From a vase drawing reproduced in *The Greek Drama,* by Lionel D. Barnett.]

the poems for chanting, or lead a special band of dancers. Still it was all very mixed, very boisterous — and perhaps it ended very wildly. For this god Dionysus, who symbolized the fields and the harvest and the red wine, who had the special power of entering into the soul of a man or a woman, had been first of all a god of all wild things, and of a magic fertility; and the ecstasy that he brought might be of many sorts. It was divine and exalting and exquisite, but there was nothing to keep it from being " loose."

There are, indeed, elements in Greek religion, and particularly in the wild god Dionysus, that are shocking to many upright and kindly people today, beyond the sheer superstition that was the foundation for all deification. For one thing, the Greek was fully aware of the beauty of the human body, counted its creativeness as part of the great creative divinity governing life, associated its beauty and its reproductive functions with the richness and fruitfulness of the earth — seed-planting, germination, vintage, and harvest — and celebrated one with the other. The phallus, fashioned in symbolic or realistic likeness to the male generative organ, was an ordinary property of vintage processionals and earthgod ceremonials. That these occasions, in those days when true drama was germinating in devotional festivals, sometimes were marked by freedoms and excesses warranting the name " orgies," can hardly be questioned. In the case of some cults, the celebrations seem to have ended in sexual orgies as well as in carousing and plain drunkenness. But to read such an extreme meaning into any great part of Dionysian celebration, or to understand drunkenness for that " intoxication " which the Greeks valued so highly, would be unwarranted and evil. The early Greeks gave due place to sex as a determining element of spiritual life, their festivals included devotions to the gods of fruitfulness, and phallic celebrations had much to do with the rise of the dramatic art. But a sense of divine cause informed all these things.

Dionysus, out of one attribute or another, is father of fullfledged tragedy and comedy as well as the more directly appropriate Satyr-play. We may consider him as the successor of those gods of fertilization and of harvest-time fullness whom we met in connection with primitive dance and ritual. But he is more. In his identification with the human, with the source of the highest ecstasy within one, he seems miraculously born to father the divine-popular art. Those earlier names of his, Bacchus and Iacchus, carried some connotation of a god who is hailed with loud cries; and what band of celebrants could utter loud cries — Iacchus! Iacchus! — without movement, dance? And that ecstasy within, would it let one go away after a sacrifice without getting up a pageant-procession? And in a procession should one merely march and sing and throw jests? No; sooner or later, one who is a god must *act* the god. Divine inspiration demanded no less than first the act of acting, then the art of acting. How did it come about?

Aristotle, the first great authority on matters dramatic, writing two centuries later, chronicles the birth of tragedy and comedy in this manner: " Both tragedy and comedy originated in a rude and unpremeditated manner, the former from the leaders of the dithyramb, the latter from those who led off the phallic songs." There is one significant emphasis here: on the *leaders* of the dance and song. From it we infer organization, and that those who led the singers and dancers became the first identifiable actors. For the essential change from mere group-dancing or processional came when one performer *separated himself* from the group of Dionysian worshippers and assumed another character than his own, impersonated.

There are various conjectural accounts how the separation came about, how it led to responses from " chorus " to " leader," how the action grew from chance repartee to incident, to story in dialogue. But we may be content if we have a clear picture of the band of revellers, ivy-crowned and with faces masked or streaked with wine-dregs, marching, dancing, singing, joshing; celebrating Dionysus, carrying grape garlands and phallic emblems, drinking the wine, working up that ecstasy which is the realest devotion to this god; and when the band is organized, for dance or for procession or for choral singing — we know not just what — we see one participant step out (most likely the poet), see him take a part different from the others.

Long before this time the Greeks had been accustomed to enjoy melic poetry. Poems had long been sung with musical accompaniment, and sometimes to the accompaniment of dance. From this source and from the great store of epic story-poem and lyric, from Homer and from his fellow-poets, the literary elements for tragedy were drawn. Joined with the mimetic elements out of the dance-revels, they served to form the dual foundation for the majestic edifice of Greek tragic drama.

The " dithyramb " mentioned by Aristotle was a special form of poetry sung by the revellers at the festivals of Dionysus, recounting the story of the god, or at least honoring him. Confusingly, the dithyramb was itself later expanded and crystallized into a truly dramatic form, was composed specifically for chorus and leader. It was this that came to be called " goat-song," and therefore this form that gave tragedy its name. For the word seems to come from τράγος, goat, and ῳδή, song — but whether in reference to the sacrifice of a goat during the ritual, or because a goat was given to the poet as prize, or on account of the goat-skins worn by the chorus as followers of Dionysus, is not certainly known (there are a dozen other guesses almost as plausible).

In these beginnings of tragedy there is an influence, too, an influence not to be measured or traced, out of straight recited poetry, poetry put over by a reciter up on a platform or in a cleared space before an audience, as distinguished from the choral dithyramb and the other song-dances. Minstrels had long ago made their recitations popular, and their materials were those out of epic poetry that later went into tragic drama. How close the declaiming minstrels may have approached to acting, no one may hazard.

Up to this time the lines of development, the streams leading into true drama, have been not only vague but scattered: from Ionian, Doric, and other sources as well as Attic. But from the first recorded acting, the story may be told by the record of the Theatre of Dionysus in Athens. This is truly the most important single theatre in all history.

Let us say that we are now in the middle period of the sixth century B.C. The Dionysian Festivals used to be held over on the north side of the Acropolis, where there were a dancing circle and some rude seats. But under Pisistratus, just after mid-century, perhaps, this potential " theatre " has been moved to the location where one may still see the half-ruined Theatre of Dionysus to-day, almost twenty-five hundred years later, in the sacred precinct of Dionysus Eleutherius on the southeastern slope of the Acropolis. Close to the god's temple a dancing-circle, the ὀρχήστρα, has been tamped hard, and some wooden seats set up against the hillside hollow. (There is no stage.) Under Pisistratus, too, the Athenian festival known as the Great or City Dionysia has been expanded, a new Temple of Dionysus has been built, and dramatic " contests " have been inaugurated.

The first decisive record of acted drama dates from this time, and the earliest name in the annals of acting. In the year 535 B.C., Thespis of Icaria was winner in the first tragedy contest. He achieved immortality more especially, however, because he is supposed to have introduced the actor as such, *in addition to* the leader of the chorus. These two henceforward are to engage in dialogue, and the actor is to impersonate various characters, with different masks and change of costumes. Thus the tragic drama is safely set on its two-fold foundation: mimetic-dramatic art and literary-dramatic art are indissolubly joined. The play text may still be very crude — hardly more than a series of poems spoken alternately by chorus leader and actor. No "plays" by Thespis have survived, though he is chronicled as both poet and actor. But the period of mere improvisation, of mere chant-and-response, is past.

The "cart of Thespis," for some reason become a world-symbol of the wandering actor, is probably wholly a thing of myth. Nor is there more than conjecture as basis for the often-repeated statement that while the chorus grouped themselves around an altar in the centre of the orchestra, Thespis mounted a table from which he addressed their leader. (This table, perhaps that on which the goat was sacrificed, was long supposed to have been the first step toward a stage, although there is no real proof of the existence of any platform stage, elevated above the orchestra-area, until centuries later.)

Greek statuette of a tragic actor. Note the mask and the rich costume. (But the blocks below the feet are not cothurnus-boots, as once believed, but merely the pegs by which the statuette was fixed into a base.)
[From Le Théâtre Grec, by Octave Navarre.]

It was only ten years after Thespis' epoch-making innovation that Æschylus was born. He was destined not only to become one of the world-masters of tragic drama — the greatest, some people still believe — but to be remembered as an innovator almost as notable as Thespis. He introduced a second actor. Sophocles, who lived his life wholly within the fifth century B.C., added the third actor. In the slowness with which the actor took on importance, during this period of developing tragedy, one may read a truth too often forgotten:

choral dance was the essential feature, the very heart of drama. The chorus was still the pivotal element in Thespis' time: the *acted* portions of the play were considered as the interludes, the dance-chants as the main design. The connected episodes only gradually took on significance as plot. Æschylus cut down the predominance of the chorus, but only with Sophocles did compact acted-spoken drama take first place.

Thespis is credited with " making up " to the extent of wholly disguising his face with paints; and then with the invention of the mask. There is conflict here with the theory that the mask was a survival from primitive ritual-dance. But there can be no doubt that from Thespis' time masks continued as an aid to impersonation through the whole story of the Greek theatre.

The two annual occasions particularly distinguished by performances of drama were religious festivals in honor of Dionysus. One, the Lenæa, in honor of Dionysus Lenæus, held in winter, incorporated more of comedy than of tragedy into its early revelry and into its later programmes; though contests in tragedy are known definitely to have been included. The other, the Dionysia, in celebration of Dionysus Eleuthereus, held in the spring in the sacred precinct containing temple and theatre, may be considered the real cradle and home of tragedy. From 535 B.C., when Thespis received the first given prize, to the decadence long after Æschylus, Sophocles, and Euripides, performances of tragedy regularly graced the City Dionysia. Very truly it may be said that on its dedicated ground Greek drama budded, flowered, and died.

The festival included, in the epochal fifth century, processions, rites, concerts, games, contests in poetry and chorus singing, and performances of tragedies, comedies, and satyr-plays. For five or six days the people of Athens took holiday from their accustomed occupations, to enjoy feasting, revelling, music, and theatre productions. The dramatic events filled the last three days. On each of these occasions, five plays were presented, probably three tragedies, a satyr-play, and a comedy (it seems that at some periods more comedies were included, perhaps on earlier days). In any case, the tragic contest consisted of three consecutive days' productions, each poet being assigned one day's programme, to which he must contribute three full tragedies and a satyr-drama as an after-piece. The Greek plays were very much shorter than is the modern full-evening entertainment; but four or five dramas must have constituted a formidable single programme. Let us remember, however, that the people of Athens were keenly devoted to literary and artistic activities of all sorts, and the contests for the prizes in tragedy and comedy roused wide public interest aside from the intrinsic theatrical values of the individual plays, and beyond the religious significance of the events. Victory in any of the games, music contests, or literary competitions brought honor and glory not only to the winning individuals but to all their relatives and to their cities or districts.

At first each tragic poet composed his plays as a trilogy, connected in subject, perhaps making them all deal with the adventures of one protagonist. Later the dramatists might present a group of unrelated compositions. During the fifth century B.C. only one performance of each play was given in Athens, except that by special decree, after the poet's death, the tragedies of Æschylus could be revived in subsequent years. It is well to remember, however, in these days of playwrights with an eye to a possible " long run," that in those earliest decades of the theatre's existence, when some of the immortal dramas were being written, they were literally designed for a day only. In a moment we shall inquire what are their special qualities, as drama, that have made them live through twenty-four centuries. First let us try to reconstruct a picture of the conditions under which they were presented.

The Greek theatre is an extraordinarily simple, but an extraordinarily pleasing place. From the tamped circle for dancing, with surrounding benches, it has now grown into an architectural bowl, graceful in outline, symmetrical, but not yet in any way ornate. About the full round orchestra, tiers of seats rise up, two-thirds of the way round, nestled into the Acropolis slope, divided by aisles into wedge-like sections. At the far side of the dancing circle an unpretentious stage-building, the *skene,* has been erected. It probably has a portico along the front, between two wings that come forward protectingly toward the auditorium. There still is no raised stage (one must repeat it, because from our knowledge of later theatres we always look first for a platform); there is no

" scenery," and very few properties. Close-by, ever a reminder that this is a sacred precinct, is the lovely little Temple of Dionysus. Not that any of the fifteen thousand spectators is likely to forget the religious significance of the occasion, of the plays to come, even of the theatre itself.

For did we not three days ago assemble with them, in the nearby Odeon, to witness the " parade " of the dramatists, actors, and chorus, all dressed up gorgeously for this ceremonial? There we heard the announcements, the names of the poet-playwrights, of the *choregi* (the patrons or " backers " of the poets, in modern parlance), and of the plays. No doubt about the seriousness, the dignity, and the significance of all this: these performers, producers, and dramatists are specially honored members of Athenian society. What they are to present during the coming holidays is to be no mere amusement to while away idle hours, but rather a sacrament — though imbedded in a festival of revelry and games. Even in this preliminary ceremony they are wearing crowns; and we are told that at the end of the contest one of the tragic poets and his *choregus* will be crowned with that more prized emblem, the ivy.

At the opening of the festival, too, we have been witnesses at a stirring ritual and procession. The citizens of Athens have gone forth in all their holiday finery to escort the statue of Dionysus back to its home.

At break of day they have begun to assemble at the shrine, till all the city seems gathered here in the precinct of Dionysus, by the theatre: the *Archon,* the priests, and the city fathers, the chosen ones who are to carry the statue and those who bear the sacrifices, the guards of honor, the choruses, the actors, the groups of contesting singers, the poets, those who later will be the audiences but who now are taking personal part in the ceremony, men, women, children, aristocrat, noble, and freedman.

Swift hands disengage the statue from its pedestal when the chief priest gives the word; the appointed carriers bear it aloft, through the city, out to a park-like place in the country near the Academy, while the procession reverently follows. Now the god's image is placed on a pedestal under the olive trees, and the sacrificial rites are held. The rest of the day is a " let-down " time, given over to games, feasting, and lighter forms of amusement. Then at night the crowd gathers again at the statue, the procession back to the city starts: the crux of the celebration, annual symbol of the first bringing of the image to Athens from Eleutheræ. Here is something out of the pre-drama days, the joyous worshippers marching by torchlight back along the road to the Acropolis, bearing the statue aloft, carrying the jars of wine and the garlands and symbolic crowns, dancing, improvising, singing. Here indeed, in the revelry and the spirited bandying, are survivals of the elements and the impulses from which the seeds of theatre sprang. Then the statue is placed in the theatre, which the celebrants now rededicate with suitable rites for the musical and dramatic events of the morrow. Sobered from their revelry, but no less " intoxicated," their demeanor promises a finer solemnity and beauty in the plays to follow.

The next day, and perhaps another, are given up to the dithyrambic contests; five hundred men and boys, come to Athens from all parts of Greece, sing in competition for the choral prizes. Ten groups in all offer their songs before the holiday audiences, not without dancing: a parallel to that other source of tragic drama, the old-time sung poetry. But it is the morning of the following day that we await.

There is still the darkness before dawn as we make our way toward the theatre. Just the first faint streaks of light have made beautiful the eastern sky, but already all Athens seems awake, excited, hurrying toward the enclosure of Dionysus.

We are soon glad that we came thus early, for we are jostled by the crowds, and it is clear that not all these ticket-holders can squeeze into the auditorium. There is room for the overflow up there on the heights above the shaped bowl, but in the dim chill light, that seems far, far away from the dancing-orchestra where the action will pass. We gaze down curiously at this consecrated circle, with the altar of Dionysus at the very centre; and beyond to the low *skene,* the background building with its pillared lower story that might be a palace front or a temple, with its three doorways facing us from the main wall, and its two " wings " or *paraskenia* thrust forward at each end — as if to enclose the acting-dancing space, so that no part of the " drama," the doings, may escape.

Light, and still more light, till the theatre seems bathed in the dim freshness, the pale clarity, the loveliest moment of the day. Ah, what a moment for a drama to begin! And indeed, everything is in readiness now. The priests of Dionysus are in their chairs of honor — their thrones — down on the very edge of the orchestra; and the bowl above them is like a teeming beehive, so alive is it with human beings.

A herald! Yes, now he is calling forth Sophocles, first of this year's contestants for the tragedy prize. And the play is on. For there, around the altar of the dancing-circle, a crowd of " supers " has gathered, Theban citizens, miserable, suppliant. And one stands a little apart, a priest. Forth to them comes an actor, majestically, masked and in kingly robes. His voice breaks into the morning silence with startling resonance, with the measured stately beauty of words severely chosen, richly intoned.

> My children, fruit of Cadmus' ancient tree
> New springing, wherefore thus with bended knee
> Press ye upon us, laden all with wreaths
> And suppliant branches? And the city breathes
> Heavy with incense, heavy with dim prayer
> And shrieks to affright the Slayer.
> . . . Seeing 'tis I ye call,
> 'Tis I am come, world-honored Œdipus.

Ah, this then will be the story of Œdipus the King, most tragic, most terrible. This actor and the priest now are telling us what we already know (our minds flash back to the old legend), how Œdipus, having slain the Sphinx and delivered Thebes, married the widowed Queen Jocasta, ruled happily twelve years, then found a pestilence destroying his city. We know more, too horrible almost for words: that this pestilence has come from the gods, because all unwittingly Œdipus has killed his own father, the former king, and now is married to his own mother. But these characters in the play, this proud Œdipus, and the Queen whom Sophocles will make so noble, so touching, they do not know. Like the gods themselves, this day we shall watch the fearful truth unfold to these two.

Œdipus and the Priest have told us now the misery of the Theban people; and the King — oh, irony! — pledges to seek out the cause of the sorrow, to cast it out at whatever cost. But now the Suppliants crowd toward the gateway beyond the orchestra, where Creon is entering. He, the brother of Jocasta, comes from Delphi with messages from the Oracle: there is an unclean one in the land, he who slew Laïus, the former king, and he is to be punished before the blight can be lifted. We watch as Œdipus and Creon build in dialogue toward the first climax: to that moment when the King goes back through the palace door — yes, that simple proscenium has become to us a palace now — vowing to search out the slayer of Laïus.

The Suppliants give way to the Chorus of Theban Elders. Half-chanting they come, half-dancing, with slow stateliness, threading their way over the dance-circle, taking up position as prayers to Apollo:

" A voice, a voice, that is borne on the Holy Way ". . . Here indeed is the old religious dancing-procession, here the old devotional pattern showing through the design of the new human drama. They chant, they repeat the story of the pestilence, they implore the mercy of the gods, they call on Apollo, Athena, Artemis, Zeus, Dionysus.

Œdipus is coming again forward from the palace. He speaks, he ponders, he calls on the guilty slayer of Laïus to come forth and be banished. He sends for the blind prophet Tiresius. We listen to these two, the King ruthlessly tracking down clue after clue, the old prophet holding back the knowledge — till spurred beyond control:

Thou art thyself the unclean thing!

We see the deluge of Œdipus' wrath at this incredible accusation, until the patient Tiresius pours forth his whole prophecy, foreshadows the tragedy to its end:

Thou dost seek
With threats and loud proclaim the man whose hand
Slew Laïus. Lo, I tell thee, he doth stand
Here. . .

> His staff groping before him, he shall crawl
> O'er unknown earth, and voices round him call:
> " Behold the brother-father of his own
> Children, the seed, the sower and the sown,
> Shame to his mother's blood, and to his sire
> Son, murderer, incest-worker."

Like a relief from storm the Chorus comes, bringing a lyrical interlude, chanting, commenting upon the ways of gods and men, affirming faith in Œdipus — and relieving the tension with the sheer visual beauty of the dance-design.

But Creon returns, eager to defend himself against Œdipus' charge that he has instigated the accusation against the King; and as these two come near to an encounter with swords, Jocasta enters before us:

> Vain men, what would ye with this angry swell
> Of words heart-blinded?   Is there in your eyes
> No pity, thus, when all our city lies
> Bleeding, to ply your privy hates? . . .

And it is she who brings to her King the first gleam of self-doubt. We see him now, losing his assurance, a dread beginning to creep in. He tells how once he killed a noble in a chariot, where three roads crossed. He was fleeing from Corinth; a prophecy had said he would kill his father and marry his mother — and so he had fled the court. And meeting this old man on the way, he had killed him and his guards. But Jocasta, stirred now by a deeper dread, sends for a herdsman, since banished to the hills, who saw Laïus murdered.

We of the audience settle back, and let the strain fall a little from us as Œdipus and Jocasta go in; we note the strophes and antistrophes of the Chorus rather idly — we have come to a human suspense that lyrics and dance cannot beguile us from. Now here is Jocasta again before us saying,

> So dire a storm
> Doth shake the king, sin, dread and every form
> Of grief. . .

But, as she prays to Apollo, a Stranger arrives by the gateway, hailing the Chorus, asking for the King. For a moment we are inclined to find relief, with Jocasta, in the news he brings. The King of Corinth, Œdipus' reputed father, is dead, and the old prophecy of patricide seems disproved. But suddenly a new dread is aroused. The Stranger discloses that Œdipus was not Corinthian at all, but was a Theban babe rescued from a wild mountainside where he had been left to die.

Ah, mark you, while this unfolds between Œdipus and the Stranger, how Jocasta turns aside, a sickness growing in her mind! Will no one there notice her as she totters? — now her head goes down into her hands. She knows! This King, her husband, is her own babe. No need to wait the coming of the herdsman. A quick effort to restrain Œdipus from seeking confirmation; then she goes, in horror, hardly daring a farewell. For us in the audience *her* tragedy is already complete. The Chorus this time interrupts only for a moment. All eyes watch for the herdsman's coming.

How crisply Œdipus questions him! On the brink of disastrous knowledge, he searches out the reluctant truth with uncanny directness, without mercy. This is an inevitable structure. We see circumstance after circumstance nailed in; till suddenly Œdipus shines out — we know it is like this in his own mind — with all the guilty knowledge on him: himself son of Laïus, murderer of his own father, incestuous husband to his own mother, brother to his own children! As he rushes into the palace, this time, we have need of the let-down of the choral interlude. Still we have little heart for the lyrical comment — for we know that at this very moment, offstage, the physical climax of the play is taking place. We know that a Messenger, as is the wont, will come and recount to us the more horrible happenings, which perchance we could never have faced in the actual acting-out, under this pitiless morning sunshine. Now the Messenger is before us speaking:

> Like one entranced with passion, through the gate
> She passed, the white hands flashing o'er her head,
> Like blades that tear, and fled, unswerving fled,
> Toward her old bridal room, and disappeared
> And the doors crashed behind her. But we heard
> Her voice within, crying to him of old,
> Her Laïus, long dead . . .

And, after that, I know not how her death
Found her. For sudden, with a roar of wrath,
Burst Œdipus upon us. Then, I ween,
We marked no more what passion held the Queen . . .
He dashed him on the chamber door. The straight
Door-bar of oak, it bent beneath his weight,
Shook from its sockets free, and in he burst
To the dark chamber.

There we saw her first
Hanged, swinging from a noose, like a dead bird.
He fell back when he saw her. Then we heard
A miserable groan, and straight he found
And loosed the strangling knot, and on the ground
Laid her. — Ah, then the sight of horror came!
The pin of gold, broad-beaten like a flame,
He tore from off her breast, and, left and right,
Down on the shuddering orbits of his sight
Dashed it: " Out! Out! Ye never more shall see
Me nor the anguish nor the sins of me . . ."
. . . Like a song
His voice rose, and again, again, the strong
And stabbing hand fell, and the massacred
And bleeding eyeballs streamed upon his beard,
Wild rain, and gouts of hail amid the rain.
. . . All that eye or ear
Hath ever dreamed of misery is here.

And then Œdipus is led in before us, blinded and bleeding. The
old men of the Chorus turn away to escape the sight. But in
a sort of sick horror we face this broken King, this abased human
being. He gropes his way forward, calling on the gods, glorying
that he has made himself a dungeon, " dark, without sound . . .
self-prisoned from a world of pain," cursing the shepherd who
saved him as a babe.

O flesh, horror of flesh! . . .
In God's name,
Take me somewhere far off and cover me
From sight, or slay, or cast me to the sea
Where never eye may see me any more.

But now he has one thought more: his children, his two little
daughters. There they are, Creon is bringing them before us and
him.

Children! Where are ye? Hither; come to these
Arms of your — brother, whose wild offices
Have brought much darkness on the once bright eyes
Of him who grew your garden; who, nowise
Seeing nor understanding, digged a ground
The world shall shudder at . . .
                              Creon, thou alone art left
Their father now, since both of us are gone
Who cared for them. Oh, leave them not alone.
        . . . So young they are, so desolate —
Of all save thee. True man, give me thine hand,
And promise . . .

For a moment only he weakens, and clings to the children. But
we see them dragged from him. Creon says, " Seek not to be
master more." And as Œdipus is led away, the Chorus chants
again. As it too disappears, we are warned:

Therefore, O Man, beware, and look toward the end of things that be,
The last of sights, the last of days; and no man's life account as gain
Ere the full tale be finished and the darkness find him without pain.

At the end of this utterly moving, purging, terrible drama, we
spectators wake gradually to the world about us. There is something absurdly trivial about the things we do when the Chorus
has finally disappeared: we stand and stretch, and perhaps turn
a little away from the sun — and titter because a man is sobbing
near us. Our feelings are very close to the surface, and we have
a tendency to lose sight of the audience around us in recurring
fits of " star-gazing." We are shaken — and yet there is a glow
of beauty in our souls, a brooding, a healing ecstasy. We have
been through high grief, have descended into terror and sorrow,
so terrible that all the pettinesses of life have been stripped away.
Now we seem to have come out on the other side, cleansed. Somehow the soul seems to stand up and take the light, naked and
glorious.

Twice more we are to suffer through tragedies of Sophocles
this day. Ah, but we shall welcome them. We await, content.

WHAT is it that puts this mood of high suffering into tragedy?
What is the secret of the majesty of these Greek dramas, that
brings their audiences close to the gods, that purges human life of

its weaknesses, bitterness, and shallowness, that inundates the spectator in exaltation and a god-like pity? The theme and story have not been pretty. We have been conducted through a tale of incest, suicide, murder — a very welter of revolting crime (we shudder to think what any playwright of our more "natural" time would make of the material). But we have not shuddered at Sophocles' telling, nor have we been revolted; somehow our suffering and grief have been kept on some loftier plane.

In the first place the combination that is *theatre* has come right, the majestic poetry matched by nobly dramatic story, the whole set forth in stately acting and in the chanting and rhythmic movement of the Chorus. The vast and nobly proportioned playhouse has some fitting appropriateness too. This is sustained theatre, without let-down to mere anecdote-telling or picturing or individual impersonation. The tragedy has passed with sweep, with unbroken passion, majestically, with a splendid inevitability. It is the art that in its completeness goes beyond dramatic literature or acting or setting or dancing.

And yet if we would know more of the secret of its effectiveness, we must ask about those elements of the art separately. Of the sheer poetic values, there is already evidence enough in the excerpts quoted. Even in translation (always a weakening process) there is obvious tragic beauty in line after line. In the original Greek there was perhaps even more of majesty than becomes evident here. In the modern "Greek Theatre" at Berkeley, I have found myself strangely moved by the beauty of the spoken Greek verse — declaimed nobly, it seemed to me, with an echo of that bigness, that solemn serenity and slowness, that must have characterized performances in the ancient theatres. It is a quality unmatched in the prettier liquid Italian as I have heard it in the old Roman theatre at Taormina, or in the more nasal French and heavier German and English, as listened to divers times, indoors and out. Let us grant, then, that each language has its special excellencies, that may or may not be capitalized for theatric uses; and that there seems to have been a perfection of adjustment in Greek tragedy, language values contributing nobly to poetic expressiveness and poetic sweep. And yet, despite the loss of those values, we may read, in Gilbert Murray's translations (from which all my quotations from the great Greek tragedians are taken) Greek dramatic works as stirring, as packed with poetic beauty as any to be found on the world's library shelves — with the one exception of Will Shakespeare's plays.

The theatre artist or craftsman, either seeing a Greek masterpiece in production or reading a text, never fails to marvel at the sheer technique of *play structure* exhibited in these works. The Greeks set up models for tragedy that have been little deviated from in any later age: a play form that induces in the spectator interest, emotional intensity, suspense and a sort of completion of sorrow, a final radiantly sad contentment. The great simplicity of the fifth century drama, as compared with later developments, the directness of action when the descriptive dithyrambs had first been transformed into dialogue and action, lends a monumental impressiveness to the play. There is something almost fragmentary about these texts, a magnificent isolation from fussing-up ornament, or pretty sentiment or rhetorical flourish. They are like sculptures chiselled out of sheer rock, massive and noble, before modelling and anecdotal subject-matter and " charm " were thought of.

But these qualities arose out of a purely theatrical genius. The conception was thoroughly dramatic, the method born of stage cunning. (The poets, remember, were leading actors.) In later ages a whole literature on the subject of " dramaturgy " has grown up, and the Greek play structure has been pulled to pieces, analyzed, made the basis for rules and " laws." These analyses are bloodless things, little useful to any later dramatist — but the fine directness and the effective action-articulation of the individual plays remain a source of inspiration and a profitable field of study for the general reader. There is in them a well-marked progression from introduction and exposition to opening movement, growth, climax, fall, or return, and finally to denouement or catastrophe. It is a structure calculated to induce the maximum of attentiveness and of emotional response. We shall come again to this subject of play-building and play-writing formulas, along with consideration of the " unities " and other " laws," when we arrive at the days of the French Classicists and their codifying of legitimate dramatic usage. At present let us only mark the Greeks as master technicians.

The subject-matter of Greek tragedy was definitely limited by the conception of the theatre as a religious institution. It simply never would occur to the dramatists to go outside the field of gods and legendary heroes for their plots or stories. The stirring deeds, the crimes, the hereditary sins, the expiations — these were the subject material, usually with a conflict of will between gods and hero or between lesser and greater gods. Every spectator knew at the beginning of the play what the outcome would be — just as we today can foresee every incident in any Christian Passion Play; but the dramatic tension and suspense were none the less sustained and powerful. And the high subject-matter, the revered gods and heroes and kings, and the piteously courageous struggles and the crushing dooms, lent a magnitude of emotion to the plays which perhaps cannot be encompassed in mere domestic tragedies and love-dramas.

The so-called " unities " were conventions observed in the shaping of the plot-action, and are supposed by some commentators to account for the qualities of grandeur and solemnity that characterized Greek serious drama.

Of the three unities, of Action, of Time, and of Place, only the first seems now to have any universal validity. It is obvious enough that the action of a play must have a unity of flow, must be of a piece, must hold together: as much might be claimed in regard to the characteristic material of any art, of the color in painting, the mass in sculpture, the flow of sound and idea in poetry. Without unity of action the stage-production fails of holding the attention, of precipitating emotion and mood, of creating sustained *theatre*.

The rules to the effect that the dramatists must compress the time of the action into one day, and show its every scene passing in one place, seem to us today to be wholly arbitrary limitations. In certain periods the superstitious reverence for these " laws " hampered playwrights and caused some of the bitterest critical battles in the history of the theatre. The Greek dramatists, so close to what had been a narrative-devotional exercise, pushed out slowly from under the limitations seemingly imposed by the conditions of dithyrambic choral performances and of the very simple form of the dance-theatre. Usually they took a single episode from a myth, dealing with an event in the life of a hero, and this they treated as if it happened in a single day; and as there was then no conception of " setting " the drama (witness the total lack of " scenery "), the action occurred in one place. But later commentators elevated these circumstances into rules to be respected by all serious dramatists. One may believe that the observance of the unities *helped* to further the monumental simplicity and impressiveness of Greek drama, without insisting that similar observance be exacted from later playwrights when theatre conditions have completely changed — any more than one should insist that gods and heroes remain the only protagonists or that a Chorus continue to comment upon or sum up the action at intervals. Aristotle in his *Poetics* codified the usages of Greek writers in a way that has been very useful and at times illuminating to the Renaissance and modern worlds, but he also embalmed some ideas in phrases that have created mischief down the ages.

Æschylus, first of the great tragedy writers, retained in his dramas more of the simplicity and literary conception out of the old dithyrambs, than did Sophocles and Euripides; certainly always a less involved plot than is illustrated in *Œdipus the King*. He was more epic in two senses: the true epic greatness, the monumental fragmentary method, with little effort to polish down to a smooth articulated dramatic flow of events, was characteristic of all his powerful and magnificent plays; and the subject-matter of the epic poets, the mythology and the legendary-historic stories, with their vast religious implications, was dearer to him than were the more human legends that Sophocles and Euripides were to weave into touching dramas.

Æschylus came when the impulse of the dramatic poets had run out along the old lines; he turned to the budding drama, but he brought his gift into the service of Dionysus on the austerer side, came sombrely, holding himself aloof from the more humanly intimate aspects of Dionysian celebration.

From the few known facts about his life, we may learn much — and presume more — about the reasons for his becoming the first great dramatist of the world. He knew intimately the rituals and mysteries from which the drama developed; for his birth-place was Eleusis, and he doubtless dreamed over the impressive ceremonies there. He had been born of a noble family, in 525, and by 499 he is known to have competed in a dramatic contest. As a soldier he distinguished himself at Marathon and at Salamis, digging down into the depths of life as is the way of poet-philosophers gone to war. He was a traveller, too, and several of his trips to far-away Sicily (where he produced some of his plays) are chronicled in contemporary records. For forty years his life was bound up intimately with the dramatic contests at the Great Dionysia in Athens and with the Theatre of Dionysus. Between 499 and 458, when the *Oresteia* was produced, he is supposed to have written ninety plays. Seven complete texts of his tragedies exist today. He won the tragic prize twelve times.

Those who have called Æschylus " the father of tragedy " had in mind not only his transcending poetic genius, by which he elevated the drama far above the level touched by his predecessors, but also his innovation in introducing a second actor. When there had been only a Chorus leader and one actor, conflict and dramatic structure had been possible within only a limited range. When Æschylus provided two actors (each capable of taking several parts successively, with change of mask and costume), he opened the way to elaboration of plot and characterization, and made the dialogue less a means of telling what had happened than a revelation of direct conflict.

Still, the earliest of his plays extant, *The Suppliants* (also the oldest Greek play that has been preserved), escapes but awkwardly out of the old limitations. It is compounded of a great deal of lyric poetry and a little dramatic action. More than half the lines are given to the Chorus, and in general the characters tell *about* what is done instead of doing it. The whole forms but a single episode rather than a chain of events with cause and effect and inevitability. The Suppliants are the fifty daughters of Danaus, King of Egypt, who have escaped into Argos, fleeing the fifty cousins who seek them in marriage. These Suppliant Maidens are the Chorus. Their leader and Danaus recount their flight and implore the gods for a favorable outcome. The King of Argos hears their petition for protection, hesitates, from fear of offending the gods or his people, goes out to consultations. Word is brought that decrees have been passed welcoming the fugitives. The ship of the pursuers is sighted and the Egyptian Herald comes to try to drive the Maidens back to the shore. But the King of Argos has arranged to take them within the city walls, and they file out of the orchestra, jubilant, going to the sought-for safety and protection. There is indeed action here in a small way —but what simplicity and slowness, what lack of suspense as compared with *Œdipus the King!* The values are largely in the lyric portions.

In the later plays of Æschylus there is growing dramatic elaboration, increase of conflict, greater theatricality. One of the finest of the tragedies, to be sure, *Prometheus Bound* is very static: Prometheus is chained to a rock, in the first scene, as punishment for giving fire to mortals, and the rest of the play consists of his dialogue with the Chorus and successive characters; till at the end he "vanishes." But conflict is implicit in the situation of a minor god who has defied Zeus. We may read here, indeed, a drama not without parallels to *Job*. And while the almost actionless play is a complete drama, the reader should remember that in the time of Æschylus each play was part of a related trilogy or tetralogy, and was presented with the others on a single programme.

But in the *Agamemnon* Æschylus has come to full-plotted and highly theatrical composition. The note of impending doom is sounded in the first speeches, and there is immediate joining of action. Clytemnestra has been unfaithful and now Agamemnon is coming home. As the action develops toward its climax and catastrophe, the speeches are long, the descriptive passages many. But here already is Greek tragic drama developed into its characteristic largeness, majesty, and inevitability. Nor is the poetry as such less telling; Clytemnestra is speaking, before her returned King, Agamemnon, who has given no sign that he knows her guilt:

> Ye Elders, Councils of the Argive name
> Here present, I will no more hold it shame
> To lay my passion bare before men's eyes.
> There comes a time to a woman when fear dies
> Forever. None hath taught me. None could tell,
> Save me, the weight of years intolerable,

I lived while this man lay at Ilion.
That any woman thus could sit alone
In a half-empty house, with no man near,
Makes her half-blind with dread! And in her ear
Always some voice of wrath; now messengers
Of evil; now not so . . .
   Aye, many a time my heart broke, and the noose
Of death had got me; but they cut me loose.
It was those voices always in mine ear.

.   .   .   .

From all which stress delivered and free-souled
I greet my lord . . .

Agamemnon is the first of the plays forming the *Oresteia*
trilogy; and there are many who hold the opinion that this group
not only marks Æschylus' greatest accomplishment but also the
supreme achievement in Greek tragic drama. There is an immensity of outline, a sweeping majesty of action, that is hardly
to be matched in the later annals of the theatre; and with it a
Miltonic greatness in the poetic garment, an austere, aloof beauty
of language. But one may still find Sophocles the better craftsman, and Euripides the more sympathetic dramatist of human
characters. Æschylus lived in a golden time, reflected perhaps a
fineness and a simple dignity that were implicit in Greek life
around him. There was a kindly faith then, linked with high
purpose and a splendor of soul. Sophocles reflects more the
polish of art in a later softer time; and in Euripides there is a
restlessness, a questioning, that seems to grow out of the early
decadence of Greek life.

Sophocles marked progress toward both stricter dramatic intensity and greater freedom of dialogue. He went on toward a
more compact and articulated play structure; and he lost a little
of Æschylus' austere beauty of line in favor of a freer, sweeter
language. All this change is in perfect keeping with what we
know of his life: that he was orderly, that he was universally
loved for his good nature and sweetness, that he put great store by
the graces of life. A nobility and stateliness of character were his;
but he could not be so perfectly the flower of the Periclean Age,
were not these attributes attuned more to the love of man and
less to an Æschylean magnifying of the gods.

Sophocles was born in 495 B.C. He died in 406 B.C., and during his lifetime had written nearly a hundred plays. Seven remain with us in complete form today. He is reputed to have given up acting at an early age because his voice was weak; but of course he " produced " his plays as well as writing them. It was he who introduced the third actor into Greek tragedy.

As to the qualities of his playwriting, we may be content with *Œdipus the King* as a characteristic example. We have seen how perfectly this built up, in dramatic suspense and intensity, from opening to close; how the order of unfoldment is consummately handled for the holding of the spectator's attention; how each bit is tied in to the main structure, each scene, each thought, each lyric contributing to the stream of living action. Where Æschylus had hewn out gigantic designs — a bit " mad " he was, they say, when he came to the writing of a play — leaving rough edges for the sake of the larger impression, Sophocles was the perfect craftsman, gaining first his proportions, then his finer adjustments, and over all a harmony of expression. Unity, symmetry, convergence, order — these he understood beyond criticism. No one in the whole history of the theatre has surpassed him as theatric technician while still compassing great beauty. (As mere skilled workmen, the " well-made-play " people of the nineteenth century may have gone farther in building a perfectly articulated play-frame, but they put nothing in that frame; and the realistic playwrights build as skilfully for sensation and shock — but there is in them little of serenity or high beauty.)

Œdipus the King is usually considered the masterpiece among Sophocles' work; and the excerpts I have quoted may stand for the quality of his poetic genius — as the outline must stand here for example of his play structure. Still it should be noted that others may prefer his *Antigone* or *Œdipus at Colonus* or *Ajax* or *Electra*. In the end, whichever plays one reads or sees produced, one will be stirred by the spectacle of man sorely tried in the grip of Destiny, man brave in the adventure of life, with a little of the divinity of those gods who make of him a plaything. And one should see always, in the mind's eye, the beauty of the Greek bowl-theatre, of the majestic acting, of the rhythmic Chorus movements; and should hear, in the mind's ear, the sonorities

Two of the great Greek theatres as they exist today. Above, the Theatre of Dionysus at Athens, the most famous in all history. Below, the theatre at Epidaurus. The Theatre of Dionysus was reconstructed during the Roman period, and therefore includes a raised stage and a semi-circular orchestra; but in the Epidaurus building there is the full round dancing circle typical of the Fifth Century B.C. [From Alinari photographs.]

A Roman tragic actor. Note the mask which he has just removed. [From an Alinari photograph of the Roman fresco now in the National Museum, Naples.]

of poetic lines declaimed, chanted, in recitative. For these are theatre works, not just magnificent poetic stories.

He who long ago wrote, "I laud Æschylus, I read Euripides," indicated in a few words a difference that scholars have discussed in hundreds of weighty volumes. Æschylus probably has suffered later from the very splendor of his works; Euripides has gained from the intimacy and simple humanity of his.

Euripides was born in 480 B.C., only fifteen years after Sophocles; but he is invariably tagged as the representative of a different age — has even been called " the first modern." Some put down to temperament his great divergence from the traditional line, poetically, dramatically, as a thinker. Born less nobly than his great predecessors, he was intended first for an athlete, then seems to have tried painting. But he turned out a student and dramatist — he produced his first play at twenty-five — and always he lived apart from civic and social interests. His predilections were for meditation rather than for a part in the life of the times.

If we were to study carefully the history of the period, we should discover many background reasons why he portrayed human beings rather than human symbols in his dramas, why he ascribed malignant as well as divine traits to the gods, why his work ended often with a questioning of life. For just then a new skepticism was creeping over Hellas. The unquestioning prostration of man before fate, the blind glorification of the gods, was no longer demanded. There is ample reason to believe that Euripides had little belief in those gods; still he was forced to include them in his plays, for theatre production and theatre-going were a form of religious exercise. Well — then he would show the gods as they are. And humans too.

Another inference or conjecture is that the audiences he catered to were less cultivated than of old. He must touch them more closely to hold their interest. They no longer listened for the traditional beauties of the chanted word, for the interpolated pæans to gods; they no longer counted beauty of eurhythmic movement a prime ingredient of drama. They must see, hear, and suffer with beings like themselves.

And so Euripides humanized the drama. Perhaps after all he did it out of the pity in his own heart; but there it is, a drama throbbing with human sorrow, with sympathy. It is no part of our present plan to inquire into the æsthetics of the matter: whether the austerity and elevation of earlier tragedy are preferable to that which is characterized rather by pathos. Euripides has been severely censured by purists — and yet most people, while they praise Æschylus, read Euripides. His works are closer to us.

He introduced some expedients that are easily challenged. His prologues seem sometimes like too-easy solutions of the problem of putting background facts before audiences. And his *deus ex machina,* brought in arbitrarily to solve the knotty problem of the drama, is clearly illogical, a trick. And there is not here Sophocles' sense of proportion and harmony, nor his inevitability.

Still, *popularly,* Euripides was the favorite Athenian dramatist at the end of his life and after. He stirred up more of criticism and opposition, but his questioning of gods and his portrayal of pitiable men were eagerly awaited and hailed. It is easy to see how *The Trojan Women,* picturing terribly the horrors of war, and the sorrows following thereon, would move a Greek audience — as, indeed, it has moved many of us in very recent times. His introduction of love, a terrible illicit love, in *Hippolytus,* would startle the Athenian audience because no such human story had ever been acted out before in a theatre. And his study of *Medea,* the spurned strong woman, her love turned to hate, murdering her own children to have revenge on her lord — there had never been a character portrait like that before.

Still, Athens as a whole was not ready for playwrights who publicly criticized war, who showed up the gods as petty and abominable, who fought for the underdog, no matter who was thereby wounded. The judges at the contests awarded him only five prizes — out of ninety-two plays presented. And finally the uneasiness over his unorthodoxy crystallized into a decree of exile. Even the greatest of dramatists were not safe from the fickle censure of the volatile audiences that gathered in the Theatre of Dionysus. Once spectators had thought that Æschylus revealed too much of the secrets of religious mysteries, in a play production, and to save his life he had been forced to take refuge at the altar of Dionysus in the centre of the orchestra, an inviolate sanctuary. (It is said that when he was tried later for the offence, it was his fame as a gallant soldier, not as a dramatist, that won his acquittal.) The earlier tragedian, Phrynichus, in a play called *The Capture of Miletus,* had so stirred bitter recollections in the hearts of the spectators that he was fined a thousand drachmas, while a law was passed forbidding further dramas on the subject. Euripides had seen his plays stormily received more than once. And finally he was driven from Athens altogether. His services to his city were not at an end, for it is recorded that the people were wont to sing his choruses in the street, and that when the Spartans were about to burn Athens they were suddenly reminded by a snatch of song that this was Euripides' city and refrained.

His last play — not quite finished, indeed — was written during exile; and to the fact have been attributed certain sentiments in it, and an increased tendency to brood on the problems of life. It is from this drama, *The Bacchæ,* that I shall take those quotations which will, I hope, indicate how Euripides carried on the noble tradition, and how he departed from it to attain to other excellencies. He made his lyric choruses such gem-like insets as no poet had achieved before him:

CHORUS OF MAIDENS

Will they ever come to me, ever again,
   The long long dances,
On through the dark till the dim stars wane?
Shall I feel the dew on my throat, and the stream
Of wind in my hair? Shall our white feet gleam
   In the dim expanses?
Oh, feet of a fawn to the greenwood fled,
   Alone in the grass and the loveliness;
Leap of the hunted, no more in dread,
   Beyond the snares and the deadly press:
Yet a voice still in the distance sounds,
A voice and a fear and a haste of hounds;
O wildly laboring, fiercely fleet,
   Onward yet by river and glen . . .

LEADER

Happy he, on the weary sea
Who hath fled the tempest and won the haven.
   Happy who so hath risen, free,

Above his striving. For strangely graven
  Is the orb of life, that one and another
  In gold and power may outpass his brother.
  And men in their millions float and flow
And seethe with a million hopes as leaven;
  And they win their Will, or they miss their Will.
  And the hopes are dead or are pined for still;
    But whoe'er can know,
    As the long days go,
That to live is happy, hath found his Heaven!

But he was no less master of the line that carried along the action. We have seen in *Œdipus the King* how the murder, suicide,
or other violence too sensational for human eyes is accomplished
offstage — an invariable rule in Greek tragedy — and how a
messenger recounts the event (often with the most moving effectiveness). In *The Bacchæ* the Messenger is telling how the luckless Pentheus intruded on the Bacchantes:

Then came the Voice again. And when they knew
Their God's clear call, old Cadmus' royal brood,
Up, like wild pigeons startled in a wood,
On flying feet they came, his mother blind
Agâvê, and her sisters, and behind
All the wild crowd, more deeply maddened then,
Through the angry rocks and torrent-tossing glen,
Until they spied him in the dark pine-tree.
            . . . 'Twas his mother stood
O'er him, first priestess of those rites of blood.
He tore the coif, and from his head away
Flung it, that she might know him, and not slay
To her own misery. He touched the wild
Cheek, crying: " Mother, it is I, thy child,
Thy Pentheus, born thee in Echîon's hall!

Have mercy, Mother! Let it not befall
Through sin of mine that thou shouldst slay thy son! "
    But she, with lips a-foam and eyes that run
Like leaping fire, with thoughts that ne'er should be
On earth, possessed by Bacchios utterly,
Stays not nor hears. Round his left arm she put
Both hands, set hard against his side her foot,
Drew . . . and the shoulder severed! . . .

It is fitting perhaps that our brief study of the great Greek dramatists should end with the closing lines of Euripides' last play; for they are spoken by the Chorus, that typically Greek theatric "character," and they show how the religious-fateful spirit had persisted through the golden and silver ages — and they occur in a play which goes back for its subject-matter to the legends of Dionysus, to whose glory the theatre had been created:

CHORUS

There be many shapes of mystery.
And many things God makes to be,
   Past hope or fear.
And the end men looked for cometh not,
And a path is there where no man thought.
   So hath it fallen here.

Or is it better to end finally on the *human* note of Euripides' work, as a foreshadowing of the future? For he rebelliously tinged high art with realism. Mrs. Browning summed up our love of him:

Our Euripides, the human,
   With his droppings of warm tears,
And his touches of things common
   Till they rose to touch the spheres!

WHEN one knows the distinctiveness of Greek tragedy, and has tasted the works of Æschylus, Sophocles, and Euripides — and has met Aristophanes in comedy — one has the essentials of the Greek drama. Reserving, then, all consideration of comedy for another chapter, we have only the lesser facts about the tragic theatre to explore: the changes in the " playhouse " and in methods of production during the later periods and decline of Greek drama.

There were a great many tragic poets,[1] to be sure, besides those

---

[1] It is curious that there should be no comprehensive and readable book in English about the Greek theatre, in the inclusive sense, treating both drama and stage conventions, to which the student can be referred. The best brief manual is Lionel D. Barnett's *The Greek Drama*, in the *Temple Primers* series (London, 1900). *The Greek Theatre and Its Drama*, by Roy C. Flickinger (3d edition, Chicago, 1926), is perhaps fullest and most accurate, but it is discouragingly cautious and disputative. Even more involved in controversy, but important regarding the origins of the Greek theatre, is *Dithyramb, Tragedy and Comedy*, by A. W. Pickard-Cambridge (Oxford, 1927). The most straightforward treatment still is A. E. Haigh's *The Attic Theatre* (3d revised edition, Oxford, 1907);

three who stand before the world as the Greek masters. Some
are known only because their names are chronicled as contestants
in the annual festivals, others from chance references or from extracts quoted by later grammarians. But the general reader, even
the student of theatre history if he is not specializing on the Greek
period, need not burden his memory with further names. He

The stage building at Oropus, as conjecturally restored by E. R. Fiechter.
[From Fiechter's *Die Baugeschichtliche Entwicklung des Antiken
Theaters.*]

should know merely that the great tragedies were endlessly imitated. For five or six centuries the contests were continued, and
new plays were offered as late as the Roman Hadrian's reign in
the second century A.D. After the great fifth century B.C., revivals
of the early masterpieces became commoner, and in the third
century customary. As time went on, the festivals of Dionysus

but in mentioning it one must add that the author had not the benefit of knowledge
gained by recent excavators, and describes the typical Greek theatre as having platform
stage, painted settings, etc. The most readable brief treatment is James Turney Allen's
Stage Antiquities of the Greeks and Romans (New York, 1927), though consideration
of the drama as such is almost excluded. Of books treating primarily the literature of the
Greek theatre, the most useful are perhaps *Greek Tragedy*, by Gilbert Norwood (London,
1920), *The Tragic Drama of the Greeks*, by A. E. Haigh (Oxford, 1896), and *Athenian
Tragedy*, by Thomas Dwight Goodell (New Haven, 1920). I am indebted, for information, to all of these books. Of translations of Greek tragedies, those of Professor Gilbert
Murray are to be recommended beyond all others. If they depart occasionally from a
strict transcription of the original texts, they more than compensate in their authentic
poetic loveliness.

in other cities or towns drew on the treasury of Athenian drama, and the more significant plays were thus shown time and again. As early as 472 B.C., Æschylus presented at Syracuse the plays with which he had won the tragedy contest at Athens the year before.

Ultimately troupes of players went out to provincial celebrations to present the more " popular " dramas. These " artists of Dionysus " may be considered the first players' guild — or " actors' union." When the Roman theatre had been securely founded, the Greek tragedies were given in Rome, both in the original tongue and in translation; and ultimately the plays of the master dramatists were heard through the vast territory of the new Roman Empire as well as in the old Greek colonial cities. In Athens itself productions are recorded as late as the fifth century A.D.

Thus within a century of the birth of drama, Athens had claimed a group of dramatists who stand in the small company of stage immortals: Greek life had come to full expression in the religious-artistic compositions of three playwrights, in whose work is the very flowering of Hellenic civilization and genius; whereas the Greek theatre for eight or nine centuries after their era subsisted on dramas wholly inferior or on revivals of the works of these masters.

The Greek physical playhouse, however, continued its development throughout the decadent period of drama, toward that Greek-Roman form which was a direct forerunner of the Renaissance theatre, and unmistakably ancestor of the theatre of today. In the golden age of Greek playwriting, it had been a comparatively simple arrangement of ringed seats, flat space for choral movement and acting, and a low porticoed *skene* at the back. The auditorium and *skene* were separated by wide entries, and the whole layout had an openness which was never again to be characteristic of theatre building.

Gradually, however, the dancing-space, the orchestra, was contracted, and the stage building brought in closer, enlarged, made more important. Finally the top of the portico became a platform stage, added to the orchestra for acting, and behind it the second story of the *skene* began to be elaborated toward that immense stage wall which is so typical of Greek-Roman and Roman theatres.

There is no example that can be called the typical Greek or the typical Roman playhouse; designing of the buildings was always subject to local conditions and to changing demands of the play-producers. But when the platform stage had been added, the theatre exhibited those features considered fundamental to theatre building in all later eras; features whose arrangement in relation to each other determine the world's general grouping of theatres

The theatre at Ephesus in Hellenic times, as reconstructed by Fiechter. Note that the orchestra is still large, but that the platform stage is added. A transition example, between true Greek and true Roman types.

into named types. The auditorium (*theatron*) or place for seeing; the *orchestra,* at first the place for dancing and acting, then dividing that function with the stage, and ultimately to be contracted and absorbed into the auditorium; the *stage,* at first a mere platform for lifting the actors into view, but in later times to become the floor of a stage-box; and the *scene,* at first a stage building beside the dancing circle (the word *skene* meant merely hut or tent), then more strictly the wall behind the platform stage, neutrally architectural but increasingly ornamental. (When the stage is finally pushed through an opening in the wall, the term "scene" will be transferred to the picture surrounding the acting space, within the stage-box — but that will be long after classic times.)

There was so little " scenery " in the Greek orchestra, or on the Greek stage, that more than brief mention of the subject would be unwarranted. For a very long time scholars took for granted that the Greeks utilized painted settings. But no contemporary descriptions survive, and most scholars today agree that conjec-

Reconstruction of the Roman theatre at Aspendus, showing the true Roman bowl-like form. Note the contracted orchestra, raised stage, and decorated stage wall.
[From Durm's *Baukunst der Römer*.]

ture and misreading of vague references alone bolstered the idea of elaborate Greek scenery. If painted settings existed, it seems likely that they were merely architectural façades painted in to save the greater expense of building a composition of columns, pilasters, niches, etc. In other words the background remained wholly neutral and conventional. There was no attempt at illusion in setting. The poet's words accomplished any necessary shift in *milieu*.

In the decadent Greek theatre, when the influence of Roman love of spectacle had crept in, the story may have been different. In the same way stage machinery for " effects" doubtless multiplied in Roman times. And there is evidence that at least one machine, a crane for the ascent or descent of the gods or humans, was introduced quite early. This was apparently rigged in such a way that an actor could be lifted from the orchestra or stage-platform to the top of the scene-building. It is supposed that Euripides utilized the device — whence the phrase *deus ex machina* — but it is in Aristophanes that the chief evidence is found. It is obvious that the comedy-writers would grasp at the opportunities for fun-making in any such crude and mechanical aid to tragic drama; and we are not surprised, in *The Clouds,* to find Socrates suspended in a basket half-way between heaven and earth, reading philosophy.

There is less evidence about a machine called the *eccyclema,* though more need for it, judging by the internal evidence of the plays. It is supposed to have been a revolving platform, designed to be swung out through the central portal of the *skene,* on which actors could be shown in " tableau." In tragic drama the murder scene in Æschylus' *Agamemnon* is usually instanced: the slaying is, of course, committed offstage, and then Clytemnestra is shown standing over the dead bodies of Agamemnon and Cassandra. This group is conjectured to have been wheeled out suddenly by means of the sliding or revolving platform.

Just as all these matters of playhouse form, scenery, and machines have been subjects for controversy, so the question of the mode of acting in the great fifth century has been debated, cursed about, and endlessly written about in recent years. And here again opinion has radically changed within the decade. For it turns out that evidence about the cothurnus-boot, about extravagantly stuffed-out costumes, and about huge masks, belongs all to a later time. It now seems likely that the human figure was little exaggerated in size in the Æschylus-Euripides period, though it was richly costumed, and that the masks were not then the grotesque and high-built affairs pictured in late Greek and Roman paintings and sculptures. Acting was doubtless artificial and declamatory, but we may best imagine it as stately, free-

moving if slow-moving, and not at all incapable of naturally
affecting moments. The mask (necessary because an actor often
impersonated several characters successively in one play, if for no
other more subtle reason) made facial play impossible.

The mask was a convention, a symbol or an abstraction of the
emotion chiefly associated with the character. One who has
studied masks may feel sure that a certain range of expression
is possible, through the turning of the mask to catch the light in
different ways, through the movement of the head, etc. But the
adoption of the device is a deliberate limitation of intimate human expression in one direction to gain broader, perhaps more
god-like values in another. We may vision the Greek actor developing a language of gesture and movement far more expressive than any on the stages of today; and in our imaginative ears
we may hear him speaking, chanting, singing, through a range of
" recitative " quite beyond the capabilities of modern players.
There is evidence enough that acting was an art which exacted
lifelong study and devotion, and that shades of expressiveness were
diligently sought after. Not realistic shades, to be sure, but emotional nuances within the conventions of mask, harmonious
movement, and designed voice-pattern.

Acting had become a recognized profession even in the time of
Æschylus, and grew in importance through the fifth century.
After the decline of playwriting, acting was still further elevated
as a separate art, until the contests of actors came to be considered
more important than those of the dramatists. The Actors' Guild
became a powerful economic and social organization, and members enjoyed special privileges, as " religious " workers.

As the drama declined, the Chorus receded in importance. It
had been the connecting link between pre-theatric revels and full
literary drama. The interludes of music, poetry, and " dance "
that it provided were an enrichment of the dramatic design
through the time of Euripides. The tragic tension seemed to demand these let-downs — like our entr'actes, but with an added
value. The Chorus moved in procession or mass formation,
rhythmically, harmoniously, like a visual re-enforcement of the
meaning of the choral odes. The words were chanted or sung.
In sense they were a comment on the action to come or a sup-

plication to the gods, or a lyric decoration. Throughout the great period they added to the emotion aroused by the action; or perhaps it is better to say that they deepened the emotion while offering relief from the stormier heights of the action. We have seen how in Æschylus' first play the Chorus claimed attention more than half the time — survival from the period when the drama formed the interludes, and the dancing-singing the main design. We have seen too how Euripides imbedded the most beautiful lyrics in his plays, for the Chorus; but we should note that these were put in more like added decoration than had been the case with Æschylus and Sophocles. And indeed, one infers that Euripides added odes as a matter of custom and tradition, without any conviction that they belonged to his dramatic structure which unfolded the fortunes of human beings. From that time the Chorus was unnecessary to drama. The Chorus Leader had been one of the chief actors ever since Thespis added the first player to bandy words with him. But now we shall never meet him again — although in later-day expositors, prologue-speakers, *premières danseuses,* and end-men, we may find certain of his duties performed.

Some pages back mention was made of the Choregus, the financier back of play-production. Athens developed a system under which a wealthy citizen could be called on to produce the play-programme of a certain poet, bearing most of the expense of the performance. If his poet was successful in winning the contest, the Choregus was crowned and shared the honor with his dramatist. He helped the dramatist to pick the actors and chorus members, paid salaries to cast, musicians, trainers, etc., and provided costumes. But as he was thus sharing with the actual theatre-workers in religious service, he seems to have been content.

The touch of the ridiculous that always followed the sublime experience of the tragedy productions in Athens is to be found in the satyr-plays. Each programme on each of the three days dedicated to the tragic contests included three tragedies and a satyr-drama. Thus all the great dramatists were forced to write these burlesque and apparently licentious pieces. Comedy had long ago gone its separate way and had crystallized into a set form. Perhaps neither tragedy nor comedy seemed to the Athenians to carry on directly the traditions of the old Dionysian phallic-revels. At any rate, the satyr-drama survived as a separate entity through the entire fifth century. The invariable central feature was the Chorus of Satyrs, hairy fellows with horns, tails, and phalluses, who could be relied upon to convulse any audience by their antics. For the rest there seems to have been the strangest mixture of heroics and buffoonery. Sometimes the tragedies would be followed by one of these ludicrous burlesques in which the very same protagonists, heroes and kings, would be seen from a comic angle, brought down to the grotesque and often indecent by-play of rough-and-tumble farceurs.

Masks for satyr-plays. [From *Dissertatio de Larvis Scenicis*, by F. Ficoronius.]

Today the juxtaposition of the two extremes, the noblest tragedy the world has ever known and farces physically so licentious that we have no parallel to them in the present world theatre, seems inexplicable unless, perchance, we remember that Dionysus had two sides, that if the divine ecstasy that he evoked might well lead over from song, dance, and music to serene drama, the wildness of him might lead away in another direction to loose dance and mimicry. The satyr-drama was the old phallic dance — so appropriate to the god of wine and of fruitfulness — made dramatic but not elevated. The Athenians were loath to leave out of the Dionysia anything so perfectly expressive of that so-beloved god. Besides, the god himself might not like it if his satyrs were discarded.

Roman tragedy was never more than an adulteration of the Greek. The only name that is accounted worth remembering out of the thirty-odd known Latin tragedy-writers is that of

Seneca; and his are the only plays preserved. They have achieved world-wide fame less for inherent virtues than for the influence they exerted in later eras as models for successive groups of Neo-classicists.

Seneca lived in a time when simplicity and serene splendor had gone out of the Western world. In the first century of the Christian era, in the reigns of Caligula and Claudius and Nero, a man who was politician, Senator, Consul, lover to empresses, philosopher, and a prolific writer in many fields, would have little chance to compass the high beauty of Æschylus or the brooding human pathos of Euripides. There was brilliancy in the time and a brilliancy in Seneca — but it was wholly a surface quality. He rewrote in drama the old tragic stories of Œdipus and Medea and Agamemnon; but the Greek elevation of feeling is gone, sincerity has fled, poetry is lost in rhetoric. Life has gone out of tragedy; the characters are vehicles to carry moral ideas, the action is violent, the verse is shaped to the uses of exaggerated declamation.

This is florid, even dull art, full of bombast and mannerism; and yet for a period covering centuries it was esteemed as the supreme body of tragedy in the world's dramatic literature, above Æschylus, Sophocles, and Euripides. It is doubtful whether these rhetorical tragedies were ever produced in the "regular," the popular theatres at Rome: those turbulent audiences would hardly relish the long didactic speeches, the overload of ornament and the slow action. But there they are, a curiosity of the world stage, important because Italian and French critics of the Renaissance almost persuaded the whole Western world that tragedy must remain Senecan for all time.

Tragedy was never again to be quite as monumental, as serenely splendid, as soul-cleansing, as it was in the fifth century before Christ. A further extension of *humanity* is to grace it in Shakespeare's time, and gloriously fine poetry; but there are those who will tell you that in turning away from Greek tragedy we are setting our backs upon the finest that the tragic stage has known.

CHAPTER IV

Comedy: Greece and Rome

IF WE had been in the audience at the Theatre of Dionysus on that spring day in 423 B.C. when an actor impersonating Socrates was suspended in a basket midway between the earth of the orchestra and the heaven of the proscenium-top, we might have found in the episode a key to the understanding of a broader truth about Greek comedy; in short, that this was a drama of action and of situation, not of character-conflict. If we had heard declaimed those lines in the play that portrayed the great Socrates as little better than a quack-philosopher and mischief-maker, we might have inferred, quite justly, that caricature and personalities made up a generous part of what little " characterization " there was in Old Comedy. (If a none-too-well-authenticated legend is accurate, we might also have seen the real Socrates — so like a comic actor, with his pot-belly and his jovial satyr-face — rise up among us and stand for the crowd to look at, to show that he too enjoyed his caricature.)

That same day we should have witnessed, too, a production of *The Wine-Flagon* by Cratinus, which won the prize over Aristophanes' *The Clouds;* a play doubtless well suited to the Dionysian Festival, in which the respective virtues of wine-bibbers and water-drinkers were (none too solemnly) explored. We may imagine how the fun of drunkenness was capitalized there. The following year we could have witnessed at the Lenæa a production of Aristophanes' *The Wasps,* and at other times *The Birds* and *The Frogs,* each with its Chorus appropriately dressed, and coached to all the comic antics that could be built on the imitation of wasp and bird and frog; from which we might have been convinced that comedy, even after Euripides' death, had not advanced

69

so very far from the old masquerade processionals of vulgar
phallic-revellers. In these several plays, moreover, we might have
marked in the dialogue not a little of ribald jest and downright
dirty allusion; for vomitings and bedbugs and manure-heaps and
worse supplied some of the motives now bound up with custard-
pies, bladders, and banana-peels, and the mention of mothers-in-
law; and the triangle relationship was handled not with delicacy
but with Rabelaisian heartiness.

Out of such materials was the comedy of the fifth century compounded, with little continuity, less inevitability, and no serious
character-drawing. From which you will judge, dear reader, that
the Athenians did not have " high " comedy.

If we distinguish " high tragedy " from a less elevated sort, we
must grant that the Greeks were masters beyond all others. They
lift the reader or spectator, they kindle the imagination, open the
gates to a divine pity, light up the soul, exalt the emotions in
sorrow — and leave one cleansed. With orderly action and noble
poetry they lead us through from a beginning expectancy to a
radiant satisfaction. Someone has said that any petty playwright
can agitate the soul, but only a master of tragedy can exalt it —
and the saying is one to be remembered as we progress from Greek
drama to modern realistic play; and exaltation is the key-note of
fifth century tragic drama. This was indeed " high " tragedy.

But in comedy, where we are told that the test of the best is
" thoughtful laughter," and that seriously important comedy
grows out of logical character-development, we can only mark
the Greek sort as *low*. It never in all its history rose to unity
of feeling, sustained satire, or sympathetic tilting at the foibles of
human character. So far as we know it at first hand, in surviving
texts and fragments, and in pictures, it retained the more vulgar,
violent, and farcical elements out of the fathering comus-revels.
During the " great " period of Athens it paralleled modern burlesque and musical comedy closer than modern legitimate comedy.

Remembering the singing, joshing bands of revellers that used
to celebrate Dionysus at the seasonal festivals, bantering back and
forth, carrying the wine-jars and the phallus, dressed up in outlandish costumes and masks, we may see how these marchers
became a " Chorus "; and how, either through a leader stepping

out to impersonate or a clown or mime joining the group, comic repartee was born. The dressed-up revellers were common to many festivals in many places, but somewhere their impromptu celebration — or masquerade — came to be called a " comus "; and when the dramatic element had entered, the name " comedy " — comus-ode or " revel-song " — was passed on to designate amusing drama for all time.

The roots of *Athenian* comedy are obscure; the comus-performances seem to have been brought to Athens in the first

Performers in a Comus. [From a vase drawing reproduced in *The Greek Drama,* by Lionel D. Barnett.]

half of the sixth century, but it is uncertain which villages or districts gave this or that ingredient or influence. It is only certain that phallic processions were at the source of it, that the more obvious costume elements — disguises as birds, animals, etc. — and the masks persisted in the comedy-choruses, that the celebration found its way from the sacred groves and the town streets into the theatre; and that there the outward form already assumed by tragedy (dialogue with choral and lyric interludes and dances) influenced it toward the structure we find in Aristophanes' plays. The actor, some say, was a Dorian clown; others, that he simply developed out of being the wittiest and loudest shouter among the revellers.

Before Aristophanes, who we may feel was coarse enough, in all conscience, the Dionysian comedy went through some sort of refining process. The Chorus was organized until it had the set number of twenty-four members; a loose continuity was adopted, from prologue to *exodus,* with action-scenes and lyrics alternating between; and a point was established at which a contest or debate was added, and another at which a *parabasis* or author's speech was set in. Plot, or something approaching it, was introduced. As the dramatic scenes gained in relative importance, over mere processional and song, sketches and "turns" like those in our vaudeville were increasingly added, or travesties and comic dialogues like those in our revues. Until, when "contests" in comedy were instituted, with three dramatists each offering a group of three compositions, the thing now known as " Old Comedy " was as much a set form as was composed choral tragedy.

Even before Aristophanes, in the works of Cratinus and Eupolis, comedy came to have purpose. It might be political satire, or travesty on a literary or social figure, or ridicule of a cult — and in this direction the violence of the attack, the intensely personal invective, the wildness of the charges, seem to us to go beyond the bounds of reason. Of course this was understood to be farce and foolery, where truth was stood on its head. The gods themselves were caricatured; and a demi-god like Heracles might afford great fun when brought on drunk. But constantly through the framework of satire and purposeful ridicule obtruded those older buffoon elements, the grotesque parades, the licentious dances, the mere monkey-shines. And — sometimes these obtrusive and little-related elements or snatches of satire were lifted to the realm of stirring poetry or imaginative incident.

It is there that Aristophanes comes in. It is not the " thought " or the incisive parody in his works that is generally important — indeed he shows himself a good deal of a reactionary in his plays, sighing vaguely for the good old days, and damning progressive tendencies along with the precious posing cults. But he was a poet, and his lyrics are often of surpassing charm, and his imagination often carried him out on amazing flights; he had, moreover, a masterly touch at light verse, wherein he seasoned with wit the flowing lines and passing pictures. He by no means escaped the " gigantic indecency of Old Comedy," and his graceful verse turns easily into channels of brutal caricature and heavy buffoonery. But by grace of a poet's gifts he rose above all his fellow dramatists in his own time, and has been a touchstone down the ages. " Aristophanic " is the term we still use for witty and biting comedy clothed in free-flowing verse.

It happens that eleven of Aristophanes' plays are the only complete comedies that have survived to us from Greek literature, out of thousands written by scores of authors. He is credited with more than fifty plays in all. He lived from about 448 to 385 B.C.

As an example of the structure of Old Comedy, we may take *The Wasps,* which Aristophanes brought out at the Lenæa in 422, probably receiving the first prize for it. The immediate

Roman comic actors. [From Ficoronius.]

subject-matter is the Athenian jury-system, but the attack is aimed at Cleon, the demagogue to whom the " jurors " were politically bound. Philocleon is an inveterate jury-server; but Bdelycleon is trying to break up his mania by keeping Philocleon imprisoned in his house. The door is guarded by two slaves, but the prisoner almost escapes by one ruse or another, crawling out windows or chimneys or along the roof, or hanging under the belly of a donkey. He is aided by the Chorus, his fellow jury-maniacs, who are symbolically dressed as Wasps. The action is interrupted by the " contest," a debate for and against the dignity and importance of jury-sitting. The Chorus is convinced by Bdelycleon's arguments, but Philocleon is heartbroken at the prospect of giving up

his pleasures of the court-room. So Bdelycleon arranges for him
to have a trial at home. A dog is tried for stealing a cheese; and
is acquitted by a trick, to the horror of Philocleon. The *parabasis*
is now introduced, in which Aristophanes takes the audience to
task, reviews his life as playwright and explains points about the
present play. The chief characters go off to a feast and drinking
party. After a choral interlude Philocleon comes back drunk.
He is pursued by other guests who bring charges of abuse against
him; and particularly he is threatened with action for carrying
away the flute-girl from the feast. But now Philocleon believes
no longer in law-courts and juries.

PHILOCLEON

Yah! Hah! summon and cite!
The obsolete notion! Don't you know
I'm sick of the names of your suits and claims.
  Faugh! Faugh! Pheugh!
  Here's my delight!
Away with the verdict-box! . . .
                              Mount up, my dear.
See now, how cleverly I fetched you off,
A wanton hussy, flirting with the guests.
You owe me, child, some gratitude for that . . .
Be a good girl and don't be disobliging,
And when my son is dead, I'll ransom you,
And make you an honest woman. For indeed
I'm not yet master of my own affairs.
I am so young and kept so very strict.
My son's my guardian, such a cross-grained man,
A cummin-splitting, mustard-scraping fellow . . .

BDELYCLEON

You! there! You there! You old lascivious dotard!
Enamored, eh? Ay, of a fine ripe coffin.
Oh, by Apollo, you shall smart for this!

PHILOCLEON

Dear, dear, how keen to taste a suit in pickle!

BDELYCLEON

No quizzing, sir, when you have filched away
The flute-girl from our party.

PHILOCLEON
Eh? What? flute-girl?
You're out of your mind, or out of your grave, or something.

And so on. One of them claims this is the flute-girl beside them,
the other that it's only a torch; they examine the girl to make
sure. They set to dancing, and the Chorus ends the action by
dancing out of the orchestra after Philocleon, singing:

Come draw we aside, and leave them a wide, a roomy and peaceable
    exercise ground,
That before us therein like tops they may spin, revolving and whirling
    and twirling around . . .
On, on, in mazy circles; hit your stomach with your heel;
Fling legs aloft to heaven, as like spinning tops you wheel . . .
For never yet, I warrant, has an actor till today
Led out a chorus, dancing, at the ending of the play.

There are other comedies of Aristophanes that would illustrate
better his imaginative reach — *The Birds* and *The Frogs* in particular; and it would be unfair to go on without quoting a few
lines of his more felicitous choral lyrics. In *The Peace* there is
the understanding eulogy of country life:

Ah, there's nothing half so sweet as when the seed is in the ground,
God a gracious rain is sending, and a neighbor saunters round . . .

Then we'll sit and drink together,
God the while refreshing, blessing
All the labors of our hands.

Oh, to watch the grape of Lemnos
Swelling out its purple skin,
When the merry little warblings
Of the Chirruper begin . . .

One might quote almost endlessly from the pleasant jingles in
the eleven plays, and vary the fare acceptably with a serious ode
here, a serenade there, or a rollicking song. That would indicate
the comic richness — and quite rightly suggest that the richness
is patchy. But only the reading of complete plays can convey the
variety and spice that kept the festival audiences in gales of laughter. The very freedom of the play form permitted an exuberance
and an extravagant fancy seldom again enjoyed in comedy. The

slap-stick elements later descended into farce, while the poetic felicity and the satirical elements were carried up and into the dignified realm of thoughtful comedy. It may be added that we have in English a series of exceptionally spirited and understanding translations of Aristophanes' plays, by Benjamin Bickley Rogers (from which the excerpts here are taken).

Of the conditions of representation in the time of Aristophanes, there is scant authentic information. Here, as in tragedy, the

A comedy scene on a platform stage. [After a vase drawing.]

actors all were men. Their costumes were extravagantly unreal, fanciful, or grotesque. The vase-paintings indicate a common use of animal disguises in the Choruses. The actor's figure was heavily padded out, on the stomach in front and lower down behind. A phallus was commonly worn. Actors and Chorus were masked, and here grotesqueness seems to have been carried to extremes. Where an actor impersonated a well-known person — like Socrates in *The Clouds* or Euripides in *The Frogs* — the mask would be a recognizable caricature. Elsewhere a wild fancy reigned. The wide mouth in certain of the masks indicates the use of a sort of short megaphone, built in to aid the actor in making his voice carry to the uppermost rows of the vast auditoriums. In certain theatres of this or a slightly later time, there was a raised platform stage (perhaps not in Athens, perhaps only in the Italian provinces at first — and perhaps not in the " regular " theatres at all, but only where comedy stages were improvised for fairs or street productions).

So much we know from the small sculptures and the vase-paintings that have been preserved. But there is nowhere a description of the complete theatres, or of stage settings, or of the choral manœuvers. Nor do we know more than the meagrest facts about the music that was so important a feature of early comedy.

There is equally a gap in our first-hand knowledge of the literary form of comedy after Aristophanes, for no complete texts

A comedy scene on a platform stage. [After a vase drawing.]

have survived. For more than a half-century a transitional type flourished which has sometimes been termed Middle Comedy. At this time the plays became less topical, less extravagant — and less insulting. While men in the public eye might be butts, and while social or political movements might be parodied, it was rather home life or street life that provided the comic materials; and the type characters that we shall meet down into Renaissance times were introduced: the parasites and the testy fathers and the cunning slaves, the procuress and the country bumpkin. The Chorus was set back into a minor position, as interlude; the debate and the *parabasis* were shorn off the play-frame; and with these changes, of course, vanished the lyric beauty of true Aristophanic comedy. What may be called the ballet-burlesque elements disappeared too. Comedy gained in dramatic continuity, in plot-complexity, in human interest. But the old grotesque farcical masks persisted.

Menander, chief dramatist of the New Comedy, who lived from 342 to 291 B.C., crystallized playwriting into a new mode. He picked up the Middle Comedy where its thirty-nine more or less obscure practitioners had left it, and he gained something also out of Euripidean tragedy. He is the culminating figure in the late Greek theatre.

Euripides, you will remember, had brought tragedy down from the regions of gods and legendary heroes to a preoccupation with human emotion. Comedy was now ready to abandon its old irresponsible gaiety and extravagance, to be curbed with the bridle of unified human story. Menander made plays that obviously dealt with real everyday life; characters might still be types rather than individualized human beings, but types that you might meet just around the corner; plotting became an art; even a certain sentiment and pathos were introduced. In short, here was a long stride toward modern character-comedy; toward a comedy of manners. Physically, too, this more personal drama indicated a step toward the smaller, more intimate modern playhouse, for the play was less extensive, demanded less space for the acting. The Chorus had all but died, was merely an entr'acte diversion.

Though the names of sixty-four writers of the New Comedy are known, not a play-text in the mode has survived. Reports agree that Menander was head-and-shoulders the outstanding practitioner. He achieved a further fame from the imitations or adaptations of his comedies left to us by the Romans Plautus and Terence. From these have been gained most of our knowledge of the New Comedy. Scholars are always hoping that a text of Menander will be turned up out of the sands of Egypt or a Greek tomb. If so, we may find that Aristophanes is not the only superlatively great name to be remembered out of the Greek comic theatre.

ROMAN comedy, insofar as it took lasting literary form, was hardly more than a reflection or survival of Greek types, with only minor native elements; and it is a question whether the more " serious " comedy ever found its way deeply into the affections of the Roman people. The really popular forms were those that we would term " slap-stick " — without continuity, and with the elemental appeal of knockabout antics, raw jests, and banana-peel episodes. It seems worth while, then, to go back to the several sources of popular farce, before looking for real Roman comedy.

Although there was little connection between religion and drama at Rome in any known period, the first introduction of actors into the city occurred in 364 B.C. as an attempt to propitiate the gods who just then were inflicting a pestilence upon the people. In nearby Etruria a form of drama already had been developed out of the rituals of an agricultural people honoring rural gods at harvest and vintage time, or celebrating festivals of marriage, birth, etc. The Etruscans had parallelled the Athenian progression from mere processional with singing and dancing to responsive improvisation, and then to separation of actor or actors from the main body of celebrants.

The earlier of two distinctive Etrurian forms, known as the Fescennine Verses, may have been hardly more than a chant at first, but developed into a sort of counter-play, with ample opportunity for interpolated dialogue, jest, and banter. It was a farcical, half-improvised amusement form, elaborated casually from group revelry. The word " Fescennine," according to some, comes from *Fescennium,* the name of an Etrurian village where the entertainments may have originated, or according to others, from *Fascinum,* a phallic symbol. If one accepts the latter view, there is again a remarkable parallel to the dramatic beginnings at Athens. In the opinion of some scholars the Fescennine Verses were only incidentally a *step* on the way to full-fledged theatrical production; they were more especially a species of entertainment developed in connection with marriage rites. Weddings, of course, have afforded more material for comedy, down the ages, than any other one subject — I say it in all seriousness, referring to comedies on the stage. And they may well have provoked in Etruria a hilarity that became organized, found itself set down in verses, was chanted in the form of responses, and thus contributed to the stream of true dramatic development. Somewhat later this form was introduced into Rome, and it became so licentious and abusive that ultimately laws were passed to suppress it.

But meantime the later Etruscan entertainments known as *saturæ* had found favor with the Roman people, forming the real bridge to Roman dramatic beginnings. Based perhaps mainly on the Fescennine Verses, but with some relationship also to recited comic story, the *saturæ* had been the earliest truly dramatic type to develop on Italian soil. They apparently had little plot; they were acted comic scenes or sketches, in verse, performed with dancing and music. The form was still not so far removed from those of the vintage celebrations: the very name *saturæ* has a connection with one of our synonyms for "full." The actors were known as *istri,* which through the Latin *istriones* gave us ultimately our still current word "histrionic."

When the Romans brought a company of Etruscan performers to their city in 364 B.C., erecting for them in the Circus Maximus the first Roman stage, it was perhaps only a music-and-dancing entertainment or perhaps a production of *saturæ* (in an unintelligible tongue) that was added to the *Ludi Romani* or city games and merged into a genuine Roman popular comedy. The Etruscans, a people of still debated origin, thus gave to the then uncultured Romans their first dramatic activities, in addition to such epochal gifts as arch-construction and contact with Greece and the Orient. The Romans long since, before Republican days, had known how to borrow profitably from the Etrurians: had had Etruscan kings for a century, had ended that line of kings when Rome was strong enough to stand against all enemies, had absorbed some knowledge of, if not taste for, the arts, even while distrusting Etruscan luxury and culture.

The entertainments that most clearly stand for a people's comedy in Rome itself, that will persist through both Republican and Imperial periods and lose themselves only in the darkness that finally settles over decadent Rome, are the *mimi* and the *pantomimi.* The *mimus* — for which our word "mime" is hardly a fair equivalent — was a combination form in which the farce-sketch in dialogue was accompanied by dancing and songs, with

occasional acrobatic and other trimmings. Its subject-matter
seems always to have been taken from low life (the authorities all
use that term), there was definite plot, and in time such stock
characters as the parasite and the knave appeared. The *mimus*
may be considered substantially a native Roman development, although it inherited elements not only from the *saturæ,* but from
another imported form called the *Atellanæ,* and doubtless from
chance importations of performances from the Greek colonies in
Sicily and the extreme South of Italy — places soon to be parts
of the Roman Empire.

Comedy masks. [From Ficoronius.]

The rustic Atellan farces, so-called because brought to Rome
from Atella in Campania, are among the most distinctly defined
types in all the puzzling array of popular comedy, and notable
as foreshadowing a Renaissance form. They regularly dealt in
brief compass with rural life, and although the plots were of set
mold, the actors indulged freely in improvisation. The plays
were peopled by stock characters, the stupid husband or father,
the glutton, the knave, etc. — here again we meet clear forerunners of the characters in the fifteenth and sixteenth century *Commedia dell' Arte;* and like the players of the *Commedia* the
Atellan farceurs wore masks. This type ran its course of popularity in Rome, from the late third century on, sometimes on its
own stages, later as afterpieces to the Greek-style dramas; until
the similar *mimus,* which had derived generously from it,
crowded it out. But before adding my last word about *mimi*
and *pantomimi,* let me go back and tell about the more literary
comedy, based on Greek models, that ran its course between the

early popular farces and the final triumph of *mimus, pantomimus,* and spectacle. The reader should keep in mind, however, that it was at all times the cruder comedy that was a more natural, and probably a more appreciated growth at Rome. Leaving no traces of a dramatic literature, it was still, on its own ground, a more vigorous and a more distinctive development than the still surviving literary drama of Plautus and Terence.

When the Romans conquered the Greek Tarentum, in 272 B.C., they opened the way for the introduction of true Greek drama into their capital city. There were as yet no Roman theatres: the popular farces were being presented on stages temporarily erected. (Another full century was to elapse before the building of the first complete theatre in Rome, auditorium as well as stage, and then only of wood, for temporary use.) There were no " cultivated " audiences; the Romans of the time were hard-headed, materialistic, unimaginative fighters, with the admirable qualities of courage, enterprise, and a sense of integrity and justice (when these did not interfere with patriotism and conquest), but with no taste for any but practical education, none for the arts, none for personal refinements. But Greek influences began to run in a strong tide, and in 240 B.C. there was added to the festival of the *Ludi Romani* a performance of a tragedy and a comedy in the Greek fashion. Livius Andronicus, come to Rome from his native Tarentum, presented the two plays, in Latin, in adaptations that he had made from the Greek. At Tarentum the Dionysian Festivals had been modelled on those of Athens, and the actor-author was well able to introduce correct Athenian methods. From that time forward theatrical representations were part of holiday festivals, and Roman literary drama was committed to Greek forms.

When the greatest of the Greek plays, now already centuries old, were presented, even in translation or adaptation, their brilliancy and vigor were such that the beginning Roman dramatist might well despair of creating new forms so telling, even with his greater liberty in subject-matter and in conditions of presentation. At any rate, he elected to follow Greece. We have already seen how the tragedy writers of Rome weakened the play, mistaking rhetoric for passion, melodramatizing and debasing the Euripidean type. The comedy writers, picking up the " New

Comedy " of Greece as model, came off not quite so badly; but certainly they left little that was brilliant, or startlingly original, or essentially Roman. Out of the score of known names of Roman dramatists, Seneca alone is generally remembered in connection with tragedy, and Plautus and Terence as writers of comedy. A post-Terence type of literary comedy — the *fabulæ togatæ* — although more native in materials, ran its unimportant way to an early death.

So frankly Greek were the characters in the Latin plays of Terence and Plautus that they were regularly interpreted as Greeks, wearing Greek clothes, and the scene was usually Athens. But profiting by the divorce of the theatre from religion, and observing life more independently, Plautus succeeded in adding something of Roman vigor and swiftness of dialogue to the borrowed Greek plots. One might have expected Plautus and Terence to succumb to the popular demand for coarse humor and farce in their adaptations. But there was a very distinct break between the few at the top and the masses below, in Rome, culturally as well as in political-economic-social life. The " literary " dramatists, resisting the pressure of the masses for a wholly gross type of comedy, continued to imitate Greek originals, adding at first nothing cheaply topical or sensational or suggestive. There are freedoms of speech and frank recognition of facts of living that often made their plays distasteful during the polite nineteenth century; but compared to what the *mimi* and *pantomimi* are described to have been they are pure as the drifted snows.

Titus Maccius Plautus was born in 254 B.C., just about the time when the first Roman dramatists were forsaking mere translation and adaptation for a more serious attempt to write Latin plays (but still according to Greek pattern). He soon took rank as first, and at that time the only, Roman comedy-writer of importance. His plays are still extant to the number of twenty, out of a possible one hundred and thirty in all. One or two of them are familiar to every college student who has reached sophomore Latin; and *The Menæchmi* has achieved an even wider fame as the model for Shakespeare's *Comedy of Errors*.

Plautus (the name means " flatfooted ") owed to Menander and his fellow-dramatists a debt that cannot be computed in the absence of the Greek originals. But it is certain that although the Roman playwright retained even the scenes and costumes of the Athenian models, he added much of life by way of local color, of Italian fashions and manners and landmarks.

The Menæchmi is laid in Epidamnium. A stolen twin boy has been brought there in childhood, has grown up, married, inherited wealth. Thither comes unknown his brother, whose name has been changed to that of the lost boy. So the local Menæchmus and his twin are both roaming the same town. The one has a wife with whom he has quarrelled, and he is now going to visit a courtesan, to whom he carries one of his wife's dresses. Into this situation walks the other twin, is welcomed warmly by the courtesan, and dressed down by the wife. The fun arises chiefly out of the position of the local twin when the other has queered him with both courtesan and wife, with the aid of a tattling parasite, a doctor who is called in to pass on his sanity, etc. Complication follows complication till the twins meet and happily recognize each other.

In the reading, this five-act comedy seems bald and obvious; the real values in it can be detected only when one carries along in the mind a picture of skilled, heavy-hitting farce-actors filling in the character outlines and the situations with a wealth of telling action, stage tricks, and " business." That, of course, is just what one would expect in a time when there were no theatre auditoriums, when stages were street platforms, and audiences street idlers or the jostling crowds at " games " or fairs. And yet let us give Plautus his full due: to invent or adapt the framework for such players, and to make the dialogue after a fashion literary, without clogging the action, is a distinct achievement. And the more credit is his because he lived in a time when the Latin language was still, so to speak, in manufacture; he helped, indeed, by his comedies, to crystallize it in its finer form. But perhaps it is more significant to us that he was himself an actor — and in all probability, also " producer " of his plays. From this we may know why Plautus rather than the more refined Terence was the oftener revived on later stages — though less studied in the schools.

A captive brought to Rome about 200 B.C., named Statius

Cæcilius, is sometimes named as the next important dramatist; but no texts of his have survived. It is rather Publius Terentius Afer, a native of Carthage, born a few years before Plautus' death (184 B.C.), who is invariably bracketed with Plautus in any review of Roman comedy-writing. Six plays of his making survive, though none is wholly or even substantially original. He went back to Attic comedy and took freely what he needed, particularly from Menander. But he is a link between Greek and modern comedy in that he made the play-form more compact, and added a certain ease of manner. Where Plautus is considered an inferior craftsman to Menander, careless and over-vigorous, though livelier, Terence carried on the refining, character-humanizing process.

Terence was a slave, but was early manumitted. At an early age he won sudden interest among the litterati of Rome through the reading of his first play, the *Andria*. But his short later career was checkered. Enamored of Greek perfection, in a gross time, and stung by charges of plagiarism, he is supposed to have fled Rome for his idealized Athens, and to have died in Arcadia of heartbreak when his manuscripts were lost.

He is in one sense out of time and place. Local color is notably absent from his comedies. An African by origin, a Roman by circumstance, his whole aim was to revive something fine out of Greece in the new Latin language. Elegance, refinement, style, were his goals. Plautus had taken the Greek New Comedies as ready framework for farce-comedy suited to Roman crowds; Terence reverently preserved all that he could of Menander's virtues in finely literary Latin. His polished metrical texts marked almost the earliest Latin poetic achievement with real stylistic beauty. He was literary creator in the technical surface sense without any inner originality. Perhaps his whole accomplishment is more important as preserving Menander indirectly, in some sort of adaptation, than from any typically Roman aspect. And yet who shall say whether the clear-flowing light-footed verse is transmitted from the Greek or added by the Roman adaptor? Even the saws and proverbs that are so common in the six plays — "Fortune favors the brave," "Many men, many minds," "While there's life there's hope," etc., etc. — may be from the one or the other. In any case, as written, Terence's plays were little to the liking of Roman audiences. This fastidious art was too delicate for its era.

As an example of the progress made at this time toward the modern human plot, one might cite *The Eunuch,* best known of all Terence's plays. The comedy was placed (as was usual) at a street-crossing, with a house on either hand; the one belonging to Thaïs, a courtesan " of the better class," the other to the father of her favored lover Phædria. Thaïs is trying to protect a girl whom she has brought up, who was taken away from her and sold as a slave but is now restored as a gift by Thraso, an old soldier and an unwelcome admirer. At the same time Phædria is presenting her with a Eunuch. But Phædria's younger brother, having fallen in love with the girl, takes the Eunuch's place, is set to watch over her, and improves the opportunity to seduce her. All plans now seem wrecked, until Thaïs proves that the girl is not a slave but free-born; so that the seducer marries her, while Phædria scares off Thraso, takes Thaïs under his protection, and only lets the old braggart soldier into the happy circle at the price of paying for much entertainment all round.

This is obviously a fable with more than usual of human relationships wound into it. And there is some little characterization, of a skilful, even tender sort. It is an indication of Terence's aloofness from current coarseness that even the scene of the deflowering of the girl is handled delicately. But the stock characters of parasite, soldier, and interfering father stalk in and out of the action. The boisterousness of Plautan action and vulgar incident is lacking; in spite of the free relationships indicated in the plot, comedy is becoming " refined."

The period during which Latin comedy-writing flourished — the word perhaps implies too much — lasted hardly more than a hundred years, roughly 250–150 B.C. The plays of Plautus and of Terence (who died very young, 159 B.C.) persisted in occasional production until the Augustan era, and exceptionally under the late Emperors. But the sort of comedy that is serious enough in thought, in values, to be perpetuated in written texts, was practically crowded off the stage by farce and spectacle a hundred years after its birth — or introduction.

Two contemporary depictions of Roman theatre scenes. Above, a mosaic panel of masked performers on a Roman stage. Below, a scene with a slave and two women in a New Comedy. [From an Alinari photograph of the mosaic now in the National Museum, Naples; and from a reproduction of the fresco, in *Die Denkmäler zum Theaterwesen im Altertum*, by Margarete Bieber.]

Two exciting substitutes for the dramatic theatre in Roman times. Above, a painting by C. Ademollo of a chariot race in the Circus Maximus. Below, a painting of a man-and-beast spectacle in an amphitheatre. [From Alinari photographs.]

In Roman-Greek comedy the Chorus had disappeared. Therefore one may be sure that the theatre will no longer be the old
Greek structure in which the orchestra, as dancing-place, is the
essential feature. The exact form of the later Roman playhouse
is known, from only partially ruined examples existing today.
But there were no permanent theatres in Rome in the days of
Terence and Plautus. It was five years after Terence's death,
indeed, that construction of the first stone theatre was started;
and when half-completed it was torn down by order of the Senate,
being considered a menace to the strict self-discipline and flint-
like character which the government was attempting to conserve
in the Roman citizen. It had even been decreed by law in an
earlier time that no auditorium seats should be erected in Rome,
lest the spectator at a play find himself too comfortable! Nevertheless, despite old Cato's bitter fight against anything Greek,
against anything smelling of self-indulgence, anything new,
anything imaginative, the Romans were already slipping toward
worse forms of luxury, toward a taste for display, and art of a
soft exhibitional sort.

At any rate, the Roman theatre of the period was essentially
a stage and a place for seeing, where the Greek had always
been shaped primarily around a circle for dancing. The Etruscan
dancers and actors had had stages, the Atellan farces were acted
on platforms, it may even have been an Italian influence that
led to the introduction of a raised stage into the late Greek playhouses. Certainly it was a platform stage for which Terence and
Plautus wrote.

But rather than try to reconstruct in detail the Plautan stage,
production, and audience, upon incomplete evidence, let us turn
instead to the theatre of the Imperial age. In every sense it is
more characteristically Roman. Its plays perhaps still are reminiscent of something in Euripides and Menander, but playwrights
have been found to bring the drama down to the taste of the
spectacle-loving populace; theatres have been built in keeping
with the showy temples and palaces of a magnificent world-
capital; and the audiences — well, let us spread out the whole
detailed picture:

The population of Rome is no longer that hard-headed, abstemious, practical race of citizen-soldiers, trained first of all to courage, personal integrity, and love of state, which has carried the city by the Tiber well on the way toward world conquest. Long ago the old authority has crumbled, character has weakened, the dikes put up against luxury have been at first undermined, then swept away. The ruthlessness necessary for conquest has turned to cruelty, in government, in amusement, in each man's struggle against all others. Corruption and greed among the rulers are matched by dishonesty and fawning in the great mass of plebeians.

The small group of patrician families of old has been all but decimated by literally centuries of terrible wars; not least destructive, the civil wars within Rome. New patricians have been elevated from the ranks of the lower classes, even freedmen not long since slaves. Adventurers have flocked here from all the vassal cities held by Rome. The old stock, that once held to itself all privileges, all wealth, even while holding to the old virtues and discipline, is gone. The corrupt, the cheap-minded, the sensation-lovers, are as often as not at the very top. Old vices permeate all circles, new vices are welcomed. Religion is a superstitious observance — to be remembered as an excuse for holidays, or, suddenly, as something to be indulged in after a bad dream or a thunder-storm. Anyway, the gods are known to have given in to those very weaknesses and desires which man wishes to indulge. Where in other days, without marriage laws, the Romans had practised monogamy and sexual continence as part of a well-ordered life and the obvious road to happiness, promiscuity is now hardly frowned upon. The theatre, in times of excess, ever makes infidelity its favorite theme, and panders openly and brazenly to the sexual appetites.

For a time Cæsar Augustus has put an end to anarchy, plundering, and unhindered corruption. He has brought back system, law, and, in a sense, justice. He has ended Republicanism by making himself the State. He has set out to dignify Rome with monuments worthy of the capital of a world empire. He has built or restored innumerable temples, basilicas, public buildings of every sort. These are larger, more massive than any known before, thrown skyward with Roman engineering genius. But the ornament is from Greece, made more elaborate, more showy, more finicky. Colored marbles from all lands, creamy travertine, colored stucco; bronze statues, rich mosaics, gilt traceries; arches of triumph, fountains, pools, parks. Augustus boasts that he himself has rebuilt the magnificent Pompey's Theatre, has erected a stone theatre in honor of his adopted son Marcellus,[1] has en-

The decorated stage wall of the Roman theatre at Aspendus.
[From a drawing by Niemann in Lanckoronski's *Städte Pamphiliens und Pisidiens*.]

couraged Balbus to build a theatre. And these are supplemented by hippodrome, amphitheatre, circus, and *naumachia*.

Augustus tries to bring back the old character, the old virtues; even while his poet Horace sighs over the lost simple country pleasures. Augustus puts into lasting banishment his own

[1] Fortunately this Marcellus who gave his name to a still outstanding theatre in Rome is not the soldier of the same name who laid siege to Syracuse and destroyed its theatres; dramatic irony goes not so far. But I add a pertinent note from my guide-book to Sicily: " The Romans raised the siege against the city, which had been strengthened by Archimedes, and at last after two years of terrible sufferings, it fell into the hands of Marcellus in 212. The Roman soldiers plundered the city and murdered the inhabitants. Archimedes, engaged in his mathematical studies, was killed. The temples and theatres were destroyed and an enormous booty of valuable works of art taken to Rome. Most of the inhabitants were massacred, the remainder fled across the sea. The parts of the city on mainland [including the sites of theatre and amphitheatre] were deserted and soon the place where magnificent Syracuse, ruler of the Greek world, had

daughter Julia when he finds that she has become little better than a woman of the streets; but he cannot more than frown upon the other noble courtesans, wasters, degenerates — there is indeed some question about his own indulgences. Sudden wealth, that greatest of all tests of a man or a nation, has poured in and overwhelmed the resistance of those in high station in Rome, wealth and the soft luxuries it buys, and the soft vices that come fawning after it. And below is a populace driven by despair, unreligious except when scared into some sort of observance, preferring idleness to any sort of industry — the actual slaves do the hard work — living as far as possible off the bounty of the rich, and expecting those rich to furnish periodic amusement in theatre, arena, or circus. The government distributes grain, its last means of staying in power, and decrees games and theatrical productions, paying out of the public funds to contractors who arrange the shows for the people (quite far are we now from Athens, where the drama was religious, and those presenting it an honored and privileged class!).

Or else private citizens pay for productions free to the public, as part of their show of wealth, or to celebrate triumphs, or even for funerals. Candidates, too, win favor by supplying a day's entertainment. Of course they all give " what the public wants " — a phrase almost invariably interpreted by " managers " in terms of the worst element in any potential audience. When the Republic had faded into the Empire there were already seventy-six holidays in the year, with fifty-five given up to theatrical productions. This is to grow later into a total of practically six months of holidays in the year, with one hundred and one given up to dramatic performances, ten to gladiatorial contests and sixty-four to chariot-racing.

On one of these holidays, when theatre performances have

---

stood, became a wilderness." I add the quotation here for the reference to Marcellus, but it illuminates the background against which the Roman theatre developed: the violence and insecurity of life, the frequent destruction of theatre buildings, and the way in which Rome " secured " art. This was the time of Archimedes and Theocritus in Syracuse, about two centuries after the picturesque ruler Dionysius I, himself a tragedy-writer and poet, who had built magnificent buildings and fostered all the arts. The theatre destroyed by Marcellus was presumably of the Greek type; but after this time a magnificent Roman theatre, the largest of all known examples, was constructed on the site. A great part of the auditorium may be seen there today, as well as parts of the stage and the under-stage passage-ways and construction.

been announced — let us say at about the time when Jesus of
Nazareth is preaching in far-away Palestine, a country not too
distant to be under Roman rule — we set out with thousands of
other Romans to find our seats in Pompey's Theatre. From
someone privileged we have secured " tickets," little bone tablets
stamped with seat and section numbers. Down through the great
Forum we go, between rows of porticoed temples, grand basilicas,
fountains, arches, with the sun flashing on marble and bronze
and gilt — a little proud we are to be a part of all this magnificence
and show, proud that our Rome is now the most obviously " artistic " city in all the world. We meet processions: actors going
early to the theatre, with their chariots and horses and other
" properties," and hundreds of supernumeraries; priests, whole
colleges of them, going to celebrate rites and offer sacrifices in the
temples of the gods, with their sacred implements borne along
by surpliced helpers; a chorus, perhaps, boys and girls of noble
birth, chanting votive songs; the procession of the horses, chariots,
and charioteers on the way to the Circus Maximus, where tomorrow they will race. And everywhere the people hurrying
along, bedecked for the holiday, mixing with the uniformed
soldiery, the thousands of police, the picturesque " colonial "
officers. Here are patricians carried in gorgeous palanquins by
slaves, and one must jump quickly at times to keep out of the
way of the heedless private chariots.

Perhaps there are three theatres offering plays this day — it
was often so — but it is to Pompey's Theatre that we are going.
We remember with a chuckle that Pompey had to employ a
shrewd ruse to get this playhouse built at all, only a generation
or two earlier. To build it was against the law. But he erected
a tiny temple to Venus at the top of his auditorium, which
technically made the curving rows of seats merely steps to a
shrine — and the whole was dedicated as a temple! But the
theatre seats are there, added Pompey, in his invitations . . .

What a magnificent theatre! We note as we take our seats that
the shrine is little more than a niche in the stately colonnade that
runs around the top of the " bowl " — really a half-bowl, with
rows and rows of seats in widening semi-circles, so many that
fifteen thousand of us are to find places in it today. Down in the

centre, on the flat, like half of the old outgrown Greek " orchestra," chairs of honor have been placed, not for the priests any longer but for the Senators. That, indeed, will add to the show; you know what Senators are, swollen with power and riches, coming in with their slaves and their over-dressed womenfolk, lording it around!

The stage has grown from that tiny scaffolding once set up in the Circus Maximus, to this massive stone platform, three hundred feet long, bounded at back and sides with a wall as high as the colonnade about the auditorium, a wall ornamented as richly as a temple or palace façade, story on story of columns, porticoes, niches, with colored marbles, statues, gilded edgings; and above it, a richly decorated stage roof. The auditorium is still open to the sky — this is distinctly an open-air structure — but the Greek separation of " scene " and " cavea " is gone; the theatre is more solidified, massive, integrated. But most noticeably, it is more decorative, more displayful, with a gorgeousness now deemed a proper addition to drama. We are reminded, indeed, that this stone theatre is not the most gorgeous of all: that not long since, in that time when temporary wooden theatres were erected for each new occasion, M. Æmilius Scaurus put up a playhouse in which the wall behind the stage displayed no fewer than three hundred and sixty columns and three thousand statues, together with " relief-plaques of glass " — and the gods only know what additional decorative plunder from his Eastern conquests.[2] Was it Pliny who remarked that in Rome there are as many statues as inhabitants? But after all, this bowl of Pompey's, rich and colorful enough, and just now filled to overflowing with excited and brightly garbed people, is proper setting for our taste of Roman Imperial drama.

A hush, while the announcements are read, of what is to be played or presented, with possibly just a little propaganda for him

---

[2] I am indebted for many figures and descriptions to James Turney Allen's *Stage Antiquities of the Greeks and Romans and Their Influence* (New York, 1927). If the student will read that book and selected chapters from *A Literary History of Rome*, by J. Wright Duff (London, 1909), he will have a broad view of the subject sketched in this chapter. Most of the books on the Greek Theatre include chapters on the Roman; but nowhere are drama, theatre, and acting treated together. For many details of the background of Roman life I am indebted to Grant Showerman's *Eternal Rome* (New Haven, 1924).

who spends a fortune to afford the esteemed people a holiday. The announcer adds an appeal to the audience to give their attention quietly and respectfully. One looks at one's fellow-spectators curiously — God! what a mob! Why haven't they gone to the bloody arena contests instead?

What plays are announced? We fill out our picture a bit conjecturally here, for the programmes have not been transmitted to later historians. Let us take it for granted, conveniently, that the morning is given up to a drama, or say two, of the old Greek pattern — but they will be debased now so that this audience will stay — and the afternoon to the popular forms, to *mimi* and *pantomimi*.

What is this opening procession, this parade across the stage, filling it with pageantry, with movement, color, crowds? The play? Not yet. The actors? Yes — we know the chief ones by their masks and their stuffed-out costumes (for this is a vast auditorium for a mere man to dominate). But these others seem to be not at all acting — men driven, rather. That's it, of course! The procession of captives from So-and-so's latest Eastern triumph. Hundreds of them. Here come the horses too. Perhaps there will be camels, even elephants. Maybe a king in chains will be led across the stage — many another has. Theatrical? One should remark!

And the play itself is interrupted by just such pageants at intervals: sometimes frank unrelated spectacle, gorgeous or sensational, other times filling out the dramatist's intention. Is a handful of supers a fit stage mob for a Roman audience? No, bring them on by the hundred and the thousand. Shall a score of horses suffice when a hero-protagonist rides out at the head of his cavalry? A half-thousand crossing the stage will better fill the eye. So here we have them, to tremendous applause, marching through a drama that we faintly recognize as descendent from a noble Greek model. Realistic battles, floods, processions of exotic animals, interrupt the flow of action.

One wonders a little whether the Roman dramatist seriously wrote this for tragedy, whether he may not have taken a grand theme in burlesque spirit. Still, here are noble speeches, delivered with telling gesticulation and spirited vocal display. Here are passionate appeal, violent murder, and rhetorical revenge. These players — slaves, freedmen, foreigners — may be little better than outcasts and thieves in real life, but they know how to tear a passion to tatters. The chief among them, the fellow with the deep powerful voice, rises to the position of opera soloist at the most perfervid moments of the play. There is accompanying music too. Then there is something reminiscent of the old choruses, and it helps the entr'actes to pass painlessly.

In the following comedy, there is hardly more left of Greek pattern than in the tragedy. The change this time is not toward spectacle, but rather in the direction of cheaper horse-play and broader jests. These later adapters have known how to borrow profitably from the local mime-makers. The masks too are more caricature-like, more grotesque, more obvious. Old-favorite characters have become stock figures that appear in play after play: we look for our favorites, the inevitable hoodwinked father, the courtesan, the parasite, the pimp, the heiress. Here they all are, spread out in complication after complication. We laugh. It is not the "thoughtful laughter" that true comedy is supposed to inspire. It is hardly a healthy animal laughter. There is something unworthy, even dirty, about it. The comedy-writers have gone too far.

Then after lunch, returning to the theatre for the performances of the *mimi* and *pantomimi,* we learn that the comedy-writers and the actors of the morning had, comparatively, not gone far at all. Given the low-life theme of the *mimus,* the license of improvisation, and the gross taste of this audience, literally anything goes. No jest is too broad, no situation too suggestive, no gesture too disgusting, to "get by" with these spectators. The actors wear no masks — the obscenities somehow come nearer thus. There is a Chorus which sings appropriate songs and dances appropriate gestures. The whole entertainment is a medley of dialogue-sketch, ballet, and song, strung on a farce idea. For the first time women have come on to the "regular" stage as actors and dancers, and their performance is as like as not a shameful display and an invitation. Along with these things that seem to us today so inexplicably degrading in a mass entertainment, there is much that is merely farcically funny, characters and

caricatures that evoke spontaneous laughter, old tricks that un-
failingly "knock 'em off the seats." Again we laugh. But we
know that comedy has kept pace with Roman degeneration
and licentiousness.

Now follows a "pantomime" — and one of those miracles so
common to the stage. A single masked performer comes before
the audience. Behind him a chorus takes its place, and an
"orchestra." Alone the actor gesticulates and dances a short
mythological play, while the chorus sings the text. With a
"clapper" on his foot he emphasizes the cadence of the verse to
the rhythm of the music. He develops a surprising theatrical
intensity, induces a mood that holds this entire uncouth audience
spellbound. Perhaps he has changed mask and costume as he
impersonates various characters. At any rate, for a time true
drama has reigned again, in a single player's performance.
Through sheer virtuosity, an audience has been made attentive,
has been swayed, has been deeply satisfied.

It is, indeed, a full tragic drama reduced and intensified into
the performance of one actor standing for many actors. Long
ago Livius Andronicus, the story goes, finding himself hoarse after
too many consecutive performances, gave over the singing of the
songs to a boy, and thereby suddenly found himself free to accomplish a much more expressive and effective performance of the
meaning through silent acting alone. The boy's part grew to a
chorus, the actor's gesticulation became a rounded-out and completely theatrical thing. The Roman pantomime had taken form.

But if this two-century-old sort of drama held the audience on
this particular day in Pompey's Theatre, the same actor's next
number, bringing the *pantomimus* closer in spirit to the *mimus,*
pleased them better. Why couldn't he stop after that one
triumph? Even in the more serious pantomime the scenario had
necessarily taken only the more effective parts of the legendary
story, with a leaning toward the violent and the amorous portions. But now, in this second piece, with this vigor turned
toward the coarse and suggestive methods of the *mimus,* with
the single actor's added opportunity for physical display, one has
a new sort of sensational display — yes, vulgar beyond words . . .
If we have a real love for our Rome, we walk back through the

Forum with something approaching melancholy in our hearts. We have felt, in the theatre at first, something of the old glamour of the stage, of the stilled expectant auditorium. But by late afternoon it is worn down to a feeling tattered, drab, uncomfortable. Is it only imagination that leads us, here among the temples, shrines, and triumphal arches of the Forum, to see in the encrusted decoration, gilt, and sculptured stone and colored stucco, to detect in all this magnificence, a note of insincerity, of pretence, of tawdry and vulgar showiness? How wholesome is this art of conquering Rome? Is it really noble, fine, soul-stirring, breeding an ecstasy of the emotions, like the early Greek? Or is it showy, a bit sensational, wearying?

The better theatre, the theatre not too mixed with sensuality, continues in a small way, even in the Rome of the Empire; though small audiences mean curtailment. Plays in the earlier styles are still written; but there is very little of originality, of lasting value in them. The original Greek plays are presented too, in the Greek, for a small group of educated Romans, for the resident Greeks, for other special groups in Rome.

In the one matter of acting, considered as an individual exhibition, the Romans have probably made progress beyond their teachers. The great actors even take students for training in the intricacies of the art. Late in the Republican days, Quintus Roscius has trod the stage, creating a lasting tradition of effective acting. He is said to have appeared one hundred and twenty-five times in a single year. He became a friend of Cicero, was honored by Sulla, and outgrew the stigma attaching to the playing profession in general. Why that profession was dishonored in this particular period of history becomes clear from our study of the mimes and pantomimes, and from our knowledge that most actors were slaves. The actor was denied the rights of a citizen, he was legally *infamis,* socially an outcast. There is reason to believe that before the time of the late Emperors, at least, he deserved his classification with panderers and thieves.

It was at Rome that the first dramatic performances by night took place. Plays were acted by the light of flares; though we may put this down as more a " stunt " for the sake of novelty than as a step toward the artificial-light stage of today. The

Romans introduced, too, as a regular thing, that paid claque which has proved a nuisance in more than one later era. When productions were so frequent, it became necessary to hire theatrical " contractors "; at so much per performance, they would undertake to deliver a " show " to the people. Often the contractor was an enterprising young actor, who played leads and hired or owned other actors for support. It meant money to him if his production was properly appreciated and acclaimed. He may even have been paid in accordance with the apparent success achieved with his audience. Therefore bands of paid clappers were organized, whose business it was to whip up enthusiasm and if possible stampede the audience into demonstrations. There are reports of the reverse activity: crying-down of the productions of opposition actor-managers. Riots occurred in this connection. One may be sure that it is a decadent or artificial art to which a claque must be called in; the productions in the degraded Roman theatres show some analogy to the " grand " opera houses of today, where the claques are often brazen, and disturbing to any artistic atmosphere.

But the changes instituted in matters of production, in the late Roman theatres, are grouped largely around the growth of spectacle as an element. Stages had been greatly enlarged, mass effects were common; but beyond this, there was a love for trick effects and surprise. Rome had for centuries displayed unfailing appreciation of tight-rope walkers, jugglers, and similar entertainers, as evidenced in many a fresco and mosaic. The machinery of the Greek stage, which had been developed for a few stock effects, most notably thunder at the entrance of a god, and the *deus ex machina* appearing to resolve the drama, was now elaborated to include devices for apparitions, trap-door disappearances, flying figures, thunder and lightning, etc. Vitruvius gives contemporary evidence about stage conventions, and Pollux, writing in the second century A.D., listed a great amount of mechanical paraphernalia for spectacle-making.

No complete accounts of painted stage scenes are extant, but references indicate that at least essays had been made in this direction. In general, the reader should dismiss the idea of localized background as an element of staging in ancient times:

it simply had not been thought of. The stage was obviously a
stage, not a representation of a place. The dramatist told in the
dialogue where the actors were supposed to be, or else it was
self-evident from the relationships of the characters present; and
that was enough for audiences not trained to expect " real " backgrounds. Before Vitruvius' time a device had been introduced

Stage of the Roman theatre at Orange, as reconstructed by
Camille St. Saëns. Note the vast scale of the building and
decoration in relation to the actors on the stage.

for *indicating* change of scene pictorially: three-sided sign-boards
on pivoted standards bore on the three faces differing pictured
scenes, two architectural (one for tragedy, one for comedy) and
the other pastoral. There is very little evidence as to the extent
to which these *periacti* were in use. But in his famous *Ten Books
on Architecture* Vitruvius wrote of them: " When the play is
to be changed, or when gods enter to the accompaniment of
sudden claps of thunder, these may be revolved and present a
face differently decorated." We shall hear of Vitruvius and his
descriptions of the scenes again, in the era when artists of the
Renaissance apply his directions specifically to the designing of

full-stage settings. But the whole matter is too involved, the authorities too contradicting, to permit us to infer changing painted settings in Roman times.[3]

One can only conjecture how far the Romans went in developing spectacle as a separate complete stage art, independent of other elements. Most of the contemporary references involve it on the one hand with the presentation of debased literary drama, or on the other with such events as triumphal entries and funeral celebrations. Protests against the intrusion of unrelated spectacle into plays were frequent and sometimes bitter. Cicero exclaims, " What pleasure is there in seeing six hundred mules in the *Clytemnestra,* or three thousand bowls in *The Trojan Horse,* or infantry and cavalry engaging in battle in gay-colored armor ? " — and this on the occasion of the opening of Pompey's Theatre, as early as 55 B.C. Horace uttered scathing criticisms of the audiences of his day, because they preferred spectacle and sensational exhibition to poetic and literary drama. In the Epistles he wrote: " For four hours or more the curtain is kept down while squadrons of horse and bodies of foot are seen flying; presently there passes the spectacle of unfortunate kings dragged with hands behind their backs; chariots of every kind and shape hurry along."

The reference to " the curtain kept down " is indication that certain of the Roman theatres had front curtains, raised from slots along the edge of the stage, which were let down when the play started and raised up when the action was done. In the larger theatre at Pompeii and at Arles one may still see the slots into which the curtain-rollers fitted. Every play producer knows that when it comes to the question of " effects," one may astonish more by the sudden disclosure of great masses of actors, or a fight

[3] I disagree with many other writers on this subject, in that I see in several references to painted stage scenes only an indication that the usual *neutral* architectural background occasionally was frescoed on the stage wall, instead of built out in relief. In many old churches in Italy one may see a chapel with a painting surrounded by elaborate architectural stonework, topped by sculpture in the round. The adjoining chapel, however, may have the central religious painting, but around it only a *painted semblance* of columns, pediments, and sculpture — the means to add the decoration in actual stonework having failed. It seems to me wholly likely that the mentioned " painted scenes " in theatres of Roman or late Greek times were entirely or mainly of this sort: a flat wall with a conventional architectural and sculptural composition frescoed in, without reference to realistic *placing* of the play. This is not scene painting or play setting in the later accepted sense.

in full swing, than by showing actors coming in or the fight just commencing. Thus the curtained stage may fairly be considered an outgrowth of the Roman love for sensational intensive incident.

At any rate pageantry, interspersed with thrilling effects, flourished in Rome as we know it to have flourished only once in later history, in the melodramas of the *Boulevard du Crime* in Paris, and the closely connected spectacles of the London stages of the nineteenth century. But the Romans had an advantage for the audiences of a bloodthirsty epoch: they could mix a realism into their stage battles, murders, seductions, etc., that later civilizations forbade. The conqueror returning home, ordering a show for the people, was able to supply thousands of real soldiers, horses, chariots, thousands of captives in strange garb, thousands of slaves bearing trophies, real gold, statues, costly stuffs. Against this background their theatrical managers might sacrifice lives in real battles to the death, and no one to object — or employ slave girls for who knows what exhibited iniquities. (One might a worse tale unfold!)

Now spectacle may be a legitimate enough form of theatre art. We must recognize that there are many forms of " theatre," and that each may be right in its place — so long as it is true to stage materials. But the Roman mind, we feel, was too realistic, too-sensation-seeking, and the theatres too large, perhaps, for any sort of subtle spectacle. For that era of violence, conquest, and decadent living, the sensational episode, the cruel personal strife, the astonishing piled-up magnificence were right. The theatre shaped itself to the violence, the license, that was Rome. At first the producers had taken the regular drama and interpolated unwarranted spectacular incidents; then they mixed in the thrills of *real* battle, real crises, with theatre elements. So real were the dangers of the " drama" toward the end, indeed, that the Romans, in making over the Greek theatres, erected barriers between orchestra and auditorium, lest spectators be injured or killed by error.

That the theatres designed for drama were later utilized for out-and-out gladiatorial contests is amply proved by the evidence of late Roman writers and by traced changes in still existing stages. The arenas were not enough for the bloody spectacles;

the theatres must be taken over.   There is even reason to believe
that the lower portion of the Theatre of Dionysus in Athens, most
glorious of all ancient playhouses, was reconstructed under a
Roman Emperor to be rendered water-tight, so that mimic naval
battles might be staged there.   Already Rome had several amphitheatres specially designed for such sea fights.

A Naumachia or theatre for mimic sea-fights.
[From *La Machinerie au Théâtre*, by E. M. Laumann.]

In these *naumachiæ* — really auditorium bowls with lake centres — two fleets of triremes of equal " tonnage " were manned
by warriors and set against each other.   A friendly parade of the
vessels (and they were truly decorative) preceded the main event;
and it is recorded that the participants were instructed to win
the battle with as little damage as possible to ships and combatants.   But in a country where slaves and captives were
regularly set to fighting against each other to the death, or against
wild beasts, in vast amphitheatres for the edification of the public,
the sea battle was sure to be bloody enough.   One commentator
adds the illuminating note that when the lake was emptied after
a production the bodies of the *naumachiarii*, the actors, were
dragged away without ceremony to the animals' dens.   The form

of amusement here is not to be considered too seriously as a type
of drama; but one may pause with real admiration for the logical
buildings developed for the mimic battles. The *naumachia* of
Julius Cæsar is reputed to have been nearly two thousand feet long
and two hundred wide, with an encircled lake on which a battle
with fifty triremes might be staged. The little picture of a
naumachia shown here is cut down for the better showing-out of
the detail, and is perhaps conjectural in many ways. But what
a pretty and logical "theatre" for its special purpose! The
Colosseum at Rome has aqueducts which archæologists say were
used to flood the arena for sea fights, and at the amphitheatre at
Pozzuoli one may trace out today just how the arena was filled,
how large the lake was, and how emptied.

The views several pages back of the Colosseum and of the Circus
Maximus show the more usual activities of man-and-beast fights
and chariot-racing. There we may safely leave the subject of
Roman spectacle. Stage tragedy had ended in plain butchery —
itself indeed had been "butcher'd to make a Roman holiday."

Comedy, as we have seen, had come to knock-about and often
indecent farce and dance. Insofar as the truly gorgeous theatres
of Rome were used under the late emperors, their stages saw
only spectacle, vulgar antic, and suggestive jest. Over most of
the lands conquered by Rome those magnificent playhouses were
built, in Italy and Sicily, in Greece and Asia Minor and Syria,
in Northern Africa and in France and Spain. Today one goes
to the half-ruined theatre at Orange and tries to reconstruct the
picture of the original audience assembled there, and the plays
on the stage. The auditorium and the scene are modelled after
the grandest and most lavish of the ornate theatres at Rome. But
the date of its opening was in the second century A.D., many years
after the decadence of Roman taste, when spectacle and farce were
all that remained in place of dramatic art at the capital. Did these
palatial colonial playhouses, then, see nothing else? One hopes
that some day evidence will be uncovered to the contrary. In the
cities that were first Greek, then Roman, like Taormina and
Syracuse in Sicily, the whole pageant of Greek drama at its height,
changing Greek-Roman plays, and finally degraded Roman production, naturally would be seen.

A new protagonist comes into the story of the last days and eclipse of Roman drama. The record of the increasingly obscene mimes and pantomimes is spotted with reports of attempted official censorship; but the censors had neither nobility of character nor conviction behind them. Then came the Christian Church, with conviction, moral courage, militant antagonism to sin and personal indulgence. As the darkness of decay falls over Rome, the drama is seen fleeing before the righteous wrath of the Church fathers. Actors become wandering vagabonds — though their tribe and their art never quite disappear. The Greek and Roman theatres fall into decay, are made over into fortresses, are built full of huts, are torn down stone by stone for the sake of the rich building materials in them — until in the nineteenth and twentieth centuries a few are cleared out, reclaimed, rededicated with Greek tragedy and comedy, or modern drama and opera. The play texts of the Greeks, and of Plautus and Terence, are forgotten, except as they afford study to monk-grammarians — until a nun of Saxony writes ecclesiastical plays after their pattern in the tenth century. Indeed, it is the Church that drives the drama into outer darkness, deservedly anathematized and despised, before Rome's story is wholly done, and it is the Church that will bring back drama as a preceptor of righteousness, an aid at the altar, when centuries have passed in penance.

CHAPTER V

Sensuous and Intellectual Theatres: The Orient

IN LIFE there are pleasures that we call sensual and sensuous, pleasures of the senses, varying from wholly animal satisfactions to something bordering on the æsthetic and ecstatic. This range of pleasures cannot easily be set off from those deeper sorts that we term spiritual and intellectual; though the Puritans tried to mark out limits to legitimate enjoyment, barring as guilty all the sensuous as well as the animal-sensual sorts: pleasure in rich color, dancing, imagery, erotic excitement, brilliant design, gay music, etc. In recent centuries, particularly, our rigid Anglo-Saxon Protestant civilization has tried to taboo the sense-activities; it brought about a colorless epoch culminating in the drab nineteenth century.

Now it is a fact that this civilization did not result in a real prohibition or suppression of the baser sensual pleasures: there are signs enough in German, British, and American life of coarseness, of realism, and materialism. But it did largely kill out the more admirable sensuous enjoyments in life and in art. And so, since our discovery of the harm wrought by a too-rigid Protestantism, of the evils of moral hypocrisy, ethical formalism, and thin sentimental or ponderously didactic art, we have been reassimilating color, brilliance, tactile values, melodious movement, fantasy, and music. While trying to avoid what seem like refinements of sensuality in Oriental life, the European-American has been consciously studying those elements that afford the sensuous glow and fulness to Eastern art. For we had obviously gone too far the other way, toward a dark and stark coded life, had denied the senses too intolerantly, had made our arts too rigid, realistic, and pale.

Personally I feel that life may be enriched for us by an indulgence of our instinct toward color, light, dreamy music,
imagery, and form-enjoyment. Our theatre might gain — I believe is gaining — much from the reintroduction of the discarded
sensuous elements. And indeed, Western art would have been a
darker and more meagre affair without the colorful influences
from the East that came with a succession of " calamitous " invasions through a long period of history. I feel that the greater
ease of communication today may help us, not to import — God
forbid! — some of the elements of Oriental art into our own, but
to awaken again our æsthetic sensibilities, to absorb the feel for
imagery and color, and to express ourselves more fully in the
richer overtones of dramatic performance. Nor do I see in such
a change anything incompatible with our Western idea of drama,
as an activity touching on spiritual crisis and purgation of the
emotions. All the depth, the emotion, the high beauty, the poetry
of the finest European plays might remain and yet the lighter
elements be woven into the pattern of the action. I imagine,
indeed, that the plays of Æschylus and Euripides as performed
in the Dionysian tradition at Athens were characterized by an
abounding life and colorfulness not at all in keeping with the
nineteenth century conception of a white classicism; with a gloss of
music, measured rhythm of movement, and conscious voice-play;
and that the productions of the Elizabethan theatre were rich
and full and glowing far beyond the comprehension of the nineteenth century scholar-producers.

The Oriental theatre and drama, doubtless, hold elements which
will never be wholly understood by the spectator out of the West.
It is difficult to understand the reaction of the audiences to the
Chinese twelve-hour plays or to the brief Japanese *No*, in all the
facets of their enjoyment. The Orientals, in avoiding almost
entirely the range of tragic emotion, as it is expressed in a compact,
ascending-descending action-structure by our most skilful dramatists, may build into their productions some other central effectiveness which we miss. But there can be no doubt of the
superiority in the two ranges lying on either side of ours: the
sensuous, decorative, image-making field and that at the other
extreme, of formalized intellectual art, where the effectiveness lies

in traditional precisions, a widely understood symbolism and a meticulous fastidiousness — the field of a skilfully thought-out and embroidered art rather than a spontaneous expression.

Our survey of Oriental drama here, then, may well begin with the reservation that there are some depths that our minds may not reach, and with the understanding that we shall only flounder futilely if we try to judge its excellencies by the standard of our own essentially and starkly emotional theatre; and further, that there are sensuous qualities that we may learn about with advantage to our own civilization. Even the only half-Oriental Hindu theatre has been so often written about unsympathetically, from the set viewpoint of what the European theatre *is,* that a caution against closed-mindedness seems necessary.

The origins of the theatre in India are lost in a haze of myth and speculation. If we set aside the legend of divine and deliberate creation of the drama, and the conjectures about the emergence of dramatic story from dance-and-song, we find that we cannot go back of the second or first century B.C. with any certainty; and it is only with the emergence of Bhasa's and Kalidasa's plays that we learn about theatrical activity in any detail. In other words, we find ourselves immediately in the golden period of Sanskrit dramatic composition, without knowing more than stray facts about the preceding birth and rise of the art. Nor is it possible to declare certainly, within a century or so, when Kalidasa lived. The Hindu people are careless about recording such details: it is characteristic that a mere fact of this sort, so prized by the Western mind, escapes the East in favor of the spirit, the enjoyment of the work. But roughly we may say that Indian drama flourished from the fourth century A.D. (which is probably just before Kalidasa's time) to the tenth century. It was probably a growth independent of Greece, Persia, or other countries with which India had commerce in the formative period in the several centuries on either side of Christ's birth, although there is definite proof of Greek influence on some of the other arts. The Indian drama is characterized most notably by great poetic-idyllic beauty, is preoccupied with the loves of men and women or with heroism, always ends happily, avoids unseemly or violent emotion or incident, and is innocent of the unities of time and place, and of that inevitability and dramatic drive which is so typically Greek.

But let us go back to the legend of divine and miraculous origin. During the Golden Age there could be no need for drama, because the sadness that is a part of every dramatic story could mean nothing where sorrow and pain are unknown. But in the following Silver Age, the gods asked the All-father to create a new art which would give pleasure to the eye and the ear alike. So Brahma took from the four existing Vedas the elements of recitation, song, mimetic art, and " sentiment " or " passion," and combined them in a new art-form.

The other gods contributed further elements — Shiva, sometimes identified as the Indian Dionysus, gave the dance — and Brahma caused the divine architect to build a playhouse where the sage Bharata would set forth the new-born drama in production. " Bharata " became, indeed, one of the names for " actor."

If we refuse to accept this account as gospel truth — *our* gospel — we may yet let it serve as indication of a religious origin of Hindu theatric art. There are dramatic elements in the sacred books, and we may again conjecture that dance-ritual (the gods themselves are conceived of as dancing) and dialogue-hymns had to do with the beginnings of drama. But as in Greece it was probably the element out of recited epic that ultimately resolved the form of the new art. A typically religious touch long survived in a brief ceremony or benediction before the beginning of the play proper, and scraps of " Mystery " plays survived down the centuries even to our times. At any rate drama emerged, after dance, song, ritual, recited poem and epic. And if you prefer to consider this the real story of the birth of the Indian theatre, you can see how the native impulse to ascribe everything to a divine creator might have taken the word for actor as the beginning point of a legend, and from that imagined a sage named Bharata who received the art from heaven, and who became the tutelary deity of the Hindu drama. As a matter of fact the work on dramaturgy which is associated with Bharata's name became as a bible to all later Sanskrit dramatists. No body of drama has been more rigidly held within a set of rules.

The language in which the earlier dramas were cast was perhaps the Prakrit, a popular form, as distinguished from the Sanskrit, a language then reserved for the use of the Brahmins and for learned works. It is not clear when Sanskrit became the language of literature; though we know that after its introduction plays were translated out into the vernacular tongues. For a long time Sanskrit and Prakrit were mixed in the same play, according to the superiority or inferiority of the characters speaking: Gods, kings, nobles, Brahmins, and the like spoke in Sanskrit; women, thieves, policemen, etc., spoke in Prakrit. Even in later times there were characters who spoke appropriate dialects. But when we come to the first plays that we can label complete literary dramas, Sanskrit is predominantly in use. The text was ordinarily composed in prose with a great deal of verse inset, the verse varying widely in form even in a single play.

The first great name in Sanskrit drama is Bhasa, a dramatist to whom thirteen recently discovered plays are attributed. But because a controversy still rages about this attribution, and because two later plays are generally considered the masterpieces of the Indian theatre, we may turn directly to Kalidasa, the author of *Shakuntala,* and then to *The Little Clay Cart,* which is attributed to a legendary king-dramatist named Shudraka.

According to the Indian scholars, Kalidasa was the brightest of the " nine gems of genius " who adorned the court of King Vidramaditya, in the first century B.C., but unromantic English and German scholars have apparently destroyed this pretty legend and have placed the dramatist in the fourth, fifth, or sixth century A.D., with the latest evidence inclining the casual reader to say " 400 A.D. is close enough." His first play, called *Malavik-agnimitra,* which has mercifully been translated into *Malavika and Agnimitra,* contains references to Kalidasa's illustrious predecessors, Bhasa, Saumilla and Kaviputra, indicating a large body of highly esteemed earlier dramatic works, now mostly lost. The prologue contains two lines that have perhaps been too seldom quoted:

> Wise men approve the good, or new or old;
> The foolish critic follows where he's told.

The play is a conventional comedy, with fairly good characterizations, and pretty love passages. The second of Kalidasa's plays

is variously called in translation *The Hero and the Nymph* and
The Tale of Urvashi Won by Valor, and is said by those who
have read it in the original to contain one act of surpassing idyllic
loveliness; though Kalidasa seems to have debased a legendary story of great tragic beauty to the estate of a pleasant love-
comedy.

Shakuntala, however, is the masterpiece not only among
Kalidasa's works but perhaps of all Oriental drama that has been
translated out into European tongues. It exhibits many essential
characteristics of the Hindu drama: in its long prose passages
embroidered with the prettiest of poetry, its idyllic setting, its
pleasing imagery, its story of love and misunderstanding and
languishment, its decorous avoidance of violence, its happy ending
so obviously devised to leave everyone in the best possible humor
after the last lines.

The rather slight story opens with a woodland scene. King
Dushyanta and his Charioteer have pursued a spotted deer into
an idyllic grove. Just as the King is about to bring the deer
down with an arrow, a voice calls on him to spare it, for this
is the sacred precinct of a hermitage. While resting, the King is
smitten with sudden love of Shakuntala, a maiden of surpassing
loveliness, ward and supposed daughter of Kanva, the pious
hermit-father; and without revealing his true identity, he finds
occasion to serve Shakuntala, establishes that she is of divine not
lowly birth, and exits feeling that

> She would not show her love for modesty,
> Yet did not try so very hard to hide it.

In Act II there is hardly more action than a summons to the
court, which Dushyanta evades by sending back his Clown, and
his decision to remain at the sanctuary grove in order to be near
Shakuntala. The rest is lyric retelling of the meeting, and praise
of the hermit-girl. A third act shows the King invading the
hermitage garden, overhearing the sweet confidences of Shakuntala and her girl-companions; and then his declaration of love —
ending in a notably delicate and poetic scene of dalliance. In the
following act the audience discovers that Shakuntala gave herself
to the King in "voluntary marriage," and that he went back
to his court; and now there seems some doubt whether he will

keep his promise to recognize her publicly. She is with child, and after pious offerings are made, she sets out with attendants for the distant capital, to claim her right as wife and queen.

But the King's memory has failed him. He renounces her; and she is unable to bring proofs because she has lost in the sacred river the signet ring he had given her. Just after she leaves the King's presence in misery she is reported as miraculously snatched away to Heaven. The King is left uneasy in his conscience.

In the next act a fisherman who has found the ring brings it to the palace; whereat the King's memory is restored, and thenceforward he spends his time sorrowing, languishing for his lost love, and brooding over her beauties and virtue. All this is seen by a heavenly nymph sent to find out for Shakuntala whether the King has repented. His repentance has indeed been so sincere that the Heavenly Charioteer appears to convey Dushyanta to the celestial regions. The last act shows the King come to Indra's realm and welcomed by the gods. He is touchingly united with his son, now a manly little boy; and then with the forgiving Shakuntala. It is discovered that the loss of the ring and the renunciation grew out of a curse, and that the King is not to be blamed for his apparently ungallant behavior. The reunited King and Queen set out with their boy to rule over their land with Indra's blessing.

Here is a tale that might be out of a child's fairy-book. But in the tenderness of the sentiment revealed in the telling, in the poetic garments in which it is clothed, and in the noble characterizations, there are notable virtues and many of the devices that are typical of the Hindu theatre.

At the very beginning, before the play proper, is the blessing to the audience, the invocation to Shiva. And immediately one is transported into an idyllic region (called up by the poet's words and not provided by scene-painters with muddy canvases). The characters who tread through these pious groves and sanctuary gardens and royal courts are more than humanly beautiful, the King quite wonderfully handsome, good, and gracious, a resplendent knight and yet a chivalrous protector of his humblest subject; while Shakuntala runs the entire range of feminine loveliness, from a flowerlike maiden-shyness to womanly fortitude and nobility. Even the child in the briefest of scenes is nobly sketched. And by contrast there is that usual figure, the Clown, confidant of the King, not too obtrusively humorous here, but serving as foil and as dramatic tool: the half-insolent servant-companion who in effect says, Hurry up and sit down, King, because "I can't sit down till you do," and who half-mocks while showing out to the audience the King's nobility and his sentiments.

Here too are the usual opportunities for telling "asides"; two parties on the stage unknown to each other. Almost at the opening the King hides in the forest to watch Shakuntala and her friends at their girlish amusements, discovering and retelling to the audience in poetic descriptions the loveliness and nobility of this hermitage child. Again in the garden scene Dushyanta is concealed, and tells the audience first of his fears, then of what the girls on the bench are doing, then of his joy when Shakuntala confesses to the other girls her love of the King. This byplay, this poetic retelling, is one of the most typical devices employed for more richly embroidering the action with lyric beauty. In the first act, too, is an opportunity set in for pretty bits of individual acting, when Shakuntala is troubled by a bee and has opportunity for graceful pantomime, while the King comments on it in an eighteen-line lyric. There is also one notably humorous scene, by way of comic relief, when the fisherman is brought in by abusive policemen, who switch suddenly to considerate friendliness when they see the King's rich reward for the return of the lost ring.

The most notable quality of the play, however, is the .high level of the verse — and this is very difficult to indicate briefly, because part of the charm is in the pervasiveness of the sentiment, re-enforced by continual felicitous allusion to the beauties of nature, by imagery, and by literary music cues. In the garden, Shakuntala has pretended to go away, hiding in an amaranth hedge — she will see how long the King's love lasts. He lifts reverently the lotus-chain she has dropped.

KING

The perfumed lotus-chain
That once was worn by her
Fetters and keeps my heart
A hopeless prisoner.

SHAKUNTALA *(looking at her arm)*

Why was I so weak and ill that when the lotus-bracelet fell off, I did not even notice it?

KING *(laying the lotus-bracelet on his heart)*

Once, dear, on your sweet arm it lay
And on my heart shall ever stay;
Though you disdain to give me joy,
I find it in a lifeless toy.

SHAKUNTALA

I cannot hold back after that. I will use the bracelet as an excuse for my coming. . . .

So she returns to him. But he makes conditions before he will return the bracelet.

SHAKUNTALA *(feeling his touch)*

Hasten, my dear, hasten.

KING *(joyfully, to himself)*

Now I am content. She speaks as a wife to her husband. *(Aloud)* Beautiful Shakuntala, the clasp of the bracelet is not very firm. May I fasten it in another way?

SHAKUNTALA *(smiling)*

If you like.

KING *(artfully delaying)*

See, my beautiful girl!
The lotus-chain is dazzling white
As is the slender moon at night.
Perhaps it was the moon on high
That joined her horns and left the sky,
Believing that your lovely arm
Would, more than heaven, enhance her charm.

SHAKUNTALA

I cannot see it. The pollen from the lotus over my ear has blown into my eye.

KING

Will you permit me to blow it away? . . . *(Shakuntala darts a glance at him, then looks down. The King raises her face. Aside)*

Her sweetly trembling lip
With virgin invitation
Provokes my soul to sip . . .

And so on. This lyric lightness lies over the play like a rosy glow. Even Shakuntala, denied verse utterance, clothes her prose occasionally in poetic form and meaning. When the lovers have been interrupted, and Shakuntala is being led away by her guardian, she turns to the hedge concealing the King: " O bower that took away my pain, I bid you farewell until another blissful hour."

The " theatres " in which such plays were presented in the time of Kalidasa can be reconstructed only half conjecturally. So far as known, there were no permanent playhouses in India before the nineteenth century. But the many royal palaces afforded perfect facilities for producing plays before select audiences — and drama was distinctly a caste development, for the educated few. Usually a great hall or the central outdoor court was chosen. The king or prince, his retinue and his guests were grouped at one side, perhaps around a throne or royal box; a space would then be appropriated to the actors, dancers, and musicians.

No special background was erected, except for one curtain (behind which were actors' quarters, from which came offstage noises, Voices, etc.). The rest would be the naturally pleasing architecture and decoration usual to the palace: rich, neutral, perfectly fitted to the sensuous-sentimental lyric-drama to be presented. Doubtless the arrangement varied in numberless minor ways at different times and in different places, but the stage seems always to have been simple, open, and perhaps not even raised above the level of floor or pavement. One might argue a platform stage from the fact that the word used to designate the chief-actor or director originally meant " architect " or " carpenter." But such impermanent stages were bound to be simple.

Not only was there no attempt at illusive scenery, but the play-text was such as to forbid " settings " even in revivals where " stage decoration " is usual. Shakuntala opens with the coming of the King and his Charioteer into a wood; but neither they nor the surroundings remain stationary. The King is pursuing a deer. "Pursue as I may," he exclaims, " I can hardly keep him in sight." To which the Charioteer replies: " Your Majesty, I have been holding the horses back because the ground was rough.

Now we are on level ground, and you will easily overtake him."
A moment later he adds:

> The lines hang loose; the steeds unreined
> Dart forward with a will.

Apparently they gain on the animal; then a Voice tells them the
deer must not be killed. The chariot stops. The King and a
hermit hold converse. Then again they drive on; till finally they
come to that part of the pious grove where the main part of the
act is played.

It would be my judgment that even the chariot here is imagined,
along with the settings; and that a very little physical movement
would be employed to suggest the journey. But there are many
guesses as to that.[1] If the *acting* must carry the whole burden
of narrative and picturing, it must be notably skilful in both
gesture and voice-expression. And we know that these branches
of the art were diligently studied. Like every other subject in
the realm of the arts and philosophy, acting was analysed, its
excellencies and vices pigeon-holed, and elaborate structures of
rules erected for the guidance of those who practised it. The
actors wore no masks, and women played the female characters.
As in Greece, the actors in the literary theatre were an honored
group in society, at least at one time; though through the ages
there was also an obscure street theatre in which performed a
class of actors and tricksters little better than vagabonds and
thieves.

Whether Shudraka was only a mythical king or a real one,
whether he wrote *The Little Clay Cart* or had a court poet write
it, whether the play is mainly a recasting of an earlier work by
Bhasa: these are questions for the Sanskrit scholar to puzzle

---

[1] A romantic picture of the first production of *Shakuntala,* conceived of as played
in operatic settings, is to be found in *The Indian Theatre,* by E. P. Horrwitz (London,
1912); but the whole book seems half-fanciful. Much more trustworthy is *The Sanskrit
Drama in Its Origin, Development, Theory, and Practice,* by A. Berriedale Keith (Oxford, 1924). It seems to me the nearest accurate and best-reasoned work in a very
difficult field; but it is far from readable, very disputatious, and filled with detail that
only the Sanskrit scholar will value. In view of the lack of a popular volume on the
subject, the reader may best be referred to the brief treatment in the Encyclopædia
Britannica, or to a chapter in *A History of Sanskrit Literature,* by Arthur A. Macdonell
(London, 1900). The most accessible and probably the best translation of *Shakuntala*
can be found in *Kalidasa: Translations of Shakuntala and Other Works,* by Arthur W.
Ryder (London & New York: Everyman's Library); equally good is *The Little Clay
Cart: A Hindu Drama Attributed to King Shudraka,* translated by Arthur W. Ryder
(Cambridge, Mass., 1905). I am indebted to the Ryder translations for all my excerpts.

over. We may better enjoy the drama on its merits. It is somewhat less typical than *Shakuntala:* it deserts the usual kings and
high-born maidens for less exalted protagonists, a ruined, if noble,
merchant and a comparatively virtuous courtesan; it comes nearer
to violence than any other well-esteemed play (but the " murder "
proves not to have been successful); it combines the love plot
with a story of political change; it is less idyllic than usual, nearer
to the domestic-drama type; it employs less of verbal decoration
and imagery. By these very tokens, it escapes a certain monotonous harmony and laziness that sometimes pall on the
Western reader or spectator; is livelier, more inventive, more
varied, more vigorous. The characters, too, are more human and
more humorous than is usual.

The noble-minded courtesan, Vasantasena, is driven to seek
protection in the house of the virtuous Brahman-merchant Charudatta, to escape the unwelcome attentions of Sansthanaka, brother-
in-law of the perfidious King Palaka; and at nightfall she leaves
her jewels in Charudatta's keeping. They are stolen, and Charudatta honorably gives his wife's necklace to Vasantasena by way
of restitution; but the stolen jewels are also returned to her
through her maid, who has taken them from the thief. Meantime a virtuous young herdsman has been imprisoned by the
wicked King, but escapes. Vasantasena goes to Charudatta's
house and while there she generously gives to his small son gems
with which to buy a new gold cart, because he doesn't like his
one of clay. In leaving, Vasantasena steps into the carriage of
the hated Sansthanaka, mistaking it for that of Charudatta —
which, indeed, is immediately occupied by the escaped herdsman.
Vasantasena is dishonorably wooed by Sansthanaka, virtuously
repulses him and apparently is murdered by him. Sansthanaka
then denounces Charudatta as the murderer, and the latter is condemned by the King to death. The headsmen are about to do
their duty by the unfortunate, when the revived Vasantasena
appears, thus proving Charudatta's innocence. Immediately news
is brought that the herdsman has killed the King, has proved
his own right to the throne, and has granted a principality to
Charudatta. Vasantasena is legally raised out of the estate of
courtesan, and is therefore free to marry Charudatta.

Within the ten-act plot, of which this is a bald outline, there are minor intrigues, comic scenes, elaborated social incidents, what-not. One of the most amusing scenes, though an interruption of the story, is that in which a burglar, at his working, sets forth the principles of robbing as a fine art, quoting freely from the revered treatises on robbery. It would be possible to quote lyric bits as sweet as those from *Shakuntala* — though it is said that we who do not know Sanskrit at first hand, not realizing the difficulties of translation from the infinitely rich variations of the language, can only guess at the lyric beauty of the originals.

But even in translation it is evident that the brooding gentle-ness of Kalidasa, his pervasive felicity, cannot hang over a varied and intimate tale like this. *The Little Clay Cart* is, indeed, an isolated phenomenon, an achievement in a type of play unfamiliar to the place and the time out of which it was born.

With their passion for intellectual order, the Indian theorists divided the field of the drama into a number of types based on the use of the different legitimate elements of composition, the caste of the protagonists, supernatural elements, the employment of legendary or real-life plots, the intensity of the erotic emotion, etc., etc. At first there were ten divisions of the " higher drama," and eighteen of the " lower." But even the names of these types are confusing, and we need note them only as an indication of formalization in playwriting — a sort of caste test in dramaturgy. Such coded rules doubtless had much to do with making the Hindu drama the limited though lyrically beautiful thing that it is.

Nor need we pause over the later dramatists — except Bha-vabhuti. This writer, of the eighth century, composed three plays that have survived to us. They are not characterized by that sweet harmony and that smooth-flowing action so notable in earlier drama. The poetry in which the action is clothed rises to more stirring moments: there is more vitality in the emotional scenes and more grandeur in the descriptions of nature. Bha-vabhuti is, too, closer to the realities of life than Kalidasa, has deeper insight, more forceful imagination; he even escapes from the old prohibitions in regard to violence. But the pretty fancy, the meticulous workmanship, the lyric delicacy are gone. Gone,

Malwa dancing girls entertaining Akbar in 1560: a painting by
the artists Kisu and Dharm das. Most of the pictures of Hindu
and Persian "theatres" centre upon the throne of the royal spectator rather than upon a stage and shaped auditorium; and we
may infer that the average theatre was an informal arrangement
of platform, throne, and surrounding space for less important
spectators, in a palace court or hall, instead of the rigid bowl-
facing-a-stage of the Western nations. [From a painting in the
Victoria and Albert Museum, London, by courtesy of the
Directors.]

Japanese actors in costume. The lower left-hand print is of a dressing-room scene, not on the stage. All the actors are men. [From the Haviland Collection Catalogue.]

too, is literary simplicity, for in the descriptive passages are elabo-
rations and exaggerations that foreshadow the decline of Hindu
drama into the grandiose and the artificial. Native commentators
have called Kalidasa " the grace of poetry," and Bhavabhuti " the
master of eloquence."

And indeed, the period from the ninth to the fourteenth century is one of decay; and after the fourteenth, India is to contribute practically nothing to the history of the world theatre.
The confusion of changing languages, the rigidities of the caste
system in social life, the codification of rules of practice for the
artist — these are circumstances hostile to the art that above all
others is social in its implications, direct in appeal, and more
emotional than intellectual. The drama got lost in refinements
and verbal ornament, went away into strange regions of florid
rhetoric and literary jugglery.

The Indian theatre, indeed, may owe its worst as well as its
best features to the fact that it was a *class* institution. The
director of a play asks, " What are those qualities which the
virtuous, the wise, the venerable, the learned and the Brahmans
require in drama? " and is answered: " Profound exposition of
the various passions, pleasing interchange of mutual affection,
loftiness of character, delicate expression of desire, a surprising
story and elegant language."

The description indicates at once the slightness or shallowness
of Sanskrit drama, and the delicacy, elegance, and harmony attained by its greatest practitioners. In accepting the injunction
to please only the most learned and the most fastidious minds
in the land, the dramatists cut themselves off from all that is
deeply stirring, that moves the soul and cleanses the spirit — the
very thing that we of the Western world consider essentially
dramatic. Instead they please us graciously, dreamily, sentimentally, and sensuously. They are masters in that little bit of
the dramatic field that lies over against lyric poetry and decorative
painting. We may find the perfect analogy in Indian and
Persian painting: in the child-like fancy, the transparent coloring, the delightful freshness, the dew-drenched sweetness; but
having experienced this slight and utterly disarming lyric beauty,
we may on occasion want to get back to our own Michelangelos

and El Grecos, to our Æschylus and Euripides and Shakespeare. For Indian drama is gentle and lulling but never splendid.

Those who are its unreserved apologists point out that it attains to the peace of the East and avoids the restlessness of the West. We others, finding that peace pleasurable, yet doubt its profundity. We see in drama and in theatre at their highest some implication of peace attained only after gripping struggle, the more radiant calm of serenity after storm. Perhaps a racial difference will always prevent us from judging eye-to-eye with the Hindus.

THE CHINESE theatre offers even greater difficulties to the Western mind. Chinese drama has no literary values for us, and the conventions of presentation are so different that almost insuperable barriers to understanding are set up. It is significant that the only so-called Chinese play that has made a considerable success in the West is a pieced-out romance with only vague relationship to any existing Chinese drama, with certain naïve customs of staging played up for prettiness or for humor. Memories of *The Yellow Jacket,* indeed, may well serve as guide to what will prove of interest to the Western student in approaching the Chinese stage: not plot or dramatic intensity or spoken poetry, surely, but a child-like fairy-tale freshness, surface glamour, patches of theatric-poetic invention, and a naïveté that to us is too often humorous.

It is the stage conventions, then, rather than the drama, that may give us pause even in a brief survey of the important theatres of the world. We may sit six or seven hours at a stretch in a Chinese playhouse and suffer fearful periods of boredom between pleasant periods of wonder and delight — but afterwards we shall always hold in memory the *way* in which poetry was occasionally conjured up for us, and the theatric brightness of the stage.

The playhouse itself is typically a platform for acting and a place for seeing. The stage is open, without concealing curtains, uniformly lighted throughout the show and wholly innocent of wings, scenery, or machinery. This is a place for acting, undisguised, but pleasantly designed. The wall at back has two doorways, one for the actors to enter from, the other for their return to the green-room (the actors' common room). There are fairly elaborate playhouses in the larger cities, but the greater number of Chinese theatres are temporary or movable structures which can be set up in street or field. Always, however, for audiences made comfortable in boxes or for those standing in the street, the simple projecting stage with two doorways at back is standard. Indoors or out, this stage has a roof, usually ornamental like that of a temple.

It is in the temple, of course, that we may seek the origins of the Oriental theatre. The Chinese have always been lovers of ritual and ceremony. Dance and music in religious exercises go back beyond historical evidence, into legend and myth. Certainly near-dramatic dancing was common here in temple and palace long before the era of Thespis and Æschylus. One need only remember that the Golden Age in China is supposed to have been at the time we would designate the twenty-third and twenty-fourth centuries B.C. Nearer to historical certainty, perhaps, is the report that the Emperor Ming Huang, of the eighth century A.D., after a trip to the Moon where he saw skilled actors, formed the first dramatic company and erected a stage in his pear orchard; whence the name still assumed by many players, " Members of the College of the Pear Garden," or " Youths of the Pear Garden."

Truly literary drama, however, seems to have come into its own only in the late Middle Ages. At least the types of play still predominating today on Chinese stages appeared in great number, and apparently without earlier imperfect or transitional forms, during the Yuan Dynasty, 1280–1368. It happened at just the time when a conqueror had thrown out all the old court literary men and scholars. Suddenly the theatre, theretofore held inferior to poetry and other intellectual arts, blossomed. It might be better to say that the theatre came up part way to meet literature, and that high literature (then in the learned classic language) stooped part way to meet the vernacular stage.

Truth to tell, dramatic literature in China never reached the importance a Sophocles or a Shakespeare endowed it with in the West. The Chinese themselves make no claims for it; and even allowing for the lack of language-embroidery values possibly lost in translation, the Western reader may agree that Chinese plays are little more than melodrama or hack journalistic plays — or grand opera *libretti*. The situations are pretty well standardized, the characters run to obvious types, the "effects" are neither deeply dramatic nor cumulatively emotional. All that the Western mind craves in tragedy is overlooked or dissipated: taut dramatic structure, suspense, psychologic truth. The casual nature of the plot, indeed, explains that apparently shattering confusion in the auditorium, the constant coming and going of spectators, the tea-drinking, the conversations and eating and even games while the actors are getting through a particularly unimportant passage. There is no continuity of mood, no built-up tension. The performance probably lasts from late afternoon till after midnight; but the programme includes several plays. As the actors from one go out the exit door, the players of the next enter by the other, so that action is continuous. And so is the music that sounds so squeaky and clangy to Western ears. (The extremely long plays, we are told, running to thirty-two and forty-eight acts, are reading rather than acting versions.)

Watching the Chinese audience at times, one knows that the spectators are enjoying values largely lost to the outsider. One guesses that these are of two sorts: first, the *acting* — the Chinese theatre, from projecting bare stage to conventions of playing, is designed to give first prominence to acting as an art; and second, a sort of operatic effectiveness induced by the music and the chanting delivery combined with the more truly histrionic virtues. In addition there is the sensuous richness of costumes, properties, and imaginatively evoked *milieu*. The instrumental music, of course, adds value only for the initiated. To those trained in appreciation of the European scale and to harmony and melody, it seems monotonous, harsh, and shrill. The musicians sit at the back centre of the stage, always in sight of the audience. The dialogue is at times spoken, but mostly chanted. The delivery is absolutely unreal, and a world of convention exists in the gestures, posturing, intonation, and shadings of artificial expression.

In the subject matter of the plays there is a range almost as broad as in the West. No arbitrary line is drawn between tragedy and comedy. In the one direction, deep tragedy in our sense is lacking, though pathetic situation and sob-scenes may be witnessed. But heroic deeds, most often built around filial piety, or historical-military exploits, are commonest in serious drama. And in the other direction there is every sort of humor, from a tender sort to slap-stick. " Broad " jests go well; but it is common knowledge that the playwright who takes to indecency to hold his audiences is tormented by evil spirits so long as his play holds the boards.

Chinese plays are sometimes classified as either " historical " or " civil," with farces as perhaps an extra and unimportant sort. Military and patriotic plays, and heroic legendary ones, are, of course, historical. The civil group is largely domestic drama, wherein virtue triumphs. " Criminal " drama forms a considerable subdivision. But sometimes there are plays of satirical purpose, often with the priests or old superstitions as target. When all is said about the literary side of Chinese drama, however, the fact remains that there is no serious effort to match great action with great poetry, to re-enforce the dramatic emotion by the revealing word. The actor, moreover, takes what liberties he likes with the written text, cutting and improvising freely.

The characters tend to standardization: Emperors and generals and heroes in the historical genre, together with demons and spirits; the honest wife, the jealous husband, the light woman, the villain, etc., in the civil plays. The poor student who ultimately overcomes all difficulties and rises to high office is a favorite. The military hero performing marvels of valor is another. Traditional make-up and costuming, known to every theatre-goer, characterize many figures in dramatic literature — almost as definitely as in the Italian *Commedia dell'Arte,* though with less of caricature. An understood convention is the coloring in face-painting (the faces are often made-up until they are to all practical purposes masks): a whitened face denotes a wicked person, a red face is honest, a gold face heavenly, a streaked face belongs to a robber,[2] and so on. A bride wears a red veil, deceased ancestors

[2] I have followed here the account of A. E. Zucker in *The Chinese Theatre* (Boston, 1925), the best available treatise on the subject; but other authorities give different though no less exact rules. See also *Studies in the Chinese Drama,* by Kate Buss (Boston, 1922), and the admirable chapter on drama in *A History of Chinese Literature,* by Herbert A. Giles (London, 1901). For Japanese drama, see Frank Alanson Lombard's *An Outline History of the Japanese Drama* (London, 1928), and the introductory chapters of Asataro Miyamori's *The Masterpieces of Chikamatsu* (London and

wear black veils or else strips of paper hanging from their right ears, a sick person wears an opaque yellow veil. Corrupt officials wear round hats.

Despite these elementary aids to understanding, much more is left to the spectator's imagination than in the theatres of Europe — even more than was left before Realism brought in detailed scene and photographic fidelity to " life." Out of a stage with a few rich hangings, a rug underfoot, and a half dozen properties, the Chinese actor and a Property Man will suddenly conjure up a cherry orchard in blossom or an idyllic lake with boats on it or Heaven. And you see these places believably, far more believably than in the elaborate painted settings of the " illusive" scene designer — in the shape and colors of your own ideal vision of the places. A handful of bits of paper fluttering down, after the property man has tossed them up, evokes the whole " feel " of a snowstorm; when once you know that a banner carried behind a general denotes a thousand soldiers in his army, you subconsciously count the banners and know that to all intents and purposes one, two, or three thousand men are following him into battle; when a character paddles the air rhythmically with an oar, the whole pretty scene of placid water and boating flashes into the mind. Sometimes the means are more concrete: the Property Man sets up two poles, a cross-bar and a silken hanging — and lo! the stage has become a throne room; or he sets up a little piece of wall, and the General acts out elaborately the convention of taking a city.

This Property Man is, indeed, the very symbol of the noble artificiality of the Chinese stage. He is dressed in black or blue, and therefore is, symbolically, invisible to the audience. He is always on the stage, and may even have assistants; but the audience never thinks of him as entering into the play. He is the wizard who sets down a ball of red cloth to show that the actor's head has been cut off, he may help the General off with his priceless coat before a piece of business that might soil it, he touches off the fireworks to indicate that this latest entrant is a ghost

New York, 1926). An excellent treatment of the popular theatre alone is *Kabuki: The Popular Stage of Japan*, by Zoe Kincaid (London, 1925). Accounts of the *No*, with translations, can be found in *Plays of Old Japan: The No*, by Marie C. Stopes (London, 1927), and in Ernest Fenollosa and Ezra Pound's " *Noh*," *or Accomplishment* (New York, 1916).

from Heaven, he places the chair which becomes a mountain over which the hero laboriously climbs. But never does he interfere with the illusion of the scene.

If suggestion and convention thus work wonders in evoking something more subtly theatrical than picture scenery, the actor does his part in creating atmosphere and belief. A ritualistic stage fight shows not one blow struck, but all the activity and excitement of battle; and no one doubts which is victor, when vanquished sneaks off and the hero proudly follows. This actor will climb stairs by merely lifting one foot high off the floor after the other, or else go all the way from Peking to Thibet by walking a few times around the stage rug (though he may then announce where he has arrived). Then, too, he can leap off the table in such a way that you know he has jumped down the well, a suicide. He mounts and gets down from horses, or gallops on them, and washes his hands in imaginary pools, and backs up to a bamboo pole and throws his head back to show he has been hanged. But it is the drummer who tells you the time of night by beating out the hours the while all other instruments are still.

The one unfailing physical richness of the production is in the costumes. The wardrobe of a Chinese troupe is costly even when judged by Western " revue " standards. Minor characters dress magnificently, literally beggars in silks, and chief characters are no less than gorgeous and resplendent. Thus in one detail there is material basis for the imaginative splendor, the glamour, of the Oriental stage. But it is from the imagination of the spectator that the larger richness and the more poetic achievement come.

The actors for such a theatre must be long and carefully trained, and many years are spent by the young player in specialized education. It is obvious that something more than the casual European training is necessary when an actor must be able not only to die gracefully on the stage but then to get up and exit with exactly the stoop that will tell the audience his body is being carried off by four bearers. Incidentally many young men must be trained to the simulation of feminine charms — even to dainty walking in cramped shoes; for the women's parts until very recently have been taken by men — at least since the eighteenth century when women were banished from the stage by royal decree, after an

Emperor took an actress to wife. (One is puzzled a bit to know whether actresses were then considered too good for the theatre, or if the measure was a precaution against possible repetition of a misalliance.) The most famous player in China today, Mei Lan-Fang, is known chiefly for his masterly playing in

A Chinese actor in typical gorgeous costume.
[From a drawing by Kenyon Cox, in
Century Magazine.]

feminine rôles. There are those who call him the world's greatest living actor; and when one considers how much more of creativeness there is in Oriental acting, and how little of photographic imitation, one hesitates to dispute the opinion.

As a matter of fact, Chinese plays are not so exclusively non-realistic and imaginative as I have perhaps suggested. The means is always imaginative and conventional, as compared with stag-

ing in the Occident.   But sometimes grossly realistic incident is
included in a play — and of a sort very distasteful to Western
spectators.   But perhaps that is a matter of "taste": our own
tragic heroines, suffering from too much love, though emotionally
moving to us, would be distressing if not ridiculous to the Chinese.

Since Western influences have flowed strongly in the Orient,
the customs of the theatre have changed.   Actresses now appear,
there are companies that adopt more and more of Realism in
staging, there are even "little theatre" groups devoted to Western
"ideals."   But China is too big a country, and too sluggish, to
swallow alien art at one gulp.   And it is more than possible that
the old stage, with its childish fairy-tale quality, its rich glamour,
its way of making poetic incident and imaginative beauty appear
out of acting and a platform and a few properties, has virtues unknown to the theatre farther west — and essentially theatrical
virtues.

IN JAPAN caste determined a sharp division between aristocratic
and popular theatres.   For the nobles there came into being a
drama highly intellectualized, rigidly formalized; for the people
there was a freer drama.   Over both sorts was the sensuous richness, the calculated decorativeness, that is of the very spirit of
Japan.

The noble drama, the No-play, is today the most important
survival in the world from the ritualistic theatre of elder times,
from the days when ceremonial beauty was more important than
plot or emotional content.   The No — the word corresponds to
our "drama" in the larger sense — has at once an austerity inherited out of the religious rites at the temples, and a formal delicacy and a colorful richness added out of the feeling for æsthetic
expressiveness.   Drama never eschewed more completely Realism
in all its aspects: surface truth to appearances, imitative mimicry,
and transcription of human emotion.   As soon as it developed out
of ritual dance into a form compounded of music, dance, incident,
and words, the No took on rigid conventions.

The single No-play is brief, shorter than the average Western
"one-act" drama; and in the reading it is often so slight that it
seems merely a reminiscent bit, of great lyric charm but undra-

matic and even bald. The secret is that the text is only a framework hung with poetic allusion and pretty words. What we would call the dramatic element, the tension-and-clash, is either non-existent (as in many examples) or comes from some traditional and racial reaction to a given situation or deed. The values that the educated Japanese expects in a *No*-drama are utterly different from those that we rate highest in our theatre: they depend for their effectiveness both upon a recondite knowledge and upon appreciation of ceremonial excellencies.

Several plays are produced on one programme, and it is typical that the arrangement, the order, of the plays is considered of greater importance than the individual content. A programme is as carefully constructed, balanced, as a religious ritual. It presents, indeed, a " service." The several parts are chosen and placed with a view to total harmony, to decorative pattern, to a sequence of feeling as subtly estimated as is the arrangement of movements in a complex musical work. There is here something approximating the Western formula of preparation-rise-climax-and-fall; but the emotional sequence is but the smaller consideration: the greater importance is in the adjustment of the poetic, imaginative, and decorative details.

One may find a hint of the care taken in these matters and of the delicacy of enjoyment, by recalling that in Japan flower-arrangement is a highly developed art, and that the nobles used to have a ceremonial game known as " listening to incense," wherein blended perfumes were distinguished and brief allusive titles written to fix the poetic thought evoked by each sort.

In explanation of the insubstantial character of the *utai,* or *No*-play text, it might be said that the object is to present an image rather than to lay out an action; and those who have got at the purpose of the modern " Imagist " poets will understand more exactly the creative intent of the dramatist. The play was written for the few, for discriminating art-lovers, for select audiences traditionally trained to subtleties and to a set of conventions.

A legend tells that the dance from which the *No* evolved was invented by the gods: when one of their number, the all-important Sun-goddess, hid away for a long time in the rock-cave of Heaven, causing universal darkness, the others invented a dance which one of them performed on the top of an inverted tub; and the **Sun**-goddess came out to see what was the hollow noise made by the dancer's feet. (The sound of the dancer's stamping on the wooden floor is still a characteristic touch in the No-play.) But later the other elements were added to the pantomimic dance, and it is probable that Buddhist priests were the first " playwrights." In the fourteenth century Kwan-ami Kiyotsugu crystallized the form of the No, and it was due to him that it was taken under court protection. Thereafter specially honored poets and specially dedicated companies of actors created that store of No-plays and No-rules that has been the treasury of the aristocratic players for five hundred years since. Always the limitations and the finenesses of noble origin — of the association with gods, priests, emperors, lords — have persisted.

It is said that almost every word in a No-play means far more than the word alone says: there are traditional associations through centuries-old use by poets; overtones, double meanings, and vague indications. The values are heightened by the delivery, in a sort of chant. But the movements of the actors and dancers are no less rich in symbolism, allusion, and suggestion. Music (the musicians here again are placed on the stage) binds the whole performance together. The usual instruments are a flute and three types of drum.

The stage is as unvarying as the methods of delivery: a rectangular platform with a temple roof. At the back is a conventional representation of a pine-tree. A bridge or trestle runs off at one side to a green-room. The auditorium is on three sides of the projecting platform. The wooden stage floor is specially constructed to afford a drum-like resonance to the dancer's stamping. The entire stage is ornamental but without any illusive scenery or machinery. Properties are but sparingly used. The fan, according to an accepted symbolism, may stand for many things: the spectator transforms it into this or that object called for by the action, just as he constructs his own imaginative setting in accordance with the poet's words.

The actors are supplemented by a Chorus of six men or more who squat on the stage throughout the play, chanting at intervals. In the design of the drama the Chorus serves practically the same function as in the Greek theatre, as re-enforcement or commentary or to instruct the audience. The main actors, all men, are two, three, or four in number. They enter with ceremonial slowness, and every gesture for every feeling or thought is prescribed by rule. All characters except young men are represented by masks, the impersonality of the acting being thus increased by suppression of facial play. The masks are beautifully carved, and are wholly formalized; but within non-realistic limits they have a considerable range of expressiveness. The gestures and posturing of the actors are equally unreal, symbolic, and according to an understood formula. The danced portions of the action are wholly unlike the freer dancing of the West — call it " Greek " if you like — and yet wholly unlike the artificial gyrations of the European ballet. Again it is the ritualistic, ceremonial element that predominates. The actors' costumes are of sumptuous richness; and the magnificence of the costumed figures has full effect on the simple stages, quietly decorative and a perfect background. It may be added that in olden days the audience likewise came in full ceremonial dress, as they would if the No were still only a ritual dance at a temple on a holy-day.

It is difficult for the Western mind to recognize such acted-danced art as essentially drama. We of the Occident demand the free play of emotion for full appreciation of acted drama; and here the intellect seems always to control. But after all, " drama " merely means something done, an act; and assuredly there is no authority to say that the ritualistic, formalized action is less noble than the imitative-emotional sort. We shall do better to grant that here is a sort of dramatic art different from ours, finely decorative to all eyes, and affording even to unaccustomed spectators sudden glimpses of a different beauty, intellectual, fanciful, subtle, poetic. At one side a sort of sensuous harmony, of color, music, and movement, lulls one; at the other, there is the constant play of pretty meaning, of description, metaphor, philosophical thought, which we may understand when our wits have been sharpened by long training — the whole rendered clearer by being lifted above human emotion to a region of impersonality.

The No has existed six hundred years or more as the privileged art of an aristocratic class. Today it is played by descendants of

Two No stages. [The drawing above from *Plays of Old Japan: The No,* by Marie C. Stopes; the painting below from a screen in two parts, reproduced in the Charles Haviland Collection Catalogue.]

Two Kabuki theatres. Above, a seventeenth century theatre, with a stage roof of the old temple type. Note the realistic properties. Below, a theatre in 1798, when the roof had become a symbol only. Here the floor boxes for spectators are clearly seen. [The print below is by Utagawa Toyokuni, reproduced in *Kabuki: The Popular Stage of Japan*, by Zoe Kincaid.]

the actors of Kiyotsugu's time. But with the almost chaotic changes in social life in Japan during the last half-century, lines between classes have been broken, and no one may foresee the future of such a very special type of art. Perhaps there will be an aristocracy of the spirit — or of the intellect — to keep it alive. Meantime certain of its elements, its utter precision, its decorative richness-in-restraint, its stylization, its poetic intensity, have been well studied by certain Western artists who have guessed that the conquest of Realism is not the whole battle of the theatre.

In one sense the No exists like a curiosity out of the past. The hereditary guardians let no changes be made after the sixteenth century. The old methods, the old subjects, the old costumes and masks, are preserved, so that one views a No-play as one views a survival of Mediæval art — but Chartres Cathedral or the Sainte Chappelle is none the less beautiful for not being modernized.

There is, however, a popular theatre in Japan which has changed with the times. The *Kabuki* was scorned by the nobles and the intellectuals through all the earlier centuries. This more vulgar theatre, less intellectual, less bound by aristocratic code and traditional methodism, compromised with popular taste, with sensationalism, with Realism. Even so, it is characterized by formalities in presentation that place it worlds apart from European drama; but it is less distinctively different — and for that very reason less interesting to the spectator out of the West.

The *Kabuki* theatre is supposed to have originated out of the performances of a woman dancer, O-Kuni, about 1600; to her dancing — perhaps religious at first — were added elements out of the No-plays and out of the exhibitions of popular entertainers. It is chronicled " that O-Kuni was beautiful, that she was skilled in calligraphy, that she had a sympathetic nature, loved flowers and the moon, and that a snowy evening or a maple scene in the autumn inspired her to poetry." We may take the description as warrant that, as the *Kabuki* developed, it did not swing *very* far toward the unrelieved Realism of the West. Indeed much was taken over bodily from the No theatre: the playhouse was but slightly changed, the conventions of staging were made less rigid, even while a similar ceremonial beauty was exacted, music continued to make the play almost operatic, and plots began to touch on common life as well as legendary deeds. Just after O-Kuni's time the women performers predominated; but their alarming popularity, and perhaps some moral laxness, led the government to forbid all but male players. By the mid-seventeenth century men's companies were firmly established, and thenceforth the *Kabuki* was the accepted entertainment of the common people.

The few changes in the playhouse, from the *No* model, indicate the direction of change in the performance. (There was, incidentally, a strong influence from the Chinese theatre too.) The stage was still the rectangular platform with audience on three sides; and for long the ornamental roof persisted in actuality — though later a painted representation or symbol of it sufficed. But in addition to the bridge from the green-room, one or oftener two bridges were built forward from the stage through the auditorium, for more effective entrances: the "flower paths" which have recently come in for wide discussion after adoption into European and American "revue" theatres. Thus pageant-like and spectacular effects were facilitated. Trap-doors in the stage floor added opportunity for tricks and surprises. To the stately acting and the old measured posturing out of ritual were added extraneous effects quite like those known to Western melodrama and opera. The form of the auditorium is sufficiently shown in the several illustrations, except that it should be added that the audience squats in the many boxes: there are no seats. Mats and cushions provide "comfort," and small stoves are sometimes utilized by more fortunate spectators. Since the performance lasts from early morning (originally from dawn) to late afternoon, there is inevitably considerable coming and going, not to mention eating and drinking.

The properties for such a stage naturally became more elaborate, and the settings grew from mere suggestions to fairly explicit indications of reality. The drift toward illusive setting became so strong, indeed, that the Japanese invented the revolving stage (originally for the doll-plays), for swift change of background, long before the idea was developed in European theatres. But the search for novelty and for natural effects on the *Kabuki* stage went on even while the producers adhered to the Chinese convention of the "invisible" Property Man. He still comes and goes in a way that would shatter the illusion in any Western playhouse.

With the austere example of No-acting before him, and yet in a theatre where novelty and sensation counted, the *Kabuki* player necessarily found himself pulled in the two directions of a high conventionalization in acting and of naturalism. So it is no matter for surprise that two schools grew up, distinguished by their devotion to the one or the other ideal. And yet all Japanese acting (up to the experiments in imitation of the Occident in the twentieth century) must be visualized as unreal and at times ritualistic. An actor may play a death scene with a dragging-out of the agony very distressing to the uninitiated — twenty minutes of dying in the midst of his gore — but the naturalism of it is not that photographic sort affected by Western actors today. The measure of progress away from the high stylization of the No is indicated by the abandonment of the rigid mask in favor of a conventional painted make-up: faces are painted in traditional ways to symbolize traditional characters. The *Kabuki* actor must be a dancer and a pantomimist as accomplished as the players of the No, though his posturing is less tightly restricted by code.

The plays are not of great poetic value, and are considered rather as "vehicles." Still at least one dramatist whose works are popular on the *Kabuki* stage, Chikamatsu, who lived from 1660 to 1724, has been called by recent commentators "the Shakespeare of Japan" — though one awaits better translations than are now available before endorsing the title. The range of plays is from heroic tragedy to melodrama, and from satire to farce. Farcical interludes, one might add, are played in Japan even between the most serious numbers on a No programme. The most famous play in the *Kabuki* repertory is one dealing with the legend of the Forty-seven Ronin.

Perhaps one detail will serve to fix the *Kabuki* drama in our minds — as conventionalized theatre making concessions to Realism — better than any other. Among the common properties is a velvet horse. You will remember how the Chinese actor mounted his wholly imaginary steed and galloped away. But for the Japanese audiences this make-believe was not enough. So the *Kabuki* horse is constructed and walks around on the four legs of two minor actors; their bodies and heads are completely hidden within the body of a quite realistic animal, that knows every trick of kicking, plunging, trotting, etc. There are even actors who specialize in being horses' legs. This velvet-covered living property, common to all *Kabuki* stages, is the very indicator of the degree of their Realism. *Kabuki* lies half-way between Chinese imaginative theatre and Western photographic theatre.

In Japan a third theatre is important, but too " special " to demand more than a paragraph here. The " Doll Theatre " or puppet theatre has held its place for centuries. Chikamatsu and other important playwrights wrote more plays for the dolls than for the *Kabuki* companies (though their puppet-plays were soon absorbed into the other theatre); and there has been constant give-and-take between the marionette-stage and that of the *Kabuki* players. It is said that historically, dancing dolls preceded the doll-play. But music, acting figures, and recited story were brought together in one entertainment, about 1600, and marionette shows have been popular ever since. In Japan far more of talent was expended in making the puppet performance sensuously beautiful and the lines poetically engrossing than ever was the case in Europe. Without making the mistake of judging by the Punch and Judy shows or other degraded descendants of the old Italian (originally Greek and Roman) puppets, we may feel sure that the West never knew a doll theatre quite so elaborate, quite so definitely patterned to æsthetic considerations, as the Japanese. The traditional fine craftsmanship, the perfection of decorative adjustment, the love of impersonal art, the delight in miniature loveliness of any sort — all these elements went into the making of the world's most skilful, and most esteemed, puppet theatre. But it is a far cry to that very specialized stage, from the emotionally intensified drama, and the human actor, at the heart of our present story.

In Java there exists a national dramatic activity almost wholly shaped by puppet-invention. Side by side are a theatre of shadow-figures (old beyond history), a theatre of manipulated puppets, and a theatre of dancing human-actors whose movements are conventionalized out of the mechanical doll-gestures. Thus at least one country gained its mimetic art not from humans imitating nature or dancing instinctively, but from a ritual-toy originally made in a formal-decorative likeness to man.   This curious round-about development, from convention to convention, may well leave to us, as our last — and most memorable — thought about the Oriental stage, an impression of purposeful unreality, of formalized theatric beauty.

Javanese puppets.   [From *Javanische Schattenspiele*, by Otto Höver.]

CHAPTER VI

The Theatre in the Church

THE THEATRE is especially the shrine of Venus. In fact it was in this manner that this sort of performance came up in the world. For the censors were often wont to destroy, in this very birth, the theatres more than any other thing, consulting for the morals of the people, as foreseeing a great peril accruing to them from licentiousness. Pompey the Great, less only than his own theatre, when he had built up that stronghold of every vice, fearing that the censors might one day cast reflections on his memory, placed over it a temple of Venus, "under which," said he, "we have put rows of seats for the shows." Thus did he cloak this damned and damnable work under the name of a temple, and by the aid of superstition eluded the rule. . . Whatever there be peculiar and proper to the stage, with respect to the dissoluteness and postures of the body, they consecrate to the soft nature of Venus and of Bacchus, the one dissolute through her sex, the other through his wantonness; while such things as are done by the voice, by music, by wind and stringed instruments, have for their patrons Apollos and Muses and Minervas and Mercuries. Thou must hate, Christian, those things, the inventors whereof thou canst not but hate . . .

In like manner also we are commanded to love no immodesty. By this means therefore we are cut off from the theatre likewise, which is the private council-chamber of immodesty, wherein nothing is approved save that which elsewhere is disapproved. . . The very harlots also, the victims of the public lust, are brought forward on the stage, more wretched in the presence of women, from whom alone they are wont to conceal themselves . . . Blush the Senate! Blush all ranks! let the very women, the destroyers of their own modesty, shudder at their doings before the light and the public, and blush this once within the year . . .

Nay, in all the show, no offence will more meet us, than that very overcareful adorning of the men and women. The very community of feeling, their very agreement or disagreement in party-spirit, doth, by their intercourse, fan the sparks of carnal lust. Finally, no one in entering the show, thinketh of any thing more than to see and to be seen . . . What manner of thing is it to go from the Church of God into the Church of the Devil? from the sky (as they say) to the stye? . . .

Why may not such men be in danger of devils entering into them? for the case hath happened, the Lord is witness, of that woman who went to the theatre, and returned thence with a devil. Wherefore when the unclean spirit, in the exorcism, was hard pressed because he had dared to attack a believer, he boldly said, " and most righteously I did it, for I found her in mine own place." It is well known also that there was shown to another in her sleep, on the night of the day in which she had heard a tragedian, a linen cloth upbraiding her with that tragedian by name, and that this woman at the end of five days was no longer in the world. . .

What wilt thou do, when discovered in this estuary of impious voices? . . . think what becometh of thee in heaven. Doubtest thou that in this crisis, in which the Devil is raging against the Church, all the Angels are looking down from Heaven, and marking every man, whosoever hath spoken blasphemy, whosoever hath listened to it, whosoever hath ministered with his tongue, or with his ears, to the Devil against God? Wilt thou not then flee from these chairs of the enemies of Christ, this seat of pestilences . . . ?

The quotation is from Tertullian, from the *De Spectaculis,* or treatise *Of Public Shows,* as the translator, the Rev. C. Dodgson, phrases it. This pious work was written about A.D. 198, just after the author's conversion to Christianity, when there was, indeed, evil enough to grow indignant about in the Roman theatres. But the descriptive portions, though they may conveniently remind us of the degradation of the classic stage, have even more value here for the light they throw on the temper of the Christian fathers, and the relationship of the theatre to the fear of devils and of the angel-spies of God. If the quotation seem over-long for such a brief book as this, let us reflect that these few paragraphs contain, by implication, practically the whole history of the theatre in Europe over a period of centuries — nay, for nearly a millennium.

Tertullian has, indeed, set forth graphically not only the iniquities of the Roman stage of his time, but also the means by which the Christian Church was to strangle theatric art and prevent its rebirth for eight hundred years to come. Note well the righteous zeal, the true Christian priest's burning indignation with the works of the Devil, growing at once out of love for the souls of men and out of intolerance. Note well the distrust of the pleasures of life, even of such apparently innocent ones as dressing-up and of congregating socially. But note chiefly the way in which the reader is warned about one who died after being seen in a theatre, and of another who was possessed by a Devil out of the playhouse. For fear is to be the great weapon of the Church in the age to come, the weapon with which drama is to be killed. The terror of Devils and of a Hell after death for those who disregard the priests — this is to outweigh love of show and of the arts.

There are, of course, other contributive causes for the long lapse before another theatre is born; in the social conditions of the times, and in the break-up of the Roman Empire under the repeated invasions by barbarous Northern tribes. (They were not so barbarous as the Romans in many ways, but uneducated to drama and the arts.) It was Christianity, nevertheless, that was most hostile, most militant, that deliberately set to work to stamp out the art sacred to the pagan Dionysus.

If you read Tertullian's treatise to the end, you may detect in his closing picture, of the Christian world as a show, a prophecy of what the theatre is to be when next the mimetic spirit in man emerges.

Dost thou breathe me a sigh for goals and theatres? . . . Behold uncleanness thrown down by chastity, perfidiousness slain by faithfulness, cruelty beaten by mercy, wantonness overlaid by modesty . . . But what sort of show is that near at hand? the coming of the Lord, now confessed, now glorious, now triumphant. What is that joy of the Angels? what the glory of the rising saints? . . . There remain other shows: that last and eternal day of judgment . . . the persecutors of the Name of the Lord, melting amid insulting fires more raging than those wherewith themselves raged against the Christians; those wise philosophers, moreover, reddening before their own disciples, now burning together with them . . .

Prophetic, because the favorite scene in the next great drama of the world is to be the realistic casting of the damned into Hell; and along with it will be the whole acted story of the coming of the Lord and the glorification of the Saints; and after that the Morality plays in which " perfidiousness slain by faithfulness " will be the end and motive. Tertullian wrote metaphorically of this Christian " spectacle "; but a thousand years later the priests of his Church will be acting out on stages the very scenes he so graphically sketches in words.

As a last reminder of the Roman stage, one may note that a later famous Churchman, Arius, of the fourth century, outlined a plan for a Christian theatre to combat the lewd ones of the pagans; but nothing tangible resulted — perhaps because Arius was excommunicated for his heretical doctrinal views. The Ro-

During the long period when the theatres were dark, this sort of show did much to entertain the people. The Church is here staging an execution of "heretics," but the Kings did their bit along the same line. Note the audience at the far left, where a severed head is held up to view.

man theatre (which then was the amusement not only of the old capital and colonies, but of Constantinople and the Eastern Empire) persisted through the fifth and into the sixth century after Christ's birth, then died in the bitter conflict with the increasingly powerful Church. Some of the later Fathers even went so far as to trace the fall of the Roman people to the influence of the depraved theatres. The last contemporary reference to the Roman stage is in a letter dated 533.

After that we may picture the wandering actors as producing

scraps of their old plays at courts, at private festivities, even occasionally at a crossroads or in a city street, surreptitiously. But they are no longer true comedians, presenting complete " dramas "; with their sketches they mix jugglery, knife-throwing, tumbling, tight-rope walking — or they lead along a trained bear to provide the " feature " act. No one can say just how far acting declined, how close drama approached toward total extinction. But before the old tradition died entirely, a new element entered into entertainment, the element of recited poetic story. It came not only from the South but from the North, from the Teutonic gleemen. Without being truly dramatic in itself — without becoming *acted* story with impersonating performers — it kept alive the *personal telling* of dramatic incident. At its best it became an accepted art — minstrelsy — which in turn gave rise to a literature that is the most important survival of the early Middle Ages, the *Chansons de geste,* the *Romans* and the *Contes;* at its worst, it afforded the miserable jugglers and " mimes " an additional item for a very degraded repertory of " turns," an item that at least preserved a vague relationship of miming to literature.

The history of the true strolling player is lost, roughly from the sixth to the twelfth century. But the history of the singer or reciter is picked up even before the Church finally succeeds in suppressing the theatre with a stage and actors; and there are records of the German *scop* almost from the time when he separated himself from communal folk-singing to his emergence as honored court-minstrel. In France, England, and Germany, the activities of the popular singer-reciter can be traced, no less in the annals of courts and feudal castles than in the prohibitions of a Church that still made no distinctions between the better and the worse sorts of entertainer.

It would be easy to read too much theatric importance into the singing of the *troubadours* and *joculatores,* of the gleemen and the minstrels — the subject is a fascinating one. But these entertainers are a link and little more. Occasionally, doubtless, an impassioned reciter impersonated a character in true dramatic fashion, and there are passages in the romances that run into dialogue; but such are exceptions to the rule. We may rather consider the minstrels as an interesting *substitute for* the theatre in the darker centuries. They sang, or chanted, the things that have been the material of drama in other times: of heroic deeds, and legendary braveries, of men and women in love, and of funny happenings. A verse in *Cursor Mundi,* a fourteenth century poem, sums up their repertory:

> Men lykyn jestis for to here,
> And romans rede in diuers manere . . .
> How kyng Charlis and Rowlond fawght
> With Sarzyns nold they be cawght,
> Of Tristrem and of Ysoude the swete
> How they with love first gan mete,
> Of kyng John and of Isombras,
> Of Ydoyne and of Amadas,
> Stories of diuerce thynggis,
> Many songgis of diuers ryme,
> As english, frensh, and latyne.

As yet there were no ballroom stages, and we may picture the gleeman and his harpist arriving unannounced before the castle gates, singing and playing a merry lay; invited in; entertaining lightly at dinner and afterward taking place at one end of the great hall, while the lord or prince (who could not read, or but painfully) and his ladies and guests would group themselves close, to hear a chanted tale of Charlemagne, or a metrical romance, perhaps the *Roman de la Rose.* This was the typical performer and the typical audience of the times.

The very flowering of minstrelsy came in the eleventh, twelfth, and thirteenth centuries, when real theatre had hardly emerged out of church service.

One other development during the centuries when the European theatre was, so to speak, "dark," demands passing notice here — in order that we may avoid violating chronology too ruthlessly: the growth of a body of more or less Christian folk-custom and folk-play bordering on the dramatic. The Church could not kill out the festival spirit in the peoples whom it gradually won to itself, partially by conversion, partly by conquest, when Christian overcame non-Christian nation. Wisely the Church compromised, and took to itself a certain number of the less ungodly and less ribald ceremonial customs. For the rest, it waged an unsucessful fight against survival of the old tribal dancing, the joyous processionals, and even the pagan superstitions as to what rites would make the new wine ferment or render the old field fertile. Through ten centuries, from the establishment of Christianity as the recognized religion of civilized Europe to the Renaissance, there are records of the outcroppings of the folk-drama instinct.

These are not enough related to afford basis for argument about a typical seventh or ninth or eleventh century dramatic phenomenon; but the examples are by no means isolated. Rather is there evidence that in many places and almost continuously people were reverting to rituals and dances that the Church had forbidden as heathenish. Perhaps the most notable feature about the known festivals is that they group themselves naturally around seasonal changes and the divisions of the agricultural year. As always in "primitive" folk-expression, the dance is at the heart of the matter. The new wine is to be tasted, perhaps; then a special day or night must be named for celebration. Two sorts of dance became common, a group-dance around a fire or a Maypole, or whatever else stands for the Dionysian altar of other days; and a processional dance through the fields and the village streets. The marchers may be costumed, and of course assuming masks adds to the fun; in some cases, chant and response between leader and chorus are the rule. Here indeed is the perfect parallel to the fertility rites in Greece at that moment when Thespis stepped forward and added the first actor-impersonator, to be followed soon after by Æschylus and Sophocles. We may almost infer, from twelfth and thirteenth century folk-custom, that if the drama were not then being reborn in the Church, a full-fledged secular drama would have developed independently quite soon. The amorous note of modern romantic comedy was already crossing with the dramatic dance — where the folk festival and minstrelsy came together. After the Mediæval Mystery and Miracle dramas, the people's Sword-dances and Mummers' Plays — both growing out of folk festivals, derived in turn from pre-Christian ritual — will lead on in a direct line to later fully theatrical, non-religious drama. One may add, too, that the Christmas Plays that grew up in the Church are characterized by elements attracted from other seasonal occasions, not entirely un-mixed with pagan custom. But let us turn to the orthodox beginning of Christian drama.

In the tenth century, or perhaps the ninth, priests in a Catholic church conceived the idea of inserting into the Mass a song with the words apportioned to two or more singers or chanters. With the strictly orthodox aim of "fortifying the unlearned people in their faith," they planned to picture an incident to their congrega-tions by the vivid means of living impersonators; instead of let-ting one stationary singer tell *about* the incident in Latin words that not one out of a thousand of the faithful understood.

The custom spread. No such aid to understanding had been introduced into the Church in ages. Soon the Mass — itself a dramatic-symbolic representation of the Last Supper, in the broader view — is divided into the read parts, the sung parts, and the acted parts. On special occasions, a whole acted episode is introduced.

At first the "scene" is very simple. A priest, specially vested, sits by "the sepulchre," while three others approach as if seeking something.

"*Quem quæritis in sepulchro, Christicolæ?*" chants the one.
"*Jesum Nazarenum crucifixum, o cælicolæ,*" chant the three.
"*Non est hic, surrexit sicut prædixerat.*
Ite, nuntiate quia surrexit a mortuis."

The seekers turn to the choir, saying "*Alleluia! resurrexit Dom-inus.*" The guardian of the sepulchre says, "*Venite et videte locum,*" and lifts a curtain to show that the "tomb" is empty. There follows the anthem, *Surrexit Dominus de sepulchro;* and then the hymn *Te Deum laudamus,* while "all the bells chime out together."

Thus the congregation has seen pictured out the incident of the Three Maries and the Angel at the tomb of Jesus. There are several varying texts of this particular "trope" (or addition to the service) dating from the tenth century, and one from Win-chester Cathedral has full "stage directions" as above outlined.

The Church service has had, of course, almost immemorially, many of the contributive elements that go to make up ritual

drama: ceremonial movement, colorfulness of setting, musical accompaniment, even an approach toward dialogue, in antiphonal
singing, in the two halves of the choir answering each other in
song. But it is the introduction of dialogue between priests representing " characters " that marks the true birth of " the theatre
in the church." Scholars call the incidents inserted into the Mass
" liturgical drama," that is, part of the liturgy or service. They
are the first steps toward the Mystery Play, or complete drama on
a Scriptural subject.

A woodcut of the Mass, indicating dramatic elements. [From
a book illustration dated 1499.]

From the tenth to the thirteenth
century there are many texts,
marked by growing elaboration,
both in wording and in directions
for acting and setting. The language changes from Latin to a
mixture of Latin and vernacular,
and finally to French or German
or other popular tongue. Singing
or chanting gives way to speech.
The single incident grows into a
series, until the Easter group provides all the materials for a real
Passion, the Christmas group for
a Nativity, and the Ascension
group for a Resurrection Play.
The " stories," of course, are taken
as directly as possible from the
Bible — it will be some time yet
before the profane have their way
in regard to " popular " concessions and additions. The natural
progression, when the first acted incident was successful, would
be to the episode next following in the legendary story: the
quem quæritis sketch, bound around the showing-out of the
empty tomb, would be followed by a scene in which the Three
Maries hold up to view the cast-off burial-clothes as token of
Jesus' resurrection. And so on until a completed story is enacted.
There is, of course, no more dramatic or theatric legend in history
than that of the Christ.

Just when or where the grouped liturgical dramatic "inserts" may be said to have become independent religious "plays," no one may venture to say. Before the first "Passion" or other Mystery Play was acted, however, there had been attempts at literary playwriting by Church people. In the tenth century a nun of the Gandersheim Abbey in Saxony, Hrosvitha by name, had written six comedies after the model of Terence, on religious themes, hoping to inculcate in her readers greater faith and love of chastity or Christian heroism. Terence had been — for reasons a bit difficult to fathom — a favorite author with the Christian scribes and scholars; and it may have been that the good nun wished to combat the dangers of the original unchaste plays with others of an opposite moral tendency. But her writing was flat, her dramatic sense defective; and it is even questioned whether her comedies ever came to amateur production even in her own prescribed orbit. Equally limited in influence was the famous Χριστοῦ Πάσγων, or *Passion of Christ,* written about the same time; which is of value chiefly because it incorporates bodily several hundred lines out of Euripides' plays, including passages nowhere else preserved. These isolated survivals may indicate a considerable monastic activity in imitating classic drama; but it was almost entirely a literary exercise and unrelated to the drama that was growing out of the tropes. Indeed, there are few phenomena in the history of the theatre more striking than the utter independence of the mediæval religious drama from classic influence — after a great dramatic tradition had once existed, and while the half-ruined classic playhouses still dotted the European world.

The Mystery Play would find in the cathedral, of course, an appropriate and truly beautiful "setting." The providing of a manger here, of a throne for Herod there, and a suggestion of the road to Egypt to one side: these simple arrangements would prepare the altar and choir area for a whole group of incidents: the Birth of Jesus, the Adoration of the Shepherds, the Three Wise Men, Herod and the Slaughter of the Innocents, and the Flight into Egypt. In a thirteenth century Orleans manuscript, there are preserved six Mysteries designed to be given in this simple way, besides four that are more properly to be termed "Miracles," that is, incidents in the lives of the Saints instead of dramatized episodes out of the Bible story. All are written very briefly, in verse and prose, and with the obvious intention that hymns and anthems be sung at appropriate intervals. The priests are the actors (the choir boys joining in when needed, as in *The Slaughter of the Innocents*).

It is useless to inquire seriously into the degree to which the acting was realistic or ritualistic at this time; but as *picturing* to illiterate people was the first aim of the religious drama, we may

Scenes in the choir area of a church.
[Part of an engraving by Hans Holbein.]

infer, in passing, that excursions toward realism occurred quite early. We shall see shortly the most curious mixture of naïve and realistic effects, when the play has been transferred to the secular guilds. At present, we may remember the impulse toward, perhaps the need for, a sense of actuality in the representation; but that in the (usually) raised altar area of the church there was an ideal "formal" stage, needing no further decoration, but already suited to the placing of a throne, a manger, or a rich sepulchre, or to serve with slightest change as a palace or Heaven or Paradise. This was the stage of the "Collective Mystery" as it was performed in the cathedral (though not to push the analogy of physical theatre and church too far, it should be added that on occasion the action and the stations were carried out into the nave or side-aisles).

The next step is the building of a simple stage outside the church, or perhaps the arranging of the "stations" on the church porch: again an ideal setting for drama, with opportunity still for church music, with the doors handy for entrances and exits. The clergy are here still the actors.

As an example of the play in the transition period, when the drama is midway between liturgical trope and guild-play, one may read the *Adam* which is accounted the oldest drama in the French language. It is supposed by some authorities to have been written in England, where French was then in use alongside the scholarly Latin and the vulgar English. (Incidentally the first play in English is said to be the *Jacob and Esau* of the Wakefield Mysteries.) Where the early tropes had been hardly more than paraphrases of a few lines of Bible text (in Latin), one finds in the *Adam,* though incomplete, an elaborated story, with sharply characterized protagonists, written out with considerable theatric ingenuity if without great literary merit. It is designed obviously to be played before a church, as indicated in one of the stage directions noting that God goes into and out of the church; and the absence of any large number of enumerated scenes would make it an ideal piece for representation on the porch.

How far drama had now travelled from mere pictured incident (not unlike a living replica of those sweetly colored wood or wax tableaux that one sees in Catholic churches at festive times even today) toward a "professional" completeness and skill in the representation, is illustrated in the *Adam* stage directions. I quote the following from E. K. Chambers' translation, with his connecting paragraphs:

" A Paradise is to be made in a raised spot, with curtains and cloths of silk hung round it at such a height that persons in the Paradise may be visible from the shoulders upwards. Fragrant flowers and leaves are to be set round about, and divers trees put therein with hanging fruit, so as to give the likeness of a most delicate spot. Then must come the Saviour clothed in a dalmatic, and Adam and Eve be brought before him. Adam is to wear a red tunic and Eve a woman's robe of white, with a white silk cloak; and they are both to stand before the Figure, Adam the nearer with composed countenance, while Eve appears somewhat more modest. And the Adam must be well trained when to reply and to be neither too quick nor too slow in his replies. And not only he, but all the personages must be trained to speak composedly, and to fit convenient gesture to the matter of their speech. Nor must they foist in a syllable or clip one of the verse, but must enounce firmly and repeat what is set down for them in due order. Whosoever names Paradise is to look and point toward it."

After a *lectio* and a chant by the choir, the dialogue begins. The Figure instructs Adam and Eve as to their duties and inducts them into Paradise.

"Then the Figure must depart to the church and Adam and Eve walk about Paradise in honest delight. Meanwhile the demons are to run about the stage, with suitable gestures, approaching the Paradise from time to time and pointing out the forbidden fruit to Eve, as though persuading her to eat it. Then the Devil is to come and address Adam.

"Then, sadly and with downcast countenance, he shall leave Adam, and go to the doors of Hell, and hold council with the other demons. Thereafter he shall make a sally amongst the people, and then approach Paradise on Eve's side, addressing her with joyful countenance and insinuating *(blandiens)* manner."

Now the last scene is at hand.

"Then shall come the Devil and three or four devils with him, carrying in their hands chains and iron fetters, which they shall put on the necks of Adam and Eve. And some shall push and others pull them to Hell; and hard by Hell shall be other devils ready to meet them, who shall hold high revel at their fall. And certain other devils shall point them out as they come, and shall snatch them up and carry them into Hell; and there shall they make a great smoke arise, and call aloud to each other with glee in their Hell, and clash their pots and kettles, that they may be heard without. And after a little delay the devils shall come out and run about the stage; but some shall remain in Hell."

Thus have we come to the dramatic stage representation of that Hell which Tertullian, one thousand years before, had sketched in his word-picture of "the Christian world as a show" — while damning out all theatre shows as works of the Devil. Here is the Church utilizing the art of drama, not as an appendage to the service, but as a complete and separate thing, pre-written by priest-dramatists, rehearsed, acted by specially trained clergy-players — educated not to "foist in a syllable or clip one of the verse," and to "enounce firmly." Others are trained even to produce the proper offstage noises, clashing the pots and kettles of Hell.

In noting this singular incorporation of the theatre into a so-long-hostile Church, we should not overlook that the Church has brought to drama theatric virtues of its own kind, of a sort not to be duplicated in later history. The pageantry of the Catholic service, the stirring sacred music, the impressive archi-

tectural background, the sincerity and conviction in delivery —
many a later theatre, though more literary and more professional,
fail of importance for lack of these.

Imagine the porch of Rheims Cathedral arranged for a play
like *Adam*. The Paradise is a simple booth built up on the top
step, within the central recessed portal; it is richly curtained, and
stands out as a colorful note against the sculptures and traceries of
the monumental façade. The other simple " stations " are placed
close by; lowest of all, the yawning Hell-mouth. The costumes
make the processionals a lovely interplay of movement and
color. The music drifting out from the cathedral is doubly impressive as one looks up at the great Rose Window; where else
could a heavenly choir be so appropriately concealed? And
whence could come the thundering voice of God so convincingly,
so nobly? The actors too — these are no mere mummers, coming
from and returning to some empty space behind canvas flats;
these are the servants of God, appearing from and returning to
his House. And do they not speak his Word? How then doubt
that this is one of the noblest theatres the world has known?

But even the cathedral-theatre can be desecrated. This time
it is the Church itself that turns wild and matches the impressive
use of drama at the altar, with ribald revelry and profane mockery
at other moments. When the common people carried on their
folk-customs in spite of prohibitions and occasional suppressions,
making heathenish glee at New Year's and May Day and Christmas, the lower clergy claimed their right to celebrate too. The
scores of minor churchmen who would be attached to a great
cathedral did not always look up reverently to their superiors
as the true and infallible representatives of God. In fact there
was often resentment or jealousy, even hatred, between the minor
and the major Fathers. And the New Year's celebration of the
lower clergy became a recognized dramatic burlesque of the
regular church service, with bitter and licentious caricature of
high priests and bishops.

The New Year's " doings " of the church underlings were
variously known as the Feast of Fools, the Feast of Asses, etc. —
sufficient indication of the irreverence involved. From the end
of the twelfth century on, the festival spread from France over

most of the Continental Catholic countries, and it had its counterpart in the later Feast of Boys and the brief rule of the " Boy Bishop," a custom that came to flower more particularly in England. At first the participants were the " sub-deacons," but these were joined by other classes of the humbler church workers; and the occasion was in the beginning the Church celebration of the Circumcision. Election of a presiding officer by the guild of vicars was at one time a feature of the occasion, and other serious purposes were often involved. But chiefly the Feast of Fools was the annual revel of the lower clergy, in which their human feelings and their cussedness broke loose — " an ebullition of the natural lout beneath the cassock," as Chambers puts it — culminating in their burlesque of sacred services with one of their own number acting the bishop or archbishop.

There were feasting (not excluding drinking) in the church, dice-playing at the altar, singing of ribald songs to Church tunes, mock sermons, etc. Rubber was burnt instead of incense, and the " Alleluia " was brayed. A parody of the Flight into Egypt is known to have been played, with a real ass brought to the altar rail. Each part of the mass then ended with a bray, and the people of the congregation responded with a " hee-haw " — oh, yes, you may be sure the townsmen came quite gladly to these sacrilegious services.

Some later writers are inclined to trace the whole Feast of Fools phenomenon to the first entry of a donkey into the church, as a natural property in the solemn Biblical plays. Anyway, the ass became a symbol of the affair, and the cowl worn by the mock high-churchman soon had donkey-ears as the distinguishing feature. There are some writers again who say that the festival can be traced back to the ninth century, when a fool at the court of Michael the Drunkard, at Constantinople, was allowed to desecrate a church, playing through a mock service in the Patriarch's robes; and that he then rode out on an ass with his revellers to meet the real Patriarch, and utterly upset the solemn procession which that dignitary was heading. This might, indeed, account for the prominence of the ass in the later feasts, and for the substitution of the chief actor for the Church head; the legend has, moreover, the advantage of lifting the guilt from Church people to a secular fool.

There exists a thirteenth century manuscript of the *Festa Asinaria* of the Beauvais Cathedral. When the ass was welcomed into the cathedral doors, and toasted with wine, the celebrants sang a nine-stanza chant, ending (in Gayley's translation):

> Say Amen, most reverend Ass, *(they kneel)*
> Now your belly's full of grass:
> Bray Amen, again, and bray;
> Spurn old customs down the way.
>   Hez va! hez va! hez va! hez!
>   Open your beautiful mouth and bray;
>   A bottle o' hay, and the devil to pay.
>   And oats a-plenty for you today.

To this feature was added the service as worked out in the Feast of Fools more strictly considered. As known particularly from the records of Sens Cathedral, it would begin with the jangling of the bells on New Year's Eve. Then at a certain point in the service, where occur the words "He hath put down the mighty from their seat, and hath exalted the humble and the meek," the sub-deacons would repeat the verses over and over, working them up into a hilarious refrain, finally ousting their superiors and carrying on the service as a burlesque. Masks would be brought out, bottles opened, and the Feast was on. Then followed a procession through the town, aping the usual solemn religious "progression," with dancing, serenading, and ceremonial visits at important houses — and the taking up of a collection. The *Dominus Festi* was variously known as the Bishop of Fools, Archbishop of Fools, *roi des fous, abbas stultus,* etc. — even the titles of Cardinal and Pope were daringly invoked.

It is only too obvious how this framework would be seized upon by the more rowdy elements in the Church, and among the townsmen for that matter, for the development of drunken and licentious scenes in the cathedral, of bitter parody of religious offices, of staging mock Mysteries, of corrupting such traditional ceremonials as the choir boys' processions. Indeed there seems no possible excess to which the Fools did not stoop during the next four centuries. The Church Fathers kept up a running fire

of prohibitions, indictments, condemnations. In the thirteenth
century the Bishop of Lincoln twice prohibited the *festum stul-
torum,* as " an execrable custom permitted in certain churches,
by which the feast of the Circumcision is defiled," and as " a vain
and filthy recreation hateful to God and dear to devils." In 1445
the Archbishop of Sens wrote that " all observers should tremble

The Fools ill received. Note the cowls with asses' ears.
[From a book illustration by Albrecht Dürer, 1497.]

and blush at the enormity of the sacrilege by which a decorous
and pleasant festival graced by the name of our Lord has been
turned into an obscenity."

In the same year the Theological Faculty at the University of
Paris issued a letter [1] to the bishops (the real ones) which summed
up the abuses:

---

[1] Translated by Chambers. The material for this and the next chapter is taken
from three excellent books. Always to be ranked first is that scholarly, heavily annotated, almost monumental work by E. K. Chambers, entitled *The Mediæval Stage*
(Oxford, 1903). Far less exhaustive, but easily readable, is *Plays of Our Forefathers,*
by Charles Mills Gayley (New York, 1907). A very good introductory account appears
with the more important play texts in *English Miracle Plays, Moralities and Interludes,* by Alfred W. Pollard (Oxford, 8th revised edition, 1927).

Priests and clerks may be seen wearing masks and monstrous visages at the hours of office. They dance in the choir dressed as women, panders, or minstrels. They sing wanton songs. They eat black puddings at the horn of the altar while the celebrant is saying mass. They play at dice there. They cense with stinking smoke from the soles of old shoes. They run and leap through the church, without a blush at their own shame. Finally they drive about the town and its theatres in shabby traps and carts; and rouse the laughter of their fellows and the bystanders in infamous performances, with indecent gestures and verses scurrilous and unchaste.

As the zealous Fathers once spent three centuries scourging the actors from the stages of Rome, they now spend three centuries ridding their own House of a semi-theatric desecration. They are betrayed often within their own walls, they make a prohibition effective here only to see the abuses flower more licentiously there; they disagree among themselves. A few, wiser than their fellows, try to divert the comedy and burlesque of the Feast of Fools into the channel of the now secularized Mystery and Miracle Plays.

The serious religious drama that grew out of the solemn trope of the Mass, and out of the Mystery at the altar and on the cathedral porch, has now absorbed more popular elements, by way of realistic incident and farcical episode and spectacle. It already is being pushed away even from the church porch, by a clergy grown suspicious of its popularity and afraid of its vividness and its humor. The theatre is going out of the Church again, perhaps for all time. We may, if we listen carefully, hear the venerable archbishop praying, "Dear God, please make doubly sure that the *Roy des Fous* and the Ass depart with the rest!" And indeed, along with the Saints and the Devils and the Biblical personages, the Ass and the Fools will turn up again, when the priests have given over the stages to the guilds and fraternities.

CHAPTER VII

The Mediæval Spirit and the Stage

THE LITTLE drawing reproduced overleaf may serve as a "text" for a brief disquisition upon the spirit of the Middle Ages, in relation to some curiously contradictory aspects of the popular theatre. It is redrawn after a miniature in an illuminated play manuscript, and it shows a stage as arranged for the Valenciennes Passion Play.

It is one of the oldest records extant of a stage with illusive settings. As such it throws light on the audiences of the later religious theatre: they are simple-minded folk who demand "picturing" of the play backgrounds. Above all, they want graphic representations of the two places that are most in their minds: Heaven and Hell. If anything, they are the more interested in Hell. Indeed, long before this time (the Valenciennes production was in 1547) Hell-mouth has become the most prominent "station" of the several that are built on a long platform to serve the actors in Mystery and Miracle Plays. And the mediæval audience demands particularly that the imps out of Hell shall be very active in hustling sinners into the belching smoke and flame, that the damned be shown in torture (as here), and that the best of all comic actors play the part of the Devil. This Devil is the favorite of all the religious characters in the mediæval theatre.

We have come now to a period when an old form of human civilization is breaking up. Politically, the feudal era is past. The society under which a lord ruled over each section of the country, when practically all the people dwelling therein were economically and legally dependent upon that sovereign — little better than slaves — is giving way to a society in which the third estate is to be powerful. Manufacturing has taken on a new importance, trade is developing, money is now in the hands of bankers instead of in the treasuries of the sovereigns (as like as not they ruined themselves by going on the crusades). A new " middle " class is claiming a place in the sun.

Just as ninety-nine out of a hundred men, in the centuries just past, had been politically subject to the feudal lord, so they had been mentally and spiritually slaves of the Church. Even now they were forbidden to think any thoughts not approved by the Church Fathers; they were taught that all intelligence began and ended with those specially appointed by God to look after men's souls; they were encouraged to believe that this life is merely a brief passage, through a vale of tears, during which one must prepare for the all-important Life-after-Death. One might seek to make this earthly visit pleasurable only at risk of spending the remaining lifetimes roasting in Hell, instead of basking in a Heaven of sweet-toned harps and golden pavements. The Churchmen, moreover, pointed out that the emissaries of the Devil in Hell and of God in Heaven are always at one's elbow, the demons trying to pluck one away into paths that lead to perdition, the Angels of God trying somewhat feebly to hold one in the ways of righteousness. The demons are the more active, and they seem to be everywhere, even in one's own being — it is they, not qualities in the man's own make-up, that tempt to lust, to anger, to impiety. Only by staying close to the Church, by obeying implicitly, by taking no chances of thinking new thoughts, can a man be sure of salvation.

Of course a demon gets him once in a while; but then there is the Confessional, and Absolution. The Church, too, has magic relics that scare away demons. And there are Saints with special powers of protection. Christ has become too awesome a figure to serve as a personal idol. These Saints are nearer to the penitent or supplicant human being; and there is the Virgin Mary, who long ago has been elevated to first place among those who intercede at the Throne for poor mortal sinners, who long since became the favorite idol of millions of men and women who obediently gave up their old tangible gods but still feel the need of praying to a seeable deity.

So there is, at this time in the history of Christianity, in these later Middle Ages, a structure of superstition, of demons and idols and magic, hardly less crude than that which impelled the savage to his ritual dancing a few chapters back. We may mark the liturgical drama as a development by which the Church hoped to bring closer to its people the reality of its multitudinous saviours (the One who is at the heart of Christianity was almost obscured in those days). Tertullian, who had argued, in the second century, that the theatre was sinful because idolatrous, might now have found a new truth in the charge. The characters at the altar were largely idols shown — as is the way with drama — in the life.

The stage of the Valenciennes Passion Play of 1547. An exact contemporary record of the mediæval stage that spread out simultaneously several Biblical localities, from Heaven through earth to Hell. [Redrawing by the author after the original miniature by Hubert Cailleau.]

Which brings us back to the audience and the Valenciennes stage. These spectators were just escaping from the estate of unthinking and fearful idolators. Whenever the Virgin Mary comes on to this platform stage, they will be reverent, thrilled, worshipful. They will cross themselves piously at this or that incident or allusion. They will accept solemnly the crudest sorts of stage " effects " for the sake of a vivid retelling of a beloved Bible-incident. But there is in them a new spirit too; the prominence of Hell-mouth on the pictured stage is the measure of it. Just as the people have escaped from under the heel of a feudal lord, they are claiming a certain freedom from Church domination. The priests, finding the comic element in the Biblical plays increasing, out of all proportion to the religious teaching, have finally thrown the drama out of many of the cathedrals and churches, with expressions of disapproval. The people take up the religious drama, disregard clerical warnings, make the productions semi-civic affairs, and turn the Devil into a comic character. They will still go to Mass on occasion, and say their prayers and make the sign of the cross at the proper times; but they will defy all attempts to interfere with what they now consider their legitimate pleasure.

We may recall, too, that this is the time when they begin putting into great secular buildings the energy, the money, and the art that hitherto have been poured into the cathedrals. The modern idea of " the state " is emerging. Man is finding scope for a certain degree of independent thought, is escaping from mental subjection. Not that superstition is erased. Physicians, for instance, the best ones — those who have royal warrants and have prevailed upon the kings to burn their rivals as impostors — prescribe dung-beetles and crickets boiled in oil for the cure of " stones," and wrappings of red flannel to drive away the smallpox.

It is only by recognizing such contradictions, of credulity and a new will to learning, of superstition and independence, of naïvety and elaboration, of piety and grossness, in the life of the times, that we shall understand the Miracle Play and the *Sottie*, the Morality and the Interlude. If we had time, indeed, it would be illuminating to trace in detail the changes in religious thought in Europe during the next three hundred years, the progressive steps toward the Reformation; and to study the racial, lingual, and political developments which later were to culminate in the Renaissance. All these had influence upon the stage. But in the multiplicity of forms of religious drama, in the gradual change from the Latin of the Priests to half a dozen vernaculars, in the progressive shifting of emphasis away from didactic elements to amusing and literary ones, we shall be sadly lost if we do not concentrate our attention on the three or four play types that stand out most clearly, considering them somewhat apart from their sources and their relationship to the seething currents of political, social, and cultural life.

For the rest, we need remember only that the theatre is in a state of flux, that the Passion as given in Italy will be different from that at Paris, or Basel, or Augsburg, or Ghent, different in language in the later days, in methods of staging, in extent of secular escape from Church domination. And yet from Florence to Aberdeen, from Seville to Riga, the European world is alive with dramatic endeavor growing out of the one source in the trope. It is not even accurate to say that in one place the liturgical drama gives way to Miracle Play at such-and-such a time, or religious play to farce; they are being acted concurrently, with countless variations shading off into ritual processions, tableaux, spectacle, etc. Even the ecclesiastic authorities are divided again and again upon the question of total exclusion of the drama from the Church. One can only note that *roughly speaking,* the fourteenth century witnessed the change from cathedral-altar or porch to market-place stage, from priest-domination to secular control.

One of the few contemporary pictures of a Miracle stage was made by Jean Fouquet, a miniaturist who lived from 1415 to 1483. From the redrawing shown here, the reader may see that the fifteenth century stage was less elaborate than that used for the Valenciennes Passion Play a century later. Hell-mouth is the only pictured setting. For the rest there is a row of raised booths in which certain of the episodes are to be played, ranged round an open stage on which an incident is now being acted out. The story is that of Saint Apollonia, the Catholic " patroness against toothache." She was one of the early martyrs who had preached Christian salvation in Alexandria, suffering therefor a violent death by burning, at the hands of the tyrant governor — her own father, some accounts say. The legend is typical of those hundreds upon which the Miracle Plays were based:

As the maiden grew up and flourished as a flower in grace and beauty, her mother ceased not to relate to her the wonderful circumstances of her birth; and thus she became a true Christian at heart. . . So he baptised her; and suddenly there appeared an angel holding a garment of dazzling white, which he threw over the maiden, saying, " This is Apollonia, the servant of Jesus! go now to Alexandria, and preach the faith of Christ."

A contemporary illustration of a mediæval Mystery Play. A scene in the drama depicting the martyrdom of Saint Apollonia. Note the booth stage in the background, as yet with little pictorial localization. [From a drawing by F. Courboin after the miniature by Jean Fouquet, in Paul Albert's *La Littérature Française*.]

She, hearing the divine voice, obeyed, and preached to the people with wondrous eloquence. Many were converted; others ran to complain. . . The governor commanded her instantly to fall down and worship the idol set up in the city. Then St. Apollonia, being brought before the idol, made the sign of the cross, and commanded the demon who dwelt within to depart; and the demon, uttering a loud cry, broke the statue, and fled, shrieking out, " The Holy Virgin Apollonia drives me forth! " The tyrant seeing this, ordered her to be bound to the column; and all her beautiful teeth were pulled out, one by one, with a pair of pincers; then a fire was kindled, and as she persisted in the faith, she was flung into it, and gave up her soul to God, being carried into Heaven by his angels."

In such a legend the opportunities for effective dramatic portrayal are enormous. The story would be known; the audience would look forward to each succeeding incident with the anticipation one feels in going back to a familiar place (*surprise,* by the way, is no valued element in drama). The characters are vivid: the beautiful virgin, the tyrant, and above all, the dazzling angels and the demons. God himself will appear to receive the martyr at the end. And, as we see in Fouquet's miniature, the torture scene can be made (in modern stage parlance) a knockout. Here are the torturers and their pincers; here is the old sure-fire dramatic incident of the innocent maiden unjustly abused. For this audience the abuse is realistically, grossly shown; but the spectators will be as deeply moved when angels out of that curtained booth-Heaven above come down to take vengeance and to carry the martyred maiden up to glory, and when the demons, after a realistic struggle, march the torturers over to Hell and cast them down into flaming perdition. Look sharp and you will see one of the imps behind the torturer at Apollonia's head; they were constantly roaming about, prodding people up, exhibiting their antics at every opportunity; even making sallies off the stage and out into the audience on occasion.

Who wrote the texts of these dramas? It is a question with many answers — and not so very important, because the written-out dialogue seldom has great literary value, or theatric values beyond a melodramatic effectiveness. Originally the text was written by a priest or a monk; there may be a dozen versions, used in this and other towns, each with its variations, each with accretions that have gathered as the play progressed farther from the Church, as new groups of secular producers and actors added bits to make the performances more popular. We may find an analogy today in the Passion Plays of the Tyrol and the Bavarian Alps. One town or village presents a play that was written by a local priest, another has a text immemorially old that has been readapted every ten years by successive producers; but over at Selzach in Switzerland, where they had no one with a flair for literary composition, they use a text borrowed with permission from the Ober-Ammergau players. Some such explanation can doubtless be made to cover the phenomenon of the mediæval religious drama of which these modern Passion Plays are survivals or revivals. Certainly some of the old English Miracles were close adaptations of French texts.

Still, there are a few names of authors known to us today, such as the French Jean Bodel, who elaborated a Miracle story, with St. Nicholas as the pivotal figure, until it contained a battle of Crusaders and Saracens, a court scene, tavern revels, a robbery, and the usual pious conversations, miracles, and final glorifications; and Rutebœf, who dramatized the story of the Priest who sold his soul to the Devil, repented, and was saved by the intercession of the Virgin Mary; and Hilarius, who may have been English rather than French, and who wrote (in Latin occasionally mixed with French) three plays that have survived, a *Miracle of St. Nicholas, The Raising of Lazarus,* and *Daniel.*

Of the French Biblical plays, Mysteries rather than Miracles, there are three groups or cycles that particularly demand mention. Those dealing with Old Testament history are known as *Le Mystère du Vieux Testament.* As collected and printed in 1500, with 44,325 verses, this work is supposed to represent a compilation from many authors. Of the collective *Nouveau Testament* Mysteries, there are several versions, that of Arnoul Greban being best known. It is in 34,574 verses, and was written in the mid-fifteenth century. The third group is known as the *Actes des Apôtres,* and the 61,968-line manuscript contains so many added Miracles that it is said to have played through all the Sundays for seven months in Paris in 1545.

Returning now to that theatre for the Valenciennes Passion Play with which we opened the chapter, we may inquire more particularly about the way in which a " cycle " is there presented. Here on the stage at one time are (more or less literally) temples, palaces, houses, city gates, pavilions, altars, towers, dungeons, a fenced field, a sea with a ship, etc., flanked by Heaven and Hell. It is obvious what a range of drama can be played, illusively, with such a " layout." By only a slight extension of the imagination, the main neutral playing space, the " downstage centre," becomes identified with one or another " station " as entrances are made from there or as actors are disposed to lead up to that station as centre of interest. In the picture, which the artist Hubert Cailleau designed for a manuscript of the play, only two of the " places " are occupied by actors: Hell with its demons and victims, and Heaven with God the Father supported by the Four Virtues.

Not all the stations were called into use in a single day. The Passion here was presented in twenty-five installments, the usual performance including two or three incidents or acts, but occasionally only one, or again four. Thus the first day saw the acting of the story of Mary's parents; the fourth day, the birth of Jesus, the Adoration of the Shepherds, and the Coming of the Three Wise Men; the tenth, the Conversion of Mary Magdalen, and the Sermon on the Mount; the eighteenth, the Last Supper, and the Orchard scene; and so on.

One with a sense of theatrical values will note that, in the division into episodes, there is little attempt to follow the emphasis of the gospel-writers: the material now is reshaped with an eye to human and spectacular values. The story of the Magdalen is generously developed, a half *journée* is given to the *Décollation de Saint Jean,* presumably the Salome story, and a full performance is devoted to *Apparitions de Jésus Ressuscité.* And again we may note the prominence of Hell-mouth on the stage as indication of apocryphal tendencies; for where in the passion proper is there such emphasis on the Devil's doings? This is borrowing from the Miracles, where the enemies of the Saints invariably and visibly went to Hell.

The text of the Valenciennes play is apparently unlike any other, and yet is a free borrower from earlier versions, particularly that of Greban. A special prologue and epilogue have been added at the beginning and end of each of the twenty-five divisions. The opening lines (as a sample of the workaday verse) are:

> Seigneurs, si vous prestez silence
> Ce jour venant demonstrerons
> La naissance de precellence
> De Marie, qu'onnorerons. . .

A contemporary report and the contracts and financial accounts of the production tell much about the performers and the methods of staging. At first thirteen " superintendents and conductors " were appointed to have charge, and the preliminary tasks were parcelled out: three undertook to arrange the text and distribute the rôles, one to construct the stage, another to arrange the *mise-en-scène,* another to see to music, another to devise the machinery and effects. Besides those among the " superintendents " there were thirty-eight important actors, each appearing in many of the twenty-five performances and often in multiple rôles; besides a great many minor players including little children " *qui étaient anges.*" The actors' contracts indicate a strict discipline: lateness to rehearsals laid one open to a fine, drinking more than one's authorized portion during a performance was forbidden — and so was talking-back at the directors. Financially, the actors could elect to win or lose with the organizers, or be content with the thanks of all concerned. (As a matter of fact there was a profit of 1230 *livres.*) The actors worked hard and even underwent danger. It is chronicled that at Metz in 1437 both the crucified Christ and the hanged Judas were cut down just in time to escape death.

Seats were provided for a certain number of the audience at Valenciennes, in temporary pavilions — but it is to be doubted whether at this time the ordinary spectator demanded more than an opportunity to stand where he could see the stage. E. Grasset has made a conjectural reconstruction of the " theatre " and performance as seen from a box in the pavilion erected for the socially important spectators. You will note that he has elaborated a little the stage and its stations as depicted by Cailleau.

At the time, what impressed the populace of Valenciennes most were the mechanical wonders that were introduced. In our next chapter we shall see how stage tricks are already, in the sixteenth century, being glorified in the masques of the Italian courts; but here we meet for the first time contemporary descriptions of mechanical spectacular effects. An account by Henry d'Outreman (quoted in Petit de Julleville's valuable *Histoire du Théâtre en France: Les Mystères*) includes mention of " strange and wondrous things " seen each day, " the secrets of Heaven and Hell being so altogether mystifying that the populace could take them as miracles." People appeared and disappeared magically; " Lucifer rose out of Hell, no one seeing how, borne on a dragon "; water was changed to wine in a way passing belief, so that " more than a hundred spectators wished to taste this wine," and five loaves of bread and two fish were apparently multiplied so that a thousand people partook thereof; the Devil changed his form; the thunder and the sundering of the rocks were like miracles anew. In connection with Hell and Purgatory, there were flames, a caldron of boiling oil, cannon, and turning wheels to which sinners were lashed (all to be seen in the sketch). In many other cases the Hell-mouth was so constructed that the frightful jaws opened and closed realistically, and we may infer as much on this Valenciennes stage.

Hubert Cailleau decorated the text manuscript with twenty-six other sketches, of scenes in the play. But he has given rein to his fancy; the backgrounds and groupings, no doubt, reflect at least the intentions of the producers, but there are figures seen in distant landscapes, and other features, impossible of accomplishment on a stage. These " painter's conceptions " may serve to remind us that mediæval graphic art is full of representations of those places and those incidents that were commonest on the Passion stages; so much so that one often is tempted to think that this or that picture must have been designed directly from a dramatic representation. Indeed, the books on the mediæval theatre are full of such might-be illustrations. It was even a favorite device of painters and sculptors to execute multiple works, with a dozen scenes shown side by side within one frame — a perfect parallel to the station stage. But it is only prudent to conclude that the influence is just as likely to have occurred the other way around, the stage people learning from the artists rather

The Valenciennes Passion Play of 1547 in progress. A recent reconstruction
of the scene, by E. Grasset, based on the contemporary sketch by Cailleau,
showing use of the " stage of the simultaneous scene."

What happened to the ancient theatres during the " dark " ages: two Roman theatres as they exist today. Above, a drawing of the theatre at Aspendus, the best preserved of all examples. [From a drawing in Lanckoronski's *Städte Pamphiliens und Pisidiens*.] Below, the Roman theatre at Ephesus —the only theatre mentioned in the Bible.

than the artists depicting the stage production. Incidentally, you will find Hell-mouth as a graphic representation of the entry to the Devil's domains in contemporary paintings, sculptures, woodcuts, tapestries, frescoes, embroideries, etc.

Now it is obvious that in the later Passions something of the old nobility has gone out of religious drama, that some cheap features have crept in. The wondrous " effects " have little to do with essential soul-cleansing inspired theatre. They are overstressed; they doubtless obscure some of the better elements that remain from the days of the simpler Mysteries. Drama has come again to a transitional period. Within a century Corneille's tragedies will be given in the regal court-protected theatres of Paris. Already Passions in the capital city are licensed only to the *Confrérie de la Passion,* an association of tradesmen-actors, forerunner of professional companies.

There are, too, a great number of secular organizations in scattered towns, producing more especially plays glorifying the Virgin Mary. Unconnected with the Church, these groups of amateur actors — " literary fraternities " perhaps better describes them — carry on that Mariolatry which Catholicism had so long officially fostered, sometimes dramatically. But the secular variations of the Mary stories ran into unadulterated romance. The Virgin came to be adored as more than an inaccessible Mother of God; rather as most lovable of mortals, as queen of beauty, as goddessmusician. On the stages of the time, she was a veritable *dea ex machina;* and often she pulled a reprehensible sinner out of the fire, as well as a worthy believer, if only he called on her in sufficiently adoring verse. Something near a strain of perversion ran through this secular dramatic glorification. The cycle of *Miracles de Nostre Dame* is as important in the body of Middle Ages' dramatic literature as the three Mystery cycles already mentioned.

In Paris and in other large cities there were also organizations carrying on *farce* from the point where the Feasts of Fools had relinquished it (if indeed they did not directly give over the impetus toward satire and comedy). Some of the *confrèries,* of lawclerks and other secular groups — known at times as *sociétés joyeuses* — produced farces with no other object than amusement and satire. Sometimes this satire was aimed bitterly at the Church;

but it also scourged those given to pretension or folly in any walk of life. It was the early gross form of later French satirical comedy — that was to bloom so finely when French vulgar comedy and Italian *Commedia dell'Arte* together fertilized the genius of Molière.

What has been, indeed, in the hands of the Fools and the Asses, mere fooling — the name *sottie* persists — is in the fifteenth century shaped, under literary influences, into something approaching true comedy. It is as early as 1470 that *Maistre Pierre Pathelin,* the masterpiece of mediæval farce-comedy, appears. It is an engaging presentation of the trusty theme of the shrewd lawyer outdone, of the swindler swindled. Pathelin, in order to outwit his draper, undertakes to defend a shepherd whom the draper accuses of stealing sheep. He tells the thief to answer " Bah " to every question asked him in court, and the draper is thus so confounded that he bungles the case and is sent away reprimanded, and the shepherd is acquitted as a nit-wit; but when Pathelin asks for his stipulated fee, the shepherd still answers only " Bah "! — and successfully sticks to it. It is to the court scene here and the draper's confusion that we owe the admonition, " stick to your muttons."

One might trace a fairly certain line in the development of French comedy from the first known author, Adam de la Halle, of the thirteenth century, through the early *sotties,* through the unknown author of *Pierre Pathelin,* to Gringoire, the famous writer of political farce-satires in the early sixteenth century. He wrote a play called *The Prince of Fools* in which he presented the Church (as *Mère Sotte*), the Pope, the King, and the Common People — really an attack on the Pope. But the treatment of these belongs rather to another chapter, when the literary play and the permanent playhouse are again solidly established in society. It is more to the point that we know here that farces — often grossly indecent ones — were acted in conjunction with the Mysteries, sacred and profane all on one platform, equally enjoyable to the mediæval mind.

In the British Isles the early history of the religious drama was very like that in France, from liturgical beginning to Mystery and Miracle. But the later cycles of plays presented by the tradesguilds were " staged " in ways that have special interest. There was, of course, a gradual change from the Latin of the Church service to the vernacular, and from domination by priests to independent production under the care of the guilds. From the fourteenth to the sixteenth century the plays were widespread; records of them exist in more than a hundred towns. In the later period the performances are no longer in or even near the churches — and out of the search for a suitable " theatre " grew the perambulatory system of presentation that is so distinctively Mediæval English: the productions on wagon-stages. It is a system that well preserves the picturing method, without the necessity of building " simultaneous " settings on an over-long stage. Larger audiences could see the plays, moreover, as each stage-wagon, with its incident, appeared at several places in the town successively, before different groups of spectators — always, doubtless, before the windows of him who gave most liberally to the pageant fund. But let a contemporary attendant at the Chester Plays, one Archbishop Rogers, writing in 1594 or 1595, describe the system for us (but in modernized spelling):

Every company had its pageant, or part, which pageant [wagon] was a high scaffold with two rooms, a higher and a lower, upon four wheels. In the lower they apparelled themselves, and in the higher room they played, being all open on the top, that all beholders might hear and see them. The place where they played them was in every street. They began first at the abbey gates, and when the first pageant was played it was wheeled to the high cross before the mayor, and so to every street; and so every street had a pageant before them at one time, till all the pageants for the day appointed were played; and when one pageant was near ended word was brought from street to street, that so they might come in place thereof exceeding orderly, and all the streets have their pageants afore them all at one time playing together; to see which plays was great resort, and also scaffolds and stages made in the streets in those places where they determined to play their pageants.

In some productions there are scenes requiring two of the pageant-wagons to appear together, and at times the actors apparently descended from the cars — " Herod shall rage on the pagond and also in the streete." Horsemen took their parts beside, not on, the wagons. For the rest, the reader will best round out his mental picture of the production by studying the reproduction of

David Jee's engraving herewith (though it was made several centuries later).

Each trade-guild that was charged with the production of an act or incident owned its own pageant-car; and we may read into

A scene on a wagon stage in an English perambulatory Miracle Play. [From an early nineteenth century engraving by David Jee, in Thomas Sharp's *A Dissertation on the Pageants or Dramatic Mysteries Anciently Performed at Coventry.*]

the circumstance an explanation of the splendor of costuming and the elaboration of stage effects. For each guild would be vying with all the others to make its act the most impressive and most magnificent. The costuming ran into regal display at times; and there are certain notable conventions, such as the Saracenic dress of Herod, the animal-headed demons, the Divinities with gilt hair and beards, winged angels, etc. The wagons and costumes were kept from year to year, and doubtless were elaborated between one Corpus Christi production and the next. The expenses were met by an assessment upon the guild members for "pageant-silver," and citizens' contributions. Productions sometimes began as early as five o'clock in the morning, in order to permit the necessary playing time — a reminder of the Greek performances that started at dawn.

The extant manuscripts of the guild-plays, of which there are four fairly complete — of the Chester, York, Wakefield (Towneley) and Coventry Cycles — indicate considerable borrowing from town to town, and not a little adaptation from French originals. It is known, too, that in each town there might be text changes from year to year, sometimes two incidents being joined together, at other times an act being subdivided to afford opportunity for additional guilds to take part. The English cycles were more extensive than the French, commonly covering the entire distance from Creation to Day of Judgment. Careful thought was given, apparently, to the distribution of the acts among the guilds: the shipwrights had the incident of the building of the ark, the barbers the baptism of Jesus, the vintners the incident of the water turning to wine, the bakers the Last Supper, and so on. It was impossible that there should be such appropriateness through all the list of incidents: among the forty-eight scenes as arranged in the York production of 1415, one may note, as sample assignments, that the tanners were to present " God the Father Almighty creating and forming the heavens, angels, and archangels, Lucifer and the angels that fell with him to Hell "; the hosiers to do " Moses lifting up the serpent in the wilderness; King Pharaoh; eight Jews wondering and expecting "; the plumbers and patternmakers offering " Jesus, two Apostles, the woman taken in adultery, four Jews accusing her "; and the saddlers and glaziers combining to present " Jesus despoiling Hell, twelve spirits, six good and six bad."

In the acting of the guild members we may infer a real spontaneity and an effective sincerity. Shakespeare made high fun out of the amateur acting of rustics in *A Midsummer Night's Dream*. But instead of visualizing the ineptitude and crudity of the playing there, we may better judge for ourselves from the performances of peasant-actors today, in Passion Play and folk-drama. The Ober-Ammergau productions are world famous; but there is an even closer analogy in the performance at remote villages like Thiersee and Erl — where peasants, woodsmen, and small tradesmen act the Passion with an absolute lack of self-consciousness, with conviction and often with grace. Simplicity, sincerity, and naturalness in amateur acting, where the perform-ance is actually lived spiritually by the player, ofttimes bring him to that region trod by the professional actor only after a life-time of training and experience.

All was not sincerity and reverence, however, in the Miracle productions (in England the term " Miracle " is commonly used to designate both plays dealing with legends of the Saints, and the " Mysteries " of the Bible story). Gross farcical scenes, humor-ous, and sometimes not too careful about the kind of humor, are intruded by way of comic relief. In choosing two representa-tive excerpts from the Miracles, it seems well to include one with a touch of comedy. In the *Noah's Flood* incident of the Chester Plays, Noah is completing the ark and invites his wife to come aboard:

> Wyffe, in this vessel we shall be kepte:
> My children and thou, I woulde in ye lepte.

> NOYES WIFFE
> In faythe, Noye, I had as leffe thou slepte!
> For all thy frynishe fare,
> I will not do after thy reade.

> NOYE
> Good wyffe, doe nowe as I thee bydde.

> NOYES WIFFE
> Be Christe! not or I see more neede,
> Though thou stande all the daye and stare.

> NOYE
> Lorde, that wemen be crabbed aye,
> And non are meke, I dare well saye,
> This is well seene by me to daye,
>   In witness of you ichone.

Goodwyffe, lett be all this beare,
That thou maiste in this place heare;
For all the wene that thou are maistre,
    And so thou arte, by Sainte John!

(They work for a time to finish the ark, and all go in except the
Wife. She refuses to budge unless she can take her gossips along.)

NOYES WIFFE

The loven me full well, by Christe!
But thou lett them into thy cheiste,
Elle rowe nowe wher thou leiste,
    And get thee a newe wiffe.

NOYE

Seme, sonne, loe! thy mother is wrawe:
Forsooth, such another I doe not knowe.

SEM

Father, I shall fetch her in, I trowe,
    Withouten anye fayle. . .

JEFFATTE

Mother, we pray you all together,
For we are heare, youer owne childer,
Come into the shippe for feare of the weither,
    For his love that you boughte!

NOYES WIFFE

That will not I, for all youer call,
    But I have my gossipes all.

SEM

In faith, mother, yett you shalle,
    Whither thou wylte or (nought).

NOYE

Welcome, wiffe, into this botte.

NOYES WIFFE

Have thou that for thy note!

NOYE

Ha, ha! marye this is hotte!

For example of the more serious parts of the cycles, outside the
Passion proper which follows closely the Bible original, one may

best read the *Abraham and Isaac* play in the Brome manuscript, or the similar *Sacrifice of Isaac* in the Chester group. In an excerpt from the latter, one feels the breath of human tragedy entering again into drama writing, not without human delicate pathos. Abraham has been commanded by God to go out on the hill and sacrifice Isaac.

ISAAKE

Father, tell me or I goe
Wheither I shal be harmede or noe.

ABRAHAM

Ah! deare God! that me is woe!
That breakes my harte in sunder.

ISAAKE

Father, tell me of this case,
Why you your sorde drawne hase,
And beares yt nacked in this place,
Theirof I have greate wonder.

ABRAHAM

Isaake, sonne, peace, I praie thee,
Thou breakes my harte even in three.

ISAAKE

I praye you, father, leane nothinge from me,
But tell me what you thinke.

ABRAHAM

Ah! Isaake, Isaake, I must thee kille!

ISAAKE

Alas! father, is that your will,
Your owine childe for to spill
Upon this hilles brinke?
Yf I have treasspasede in anye degree,
With a yarde maye beate me;
Put up your sorde, yf your wil be,
For I am but a childe.

ABRAHAM

O, my deare sonne, I am sorye
To doe to thee this grete anoye:
Godes commaundment doe must I,
His workes are ever full mylde.

ISAAKE

Woulde God my mother were here with me!
Shee woulde kneele downe upon her knee,
Prainge you, father, if yt may be,
    For to save my liffe.

ABRAHAM

O! comelye creature, but I thee kille,
I greve my God, and that full ylle;
I maye not worke against his will. . .

. . . .

ABRAHAM

Lorde, I woulde fayne worke thy will,
This yonge innocente that lieth so still
Full loth were me hym to kille,
    By anye maner a waye.

ISAAKE

A! mercye, father, why tarye you soe?
Smyte of my head, and let me goe.
I pray you rydd me of my woe,
    For nowe I take my leve.

ABRAHAM

Ah, sonne! my harte will breake in three,
To heare thee speake such wordes to me.
Jesu! on me thou have pittye,
    That I have moste in mynde.

ISAAKE

Nowe father, I see that I shall dye:
Almightie God in magistie!
My soule I offer unto thee;
Lord, to yt be kinde.

(Here let Abraham take and bynde his sonne Isaake upon the alter; let
hym make a signe as though he woulde cut of his head with his sorde; then
let the angell come and take the sworde by the end and staie it. . .)

While this human note was creeping into the Miracles — like
a foreshadowing of the Elizabethan playwrights — a radically
different sort of play was developing in the " Morality." The
form came to blossom most fully in England, and one of the best
examples is dated as early as 1405: the *Castell of Perseverance*.
In the field of drama the Morality corresponds to the Allegory in

poetic literature. The characters are personifications, and the central theme or struggle — seldom very dramatic — is between the good and the evil in man, or between Good and Evil for Man. The extant examples, with one exception, interest us less than the Miracles, for they are likely to be endlessly dull. Were it not indeed for the presence of two characters out of the older drama, the Devil and Vice, we should find the "Morals" well-nigh intolerable.

A French farce of the late Middle Ages. [From an old print as reproduced in Paul Albert's *La Littérature Française*.]

These two, like a vaudeville team introduced into a modern revue, Vice incessantly badgering the Devil, lighten up the slow-moving action, and take the curse off the greyness of the abstractions that serve as *dramatis personæ*. Of course, our ethical nature applauds when Virtue triumphs, when Wisdom, Sobriety, Charity, Obedience, draw Humankind to their side; and we equally rejoice when Folly, Gluttony, Pride, Voluptuousness, and Avarice suffer a fall. The characters are not all quite so abstract: there are Bad Habits, Imagination, Mankind, Good Counsel, Bad Luck, Bad-end, Colic, Dropsy, Pill, even Dinner, Supper, and Banquet.

Indeed there are shadings that carry us beyond the Idea to the human character standing for Hypocrisy or Snobbishness or Gossip — true beginnings of satirical comedy or character comedy.

Everyman is the exception that makes all readers pause when they are about to give over Morality Plays as nothing more than a curiosity of species. For here the moralizing and didacticism are balanced by very human conceptions of Fellowship, Good-Deeds, Death, and similar characters; and one feels a real dramatic pull in the struggle for Everyman's soul. The play was evidently a favorite of its kind, too, in the sixteenth century, for there were several early printed editions; and there exists a translation in Dutch (or, as some believe, the Dutch original from which the English version was made). The play has achieved new fame in our times, through some excellent English and German revivals; and at Salzburg the *Jedermann* performance before the cathedral is the central attraction of the annual dramatic festivals — though Max Reinhardt uses a somewhat rococo version, and loses some of the mediæval naïvety while recapturing much of the effectiveness of cathedral background, church music, and simple outdoor staging.

As in France, it is impossible to disentangle the beginnings of English secular drama from the manifestations of late religious drama. The French Feast of Fools had a later counterpart in the revels of the English choir boys: characterized by feasting, burlesque of the Church service, processions, and a *dominus festi,* who here became known as the Boy Bishop. A line may be traced down from the boy-revels to secular dramatic activity. Other lines come down from the court entertainments, not without relationship to the minstrels, and from the folk customs — particularly those that culminated in the Sword Dances and the Mummers' Plays.

When the festival of the renewal of life in the earth, the turn of the year, had grown into set form, with certain recognized dances, and with named participants (the Doctor who restored life was a regular character), it came to the estate of drama; and this drama was carried out widely, by its folk performers, into the houses of nobles and into the courts — where, indeed, the minstrel beginnings, the "mummings" and new-fangled Renaissance masque-importations from Italy became inextricably mixed. Even the court masque had had local antecedents, in the " ridings," the royal " entries," and civic pageantry.

The word " interlude " that is commonly used to denominate, roughly, the drama that came after the Moralities and before the true English comedy, is almost hopelessly vague — and almost lost in the haze of scholars' disputes over its origin and application. It has been employed to describe the early court entertainments — as a dramatic and musical interlude, or perhaps ballet, at a banquet — and a certain sort of Morality, and the earliest farce sketches that came after the Miracle Plays. In the last signification, it is seen as a main transitional agent between, say, the humorous incident of Noah trying to get his wife aboard the ark, and the comedies of the immediate predecessors of Shakespeare. John Heywood's " farces " are called interludes. They are the first group of wholly secular plays in English; they escape from the moralizing purpose and from any connection with Bible history or the legends of the Saints. They are not notable for either characterization or dramatic vividness; but with Heywood the drama has returned to a preoccupation with human people and with undisguised entertainment values. The way is prepared for the entry of the Renaissance spirit into the English theatre.

Religious drama does not die immediately, of course. The Miracle cycles are to be presented as late as Elizabeth's reign. But already in the Moralities, historical characters are appearing — prophetic hints of the coming Chronicle plays. And there are school stages whereon even classic revivals are known. But in ending our mediæval chapter it is more profitable to glance at the countries we have not found time to explore. The German-speaking nations particularly, while offering a parallel to France and England in the pervasiveness of the Mysteries and Miracles, provide at least one striking variation in methods of " staging." In addition to the pageant-wagon system that we have noted as more especially typical of the English guild productions, and the simultaneous scene on one long stage as recorded from Valenciennes and other French towns, there is here a method of transforming a whole city square or plaza into a theatre, with processional action from station to station.

Thus at Lucerne in 1583 the Easter Play was given in the Market Square, with Heaven built at one end (like a fortified and turreted castle), the Temple, the Synagogue, the tree for Judas' hanging and other stations ranged down the two sides, and Hell-mouth at

A religious play with scenes acted at separated station stages in a square in Copenhagen in 1634. Here again Hell-mouth is a prominent feature. [Drawing by Warren D. Cheney after an old print.]

a far corner beside other " localities." The diagrams for performances on two successive days leave us doubtful whether the crowd followed the actors from station to station, without any spectators ever being seated, or if there were balconies or other points of vantage from which the entire " theatre " could be seen. And by the way, for many years everyone believed that there was another sort of fixed stage for Mysteries, upon which the stations were built up in three-decker fashion, so that three episodes might be played successively in booths on (so to speak) the first, middle, and top floors. In some cases the lowest deck is marked as Hell, Purgatory, etc., the middle one as the World, the top one as Heaven and Paradise; but there is also mention somewhere of a nine-deck stage. The mistake probably arose from the fact that Heaven was commonly placed higher than the other stations in a simultaneous scene, and sometimes Hell lower; and from the confusion of a description of the *spectators'* boxes or benches with the booth stage. At any rate, the " authorities " now frown upon any mention of superimposed stages. In Italy and in Spain the pageant-cars became very popular, but usually with one movable wagon-stage serving for a whole drama. And in those countries today there are festivals in which the plays on wagons are a central feature.

Most important of all survivals of the mediæval theatre, however, is the decennial Passion Play at Ober-Ammergau in the Bavarian Alps. In this twentieth century, the rude wooden theatre in that out-of-the-way town is better known than any other playhouse in the world, is more sought out by pilgrims, is more praised for its performances by all classes of theatre-goers. The stage is an interesting — perhaps unfortunate — compromise of traditional religious-play architectural scene and modern box-stage for changing painted settings: the permanent stations for the mediæval stage appear at each side of a proscenium-arched, curtained inner stage, with nineteenth century scene-shifting paraphernalia. But the actors retain their old faith, their sincerity, their reverent devotion in acting. In the course of the years since 1633, when the first performance was given, there have been many modifications in text, in music, in methods of presentation; but the spirit of mediævalism has persisted — on its better side. Some of the crudity of those times, and much of the naïvety, have been rubbed away. We may resent the intrusion of the almost-as-crude painted settings that are now introduced; but one cannot see the production, or talk with Anton Lang and his fellow-actors, without knowing that here is some spirit of service, a conviction, a devotion — something very beautiful, something typically mediæval — that is lost out of the rest of the theatres of our times.

CHAPTER VIII

The Glorious Renaissance — with Reservations

IN THAT "Renaissance" period which is the chief glory of Italian history, the story of the theatre is not marked by the emergence of a drama in any way comparable to the amazing contemporary achievements in the realms of intellectual research, painting, sculpture, and architecture. In those other fields the Renaissance was both a rebirth of a forgotten spirit and a flowering of creative activity: first the Revival of Learning which sometimes gives the period its name, then prodigious individual feats of scholarship, startling advance in freedom of thought, the creation of the masterpieces of Giotto, Brunelleschi, Michelangelo, and Leonardo da Vinci, and others whom the world still counts among the great artists of all time.

Yet the theatre in this period, however magnificent its advance in the outward trappings of drama, however colorful its accompaniment to the opulent social life of the time, failed to bring into existence a single play of lasting world-importance. We go to Florence today to see Giotto's paintings or his lovely Campanile, and Brunelleschi's cathedral dome, or Michelangelo's sculptures; and we may, as we wander through the palaces, the piazzas, the gardens, reconstruct a picture of the lavish court productions, and a picture of the robust vulgar popular comedy; but nowhere on the bookshelves shall we find a play text comparable to the poems, the stories, and the histories that came out of the half-fabulous Italy of the fourteenth to the sixteenth centuries.

The Italian Renaissance, none the less, marks the birth of the modern stage. If the recreating process, in regard to drama, was less complete here than in the other arts, the revival, the return to ancient forms, was no less epochal. Mediæval art had sprung

177

largely from alien, unclassical origins; the theatre of the Middle Ages particularly had come from a new source, wholly Christian, a separate thing, not connected with the tradition of Greece and Rome.

The Italian Renaissance accomplished the transition from the mediæval to the modern theatre by wholly cutting off the religious drama and its type of stage; by returning the course of dramatic development to the old channel of classic times. The revived models of play forms, though failing to inspire any Italian Shakespeare, marked out the way for Spain, for England, for France — and for what followed, even down to the Realism of today. In another direction, the change was even more immediate; in Italy a new type of theatre building was developed, and the transition was accomplished from mere acting on platforms or in areas to acting in painted settings. In summary, the Italian Renaissance gave the world a new place for play-producing, and a new method of dressing the drama; and indirectly it fathered Shakespeare, Jonson, Corneille, Racine — and the rest.

" Humanism " is sometimes offered as the key word to unlock the mystery of the sudden rebirth, the flaming passion that was the Renaissance. For centuries all thought, all research, all " culture " had been dominated by the Church; the individual man could not be considered, conceived of, judged, as a being apart from his religion, from the rules of Christian conduct, from theological law and organization. Almost suddenly the time became ripe in Italy for man to turn the light of reason on himself, to dignify himself, to become creative (and incidentally, to commit all those excesses that go with sudden freedom from over-restraint). From being afraid to walk except in fixed paths, suspicious of or apathetic to beauty, accepting ignorance as a good pleasing to God and the Church, striving, if imperfectly, to be prepared for the all-determining judgment after death, the individual man emerged into a world where reason told him it was possible to live happily, to exercise the intellect, to create beauty, to determine his own destiny. With exuberant spirits, with enthusiasm, with animal vigor, he set out to triumph. From the uncovering of Greek and Roman texts, sculptures, and buildings, he gained new conceptions of life, of art, of reasonable pleasure.

He threw himself into new efforts at creation, imitatively at first, then with superb independence and originality. He indulged a very passion for all that was antique, collected and recopied manuscripts, uncovered monuments, wrote detailed essays on the ancients, picked up the lost impulses to poetic composition, scientific investigation, and philosophic speculation.

He even questioned the Church — leading not so indirectly to the later Reformation. His self-assertiveness was soon to lead to a new era of discovery, to the epochal development of the printing-press, to the invention of mechanisms destined to revolutionize war, exploration, and living. All these things followed on what was essentially a rediscovery of the freedom and the power of the human spirit.

The Renaissance was Europe-wide; but Italy emerged first from the condition of insecurity, superstition, and widespread ignorance that had cloaked the continent so long. By a conjunction of political, commercial, and racial circumstances, which we need not explore here, the Italian peoples first felt the breath of intellectual curiosity, were stirred by the new ideal of human freedom. This was no united Italy in the present-day sense: the communes or cities or minor states were still waging continual warfare with one another, the forces of the Papacy and the Empire were at each other's throats, foreign rulers held large parts of the Peninsula under Spanish or French or Germanic rule. Party strife among the nobles often made a city-state the seat of civil wars and anarchy. But amid the reign of violence, terror, cruelty, and political perfidy, the flower of learning and art somehow sprang up, grew straight and beautiful, enriched the world for all time.

Perhaps only the sword in the hands of nobles with passionate imagination could wrest from those violent times the wealth, the margin of leisure and the magnificence which made possible the creative activities of the artist, under protection and generous patronage. Certainly, it was at the courts of men we would call "tyrants" that learning flourished, that scholars from abroad were entertained, that "circles" were established for the discussion and comparison of ideas and the dissemination of knowledge; that theatres were established. Here the bridge was formed that led from the world of Greece and Rome to the world of the future; here was the new valuation of human achievement apart from Church or State. From the courts — and the popes, too, were great princes, as well as ecclesiastics, in those days — the enthusiasm spread, from nobles and artists and scholars to adventurers and tradesmen and idlers. The foundation was securely and widely laid for modern intellectual and artistic activity.

We may say that Dante, if you like, embodied the final expression of the spirit of the Middle Ages — his mysticism, his faith, his self-negation and his prophetic and exhortatory method all warrant the statement — even while he foreshadowed the intellectual freedom to come. It was rather Petrarch who opened the door full to the new spirit. He was the first great figure among those who gave humanism and liberalism to Italy, at once creator and inspirer of other men. Boccaccio was more clearly the literary artist. It would be futile to speculate why these writers and half a dozen lesser poets and novelists failed to write importantly for the stage. In a later time the material of some of the world's treasury of plays was drawn from their translated works. But it is pertinent to remember that they opened the way for the drama to treat hitherto forbidden subjects and emotions. The Church had judged the classics vicious on several scores; it had condemned literature as extolling alien gods, as inciting loose living, as failing to prepare the spectator for the life-after-death, as making attractive a human concept without theological authority. However the Italian dramatists of the Renaissance may fail to put life or effective drama into their plays, an all-important freedom had been won by these earliest writers. Human life — not merely Bible legends — would thenceforth provide the raw material for serious drama.

To understand why those who did turn to the theatre, the earliest Renaissance playwrights, wasted their substance in crassly imitational works, it is necesary to hold in mind the all-pervading passion for a rediscovered antiquity. Academies were formed for the study of every detail of Latin and Greek manuscripts and monuments. The texts of Plautus, Terence, and Seneca were brought to light, subjected to scholarly commentary, gravely and devotedly brought to the stage — probably with as complete loss of the *spirit* of the plays as is usual in " school " revivals today.

In their aim of making the theatre of the new era the most perfect imitation of that of the ancients, certain of the academies built what they deemed to be classic playhouses (an activity that profoundly affected the course of theatre-building in later times, as we shall see). In the academy theatres and on the stages temporarily erected in court ballrooms, the Latin plays were soon being given widely — and not without spectators genuinely interested, in a scholarly way. (But Perrens in his *History of Florence* shrewdly says: " the spectacle being free, nobody had the right to find fault.")

In following out first the development of literary drama — setting aside momentarily the more colorful pageant-making, spectacle, and farce-comedy — we need not linger long over those writers who slavishly copied the old play models even while attempting new subject-matter. Earlier than the true period of the Renaissance there had been isolated examples of plays written in the Roman manner; Hrotsvitha had composed her not-too-Terentian comedies, and there had been other monastic attempts to reconcile churchly and pagan literary ideals. There had been considerable activity, too, at the universities and schools in various parts of Europe, in the revival of Plautus and Terence; a general vagueness covers the subject, but there is evidence of widespread school productions, and indications that a special type of stage, entirely separate from the mediæval and possibly not unconnected with the classic, had been developed for such revivals.

But the rebirth of classic drama is generally ascribed to the fourteenth century; its full effect was felt in the mid-fifteenth, when the Roman Academy under Pomponius Lætus was producing both Roman drama and imitations in Latin, while groups at Ferrara, Florence, Siena, Venice, Naples, and elsewhere were either staging similar performances or soon to follow suit; and the first truly original works in the vernacular belong to the sixteenth century.

By stretching our definition of drama a bit, we may trace Renaissance tragedy back to 1314 or thereabouts, when Albertino Mussato produced his *Eccerinis,* a very short tragedy on an Italian subject, and his *Achilleis,* on a classical theme, both written in Latin in imitation of Seneca. Likewise, literary comedy may be traced back to a lost play by Petrarch, after the Terentian model, also of the first half of the fourteenth century. By 1450 the imitation of the ancient dramatists was in full swing. Latin long remained the preferred dramatic language; and the classic theme was favorite over local or modern story — it was part of the reaction against too much Church that Greek and Roman gods, heroes, and legends, should be given as wide currency as possible. At a time when scholarship was so revered, the study of the ancient languages so general in the upper circles of society, dialogue in Latin would find both court and Academy audiences understanding and responsive. Necessarily, however, the plays of the period are hopelessly inferior to the classic models; not a playwright's name need be remembered from the period. A curious sidelight is thrown on the limitations of the scholar-writers of this Latinized century when one reflects that even Dante and Petrarch then suffered neglect from being in the "vulgar" tongue.

With the early sixteenth century, composition of plays *in Italian* began in earnest. Gian Giorgio Trissino is generally credited as the first "regular" Italian tragedy-writer. His best-known play, *Sofonisba,* was composed in 1515, several times printed, and finally staged in 1562. In his life and in his writing this author affords a key to an understanding of the times and of the failure of Italy to produce a great dramatist during the Renaissance. Trissino was, according to Symonds,[1] "a man of immense erudition and laborious intellect, who devoted himself to questions of grammatical and literary accuracy, studying the critics of antiquity with indefatigable diligence, and seeking to establish canons for the regulation of correct Italian composition. . . He set himself to supply the deficiencies of Italian literature by producing an epic in the heroic style, and a tragedy that should compare with those of Athens. The *Italia Liberata* and the *Sofonisba,* meritorious but lifeless exercises which lacked nothing

---

[1] *A Short History of the Renaissance in Italy,* taken from the work of John Addington Symonds by Lieutenant-Colonel Alfred Pearson (London, 1893). This is a useful abridgment of Symonds' standard *Renaissance in Italy,* still, I think, the most readable book on the subject. Volumes IV and V, under the sub-title *Italian Literature,* include much material about drama and dramatists.

A diagrammatic view of a theatre for revival of the classics, in the fifteenth century. Note that the stage is of the type shown in the next illustration. [From the Trechsel edition of Terence, 1493.]

but the genius for poetry, were the result of these ambitious theories."

In short, Trissino wrote a correct, imitative, dramatically dead tragedy. In following the ancients he made the further mistake of taking Seneca rather than the Greeks for model. Most of the Italian tragedy of the time reeks of Senecan violence and horror, and of Senecan rhetoric, without the clarity, inevitableness, and poetry of the Greek.

After Trissino one may mention, as similar practitioners, important in their own time, Rucellai, Aretino, whom we shall hear about in connection with comedy, Cinthio, who first invented his own plots (whose *l'Orbecche* " is accounted the best and the bloodiest "), Dolce, and that Tasso who is to appear again when we study the pastoral drama. Through all this time, from 1502 till the eighteenth century, when the circle of development will have been completed through Italy to Paris and back again to Italy in the influence of French classic tragedy, there is a gain from mere narrated event toward acted drama, a gain in freedom of subject-matter, a gain in variety of metric forms. But until Alfieri, Italian tragedy hardly achieves a text of world significance.

The transition from productions in Latin to productions in Italian came slightly earlier in comedy than in tragedy. The close of the fifteenth century was already seeing comedies produced in the vernacular, both translated works and imitative plays by Italian authors. Almost immediately the most important playwright of the Renaissance makes his appearance: that Lodovico Ariosto whose epic *Orlando Furioso* is so much finer than any of his dramas, though of the latter several survive and are highly esteemed in Italy to this day. Ariosto lived from 1474 to 1533, in the very heart of the Renaissance, and his materials reflect the bigness, the audacity, and the moral looseness of his time. His *Lena* is especially esteemed as a picture of society at Ferrara, beyond its values as comedy. He is a main link between ancient and modern drama.

Of those whose names are offered as precursors of Ariosto, in the invention of native comedy, there is Boiardo, whose play of 1494 or earlier seems, however, to have been more adaptation than original. There is Dovizio, later to be Cardinal Bibbiena, whose " disreputable but entertaining " farce-comedy *Calandra* was based on Plautus' *Menæchmi,* but " enhanced the comic effect at the expense of morality." It was produced at Urbino about 1509, passed triumphantly through all the courts of Italy, and later so pleased Pope Leo X that he had it repeated often for his entourage and guests in Rome. And there is Ricchi, who is set aside by most commentators because his " first Italian comedy in verse " is an adaptation of the Morality Play rather than in classic tradition.

Beside Ariosto stand Niccolo Machiavelli and Pietro Aretino — as picturesque a pair of libertines as ever graced the theatre. In

Scenes from the plays of Terence, on a platform stage.
[From the Trechsel edition.]

a time when men lived and loved wildly, passionately, cruelly, dissolutely, when the shrewd fighter who cared least for personal or public honor was most likely to become ruler and to amass riches, when violence and perfidy and insolence were as ready weapons as physical courage, these two authors wrenched comedy finally free from classic limitations and used it to amuse and to portray the society about them. They chased the pedants out of the field: the men who always worked at second hand, taking other people's opinions and bowing before classic precedent. They were the first to forget Plautus and Terence. " I show men as they are, not as they should be," exclaimed Aretino; and he might have been speaking for Machiavelli as well. They both had the directness, the incisiveness, the spontaneous surface truth implied in that statement. Their plays were indubitably powerful, lively, vivid in scene or incident, absorbing for their unabashed view of sensational living, often witty in dialogue; yet they lack the final unifying, cementing, dramatic quality that might have made them comparable to Molière's portraits of a later age, or Sheridan's spirited satire.

It has been said that Aretino typified the dissolution of the genius of the Italian Renaissance, that he embodied the fault that lay at the heart of Italy's failure to develop a national drama: his inherent coarseness made impossible any eternal fineness in his plays; that his baseness and grossness, mental as well as outward, stand for the degeneration of Italy's culture as they do for the shallowness of the man's talent, and its instability. Aretino, in a magnificent gesture, struck the shackles of pedantry off drama; but his self-confidence, his malice, and his sensuality betrayed him as artist. There are those who say that he was most notable as ushering in the methods and the era of the modern press — publicity, blackmailing, reporting, *realism,* sensationalism, the newspaper drama.

One might outline the plot of Machiavelli's *Mandragola,* and quote a few passages, by way of better showing out the state of comedy in this time — we have sampled the drama of other periods in that way. But taste and custom have so changed that the play seems simply not to belong to the theatre or any body of theatre-goers today; is not important in the wider (or is it the narrower?) view. Suffice it to say that the theme is that one most beloved by the Latin races, the way in which a married woman takes a lover, this time made piquant by the husband who connives at his own betrayal — the whole set forth with unexampled cynicism.

That we should so immediately come upon two such sinister figures, so soon after Ariosto, is, indeed, an index to the life of the " scholarly " theatre of the time. Largely, the literary drama had exhausted itself in lifeless imitation. The first writers who bring vigor and originality to it are these almost incredible libertines: that Aretino " whose very name should be written in asterisks," and the Machiavelli who is permanently memorialized in our language by two equally suggestive phrases, " Machiavel-

A theatrical production in a Florentine ballroom theatre. A print by Jacques Callot of a court masque in 1616, in the great hall of the (now) Uffizi Palace. Note the performers on the dancing floor as well as on the raised stage; and the non-architectural scenery. It is said that this etching in which Callot fixed the natural ring-line of the standing spectators helped to determine the form of the later " horseshoe " auditoriums.

[From *The Theatre of Tomorrow*, by Kenneth Macgowan.]

lian " and (as some say) " the old Nick." Scores of other play-wrights' names and a list of known comedies that runs into the thousands, bear witness to a prolific period during and after the lifetimes of Aretino and Machiavelli; but literary comedy in Italy practically died with them.

THERE is, however, a brighter side to the story of the Italian Renaissance theatre. As soon as we get away from the lasting play-text as a criterion, away from consideration of literary drama, we find evidences of extraordinary theatrical activity. The popular street comedy, the improvised drama of the *Commedia dell'Arte,* developing almost without any written dialogue, is spirited, sheerly theatrical, admirably original; without escaping the coarseness and licentiousness of the times, it is, in the early Renaissance, vulgar without cynicism, expressive, and endlessly amusing. And in the court theatres, *production* as an art is developing a new elaboration, a new magnificence, in keeping with the abounding life and lavish display of the rival noble families. The stage is playing its brilliant part in the reckless and colorful advance of human freedom.

Florence, as it was the cradle of the Renaissance, also is the home of its most opulent achievements in the arts. The Florentine courts, rivalled as they are by memories of the Gonzagas in Mantua, of the Court of Ferrara under the Estes, and of others no less brilliant, still stand out in greater, in epochal magnificence. The Medici rulers are the very type of Renaissance soldier-politician, merchant-prince, and ruler-patron. The Medici popes, though less sensationally unreligious, less spectacularly dissolute, than some others, and less bloody, did most to turn the papal court at Rome into a gorgeous and majestic replica of the glittering secular courts that their forefathers had already established in the city on the Arno.

These nobles and their courtiers, their rivals who have bowed to them or who watch for a chance to assassinate and usurp, even while contributing to the pageant of social display and art endeavor, their favorite ladies and their kept poets, all these enter into a colorful show of courtly extravagance seldom equalled in other eras. Florence at one time has thirty palaces within its walls. Only a bit lower down is a population cultivated, vitally alive, mentally independent, art-loving. If below that there are circles touching on poverty, wretchedness, and crime almost incredible — never, we are told, was mere human life held at lower valuation — we may shrug our shoulders because they have nothing to do with the regal productions at the courts.

Cosimo de' Medici, corrupt tyrant, egotist, cynic, unprincipled fighter, is yet the great patron of the arts, bringing scholars from afar to his court, giving enormously generous commissions to architects, painters, sculptors, for the embellishment of Florence, meeting poets on their own ground as understanding critic, collecting works of art and manuscripts, and keeping copyists busy, making his palace the centre for literary, philosophical, and artistic societies and coteries, founding the Platonic Academy — in short, while earning politically the title *pater patriæ,* putting into his debt by wise munificence art lovers down the ages.

Then Lorenzo the Magnificent: his very name, as put down in a dedication by Machiavelli and perpetuated by all later historians, is a spur to our imagination in picturing his theatre. Lorenzo was the very incarnation of the free spirit of the Renaissance, himself a poet and scholar of no mean ability, writer of lyrics for the carnivals, the patron who did most to unite the two currents of antique revival and Italian effort, no less enthusiastic and spirited in intellectual pursuits and art patronage than in the adventures of love, tilting, and political intrigue. It is this sort of prince that we may visualize as decreeing that on a certain night a play of Terence shall be performed, exactly in the ancient manner, on the ballroom stage; on another night the newest tragedy (after Seneca) of his latest poet-protégé; or on another evening a masque, with so-and-so's dancers and perhaps those diverting " settings " which the artists have been bringing indoors piecemeal from the entries and pageants.

The *drama* that the princely theatres of these tyrants fostered, as we have seen, failed to come to world importance. What is it, then, that lends such lustre to the Renaissance stage? Chiefly the magnificence of the outward trappings; and then the perfect fitness of theatre activity to the life of the times. Rediscovery of old elements of theatrical art — in playhouse forms, in setting, in machinery — and new opulence of visual display: these are gains perfectly in the spirit of the day. The regally decorated palace ballroom becomes a theatre; its stage takes on an appropriately wasteful decorative richness.

We catch the spirit of the occasion best by seeing through contemporary eyes. (We may forget for the moment that the accounts deal with another court than the Medicean, and that the date is a year after the great Lorenzo's death: the Venetian court is equally typical.) Thus Beatrice d'Este, writing from Venice in May, 1493, to her husband, the Regent of Milan:

After dinner and a little rest, a large company of gentlemen came to conduct us to the *festa* at the palace. We travelled in barges, and, when we reached the palace, were conducted into the Great Hall. There a grand tribunal was erected at one end of the hall, in two divisions running the whole length of the walls, and in the centre of the hall a square stage was placed for dancing and theatrical representations. We ascended the tribunal, where we found a number of noble Venetian ladies, one hundred and thirty-two in all, richly adorned with jewels. . . During the dancing, I left the hall and retired to rest in another room for an hour. When I returned it was already dark. A hundred lighted torches hung from the ceiling, and a representation was given on the stage, in which two big animals with large horns appeared, ridden by two figures, bearing golden balls and cups wreathed with verdure. These two were followed by a triumphal chariot, in which Justice sat enthroned, holding a drawn sword in her hand inscribed with the motto *Concordia,* and wreathed with palms and olive. In the same car was an ox with his feet resting on a figure of St. Mark and the adder. This, as your Highness will readily understand, was meant to signify the League, and as in all their discourses to me the Prince and these gentlemen speak of your Highness as the author of the peace and tranquillity of Italy, so in this representation they placed your head on the triumphal arch above the others. Behind the chariot came two serpents, ridden by two other youths, dressed like the first riders. All these figures mounted the tribunal in the centre of the hall, and danced round Justice, and after dancing for awhile, their balls exploded, and out of the flames, an ox, a lion, an adder, and a Moor's head suddenly appeared, and all of these danced together round the figure of Justice. Then the banquet followed, and the different dishes and *confetti* were carried in to the sound of trumpets, accompanied by an infinite number of torches. . . When the banquet was finished, we had another representation, in which two youths on serpents played the chief part. A messenger arrived, riding on a triumphal car in a boat . . . and a little while afterwards the triumphal car of the League appeared again, followed by four giants. The first one carried a horn of foliage and fruit, the two next bore two clubs with gold and silver balls, or catapults, while the last carried a cornucopia, similar to that borne by the first giant in his hand. Then came four animals in the shape of Chimeras ridden by four naked Moors, sounding tambourines and cymbals or clapping their hands. They were followed by four triumphal cars, bearing figures of Diana, Death, the Mother of Meleager, and several armed men — four or five persons in each chariot, the whole intended to represent the story of Meleager, which was fully set forth from his birth to his death, with interludes of dances . . . The Bishop of Como was sitting by me all the evening, and his infinite weariness at the length of the performance and his dislike of the great heat in that crowded hall made me laugh as I never laughed before. And in order to tease him and have more fun I kept on telling him that there was still more to come and that the acting would go on till tomorrow morning. . . When at length we reached home, I supped frugally and then went to bed, as it was already three o'clock. The gown that I wore after dinner was a crimson and gold watered silk, with my jewelled cap on my head, and the rope of pearls with the Marone as a pendant. I commend myself to your Highness. Your Excellency's most affectionate wife,

BEATRICE SFORZA VISCOMTIS

Here indeed is drama subordinated to the new elements out of pageantry and decorated dance-ballet. Here are monsters, giants, serpents, chimeras, chariots, allegorical figures, mythological story, and interludes of dances, in place of unified dramatic action; and the whole is mixed with feasting, richly adorned and bejewelled ladies, bishops, lords, and such — not wholly unconnected too, with political purpose.

The Latin comedies were still being presented, and Italian ones; a few years later Beatrice's sister, Isabella d'Este, writing after performances at the Court of Ferrara, remarks: " These plays are certainly full of vain words, and are not without doubtful passages to which some persons might take objection. All the same, they are amusing, and excite much laughter, chiefly owing to the frequent changes of voice and excellent performance of these actors." And in the same year Isabella sees at Mantua productions described (by Sigismondo Cantelmo) with the new emphasis on grandeur of staging:

On Friday *Philonico* was given, on Saturday *Il Penulo* of Plautus, on Sunday the *Ippolita* of Seneca, on Monday the *Adelphi* of Terence. All of these were admirably recited by skilled actors, and received the greatest applause from the spectators. . . I should fail in my duty if I did not write to tell you what, indeed, requires a better scribe than I am — all the magnificence, grandeur, and excellence of the said representations, the beauty of which I will try to describe as briefly as possible. . .

The narrator then goes on to describe a luxuriantly decorated stage and hall, with paintings by Mantegna, a grotto, arcades, foliage, banners, and " the blue vault of heaven, studded over with the constellations of our hemisphere." Certainly Plautus and Terence and Seneca have come to a new magnificence of setting here.

Still another report by Isabella herself begins with a comment on the sumptuous costumes for five comedies, which were so many that " those which were worn in one comedy would not have to be used again," though there were one hundred and ten actors, men and women. And in 1508 Bernardino Prosperi writes from the Court of Ferrara a letter [2] that sums up the whole drift of dramatic performance away from mere play and acting toward glorified scenery, dance, and regal pageantry:

On Monday evening the Cardinal had a comedy performed, which was composed by Messer Lodovico Ariosto, his familiar, and rendered in the form of a farce or merry jape, the which from beginning to end was as elegant and delightful as any other that I have ever seen played, and it was much commended on every side. The subject was a most beautiful one of two youths enamored of two harlots who had been brought to Taranto by a pander, and in it there were so many intrigues and novel incidents and so many fine moralities and various things that in those of Terence there are not half of them; for the parts were cast to honorable and good actors, all from without, with most beautiful costumes and sweet melodies for interludes, and with a morris-dance of cooks heated with wine, with earthen pots tied in front of them, who beat time with their wooden sticks to the sound of the Cardinal's music. But what has been best in all these festivities and representations has been the scenery in which they have been played, which Maestro Peregrino, the Duke's painter, has made. It has been a view in perspective of a town with houses, churches,

---

[2] The quotation here and one at the end of the chapter are from *The King of Court Poets: A Study of the Work, Life and Times of Lodovico Ariosto,* by Edmund G. Gardner (London, 1906). This and the same author's *Dukes and Poets in Ferrara* (London, 1904) illuminate well the background of political and social intrigue against which the artists and dramatists of the Renaissance worked. Equally fascinating studies of the courts of the period are the two books from which I have taken the quotations from letters of Beatrice and Isabella d'Este: *Beatrice d'Este, Duchess of Milan,* and *Isabella d'Este, Marchioness of Mantua.* Both are by Julia Cartwright (Mrs. Ady) and both were published in London in 1903.

belfreys and gardens, such that one could never tire of looking at it, because of the different things that are there all most cleverly designed and executed. . .

What is this new " scenery " that so many of the Renaissance chroniclers wonder at and joy in? What, we may ask, is its place in the theatre art? Where did it come from? In Greek days, we are fairly certain, there was no attempt at placing a play

A typical architectural perspective stage. Setting for *Il Granchio, 1566.* [From *Scenes and Machines on the English Stage during the Renaissance,* by Lily B. Campbell.]

in illusive settings. In Roman times the architectural stage wall was elaborated into a richly decorated background; but painted picture settings were either unknown or so rare that they escaped all historians. Just about this time the producers of Miracle Plays and Mysteries were developing the simultaneous scene with grouped picture-bits; but that is an activity not likely to have influenced greatly the Renaissance architects and play producers.

The impulse toward the illusive setting and pictorial "effects" probably rose from the same source in the two cases: the priests began to picture out the Mystery incidents because they were dealing with naïve audiences with child-like minds, and gradually the picturing method spread to the backgrounds; and in Renaissance Italy the producers set out a comedy in "a view in perspec-

The fixed architectural scene for comedy as prescribed by Serlio, in 1545. [From reproductions in *Theatre Arts Monthly* of the originals in Serlio's *Architettura*.]

tive, such that one could never tire of looking at it, because of the different things that are there," for the same reason, to raise delight by clever portrayal of place and with surprising trappings. And it always seems to me that the best explanation of the strange things that happened in the name of stage decoration, then and in later centuries, is that the producers adopted the principle of putting in a lot of things to please the children. It is a question,

indeed, whether the coming of perspective-picture settings has not
been more of a curse than a blessing to adult drama (though I
believe in color, lighting, and the visual element in general as
a major contributing element in production). Anyway, it was at
this time that "scenery" flowered; and until the twentieth century the painted-perspective setting will claim its showy place on
all the stages of Europe.

The fixed architectural scene for tragedy. Note the severer architecture
here as compared with that of the comedy scene shown opposite.

The origins of the picture scene are badly entangled. Our
writer from Ferrara in 1509, Prosperi, praises "a view in perspective of a town with houses, churches, belfries and gardens"; the
designer of it, the Maestro Peregrino, may have been carrying on
a tradition of the outdoor *Commedia dell'Arte* stage, whereon a
rudely indicated street between two rows of houses was standard;
an idiom that may possibly be traced back into Roman times.
In any case we may be sure that Peregrino also was claiming
classical precedent for his "view in perspective." You will re-

member that Vitruvius had written of the *periacti,* devices by which change of scene was indicated (it didn't take place) in Roman times. He described three scenes as they appeared on the three faces of a turning prism, two as architectural views with buildings, for tragedy and comedy, and the third a pastoral view, for satyr-plays. It seems likely that the Renaissance scholars and

The scene for satyr-plays as devised by Serlio.

artists misread the description and set out to apply the principle to full-stage scenes, not merely to an indicating device. The re-discovered treatise by Vitruvius, *De Architectura,* had been published as early as 1486.

What the artists after that made of the Vitruvian scenes is best illustrated from plates in a volume of Serlio's famous *Architettura,* first published in 1545 and then reprinted and translated in

Above, the stage and proscenium of the Farnese Theatre at Parma, as seen from the "arena" floor. Built in 1618–1619, this is known as "the first modern theatre," by reason of the proscenium-framed and curtained stage — though the auditorium is still of the ballroom type. [From a drawing by J. M. Olbrich in Streit's *Das Theater*.] Below, an example of the Renaissance architectural scene, as designed by Baldassarre **Peruzzi**. [From a Brogi photograph of the original drawing in the Uffizi Gallery, Florence.]

The Theatre of the Olympian Academy at Vicenza. This may profitably be compared with the reconstructions of the theatres at Orange and Aspendus, for proof of its relationship to the classic playhouses. It is really a small Roman theatre roofed over. The perspective vistas beyond the doorways were added in 1585, a few years after the building of the theatre.

the chief countries of Europe. I reproduce the three scenes according to Serlio herewith; because no other pictures of real or supposititious settings ever had so extraordinary an influence upon methods of staging. In a sense the series went far to establish the perspective setting, architectural and landscape, as the approved thing for the theatres of Europe. Of course Serlio had had opportunity to see many perspective scenes worked out on Italian ballroom stages — perhaps saw this very one in Ferrara in 1508.

At any rate the "street perspective" became the common *play* background (the masques, interludes, etc., had another novelty in a less austere, pageanty scene, as we shall see in a moment). Two more examples are pictured to illustrate the point. And to make a long story very short, the architectural perspectives throve and throve, until in the next century operas and sometimes even plays were being exhibited in those gorgeously elaborate architectural compositions that are associated with the illustrious name of the Bibbienas, who, even to four generations, dwarfed the actor with the towering magnificence of arches, columns, cartouches, and wreathes. You will find their works illustrated in the next chapter — because they are so essentially operatic.

Aside from a misconception of Roman scenery, the architects of the Renaissance gained from Vitruvius a knowledge of the architectural form of the ancient theatre. When an academy planned to build a "classic" playhouse, the designers could read Vitruvius, perhaps explore some ruins, and construct a fairly close approximation to a Roman auditorium and stage. One such theatre survives today, almost exactly as it was constructed in 1580 and the few years following: the Theatre of the Olympian Academy at Vicenza, known also as the Palladian Theatre, after the architect. From the photograph the reader can see how like the building is to a small Roman theatre roofed over. After the death of Palladio, the architect Scamozzi added the perspective vistas seen through the doorways in the stage-wall — borrowing and intruding a feature already well developed on the free-standing ballroom stages.

And thereby hangs the tale of the coming of the proscenium arch that is the distinguishing structural feature of theatres for

Plan A is the Vicenza stage, of Roman ancestry, but with vistas added beyond the doorways. B illustrates how Scamozzi designed the theatre at Sabionetta with the stage forming a single vista. C is Inigo Jones' combination of Roman walled platform with the vista into one stage composition. D shows the first theatre in which the entire stage is known to have been pushed through the portal and curtained, that at Parma (1618–19). To the left is a sketch after Inigo Jones' drawing for his stage, the best evidence of transitional thought about the matter. (Sketches not drawn to same scale.)

AUDIENCE

STAGE

PERSPECTIVE VISTAS

1580-85

VISTA BECOMES STAGE

1588

STAGE

A B C D

CURTAIN

STAGE

The evolution of the picture scene: showing how the decorated stage-wall of the classic theatre moved forward to become the proscenium frame of the modern theatre, while the vista once seen through the central stage doorway became the full-stage scene, curtained and changeable between plays or between acts.

three centuries to follow. For there is a theory to the effect that the proscenium arch of the modern theatre is the direct lineal descendent of the central doorway of the Vicenza stage. It occurred like this: Scamozzi put five perspectives behind the doorways, making a stage plan like A opposite; other architects and Scamozzi himself wanted to preserve the useful stage-wall and yet open up the perspective to afford more acting space, and Scamozzi developed B as a stage-plan for the theatre at Sabionetta, while the visiting Inigo Jones made the plan C as a further modification. From this it was but a step to push the entire playing space through the portal, arriving at a curtained stage, D, with the decoration of the old Roman stage-wall now persisting only as adornment of the frame to the acting stage.

What we arrive at is that playhouse in Parma which is known as " the first modern theatre " — because it has the first known proscenium-framed stage. Here indeed is an acting space with new potentialities and new limitations. Acting is to be within a space surrounded by walls or "scenery," not out on an open platform. It will be quite a different thing after two hundred years of blanketing by painted settings. And now that those settings can be shown suddenly, by the drawing of curtains — and yes! even changed between acts — the scene-painter is going to be a mighty important man in the theatre.

Before going on to his story, however, let us note that the classic form of auditorium, modified by the influence of the ballroom theatres, determined the form of the seventeenth to the nineteenth century playhouses. The Farnese Theatre at Parma has the new proscenium-framed stage combined with the ballroom floor and " arena " seating of the informal palace playhouses. That arrangement was necessary as long as pageants and social dancing were mixed up with drama (see the picture of a Florentine fête some pages back). The next step is the compromise auditorium in horseshoe shape; it gives a larger number of people a view into the scene behind the frame, by cutting off the ends of the old Roman semicircular auditorium, as illustrated on page 201.

It is necessary to go back and inquire where the scene-painter came from (we have discovered the sources of the curtained stage to which he will bring his flats and back-cloth, and we have learned about the architect's built-up scene; but this is a third, independent development). A hint has been dropped about a possible influence from the Miracle and Mystery Plays — which in Italy were presented at times on ballroom stages. But the safer conjecture is that painty, though not exactly painted, settings grew out of the pageant-cars and tableau-stages that had long been a feature of the royal entry, the outdoor *festa,* and the *carrousel* (yes, in France, too). In the open-air fêtes, the increasingly extravagant pageantry called for increasingly extravagant and ingenious moving or stationary stages, as backgrounds for grouped nobles in sumptuous costumes, or for posed tableaux of amateur

A pageant car, as etched by Jacques Callot.

actors. The car etched so prettily by Jacques Callot and reproduced on this page is typical; and so is the street " decoration " shown on page 204.

The next step is the introduction of these features into the ballroom as background for masques, for the sort of ballet-entertainment so clearly described by Beatrice d'Este; and from France we have a picture perfectly illustrating the intermediate arrangement of fragmentary tableau " scenery " brought on to the dancing floor (in the *Ballet de la Royne* engraving over-page). From this it is obviously a short step to the full-stage setting on the platform at the end of the ballroom theatre, as illustrated in the picture by Callot of the Florentine masque, earlier in the chapter.

How the vista stage and the horseshoe
auditorium crystallized in a theatre form
that was standard for the eighteenth and
nineteenth centuries. Note the parallel
grooves for wing settings on the stage.
La Scala Opera House in Milan.

The scene here is typically painty; that is, it could not be built up in stucco, and is unarchitectural.

Serlio had given instructions that the buildings in his Vitruvian tragedy and comedy scenes were to be built out in relief, not painted on canvas (and the perspectives at Vicenza are properly thus constructed); but he allowed that the tiny bits at the end of the vista might be painted in perspective to carry on the lines of the carefully built, diminishing rows of buildings on his " street." We may visualize the scene painter enlarging that back-drop year after year, usurping more and more of the space given (so expensively) to the architect's constructions; until finally the painter, providing even architectural scenes so much more cheaply than architect and carpenter, and able to bring landscape effects into the theatre as well, pushes his rivals out the stage-door. The painted perspective setting, thus established in Italy in the early sixteenth century, and spreading northward in the seventeenth, is to rule on the stages of Europe until the twentieth century, when the latest Modernists will suddenly discover that too much picture scenery has been killing drama and nullifying the better sorts of visual-theatrical effectiveness.

In opera and spectacle, as we shall see, the glorified background will have triumphs of its own. But we may profitably note that it came into the theatre when drama as such was weak. Regard-ing the theatre art as a thing architectonic, we may say that the gains during the Renaissance were decorative, not structural: or-namental, not organic. As a last thought about the matter, let us remember that Italy at this time had gained something of sumptu-ousness out of the Orient.

In closing the chapter, which treats of the period immediately following those mediæval centuries when Church had killed theatre, then reared and disowned a separate " religious drama," we may glance at Renaissance theatrical entertainment as it flow-ered finally in Holy Rome. While the more strict sub-Fathers were fastidiously drawing their skirts away from the now-too-liberal, half-secularized Miracles and Mysteries, the Pope Leo X was building himself a private ballroom theatre at the Vatican. I find two accounts of a production there, which when pieced

A ballroom theatre as arranged for the *Ballet Comique de la Royne*, performed in 1581 before Henry III of France and his court. Note the fragmentary settings on the dancing floor, and the full pictorial setting on the rudimentary stage. [From a re-engraving in Pougin's *Dictionnaire* of the print published soon after the performance.]

An arch built for the entry of Charles IX into Paris in 1572, designed by
Bernard de Palissy. Typical of one of the sources of the "painty" setting.
[From Edouard Drumont's *Les Fêtes Nationales à Paris*.]

together seem to tie up the threads out of the story of the Renaissance theatre: half-original plays, half-classic; emerging painted scenery and opulent trappings; reckless social life as background. John Addington Symonds writes:

Leo had an insatiable appetite for scenic shows. Comedies of the new Latinizing style were his favorite recreation. But he also invited the Sienese company of the Rozzi, who played only farces, every year to Rome; nor was he averse to even less artistic buffoonery, as may be gathered from many of the stories told about him. In 1513 Leo opened a theatre upon the Capital, and here in 1519, surrounded with two thousand spectators, he witnessed an exhibition of Ariosto's *Suppositi*.

Here we may let Edmund G. Gardner take up the account:

His Holiness himself stood at the door to superintend the admission of his guests, letting in with his benediction those whom he thought proper — about two thousand in all. On the curtain was painted the Pope's Dominican jester or buffoon, Fra Mariano, sporting with devils, with the inscription: "These are the Japeries of Fra Mariano." Then, to the music of the pipers, the curtain fell, and revealed a beautiful scene of a city in perspective, representing the Ferrara of the play, painted by Raphael himself, which the Pope peered at through his eye-glass and greatly admired. The stage was lit by candelabra supporting torches forming letters, each letter made by five torches, and spelling *Leo Decimus Pontifex Maximus*. At the obscene equivoques of the prologue, the Pope laughed heartily but the foreigners were scandalized. The comedy was played in the usual style of the epoch, with singing and music between the acts, and at the end there was a *moresca* representing the Fable of the Gorgon. . .

And again Symonds sums up the matter and carries the thought forward:

When Leo was made Pope he said to Giuliano, Duke of Nemours, "Let us enjoy the Papacy since God has given it to us." It was in this spirit that he administered the Holy See. The key-note which he struck dominated the whole society of Rome. Masques and balls, comedies and carnival processions, filled the streets and palaces of the Eternal City with a mimicry of pagan festivals, while Art went hand in hand with Luxury. . . Meanwhile, amid crowds of cardinals in hunting dress, dances of half-naked girls, and masques of Carnival Bacchantes moved pilgrims from the north with wide, astonished, woeful eyes — disciples of Luther, in whose soul, as in a scabbard, lay sheathed the sword of the Spirit, ready to flash forth and smite.

Nothing could better illustrate the perilous position of the theatre in human society: its transitions from the estate of sub-

206 THE THEATRE

lime art to the estate of plaything of the reckless and the vicious. When we meet those scandalized " disciples of Luther " again, they will be suppressing another licentious theatre — which has just given birth to the comedies and tragedies of Shakespeare. And here is the stage of the glorious Renaissance degraded to amuse the pope and cardinals of that Church which even at the moment refused Christian burial to professional actors — as sinners and libertines.

CHAPTER IX

A Pretty Interlude — Pastoral and Operatic

IN ONE minor department of drama the poets of the Italian Renaissance developed a new form and left play-texts of lasting value. Before their era, there had been pastoral poetry but never a memorable pastoral drama. As a by-product of — perhaps an attempted refuge from — the violent and ostentatious life of the times, there came into existence a considerable body of idylls and pastoral plays. A court dramatist could serve his prince never so well else as when he turned his fancy to a dream age, created heroes and heroines who walked amid Arcadian pleasures, and brought pictures of rustic simplicity and pastoral beauty before the un-simple and surfeited ballroom audiences. Perhaps this playwright's manuscript was little more than a framework for a series of pictures, dances, recited idylls; or perhaps as important as a serviceable masque text; but in the end it was somewhat important as a full-fledged example of literary drama.

There was a special rightness, of course, in the appearance of pastoral drama just when the stage for the first time could be set with groves or villa gardens or orchards; the form does seem to need the re-enforcement of pictures — unless it is to be presented in garden or woodland playhouse. The Italian hedge theatre, however, was a second by-product of the amorous-rustic literature, and quite as pretty a novelty among theatre "buildings" as pastoral drama was among play-texts.

Idyllic poetry had beguiled the Romans even when they were at the heyday of their so unidyllic conquering and blood-shedding. But the Greek-Sicilian Theocritus remains to this day the master of the form, having given the world such lovely lyrics and dialogues of the fabled sylvan hills and valleys of Sicily that no later poet ever quite touches our emotions with the same magic. In the Renaissance as in ancient Rome, we may read some alien spirit, an insincerity, a weak romanticism, into the interest in rustic things: there seems, indeed, here, as later at Louis XVI's Versailles court, an elaborate affectation. But we may be sure, too, that there is, between violent intrigues and artificial social functions, a genuine feeling for country life, a real longing for sweeter, simpler pleasures. The villas and vineyards of Italy bespeak it, Boccaccio breathed it (his amorous tales, lingering in memory, seem always to carry something of the fragrance of their garden setting), even Lorenzo the Magnificent is best remembered (as a poet) for his rural idylls and mythological sketches. Partly in imitation of Virgil and the other ancients, partly as an echo from the Italian countryside, pastoral literature and praise of pastoral life are here ushered in, to become a lasting pursuit in court circles through Italy, Spain, France, and England for two centuries or more. If Sannazzaro had not written his *Arcadia,* it is doubtful whether Sir Philip Sidney would have written his. And we know how Shakespeare browsed through the transplanted Italian tales of this time, taking as he willed for a palace-and-garden comedy to be called *Twelfth Night* or a courtly-rustic piece to be entitled *The Winter's Tale.*

It was inevitable that the Italian drama, newly emancipated, in the sixteenth century, from the old classic forms (though not from classic characters) should absorb this pastoral impulse. As a headline for the plays of all those dramatists who led up to Tasso, we may write: *Time,* the Golden Age; *Place,* myrtle groves and rustic farms, the hills and woods of mythological countries; *Characters,* Pan and his fauns and nymphs, Polyphemus, Echo, the Cyprian, and always the shepherds and the shepherdesses with their crooked sticks — figures embodying that simple ideal for which every heart in the audience yearned.

The stories are of love, the idyllic love of old-time places and times, before life became complicated or dull or feverish. Ah, there is a charming felicity in these legends! Then the Gods had made the world for lovers alone. The time of day is eternally twilight or the clear freshness that comes just after dawn. There are no rooms, no streets; only river banks and bathing pools and cool grottoes. Arcadia on the stage.

Torquato Tasso carried the form to its perfection in *Aminta*, enriching the pastoral idyll with exquisite poetry, genuine feeling, and not a little affecting (if artificially contrived) drama. Battista Guarini in his *Pastor Fido* added strength and body to the *metier*. These two breathe the very air of those mythological fields and that Golden Age which all the true pastoral poets so delicately sighed to recapture.

The *Aminta,* first played at Ferrara in 1573, partly presents and partly tells the charming story of the love of the shepherd, Aminta, for the beautiful virgin, Sylvia, once his playmate but now a follower of the huntress-goddess Diana and cold to the call of love. The play opens, characteristically, with a prologue spoken by *Love, Disguised as a Shepherd.* In two scenes, the situation is set out, Daphne vainly reproaching Sylvia for her insensibility to the pleasures of love, incidentally painting a pretty picture of her own finding of delight; and Aminta recounting to his friend Thyrsis the story of his passion for the unfeeling Sylvia.

AMINTA

> While yet a boy, scarce tall enough to gather
> The lowest hanging fruit, I became intimate
> With the most lovely and beloved girl,
> That ever gave to the wind her locks of gold. . .
> There grew by little and little in my heart,
> I know not from what root,
> But just as the grass grows that sows itself,
> An unknown something, which continually
> Made me feel anxious to be with her; and then
> I drank strange sweetness from her eyes, which left
> A taste, I know not how, of bitterness.
> Often I sighed, nor knew the reason why;
> And thus before I knew what loving was,
> Was I a lover. . .

After these expository and descriptive scenes, a chorus — survival of classic drama — appears and sings of the Golden Age: in this time a chorus of Shepherds, of course. An uncouth Satyr opens the second act with a monologue about love, and goes in search of Sylvia at her bathing-place. Daphne and Thyrsis conspire to bring Aminta and Sylvia together, and Thyrsis tricks the love-lorn shepherd into believing that Sylvia expects him at the pool. The next act opens with the recounting by Thyrsis of the scene at the bathing-place: he and Aminta had found Sylvia bound to a tree, by the Satyr. The monster had fled at their approach; but Sylvia, instead of rewarding her rescuers, had run away like a frightened fawn.

Aminta appears, fresh from an attempt at suicide which Daphne has frustrated; and now comes a nymph — typical "messenger" — bearing word of Sylvia's death during a wolf-hunt. Aminta immediately rushes out to throw himself over a cliff. Sylvia, however, reappears, telling of her narrow escape from the wolf. She is stirred to remorse by Daphne's account of Aminta's grief, and when a messenger brings news of the shepherd's leap from the cliff, she vows she will join him in death, and pauses on earth only long enough to give burial to his supposed cold and mangled corpse. The final act opens with a soliloquy upon the strange ways of Providence — and, indeed, quite miraculously has Aminta escaped injury in his fall. And less miraculously Sylvia and Daphne, searching for his body, came upon him:

ELPINO

. . . But when Sylvia recognized
Amyntas, and beheld his beautiful cheeks
So lovelily discolored, that no violet
Could pale more sweetly, it so smote on her,
That she seemed ready to breathe out her soul.
And then like a wild Bacchante, crying out
And smiting her fair bosom, she fell down
Right on the prostrate body, face to face,
And mouth to mouth.

CHORUS

Did then no shame restrain
Her who had been so hard and so denying?

ELPINO

It is a feeble love that shame restrains;
A powerful one breaks through so weak a bridle.
Her eyes appeared a fountain of sweet waters,
With which she bathed his cold cheeks, moaningly,

Waters so sweet, that he came back to life,
And opening his dim eyes, sent from his soul
A dolorous Ah me! . . .

And Elpino sets off in search of Sylvia's father, who, he tells us, has long wanted grandchildren.

Of course this drama skims perilously close to sentimentality, and only the richness and delicacy of Tasso's imagery and verse (quoted here in Leigh Hunt's translation) keep the story from cloying. Everything is maintained on a fanciful plane; there is no reality in these suicides and dangers, no real suspense, no fear that Aminta will not melt the ice that encases Sylvia's heart. But somehow — in our mellower moods — we are touched by the incidents; and we flow along in a sort of sensuous delight at the richness of the outward form of the play. There is not the magic of Theocritus here — Daphne tells us why:

The world, methinks grows old,
And growing old, grows sad. . .

The spirit of the Renaissance has added an artificial note to pastoral poetry. The poets are sighing for, rather than delighting in, a simple age. But here is an idyllic love sung with lyrical exuberance, a simple rustic legend decorated most delicately, most appealingly; with the glow of the Golden Days spread over an imagined world.

For the original audience there was the additional delight of symbolism and local allusion. For Tasso imbedded a long description of the ideal court, in compliment to his patron; and every character can be identified with some one of the nobles or ladies of Ferrara society.

Aminta had enormous influence outside of Italy in succeeding years. It was endlessly imitated; but so seldom equalled that it may rest here as the one example outlined to serve as sample of the pastoral form, the typical rustic play. There were over two hundred editions printed in Italian, twenty translations into French, nine into English, and scores of scattered ones in all the European languages and even in minor dialects.

The Pastor Fido or *Faithful Shepherd* alone enjoyed the same fame. It is a more ambitious work, three times as long as the over-brief *Aminta,* substituting a complicated plot for the simple fable of Sylvia. The speeches are similarly long, and most of the action occurs offstage, to be recounted charmingly by lovers, messengers, and chorus. The same sincere love of pastoral life floods the speeches, however:

AMARILLIS

Dear, happy groves!
And thou all silent, solitary gloom,
True residence of peace and of repose!
How willingly, how willingly my steps
To you return; and oh! if but my stars
Benignly had decreed
My Life for Solitude . . .
No, not th' Elysian Fields,
Those happy gardens of the Demi-Gods,
Would I exchange for your enchanting shades! . . .
The rural maid how blest,
Who though but scantly drest,
In homely gown, and plain,
Unsullied with a stain;
Rich in herself alone . . .

And as final words from the pastoral drama, we may note the closing lines spoken by Amarillis, in which she touches upon the reason for the combined eternal charm and ephemeral prettiness that grace these compositions. After all, they were composed for noble ladies and gallants who were seeking no more than an afternoon's beguilement from the realities of life.

. . . And if thou'rt inclined
To share our bliss, come freely and partake
Of this our sweet Festivity!

Yes, it was the bliss of festivity that somehow shaped the pastoral drama. It is a drama of refuge, not of living. And in that connection it may be illuminating to add that these two poets who dramatized so sweetly the legends of "the golden haze out yonder," were both disillusioned and embittered courtiers: Tasso so nonsensically the idealist that he plunged over the verge into actual and imprisoned madness; Guarini withdrawing into a pedant seclusion. Plays echoing theirs will parallel all the types of drama that we explore down to the coming of the democratic

The garden theatre at Villa Gori.

The garden theatre at Mirabell Castle, Salzburg.

spirit; but not in Spain nor in France shall we find the same sensuous exuberance. In England the spirit entered rather into lyrical poetry, into Spenser who breathed it richly and sweetly, and into that Marlowe who could sum up the impulse in

> Come live with me and be my love,
> And we will all the pleasures prove
> That hills and vallies, dales and fields,
> Woods or steepy mountain yields —

and into a Shakespeare who cast the pretty glow of it over works stronger, fresher, and more diverting than any that ever came out of Italy — but not so simple.

In adding here pictures of the Italian garden theatres, seeming so perfectly fitted for the presentation of the pastoral plays, I must note that these are later in date (so far as we know); that the pastoral drama was staged in the then new and much-appreciated pageant-settings. It is recorded that Tasso, in his mad way, journeyed all the way to Florence to thank the great Buontalenti for his part in setting *Aminta* properly, and gave point to his homage by omitting to pay respects to the Grand Duke. But if the architects and painters were having their way just then on the stages of Italy, at some time later the open-air playhouses came into vogue; and villa theatres in Italian style, with wings and back-drop of gratefully green and neutral hedge, were copied in many a northern palace garden. One is pictured here from the Schloss Mirabell gardens in Salzburg, and you may see the theatre itself there today if you wish. Nor has the vogue entirely passed: in this twentieth century you will find as many garden theatres in California as in all of Italy — and, I dare say, more used.

In the house, or the palace, of Giovanni Bardi, Conte di Vernio, in Florence, in the last years of the sixteenth century, a group of *dilettanti* poets and musicians were accustomed to meet, to talk about the arts, to recite and play for one another. These amateurs were stirred by the same passion for art and learning that had impelled their more professional brethren to form academies, to study the achievements of the ancients, and to formulate rules as to what constituted " classic " practice in drama-writing, in music, in versification, etc. Happily the members of the Count Bardi's

Ground plans of four Italian garden theatres, showing various types, and indicating the toy-like nature of the smaller examples. The stage wings were usually of clipped cypress or ilex hedge, and the stage floor of turf.
[From Cheney's *The Open-air Theatre*.]

" circle " were not too bound by the rules of the pedant-academicians — or by exact knowledge of their subject — to venture upon impossibly new and unorthodox experiments. Among them were Vincenzo Galilei, father of the famous Galileo, and two younger musicians named Jacopo Peri and Giulio Caccini.

One day the talk ran upon the method of verse-declamation in the old Greek theatres. It was known that the delivery of the lines had been declamatory if not strictly musical, and that music had accompanied the chanting of the choruses. Why not restore this method in the Florentine ballroom theatres? But the music of the Greeks had wholly disappeared; nor was there any treatise to tell what it had been. And so the amateurs set out to recreate the Greek drama-with-music. They had a definite object in view, and they were beautifully unhampered by any facts.

What they arrived at was something which none of them had foreseen. (The professional musicians pointed out that they were proceeding blindly, ignorantly.) They came to a new — if hybrid — art form, *Opera*. They failed to recreate, or even to throw any light upon, the Greek method of delivery. But they founded a sort of music-drama that has been much with the world ever since; that has, indeed, pre-empted its biggest and showiest theatres for three hundred years. For while no one admits that opera can ever be a " pure " art-form, and though none of us has ever seen — or heard — a perfect opera, the operatic stage holds its important place in all sophisticated communities, through criticism, calumny, and repeated proofs of its unimportance. The word " opera," by the way, means nothing: merely " work," shortened probably from " work in music." We may adopt such definitions as " a musical form of stage play," or " a drama set to music." The point is that music is no longer merely incidental; it is intended to be of the structure of the piece.

It is possible, of course, to go back and discover some forerunners of opera: [1] particularly in church music as adapted to the

[1] See *Some Forerunners of Italian Opera*, by W. J. Henderson (New York, 1911). For the history of opera perhaps the best short account is in *Grove's Dictionary of Music and Musicians* (London, 1927). For a longer account see *The Opera*, by R. A. Streatfield (London and New York, 5th enlarged edition, 1925); or as guide to existing opera rather than as history, Gustav Kobbé's *The Complete Opera Book* (New York, 1922). For a study of pastoral, see *Pastoral Poetry and Pastoral Drama*, by Walter W. Greg (London, 1906).

Mystery and Miracle Plays, in the court productions of masque and pastoral, wherein music played a generous part (the *Orfeo* of Poliziano should perhaps be specially noted), and in the sung madrigals. But the production that is usually chronicled as "the first opera" is that of Peri's *Dafne,* with Rinuccini's libretto, performed at the Palazzo Corsi in 1597. This rather elementary piece aroused such intense interest that Peri and Caccini's *Euridice,* composed for the festivities in honor of the wedding of Maria de' Medici to Henry IV of France, in 1600, was awaited with excited anticipation by the intellectuals, amateur and professional alike, and by musicians far outside the confines of Florence. This was, incidentally, the first opera produced for "the public" — though one must note that this is not yet the playhouse whither one goes with money to buy a ticket of admission. It was a court-arranged production. *Euridice* became at once the model for imitation and the starting-point for experiment on the part of numberless composers. Opera was an accepted and established form.

In 1607, at the Court of Mantua, the Duke's *maestro di cappella,* Claudio Monteverdi, wrote the music for two libretti by Rinuccini, a *Dafne* and an *Arianna.* These were presented at the celebration in honor of the marriage of a Gonzaga Prince to Margherita, Infanta of Savoy. (I am repeating the point about court-festivity background, so that the reader may recall the richness of the physical investiture of palace productions — we are to see not only the ballet trimmings but the interludes as a whole swallowed by opera.) Monteverdi enlarged the scope of music as an aid to the dramatic story, added boldly to the orchestra, and wrote with so much of originality and imagination that he is credited with being the first of the real masters of the opera. His success with *Arianna* led to an immediate commission to compose another work, and in the following year *Orfeo* was performed. In this the composer dared to use an orchestra of nearly forty pieces. He also introduced bits of melody.

True to its beginnings in supposed imitation of Greek drama, opera had not yet branched out into that sort of melodic display that seems today so essentially the operatic thing; *recitative* was considered the key to the difficult union of drama and music. But

Two paintings of typical Venetian eighteenth century theatres, by Gabriele Bella. The one above showing a stage setting, the one below a theatre decorated for a festival.

Grand architectural settings by the Bibbienas. Above, a drawing by Giovanni Maria Galli-Bibbiena, for an exterior setting. Below, an interior by Giuseppe Galli-Bibbiena, as realized for a dramatic festival at the Court of Bavaria, 1740. [The drawing reproduced from a Brogi photo of the original in the Uffizi Gallery, Florence; the other from an original print.]

once the melodic element was given a bit of play, opera drew farther and farther away from drama presented musically, and closer
and closer to a musical exercise with a dramatic legend as its
excuse. Of course the whole history of the art in the centuries
since has been punctuated by controversies and explosions over
this distinction — as is to be expected where a form straddles two
distinct arts — and so recently as the late nineteenth century there
was an epochal swing back toward " music-drama " as against the
over-florid ornamental thing. But the history from Monteverdi,
through Cavalli, Cesti, and Scarlatti, and on to the later Italian and
French schools of composers, was a record of growing melody,
of increasingly interpolated aria, of lessened dramatic directness.
It is interesting that the Florentine inventors of opera, who had
defied the professional musicians in order to experiment in a
musical-dramatic form, were scandalized at Cavalli's innovations
in rhythmic melody; they had now become the conservatives, and
they were worried that their child, though born of the wayward
impulse, should wander out into fields so dangerously uncharted!

But when Cavalli was through it was certain that opera would
never go back to the monotony of unrelieved recitative. It was,
however, Scarlatti who determined the way for the development
of Italian opera — which even to this day emphasizes vocal melody
more than does French or German. That in Italy the music
became over-ornamental almost immediately, that there was
toadying to the singers who were more interested in display-pieces
than in furthering the dramatic expression, there can be no doubt.
Within forty years the newcomer in the theatre field had grown
from timid experimental performance to " grand-opera."

The first public opera-theatre was opened in Venice in 1637: the
Teatro di San Cassiano. It was so much a success that rival houses
sprang up almost at once; and before the end of the century there
were eleven theatres in Venice alone. No other Italian city had
so many, though this was the period when the serious drama and
the opera became professionalized, and were disentangled somewhat from the social life of the courts. In time, Venice, Naples,
and Bologna became the noted centres of opera production. In
France and England the influence of Italian opera was to be
immense, not only in the direct instigation to musical-dramatic

composition, but in its effect upon methods of staging and upon the form of the playhouse. The " Italian style " theatre that dominates throughout Europe till the late nineteenth century is really an opera house and not a theatre designed for " legitimate " production.

From the titles of the operas so far mentioned, *Dafne, Euridice, Arianna, Orfeo,* it is clear that the new art was carrying on the tradition of the pastoral drama. The *Teatro di San Cassiano* was opened with the Ferrari-Manelli *Andromeda;* and it was a long time before the librettists escaped out of the classic-story limitation. But Scarlatti (1659-1725) fixed a form for opera as distinguished from ordinary play-writing. He brought in *design*. This characteristic design was broad enough, however, to take in much that in the sixteenth century had belonged to masque and interlude. The settings, the ballets, the wondrous machine-effects, were soon claiming place between the impassioned arias of the opera singers. Perhaps the mythological libretti were doubly useful because they brought all sorts of opportunity for showy landscape and palatial scenery, and for magical transformations, disappearances, etc.

At any rate, the emergence of opera is accompanied by a continuation of that effort toward ever-more-elaborate scenery that we noted in the last chapter. On the curtained stages the settings could be changed several times in the course of a performance. The perspective setting, grown now from that little symmetrical street scene of Serlio to grand portrayals of the local " square " or many-arched ideal-interiors, was glorified by the Bibbienas into the vast halls and the expansive street vistas that you see here. Magnificent, yes! but he who is interested in drama and acting may well ask, " what has become of the actor now? " Just see if you can find him in these gorgeous palace scenes.

And stage machinery was so developed that no cloud-riding scene, no celestial apparition, no magic appearance or disappearance, no moving sun or moon, was too difficult to attempt. As early as 1486 the Mantuans had seen a court production of the *Menæchmi* of Plautus, out-of-doors, in which a boat with sails and oars, with ten persons aboard, moved across the stage. After that the ballroom stages saw many and marvellous machine-made effects, during plays, masques, and ballets. But the producers of opera made these things a regular adjunct to performance, and they outdid their predecessors in boldness and elaboration. The opera-house stage grew in dimensions and in complexity, not because music or drama or the two in combination needed so much room, but because the public wanted to gape at new miracles of piled-up scenery and of tricked magic effects.

It was these effects as much as the novelty of the musical-dramatic form that led French kings and cardinals to clamor for opera before the seventeenth century was half gone. We shall see how, after isolated importations, the French Court invites an ambitious young Italian page, Lulli by name, to direct a tentatively established official French opera house. With his elevation into authority — with, so to speak, Italian opera under his arm — a new era in staging and theatre-building is in prospect for non-Italian Europe. After some periods of high creation in Spain, England, and France, before the influence has been greatly felt, there will follow a long period during which an operatic incubus is on the theatre.

CHAPTER X

The Vulgar Popular Comedy

THERE is a figure that stands for many playgoers today as a symbol of the theatre in its softer, more romantic aspect. Pierrot, in many guises, but always delicate, gently smiling, or charmingly melancholy, is the very antithesis of that crude, violent, and prying figure that can be visioned as the symbol of the realistic stage. Pierrot the moonstruck, Pierrot the pretty, Pierrot the eternal misunderstood lover, Pierrot with a rose in his hand and a fluffy ruff at his throat — this figure represents the other half of the theatre, variously thought of as the poetic, or the soulful, the glamorous or the beautiful half.

Now to me there is something very disturbing about the identifying of the non-realistic, the " ideal " theatre, with any such milky symbol-figure. My readers already know that I put small store by the other, larger, more immediate half, the realistic theatre; but to let Pierrot represent the rest is a typical nineteenth century missing of the essence of the art — typical of dividing the theatre into a half that portrays life " truthfully " and a half that affords *escape*. There is something vaguely unhealthy about this powdered Pierrot, too gentle in an aboundingly vital world, too sentimental, too perpetually sad, too dependent upon sympathy.

The ancestors of Pierrot, curiously enough, are among the most vigorous, the most gorgeously adventurous, the most theatrical — and at times the most robustly wicked — figures in the whole pageant of the stage. Only on the theory of a very devil of a father and a beautiful adventuress of a mother begetting, by contrast, a timid and soulful offspring, can the ancestry of the modern Pierrot be explained. For those who begat him were the actors of the *Commedia dell' Arte,* playing the brilliant, vigorous, audacious, and gay buffoon-comedies that delighted the reckless Latin peoples of the Cinquecento and the Seicento.

If you had wandered into Venice on a *festa* day in, say, 1550 — the name Venezia even today will give you something of the feel of the holiday atmosphere, the sensuous color, the liveliness of the place — you might have seen some of these actors of the *Commedia dell' Arte* playing on a platform in the Square of St Mark's. The crowd about would be, as we say, picturesque; the *magnificoes,* nobly dressed, swelling around; the shrewd tradespeople and shopkeepers and country folk like enough in festival costume — or perhaps just the dress of the country was like that; gondoliers; masqueraders; the beggars and cripples that have crawled out of the incredible poverty and dirt of Venice's " back streets "; all these are mixed in the crowds that surge through the square. Everywhere are vendors, fakers, sellers of sweets, crying their wares and their shows: medicine sellers with patter men, no doubt, jugglers, clowns, acrobats, singers, tightrope walkers, dancers. And above it all the pealing bells, and the color of St Mark's. Here are a dozen theatres, a dozen noisy performances. But one is the favorite, the embodiment of the festival spirit, the very centre of hilarity in all this field of laughter and noise. For the *Commedia dell' Arte* players are up to their old tricks, improvising a farce with all their mingled vigor, art, and vulgarity. And if you watch the audience, you will see just those qualities reflected, rudely or more delicately, in each face. In a booth, at a fair, the players are perfectly at home.

Let us not try to distinguish the comedians too exactly from those conjurers, clowns, and quack " come-on " men close by; they have not, in this mid-sixteenth century, brought their art to a set form; they are still shaping the *Commedia dell' Arte* — partly by watching shrewdly how the holiday throng shrieks at this new gag or merely titters at that old spitting episode. Out of the very tricks of the swindlers and fakers, as out of an intrigue here stolen from Terence and a page of comic dialogue there out of Plautus, they are manufacturing the " Professional Comedy." As yet only the *characters* are set, vigorous sketches of the stock figures that are to win courts and market-places alike to their praise a century later: Pantalone, from this same Venice; the

Doctor from Bologna; the boastful, lying, and timorous-at-heart
Spanish Captain — once Italian, out of ancient Rome, but then
changed to Spanish because the Spaniards were the swaggerers of
Europe, the detested, overbearing overlords of Naples; the mer-
curial Arlecchino and the knavish Brighella; the maid-servants,
and the rest.

The *Commedia dell'Arte* is a thing that must be considered as
theatre or not at all. It simply does not exist, and never did, as
written drama or as spectacle; it is a platform, actors, action. Its
story [1] used to be left out of the histories — until very recently there
wasn't even a fairly full account of it in the English language,
because it obviously couldn't qualify as dramatic literature. What
else about it, the scholars asked, could be permanently important.
Well, for one thing, the glorious spirit of it; and for another, the
triumph of the actor as sheer creator.

Its name as commonly translated — the Professional Comedy,
or the Comedy of Improvisation — affords a clue to this essential
theatric quality. It is the professional's theatre, the work of the
members of a craft; not only must the player be a professional in
today's sense, but he must be so experienced as actor-producer
that he can improvise his part with nothing more than an outline
of the scenes in mind. There literally was no text of the play
for the actors of the Professional Comedy: merely a scenario
tacked up back-stage. The player must supply the rest out of his
own inventiveness, wit, and bag of tricks.

The actor today is given words to speak. He expends his talent in " interpretation " of the part. He is half reciter and half
creative artist. The comedian of Sixteenth Century Italy made
up his part as he went along. He stepped into the scene knowing

---

[1] The best brief statements are John Addington Symonds' prefatory chapter in his
translation of *The Memoirs of Count Carlo Gozzi* (London, 1890), and articles in the
issues of *The Mask* for January and April, 1911 (edited by Gordon Craig). *The History of Harlequin*, by Cyril W. Beaumont (London, 1926) is a thoroughgoing treatment
of the subject insofar as it can be tied around the Harlequin character. The student
will find Winifred Smith's *The Commedia dell'Arte* (New York, 1912) useful. Though
elsewhere I have limited my bibliographical notes to works in English I can't refrain
from adding two excellent illustrated books in French covering the subject of this
chapter: *La Commedia dell'Arte* by Constant Mic (Paris, 1927), and *La Comédie
Italienne*, by Pierre Louis Duchartre (Paris, 1924). I have consulted all these works;
but I am most indebted to the spirited if scrappy treatment in the noted issues of *The
Mask*. (The important Duchartre volume is just now announced for publication in an
English translation in New York and London.)

Two paintings of festas in Venice, by Gabrielle Bella. Above, an open platform stage. Below, a temporary theatre before the Doges' Palace.

Two wayside stages of travelling *Commedia* troupes. Above, a drawing by
Hendrick Verschuring (1627–1690). Below, a painting by Nicolas-Antoine
Taunay.

the end and aim of the action, but not what his fellow actors were going to say; he and his fellows improvised that, partly no doubt from traditional snatches of dialogue, from his own speeches grown effective from long trial, from gags and bits of standard buffoonery, covered by stereotyped "business"; but never in two performances exactly alike, and therefore in a continually changing ensemble, where wits clashed, openings must be jumped at, eccentricities and topical ideas capitalized. Facial display counted for nothing; the actor wore a mask. The mask and costume represented a traditional figure to the crowd. The player must get his fun within the character, building it out, caricaturing it, making it witty in its repartee and an object of mirth in its runnings-away, fallings-down, its mistakes, its blindness, its perverse misunderstandings, its impertinences.

(Is it any wonder that a sort of production that called for so much invention, theatrical deftness, and spirit has seemed to certain revolutionaries of the early twentieth century the very sum and summit of theatrical art? Brooding on the realistic acting of the time, particularly on the growing tendency toward *personal* acting — the player always acting a variation of himself — those insurgent leaders, delightedly digging up forgotten facts about the *Commedia dell'Arte*, held it up as a sort of rediscovered touchstone of the art. Some such development must arise out of the ashes of the literary-realistic theatre — for only thus could the actor be brought out of slavery to the playwright. There is, however — we may opine — no chance that anything like the Professional Comedy will rise out of the present theatre, or from its ashes if they could be accomplished. The *Commedia dell'Arte,* growing through centuries, before it came to flower, was an answer to a call of the times, is most interesting when studied in relation to the abounding, violent life of those times.)

If Pierrot had ancestors among the characters of the *Commedia dell'Arte,* the latter in turn could trace their lineage to Roman, even Greek forebears. Some elements were everywhere local, the characters changed continually under the impact of public approval and disapproval, creative actors built out shadowy types to well-delineated figures. But it is possible to identify several Roman prototypes; and no one has been able wholly to disentan-

gle the elements of Roman vulgar entertainment from survivals
of the Greek satyr-drama or Greek-colonial developments.

The Capitano had a clear likeness to the *Miles Gloriosus* of the
Roman literary drama. But it is to the popular *attelanæ* that the
Commedia dell'Arte is easiest traced, or likened: those short
native plays on local topics, wherein the characters were stock
figures, played with masks. The " mimes " too, entertainments
that included farcical scenes and spectacular elements along with
song and dance, utilized characters of strongly marked types, the
scheming servants, the swaggerers, and other old favorites that
are now reappearing.

Commedia dell'Arte players on a stage with curtains, as etched
by Jacques Callot. [From *La Comédie Italienne,* by Pierre
Louis Duchartre.]

No one knows to what extent the fugitive strolling player had
persisted or disappeared through the dark ages. We do know
that if his companies were broken up, there were at least clowns,
dancers, conjurers, pantomimists who bridged the great gap. Perhaps the mimes who had gone from Rome to Byzantium, capital
of the Eastern Empire, persisted in Turkish theatrical entertainment, and now were coming back to their native Italy. At any
rate, when we pick up the story again, during the earliest years
of the Renaissance, the companies are acting at crossroads, in
piazzas, at the fairs. They are roaming about, setting up their
roadside stages wherever a large enough audience can be mus-

tered. The public is their god, their only mentor, their means of living.

The Church, of course, is against them. When the religious drama, fostered in cathedrals and chapels, had become too secular, too concerned with having a good time, and too little zealous to extend the faith, it had been pushed out-of-doors, and soon the blessing and sanction of the Church fathers were withdrawn entirely. By the time the *Commedia dell'Arte* is taking definite shape we may think of the village priest and the district bishop as distinctly hostile. (Later, to be sure, cardinals are openly amused at the performances of *I Gelosi* — though there is more on the opposite side of the ledger, petitions for suppression, forbiddance of Christian burial to actors, downright persecution.)

No more sympathetic are the courts and the academies — at first. The great princes and dukes are still the patrons of the literary drama, giving encouragement and means to the scholars who vainly imitate the classic dramatists. Along with the sterile neo-classic plays the courts are fostering the masque, a pretty, queenly form of drama that is to revolutionize " staging " throughout the Western world. It is the exact opposite to the *Commedia dell'Arte* in its lavishness, in its other-worldliness, in its gentility. The staging of the street comedy is bare: a platform with curtains, hardly more than a booth, perhaps, or again a convenient roadside embankment; its lavishness is all in the acting. It is of this world, earthy; the populace love it and its only thought of gentility is to show up high pretension and gentle villainy for the enjoyment of the crowd. It has just those virtues that the cultured literary theatre of the time lacks: robustness, genuineness, theatrical zest, originality.

Somewhere during the formative years, before the courts had tired of the literary playwrights, before they invited the *Commedia dell'Arte* companies to come off the streets and into the palace theatres, certain conventions took shape. The comedy setting, developing perhaps from the tradition of the Roman comedy that so often was set " before so-and-so's house," became typically the " street scene." If the booth or platform stage was backed with curtains, these (we know in certain cases) bore a rude painted representation of houses with a space between. Garzoni speaks of " the scenes scrawled with charcoal." Later, when the wing setting came in, on the indoor stages, houses were represented by the front flats, with others indicated farther back, in an arrangement that left the actors unhampered in the central space and down front, while affording them the widest use of doorways for hidings and escapes, windows for serenades, etc. But this vignette of an outdoor stage, where all " scenery " is painted or

Razullo.   Cucurucu.

Two comedy characters, with a typical *Commedia* theatre in the background, as etched by Jacques Callot. [From the reproduction in Mantzius' *A History of Theatrical Art.*]

drawn on a curtain behind the acting space, is typical of the street-theatre days. In later years each character had his own point of entrance, and there was an orthodox method of coming to the front of the stage, bowing welcome to the audience, for the " Parade " or inspection of the actors, etc.

But if the setting became " set " in the years of gradual establishment of the Improvised Comedy as an institution, it was the characters who were crystallizing most definitely and most interestingly. Next to the fact of improvization, the most distinctive

feature of the *Commedia dell'Arte* is the limitation to a dozen
or so traditional type theatric figures, each played with a mask
and a costume different from the others, each with conventional
characteristics and limitations.   Even the character's carriage,
gestures, and grimaces became known; and a further identification was possible in the dialect he spoke — since the Dottore came
from Bologna, Pantalone from Venice, and so on.

An actor assuming a part, incidentally, devoted his life to it,
and ordinarily played no other character during his career.   One
well-known actor is said to have played the Lover at seventy.   This
concentration on one impersonation, of course, had much to do
with the player's adeptness at improvisation.

So closely were the actors identified with their parts that often
their personal life was all but lost in the theatrical character.
Occasionally an actor was strong enough to bring a new character into the restricted popular pantheon; developing a new line
of business, or adding variations in an accepted characteristic, he
made two figures grow where only one had been accepted before;
or, very rarely, created a niche and a name almost wholly out of
his own genius — as was the case with Scaramuccia.   Exceptionally a player might give his own name to an older part: as
"Flavio" was the name of the Lover for a time, from Flaminio
Scala.   Isabella Andreini played an "Isabella" part throughout
her lifetime, after which the character disappeared.   But mostly
it was a long process of experiment, experience, and adjustment
by which a figure came into being, by public impact; and the types
are as common, as easy to comprehend, as the Katzenjammer
Kids or Mutt and Jeff.

In what period the main characters became wholly identifiable
— became themselves, so to speak — it is difficult to say.   There
is a very reasonable air to the argument that the two *zannis* were
re-creations of the Roman *sanniones* — certainly their positions
as servants and their cunning-stupid ways warrant the inference.
The lineage of others is less easily traced or guessed.   But in the
time we are now considering, before the acceptance of the popular
comedy into court circles, there were already a number of set
types; and certainly those four central characters, the Dottore,
or Doctor of Bologna; Pantalone, the wheezy merchant, from

Venice — these two being old men; and the two servants, or *zannis* (our Zany), Arlecchino and Brighella, knaves of opposite temper; and the Capitano. These " masks " appear in many variations later, and under varied names.

Pantalone is the deceived father or husband, the easily-duped old man, of Roman popular comedy — by inheritance or by grace of the undying comic potentialities of senility and cupidity.

Arlecchino, as played by the actor Martinelli in the sixteenth Century. [From *La Comédie Italienne*.]

Often enough he is the cuckold, the old husband of a merry young wife, hoodwinked and deceived — and as such, perhaps the favorite comic character for Italian audiences. In this Renaissance Italy he is also the Venetian merchant, grasping, overreaching; and at the same time credulous and talkative. He is amorous in an ineffective way, outwitted in his love suits by his son, his servant, or any other. He is the typical old-fool. He wears, of course, the long trousers that bear his name to this day.

The Dottore is the boon companion of Pantalone, the second old man. He is the comic man-of-learning, the pedant, hailing from Bologna, the university town. Many of his comic effects arise from his readiness to spout Latin and his cleverness at presenting facts wrongly. He may be any learned type, physician, lawyer, astrologer, professor; but he is as much a butt as Pantalone in his love affairs and his tricks to save a ducat. If he is a father to one of the girl lovers he is easily outwitted.

The servants or *zannis* are commonly known as Arlecchino and Brighella. Through the course of three centuries Harlequin changed much in character. But in the great days of the Improvised Comedy he was the scheming and cunning valet, the shrewd-but-dull servant to one of the foolish old men, ever aiding the young lovers in their designs and ever cheating Pantalone and the Dottore. (For instance, he tells Pantalone that a noble lady is in love with him, and that a rendezvous can be arranged, but that to spare the lady's reputation Pantalone must dress as a woman. He then goes to the Dottore with the same story. He thus brings the two disguised old men together, each believing the other an amorous but coy lady — in a situation which, as any one can see, lends itself to hearty if not too delicate humor.) Arlecchino is at other times definitely the blundering or foolish servant. He seems always to have been acrobatically alive, bounding on and off stage, appearing at unexpected moments, escaping through impossible openings. His checkered suit was assumed at a rather late date, perhaps along with some of his less buffoon-like traits. In the seventeenth century Dominique lifted the character to the estate of a witty and wise commentator, at the Italian theatre in Paris.

Brighella is the second valet. He is more definitely a caricature, often a cruel one: the dishonest servant, unscrupulous and sensual. He descends to the estate of panderer or thief on occasion. Scapino is either another guise for him, or perhaps his cousin. We might say that these servants are all members of the Rascal family; and we then can add another name to the list: Pulchinella. This is the ancestor of the famous Punch of the puppet shows. Even in those days he was hook-nosed, old, and energetic. His pugnaciousness was a later accretion. He hailed from Naples.

The Capitano was the Renaissance embodiment of the swaggering officer, the soldier who puts up a bold front but is quaking inside. He tells tales of astounding deeds of valor, but dodges if another but sneezes. He blusters, threatens, parades, but runs away if a servant but puts a hand on a wooden sword. He wears fierce moustaches and carries a wicked-looking sword, and he may create terror for a moment; but always at the end he is in flight, his cowardice revealed, his pretensions pricked. Or else Harlequin thrashes him. He appeared first as an Italian officer, but the type was early changed to picture the Spanish overlords. Like most of the *Commedia* characters, the Captain appeared in a dozen variations.

The other types, as they are less caricatured, are less interesting in memory. It is necessary only to record that the elegant young lovers were indispensable to the usual plot, that the valets were regularly matched by the tricky maid-servants (Colombina was the most famous, and lived on in another guise), and that *ballerinas* carried on the dancing.

The scenario which was provided by the head of the company — he was probably the " author " too — for the actors' guidance in the larger outlines of the performance, included not a line of dialogue: only directions for the movements, and lists of the " situations." As the body of scenarios grew, certain " irresistible situations " appeared again and again and again. Naturally the intrigue was a staple basis; and there were certain clustered jokes, bits of buffoonery and gags around each incident. One account says that the actors, moreover, filled in with *lazzi* the empty spots in the scenario, *lazzi* in this sense meaning not only the jests but the tricks, turns and bits of business that the player had learned were " sure-fire " with the average audience. Out of his own repertory, so to speak, the actor provided entertainment that carried over from one planned dramatic peak to the next. He had his own line of conceits and tried speeches that were " in character "; the scenarist thus might call for his " lover's outburst " or his " soliloquy with metaphors " or his tirade in Latin.

In the latter decades of the Improvised Comedy in France, the literary element was somewhat intruded, and the skeletons are largely filled out with lines. There are, however, several extant collections of the unadorned scenario. One is the "Theatre for Fifty Days" collection, with fifty works of Flaminio Scala (Flavio), these being part of the repertory of the famous company known as *I Gelosi;* another is the Corsini Library Manuscript in Rome, which is adorned with interesting sketches of stage settings.

A version of the Capitano, as depicted by Abraham Bosse.

The scope of the drama played by the popular comedians — although most commentators describe it all as farce or buffoon-comedy — is put down by the players themselves, in petitions, etc., as very broad; for instance, an actor of *I Gelosi,* about the end of the sixteenth century, spoke of his company as " setting an example for future actors as to how to compose and interpret comedies, tragicomedies, tragedies, pastorals, interludes. . ." The plot outlines were stolen freely from old plays, from novels, from any source whatsoever; or invented on the basis of remembered incidents, fables, or the latest scandal. The knowledge that so-and-so was in the audience might change the whole drift of scene after scene and afford material for allusion and mimicry. An actor's indigestion and grumpiness might be capitalized, if not by himself, then by his fellow actors. In days when the chamberpot was a common "prop" on the farce stage, illness as a subject must have yielded more comic values than in our squeamish times.

The latitude allowed on the stage, of course, was simply a reflection of the latitude allowed in life; and the energy of the actors part of the energy of the Italian peoples. We have seen how the prince-patrons lived, how even the cardinals and bishops accepted life fully as it came, falling in with the lax morality of the time; how court poets made a stupendous joke of infidelity, playing up the lascivious priest along with the noble rotter, the easy-going wife along with the unscrupulous serving-maid — anything so long as the incidents moved swiftly, so long as the interest never lagged. The same humor was used in the street comedy; and the audiences were, at their own level, as zestfully interested as the nobles, in a hundred activities that had been unknown or forbidden to their fathers. "They found the door of a theatre as irresistible as a café," one writer tells us — and unless you have lived in a Latin country you can't imagine how wholly irresistible that is, to entire populaces.

Of the spirit, the materials, and the speed that went into the productions of the *Commedia dell'Arte,* Philippe Monnier has written, in a passage that seems to have caught in its own accents the breathlessness and swing of the stage performance.[2] He is speaking of the players:

They were all as chock-full of malice as of wit. Mimes, acrobats, dancers, musicians, comedians, all at once, they were also poets, and composed their own piece. They strained their fancy to the utmost in inventing it, and improvised it on the spot as their turn came and the inspiration took them. They were not willing, like silly school-boys, to recite only what they had learnt from a master, nor to be mere echoes, unable to speak for themselves without another having spoken before them. They did not draw themselves up in a line before the footlights, five or six in a row, like figures in a bas-relief, and wait their turn to present their tricks. Rather they were

[2] Quoted by permission from *The Mask* of January 1911.

full of impatience, imagination, devilry. They were the great artists of Laughter, the sowers of the golden grain of Gaiety, the servants of the Unseen, the kings of Inspiration. They had only to receive a scenario, which someone had scribbled on his knee, to meet their stage manager in the morning to arrange the outlines of the plot, and to hang the paper within easy reach of the wings; the rest they could invent themselves. Familiarity with the stage and their profession and their art had taught them a whole bundle of tricks and quips. They had a store of proverbs, sallies, charades, riddles, recitations, cock-and-bull stories, and songs jumbled together in their heads. They knew all sorts of metaphors, similes, repetitions, antitheses, cacophonies, hyperboles, tropes, and pleasant figures; and besides they had volumes of tirades, which they had learnt by heart, of soliloquies, exclamations of despair, sallies, conceits of happy love, or jealousy, or prayer, or contempt, or friendship, or admiration, always on the tips of their tongues, ready to utter when they were out of breath. They raised their scaffolding high into the air, and then gave themselves up to their own fertile genius and their amazing caprice. They obeyed all the intemperance and extravagance of their humours. They became nothing but retorts, sallies, conceits, paradoxes, witticisms, mental somersaults. They seized opportunity by the forelock and turned the least accident to profit. They drew inspiration from the time, the place, the color of the sky, or the topic of the day, and established a current between their audience and themselves out of which the mad farce arose, the joint product of them all. It varied at each representation, seemed different every evening, with all the spirit and warmth and alertness of spontaneous creation, a brilliant ephemeral creature born of the moment and for the moment.

The pieces went with the speed of lightning and the noise of Pandemonium. The house was consumed with shrieks of laughter, like the tumult of a whirlwind. It was all lover's intrigue, complicated by disguises, kidnappings, unexpected returns, impersonations and supposititious infants. Retorts, misunderstandings, character-sketches, jests, caricatures, blows, and kicks were their stock in trade. They groped about in the dark and ran into one another and fell down. They mutilated words. They put out their tongues, rolled their eyes, made grimaces. They boxed their ears with their feet. They sang songs and recited, and poured forth proverbs, quotations, precedents. There were scenes of tumult and uproar and inexpressible confusion, in which they were knocked down and got up again, supporting themselves as they could, tripped each other up, got in each other's way, and ran off in the midst of the clatter.

They passed the word round, for instance, to make Pantaloon believe that his breath smelt. Pantaloon blows his horn from the window to proclaim the opening of the chase. Gratiano appears holding a cock, Burattino with a monkey on a chain, and a child on the back of a bear is leading a lion. Harlequin, armed with a blacksmith's tools, draws four of Pantaloon's soundest teeth. He waits on Don Juan at table and wipes the plates on the seat of his breeches before he hands them, or produces his cap, full of cherries, from the same place, and cracks the stones with his teeth and pretends to spit them on the ground. He keeps hissing some tune through his lips or pursues a fly in the air and catches it. He counts his coat-buttons, saying, " She loves me, she loves me not, she loves me." There is only one plate of macaroni between three of them, and they eat it in floods of tears. . . Dreams were grafted on mistakes, marvels on absurdities. Pirouettes, repartees, music, dances, jests, acrobatic feats, grimaces and dumb-show, pantomime and drama, peals of laughter and peals of thunder followed in quick succession. They ran, jumped, turned somersaults, and kicked up their heels, and the piece went like lightning . . . crackled, and sparkled, and glowed, and blazed, and then died away and disappeared. Their whole bodies moved at once. Their hands and fingers, their gestures, almost seemed to speak. Their extravagant fancy broke loose before an audience and burst into fire and soared into the sky, a marvel of balance. Explosions of wild laughter followed, and wild confusion, and a medley of caricatures, dreams, buffooneries, scurrility, poetry, and love.

It was inevitable that a form of art so vital, so genuine — even if so vulgar — should ultimately displace the hothouse pageantry and the pedantic neo-classic drama in the affections of the princes and their courtiers. There are passages out of the diaries and correspondence of the fine ladies of the time, in which they rue the boring hours spent at classic and contemporary plays — relishing only the spirited dance interludes and the machine-made wonders of " the new staging," and sighing for more comedy. There are sad plaints from the local playwright-scholars who suddenly find themselves thrust out of the security of the duke's patronage, and displaced on the palace stage by " popular " travelling companies.

By 1575, certainly, the courts had tired of the imitations of the ancient plays and the dramatically thin effusions of their poet masque-writers. From then on, for a century and a half, the Italian companies of professional comedians were the favorites of all courts, the most-sought-after acting groups of all time. Wars might drive them from one locality for a time, Church pressure might bar them from this kingdom or that for a decade, plagues and hard times might thin their ranks, but throughout the next two hundred years their story weaves in and out of court and social history in a half dozen states of Western Europe. It was the magnificent courts of the Italian princes that first

Two stages of *Commedia* actors during the decadence. Above, an etching after Karel du Jardin's *The Charlatans*. Below, a painting with Pierrot and Scapin, by Martin Drolling.

Tommasino (Thomassin) of the *Théâtre Italien* in Paris, with the Harlequin mask. [After an etching by T. Bertrand from La Tour's pastel.]

welcomed them indoors, of course. The Dukes of Mantua and of Ferrara were celebrated patrons of the stage, and the magnificence of the productions in their palaces has been a tradition of all later ages. Without knowing when the actors of the *Commedia dell'Arte* were first accepted at these courts, we find that the later records delightedly chronicle their appearances again and again; and it was a Gonzaga, Prince Vincenzo of Mantua, who in 1586 honored the famous Isabella of the *Gelosi* company by acting as godfather at the christening of her child. But even richer are the records of the triumphs of the comedians at the courts of Venice and Florence, at Milan and Verona and Naples.

Travelling courtiers and prelates and scholars saw the performances and reported glowingly to the stay-at-homes of France, Spain, Austria, Bavaria; and an English ambassador even made them the subject of an official report to Queen Elizabeth. The first important performance by Italian comedians in France was at Lyons in 1548, although it is not clear that this was strictly a *Commedia dell'Arte* company. But by 1571 we find a troupe specifically summoned to Paris on the occasion of the marriage of Charles IX, and taking the French capital by storm. All, we are told, were captivated by the gorgeous fun of the plays, the unexampled spirit of the acting, and the charm of the actors — all, that is, except the officials of the Church. They made representations or something, looking to the fining and banishment of the players; but the appreciation and protection of the king served to quiet that storm. For two hundred years after, despite ups and downs, the troupes of Italian comedians were favorites of the French monarchs, were summoned to celebrate "entries," marriages, and victories, were granted exclusive licenses for certain types of production, were honored not only as artists but as individuals. From them the French actors learned; and it was out of the unliterary Italian *Commedia dell'Arte* that the genius of Molière flowered: out of an alien popular amusement an actor-playwright took elements that he shaped into the body of dramatic literature which is considered in France the supreme expression of drama in all time.

Meantime the *Commedia dell'Arte* had been carried into Spain, where apparently the boastful Spanish Captain amused more than he offended, for there are reports of the pleasure of the court of Philip II, and of a lasting influence on native playwriting and acting. Even earlier, in 1568, a company had travelled in Austria and had enchanted the court at Vienna — where Tabarino, indeed, became " Comedian to his Majesty." In Bavaria the Italian comedy was already known; and a Mantuan company even invaded the distant, and perhaps less appreciative, England. The dialogue, of course, was mainly Italian, wherever the comedians played; but this proved no bar to the enjoyment of performances in which action, buffoonery, intrigue and cartoon-characters entered so largely. We may be sure, too, that the farceurs made rich fun out of their own struggles with the alien language of their audience, mixing words and phrases ludicrously — such an opportunity for mispronunciations and comic misunderstandings was not to be missed.

While there seems much of vulgar clatter, speed, and boisterousness in the Improvised Comedy performances, as generally described, there is a finer side to both the productions and the players. Indeed, in the best period of the *Commedia dell'Arte* the actors included in their number some of the most illustrious people the stage has known, true artists with broad human and social interests. There were, no doubt, whole companies hardly above the estate of those vagabond strolling players who in three or four periods of history caused actors to be classed with rogues, thieves, and other public nuisances. These wandering troupes went back and forth over Southern Europe, setting up their scaffolds at each town on the way, luckily striking a Fair week here, or a feast-day there; but in general taking their luck with a public always eager but seldom too generous; hazardously travelling the roads over treacherous mountains or sun-beaten plains, in storm or fair weather, with their terribly slow canvas-covered ox-carts; taking the luck of the country, cheap inn or open field or smelly stable. They were not far removed from vagabonds if fortune failed to favor them for a period; and — well, yes, they did harbor in their companies petty thieves and prostitutes.

But beside these are to be placed the recognized troupes, under dignified leadership, made up of players to whom the queens and princes delighted to do honor. It is recorded that a king after a performance that pleased him called for Scaramuccia and presented his own coach and six to the actor. Kings, dukes, and cardinals gave banquets for the visiting players. There is a record that Tasso wrote most gallantly of the actress Vittoria, at whose side he sat at a banquet given in her honor by Cardinal Aldobrandini, " to which were also invited six other cardinals " — but the records fail to state whether they all came. A few of the actors were made nobles; others held court positions — one was even keeper of the privy purse, on what theory one is puzzled to decide. Tournaments were arranged in their honor, the city bells pealed when they arrived, they doubtless had a weighty collection of those symbols of royal welcome, " the keys to the city." Even these better companies, however, were not free from the hazards of the road. *I Gelosi* were captured by the Huguenots in 1577, and were ransomed by the king barely in time to give their scheduled performance before the court in the State-Hall at Blois.

The company known as *I Gelosi* was the most famous, and probably the most accomplished, through a period following 1570, and it became the favorite at a dozen courts; kings and dukes disputed over its dates and itineraries. But there were other troupes hardly less esteemed. Every member of the *Gelosi* group is said to have been an accomplished artist, such as would have stood out as " star " in many lesser companies. Its leader was Francesco Andreini, who had a rich heritage out of living, culture, and the arts, on which to base his acting. Having started out as a soldier he fell into slavery to the Turks, from which it took him eight years to escape. He was a singer, played many musical instruments, knew five languages, and wrote freely in verse and prose. As an actor he was not content with the usual single type part; he tried his hand at creating new figures, played a dozen variations of the Spanish Captain, and was cast also as the Lover.

But if this Andreini was esteemed, it was his wife, Isabella, who was most sung by the bards, the critics, and the gallants of the times. It is recorded that she wrote well in three languages, played sweetly on musical instruments, and knew much of philosophy — and all that besides being " beautiful in name, beautiful in body, and most beautiful in spirit . . . queen of beautiful and virtuous women." Tommaso Garzoni wrote of her as " an adornment of the scene, an ornament of the theatre, a superb spectacle of virtue no less than of beauty. . . While the world lasts, while the centuries endure, while times and seasons continue, every voice, every tongue, every cry will repeat the celebrated name of Isabella."

It was in 1604 that the company was travelling from Paris toward Italy, when at Lyons Isabella, newly honored by Queen Marie, fell ill and died. And in her death is one of those strange contrasts that dot the history of the stage. This woman " of supreme modesty and perfect innocency of morals," was refused burial in consecrated ground by law of the Church. But the parish priest had the grace to record: " She is deceased with the universal reputation of being one of the most rare women in the world for learning as well as for speaking in many languages." And the officials of Lyons somewhat made up for the Church's churlishness by according her all honors, including torch bearers, mace bearers, and banners accompanying her body to the grave. And from that day her husband, the celebrated Andreini, never acted again.

The story of the *Commedia dell' Arte* is rich in figures hardly less beautiful, less noble, and certainly no less outstanding. There was that Vittoria, the " Divina Vittoria," who was celebrated as " having proportioned gestures, harmonious and becoming movements, majestic and graceful action, words sweet and affable, sighs delicate and subtle, laughter agreeable and charming, comportment lofty and noble, and showing in her whole person a perfect decorum such as belongs to, and is becoming to, a perfect actress. . . Beautiful magician of love who wins the hearts of a thousand lovers with her words." There was, too, that Florinda who at the court of Mantua, when death by smallpox had snatched a famous singer and left doubtful a command performance, stepped into the rôle and played it so movingly — " drawing from a thousand hearts a thousand sighs " — that from that day on she was a favorite and honored player.

Among the men, too, was Giulio Pasquati, whom Henry of Poland termed, in a summons, the " Magnifique," known later by his stage name of Graziano, and called the " Magnifico Pantalone." There was Flaminio Scala, actor, director, and author of fifty still-extant scenarios. And that Lelio, son of the famous Andreini and Isabella, who is reputed to have written literally

The later softened types of *Commedia* characters, in France. Above, Pierrot, Mezzetin, the Captain, and Harlequin; below, Pantalon, Polichinelle, Scapin, and Narcissin. [After engravings in a work by Riccoboni, reproduced in *l'Ancienne France: Le Théâtre et la Musique*.]

hundreds of works in drama, verse, " visions," dialogues, etc., etc. These and scores of other vivid figures are lost except in the dusty tomes and manuscripts in Italian libraries; and least of all are they known to English readers.

Half a dozen figures of the period have become legendary, more or less by the caprice of fate. Scaramuccia of the seventeenth century has outlasted all his companions. He who is historically identified with the name, Tiberio Fiorillo, did not even invent the Scaramouche name — another had used it not wholly obscurely before. Nor did he create the character: it was no more than a variation of the Spanish Captain. But his playing was so vivid, his all-black costume so much a trade-mark, and his influence (particularly on French acting and Molière) so great, that he passed into the gallery of immortals. The character, as distinct from the actor, was, of course, carried on into later Improvised Comedy and French pantomime. It is recorded that without really moving and without saying a word Scaramuccia could keep an audience in roars of laughter for fifteen minutes, by " his varied manifestations of terror of the unseen Pasquariel behind his chair."

But the virtuous and vicious among the Italian comedians, both picturesque in their heyday, and spirited, went separate ways to separate sad fates toward the end of the eighteenth century. A few of the better companies, under a " reform " impulse, absorbed literary elements into their productions and compromised with refined taste. They compromised, too, with the Church and the censors, as evidenced in an address of the actors to the French Court, when Riccoboni's company became the licensed Italian troupe in Paris. After petitions that all other Italian companies and all playing of the stock comedy characters be prohibited, and that no member of the Costantini company be added to the troupe — " through whom all know that the Italian actors who preceded them fell into disgrace at the Court " — they end: " The actors entreat your Highness to, make urgent representations at the Court that they may be permitted, as in Italy, the free use of the Holy Sacrament; the more so as they will never recite anything scandalous; and Riccoboni undertakes to submit the scenarios of the plays for examination by the Minister and also by an Ecclesiastic, for their approval." That was pretty near the end of the *Commedia dell'Arte* in France. Out of it grew new glories — but not of the same burgeoning sort.

Its end in Italy was more miserable and more deplorable. In

the eighteenth century fresh invention ceased, the spirit waned, the Professional Comedy sank back toward those crude, violent, and often licentious types out of which it had flowered. Licentiousness particularly brought about the final eclipse. English travellers naturally enough, when they returned home, reported on the incredible license and disgusting dissoluteness of the plays they had seen in Italy; although this was in the time of the smutty English Restoration playwrights, when London's own stage was the scene for plays that have been barred ever since. But the tired comedians were salting their now-stale intrigue-plots and stereotyped buffooneries with the very limit of sensational incident and suggestive gesture. Even women in childbirth and mock circumcisions were material for farcical treatment, and the chamber-pot a favorite " prop." Thus went out in a twilight of scurrility, crudeness, suggestiveness, of official suppression and popular apathy, a thing that in its day had been unique, robustly expressive, gloriously alive.

The actor when he had respected his liberty — when he had utilized his freedom from the restraint of the playwright to create richly, from the materials of his times and of the theatre, vulgarly, perhaps, but not licentiously — had made himself master of the theatre to a degree unknown in the annals of playing before or after. He had created one of the most vivid chapters in stage history. But his less talented, less conscientious, and tired followers closed it with a melancholy descent and with something very close to a bad smell.

CHAPTER XI

The Chivalrous Theatre of Spain

THE SPANISH Captain strutting across the stages of the Italian *Commedia dell'Arte,* boasting, parading, recounting his conquests among fighters and among fair ladies, but starting and trembling if another so much as speaks sharply, and running away precipitately if a sword is drawn or a gun fired — this *Capitano* may well serve to carry us over from Italy to the theatre of Spain. For despite the obvious caricature elements, and allowing for Italian bitterness toward the conquering Spaniard, and the Latin tendency to spit at the stronger man the moment his back is turned, one still may find in the prototype of this stage figure much that is characteristic of the drama and stage of Spain. Indeed, none but a vainglorious figure, a lover and a fighter, a braggart and a bully, could symbolize the sixteenth and seventeenth century Spanish stage. The drama of the period is amazingly varied, but in its most characteristic manifestations it is heroic, extravagant, a bit absurdly romantic, full of physical action; but one suspects that a mere rattling of the critical sword might prove its heroism, its wisdom, and its emotion almost as hollow as the Captain's valor.

The Capitano may have been one of the cruellest caricatures in the whole history of stage portraiture. His lies about his prowess, his oaths, his insolent parading, his fingering of his moustaches, his pride, were gorgeous; but they were contrived so only to get the more fun by contrast, when he took to trembling because the leaves rustled, or paled and ran immediately someone hissed or struck a menacing attitude. But there can be no doubt that under the caricature was the real Spaniard, who entered into Don Quixote and Don Juan. That Spaniard in his nobler embodiment appears thousands of times as the protagonist of Spanish drama. His code of honor, his love-making and his fighting are the very breath of it. Chivalry not only supplied the material for the dramatists but determined the forms of the plays. Valor in battle, a punctilious personal honor, unquestioning obedience to King and Church, romantic love — these were the ideals of

The Spanish Captain, as depicted by Abraham Bosse.

the people, which must be reflected back to them out of any drama that was to flourish.

When their national theatre emerged, the Spaniards were racially conscious more than any other people of Europe. They had fought the glorious centuries-long fight against the Moor and had saved Europe to Christianity. They were the great imperialists of the time, with the entire overseas world of America as vassal. They were the chosen of God, the upholders of Catholicism. The flame of patriotism burned fiercely. The theatre must do its bit to keep this flame bright and clear.

There are those who feel that Spain has declined steadily since those brilliant days, and one may hear talk of the debased Spaniard of today. Certainly within the first hundred years of the Spanish theatre, the nation receded from its position as political and military leader in Europe to the rank of a secondary power; the chivalry and glory in the plays was the reflection of a venerated past rather than a mirror of the sixteenth and seventeenth century present. But it may be that in the abounding national success of fifteenth century Spain there were determining elements far less admirable than those to be found in the less vaunting Spain of today; and that in these elements we may find at once the causes of the decline of political power and the reasons for the secondary place now taken by the drama of Spain, despite its one-time brilliant staging and its amazing extent (Lope de Vega alone composed 1800 dramatic works).

In the first place, although the Renaissance had its effect everywhere in Western Europe, it failed to turn the Spaniards from Mediævalism wholly back to the study of the classics as in Italy and France. The Spain of the time of the Inquisition was too fiercely Catholic to welcome that new freedom of thought which was mankind's most precious gain out of the Renaissance. The country preferred mysticism and a conception of life on earth as an interlude between birth and an all-important after-life. There was no questioning of the Faith as in Italy, no new intellectual curiosity, certainly no breaking away toward pagan freedoms in human enjoyments. Curiously enough the national art had gained much of color and richness from the Moors whom the Spaniards had finally expelled, and a certain richness of life might be put on like a cloak by the individual; but the national ideal was rigid with the unbending allegiance demanded by the Church, and with the system of caste that began with the protection of the divine right of kings. These things being the mainsprings of human action, an organized religion and an artificial code of honor ruling all men's actions, drama and literature failed to take on that warm glow of humanism so notable elsewhere. The stage was set to unending duels, intrigues, imbroglios, assignations, revenges, patriotic flatteries, heroics, relieved by farcical under-plots and comic interludes. There was little place here for the thoughtful laughter of Molière, little for the so-human sentiment of Shakespeare; too much of parade and clash for the serener elements of drama to enter.

The Spanish dramatists escaped, indeed, the too-close imitation of classic models which nullified the efforts of the Italian Renaissance playwrights; but they failed to gain the compactness, the theatric directness that a study of Greek plays might have given them. A mediæval looseness characterizes the bulk of Spanish plays, and they exhibit not a little of the monotonous repetition and episodic method of the religious plays designed for credulous and unthinking mob-audiences. Their virtues lie in a vigor of action, a romantic colorfulness and a rhetorical display seldom matched elsewhere; and not at all in compact, jewel-like workmanship or delicacy of emotion. Their vigor and freedom dramatically link them with the Elizabethan; but they go not so deep humanly, are less imaginative.

Just as the Spanish Captain represented first the swaggering overlord, flaunting the pride of the Vice-regal power through the streets of Naples, but at the same time derived out of the *Miles Gloriosus* of Roman comedy, just so the Spanish drama, though more *national* than any other in Europe, inherited elements out of both the immediately preceding Miracle theatres common to all Western Europe, and out of the obscure survivals of Roman dramatic forms. When the Spanish theatre begins to emerge as an institution, shortly after 1500, the incipient drama is close to balladry, and the travelling minstrels or troubadours are already popular. The other and perhaps the stronger root of the new plant is in the Church and religious sketches. Miracles, Mysteries, and Moralities are here played, inside and outside the Church buildings, quite as freely as in France, Germany, and England, but with closer ecclesiastic supervision. Nor will the Church lose its authority over drama for a long time after.

He who is known as " the father of Spanish drama " is Juan del Enzina, who was born in 1468 or 1469; but his sketches for the stage were hardly more than dialogue bits, of pastoral or religious sort. We may pass him over as not intrinsically important and as not determining the course of the Spanish theatre; as also Bartolomé de Torres Naharro, a Spaniard who wrote in Italy a number of comedies tinged with such grossness and disrespect that the Church Fathers forbade their representation.

It is rather with Lope de Rueda, who flourished in the mid-years of that century that any brief study of the Spanish drama should begin. He was perhaps only one of a score of similar actor-directors of strolling acting-companies, but he is repre-

Performance of an *auto sacramental*.
[Drawing by Warren D. Cheney after a painting by J. Comba.]

sentative, and of him we have authentic records. It was the great Cervantes who wrote:

In the time of this celebrated Spaniard all the properties of a theatrical manager were contained in a sack, and consisted of four white pelices trimmed with gilded leather, and four beards and wigs, with four staffs, more or less. The plays were colloquies or eclogues between two or three shepherds and a shepherdess. They were set off by two or three *entremeses,* either that of the *Negress,* the *Ruffian,* the *Fool,* or the *Biscayan,* for these four characters and many others the said Lope acted with the greatest skill and propriety that one can imagine. At that time there were no *tramoyas* [stage machinery] nor challenges of Moors or Christians either afoot or on horse. There were no figures which arose or seemed to arise from the centre of the earth through the hollow of the stage, which at that time consisted of four benches arranged in a square, with four or five boards upon them, raised about four spans from the ground, nor did clouds with angels or souls descend from the skies. The furnishings of the stage were an old woolen blanket drawn by two cords from one side to the other, which formed what is called a dressing-room, behind which were the musicians, singing some old ballad without the accompaniment of a guitar.

Cervantes then goes on to describe the betterment achieved by Pedro Navarro:

He improved somewhat the setting of the *comedia,* and instead of a bag for the costumes used chests and trunks. He brought the musicians from behind the curtain, where they formerly sang, out upon the stage, removed the beards of the players, for up to that time no actor appeared upon the stage without a false beard . . . except those who represented old men or other characters which required a facial disguise. He invented stage machinery, thunder and lightning, challenges and battles, but these never reached the excellence which we see now. . .[1]

From this description we may easily picture a roadside or market-place theatre very similar to that which we have already met in connection with the less pretentious Italian *Commedia dell'Arte* companies, and which we shall meet again when we glance at the beginnings of the French theatre. Here the platform is a bit barer, the company of actors smaller, the drama very primitive indeed. The texts of some of Lope de Rueda's pieces — he was playwright as well as director and chief actor — have survived. One is called *The Olives.* A peasant and his wife discuss an olive tree he has planted this very day. The wife's imagination soars till she sees whole groves of fine trees multiplied out of this one plant, and she opines that some day their daughter will be able to sell great quantities of olives at a fancy price, say two *reals* a peck. This strikes the peasant as too high a price to ask. The mother turns to the daughter and orders her to charge two *reals*. The father counterorders. Each begins to threaten the daughter if she follows the command of the other; then they begin actually to beat her if she will or won't charge

---

[1] Quoted from *The Spanish Stage in the Time of Lope de Vega,* by Hugo Albert Rennert (New York, 1909). This is by far the most interesting of the few available works on the Spanish Theatre, though limited to a period. For the rest, one must search through the books on Spanish literature: the standard *A New History of Spanish Literature,* by James Fitzmaurice-Kelly (London, New York, etc., 1926), and *History of Spanish Literature,* by George Ticknor (in 3 volumes, Boston, 1888).

two *reals*. Her cries bring a neighbor who inquires what the trouble's about, and the parents have to admit that it is all over olives that are not planted yet.

Such a simple fable is quite in keeping with the simplicity of the plank stage and the lack of settings and special costumes; for there was absolutely nothing by way of " scenery " and apparently no change of costume from play to play. Always plenty of ballad-singing was thrown in. It is hardly necessary to dwell on the likeness of such a " play " to the ballads, in its directness, homeliness, and simple characterization. It demanded scarcely more than did a ballad in the way of stage equipment to be carried by the itinerant actors from town to town.

The company was made up of Lope de Rueda, originally a mechanic of Seville, his book-seller friend Timoneda, who likewise wrote plays and acted, and two others who are said also to have been " authors." Their plays were not always so close to the Spanish soil as *The Olives*. There are classical traces in some, others are definitely Italian, and at least one seems to have been lifted from Plautus. But this is really the first essentially and healthily Spanish popular theatre about which there is definite data.

At this time the courts were toying with adaptations of the Italian pastoral play-form and with other importations: all artificial and negligible. By the beginning of the fourth quarter of the sixteenth century, tragedies in classic form on native historical themes were being attempted. In 1574, too, an Italian *Commedia dell'Arte* company, one of the best, under Alberto Ganassa, came to Spain and performed its comedies at the court, and later in a " corral " or yard theatre, for larger audiences, to great applause we are told, and not without affecting the course of native theatrical endeavor. Lope de Vega, then a boy, remembered these spirited scenes — and characters — well, when he became Spain's greatest playwright. For while the classic revival brought in a literary play-form too rigid for the Spanish genius, and a humanism too free for the anti-libertarian ruling Churchmen, the Italian popular comedy brought elements easily grafted on to such meagre but popular sketches as those of Lope de Rueda.

The next great figure, however, is more literary than theatrical, in his approach and in his achievement. Cervantes, immortal for his creation of *Don Quixote,* and indubitably Spain's greatest writer, failed to write brilliantly for the stage or to turn the course of its development, although he was author of a considerable number of plays. Though he described appreciatively, as we have seen, Lope de Rueda's honest theatre, Cervantes failed to recognize that the qualities of directness, simplicity, and theatricality which he praised in his predecessor were exactly those which he should have built upon in his own work. Cervantes' early dramas, judged in the light of Lope de Rueda's crude but playable pieces, were weak, slow, and untheatric. One can only feel that he remained always the typical literary man, drawn by the glow of the theatre, but seeing it only as a method of making literature more pervasive and palatable, never as an art in its own right, less of words than of action. Moreover, he was under the orthodox Senecan influence.

For a long period he gave up writing for the stage, and in that time Lope de Vega determined the course Spanish drama was to take. But Cervantes, coming back to the attempt late in life, with the new play-forms before him, still wrote comparatively lifeless dramas, declamatory and diffused. His novels later served many playwrights as a rich ground for picking and stealing. But his own dramatic compositions not only are not to be mentioned with his great romance, but are inferior to the plays of his obviously less talented followers.

Perhaps Cervantes had too much knowledge of what the literary theatre was becoming in Italy and other countries, and failed to square this with the stage he saw in Spain. Although Madrid in his time was to see its first permanent theatres built, the stage of his earlier years would be a sad-looking place for dreaming romantic and decorative plays, for elegant and literary performances. The popular theatre was a few bare boards without decoration, with groundling audiences and daylight performances of rude episodes. The " corral " theatres were less crude, but the stages simple. Perhaps Cervantes had tasted in Italy the fare of the new ballroom theatres that were being decked out with pageantry and rich costuming and machine-made trick effects. At any rate, he failed to connect effectively with the existing stage of his own country.

There was another, however, who lived in Cervantes' time, destined to pick up the inheritance from Lope de Rueda and his fellow strollers, and to shape the Spanish theatre to his own genius. Lope de Vega not only paid no false homage to revived classic-literary forms; he almost leaned backward in his eagerness not to bow before them. He once wrote: " When I set out to write a play I lock up all the rules under ten keys, and banish Plautus and Terence from my study, lest they should cry out against me, as truth is accustomed to do even from dumb books. For I write in the style of those who seek the applause of the public, whom it is but just to humor in their folly, since it is they who pay for it."

Thus Lope de Vega aligned himself with those in every age who, usually dangerously, start writing with the primary aim of " pleasing the public." His success went far beyond that of most adherents to the doctrine: he not only established an immediate contact with the popular stage, and wrote for it steadily through a lifetime, but lifted that stage to finer heights and richer accomplishments. But still — and certainly his purveying to a mass-public that demanded sensation, and asked constantly for racial flattery, had something to do with it — he failed to write any drama that has lived through the years with the best out of the Greek, English, French, and German theatres. Incidentally he fractured many of the laws of probability, geography, mythology, and history — and occasionally of morality. He theoretically and openly adhered to the classic unities; but out of his first four hundred and eighty-six plays he observed them in only six.

Lope de Vega, however, *was* the theatre of an age and a country as no other dramatist ever has been. Not that he had no talented and fertile contemporaries: the Spain of the seventeenth century abounded with theatrical life. But in his versatility he practised every form of playwriting, and originated most of those practised by his contemporaries. He took the stage as he found it, handicapped by no literary theories; but he shaped, then dominated, Spanish drama because he instinctively brought literary form and enrichment to it. He began by doing things

hardly different from Lope de Rueda's dialogues, with dramatized ballads and interludes, eclogues and religious sketches. But
he went on to pastorals and allegories and chronicle plays, to
comedy, farce, cloak-and-sword mystery plays, and heroic tragedy.
He is the very mirror of the Spanish stage, and it would have
a considerable dramatic literature if no other playwright had
ever graced it — for he wrote 1500 works classed as plays, besides
more than three hundred works put down as dramatic sketches,
religious processionals, etc.

He could not have been so perfectly the protagonist of the
Spanish theatre if he had not been also thoroughly the Spanish
gentleman, adventurer, and court hanger-on. He tasted early
the sweets and the bitterness of love and of fighting; suffered
exile; sailed with the Armada; lived scandalously; became intensely Catholic, was honored by the Pope and made titular
official of the Church; took his place as a noble, and lived full
of rather stormy honors, and as arbiter of the contemporary
theatre. If he began by making the form of his dramas pleasing
to the popular taste, certainly he had every opportunity to weave
into their substance those sentiments and those passions dearest
to an idolizing and proud-hearted people. From this we may be
sure (without reading all the 1800 works) that his plays are
filled with physical action and surprise, with inventive plot and
swift movement, with flattery and romantic description, with
playings-up to royalty and religion, with farcical interlude and
relief characters, with fascinating heroes and seductive heroines.
They are, too, deft, clever, fast flowing, with the most skilful
mechanical articulation yet known to the world stage.

Their faults lie, of course, in the lack of those serener and
deeper qualities that too seldom go with such vigor of action and
dramatic facility. The last acts are often feeble. There is little
depth in the characterizations, too little of sustained poetic effect
without rhetoric, seldom the inevitable moment, the soul-stirring
scene at the end of a carefully designed emotional ascent.

We may here again go back to the life of the times for a
reason. Violence was as commonplace as in Renaissance Italy.
In Spain murder might be committed in the name of Church or
King rather than for the material gain of a prince or gentle-

A conjectural restoration of a corral theatre in Madrid in 1660. There is here a notable likeness to the Elizabethan inn-yard playhouses, in the balconies and windows utilized for the spectators of quality, the mob audience on the ground, and the half-projecting, half-curtained stage. Note also the awning over the audience. Below is the notorious gallery for women, sometimes known as "the stews," which was for long a feature of the Spanish popular theatre.
[From *Ten Spanish Farces*, edited by George Tyler Northup.]

man, but human life was rated almost as cheaply. And callousness to the value of human life is almost always an accompaniment of art that is showy but fails to go deep. Violence begets a drama rich in conflict and clamor but poor in serenity and spiritual overtones. It may be added that the serious Spanish theatre was kept fairly free of those obscenities that were just then abounding on the Italian stage, even in the court theatres. A natural delicacy seems to have determined a true propriety in both dramatist and actor. There are matters connected with the physical passion of love, and with the sewage problems of the individual, which the Italian parades on occasion with coarse enjoyment, and along which the Frenchman skims with a cynical fascination; but there were no chamber-pots or bridal beds on the " higher " Spanish stages of the time. The street theatres might tell another story, what with the vaudeville sketches and the dancers — and Lope de Vega sometimes wrote for them too.

Among the contemporaries of Lope there were many dramatists both prolific and able, but none who is not overshadowed by his achievement. Ruiz de Alarcon (really a Mexican), Guillen de Castro, who wrote the plays upon which Corneille was to base his epochal *Cid*, Perez de Montalvan, and Tirso de Molina, who is generally credited with creation of the now universal Don Juan character: these are the chief figures among many practitioners. They might warrant closer study had they not lived just at the time of Lope de Vega and just before Calderon. The titles of some of their plays indicate how closely they were following the models set up by their great contemporary: *The Deceiver of Seville, Don Gil in the Green Breeches, The Youthful Adventures of the Cid, Mismatches in Valencia, The Lovers of Teruel, Mercy and Justice, A Bashful Man at Court,* and *Double Vengeance.*

The special conventions of the Spanish theatre at this time include an almost absolute disregard of change of physical setting. Lope de Vega even inveighed against the invading " scenery." The dialogue might carry an indication of change of scene; or the spectator might become aware where the action was taking place simply from the characters present. In the popular or public theatre scenery was practically unknown. The language of the plays lent an enrichment, there being an unusual prettiness for the ear in spoken Spanish; though the lyric loveliness often ran into rhetorical extravagance. The loosely constructed plays might alternate highly flowery passages with the prosiest of commonplace scenes; the play was, indeed, one situation after another, of one sort and another, rather than the carefully articulated, carefully unified and sustained thing that the Greeks had once made it, and that the Elizabethans and the French were to make it again (with Lope de Vega's mature works, we are well into Queen Elizabeth's time). Even the verse in a single play might be in a variety of metres, at the same time admitting prose.

The acting on the Spanish stage was well suited to carry on the swift-moving plots, to register the florid speeches, and to cover over successfully the shallow characterizations. For no such vivid acting was known in all the rest of Europe, nothing so spirited, so all-compelling. Even the Italians praised it as vivid and stirring beyond comparison.

The favorite and perhaps the most representative type of play was the " cloak-and-sword " drama, so named from the class of characters chosen for the main plot. No matter how serious or tragic this plot might be, there would be a comic underplot, played by " relief " characters. The most distinctively Spanish figure in theatre history, indeed, is the comic-relief *gracioso,* servant, clown, and chorus, adding fun to the action, sharpening his master's sayings and doings by contrast, keeping up a running fire of comment, not seldom philosophical, being to the leading characters and to the play what Sancho Panza is to Don Quixote. Perhaps the favorite " device " — by which the dramatic knot is untied — is the king-in-disguise.

If Lope de Vega and his fellows could train their muse to the demands of the crowd, in secular drama, they no less easily turned to pleasing the Church on occasion. About four hundred of Lope's dramatic compositions are *autos sacramentales,* a sort of masque combining prologue, farce and religious allegory, designed for acting on the pageant-cars during the Corpus-Christi processionals, and dealing presumably with the Eucharist. In his time the " religious plays " had become very elastic, very mixed, with plenty of features introduced to please the mob; but there is no doubt that the Church sanctioned them, and could have suppressed them.

The *auto* proper was preceded by a decorative procession, probably with monsters, giants, etc., followed by choirs, dancing choruses, priests bearing the Host under a canopy, the king and his courtiers, and finally cars full of actors. At an open-air stage the procession stopped, the crowd knelt, the religious devotions were gotten out of the way, and the acting began. First would be an acted prologue: perhaps a peasant is represented as having come to town for the shows, has lost his wife in this very crowd, decides it is no use to hunt her further and is about to console himself with another when she turns up; then she begins telling him all about the wondrous procession she has seen — which is, of course, the very one the audience has just witnessed. Next comes a farcical sketch: one of Lope de Vega's tells a story not unlike that of *Pierre Pathelin,* of a peasant who outwits a shrewd lawyer, and escapes in the disguise of a blind ballad-singer — giving the audience, of course, a sample of his art.

The *auto* itself is a nominally religious sketch. To take an example from Lope de Vega's works again, we may visualize the actors as presenting *The Bridge of the World.* The Prince of Darkness places Leviathan (" Hell-mouth " is none other than the Biblical Leviathan — or at least his jaws) across the bridge of the world. None can pass without admitting the supremacy of the Prince. Adam and Eve, " dressed very gallantly after the French fashion," agree and pass on. Others of the familiar Bible characters — Moses, David, Solomon — weakly submit. But then comes the Knight of the Cross, who routs the Dark Prince and opens the passage of the world to the Soul of Man. A dance or songs follow.

Lope de Vega also wrote innumerable other religious sketches and plays, including a group of Miracles based on the lives of the Saints and some more strictly Biblical dramas — these latter having occupied his attention during the two years of the ban laid by the dying Philip II in 1598 on all but religious theatrical activity. But whatever the materials and the forms of the drama it remained always close to the people, always popular, and somehow always Spanish. Even during the years of the prohibition, it was a case of making the religious plays popularly appealing, rather than a case of actual suppression of the glamorous and profane elements in drama. The terrible insincerity of the Inquisition is nowhere more apparent than in the evasions it permitted in theatre and in literature.

There is only one Spanish name that transcends Lope de Vega's in any department of dramatic mastery. Calderon — more properly Pedro Calderon de la Barca — is usually cited as the greater poet. Less spontaneous and less inventive, and certainly less fecund (he wrote only a hundred plays), Calderon is more imaginative and the richer writer. Spanish to the core — he too is soldier, nobleman, and ardent and narrow Churchman — he exhibits all the brilliant and romantic characteristics to be found in the theatre of his predecessors; but in his tragedies he cuts a little deeper into life and decorates the dramatic skeleton more richly. To know Spanish poetic tragedy or neartragedy in its highest flights, we must read *The Constant Prince (Don Ferdinand of Portugal)*, *Life Is a Dream*, *The Mayor of Zalamea*, *Love Survives Life*, or *The Physician of His Own Honor*.

The story of this last illustrates that " point of honor," the over-punctiliousness that excuses even murder, which is so favorite a theme in Spanish drama and romance. Don Gutierre de Solis has married a noblewoman, who is true to him in thought and deed. The King's brother, who had admired her before her marriage, finds his passion rearoused through a chance meeting; and it so happens that the husband's suspicions are stirred, and the wife's efforts to cut off any further misunderstanding only lead to Don Gutierre's certainty of her infidelity. He gives her two hours to live; during which she lays herself out for a holy death, with candles and crucifix over her. Don Gutierre brings, blindfolded, a surgeon who bleeds away the wife's lifeblood. But this surgeon, in order to know the house again, imprints his bloody hand upon the door, and straightway reports to the King, who comes to the house. Don Gutierre, from desire to protect his own honor, explains his wife's death as accidental; the King requires him to marry one Leonore, to whom he is

already somewhat bound, and who is present. The only delay
is over Don Gutierre's desire to leave no doubt that he would
defend his honor if a case like that not yet explained to the King,
but understood, should arise. The ending is thus translated
by Ticknor:

KING

There is a remedy for every wrong.

DON GUTIERRE

A remedy for such a wrong as this?

KING

Yes, Gutierre.

DON GUTIERRE

My lord! What is it?

KING

'Tis of your own invention, sir!

DON GUTIERRE

But what?

KING

'Tis blood.

DON GUTIERRE

What mean your royal words, my lord?

KING

No more but this; cleanse straight your doors.
A bloody hand is on them.

DON GUTIERRE

My lord, when men
In any business and its duties deal,
They place their arms escutcheoned on their doors.
I deal, my lord, in honor, and so place
A bloody hand upon my door to mark
My honor is my blood made good.

KING

Then give thy hand to Leonore.
I know her virtue hath long deserved it.

DON GUTIERRE

I give it, sire. But mark me, Leonore,
It comes all bathed in blood.

LEONORE

I heed it not;
And neither fear nor wonder at the sight.

DON GUTIERRE

And mark me, too, that, if already once
Unto mine honor I have proved a leech,
I do not mean to lose my skill.

LEONORE

Nay, rather,
If *my* life prove tainted, use that same skill
To heal it.

DON GUTIERRE

I give my hand; but give it
On these terms alone.

Perhaps nothing could better illustrate the fault that lies under the great mass of serious Spanish drama: a falsity that seems often to vitiate the atmosphere of great deeds and heroic sacrifices. The human element suffers eclipse in the holding up of a code.

Another fragment may serve to illuminate the point, a bit with the best and the worst of Spanish drama in it — the famous soliloquy of Isabel in the last act of *The Mayor of Zalamea*. Edward Fitzgerald despaired of catching the fulness of the original in English verse, and transposed it into prose thus:

ISABEL

Oh, never, never might the light of day arise and show me to myself in my shame! Oh, fleeting morning star, mightest thou never yield to the dawn that even now presses on thy azure skirts! And thou, great Orb of all, do thou stay down in the cold ocean foam; let night for once advance her trembling empire into thine! For once assert thy voluntary power to hear and pity human misery and prayer, nor hasten up to proclaim the vilest deed that Heaven, in revenge on man, has written on his guilty annals! Alas! even as I speak, thou liftest thy bright, inexorable face above the hills! Oh, horror! What shall I do? whither turn my tottering feet? Back to my own home? and to my aged father, whose only joy it was to see his own spotless honor spotlessly reflected in mine, which now — And yet if I return not, I leave calumny to make my innocence accomplice in my own shame! Oh that I had stayed to be slain by Juan over my slaughtered honor! But I dared not meet his eyes even to die by his hand. Alas! — Hark! What is that noise?

CRESPO *(within)*
Oh, in pity slay me at once!

ISABEL
One calling for death like myself?

CRESPO
Whoever thou art —

ISABEL
That voice!   *(Exit)*

In ranking Calderon higher than Lope de Vega as a poet, we should remember that his superiority is notable chiefly in a literary way. Lope is by so much the superior craftsman of the stage, so clearly the creative inventor of theatric forms, that there can be no question which is the greater figure in stage history, which the outstanding representative of the Spanish theatre in the eyes of the world.

The contemporaries of Calderon included that Agustin Moreto who wrote (partially by plagiarizing Lope de Vega) *Disdain against Disdain,* a drama often translated, and as near to the type of *human* play then being composed in England as any ever devised in Spain. Many others continued the popular-romantic play tradition: a few wrote in styles introduced from other countries, quite hollowly; and opera was imported — even Calderon wrote certain pieces with music in mind. Italian scenery and Italian ballroom theatres came in. But only the very popular forms of drama and those in their cheaper aspects, persisted seriously after Calderon. For the political decline of the nation was rapid, and the old brilliancy faded out of life and letters. The stage of the people was too vigorous to disappear — there were forty theatres in Madrid by 1675, and the country was fairly teeming with dramatic endeavor — but no new Lope appeared to lift it again; rather the playwrights went down to it. In the eighteenth century theorists tried to introduce classic writing according to the French formula, and some tried to reconcile the supposed " Greek " dramaturgy with the Spanish national forms as exemplified in the seventeenth century masters; but futilely. Indeed there is precious little to draw our attention back to the theatres of Spain between the late seventeenth century (Calderon died in 1681) and the early twentieth century.

The Spanish stage had been as vividly alive as any in Europe for two hundred years. In that time it developed a national dramatic literature that is both brilliant and distinctive. And yet, as a body of reading texts and as material for translation and revival, this mass of plays assays rather thin. Spain failed to bequeath to the world works that will stir audiences everywhere by their universality, their humanity, and their inevitableness. The virtues of the Spanish were those that interested, amused, surprised, and flattered its spectators, and those that flamed with sudden bursts of rich fun, tragic feeling, and lyrical exuberance. Serenity and sustained intensity of emotion were not here.

As a tag to one of his own plays Calderon wrote four lines translated by Ticknor as follows:

> This is a play of Pedro Calderon,
> Upon whose scene you never fail to find
> A hidden lover or a lady fair
> Most cunningly disguised.

And indeed upon the whole Spanish scene those are the standard ingredients: hidings, fair ladies, lovers, disguise, and cunning structure.

LOPE DE VEGA

Queen Elizabeth viewing an allegorical group of the sort common in the masques and garden entertainments arranged in her honor. The painting is called *The Masque of Zabeta,* and the figures represent Juno, Minerva, and Venus. [From *The Queen's Progress,* by Felix E. Schelling.]

An example of the Italian architectural perspective setting, of the sort introduced into England during the Elizabethan era. The scene represents the cathedral square at Siena, and is set behind the usual proscenium frame. Compare this with the proscenium and forestage arrangement in the drawing by Inigo Jones for *Florimène,* page 295.
[From a wood engraving by Andrea Andreani after B. Neroni.]

CHAPTER XII

Shakespeare

WHEN Elizabeth came to the throne in 1558, England had responded but timidly to the freshening breath of the Renaissance. Already there had been a king with Italian tastes, but Henry VIII, however he may have encouraged the more precious arts of music and masque-making, had done little to popularize or to better dramatic productions or to further intellectual research. He had been too busy, perhaps, politically — freeing the English Church from Rome was more a political than a religious matter — too busy to stir his people to emulation of those Italian accomplishments that he so admired. When Elizabeth became queen, London had not one theatre, amateur dramatic performances were still more important than professional, the age of Miracles and Moralities had not passed. And yet within fifty years we are to see the flowering of a theatre surpassed by none in history as regards spirit and accomplishment — and everlastingly important for the dramatic texts it bequeathed to posterity. We are, indeed, at the threshold of the most vital and (with that of the Greeks) the noblest theatre the world has known.

The push forward during Elizabeth's reign was integral to a larger national and economic advance. The Renaissance, in freeing men's minds from domination, had resulted indirectly in the invention of printing, and a consequent enormous spread of knowledge; and had brought an era of exploration and discovery that remade the map of the world, destroying once and for all the concentration in the Mediterranean of trade and cultural routes, leaving that sea, indeed, at the fringe rather than the centre of a new European-American world. In the period of expression and expansion that followed the Renaissance, the torch of progress was passed successively from Italy to Spain, from Spain to England. Amid the comparative peace of Elizabeth's reign, the English were better able than any other people to keep the flame brilliantly alight. In the theatre it burned most gloriously.

If there was no playhouse in London in 1558 — nor for eighteen years after — we are not to infer that there was little theatrical activity. The Guilds have not entirely given up their plays, though professional travelling troupes have multiplied greatly; the schools and universities are acting Latin plays, translations of Italian plays, and even native plays; the court has had a taste of Italian masques and native mumming, and even an occasional glimpse of imported professional troupes; pageant-like productions are a concern of the civic authorities, particularly on the occasion of a sovereign's visit or a Lord Mayor's induction.

We have already seen how the humorous elements (or humorous intrusions, if you prefer) in the Miracles led on to witty interludes as secular as those of John Heywood. The Moralities, too, were changing toward the form known as *Chronicles*. A transition type between Morality and Chronicle arose in the plays of political purpose: *Upon Both Marriages of the King,* and *Kyng Johan* (wherein the character Sedition is supposed to represent the Archbishop of Canterbury, Usurped Power the Pope, Imperial Majesty the King, etc.); and, as an example which affords a clue to its purpose in the very title, *The Three Laws of Nature, Moses and Christ, Corrupted by the Sodomites, Pharisees and Papists.* (This last piece, of the early sixteenth century, has the following directions for the costuming of certain characters: " Let Idolatry be decked lyke an olde wytche, Sodomey lyke a monke of all sectes, Ambycyon lyke a byshop, Covetousnesse lyke a popysh doctour, and Hypocresy lyke a graye fryre.") We might spend chapters on tracing out how plays of this type led on, with the aid of the ballad influence, to the purely historical Chronicle plays — and Shakespeare's early dramas were in that genre — and how similarly the Devil of the Miracles became the Vice of the Moralities, and finally turned into the

Jester who appears so frequently in Elizabethan secular drama. For England at this time is full of transitional dramatic activity, and a multitude of play types and sub-types have been described by historians and scholars. But for us, in a brief tour of the world's theatres, it is better to mark only the pervasiveness of the spirit of experiment in putting the drama to use, as amusement, as political and religious propaganda, as a decorative adjunct to court and civic functions. The theatre has come alive, even if it has not a playhouse, nor yet a memorable artist.

Queen Elizabeth was a patron of the theatre only in a limited way. She had an insatiable appetite for the pomp and show of pageantry and masque; and a comedy was to her liking. But here was no lavish encouragement to dramatist and " decorator," like that of the Italian princes; no commissioning of playwrights to pen serious dramas, no building of magnificent theatres. Indeed, the Court continued to harbor some narrow prejudices: Chronicle plays were suspect, as not certain to hold kings up in the most favorable light, and soon all religious plays were banned — for no one could tell how some provincial guild might forward heretical doctrine by an uncensored Miracle or a wrongly political near-Morality.

Still the Court was at least passively favorable to the actors and playwriters; and certain of the titled nobles lent their names and a sort of protection to the acting companies. The number of travelling troupes so increased that restrictions were passed on " common players," as distinguished from those under patronage. The Puritans were already attacking the drama — the beginnings of a fight destined to end with the closing of the theatres and absolute prohibition of plays in 1642; but the Court and nobles resisted the pressure brought by the clergy — thus favoring the dramatist at least to the extent of opportunity if he could please public audiences. And it is the popular public theatre that is to give us Marlowe, Shakespeare, and Jonson. Noting the productions in castle halls and palace ballrooms, like those at the colleges, as a separate and somewhat removed activity, we may say that the typical " playhouse " of the time is the inn-yard. It is for the emerging companies of professional strolling players that the young playwrights, the gentlemen-scholars who find conservative literature too tame in a spirited world, exert their energies.

The dramatists known as " Shakespeare's predecessors " exhibit common characteristics which may be marked as reflections of the national life of the times, and of the conditions of inn-yard and roadside representation. A vigor and a richness that often ran into extravagance, a freedom and a sweep that brought into drama unmatched variety and stirring emotional climaxes, without a great deal of cunning in the finer points of craftsmanship: these are qualities easily explained by reference to contemporary living. And where audiences were such that no woman ever went to a public play unmasked, there was double reason for vigor of writing, grandeur rather than intimacy in story, for sacrifice to " acting effects." The early playwright, indeed, reached straight for the strong and the picturesque: " In three hours runs he through the world: marries, gets children, makes children men, men to conquer kingdoms, murder monsters, and bringeth Gods from Heaven and fetcheth Devils from Hell." The professional dramatists treated Italian Renaissance literature as a first-class raiding ground for story, but they put their stealings into the old mediæval form of loose-knit chronicle, with emphasis on violent actable incident.

The first English tragedy that has survived is *Gorboduc,* by Thomas Sackville and Thomas Norton, acted in 1562, a Senecan play on an English theme, in that " blank verse " — unrhymed iambic pentameter — which is to become so glorious an instrument in the hands of Marlowe and Shakespeare. *Gorboduc* is characterized by rhetoric in place of action, and by the old inserted device of " dumb show," passages of explanatory pantomime without words. The earliest " regular " comedy is *Ralph Roister Doister,* a Plautan imitation by Nicholas Udall, of somewhat earlier date, and this was followed quickly by Bishop Still's *Gammer Gurton's Needle,* a racy farce-comedy. Having established these, so to speak, date-marks, we may turn to the dozen dramatists who more definitely established playwriting as a profession, determined the direction of English dramatic endeavor, and wrote the plays to which Shakespeare was to shape his less

mature genius — plays, indeed, touching heights that only Shakespeare afterwards passed.

John Lyly was first, and most independent of the early dramatists, and by that token less a true Elizabethan. Or perhaps because he spent his talent chiefly in writing for the Court, and with
the companies of boy-actors in mind, he was merely less of the
public theatres, and therefore less aboundingly virile and theatric.
His work is romantic and elegantly artificial, dealing with legendary themes and characters — sweetly lyrical at times, but tame.
Perhaps Lyly's service to the drama was greatest in his " domesti-
cation " of prose in English comedy: he marked out a path to be
trod by far greater dramatists during his own lifetime. As a
notable contrast to him there is that Thomas Kyd who wrote
The Spanish Tragedy, a melodramatic play which was the best
seller of the years around 1590, and which had influence far outside England. It is a violent but readable and playable piece,
the perfect example of the tragedy-of-blood then so in vogue.
We may exclaim with its King,

> What age hath ever heard such monstrous deeds!

but we cannot help marking the fresh vigor of Kyd's writing, and
the dramatic directness of the tragic story. Although the Senecan
Ghost appears in *The Spanish Tragedy,* the play exhibits an amazing advance, theatrically, beyond *Gorboduc,* which had substi-
tuted narrative and description for action, and in interminable
speeches. Kyd is the typical professional playwright, hack-writing
to the needs of a vigorous popular theatre, where the authors of
Gorboduc had been courtiers, amateurs, and imitators of clas-
sically correct authors.

George Peele was a popular playwright, too, but he wrote at
least one Court play that surpassed Lyly on the latter's ground.
Where Lyly had delicately flattered Queen Elizabeth in allegory
and thinly-veiled legend, Peele stepped in with *The Arraign-
ment of Paris,* wherein one saw Jupiter cancel the award of the
golden apple to Venus, in order that Diana might step forth at
the end of the masque, kneel before the Queen, and present the
prize to that paragon of chastity, etc., on earth, the peerless
" nymph Eliza." In the public theatre Peele is hardly more than

a hack-writer with sound education and a considerable literary gift making progress toward a greater time.

Robert Greene deserves credit for more than such contributory achievement. If he marred his plays by careless workmanship — just as he marred his life by reckless living, going down to a premature and ugly death — he nevertheless exhibits powers that more than foreshadow those of Shakespeare, in variety, freedom and freshness of invention, that make his own works permanently significant. *Friar Bacon and Friar Bungay* perhaps best illustrates his humor, tenderness, and freshness.

It has been estimated that of the immense output of the Elizabethan playwrights, not more than one-third has survived in printed form. Plays were quickly written, performed, quickly forgotten. Only the exceptional drama was composed with the thought of book publication; even Shakespeare seems to have considered little the question of preserving the uncorrupted texts of his stage plays. Among the many dramas that have survived, however, those of three other dramatists demand mention. Thomas Lodge only dabbled in playwriting, but did well what he did; and he wrote a non-dramatic *Rosalynde* which has achieved a greater fame as the source of the story which Shakespeare utilized in *As You Like It.* Thomas Nashe likewise was the figure of the versatile Elizabethan writer; and he was dramatist to the extent of being jailed for the too licentious criticism he had written into *The Isle of Dogs* — which may serve to remind us that literary work in this period often involved the author in controversies, forced exiles, imprisonment, and physical encounter.

Last among the predecessors of Shakespeare, and most important — nay, the only true genius among them — is Christopher Marlowe. Had there been no Shakespeare after him, here would have been ample reason for calling the Elizabethan theatre glorious — in four plays composed before Marlowe was killed, at thirty, in a tavern brawl. It is idle perhaps to speculate upon what masterpieces might have been born out of Marlowe's matured genius; and yet one cannot but pause to sorrow over what here was cut off by folly. No other known actual tragedy of theatre life seems quite so grievous, so blighting.

Ben Jonson wrote of " Marlowe's mighty line," and the phrase prepares the reader or spectator for the power and greatness of the dramatist's verse. The qualities are echoed even in the prologue of Marlowe's first play, *Tamurlaine the Great:*

> From jigging veins of rhyming mother wits,
> And such conceits as clownage keeps in pay,
> We'll lead you to the stately tent of war,
> Where you shall hear the Scythian Tamurlaine
> Threatening the world with high astounding terms,
> And scourging kingdoms with his conquering sword . . .

As if to match the sensational excesses of the action, the high astounding terms run off into bombast on occasion; but there is high poetic beauty too — and sometimes human pathos with it. When Zenocrate is dead:

> THERIDAMAS
> . . . Nothing prevails, for she is dead, my lord.

> TAMURLAINE
> " For she is dead! " Thy words do pierce my soul!
> Ah, sweet Theridamas, say no more;
> Though she be dead, yet let me think she lives,
> And feed my mind that dies for want of her. . .

Marlowe's second play, *The Tragical History of Doctor Faustus,* if fragmentary as drama, nevertheless treats the Faust legend with magnificent boldness and not seldom in glorious verses. When Helen is conjured up before him, in those last tormented hours, Faust speaks:

> Was this the face that launched a thousand ships
> And burnt the topless towers of Ilium?
> Sweet Helen, make me immortal with a kiss. *(Kisses her.)*
> Her lips suck forth my soul; see where it flies! —
> Come, Helen, come, give me my soul again.
> Here will I dwell, for Heaven is in those lips,
> And all is dross that is not Helena.
> I will be Paris, and for love of thee,
> Instead of Troy shall Wertenberg be sacked:
> And I will combat with weak Menelaus,
> And wear thy colors on my plumèd crest:
> Yea, I will wound Achilles in the heel,
> And then return to Helen for a kiss.
> Oh, thou art fairer than the evening air

Clad in the beauty of a thousand stars;
Brighter art thou than flaming Jupiter
When he appeared to hapless Semele:
More lovely than the monarch of the sky
In wanton Arethusa's azured arms:
And none but thou shalt be my paramour.

A reconstruction by Walter H. Godfrey of the Fortune Theatre. An Elizabethan playhouse depicted in accordance with the original building contract. [From *Shakespeare's Theatre*, by Ashley H. Thorndike.]

And at the end of this play the Chorus speaks those lines so often quoted in regard to the poet himself — murdered while still almost a youth:

Cut is the branch that might have grown full straight,
And burnèd is Apollo's laurel bough. . .

The Jew of Malta and *Edward II* are more mature works, characterized by a dramatic unity that the earlier plays lacked. *The Jew of Malta* is often studied for its likeness and contrast to *The Merchant of Venice;* the central character is equally vivid, but far less human, and the action is more violent than in

Shakespeare's carefully balanced, if loosely knit, drama. *Edward II* is usually termed Marlowe's masterpiece, for its superior craftsmanship and characterization. But after all it is the dramatist's poetic richness that entitles him to a place up near Shakespeare. No one before him had written blank verse with such mastery. And, what served equally to endear him to Elizabethan audiences, no one else had packed quite so much of passion into the play form.

The theatres for which Kyd and Greene and Peele and Marlowe wrote were an outgrowth of the old inn-yard to which the strolling players were wont to resort. In 1576 James Burbage, head of the Earl of Leicester's company of players, opened a playhouse, known as the Theatre, in the suburbs of London, outside the jurisdiction of hostile Lord Mayor and unsympathetic civic authorities. Almost immediately another, known as the Curtain, was built close-by. The houses were constructed on the same open-air model, and it was not until considerably later that a roof was thrown over a building intended exclusively and specifically for dramatic performances. (Don't forget that during all this time the *occasional* performances were going forward at Court, at university, and in the inns of court or halls of the legal societies.)

The public theatres were somewhat like the pictures shown here (I have particularly noted which is contemporary evidence and which a later conjectural reconstruction). One may remember that the building as a whole was more or less in doughnut-shape — "a wooden O," as Shakespeare phrased it — and that the tiers of balconies with pit below were an inheritance from the inn-yards, the only play-places the companies had known. The stage naturally varied in the several houses, though its half-roof and its curtained "inner stage" seem to have been fixed features. This is obviously a type of playhouse suited to virtuoso acting, with a platform thrust out into the midst of the audiences. Only a small area is curtained, and there is no opportunity for compelling scenic effects; it is a neutral architectural stage as distinguished from the Italian picture stage.

The changes of scene are accomplished in the imagination of the spectator, stirred by the descriptive verses of the dramatist.

In a single act of Kyd's *The Spanish Tragedy*, for instance, there are fifteen scenes played presumably in nine " places." Some times, it seems, signboards were put up to tell the audience the scene of the action; but it is likely that ordinarily the lines and the spectator's wit were sufficient guide. Stage " decoration " was not then a consideration. And yet the whole aspect of the theatre, stage, auditorium, actors, and rich costumes, must have been gay, spirited, rich. Nothing else would have served in an era so abounding in life, so adventurous, so self-assertive.

Playgoing was not the orderly activity that it is today. We go to the theatre quietly, to listen attentively to a half-literary exercise. The Elizabethans went to the public theatres boisterously, with little reverence or consideration for dramatist or actor, the dandies anxious to show themselves superior to the entertainment by which they were passing idle hours, aiming at *conspicuous* attendance, and the groundlings in the pit offering vociferous approval or disapproval at every opportunity.

The flag flying over the building to signify " a play is on " brought, indeed, a strange audience: a pit crowd of apprentices playing " hookey," town idlers, a few shameless women, travellers intent on seeing the sights, fighters off duty, seafarers ashore, etc.; and above in the balconies students and poets and a few shrewd burghers or minor Court hangers-on (perhaps with ladies, who dared come only under masculine protection); and on the stage itself the fops and beaux and noblemen, as anxious to be seen as to see, interrupting the action if they willed, smoking and talking and displaying their figures and their finery. To this queer mixture of cultured and uneducated, of lowly and exalted, of those who came for love of drama and those who came to show their superiority, the Elizabethan drama was shaped. No doubt about this vigorous audience enjoying spirited verse or swift action. No doubt about its vociferous reaction if the lines or the action became too slow or too tame. Coarseness went down agreeably, but literary fineness might kill comedy or tragedy. If anything on the stage bored, the audience took to the dice or cards; and always there was much drinking of ale and widespread eating of fruits and sweets.

There are evidences enough, too, that audiences made more di-

A drawing of the Swan Theatre in London about 1596, by Johann deWitt. One of the few uncontested bits of contemporary evidence regarding the form of the Elizabethan playhouse.

rect and violent protest if they really disliked the performance; and it might be a quarrel that had nothing to do with play or actors that ended in disorder and blood-letting. The theatre was part and parcel of the active, feverish, and reckless social life of the time. It has already been noted how Marlowe and Greene went down to deaths attributable to the license and recklessness of the age; many another, playwright and actor and theatre patron, was involved no less in wild adventure, tavern profligacy, and violent quarrel. The theatre that knew how to value gentle Will Shakespeare's dramas, was little short of riotous — next of kin to the nearby bear-baiting rings (structurally related, too) and not too far removed from the " stews " — which the nineteenth century more delicately and illuminatingly termed " the disorderly houses."

The actors however were no despised class, as had been their lot in other places and times. At present they were men's companies, with specially trained boys to take the female parts. In Spain, already women had come to the " regular " stage, even in the none too decorous corral theatres; but not in England. To be sure, there had been amateur actresses in the Miracle plays, and Court ladies played in the masques, but the public playhouse was considered no place for them. The guild actors had often been paid — there are records like " 6d for God," and " 8d for acting Lucifer." But these Elizabethan players are professionals, men studying their art with the double aim of pleasing the groundlings and satisfying that discriminating taste that had somehow grown up vigorous and true.

From Hamlet's famous speech to the actors, we may gather an impression of the playing of the times, from the player who " outHerod's Herod," the " robustious periwig-pated fellow " tearing " a passion to tatters, to very rags, to split the ears of the groundlings," from him to the actors who " in the very torrent, tempest, and, I might say, the whirlwind of passion . . . acquire and beget a temperance that may give it smoothness " — and who speak the speech " trippingly on the tongue." No doubt Shakespeare suffered from fellow-actors who " have so strutted and bellowed, that I have thought some of nature's journeymen had made men, and not made them well, they imitated humanity so abominably."

But while acting then was certainly artificial, stilted, and bombastic if judged by any realistic standard, we may note Hamlet's words about discretion and modesty and temperance as indications of a true interpretative art.

To this vigorous-violent theatre in 1588 or thereabouts came William Shakespeare, from his idyllic home village, Stratford-upon-Avon. One might be wiser to begin, *perhaps* he came to London in 1588 or thereabouts; for a great deal that is commonly put down as fact about Shakespeare's life is inference or based on vague documents and opinions. The story goes that William Shakespeare was born in 1564, son of a butcher who also was a respected town officer, and business-man in several collateral lines; that he attended the local grammar school for a few years, probably gaining a knowledge of Latin; that he worked as apprentice to his father in the butchering business, when the latter was reduced to that trade again by losses in other fields; that he married Ann Hathaway, eight years his senior, when he was a youth midway between eighteen and nineteen; that he was not very happy in family life, and that he ran wild for a time and capped his misdemeanors by poaching on the neighboring estates of Sir Thomas Lucy — and that therefore he ran away from Stratford and eventually found his way to London and the doors of the theatre. There is even less substantiated evidence that he began by holding the horses outside the playhouse (the dandies came from town on horseback); but the tale offers a pleasant starting-point for a dramatic rise-from-the-lowly story. For Shakespeare was soon play-tinker to Burbage's company, and soon an actor.

That he began his serious literary activity by doctoring and adapting old plays, there seems little doubt. It was a common occupation; and there is so much working over even of new manuscripts that some plays seem likely never to be properly ascribed. Peele, Greene, and Lodge have so puzzled later scholars by their collaborative work that no peace is possible where they are studied; and to this day there is only conjecture as to what parts of *Henry VI* came from Shakespeare's pen, and what from Marlowe's or perhaps from those of Greene and Peele, and as to the extent of Shakespeare's service in preparing *Titus Andronicus* for the stage. In that day the manager bought a play outright from an author, for a lump sum; and it was his privilege to have it improved as much as possible before performance.

But Shakespeare became known as an actor before he gained fame as a playwright. He seems to have been a good actor — that about sums up our knowledge of his playing. His name appears in several lists of players, and someone recorded that he " did act exceedingly well." There is almost unanimous praise of him off the stage, however, and we may picture him as amiable, witty and well-liked, as, indeed, the " sweet master Shakespeare " mentioned in a play of 1601. As to the measure in which he had studied his craft of acting, we have already found indication in the speech of Hamlet to the players. To complete what little we may have here of biography, Shakespeare worked for twenty years on the London stage, as actor and playwright, prospered, bought a part ownership of the producing company that had aided his major triumphs, and retired to Stratford-upon-Avon to spend the last five years of his life in respected ease. He died in 1616.

Shakespeare as dramatist is by so much the greater figure than any other mentioned in these pages, that one despairs even of suggesting the many aspects of his genius. If we are to follow out our plan of glancing at all the theatres of all the nations, we needs must be content with a few words about his mastery in each of the major fields of playwriting, and in each of the forms of theatrical effectiveness, and with a very few quotations to remind us of his " poetry in drama " that so surpasses any other in the language. One's bewilderment arises not so much from the number of plays that may justly be termed masterpieces and immortal — there are hardly a half dozen of the thirty-seven that we would willingly omit from any compilation of the world's best half-hundred dramas; it is rather the infinite variety of them, the richness within each play in its own kind; and perhaps most of all the extraordinary gallery of human portraits formed by the " characters."

For who should say that Hamlet, the most-played figure on the world stage, noble, complex, grievously mad or terribly sane, is more theatrical and more familiar than Falstaff, drunken brag-

gart and beloved sensualist; that tragic Othello or piteous Lear
is more immortal than Rosalind or Portia or Viola. What other
figures crowd into the mind's eye! — clear, human, bringing dark
shadow or smiling reminiscence, as brightly etched as if we had
met them but today: Romeo, Juliet, the Nurse, Shylock, Macbeth
and Lady Macbeth, the Witches, Bottom, Puck, Iago, Desdemona,
Dogberry, Sir Toby, Sir Andrew and Malvolio, Petruchio and
Kate, Ophelia, Polonius, Ariel, Prospero, Cæsar, Cassius, Brutus,

Portion of Visscher's pictorial map of London in 1616, showing the exteriors of two theatres. The flags up mean "performance today." [From
a reproduction in *The Stage Year Book*, 1927.]

the Merry Wives. Even then one has not mentioned the gallery
of noble historical portraits, in a series of Chronicle Plays that lifted
the form to a place beside human-life tragedy. And yet what an
amazing variety, what unforgettable characterizations! These
figures have gone into everyday currency, are of our daily living
as no others save those of the Bible. Every schoolboy knows them,
philosophers sustain themselves by rereading their adventures
year by year. And, oh, yes! the plays in which they appear are
performed quite regularly in those countries where the artistic
sensibilities of audiences are keen, and minds eager.

I take it that I would only be insulting my readers by retelling the story of the half-pastoral, half-comedy *As You Like It,* or the part farce-comedy, part tender idyll *Twelfth Night, or What You Will,* or the tragi-comic tale of those so-jumbled characters in *The Merchant of Venice.* One might, indeed, outline a drama in each of those sorts so ably listed by Polonius: " tragedy, comedy, history, pastoral, pastoral-comical, historical-pastoral, tragical-historical, tragical-comical-historical-pastoral, scene individable, or poem unlimited." But you know them all in Shakespeare's originals; and besides, no other plays quite so successfully defy retelling — escape, in their flavor and essence, so completely from the bare recounted structure.

Indeed, there are those who say that Shakespeare's dramas exist too much in characterization and poetry and telling incident and felicitous conceit, that by that token the structure is weak, the play as a whole not truly theatrical. But if one has a perspective on the history of the stage in all times, one may well conclude that it is the theatre of today that is too limited, too restricted, to hold so much of dramatic incident and rich embroidery and far-riding imagination. The box-stage, the picture setting and the proscenium-frame playhouse are inadequate to compass so much that transcends painted picture, realistic situation, and personal acting. Shakespeare is a challenge to any producer; and the man who sticks by the limitations of the still-lingering nineteenth century theatre is impotent in the face of that challenge: and usually he sidesteps by simply saying that Shakespeare is untheatric. But in his own time his plays were supreme upon the stage, were known in performance only — were designed in every feature to *acting.* And they give promise today of becoming supreme again, till some new Shakespeare arises, when the modern stage completes the process of making itself as free, as sheer-for-acting (though not necessarily as bare) as was the Elizabethan. Meantime Shakespeare's texts upon the shelf transcend most other poetry, theatrical and untheatrical; and we do see the plays performed occasionally, well or indifferently.

We may grant, indeed, that the poetic genius, welling up, stretched the dramatic structure awry at times. *A Midsummer Night's Dream* seems mixed and formless and *The Tempest* hardly achieves dramatic unity; but were ever gigantic faults so greatly atoned? For the rest, let us recall, by Shakespeare's own lines, the excellencies of the verse and the perfect fitness of that verse to characters.

Even the "lyrics" are expressions of feeling integral to the character-plot. For what could better sum up the pastoral spirit that freshens *As You Like It* than the song:

> Under the greenwood tree
> Who loves to lie with me,
> And turn his merry note
> Unto the sweet bird's throat,
> Come hither, come hither, come hither. . .

Or at the very extreme from this, call to mind those lines of Lear that so picture a King basely abused, gone mad, but still a King, in the scene beginning:

> LEAR
> Ay, every inch a king:
> When I do stare, see how the subject quakes . . .

And the change in the next scene:

> LEAR
> Pray do not mock me:
> I am a very foolish fond old man . . .

The opening lines of a play may reveal in their overtones what is to be the "feel" of the drama; as these in *Twelfth Night:*

> DUKE
> If music be the food of love, play on;
> Give me excess of it, that, surfeiting,
> The appetite may sicken, and so die.
> That strain again! it had a dying fall:
> O, it came o'er my ear like the sweet sound
> That breathes upon a bank of violets,
> Stealing and giving odor! Enough; no more. . .

But when one begins to quote, and starts thinking after these revealing character-passages, so many come that surely one may see there is no more of wonder in the gallery of portraits than in the written verses. Shall it be Portia's "The quality of mercy

is not strained," or Othello's " Speak of me as I am," or that scene
between Macbeth and Lady Macbeth wherein he fears his hand
will " the multitudinous seas incarnadine "; or his cry at her death:

> She should have died hereafter;
> There would have been a time for such a word.
> To-morrow, and to-morrow, and to-morrow,
> Creeps in this petty pace from day to day,
> To the last syllable of recorded time;
> And all our yesterdays have lighted fools
> The way to dusty death. Out, out, brief candle!
> Life's but a walking shadow, a poor player
> That struts and frets his hour upon the stage
> And then is heard no more; it is a tale
> Told by an idiot, full of sound and fury,
> Signifying nothing.

For the rest, let us take one play, the *Hamlet* that is so compact as drama, as theatrical tragedy-of-blood, as character-study,
and yet so packed with thoughtful phrases that no other mine
yields so much that goes into street usage, that comes with familiar
ring to the common ear, that sustains so richly him who rereads a
hundredth time. Let us note merely how the thought, the beauty,
the human pathos belong theatrically to the stage character speaking, and to those in dramatic impact with him.

OPHELIA

> O, what a noble mind is here o'erthrown!
> The courtier's, soldier's, scholar's, eye, tongue, sword:
> The expectancy and rose of the fair state,
> The glass of fashion and the mould of form,
> The observed of all observers, quite, quite down!
> And I, of ladies most deject and wretched,
> That sucked the honey of his music vows,
> Now see that noble and most sovereign reason,
> Like sweet bells jangled, out of tune and harsh;
> The unmatch'd form and feature of blown youth
> Blasted with ecstasy: O, woe is me,
> To have seen what I have seen, see what I see!

And the King characterizes himself in two lines:

> O, my offence is rank, it smells to Heaven;
> It hath the primal eldest curse upon it. . .

But nothing in the language equals, for meat, the soliloquies of Hamlet. I pass over the longer one beginning " O, what a rogue and peasant slave am I," in order to quote another in full, together with its context; this to illustrate finally how Shakespeare wedded poetry to drama, not merely decorating a plot but so binding up character, story, action, and beauty of verse that here is a very summit of the theatric art:

HAMLET

To be, or not to be: that is the question:
Whether 'tis nobler in the mind to suffer
The slings and arrows of outrageous fortune,
Or to take arms against a sea of troubles,
And by opposing end them. To die: to sleep;
No more; and by a sleep to say we end
The heart-ache, and the thousand natural shocks
That flesh is heir to, 'tis a consummation
Devoutly to be wished. To die, to sleep;
To sleep: perchance to dream: aye there's the rub;
For in that sleep of death what dreams may come,
When we have shuffled off this mortal coil,
Must give us pause: there's the respect
That makes calamity of so long life;
For who would bear the whips and scorns of time,
The oppressor's wrong, the proud man's contumely,
The pangs of despised love, the law's delay,
The insolence of office, and the spurns
That patient merit of the unworthy takes,
When he himself might his quietus make
With a bare bodkin? who would fardels bear,
To grunt and sweat under a weary life,
But that the dread of something after death,
The undiscover'd country from whose bourne
No traveller returns, puzzles the will,
And makes us rather bear those ills we have
Than fly to others that we know not of?
Thus conscience does make cowards of us all,
And thus the native hue of resolution
Is sicklied o'er with the pale cast of thought,
And enterprises of great pitch and moment
With this regard their currents turn awry
And lose the name of action. Soft you now!
The fair Ophelia! Nymph, in thy orisons
Be all my sins remembered.

OPHELIA

Good my lord,
How does your honor for this many a day?

HAMLET

I humbly thank you: well, well, well.

OPHELIA

My lord, I have remembrances of yours,
That I have longed long to re-deliver;
I pray you, now receive them.

HAMLET

No, not I
I never gave you aught.

OPHELIA

My honor'd lord, you know right well you did;
And with them words of so sweet breath composed
As made the things more rich: their perfume lost,
Take these again; for to the noble mind
Rich gifts wax poor when givers prove unkind.
There, my lord.

In this play, too, one sees prose (which had been brought to the uses of the stage but a few years since) become an instrument flexible, expressive, pat. You may browse through the Polonius and the grave-digging scenes, and find the thoughtful humor in this prose. Nor let us forget, our study being theatre, not mere texts, that the last line of this tragic play of Hamlet is " Go bid the soldiers shoot " — and after, there is the procession bearing the bodies, and a peal of ordnance without.

The dramatists who followed Shakespeare in the Elizabethan age have suffered in history by being directly overshadowed by his fame. It is wholly natural that students should turn first to him who sums up in one group of plays the tendencies of the age, who packs into his dramas every sort of stage excellency of the times. And yet Ben Jonson and John Fletcher and John Webster would be outstanding giants in any other era.[1] When one puts down,

[1] The theatre and drama of this period are no more bewilderingly rich than the books on the subject. Most exhaustive and scholarly, about the theatre, is E. K. Chambers' *The Elizabethan Stage* (Oxford, 1923); but the student should consult also the more specialized studies by W. J. Lawrence, by Victor E. Albright and by William Poel; as also Ashley H. Thorndike's *Shakespeare's Theatre* (New York, 1916). The

also, the names of the additional practising playwrights — George Chapman, Francis Beaumont, Thomas Dekker, Thomas Middleton, John Ford, James Shirley, Philip Massinger, Thomas Heywood, Samuel Rowley — there is such a range of rich achievement as no later age can match. There will be not so many names of notable dramatists to record out of the following three centuries of English theatre history. But again, Shakespeare tops them in every field, tragedy, comedy, chronicle. They are of the same richly active theatre, vigorous, wide-riding, fearing limitation and dullness more than extravagance and violence. As a matter of fact they began to step out of the realm of gorgeous adventure and fun into the field where coarseness and license and melodrama rule. But there was immortal achievement too.

Ben Jonson, more learned than Shakespeare, more a commanding figure among his contemporaries, more a man of the world, was decidedly inferior as a tragedy-writer. Perhaps he knew too much about the classics, and let theory interfere with practice. Thus there is point to the old epigram about Shakespeare being sent from Heaven, Jonson from College (though really he attended neither University). In comedy, on the other hand, he scored a success almost comparable to that of Shakespeare. His plays were less human, less tenderly memorable, less nobly clothed; but in a new field, satirical comedy, they were supreme — and they marked out a path for future dramatists.

The "comedy of humours" which Jonson put forward, no less in practice than in broadcast theory, was a genre in which the sources of action were sought in character rather than situation. Incident grew out of character, was no longer developed for its own sake. Moreover, Jonson maintained, in every man there is a ruling trait, a bias of character — in short, a "humour" — which is the very fountain of comedy. And with *Everyman in His Humour* and *Volpone* and *Poetaster* he proceeded to

---

standard history of drama of the time is Adolphus William Ward's *A History of English Dramatic Literature to the Death of Queen Anne* (London and New York, 1899). *The Cambridge History of English Literature*, edited by A. W. Ward and A. R. Waller, in 15 volumes (Cambridge, 1907–1916), contains many excellent but scattered chapters on English dramatic literature. The most useful complete view of British drama is in Allardyce Nicoll's excellent and authoritative *British Drama* (London, 1925). The standard biography of Shakespeare is Sidney Lee's *A Life of William Shakespeare* (London, 1925).

satirize such weaknesses, leaving to posterity dramas that interest today almost as much as they did in Elizabeth's reign; and *The Alchemist* and *Bartholomew Fair* are hardly less read. It happened that some of Jonson's contemporaries thought they detected in the humours of certain of his characters some of their own less admirable traits, and he soon found himself involved in a bitter stage quarrel, play satirizing rival playwright and rival answering in kind. But Ben Jonson lives for posterity, whereas most of the competing " comedies of humours " remain undisturbed on the shelves, if they got into print at all.

Still Dekker and Marston, the particular antagonists of Jonson in " the War of the Theatres," wrote plays that not only were important in their time but have outlived those of many fellow dramatists. Dekker's *Shoemakers' Holiday,* a realistic comedy, and his *Old Fortunatus,* a romantic comedy, still afford good boisterous fun, and *The Honest Whore* lives by right of sincerity and unusualness. Marston, however, is best remembered for his collaboration with the recently hostile Jonson, and with George Chapman, on the comedy *Eastward Ho.* Chapman approached Jonson in the field of satirical comedy, and put exceptional vigor without very deep characterization into his tragedies — but his name has been repeated oftener for his translation of Homer than for his plays. That he occasionally touched heights in his verse may be illustrated briefly in these lines from the comedy *All Fools:*

> How blind is pride! What eagles we are still
> In matters that belong to other men —
> What beetles in our own. . .

Thomas Heywood, dubbed by Lamb " our prose Shakespeare," contributed to the stage a domestic play so direct and human that it is marked as the best of its type in those times, *A Woman Killed with Kindness;* and in comedy Massinger contributed *A New Way to Pay Old Debts,* built around the character of Sir Giles Overreach, which holds its place on the boards today. One other more or less isolated play, Webster's *The Duchess of Malfi,* has stood out in later years; it is a violent but often moving drama, the very play to mark for us how tragedy, which had been ennobled and refined by Marlowe and Shakespeare, now turned back again toward melodramatic and rhetorical ways.

Francis Beaumont and John Fletcher are the most notable team of collaborators among English dramatists. There are those who say that Massinger had more to do with " Beaumont and Fletcher " plays than ever did Beaumont. However the credit be divided, here was joint work that left no mark of the double origin. Nor did the partnership result in drama in a limited field. *The Maid's Tragedy* may be surpassed in fame by the mock-heroic *The Knight of the Burning Pestle* or the tragi-comedy *The Knight of Malta,* or by the straight comedy *Rule a Wife and Have a Wife* (which is more often ascribed to Fletcher alone). But here is the most successful collaboration in the history of the " regular " stage. If there was the late Eliza-bethan excess of passion in some of the resulting dramas, we may call Beaumont and Fletcher blessed for their burlesque of that very quality in *The Knight.* Still, let us realize that we are well down the other side from the eminence that was the high Elizabethan drama.

In thirty years, roughly from 1590 to 1620, the stage had flowered, had seen Shakespeare triumph and go, had seen almost all the playwrights and plays that have been mentioned. Life in those years had moved swiftly, adventurously, gorgeously. The theatre had risen to be, *par excellence,* the interpreter of the time and its mirror. The great poets were dramatists; often the great dramatists were actors, or resident play-doctors. The stage was at the heart of life. London was still a mediæval town of fewer than two hundred thousand inhabitants; but the playwrights brought to its doors Italy and France and Spain, and the fabled lands of the ancients and others unknown to either earlier poets or contemporary geographers. Nor was their offered treasure more notable for these exotic riches than for those mined from a new understanding of the human heart and human foibles. Eng-land had had her era of exploration, expansion, richer living. The dramatists had explored and found riches matched in no other field.

During all these years when the public theatres were so pros-pering, so enriching London life, there were other theatres at court and other productions by students, boy companies and amateur groups, as we shall see when we inquire into the masques and plays at court. But it was the drama designed for the original " wooden-O " playhouses, and a half dozen others designed almost in their image, for groundling apprentices and balconied burghers and fops on the stage, that the greatest of English plays were written.

The exceptional new roofed playhouse had come in, and doubtless there were increasing concessions to the demand for richer Italian-style settings — perhaps only more costumes and properties at first, then attempts at suggestive " scenery." But in general the Elizabethan platform-for-acting persisted through the great days. The play was markedly a drama-for-acting, designed with little thought for scenic dressing or for reading. At this time playwright, actor, producer, and audience were at one in spirit, collaborated together for entertainment, somehow opened the channels from the well-springs of genius — became part of the high, noble, poetic theatre that our minds conjure up at the mention of Shakespeare.

Two contemporary drawings of seventeenth century stages.
[From title pages of *Roxana and Messalina.*]

CHAPTER XIII

The Puritans and the Chapel of Satan

AS THAT portion of the kingdom of Anti-Christ known as Theatre-land was further and further explored by the Puritans of Sixteenth and Seventeenth Century England, such iniquities and blasphemies were found seated therein as had scarcely been hinted at by scandalized Tertullian back in Roman times. And indeed the problem of " the theatre evil " had become more complex. The moralists under the late Emperors, after all, had been fighting against a stage inheriting directly from paganism — if religious in origin, then only by grace of Heathenish Gods. But the Elizabethan stage inherited from the Christian Church, was successor to Christian shows, and the Puritans were Christian if anti-Papist. Unlike the decadent Roman stage, too, this one linked up with learned people, with poets, with nobles. But how much more horrible, then, that it should be so lewd, so profane!

The crimes of the theatre, as set forth in Puritan sermons and pamphlets, included these: emptying the churches, perpetuating pagan custom, distorting truth, showing forth profane, seditious, and bawdy stories, teaching knavery and lechery, causing God to visit the plague on London, leading youths into idleness and extravagance, affording meeting-place for harlots and customers, aiding the pope, currupting maidens and chaste wives, undermining fortitude and seriousness, etc., etc.

The theatre was now thrice damned from the theological standpoint, and even if it had any merits it would be offensive in the sight of God: for had not the Devil invented it, had not he given it to the pagans, had not these pagans bequeathed it to the papists, who allowed it in the House of God? " The ungodly Plays and

Interludes so rife in this nation: what are they but a bastard of
Babylon, a daughter of error and confusion, a hellish device (the
Devil's own recreation to mock at holy things) by him delivered
to the Heathen, from them to the Papists, and from them to
us? . . . Now they bring religion and holy things upon the
stage: no marvel though the worthiest and mightiest men escape
not, when God himself is so abused." Thus spoke William
Crashaw in a sermon, in 1607 — when Shakespeare was acting and
writing plays. And as early as 1577 Thomas White had preached
as follows:

Look upon the common plays in London, and see the multitude that
flocketh to them and followeth them: behold the sumptuous Theatre houses,
a continual monument of London's prodigality and folly. . . Shall I
reckon up the monstrous birds that breed in this nest? without doubt I
am ashamed, and I should surely offend your chaste ears: but the old
world is matched, and Sodom overcome, for more horrible enormities, and
swelling sins are set out by those stages, than every man thinks for, or some
would believe, if I should paint them out in their colors: without doubt
you can scantly name me a sin, that by that sink is not set a-gog: theft
and whoredom; pride and prodigality; villainy and blasphemy; these three
couples of hellhounds never cease barking there, and bite many, so as they
are uncurable ever after. . .

Mentioning the Theatre and the Curtain, then just built, John
Northbrooke in 1577 wrote:

Satan hath not a more speedy way, and fitter school to work and teach
his desire, to bring men and women into the snare of concupiscence and
filthy lusts of wicked whoredom, than those places, and plays, and theatres
are . . . It hath stricken such a blind zeal into the hearts of the people,
that they shame not to say, and affirm openly, that plays are as good as sermons, and that they learn as much or more at a play, than they do at God's
word preached. . . Many can tarry at a vain play two or three hours,
whenas they will not abide scarce one hour at a sermon. . . In their
plays you shall learn all things that appertain to craft, mischief, deceits and
filthiness, etc. If you will learn how to be false and deceive your husbands,
or husbands their wives, how to play the harlot, to obtain one's love, how
to ravish, how to beguile, how to betray, to flatter, lie, swear, forswear, how
to allure to whoredom, how to murder, how to poison, how to disobey and
rebel against princes, to consume treasures prodigally, to move to lusts, to
ransack and spoil cities and towns, to be idle, to blaspheme, to sing filthy
songs of love, to speak filthily, to be proud, how to mock, scoff and deride

any nation . . . shall you not learn, then, at such interludes how to practise them?

Besides this liberal education offered at the theatre, there were
other teachings and effects that seemed to the Puritans conducive
to evil — including, one knows not why, the sorrow evoked by
tragedy, and laughter. In 1582 Stephen Gosson wrote:

The beholding of troubles and miserable laughters that are in Tragedies,
drive us to immoderate sorrow, heaviness, womanish weeping and mourn-
ing, whereby we become lovers of dumps, and lamentation, both enemies
to fortitude. Comedies so tickle our senses with a pleasanter vein, that
they make us lovers of laughter, and pleasure, without any mean, both foes
to temperance. What schooling is this? Sometime you shall see nothing
but the adventures of an amorous knight, passing from country to country
for the love of his lady, encountering many a terrible monster made of
brown paper. . . When the soul of your plays is either mere trifles, or
Italian bawdery, or wooing of gentlewomen, what are we taught?

What indeed!

Anthony Munday (or another) in the famous *A Second and
Third Blast of Retrait from Plaies and Theaters*, of 1580, wrote
concerning Sunday performances:

The Lord is never so ill served as on holy-days. For then hell breaks
loose. Then we permit our youth to have their swing. . . Whosoever
shall visit the Chapel of Satan, I mean the Theatre, shall find there no
want of young ruffians, nor lack of harlots, utterly past all shame: who
press to the forefronts of the scaffolds, to the end to show their "impu-
dencie," and to be as an object to all men's eyes.

But let us see the indictment summed up in Phillip Stubbes'
The Anatomy of Abuses:

Do these mockers and flouters of his Majesty, these dissembling *Hipo-
crites,* and flattering *Gnatoes,* think to escape unpunished? beware, therefore, you masking players, you painted sepulchres, you double dealing ambodexters, be warned betimes, and like good computists, cast your accounts
before, what will be the reward thereof in the end, lest God destroy you
in his wrath: abuse God no more, corrupt his people no longer with your
dregs, and intermingle not his blessed word with such profane vanities. . .
If their plays be of profane matters, then tend they to the dishonor of God,
and nourishing of vice, both which are damnable. So that whether they be
the one or the other, they are quite contrary to the word of grace, and
sucked out of the Devil's teats to nourish us in idolatry, heathenry, and

sin. And therefore they, carrying the note, or brand, of God his curse upon their backs which way soever they go, are to be hissed out of all Christian kingdoms, if they will have Christ to dwell amongst them. . . For so often as they go to those houses where players frequent, they go to Venus' palace, and Satan's synagogue, to worship devils, and betray Jesus Christ. . . Do they not draw the people from hearing the word of God, from godly lectures and sermons? for you shall have them flock thither, thick and threefold, when the church of God be bare and empty. Do they not maintain bawdery, infinite foolery, and renew the remembrances of heathen idolatry? Do they not induce whoredom and uncleanness? nay, are they not rather plain devourers of maidenly virginity and chastity? For proof whereof, but mark the flocking and running to Theatres and Curtains, dayly and hourly, night and day, time and tide, to see Plays and Interludes; where such wanton gestures, such bawdy speeches, such laughing and fleering, such kissing and bussing, such clipping and culling, such winking and glancing of wanton eyes, and the like, is used, as is wonderful to behold. Then, these goodly pageants being done, every mate sorts to his mate, every one brings another homeward of their way very friendly. . . And whereas you say there are good examples to be learned in them, truly so there are: if you will learn falsehood; if you will learn cosenage; if you will learn to deceive; if you will learn to play the Hypocrite, to cog, lie, and falsify; if you will learn to jest, laugh, and fleer, to grin, to nod and mow; if you will learn to play the vice, to swear, tear, and blaspheme both Heaven and Earth: if you will learn to become a bawd, unclean, and to devirginate maids, to deflower honest wives: if you will learn to murder, slay, kill, pick, steal, rob and rove . . . if you will learn to play the whoremaster, the glutton, drunkard, or incestuous person: if you will learn to become proud, haughty and arrogant; and, finally, if you will learn to contemn God and all his laws, to care neither for heaven nor hell, and to commit all kind of sin and mischief, you need to go to no other school, for all these good Examples may you see painted before your eyes in interludes and plays. . . Away therefore with this so infamous an art! . . . The Lord of his mercy open the eyes of the magistrates to pluck down these places of abuse, that God may be honored and their consciences disburdened.

In answer to these blasts that the terribly sincere and militantly righteous Puritans loosed against the theatres in the years 1550–1620, the dramatists wrote pamphlet after pamphlet; [1] but after all,

[1] E. K. Chambers in his invaluable *The Elizabethan Stage* (4 vols., Oxford, 1923) prints extracts from sixty-three defences and attacks (from which I have taken my quotations), and adds one hundred and sixty extracts from " documents of control." The books listed in the last bibliographical note all cover the matter briefly; but for a more exhaustive treatment of all elements in the period we are now entering, the reader should consult Allardyce Nicoll's *A History of Restoration Drama* (Cambridge, 1928), and the same author's supplementary works *A History of Early 18th Century Drama* and

the best answer is in the plays of Marlowe, Shakespeare, Jonson. (Other and more bitter answers were in the caricatures of Puritans in scores of played comedies.)

Here we have come to a time when the line is more sharply drawn than ever before between pious workers and those who live loosely or are complacent about their easy-going neighbors. Just after the English Church had accomplished its divorce from Rome, the reformers had used the drama as a weapon for flaying the Pope and Papists (you remember *Kyng Johan,* written by the Protestant Bishop of Ossory, known as " Bilious Bale "); but now the theatre is definitely down on the side of the anti-Puritans. If it is on the side of the loose-livers, it is also on the side of laughter and high poetry and purging tragedy.

Crashaw in 1610 grouped together " the Devil, Papists, and players." This new alignment may serve to remind us that the Chinese had put special legal restrictions upon actors, barbers, and slaves, while the Romans grouped thieves, panderers, deserters, actors, and reciters in an *infamis* class; while in India, where there was a noble class of players, another group was rated with butchers, fishermen, hangmen, and scavengers, and thus had to live outside the town and pass on the far side of the street from the nobles. In England as early as 1545 " common players " had been officially classed with " ruffians, vagabonds, masterless men, and evil-disposed persons." And almost throughout the glorious time of Elizabethan drama, the civic authorities were with the preachers in the desire and effort to " hiss out of all Christian kingdoms " these " double-dealing ambodexters." What, then, saved them from suppression, exile, and extinction?

The Court of Elizabeth, by tolerance and occasionally by protection, gave the theatres a certain standing, gave the dramatists confidence, permitted gentlemen to go to the play with ease of conscience. This Court was quick enough to strike at a play-

---

A History of Late 18th Century Drama (Cambridge, 1925 and 1927). Another volume by Professor Nicoll, the richly illustrated *The Development of the Theatre* (London, 1927), contains the best treatise on the changes in the physical theatre and stage decoration at this time — as throughout the story of the English theatre. For a brief record of acting and actors, see *A Short History of the English Stage,* by R. Farquharson Sharp (London and New York, 1909). Lily B. Campbell's *Scenes and Machines on the English Stage during the Renaissance* (Cambridge, 1923) contains exceptionally rich materials about the staging of the masques.

wright or to punish actors if an unseemly criticism of royalty or any seditious utterance cropped up in a play. But the Queen and the nobles were, in sympathy, on the theatre's side. (Later, of course, the consideration became political: Court against Puritan for control of England.) And in at least one notable case a little later, the governing powers stepped in to punish terribly a heckler of the stages:

In 1632, after seven years' labor on the work, William Prynne, an intolerant moralist and zealot, the very type-figure of Puritan, published *Histrio-Mastix,* an eleven-hundred-page blast against the stage and its immoralities. If any sort of crime had ever been committed in or about the theatre or by persons to be connected in name with the stage, Prynne was sure to find the record — and embalm it for all time in this classic of abuse. The material was not new, of course, to the post-Elizabethan readers. But it happened that the luckless author inserted — in reference to a disturbance over one of the earliest appearances of professional women actors in London (*French* ones, of course) — a remark that women players were " notorious whores." At the moment of publication, Queen Henrietta Maria was rehearsing for an amateur performance of a pastoral. Prynne was stood in the pillory, condemned to life imprisonment and a fine, branded S. L. (seditious libeller) on both cheeks — and his ears were cut off.

From which one may judge that not all the hatred, intolerance, and militancy existed on one side. And, indeed, one who loves the theatre with more than a passing or a commercial affection, who wants to see the stage unfettered, may still shake a head dubiously over what happened in the Chapels of Satan within the fifty years after Shakespeare's time. For there is little after Ben Jonson and Shirley and Beaumont and Fletcher that has its value today; except those comedies of the Restoration which mix graceful wit and corruption of the spirit more cunningly than any other body of drama in the world.

The bitterness that has existed between theatre-artists and moralists since the period immediately preceding Christ's birth would not have persisted so unremittingly if there had not been wellnigh unbridgeable gulfs between the two parties. For one thing, Christian mankind is temperamentally divided, one half mistrusting the pleasures of the senses, suspicious of laughter, eager to prohibit and suppress the lighter, gayer, more colorful elements of life; the other half clinging to pagan enjoyments, willing to take chances with life, adventurous, valuing sensuous and emotional experience as among the sweetest joys in living. The Puritan, moreover, distrusts frankness; and he knows there is nothing so dangerous as truth. His first impulse is to limit knowledge and experience to a small range, bounded according to a conception of righteous conduct as permitted in the books of a revealed religion.

The artist knows that art, and particularly the theatre, dies of prohibitions and limitation. He fights instinctively against censorship. And yet his battle is made confusing because of betrayals within his own camp. In seventeenth century England, the voluptuaries, the cynics, and the commercialists carried freedom to an extreme that makes many plays of the period unpleasant reading to 999 out of every 1000 readers today. In our own twentieth century managers and playwrights, with nothing but money in mind, put on the stage sensational pieces, parading violence, nudity, and sexual perversion — and render infinitely harder the way of those who want simple freedom. For us here, the point is that these commercialists carry drama out to a topical or expositional region where subject-matter so intrudes, so absorbs the spectator, that there is no longer any question of the art of the theatre. And if one reads through some of the more successfully suppressed plays of the time of the Stuarts — not only those that by their finer qualities have survived in the Mermaid editions and similar collections — one may feel that then a great many people were using the stage simply for the exhibition of pornographic situation and filth; that the battle of those who wanted only freedom for the flowering of an art was badly complicated by the pushing pack that smelled gold in the exploitation of bawdy tales and suggestive situation.

The temper of the Puritans was such, of course, that a dozen Shakespeares could not have excused the existence of the theatre; but on the other side there seems to have been an unfortunate pouring of all energy into counter-blasts, when a little might so well have been spent in excluding the crowds of harlots from the audiences, and in driving the filth-exploiting producers and actors from the stage. But whatever had been the truth in Shakespeare's time, the theatre was now on the down-track, in many senses. Curiously enough, the plague that periodically swept over London proved the best ally of the Puritans. Several times it accomplished the temporary closing of the playhouses.

In the long history of the contest between those who believe in a free stage and those who favor prohibition or censorship, this seventeenth century England provides the most vivid chapter. Puritanism never else was either so inexorable or so powerful; the stage was never else so licentious while still sheltering great dramatic art. The struggle ended with the Puritans closing all theatres in 1642; and except for the hang-over to Restoration times, there was never afterwards a period of such bitter battle. We have today our exploiting producers who cloak pornography under " realism "; but they are so much the exception that we may feel sure that " the common authorities " will find ways to suppress them without burdening the whole theatre with censorship. We may wonder at the open and apparently officially arranged soliciting by prostitutes that is customary in some of the larger theatres of Paris even today; but we shrug our shoulders because the matter touches upon the serious drama not at all, is an adjunct to revue-producing. In short, the problem of the evil stage has been greatly simplified with the coming of orderly democratic government and the growth of the spirit of individual responsibility and freedom.

England alone has tried the solution of continued government censorship; and has thus denied its theatre-goers much that has given great, and presumably unharmful, pleasure to audiences in other countries — particularly in the case of plays by Ibsen, Shaw, and other thinker-dramatists. The system has helped to make the English stage the tamest in modern times, with the virtues and the limitations of tameness. But no republican country today would permit such arbitrary censorship. Nothing but general moderation and individual decency can finally solve the problem.

With just a word about the " regular " theatres, let us turn to that queen's pastoral that happened to bring a cruel wrath down upon him who called loudest upon God to destroy the players.

The public theatres continued without important change in form of playhouse or acting or plays until 1642. Boys still acted women's parts in the men's companies. The troupes made long tours outside London. Playwriting gradually lost the old fire, the old poetry, the high Shakespearean and Jonsonian humor. The swift and tricky Spanish plays particularly afforded materials for adaptation. Violence increased in tragedies, coarseness abounded in comedy. The popular theatres made no effort to escape those evils that linked them too closely to the stews. The war with the Puritans went on, until inevitably there came in 1642 the law suppressing all stage plays — and enforcement, since the Puritans now were in power. At the universities playwriting of an academic sort continued, in both English and Latin. But what overshadows the public theatres in interest, out of the times of James I, is the masque-making, and productions at court. For here there came new elements into English staging, and even a text or two that lasted as literature.

Elizabeth in her time had been fond of masques and of the pageant-like shows that celebrated her comings and goings at the towns away from London. She was an inveterate visitor, and many a noble lived impoverished through succeeding years because he entertained his Queen so lavishly during one of her triumphal pilgrimages. Special pastoral plays were staged in her honor; tableau groups were arranged in the castle garden or woods where she might come upon them (see plate at page 261); masques with dancing and music were presented in the castle ballroom; and sometimes the spectacular elements of Italian staging found their way into these English productions. Ever since the time of Henry VIII there had been a taste at court for French and Italian art, and among the expense accounts of Elizabeth's own Master of Revels there are entries indicating built-perspective settings, trick clouds, painted landscape back-drops, grottoes, and similar features in the approved Renaissance tradition. During the time of Henry VIII, Italian architects and painters had been resident at the English Court.

The pastoral drama, so closely related to the masque in its beginnings, is here again bound up with the court entertainments. In Shakespeare the impulse mixed with others, and his romantic comedies became true dramas with a pastoral freshness and sweetness over them. John Fletcher alone mastered the form in that time; he put more real loveliness into *The Faithful Shepherdess* than went into any other English pastoral play. Even while imitating the Italian *Pastor Fido* directly in some particulars he showed originality and above all, great poetic felicity. The work is generally spoken of as a poem rather than drama; and indeed its virtues are largely literary. Ben Jonson wrote *The Sad Shepherdess,* an unfinished play, in which he more successfully domesticated the pastoral into an English scene (Sherwood Forest) and to English characters. But with Jonson as with other English dramatists the impulse passed over into the field of masque-writing: if, indeed, we grant that the yearning for unreal prettiness and an artificial simplicity is at the basis of both these sorts of delicate and decorative "drama."

Jonson wrote more than thirty masque-texts, and endowed them with a lyric charm seldom equalled; but he felt in the end — as perhaps every masque author is certain to do — that his work was badly overshadowed by the showier elements of scenery, costuming, and dancing. After him John Milton wrote *Comus,* distinguished by flowery allegorical verse most amazingly bound up with sublime moral passion. And of a truth, a form of drama usually quite trivial or merely pretty is here elevated to the region of majestic poetry and immortal imagery. It is one of the superb tributes to Purity. If it suffers a little in stageworthiness, seems none too deftly shaped to acting, we may recall that masque-texts are likely to be formless anyway — and forget the fault in delighted reading. As an example of how the masques were shaped to occasions, *Comus* was written for performance at Ludlow Castle, and was produced, in 1634, as part of a long series of festivities in honor of the appointment of the Earl of Bridgewater to the Lord-Presidency of Wales. The players were amateurs, including the three children of the Earl, while the staging was superintended by the composer who wrote the masque-music.

By this time the courts had quite gone mad over masques, and no "occasion" was complete without one. The more elaborate productions were lavish and wasteful almost beyond belief. And

in connection with the " trimmings " of the productions, as the
disgruntled Jonson might have put it, we come to that singular
figure in English theatre history, Inigo Jones. Long ago, in the
very earliest years of the seventeenth century, this eminent architect had started to experiment with " Italian style " stages and
stage-setting. He travelled in Italy, learned the advantages of a

A mask setting by Inigo Jones, for a production in 1635 of *Florimène*
in the Italian style. [From *The Theatre of Tomorrow*, by Kenneth
Macgowan.]

curtained stage, and picked up knowledge of all the " effects "
that were then delighting Italian audiences. He wrote out detailed descriptions of the Palladian stage at Vicenza, and he made
drawings for similar perspective-vista and Roman-*skene* theatres.
He introduced the proscenium-frame into England, and ushered
in the approved " painty " scenery and allegorical-florid costuming. He is an important theatre-artist because he, more than any
other, determined the direction of development of the English
theatre after the extinguishment of the inn-yard type of playhouse in 1642. He more than any other established the

proscenium-frame theatre and the picturized stage as a substitute for the Elizabethan acting-platform. A few features of that platform stage (most notably the apron-doorways) reappeared in the eighteenth century theatres; the rest went down under the popular demand for Italianate " scenery."

Even in Shakespeare's day there had been in London a roofed theatre, the Blackfriars, to which his professional company had resorted at times; but there is little evidence to tell us how far this departed from the Globe-theatre type, how close it may have approached toward masque-stage elaboration. " Regular " plays were often presented for the court, sometimes by the professional men's companies, oftener by the favorite boys' companies. Long since it had been a custom to train grammar school students into acting troupes; and for two hunded years the choir boys had combined music and drama on occasion — there is a more or less vague relationship to the Boy-Bishop activities.

At any rate, in time the acting companies out of the schools and choirs became favorites. Plays were specially written for them, with special care put on the interpolated songs; and the Children of the Royal Chapel, and Paul's Boys, are mentioned again and again in the records of theatrical events of the period; and no less in the protests of the Puritans. In 1597 the master of the Chapel Children had been officially empowered to "take up " boys to fill his company, and to provide living accommodations for them; and he made the group into a professional troupe that appeared at the Blackfriars' Theatre, apparently with the direct approval of Elizabeth.

But in general we may think of the boy companies as playing at " special " functions, and particularly for court circles. They link up less with public entertainment than with the privately arranged " social " productions. (The Blackfriars, to be sure, was called a " private " theatre too, but more for the sake of evading the law against theatres in town than as a restriction against the general public; it was more " select " than the open-air playhouses, but not truly exclusive like the court ballroom productions.) The phenomenon of The Boys, indeed, belongs to that half of the late Elizabethan and the Jacobean theatre that we have found more interesting than the fast-declining public stage: the masque-making, the command performances in exotic settings, the ornamental theatre.

After the suppression of stage-plays by Parliament in 1642, there was a scattering of the professional actors (not unaccompanied by some historic plaints), and a long silence on the part of play-wrights. Until the Restoration in 1660 there was practically no activity on the London stages — if indeed they were not all pulled down. Sir William Davenant alone had the temerity to force an opening for dramatic productions in the interim, and he succeeded only by pleading that he intended musical and not strictly dramatic offerings — that is, opera. Davenant had been poet, playwright, and theatre manager, and Royalist to boot, and had no reason to expect special favors at the hands of the governing Puritans. His were the first productions, nevertheless, to break the long silence. In 1656 at Rutland House he cautiously staged an " Entertainment, by Declamation and Musick, after the Manner of the Ancients." Immediately after, he put on the boards his *The Siege of Rhodes* — rather a play with music than an opera.

It was the masque tradition that led on to this event, rather than the tradition of the Elizabethan public theatre. And there is a notable separation of all succeeding theatrical activity from what had been known in the Shakespearean playhouse: not only a different type of stage and of scenery but a new sort of literary drama, generously influenced by the dramatists of France. Opera, to be sure, did have a fitful flight in England soon after this; but the next chapter in *that* story, after Italy, belongs rather to France, as we shall see shortly. Davenant's courageous experiments, moreover, have greater importance here as leading on to the next form of non-musical tragedy. For evidence, one may note how Dryden, the only great or near-great tragedy-writer in post-Elizabethan England, wrote of Davenant as the initiator of the Heroic Drama:

For heroic plays . . . the first light we had on them, on the English theatre, was from the late Sir William Davenant. It being forbidden him in the rebellious times to act tragedies and comedies, because they contained some matter of scandal to those good people, who could more easily dispossess their lawful sovereign, than endure a wanton jest, he was forced to turn his thoughts another way, and to introduce the examples of moral virtue, writ in verse, and performed in recitative music. The original of this music, and of the scenes which adorned his work, he had from the Italian operas; but he heightened his characters, as I may probably imagine, from the example of Corneille and some French poets. . .

And no one should know more than Dryden about this same heroic drama; for no other name, save possibly that of Thomas Otway, who wrote *The Orphan* and *Venice Preserved,* and starved to death, needs to be remembered out of the history of this Restoration play-form.

If we approach the heroic *genre* with an eye to the continuity of the English tradition, we may find reason, by virtue of the seriousness of the times, to say that the irresponsible violence of the late Elizabethan tragedy-writers was here rendered *serious:* that here was a grave extravagance. But it takes no eye at all to see some operatic awkwardness and floridity in Dryden's rhetorical plays; and the influence of French classic drama is obvious in the greater formality in both structure and verse. Extraneously, too, there is plenty in Dryden's writings to prove devotion to the purists across the Channel. Tragedy lost all the Elizabethan rambling freedom; the tendency to mix comedy into tragedy came to an abrupt end; and blank verse went out in favor of the rhyming couplet. If acting had been artificial before, the actor now had just the stuff for rant, and just the characters for high strutting. The persons in the heroic tragedy were largely princes and conquerors and great ladies. The stories were of love and war. The virtues of the drama no longer lay in emotion and sympathy and adventure, but in neatness of versification, didactic purpose, heroic story, and display of rhetoric.

John Dryden's *The Conquest of Granada* is the type example of heroic drama. It is not without a greatness: in outline, in a certain mighty heedlessness of nature, and in gorgeous declamation. It achieved a bigness that swept it to popularity in its time; it might have continued to move audiences even down till today, were not the faults of rhymed speech as a medium for drama, and of operatic conception, bound to vitiate any play for other than artificial eras. In his Epilogue Dryden claimed that he wrote " to please an age more gallant than the last "; excusing earlier poets for being not so good, he saw his own play as reflecting a higher taste:

> If love and honor now are higher raised,
> 'Tis not the poet, but the age is praised.
> Wit's now arrived to a more high degree;
> Our native language more refined and free.
> Our ladies and our men now speak more wit
> In conversation, than those poets writ.

If both language and taste were now more " refined " than ever before, morals were not. And the sophisticated audiences that welcomed the heroic tragedy demanded an equally unlifelike sort of comedy, with dry wit taking the place of dry rhetoric; and with that wit spiced out of town tattle and boudoir scandal. Before turning to the sparkling " Restoration comedy," however, one may recall, not without pleasure tinged by malice, that some contemporary playwrights saw through the pretensions of Dry-denesque tragedy, and concocted a mock-heroic entitled *The Re-hearsal,* which burlesqued all the noble " effects," and quite took the town. It was long attributed to the Duke of Buckingham, but is probably a collaboration from several hands. It well-nigh put an end to heroic tragedy in England. One should add that Dryden later turned to blank-verse drama, and frankly imitated Shake-speare. He also directly adapted some of the latter's plays. Con-sidering how bad most alterations of Shakespeare are, Dryden's, while inferior to the originals, seem occasionally very good. And in *All for Love or The World Well Lost,* a reworking of the story of *Antony and Cleopatra,* he wrote, in more or less Eliza-bethan manner, a play that some critics still consider very great.

In approaching Restoration comedy, one does better to check one's moral sensibility, one's conscience, one's " taste," at the door. These brilliant plays are shocking, contrary to all later conceptions of what is " in good taste " — quite indefensibly un-moral in outlook and licentious in expression. If the playgoer cannot achieve a detached point-of-view, he had better stay away. And yet what brilliancy, what wit, what sustained style!

A quarter-century ago Brander Matthews wrote that " Congreve and Wycherley, Farquhar and Vanbrugh helped themselves to Molière's framework only to hang it about with dirty linen." And with hardly more mention than that, he dismissed the Restoration playwrights out of his history of drama. The world has so far "broadened," since then, that today Congreve's plays are staged, new editions appear, the Restoration dramatists are touted as veritable masters of comedy-writing. In this age of greater intellectual emancipation, of extended moral freedom — and of cynicism — Congreve and Wycherley have come back into their own. The point is, perhaps, that they wrote for a very small "advanced" audience in their own time; and today a similar audience has come into existence. Those who belong to it will explain that it is composed of the only truly "civilized" spectators: the open-minded, the men of the world, the intellectually emancipated. The others will say that it is an over-sophisticated audience, to whom only the affected and the over-spiced can give delight. And, indeed, here is typically the drama for the few: graceful, witty, with extraordinary style and finish; but totally unnatural, losing its lustre the moment one tests it by the touchstone of human feeling.

The audience for which the Restoration comedy was written was the elegant and limited court "society." There were no theatre activities outside London — the Puritans could still control everything except the King's own circle — and only two playhouses in London. There the fops and beaux were wont to gather for entertainment, with their equally light-thinking and easy-living court-ladies and fashionable courtesans. There were scarcely any theatre-goers outside this circle of gallants and town wits and court hangers-on. For a debauched society, headed by a debauched king, the playwrights shaped their entertainments. Nothing could then be in worse taste than a show of human feeling, a suggestion of moral concern, an honest heartiness. Everything must have a hard surface glitter, the artifice of wit alone could continuously please, brilliancy and style and grace were the only virtues worth achieving.

There were more or less transitional figures, carrying on from Jonsonian comedy, and not wholly committed to the artificiality of the time of Charles II. Dryden wrote some in-between plays, and George Etherege harked back somewhat to Jonson and Fletcher; still his three comedies, *The Comical Revenge, or Love*

Interior of the Duke's Theatre in Lincoln's Inn Fields, as shown in a print of 1809 based on an engraving of 1673 — there captioned "The stage of the above theatre and its very elegant frontispiece". — indicating the appreciation in England of the Italian prosceniums then just introduced into the "regular" theatres.

in a Tub, and *She Would if She Could,* and *The Man of Mode, or Sir John Fopling,* sufficiently indicate in their titles the trend of playwriting. It was rather William Wycherley who established the smart dialogue and sparkling style for the period to follow: in *The Country Wife* and *The Plain Dealer,* coarse plays both but greatly amusing. After him came the truly typical group of dramatists, composed of William Congreve, Sir John Vanbrugh, and George Farquhar.

Of these, Congreve proved himself the possessor of the most sustained style, the readiest flow of wit. And in *The Way of the World* and *Love for Love* he wrote the most famous of English artificial comedies. In his affected pose of not caring about his plays, he is, again, the soul of his age. If morals are mentioned in his plays it is only because by their inversion a certain effect is gained; if life is reflected, it is only the life of the trivial-minded and licentious court society. No human being stalks through the artificial plots. And yet here are verbal repartee and witty dialogue unmatched. *Love for Love* comes nearer to being pure comedy; some of its characters are Scandal, Tattle, Foresight, Trapland, Mrs. Frail, and Miss Prue. But if the reader — our players no longer have the right artificiality to put these brittle pieces on the stage — if the reader will spend two hours over *The Way of the World,* he will have the *genre* at its best, and with almost a seriousness beyond the wit, and such spirited characterization as never else happened within the limits of pure artifice. Indeed, here Congreve stripped the Restoration comedy of half the grossness of its other practitioners; and he sharpened the sword-play of wit till the flash of it well-nigh blinds us to all other considerations. Two lines of the character Witwoud touch to the heart of the matter: " A wit shou'd no more be sincere, than a woman constant; one argues a decay of parts, as t'other of beauty." There one has a summary, almost: as regards truth, style, sincerity, epigrammatic dexterity, artifice, inversion, cynicism, skill.

The company that acted Congreve's comedies included, according to Colley Cibber, " thirteen actors standing all in equal light of excellence "; and though we moderns suspect that often an actor high-praised in his day would ill please us now, we may visualize Betterton's company as perfectly formed to show out the Congreve rapier-thrust of wit and parade of brilliancy. Perhaps the ladies of the stage — this is the first time we meet them in the story of the English theatre — were even better fitted than the men to give authentic ease and flippancy to the parts: they lived like the heroines and courtesans the comedies portrayed. Most famous for her acting was Mrs. Bracegirdle; though Nell Gwyn's name is writ the larger in history, partly for her adorable pertness, partly because the King took her under his protection; so that theatrical blood crossed with Royal, to the great enrichment of England's later illegitimate nobility.

The "King's Servants," one of the two companies in London just after the accession of Charles II, had been made privileged members of the Royal household, with the title "Gentlemen of the Chamber"; while the other troupe was known as "The Duke of York's Company" — ample indication of standing quite different from that suffered by the "rogues and vagabonds" of other days. The stage at this time was the Italian proscenium-frame affair and the masque-settings had found their way into the regular playhouses for good. Stage costuming was a strange mixture of conventions. Some characters must have romantic and plushy "historical" costumes, while in the same play others might appear in any stylish robes of the day or recent fashionable French dresses. This mixing of conventions and styles had been a curiosity of Elizabethan times, and is to last for almost a century yet.

In 1682, the two companies were merged, assuming the title "King's Company," and Drury Lane Theatre became its first home. In the engraving of the Duke's Theatre (or Dorset Garden Theatre) stage, the reader should not be misled into thinking this is a modern "box-set" scene. Back-cloth and flats (of which more later) were designed to give this effect when viewed from one point in the house, the Royal box, but never achieved the ideal from any other viewpoint. The fore-stage and boxes, too, are here cut off.

The drawing by Sir Christopher Wren, generally supposed to be a design for Drury Lane Theatre, sufficiently indicates how London at this time fell into line with continental practice in theatre design. Here are the raked stage, designed for perspective scenery, and the horse-shoe of hen-coop boxes, and the Renaissance pilasters and moldings; with only the apron before the curtain and the doors under the stage boxes as heritage from the Elizabethan acting-platform. Indeed, in more ways than one the British stage had become internationalized. If the heroic tragedies had owed both to Italian opera and to the French school of Corneille, no less had Restoration comedy been influenced by Molière. And it had been the French example that led to the banishment of boys from the stage, and the appearance of actresses.

A theatre design by Christopher Wren, probably for the 1674 Drury Lane Theatre. Note the raked stage, wings, stage portals, the many boxes and the small pit with benches.
[Redrawn after the original sketch now in the Library of All Souls College, Oxford.]

And oh, yes! there was a lady playwright, too — an authoress who is vividly, almost epochally, remembered. Mrs. Aphra Behn was one of the many near-great dramatists who made Restoration audiences laugh; and this first woman among English dramawriters yielded nothing to the men in her racy treatment of scandalous themes. Her immodesties seem, in the light of today, no less than stupendous. (They gained for her, incidentally, the honor of burial with England's immortals in Westminster Abbey.)

But this sort of vicious pandering to the taste of King and nobles, brought a reaction that completes the circle to the point at which the chapter started. In 1698 Jeremy Collier issued his *Short View of the Immorality and Profaneness of the English*

Stage. This time it was no bigoted zealot speaking, no blindly-raging extremist. A man well-informed, somewhat humorous, even-tempered, simply showed up what he knew to be true about the depravity of the stage in his time. And the effect was immediate and far-reaching. Serious indecency was almost cut off; or at least the theatres developed no new artificial dramatists after Congreve, Farquhar, and Vanbrugh. The literary value of drama

Two formal stages of the Rederijker societies, at Ghent and Antwerp, in the mid-sixteenth Century. [From *The English Drama in the Age of Shakespeare,* by Wilhelm Creizenach.]

also declined; one can hardly count Colley Cibber important as a playwright, though he was an outstanding figure as actor-writer-manager — "an industrious poet and an honest man," someone has called him, in addition. Richard Steele wrote some plays that ushered in the sentimental note, the one note most foreign of all to the true Restoration writers; and Joseph Addison wrote a correct tragedy entitled *Cato* that enjoyed a vogue. But these pieces interest us today chiefly as indicating the extraordinary reaction to Restoration freedom. Collier was already triumphant within the first quarter of the eighteenth century. Dryden even publicly apologized for having dirtied his hands with indecent comedies.

To FRANCE, and the last of the Renaissance stages, in a moment. First, we must pause to note that, in a brief story like this, the theatres of the minor countries suffer from a perhaps undeserved neglect. There is Denmark, where the theatre suddenly appeared at this very time, under the direction of that Holberg who is accounted one of the leading two writers of all Europe in his generation. His comedies are played to this day, not only in Scandinavia but in Germany and occasionally in even more distant lands. And then there is Holland, which had had a vigorous theatre in the days of Christian religious drama, and which felt the breath of Renaissance freedom and experiment as early as England. For the world historian, the Dutch theatre is particularly interesting by reason of some strangely Italian stages that appeared in the fifteen-hundreds and may have influenced the English; and for a curiously mixed playhouse that shows more kinds of influence, classic, mediæval, and local, than any other ever recorded. On this page and the page previous I reproduce illustrations which tell the story and will allow us to hasten across to France and the main show.

The strange stage of the Amsterdam *Schouburgh* in 1638, wherein one may see elements reminiscent of the mediæval simultaneous stages, the Elizabethan platform with balcony, and the Italian vista stage. Note the curtain, and the gallery benches above the boxes. The auditorium was of the ballroom type, with flat floor and a double tier of boxes all round. [From a contemporary engraving by Nicolaes van Kampen, as reproduced in *Das Bühnenbild,* by Carl Niessen.]

CHAPTER XIV

Kings, Courtesans, and Dramatists of France

PICTURE to yourself, if you please, the Court of Louis XIV: the pageant of magnificence: the great King himself, Louis the Grand, The *Roi-soleil* — " *l'Etat, c'est moi* "; the vast palaces and gardens at Versailles and St. Cloud, the Louvre in Paris; the retinue of Gentlemen-in-waiting and fine ladies, the pretty and accomplished courtesans, the dandies; the laces and frills, the love nests, the satin and silk clothes — like a perpetual masquerade; the fêtes, the fireworks, the ballets, the ceremonies; the circles of literary men and artists, aspiring to be courtiers too, just as the courtiers must dabble in the arts to be fashionable. Bring to focus the picture of this gay and elegant society, consistently artificial, overdecorated — overstuffed, the upholsterers might say — and you will have the key to the changes that came into the theatre in the seventeenth century. For courtliness is to be a characteristic of the stage art for two full centuries.

Soon after 1600 Paris becomes the centre and all of French life: France is thereafter to be milked to support this capital city. And the Court is to rule brilliantly all activities in Paris. The form of the playhouse and the methods of stage setting are to be determined by the needs and tastes of the royal family and favorites; even playwriting is to be controlled. The surface aspects of a fastidious and frivolous courtliness are to be imposed on the theatre, so effectively that they will hardly be questioned until well into the nineteenth century — and so glamorously that even today, in this new machine-era, we find them hovering over the playhouse and hindering the attempt to evoke an art appropriate to this so-uncourtly age.

At the beginning of the seventeenth century, France emerged from a period of chaos, wherein there had been little leisure for serious attention to the arts, no centralization of social or cultural life, not even an unchallenged political capital. Theatrical conditions were almost as crude and unformed as in the neighboring Germany; whereas the golden age of the Renaissance had already come and almost gone in Italy, Spain, and England. France had lagged, knew only a rude native stage, or an occasional imported troupe from one of these more favored countries. Yet within sixty years France is to see its most glorious theatrical achievements, its most magnificent plays; is to become the most brilliant centre of the stage arts in all of Europe, is to be recognized as arbiter in matters dramatic over all the Western world. The glory of this accomplishment is to prove so dazzling, indeed, that there is nothing but imitation of it till the end of the eighteenth century; and then when Democracy brings a real challenge, the little democratic artists will still be so under the spell that unconsciously they will imitate and perpetuate the very qualities imposed on the theatre by the kings — and, only too often, by the kings' courtesans. Indeed the whole bourgeois conception of art, up to a time perilously close to the present day and hour, has embraced something romantically different from ordinary life, romantically royal, decorated, befrilled, and plushy. Instead of art as an intensification of life, Democracy has visioned it as an escape back into the soft days, as the privilege of a few, as a basking in the effulgence of an orientally wasteful diversion. The theatre most of all has suffered from the aristocratic incubus; and it is therefore somewhat important to know from the start this " courtliness " for the thing it is.

We may remember, if we wish, that it was the opulent Italian courts that brought in the ballroom theatre and pictorial settings, and that it was under their protection that the neo-classic drama developed, and that opera was invented. France picked up all these impulses, and the one great centralized Parisian Court gave new authority to classicism, stamped with approval the Italian playhouse and lavish Italian stage decoration, and imposed operatic elements on theatre art for, apparently, all time.

The legitimate theatre was affected by the French Court activity in two ways: The whole idea of a ruling class with powers and laws divinely guided was imposed on playwriting. And the outward glow of court life, including not a little of the element of tinsel-and-fine-clothes demanded by the courtesans, was thrown over the productions on the stage.

In the matter of playwriting, the Italian rules were diligently codified and set forth as an inalterable basis for future composition of drama. The term "classic" was rigidly defined; thenceforward there was separation between the orthodox practitioners, within the rules, and reckless experimentors who would bring playwriting closer to life, or perhaps only let playwriting and life develop hand in hand. Academies were created whose function it was to endorse and honor those authors who conformed, and to resist all apostates; and special theatres were subventioned, made the official homes of classic drama, and often given monopolies on legitimate tragedy-and-comedy production.

This codifying of rules and granting of privileges had great effect on playwriting: for even while the dramatist was stirred, by the brilliancy and the patronage of the courts, to give his best substance, he found himself hampered by the arbitrary "laws" of composition. He generally, moreover, fancied the idea of being part of the aristocracy of the intellect, and thus akin to the aristocrats of the blood. Of course the one greatest genius of the period broke all the laws, was refused admittance to the Academy, and challenged the privileged acting company — but found a king who was discerning enough and broad enough to stand against his own court-made distinctions. Still, in general, the whole period is marked by the characteristic knuckling to authority; there is deference to rules, an artificial formality and reserve in playwriting, a lack of depth of feeling. Etiquette is more important than creation. The dramatist worked within the limits of an artificial decorum, a hollow elegance, in serious mood, or else descended to fashioning pretty trifles for the amusement of the court at garden parties, balls, and royal command performances, in the spirit of masquerade and pageantry.

The courtesan element crept more insidiously into the physical playhouse. An exuberance and delicacy of decoration, more fit to wrap a king's mistress in than for the fitting up of a theatre, came to be the accepted thing in playhouse ornamentation (though it only reached its apotheosis two hundred years later in the Paris Opera House and a hundred more tinselly imitations); the auditorium became practically tier on tier of private boxes; and stage decoration became soft and luxurious. A lot of other playthings were added — as we shall see in another chapter. With all these concrete additions there came the more subtle one, the casting of a courtly "glow" over stage life. The gorgeous dressing extends to the performers, and elegant manners, and courtly vivaciousness. There is constant interchange between the few regular theatres and the ballroom stages, until finally the old platform stage is lost in the court theatre building, and production has become a privileged function by royal grace. Here the ancient Dionysian joy of the theatre gets mixed with some of the surface glamour and the petty intrigues of the less-royal hangers-on at court. But at any rate the brilliancy of the great kings is on the theatre for a time.

In 1600 there is only one theatre in Paris: a rather rude affair known as the *Hôtel de Bourgogne,* modelled in part after the old outdoor Miracle stages, and retaining their arrangement of "station" settings. There is no permanent troupe of actors in the city. Playwriting activity is practically non-existent, though there is a body of old religious plays and farces, and a few literary men have written tragedies in imitation of the neo-classic Italians. The theatre itself exists only in the visits of strolling comedian troupes, particularly at the seasons of the fairs — though a quack may bring a company with him at other times of year, to act on his outdoor platforms. In England this is the very heart of the glorious Elizabethan flowering, when Shakespeare's *Romeo and Juliet* and *As You Like It* have been enlivening the London stage, and just when the poet is turning to *Hamlet* or *Othello* or *King Lear.* In Spain Lope de Vega is at the height of his brilliant power. The crest of the wave of creative activity that followed on the Renaissance is past in Italy; and indeed it is the infrequent visits of Italian acting companies that occasion the few bright entries in the dull theatrical annals of the times. Even on the *Hôtel de Bourgogne* stage as recently as 1599 a visiting Italian company has so shown up the crudeness of a native competing troupe

that Paris is left again without any offerings. And as late as
1622 there will come a season when the city is without theatrical
entertainment.

In the years between 1600 and 1622 there are to be frequent
starts toward permanently settled theatrical activity, as we shall
see. But the more interesting productions for long will be those
of the strolling players. We may picture them setting up their

The stage at the *Hôtel de Bourgogne,* from an engraving by Abraham Bosse.
The central figures in the scene are Turlupin, Gros-Guillaume, and Gautier-
Garguille.

temporary curtained stages in the grounds allotted to the *Foire
St Laurent* and the *Foire St Germain.* These fairs are gala occasions, and even kings are known to frequent the gambling booths,
the sales pavilions, the stage productions, and the strange side-
shows. Sometimes an acting troupe has come here independently,
bringing old farces or new, harlequinades or jugglery and tumbling. More likely the actors are part of the retinue of one of the
great quacks of the period (who are much more important personages than any licensed doctors), and they give their plays as an ad-

junct to medicine-selling. Perhaps their exhibition is only of a vaudeville sort, with the emphasis on clowning, conjuring, and the showing of freaks; but again a complete farce is presented. Even so important a company as *I Gelosi* is known to have been brought into France by a quack.

The prints of the period show oftener than not the medicine-sellers and their bottles on the stage, along with the actors: as in this illustration of the platform of Tabarin in the *Place Dauphiné*. An audience of the time, the group of buyers, the great quack Mondor, Tabarin himself, and other performers and musicians, all these are shown, as well as the plain platform with a curtain back-drop. The more pretentious booth theatre of the Italian

Mondor and Tabarin on their theatre in the Place Dauphiné, Paris, as etched by Abraham Bosse. [From *Les Rues du Vieux Paris,* by Victor Fournel.]

farceur-quack Orvietan is pictured a few pages over, along with a later street stage. His stand often was a feature of the Pont Neuf. The popular vogue of the outdoor productions is to persist long after the "serious" drama has become the plaything of courts, and after indoor stages in the Italian style have become the proper frame for both tragedy and comedy.

Even in 1600 the *Hôtel de Bourgogne* was a privileged theatre, though it had no actors and was a mere way-station for this and that travelling troupe. As early as 1402 Charles VI had granted the Brothers of the Passion permission to act holy Mystery Plays in Paris, and the seasonal performances had been highly esteemed for years. But when the Church, alarmed by the freedoms that had been brought into "religious" play production, at first withdrew approval, then actively fought against further performance, the privilege was modified. In 1541 the actors of the Brotherhood were officially termed "ignorant workmen," and it was charged that "in order to lengthen *The Acts of the Apostles* they have added several apocryphal things, and at the beginning and end of it have introduced loose farces and pantomimes, and have extended their play to the length of six or seven months, which led and leads to neglect of divine service, indifference in almsgiving and charity, adultery and incessant fornication, scandals, mockery and scorn." Moreover it was shown that during the plays "all preaching stopped," and even members of the clergy hurried through their offices to get to the performances. By 1548 the agitation against the Brotherhood had been so strong that they were thenceforward restrained from presenting sacred Mystery Plays, though their privilege to present profane drama, "decent and lawful," was continued and their monopoly on production in Paris and suburbs officially endorsed. Protests continued, and in 1588 the King had been petitioned to do away with "a cesspool and House of Satan, named the *Hôtel de Bourgogne.*"

Now, however, in 1600, the Brothers of the Passion have given up acting — after all, the members are artisans and tradesmen, the theatre is becoming professionalized, and audiences are demanding something up to the standard set by the Spanish and Italian companies. But no one is allowed to present plays in Paris except under the *name* of the Brotherhood and to their profit. They determine to work their royal privilege for all it is worth, closing any performances outside their own house, and collecting tribute from every troupe that operates in it (though they can't put an end to the special dispensations to provincial companies to act in Paris at the fairs; and the court occasionally has its own command performances, by any company it likes). But the *Hôtel de Bourgogne* is the first "regular" theatre in Paris; and within a few years we find it let out to this and that courageous provincial company, to the Italians (including *I Gelosi* and the Andreinis); and finally, about 1610, to the first company that could claim anything like permanence in Paris. This troupe, headed by Valleran Lecomte, stayed in the house a dozen years, was known as "The King's Players," made a real place for itself

in the community, and helped to develop a true dramatic literature. And after the cupidity of the Brotherhood drove the actors
out of the theatre again, resulting in a playless season, and then
a brief tenancy by a second company, known as the Prince of
Orange's Players, Lecomte and his King's Players returned and
settled down to a half-century occupancy.

In 1629 Paris is ready for a second, competing company; the
Prince of Orange's Players establish themselves as permanent
rivals to the royal troupe; and soon they open the second famous
Parisian theatre, the Marais. And more notable, the rival group
has turned up a new dramatic author, Pierre Corneille, whose
first play, *Mélite,* is acted in 1629.

Playwriting has been almost as chaotic as stage conditions.
Since the tradition of the old amateur farce-writing ran out in
the last century, everybody has been influenced by the Italian
comedies. There was, of course, no native French tradition in
tragedy, and it is the Italian neo-classic form that has been reflowering in France. Shortly after 1550 the dramatist Stephen
Jodelle, a disciple of Ronsard in the famous literary group called
the " Pleiad," composed *Cléopatre Captive,* a Senecan tragedy,
very rhetorical and trailing such classical remnants as ghost and
chorus. Jodelle is called " the Father of French tragedy"; and
he not only established the Italian neo-classic form as model, but
introduced (though he did not use exclusively) the Alexandrine
verse-measure, the six-foot line rhymed in couplets, which is to be
the characteristic French dramatic medium for centuries thereafter. Among many imitators only one, Robert Garnier, rose to
eminence: he wrote tragedies that are the least rhetorical and
stilted up to the time of Corneille's appearance.

As in Italy, the group of early literary dramatists in France had
only contempt for the current popular theatre, and there was
little connection between the stage and tragedy-writing for a
considerable period. The men-of-letters clung to the chorus, the
rhetorical account of action instead of the thing itself, and similarly inappropriate and deadening dramatic heritages. They
acted their own plays, in amateur groups. They stayed wholly
aloof from the dramatic activities of the fairs and market-places.

But it was inevitable that the currents should flow together in

Two seventeenth century paintings of outdoor platform stages. Above,
Charlatan sur une Place de Paris, by Pierre Wouwermans. Below, a painting of the stage of Orvietan, by Gerrit-Adriaenaz Berckeyden.

French and Italian farceurs of the Paris stage in the sixty years preceding 1670. Molière is at the extreme left. Besides Jodelet, Gros-Guillaume, Scaramouche, and other famous actors, still others are represented merely under the names of their masks. [From a painting in the collection of the *Comédie Française*.]

time. Perhaps the pastoral and the romance, bearing in from Spain and Italy, brought a softening influence on the rigid tragedy. At any rate tragedies begin to appear in not unliterary form on the popular stage; and a new type that is neither comic nor tragic, strictly speaking, and that pleases a wide public with romantic-literary materials. There has had to be no radical change in comedy to reconcile it with slowly improving public taste; for there was no great gap between popular French farce and the Terentian comedy that was brought out of Italy by the literary comedy-writers. Indeed the popular stage long since had absorbed from visiting *Commedia dell'Arte* companies the characters and the masks of the *Dottore, Pantalone, Arlecchino* and the others; while distinguished authors were putting these very characters, and many " stock " situations into their comedy-texts. A good deal of the recorded comedy-writing, indeed, was merely a transcription of the late Italian Renaissance product, none of it very important to begin with.

The writer who came to Paris with the troupe that entered the *Hôtel de Bourgogne* in 1610, as The King's Players, was Alexandre Hardy, who " thanked Heaven that he knew the precepts of his art while preferring to follow the demands of his trade." No other notation is necessary to indicate his perfect fitness to bring together the literary and popular currents. He combined something of solid structure and poetic language out of the aloof literary product with the ease of story-telling out of chronicle-play and romance (particularly Spanish); and he knew how to point up a situation with speeches that would register tellingly in the delivery. It is said that he invented tragi-comedy. All the way along he seems to have been the joiner-together and the compromiser so needed at just this moment. His poetry as such — he finally adopted the Alexandrine verse — leaves something to be desired. Perhaps his greatest service was as model: for the actors he was a guide toward the literary (there were to be an exceptional number of actor-playwrights), while doubtless the poets let down the bars a little to join him as purveyor of plays to the royal troupe or their rivals at the Marais Theatre.

Those poets did not, however, stray outside the more sanctified rules of the drama as understood from the ancients. Nor did they give up declamation in favor of Hardy's free-flowing dramatic action. What they did was to accept the conventions of the current stage, drop out such obviously anachronistic elements as the chorus, and train the classic form a *little* closer to human motive and individual character. But still it was a stiff, artificial thing that emerged, and only redeemed — according to our modern notions — by the nobility of the poetic investiture. The court element is strong upon it.

A tennis-court theatre, showing the simple " shelf for acting," in this case without the simultaneous scene. [Drawing by Warren D. Cheney after a contemporary sketch by F. Chauveau.]

The physical stage to which the nobler poets came down, so to speak, was crude enough. We do not know exactly what were the architectural antecedents of the *Hôtel de Bourgogne*. But the other theatres in Paris were converted tennis-courts. When it seemed that the time had come to take the drama indoors, the producers had sought nothing else than a convenient " place for seeing," and the covered courts, with balconies and benches for spectators, were exactly that. The Prince of Orange's Players occupied three tennis-courts in succession, between the opening of *Mélite* in 1629 and 1634; the last being the Marais Tennis-Court that gave the troupe its name thenceforward. We may

picture the auditorium as long, narrow, and almost bare, with
balconies along the side walls, the benches placed on the main
floor, facing a platform stage at the end. The sketch on page
316 indicates the somewhat cramped intimacy and the arrangement of the place. The *Hôtel de Bourgogne* was similarly long
and narrow but the only portion about which there is undisputed
evidence is the stage. This was modelled on the Mystery or
Miracle platforms, whereon a neutral acting space was bordered

A simultaneous setting at the *Hôtel de Bourgogne,* showing how the influence of the religious plays persisted on the secular stage. [Redrawn from the
design by the stage artist Mahelot, preserved in a book of drawings in the
Bibliothèque Nationale, Paris.]

at back and sides by representations or suggestions of the several
localities in which the action was supposed to pass. A whole book
of sketches for these composite settings has been preserved. It
shows exactly how the stage " decorator " at the *Hôtel de Bourgogne* set about to provide " simultaneous settings " for each
new play of Hardy or his fellow-dramatists — even up to
Corneille.

At the Marais Theatre on an afternoon late in November 1636,
Corneille's *Le Cid* was acted for the first time. The date is under-
lined in all histories, for the great era of French tragic drama is
supposed to have been ushered in that day. Corneille's comedies

had been popular, but no tragedy had yet come from his hand. If we had been present at this most noted of Paris premières, we would have seen something like this:

Within the dim candle-lit auditorium is an audience of the most mixed sort. Courtiers and dandies fill the balcony boxes, and on this special occasion have the best benches on the main floor; and close by them are litterateurs, officers, travellers, tradesmen, even down to the court pages, idlers, and adventurers — an element so unruly that the actors will be lucky to get through without disturbance or battle. This audience has been admitted by a brawny and heavily armed doorman, whose duty it is to exclude by violence all who refuse to buy tickets — all, that is, except the nobles, against whom a mere theatre proprietor or ticket-taker must not stand out. (Had not Battistino, the actor-proprietor who undertook to dispute with a courtier who refused to pay — had he not been openly murdered, and nothing ever done about it?) The stage is curtainless; on it are spread out the several " mansions " or " stations " indicating the locale of the action, each touching upon that central space where the actors will stand. Here are indicated a king's council-room, a woman's apartment, etc. There are practically no properties.

When the auditorium candles have been snuffed, two actresses appear, richly apparelled. They break immediately into the verse-dialogue, strongly, sonorously; there is no pretense of nature here. Indeed the Confidante's second speech is thirty-six lines in length. But now the women have gone, the men enter — this one will be Mondory, chief of the troupe. These actors are violent fellows. Mondory's plan of attack is to startle the audience with a sudden explosion, pause, then wear it down by a series of lesser detonations. This is acting and no mistake. Of course, there have to be quieter passages. But the French verse runs swiftly, fluently. And the poet continually comes back to those rhetorical fireworks that Mondory so relishes.

The fable is a borrowed one, taken quite directly from a Spanish play of almost the same name. It revolves about the old favorite theme of the point of honor. Don Rodrigue, to avenge an insult to his own father, kills the father of Chimène, whom he loves. How shall the two lovers be brought together despite this barrier?

We see Don Rodrigue torn between duty and love. Then we see Chimène fighting against her love, for a decent regard to convention, while her hero goes off to wondrous deeds in the wars. Well, we know how it will turn out; but what chance for high acting!

And indeed this performance takes the house. For days and weeks *Le Cid* is on every tongue. All Paris is buzzing with the sensation of a new type of play, by the young *avocat* of Rouen, Pierre Corneille. The older established playwrights are furious. A great controversy is waged. Cardinal Richelieu throws the weight of his authority against the youthful dramatist — even orders the Academicians to turn thumbs down. It seems the three unities have not been observed. But the public and the Court take Corneille's side. The new French dramaturgy is established.

What is it that Corneille has brought to the French stage which has not existed before? Out of Spain he has caught a new hint of heroic dramatic situation, of largeness, of nobility. He has brought this under control, under French discipline. Instead of Spanish succession of incident he has put a stirring human story into the heroic framework. It isn't human in the present-day personal sense, nor stirring except in a detached grandiose way, and no near neighbor to probability; but infinitely closer to the audience than the academic exercises of the earlier French classicists had been. And if rhetoric still remains, at least the verse — the rhymed Alexandrines, of course — is swift-flowing and at times majestic. It is the perfect verse-medium for the tirade-loving actors, for the formality-loving courtly audience. And the stripping of the dramatic story to one main conflict, without ramifications or sub-plots, to a climactic simplicity, sets up a model for future French tragedy.

Corneille goes on to other successes: *Cinna, Horace, Polyeucte.* He squirms a little under the necessity of confining his art within the limitations of the three unities and other Aristotelean " laws "; but perhaps he sees that what he brings by way of heroic framework and grandeur and concentration, when married to the older classicism, may result in a play-form for all French stages — perhaps for all tragedy-writing everywhere, for all time. He accepts the rules. Perhaps the discipline of bringing his action into one day and one place made him a greater dramatist; or perhaps he would have written more magnificent plays if left unhampered. No one will ever know. But Corneille became the

Pierre Corneille. [From an old print.]

very type dramatist for that Academy which had tried at first to exclude him. Through him the French became the guardians and exponents of the Greek tradition.

What it was that French classicism thenceforward demanded of every " legitimate " dramatist in Europe may be summed up in a few brief rules: the unities of time, place and action must be observed; every play must be in five acts; every play must be in verse; all violent action must be accomplished offstage, must be merely recounted to the characters and the audience; no comic relief or sub-plot could be included; the themes must be lofty, and the characters noble.

Corneille fashioned dramas after this code; and his characters are indeed so lofty, and the verse so fine, that one goes to the *Comédie Française* to this day to enjoy the glitter and parade of them. It is only when one compares them with Shakespeare's more human creations that one discovers a well-nigh intolerable formality and bareness. For this French classic art is for a time and a place and an intellectual mood. It is a very great art within narrow limits, a dry art, an art that demands detachment from sentiment and personal emotion. Its excellencies are formal, to be intellectually relished and appreciated.

After Corneille came Racine, who made passion less intellectual, but further simplified and concentrated the play-form, accepted all the rules — and established indisputably the type-tragedy that Corneille had somewhat fumblingly initiated. As a writer Racine was a meticulous craftsman; and he understood perfectly the shaping of action and dialogue to acting — to declamatory delivery. In the field of an art somewhat cold, never unbending, flawlessly literary, decorous, he still somehow managed to build dramas with tremendous climaxes, with superbly moving situations. *Phèdre* is the greatest " acting part " in the French language: that is, it gives the actor richest opportunity for scoring by a display of rhetorical passion.

With a few characters, and a plot simple but perfectly proportioned — nearly always chosen from orthodox Greek or Roman sources — Racine built majestically and surely. In one sense, his was a psychological method: he was more interested in showing forth what his characters suffered than what they did; but it was oceans apart from what the modern world understands by the term " psychologic drama."

It is unfortunate that the English language is incapable of translations preserving the values of the French verse; we are thereby incapacitated from judging wholly fairly, will always feel a sense of fragmentary grandeur. In the original, one of Phèdre's many soliloquies runs thus:

> O toi, qui vois la honte où je suis descendue,
> Implacable Vénus, suis-je assez confondue?
> Tu ne saurois plus loin pousser ta cruauté.
> Ton triomphe est parfait; tous tes traits ont porté.
> Cruelle, si tu veux une gloire nouvelle,
> Attaque un ennemi qui te soit plus rebelle.
> Hippolyte te fuit; et bravant ton courrous,
> Jamais à tes autels n'a fléchi les genoux.
> Ton nom semble offenser ses superbes oreilles.
> Déesse, venge-toi: nos causes sont pareilles.
> Qu'il aime. . .

But in the English this proportioned verse, so perfectly fitted to the French recitative-acting, so swift-flowing, becomes, even at the hands of a generally satisfactory translator:

PHÆDRA (alone)

> Venus implacable, who seest me shamed
> And sore confounded, have I not enough
> Been humbled? How can cruelty be stretch'd
> Farther? Thy shafts have all gone home, and thou
> Hast triumph'd. Would'st thou win a new renown?
> Attack an enemy more contumacious:
> Hippolytus neglects thee, braves thy wrath,
> Nor ever at thine altars bow'd the knee.
> Thy name offends his proud, disdainful ears.
> Our interests are alike: avenge thyself,
> Force him to love. . .

Thus we are always at one remove from the drama that Racine wrote. We know the dignity and majesty of theme and story; but only imperfectly the rightness of the word-vehicle. Perhaps some day the miracle of an adequate transcription into English will come, not with the same values — of rhymed couplets — but with others, compensating by stirring poetry. Gilbert Murray has accomplished as much in his transcription from the Greek of the very play upon which Racine modelled *Phèdre*, the *Hippolytus* of Euripides.

Racine based others of his famous tragedies on the works of Euripides or the earlier Greeks, most notably *Iphigénie, La Thébaïde* and *Andromaque;* but at times he ranged farther afield, to the Bible for the materials of *Esther* and *Athalie,* and to almost contemporary history for *Bajazet;* though he never strayed beyond themes that were great and noble and characters of a sufficient stature.

The dramas of Racine and Corneille are, of course, typically of the theatre, shaped for acting; but of a particular and rather limited theatre, that of a select and educated audience to whom the literary polish and an actor's virtuoso delivery weigh heavily. They belong to the simple platform-for-acting theatre, and not

The ballroom stage in the palace of Cardinal Richelieu, with a setting for *Miramé*. [From a print reproduced in *l'Ancienne France: Le Théâtre et la Musique*.]

to the lavishly pictorial stage that was even at this time being introduced. Richelieu already had his ballroom theatre by 1641, with a stage proscenium-framed, as here shown, and with all the improvements that could be imported from Italy by way of machinery and scenery — and by the way, the great Cardinal more than any other one man established French dramatic art firmly, by his encouragement and patronage, though he failed to touch greatness in his own efforts at playwriting. The King, too, had a theatre fitted up at the *Petit-Bourbon* palace, of the same Italian sort.

At a later time Racine's *Alexander the Great* was acted by rival companies on the two types of stage, that of the *Hôtel de Bourgogne,* and that at the *Palais Royal* (formerly Richelieu's palace), then given over to Molière's company. The audiences at both sorts of theatre, however, may be thought of as courtly. It was the gallantry and brilliancy of court life that determined the language and the mould of Racine's plays.

In the literature of the French tragic stage there are no names beyond those of Corneille and Racine that are internationally important. Voltaire is sometimes added as a third figure in a triumvirate; but it was assuredly his battle for the unities that made him famous in theatrical annals, and not his plays. He believed, as did some of his contemporaries, that he had surpassed Racine; but even the French theatre has allowed his uninspired tragedies to sink into a probably permanent neglect. The clever and versatile Voltaire, nevertheless, dominated the theatre of his time as he dominated literature and thought. And he put down a definition of tragedy, or rather a statement of the tragedy-writer's duty, which deserves to be kept forward:

To compact an illustrious and interesting event into the space of two or three hours; to make the characters appear only when they ought to come forth; never to leave the stage empty; to put together a plot as probable as it is attractive; to say nothing unnecessary; to instruct the mind and move the heart; to be always eloquent in verse and with the eloquence proper to each character represented; to speak one's tongue with the same purity as in the most chastened prose, without allowing the effort of rhyming to seem to hamper the thought; to permit no single line to be hard or obscure or declamatory; — these are the conditions which nowadays one insists upon in a tragedy.[1]

And be assured Voltaire did insist upon them. He became the very pope of the Theatre-realm. He had his bishops and his minor clergy in France, in Italy, in Germany, even in England, as we have seen (though drama was " down " at the moment over most of Europe). Everywhere tragedy was made to bow

---

[1] Translation of Brander Matthews, in his *The Development of the Drama* (New York, 1906). One may recommend also, in connection with the subject of this chapter, his study of *Molière: His Life and His Works* (New York, 1910). The story of the French drama and theatre of the period is told, in an interesting if not a scholarly way, by Frederick Hawkins in *Annals of the French Stage from Its Origin to the Death of Racine* (London, 1884, 2 vols.) Equally interesting and more unscholarly is Volume IV of Mantzius' *History,* entitled *Molière and His Times.*

to the French rules. For had not the French dramatists become the successors of the ancients — nay, had they not improved upon the Greeks? Certainly. At least, for those courtly times, for those stiff audiences, it was an improvement.

The dictator, nevertheless, being broad-minded, took a liking to the plays of Shakespeare — as one sure of his own civilization will

The crowning of Voltaire at the *Théâtre Français* at the sixth representation of his *Irène,* March 30, 1778. [Portion of an engraving by Gaucher after the design of Moreau le Jeune.]

take to an attractive barbarian — one of those diamonds in the rough. While chiding the dead bard for his forgetfulness of the rules, Voltaire found in him qualities to praise: even essayed some adaptations in which Shakespeare's worst faults were corrected. But he found in Racine's *Iphigénie* the " chef d'œuvre of the stage." And of course his own correct dramas were played and discussed wherever civilization had reached.

But not to spend too long with one whose influence soon after waned (Lessing was born before Voltaire wrote his second play, and launched his attack on French Classicism long before Voltaire wrote his last), the reign of this dictator was long and adventurous and infinitely exciting. And after the little man had been exiled again and again — for his political and religious opinions that were far less orthodox than his playwriting prac-

A scene with spectators on the stage, at the theatre of the *Petits Comédiens*. [From Gravelot's engraving as reproduced in *Shakespeare in France under the Ancien Règime,* by J. J. Jusserand.]

tice — he was recalled to a triumph in the theatre. He went back to Paris in 1778, at the age of eighty-four, attended a performance of his tragedy *Irène* at the *Comédie Française,* and saw a portrait bust of himself crowned at one of the most brilliant assemblies in the history of the French stage. But we have now gone forward to a time long after the triumph of Molière and the glory that was French comedy.

There is, however, one matter of theatre custom which demands mention before Voltaire's name is dropped: for every later playwright, actor, and stage worker owes him a debt.   By his persistence he drove spectators off the stage.   You will remember how the dandies in Shakespeare's theatre had made themselves obnoxious by parading up on the platform beside the actors, how they detracted from the drama.   In Paris, it is said that seats were first set upon the stage when Corneille's *Le Cid* scored its epochal success.   The abuse grew until the actors had hardly more than a strip of playing space between two rows of benches as shown on the opposite page.

And the beaux and fops who claimed the privileged platform seats were no silent and attentive group; they strolled in and out when they pleased, made audible comments, took delight in showing superiority to the play, the players, and the audience. Voltaire is credited with driving them out permanently, with freeing the stage for acting.   God bless him!

In 1643 a company of amateur and semi-professional actors known as *Les Enfants de Famille* made the momentous decision that they would enter into competition with the " regular " theatre groups in Paris.   They hired a tennis-court, obtained a noble patron, and announced productions of tragedy under the name " The Illustrious Theatre."   The venture promptly, and apparently repeatedly, failed.   The Illustrious ones were driven to touring the provinces.   Among them was a young man of native wit and education above the average.   His name was Jean Baptiste Poquelin, and he was the son of an upholsterer.   For the purposes of the stage he took the name " M. de Molière."   Perhaps he would not have made that name the greatest in the story of the French theatre if he had not so promptly failed when he first came to the stage.   At any rate, we may well believe that he gained out of twelve years of " trouping " in the provinces two things that went into his equipment as first of the world's comedy-writers: a first-hand knowledge of the stage effects that infallibly amuse audiences; and a seasoning of philosophical humor and gentle wisdom, born out of struggle, companionship, intrigue, poverty, and checkered success.

Molière, the actor, returned with his company to Paris in 1658, and at this time he was already Molière the playwright, with a record of several farces or comedies tried out and found effective. If they were little more than adaptations from the *Commedia dell'Arte,* still there must have been a freshness about them. At the first Paris performance, before the King and the Court in the theatre at the *Petit-Bourbon,* it was not the tragedy but the farce after-piece that won approbation; so much so that the company was accorded the privilege of playing regularly at the royal theatre, alternating with the Italian Comedians. From that day to the end of his life, though he was compelled to fight through personal disappointments and intrigues arising out of professional jealousy, Molière marched forward to success after success, recognized as a chief figure in the theatre of France.

For one thing, those who valued restraint in acting above the old tragic declamation or comic buffoonery, began then to count him the best of actors, particularly for comedy. He was also a shrewd manager and director. And by 1659 he had written and presented *Les Précieuses Ridicules,* a brief satire on the groups of affected ladies who made pretence to a superior culture; and this witty take-off on the dilettanti, the *précieuses,* met with enormous success. (Indeed, the theatre immediately doubled its prices of admission.) The plot is negligible; the trick by which two servants play the substitute to their masters in wooing vain ladies is an old one; and the characters are hardly more than borrowings from the stock figures of the Italian Comedy. But Molière put rich fun into the farcical trifle, a swift gaiety and a freshness of humor quite uncommon; *and* social point. *That* the comedy of France had not had before. Other minor pieces followed; and in 1661 Molière brought out the *Ecole des Maris,* first of a long series of masterpieces in satiric comedy.

It is possible to trace back and discover the origin of many of the materials and qualities that had gone into Molière's " stock in trade." There was the old native French farce, the honest drollery of *Pierre Pathelin;* there was the imported Spanish play of piled-up incident and stressed intrigue; most of all, there were the improvised farces and the stock caricature-figures of the Italian *Commedia dell'Arte.* To these last Molière had gone directly for tutelage; he had competed with them for popular favor; since boyhood he had been laughing at their tricks and

RACINE

Molière and his troupe playing before the King and Cardinal Mazarin. [A reconstruction of the scene by the nineteenth century artist V. A. Poirson, in Moland's *Molière: Sa Vie et Ses Ouvrages*.]

their genius. (Even in *Les Précieuses Ridicules,* Molière's fellow-players Jodelet, La Grange and Du Croisy appeared as characters bearing those names, a convention taken from the Italians.) Corneille, too, had written a forerunner of later comedy, *Le Menteur,* in which he had made over a Spanish original into a true comedy of character.

But here is the miracle of one man picking up all these borrowings and influences, and so transcending them that he creates a new form of art, reaches a height in comedy-writing that never after is touched by any dramatist of this or any other land. Just as Shakespeare borrowed material with a freedom quite amazing, and began writing in a style that he found ready-made to his hand, and yet transcended all his fellows in all ages in the range and richness of his achievement, so Molière in comedy imitated and took, but lived to create with an originality unequalled in the entire comic literature of the stage.

Shakespeare, to be sure, had written unmatched comedies in a limited field, in addition to his incomparable accomplishment in the realm of tragedy; or perhaps it is better to say that he had written the finest plays ever produced in a mixed form that is half comedy, half fantastic drama. It is usually termed, inexactly, "Romantic Comedy," and embraces, of course, the plays of the type of *Twelfth Night* and *As You Like It.* There is, too, the comedy-nearer-farce — *The Merry Wives of Windsor.* But in the sort of dry comedy that usually is considered to contain the very essence of the comic spirit, Molière is accounted supreme.

Demanding a certain seriousness in all drama that raises claim to importance, and setting aside the old crude test of happy or gloomy ending, we may usefully distinguish comedy (from tragedy) as a form of dramatic action which touches upon our sense of the laughable, rather than upon the emotions of pity and anguish. Comedy is the drama of laughter, be that laughter in the manner of sympathy or of ridicule. The usually applied test of the excellence of any given comedy is the extent to which it evokes " thoughtful laughter." The play that begets thoughtless laughter, by sudden improbabilities, by extravagant coincident, by physical by-play, we call farce.

True comedy arises rather out of character — usually the clash of foibles in character against common-sense truth; out of the vices and weaknesses of human nature held up to ridicule. If at the same time sympathy is aroused, the play borders on sentimental comedy — which may run off into tenderness and sweet vaporings quite cloyingly trivial and empty, without ever getting into farce or burlesque (wherein the laugh arises out of contrast between characters and the action in which they are placed). But what is generally accepted as essential comedy, " high " comedy, is the satiric sort, untinged with sympathetic appeal.

The French feel that they are the guardians of the true comic spirit. In discussing these matters, they claim that other nations vitiate comedy by tagging along sympathy and personal emotion. They, instead, place life on the rack and watch the result from an aloof viewpoint, without becoming entangled in an emotional or human reaction. We need not debate here whether a more human type of comedy is more enjoyable — whether it is " legitimate." We shall do better to grant to the French spectator a detachment which permits him to enjoy the pure wit of satiric comedy as we Anglo-Saxons cannot. He comes to the playhouse dispassionate, he leaves his personal emotions at home. And in the field of the detached comedy his Molière is supreme.

The distinction is a difficult one — for all drama is human — it is action by human beings before us, up there on the stage, that conditions the art. The theatre is trying out today the experiment of making the action very intimate, the character very personal, in realistic plays. But we read Molière with the feeling that here is a fine lofty reserve, a view of the foibles and follies of human beings that never descends into the mud or the easy sentimentalities of their personal lives. Somehow types are fixed, are held for our view, act their ridiculous bits, are gone. The characters are gracious and real, vigorous and socially true, but they never ask that we take them to our hearts. Let us grant that this detached comedy is " high " comedy.

Molière painted such a gallery of these social characters that only in Shakespeare may one find more figures that are universally used as touchstones. Molière quickly developed the serious critical note that he had added to the rich fun, the lively intrigue, of the older comedy. The social point that had distinguished *Les Précieuses Ridicules* became the distinguishing feature of his dramaturgy. The ridiculous conventions in life, the faults in the structure of society, the frailties of human nature, these became his targets. With good-natured humor, with barbed wit, he held up to view pretensions, absurdities, habits, religious superstitions. Beyond the playwright there came to exist the

Le vray Portrait de Mr de Molière en Habit de Sganarelle.

Molière in the character of Sganarelle.

philosopher, the moralist, the flayer of folly. And he brought his satiric gift to bear in searching out the weaknesses of *contemporary* society; in that, he brought drama one step closer to realism. No one had written so seriously before of the life at one's elbow. And Molière wrote with a marvellous finish, a superb grace, whether in prose or in rhymed couplets. The verse is not "poetic" in either the lyric or the florid sense; it is rather distinguished by ease, flow, and flexibility. His range of comedy — though the satirical comedy-of-manners is at the heart of his achievement — is extraordinarily wide; from farce through comedy of situation to comedy of character; and beyond that, excursions into tragi-comedy, ballet, and interlude.

From his very titles the world has taken by-words: *Le Bourgeois Gentilhomme, Les Femmes Savantes, Les Précieuses*. And from his characters we judge a man today as a Tartuffe or an Alceste. But rather it is the range of comic characters that is most notable: for here are the most memorable of hypocrites, humbugs, quacks, and snobs in all theatre literature. The ladies with pretensions are shown up in — to switch to the Englished titles — *The Affected Misses* and *The Learned Ladies;* the tradesman putting on airs, in *Le Bourgeois Gentilhomme;* the holy hypocrite in *Tartuffe;* the doctors in *Le Médecin Malgré Lui* and *l'Amour Médecin;* "the best society" in *Le Misanthrope;* the miser in *l'Avare;* and so on.

Tartuffe is an example of Molière at his best. The action passes in the house of Orgon, a French gentleman of assured position, with two grown children, who has taken a second wife, a charming and beautiful young woman (a part written by the author, as so often, to the measure of one of his actors, in this case his own wife who was hardly half his age). Orgon has taken up religion, and has brought into his house a pious impostor named Tartuffe. The young people, with the aid of an astute maid, are struggling to dislodge the hypocrite, while the credulous Orgon and his old mother fight back. Through two acts we see this situation explored, with special attention to the love affair of Orgon's daughter Mariane, which he breaks off in order to give her to Tartuffe.

But the impostor (he is known as such to the audience from the start) has other and more wicked plans: besides annexing Orgon's wealth, he will seduce his wife. He enters first in act three, and from that time his power seems to grow — the comedy is mixed with a sinister seriousness here. He immediately makes love to Elmire, Orgon's wife; and when the son exposes his duplicity to Orgon, the latter's only answer is to turn over to Tartuffe a deed to his property as a mark of confidence. Finally, to break through her husband's blindness, Elmire hides Orgon under the table and permits Tartuffe to continue his advances. And then when Orgon, convinced, faces Tartuffe and orders him from the house, the latter brazenly claims that the deed of gift has made the house his and that Orgon is rather the one to go. In the final act, when calamity seems to have come to completion, the dramatist solves the difficulty a bit mechanically, by having the King send in an officer to apprehend Tartuffe as a wanted criminal. The house is thus cleansed; and Mariane of course is restored to her rightful lover — while Orgon presumably will let pious phrases dupe him no more.

A bit of the scene when Tartuffe is making love to Elmire may serve to illustrate the surety of the characterization (quoted here in Curtis Hidden Page's translation):

TARTUFFE *(handling the lace yoke of Elmire's dress)*
Dear me, how wonderful in workmanship
This lace is! They do marvels nowadays;
Things of all kinds were never better made.

ELMIRE
Yes, very true. But let us come to business.
They say my husband means to break his word,
And marry Mariane to you. Is't so?

TARTUFFE
He did hint some such thing; but truly, madam,
That's not the happiness I'm yearning after;
I see elsewhere the sweet compelling charms
Of such a joy as fills my every wish.

ELMIRE
You mean you cannot love terrestial things.

TARTUFFE
The heart within my bosom is not stone.

ELMIRE
I well believe your sighs all tend to Heaven,
And nothing here below can stay your thoughts.

TARTUFFE
Love for the beauty of eternal things
Cannot destroy our love for earthly beauty;

Our mortal senses well may be entranced
By perfect works that Heaven has fashioned here.
Its charms reflected shine in such as you,
And in yourself its rarest miracles; . . .
I could not look on you, the perfect creature,
Without admiring Nature's great Creator,
And feeling all my heart inflamed with love
For you, His fairest image of Himself.
At first I trembled lest this secret love
Might be the Evil Spirit's artful snare;
I even schooled my heart to flee your beauty,
Thinking it was a bar to my salvation.
But soon, enlightened, O all lovely one,
I saw how this my passion may be blameless,
How I can make it fit with modesty. . .

But one needs the full-length portrait to know why the play precipitated a years-long controversy in Paris. There were those, it seems, who read into the deceitful Tartuffe a symbol of the Church, or perhaps of one of the powerful Religious Societies, and for a time even the King who had been Molière's generous protector felt compelled to ban the play. It was five years later that *Tartuffe* was unreservedly given to the public.

Molière had fought through many another quarrel and intrigue — not least, a competitive war with the troupe at the *Hôtel de Bourgogne*. And he fought against unhappiness brought upon him by his young wife, against libellous accusations, against court cabals. Through it all he kept on with his management of the theatre, with his acting, with his writing of plays. But fifteen years after his return to Paris his health broke under the strain. Returning home after stumbling through the fourth performance of *Le Malade Imaginaire,* he went to bed and died within a few hours. The local priests refused the last rites of the Church and opposed burial in the parish cemetery. An appeal to the Archbishop of Paris, who happened to be a notorious waster, only resulted in a confirmation of the ban. Finally the King's intercession brought permission for interment, provided that there were no ceremonies or pomp; and this great man, beloved and gentle and generous, as Shakespeare and Sophocles had been, was sneaked into an obscure grave in the middle of the night. But his genius has lived on, until his fame is greater than that enjoyed by any other artist out of France. Even the French Academy discovered and honored him a hundred years later.

After him there came no other comedy writers of first magnitude. The only one who demands mention is Jean-François Regnard. His plays have survived, and have a liveliness and a heartiness; but he is Molière's imitator, by no means his companion.

Molière wrote often for the Court of Louis XIV: ballets, interludes, "improvisations." He was too busy with his theatre to join regularly in the activities of " society " (he had the stage in the *Palais Royal* after that in the *Petit-Bourbon*); or else he was temperamentally not fitted to live the decorative life of a courtier. He was of the court, but always strangely a stranger there. And yet there are records of his contributions to the fêtes and the ceremonies. And this weaker side of his art got mixed up with the frills and furbelows that the fops and courtesans were just then mixing into opera and ballet.

More than any other dramatist, however, Molière held his serious comedies clear of the courtly influence. Neither the demand for scenic aggrandisement nor the threat of disbarment from the Academy if he defied the rules, led him to compromise in his comedy-writing. His plays demand no scenery, and no properties except for a table in *Tartuffe* and an occasional chair elsewhere; and he wrote them as seemed to him right, without regard to rule, genuine, hard, precise, with what characters he willed. He was of a court and a courtly age, yet above it; he shaped his art to a rude theatre as he first found it, yet transcended it with an art that fits all theatres. He was indeed greater than his time.

But aside from him, the limitations of those times settled down over all stages. The kings and courtesans and Academicians and dilettanti-artists with whom the chapter started are still ruling France. They are making the theatre courtly. They are building private theatres in palaces and country houses, and they are acting on those stages. Even the King himself has appeared in ballets. They have made a vogue of decorative " theatricals."

Machine-effects, scenery, dance, all have been imported from Italy. Look at this chapter's pictures, to see how the courtly glow has spread over the playhouses. Then turn to a new chapter, and the continuation of the story of operatic influences.

The French theatre as designed for the aristocracy. Note the very low orchestra floor which throws the best seats into the balcony. [Drawing by Warren D. Cheney after the water-color by Gabriel de St Aubin.]

CHAPTER XV

Opera, Picturing, and Acting

THE MEAT of this chapter, I warn you, is in the pictures. For my purpose is to show how the trappings of drama came to glorification; and then to name the personalities that shone out in " the Age of Great Acting." There is little to record about the essential theatrical thing, the dramatic play, the rounded stage performance. After Molière, France hardly turns up a world-dramatist until 1830; and this is a dull age in the playhouses of Spain, Italy, and Germany. Ballet, opera, spectacle, great actors — these are the outstanding phenomena.

Ballet — which we may define as dramatic dance in a musical and scenic investiture — has been a favorite court pastime for nearly a century, at the time of Molière's death. In 1581 the French Court of Henry III had enjoyed the more or less Italian *Ballet Comique de la Royne* at the Château de Moutiers; and there is a record of the event in the picture which you will find back in the chapter on the Renaissance and the beginnings of scenery. After that, attempts at the founding of native opera alternated with importations of complete Italian operatic productions. But at last Louis XIV so enjoyed a musical-dramatic performance of a pastoral by the Abbé Pierre Perrin that he lent official encouragement; and in 1669 Perrin was granted a royal charter under which the *Académie de Musique* (the present-day Paris *Opéra*) was founded.

Meantime, however, there had risen to power at the court that Italian who was destined to write his name as first among the great opera-producers of France: Jean Baptiste Lully. He had come away from Florence, as Lulli, when he was ten or twelve years old, had been either page or kitchen scullion in the service

337

of the King's niece, had risen to be leader of *les vingt-quatre violons du Roi* and accepted court composer. By 1671 he had composed music for no fewer than thirty of the court ballets — including several by Molière — had acted in some of them alongside the King, and had wormed his way into the position of favorite, partly by very dubious devices. And so it is not surprising that in 1672, by conspiring with one of the King's

Ballet costumes of Neptune and an African, by the decorator Martin
[From *l'Ancienne France: Le Théâtre et la Musique.*]

mistresses, Mme de Montespan, he succeeded in wresting the *Académie de Musique* charter and privileges from Perrin. From then on Lully *was* French opera for fifteen years. And the ballet element was strong in operatic production ever after.

Italian opera, you will remember, had already escaped from the courts and had claimed public theatres of its own. But in France it remained at least a court-protected, if not a privately shown art, operating under an official monopoly. It is said that Lully limited his art to please the taste of Louis XIV, who disliked brilliant and over-melodic music; and we may allow that here a real French decorum restrained the operas from an exuberance that sometimes ran wild farther south. At any rate Lully preserved Italian grace, added some orchestral elements, and fitted the recitative perfectly to the French verses of his collaborator Quinault. He established the type-form of French opera. With his great knowledge of practical stage technique, gained out of his long experience in presenting ballets, he made opera stageworthy; and of course he made ballet numbers a

Costumes for an eighteenth Century ballet. [After Gillot.]

fixture in every musical-dramatic production. (So if today you go to a performance, and wonder why they stop the play for that dance-divertissement, you may think back to this excitable French-Italian, who transformed the amateur diversion of the court ladies and gentlemen into a professional operatic interlude.) And aside from the shaping of the opera-structure and the tasteful improvements in the music as such, the court artists added to those extraneous scenic effects that have weighted down "grand" opera ever since.

Because the ballets had long been danced by the nobles and

the ladies, the costumes had been royal approximations of the dress of ancient kings, goddesses, shepherdesses, sorcerers, and such; with occasional excursions into contemporary exotic costume, Oriental, American, etc. In a contemporary engraving the Duke de Guise appears in amazingly elaborated "American" regalia; and that sort of glorification seems to have been common in all stage dress of the time. The progress of dancing in opera-ballets during the fifty years after Lully was conditioned by the reluctance of producers to give up the stiffly ornamental and weighty garments inherited by the professional dancers from the court ladies. It was not until the time of the famous *danseuse* Camargo (about 1730–40) that a gradual stripping process ended by bringing the foundation of costuming down to tights; and twenty years more before Noverre fully "reformed" stage dancing. Even so the ballroom slippers persisted, along with many another artificiality, down to our own century and the revolution accomplished by Isadora Duncan.

Nor was the costuming on the legitimate stage less scrumptious than that on the operatic. Drama must not fall behind this new rival, in appointments, in appeal to the courtly eye. So one sees characters in quite ordinary plays remarkably upholstered in silks and satins and plush, with truly monstrous head-dresses, their heads bowed under helmets and plumes, their bodies trailing vast quantities of brocaded stuffs. The mode was not out of keeping with that of serious acting, which was slow-moving, stately, stilted. Or was the acting partly conditioned by this costuming?

Watteau, who himself designed for the stage in the early years of the eighteenth century, fixed, with his inimitable courtly touch, portraits of the actors of the *Théâtre Français* in all their finery, as shown here. The *Théâtre Français,* by the way, was the new name given to the privileged royal acting troupe in 1680, when Louis XIV ordered the two existing companies, that at the *Hôtel de Bourgogne* and that of Molière (still carried on by his widow) to amalgamate. To the combined group he gave the sole right to present plays in the French language in Paris; though this did not work to the injury of either the Opéra producers or the ever-popular Italian Comedians. The date of the amalgamation of the two legitimate companies, 1680, is usually

Two paintings by Watteau, typical of the decorative French theatre of his time. Above, "L'Amour au Théâtre Français." Below, "Les Comédiens Français." [After engravings by C. N. Cochin and J. M. Liotard, reproduced in Dacier's *Le Musée de la Comédie Française.*]

The King's ballroom theatre in the Petit-Bourbon Palace. The group of spectators includes Louis XIII, Anne of Austria, and Cardinal Richelieu. Note how the proscenium frame has been permanently introduced here, by the imported Italian artists. [From the painting in the Louvre Gallery.] Below, a painting by Lancret, entitled *Scene from an Opera*. [From a photograph by courtesy of Wildenstein and Company, New York and Paris.]

recorded as foundation-date of the present *Comédie Française*.
(The terms *Théâtre Français* and *Comédie Française* are
often used interchangeably, when the larger *institution* is in
question.)

If the ballet costuming spread to the regular stage, that other
plaything of court-artists, scenography, was equally exploited on
both legitimate and operatic stages. The Italian perspective set-

Scene with elaborate machine effects of cloud-riding figures, moving ships,
etc., in the opera *Les Noces de Thétis et Pelée*, Paris, 1689. [From
l'Ancienne France: Le Théâtre et la Musique.]

tings were adopted, and Italian influence determined the form of
the French playhouse — though the Paris-Versailles Court added
luxuriousness in decoration. The painted settings grew to an
elaboration never surpassed (though they were made more natural and credible in later eras), and stage machinery for trick
effects again gained in range and complexity. We may believe
that some of the scenery was gorgeous, and compelling of admiration, however much we may deplore the spread of showy settings
to the dramatic as well as the operatic stage; and we may grant,

too, that the apparitions and the wire-riding and other trickery provided sensational moments.

The artist Giacomo Torelli produced at the theatre in the *Petit-Bourbon* Palace some of the most elaborate stage-pictures and effects of the times. He had come to Paris from Venice, it is said, because in the latter city he had staged some tricks so mystifying that spectators put on masks and tried to kill him, thinking he must be in league with the Devil. And he established a new standard of gorgeousness, as well as a new efficiency in rapid scene-changing. I have chosen my illustrations here to remind the reader that the proscenium-frame came from Italy along with scene-painting, as well as for the depicted scenic wonders.

After Torelli, who left Paris in 1660, came another Italian, named Gaspare Vigarani, who fitted up a palace theatre for the King, wherein the scenic features so far outweighed all other considerations that the place was called *Salle des Machines*. On the stage there, any known effect could be staged; and the settings might aspire to rival even the marvellously piled-up creations of the Bibbienas. A little later Paris was to have that famous follower of the Bibbienas, Jean-Nicholas Servandoni. But also the French artists were learning to design in the new style.

In theatre architecture, the horse-shoe type of auditorium was being perfected: it was the logical accompaniment to the V-shaped perspective scene, in a time when audiences wanted exclusive boxes rather than solid banks of seats. The opera-house in the Château at Versailles, though built later than the time of Louis XIV that we have been exploring, is representative of the French variation of the Italian originals. The later opera theatre, familiar from many prints of the period, shows how the audience in a large theatre was disposed in relation to the stage; and also how perfectly the stage had become a picture — how far it had changed from that platform, that shelf for acting which had served up to the time of Corneille. In truth, all theatres had become opera houses. (See pictures at pages 216 and 336.)

THE IDEAL of theatre art as a synthetic form, in which no one element predominates — neither acting nor literary drama, and certainly not setting — has so far engaged the artists in the theatre in this twentieth century, that there is even a sentiment against discussing acting as a separate art.   Certainly the greatest gain made in the playhouses within the last thirty years has been the new standard of ensemble production, the progress toward seeing the performance *as a whole.*

But in past times there were eras when story and poetry weighed heaviest, others when spectacle and trick-effects alone satisfied the audiences; and still others when a vigorous show of virtuoso acting was the *clou* of the stage art.   To us today there seems no doubt that acting should be considered a *contributive* art — perhaps the central one of those grouped to make whole the stage production, but still a craft within an art rather than an independently important manifestation.   Yet in a period covering the late seventeenth and most of the eighteenth century, acting was the most conspicuous element in the theatre's activity, and the only element about which a history of the playhouses of the times could be written.   Dramatists of world significance are not met with in France for a long time after Molière, nor in Spain after Calderon, nor in England after Dryden; and Germany won't bring forward any contribution till the star of Goethe and Schiller rises a century hence.   The actors are left to carry on the story.

In France there has been a steady progression from the days when actors were amateurs or near-vagabonds to the brilliant time of the honored *Comédiens du Roi*.   Richelieu particularly deserves remembrance for bettering the estate of the players.   But when a princely actor like Molière represents the stage, it is natural that great honor be done to players.   And it is in Molière's time that we meet the figure that comes earliest in the list of great French tragic actors.   (Those who have played tragedy nobly seem better remembered than those who shone in comedy; though there is a general belief that comedy-playing is the more difficult art.)

Michel Baron rose to eminence by opposing to the old stilted and pompous playing a sort that measurably reduced the unnaturalness and woodenness.   It was difficult, nay impossible, to escape artificiality when acting the rhymed-couplet plays.   But where his predecessors (of whom Mondory had been the greatest) had declaimed the lines with sing-song regularity, emphasizing the rhyme, Baron broke the lines, and threw the words into a more natural rhythm, at the same time modulating his voice to natural emotions. He was the first great fighter in that progressive battle between convention and naturalness, which has continued down to our own day. His facial play was expressive beyond any known before his time; and he refused to be bound by the rules for gesture which had grown into a tradition. Once when criticized for his over-natural movements, he answered: " My comrades contend that even in bursts of passion I ought not to let my arms go above my head. But if passion carries them there, I shall let them go. Passion knows better than the rules." And that, indeed, was highly revolutionary in a time when there were laws about everything, and Academies and such to enforce them. Acting had become a recognized separate art, and courtiers, writers, and the *précieuses* went to the playhouse to see how so-and-so handled such-and-such a passage out of Corneille or Racine. And every effect and method had been tabulated.

Baron quite recognized that he had gained the peak in his art. " The world," he said, " has seen only two great actors: Roscius and myself. Every century has its Cæsar; two thousand years are necessary to produce a Baron." But when he had made himself the greatest figure in the French theatre, he suddenly retired, at the age of thirty-eight. Apparently he felt that the world of the stage was too small for a Baron. Conceit, of course, has never been lacking among players — I could name you a few even to-day! — but it is seldom that the superiority is so ingrained that an actor feels impelled thus to quit the stage.

After thirty years in private life, Baron returned to the boards; and he scored again almost as notably as before, and with further innovations. And it was he who handed on the torch to another generation of players.

Among those who made their reputations in the older sort of acting, the frankly declamatory, the most famous were Mlle Champmeslé and Mlle Duclos. The former was particularly celebrated for the skilful use of her voice. " She shows so much art in the use of it," a contemporary wrote, " and she accommodates its modulations so well to nature, that her heart really seems to be full of the passion which is only in her mouth." And, indeed, *there* is a key to the fault in "majestic" acting; after all our praise of the effects, our thrill at the bigness and force of it, in the end it is remembered as only "in the mouth." If we would make out an excuse or a reason for the steady advance of "naturalness" since that day, we must study how the actors spoke increas-

Diagram of a stage with machinery for shifting painted scenery and for staging cloud effects, apparitions, etc. [From Grobert's *De l'Exécution Dramatique*.]

ingly from the heart, from the emotional centre. The appeal to an artificial taste, even the appeal to the intellect, may ride over on the declamatory method; but the deeper emotional-spiritual message that we believe today to be the essence of serious drama — *that* cannot be carried on verbal rockets or mannered gesticulation. Mlle Duclos continued on with the recitative sort of thing, to even greater extremes than her tutor, Mlle Champmeslé; and she gained fame with many, though she lingered on into a time when the pompous style was pretty well discredited — temporarily.

In the gallery of celebrated French actors of the time we might linger before the portraits of the Quinaults. Best-known out of that stage family was Quinault-Dufresne, who seems to have been the " matinée idol " of the early eighteenth century. But it is rather Adrienne Lecouvreur who soon commands all eyes. And she brings us back into the full tide of the reforms instituted by Baron. She came to the stage with a distaste for the bombast, intrigue, and pretense that were so large a part of " artistic " life. When the most celebrated actresses were mannered and stilted, she was simple and sincere (that is, within the limits allowed by Alexandrine verse); where the accepted tragediennes were fullsome and florid, she was slender and gentle and undecorative. She added to her native sincerity and feeling the schooling of Michel Baron; and she seemed to the spectators to " live " her part as no one before her had done. As distinguished from the passion that was in the mouth only, Adrienne Lecouvreur gained hers from the heart and the soul. And in a very short time she became leading actress at the *Théâtre Français*.

Her success offstage was hardly less brilliant than on, and her *salon* became a meeting-place for the élite in the social-artistic life of Paris. But unfortunately her semi-royal lover divided his attentions between the humbly-born Adrienne and one who had been born a princess; and when jealousies had been aroused, a plot to poison the great actress was uncovered. One day in 1729 Lecouvreur took a theatrical revenge: in playing *Phèdre* she stepped to the box where her rival was sitting, and delivered full-face the lines about those who, resting secure while committing crime, have learned to show an unblushing countenance. The audience rose to this drama within a drama, and left no doubt where *their* sympathies lay. But within the half-year the beloved Adrienne was suddenly dead — of poison, everyone said, but nobody dared seek out the poisoners.

Once more was repeated the old injustice: the greatest artist of her era, though an honored favorite but yesterday, in death was borne from her house at midnight, having been refused burial by

Adrienne Lecouvreur, as painted by Charles Coypel.
[From Dacier's *Le Musée de la Comédie Française.*]

At left, Giuseppe Biancolelli, known in France as Dominique, in the role of the Doctor. [From the catalogue of the Sambon Collection.] At right, Talma.

the Church and the law, and laid in a grave so obscure that no one has found it out even to this day. And yet the great Voltaire wrote of her as " this incomparable actress, who almost invented the art of speaking to the heart, and of showing feeling and truth where formerly had been shown little but artificiality and declamation."

Voltaire did much to aid the advancement of the theatre, outside the playwriting field. (You will remember that he freed the stage of spectators.) Perhaps his long residence in England had something to do with it, but certainly he saw through the worst mannerisms of French playing; and when acting seemed to be slipping back into the old pompousness, after Lecouvreur's death, he stimulated the *Comédie Française* players to further efforts after some sort of restraint. If he had a certain success with Mlle Dumesnil, who nevertheless overdid passionate nature at times, he failed to keep her co-star, Mlle Clairon, from being very rhetorically " sublime." Indeed, it was Clairon's self-consciousness and grandiloquence that carried on to the pre-Revolution theatre and made necessary Talma's new fight for restraint and naturalness. Unfortunately Mlle Dumesnil's weakness was such that toward the end " Bacchantes were the only ones she could play naturally "; and her influence waned.

Meantime, however, Voltaire had found a young actor named Lekain whom he could train after his own ideas. In the end Lekain became leading actor at the *Comédie Française,* could hold up his end of a grand scene with the florid Mlle Clairon, but withal tempered outlandish convention with an individual natural charm. And it was Lekain who handed on the torch to the young Talma, who, fifteen years later, is to make the fight for nature while France is in the throes of political revolution. But in the meanwhile the *Comédie Française* company is to suffer a sad relapse into " high " acting. With the passing of Lekain the " Era of Great Actors " in France is gone.

Generation after generation the Italian Comedians had been a fixture in Paris, and the fame, even the popularity, of their troupe had been more sustained than that of the French actors. In general their subsidies had been more generous. They had not always escaped persecution at the hands of their jealous rivals;

and by 1697 the King was prevailed upon to withdraw their "privilege," and they left France. But twenty years later a new company was summoned to the capital, and continued till the Revolution to delight the Parisians with farce-comedies, and, in later days, operas.

In the time of Molière, the Italians claimed two actors whose

Two productions with Harlequins, of the time when the Italian improvised farces were being turned into "Harlequinade" plays. [From old title pages.]

names have gone down in the annals of the great: Scaramouche (Fiorilli) and Dominique. It was Fiorilli who broadened the Italian Scaramuccia part into the celebrated character that has gone down in history under the Scaramouche name. Others played Scaramouche after him, but his will always be the glory of the creation and of the supreme playing of the character. One of his biographers wrote: "We may say that every part of his body spoke, his feet, his hands, his head, and that the most insignificant of his gestures was studied." And Gherardi, who is

remembered because he published a collection of the plays of the
Théâtre Italien, speaks of " the incomparable Scaramouche, who
was the adornment of the theatre, and a model to the most celebrated actors of his time. . . He made people nearly die with
laughter for a quarter of an hour by a scene in which he expresses
his fright without saying a single word. He touched more hearts
merely by simple natural means than the ablest speakers by the
beauties of the most persuasive rhetoric."

Dominique, who was really Giuseppe Domenico Biancolelli,
greatly broadened the part of Harlequin, from the limits within
which it had previously been played. Indeed, there is some
reason to believe that he made the character more serious than
the true *Commedia dell' Arte* troupes would have wished;
the Italian company in Paris was being influenced by French
surroundings. But he was enormously popular, and when he
died in 1688, the theatre was closed for a month. And after
him there was never again such an outstanding figure in the
troupe. The King exiled the Italian players only nine years
later, and the eighteenth century company never reached such
heights.

The Italian comedians had served Paris exceedingly well, not
only in purveying entertainment, but in their determining influence upon the genius of Molière.

THOMAS BETTERTON's company of actors, that so perfectly presented the artificial Restoration comedy in London, has already
found mention; and the names of Mrs Bracegirdle and of Nell
Gwyn have been accorded all the space proper in a brief survey
like this. In their time Betterton acted tragedies with Mrs Barry,
who perhaps should be the better remembered, since she helped
to carry on the tradition that was to lead over to the later
eighteenth century players.

Here again there is a fascinating gallery of portraits: Colley
Cibber and his fellow actor-managers at Drury Lane, Booth and
Wilks; Anne Oldfield, Kitty Clive, and Peg Woffington; James
Quin and Charles Macklin. Of these, however, only the last-
named can be said to have made progress toward the future — a
future summed up in the person and personality of one man:

David Garrick. In the Age of Great Acting, in England, all other names pale beside his.

Acting, indeed, was properly artificial in comedy, but pompously artificial in tragedy. The sonorous line, the strutting effect, these were the esteemed qualities, from Betterton to Quin. Then came little David Garrick, to prove that the natural thing was more pleasing, more stirring, than the most elegant declamation. Here was a man not too well-favored physically, who by sheer mobility and expressiveness moved spectators to a new understanding of Macbeth and Lear and Hamlet; who by a native brightness and vivacity put new spirit into comedy. And off the stage, Garrick was as well liked as on: he was amiable, intelligent, well-read, witty. Indeed, his success on the stage as actor was, if one may so express it, very little due to his being a born actor; to an undoubted natural gift for mimicry he brought influences out of wide learning, out of intelligent training, out of a broad purpose to meet life nobly. His first connection with the theatre was as dramatist, not player: his first dramatic effort was staged at Drury Lane Theatre in 1740.

In 1741 he acted at the Theatre in Goodman's Fields the part of Harlequin, incognito, as a substitute for the regular player; probably half as a lark, half as a test of his own fitness for a profession to which his desires impelled him — though his respectable family connections deterred. But only seven months later he appeared as Richard III, to an extraordinary popular success. And soon after, he gave over his wine business and turned all his energies to acting and playwriting. So great was his appeal that he leaped into first place in the theatrical world in England; within six years he was enabled to buy a two-thirds ownership of Drury Lane Theatre, building as well as business, and for thirty years reigned over the foremost London stage.

As player, Garrick brought actual revolution with him. Richard Cumberland wrote: " Old things were done away, and a new order at once brought forward, bright and luminous, and clearly destined to dispel the barbarisms of a tasteless age, too long superstitiously devoted to the illusions of imposing declamation." In short, by an intelligent reference to nature, Garrick avoided the grandiloquence, stiffness, and rant of the old school of acting. He turned the art into the channel known as " character acting."

D. GARRICK.

Acteur Anglois.

DAVID GARRICK
[From C. N. Cochin's engraving as reproduced in Jusserand's
Shakespeare in France under the Ancien Régime.]

Just as true comedy can be tested by its rise out of the clash of character, rather than out of mere situation, so genuine acting may be judged as having character-depth — and not merely the hollow shell of type-impersonation. Garrick brought mimicry into touch with life. Quin said, " If this young fellow is right, we are all wrong." He spoke more truly than he knew.

As manager and director Garrick created a new standard in many directions. He reduced the coarseness and grossness (there had already been progress from the time of Jeremy Collier's attack, but there was plenty of room for improvement still). He brought costuming and scenery more into line with the dictates of common sense; though here we may feel that the advance was but half-way out of the woods of showiness and artificiality. And he made for the theatre a sure place among the recognized arts of his day in England. Seldom else have actors enjoyed so much of equality and consideration in respectable society and among artists (though often before they had been accepted by none too virtuous court circles). And in choice of plays Garrick went back to the Elizabethans; he scored his own greatest success in Shakespearean parts, and he made productions of no fewer than twenty-four of Shakespeare's plays. The less said about the way he adapted these plays, the better. Let us grant that it was a step toward a more dignified and nobler stage that he should revive the great Elizabethan so fully, after the vogue of Restoration comedy and heroic tragedy.

In shaping his playing company Garrick let a natural fairness and breadth of view outweigh his own desire to shine as actor. He sacrificed much for ensemble, he introduced strict discipline, and before any other he foreshadowed that modern ideal which has determined the finest achievements of the acting art in this twentieth century. He created an acting machine. It was as a means to give this machine a fair road that he banished spectators from his stage.

The one-sidedness that is implied in the very term " Age of Great Actors " is thus somewhat belied by Garrick's conduct of his theatre. Even he cannot be exonerated of the charge of " writing up " the good acting parts in Shakespeare; but that dramatist suffered less then than in the hands of many a less gifted player-adapter in later times. And we may, with pleasure, mark Garrick

as the one great " star " of the eighteenth century who did most
to advance the theatre toward that ideal which has found such
wide acceptance within our generation, the ideal of " the acting
company " as against star-and-support.

But it would be unfair not to end the chapter on the note of his
individual achievement as an actor; and since I have mentioned
his tragic parts, I will choose an account,[1] by a German traveller,
of one of his comic characterizations:

At first he wears his wig straight, and you see his round, full face.
Afterwards when he comes home quite drunk, his face looks like the moon
a few days before its last quarter, as nearly half of it is dimmed by his
wig. The uncovered part is bloody and shining with sweat, yet most
benevolent, so that it entirely compensates for the loss of the other half.
The waistcoat is open from top to bottom; his stockings hang in wrinkles;
the garters are loose and — very significantly — are not a pair. It is a wonder that Sir John has not put on shoes of different sex.

In this sad state he enters his wife's room, and to her anxious question
what is the matter with him (and she has good reason enough for her
question) he replies: " Sound as a roach, wife! " Yet he does not move
away from the door-post, against which he leans as heavily as if he wanted
to rub his back against it.

Then he becomes alternately brutal, drunkenly wise, and again, kindly,
all amid the loud applause of the audience. In the scene where he goes
to sleep he astonishes me. The way in which, with closed eyes, swim-
ming head and pale face, he quarrelled with his wife, and mixing up his
r's and his l's to a kind of inarticulate sound, now scolded, now babbled
out scraps of moral sentences with which his own state contrasted most
abominably; then the way in which he moved his lips, so that you were
at a loss to say whether he was chewing or tasting or speaking — all this
surpassed my expectations as much as anything else I have seen this remarkable man do. You should hear him pronounce " prerogative " in this
part. It was not till after two or three efforts that he was capable of getting
to the third syllable.

This illuminating bit is quoted from a German critic, and is
the first indication we have had of dramatic interest or activity in
that country since the era of the Miracles. But now, in the
eighteenth century, Germany's day has come.

---

[1] By G. C. Lichtenberg. The translation appears in Vol. V of Mantzius' *History*.
This volume treats the English stage but briefly, though very interestingly. The reader
will find the richest material about the period in Dr. Doran's discursive *Their Majesties'
Servants: Annals of the English Stage from Thomas Betterton to Edmund Kean* (Lon-
don, 3 vols., 1888). A shorter outline history, covering all periods, is H. Barton Baker's
History of the London Stage and Its Famous Players (London and New York, 1904).

CHAPTER XVI

Sturm und Drang

FOR AN extraordinarily long period following the Renaissance, the theatres of Germany remained rude, clownish, and wholly unliterary. This was the country where the first surviving Christian plays had been written after the eclipse of the Roman theatre; and a country second to none in the vigor of its mediæval religious drama. But from the late fifteenth to the mid-eighteenth century the theatre existed only in an incredibly crude form: the stages were outdoor booths or platforms, or at best a vacant hall; the dramas were sheerest farce or coarsened foreign plays, with added acrobatic turns and Hanswurst or Pickle-herring characters; the acting was clownish or stilted, exaggerated and unstudied. The other theatres of Europe had experienced a period of this sort of thing, during the generations when the secular drama was refinding itself in Spain, England, and France. But nowhere else was the period so prolonged or so unrelieved by flashes of truer theatrical genius. Literally for centuries the cheapest theatre, the clown theatre, was all the theatre in Germany.

This crude popular stage is continuously vigorous, from mediæval times on, manifoldly active, widespread over the German nations; but it is so poor in achievement that it leaves not a single play that is important to later times, and hardly a memory that is of more than local significance — up to 1750. Then, almost suddenly the cross-currents will be turned into one channel, the stream of German national drama will begin flowing strongly and irresistibly — the stream that is to wipe out French domination, and within a few decades to send German plays and German influence into all the theatres of the Western world. But in these

354

earlier times there is no literature of the stage — and much less any theory of the theatre. In short, a remnant of theatrical activity hangs on: the stage, with its ignorant and suspected actors and its coarse audiences, exists in a world wholly apart from that of the scholars, the literary men, the cultured, the ordinarily progressive.

Reasons enough for this condition are to be found in the broader history of the Germanic peoples before the eighteenth century. There is no national unity, no national consciousness, no centre of cultural or artistic life. The " society " of the times is itself uncentralized, even chaotic. A terrible war blights the land, kills out budding literary endeavor, makes established theatres an impossibility. When the many independent courts turn to amusement, it is seldom that of the stage — despite their aping of the French kings — except as a foreign troupe may be invited in for an isolated engagement. In the capital cities nearer to Italy — Munich or Vienna — an Italian opera-theatre may flourish for a time; but it remains an exotic.

In one sense foreign acting companies overran Germany more than any other country, as we shall see; but no one country's drama and actors formed a single coherent thread upon which to tie the few notable phenomena of the times.

Religious drama in Mediæval Germany had been, toward the end, turned from its normal course to the uses of the Reformation. Not seldom it served for attack on the Catholic Church that had given it birth. Thus a play by Niklas Manuel, of the early sixteenth century, entitled *The Pope and His Priesthood,* showed the Pope parading in all his worldly splendor and display, accompanied by his court and his soldiers, while the simple Peter and Paul walked behind, speculating as to who this regal man might be.

But it may be said in general that the Miracles, which at first had admitted spectacular and farcical features as a concession to an ignorant public, ended by turning into popular farce-comedies. The German Shrovetide or Carnival-play is a perfect parallel to the transitional French farce of the late Middle Ages; with this one difference, that where the French playwrights concerned themselves largely with cuckold stories, the Germans found their materials more in the comic aspects of peasant coarsenesses. The sketches in either case, viewed in the light of modern taste, are degraded and offensive — with the exception of a few wherein the naïvety and shrewd humor outweigh the coarseness. Usually the Shrovetide play preserved, as a survival from its ancestor-Miracle, a tail-end justification, a few verses in which the author trusted that he hadn't offended too greatly against those moral principles that were his real concern. (That dodge of excusing a filthy play for the sake of a tagged-on moralistic ending is still being practised by some slice-of-life playwrights today; is, indeed, a newly-recurring evasion of responsibility down the ages.)

A stage as arranged in a church, for the Meistersingers. [Drawing after a reconstruction by Albert Köster.]

From the Shrovetide plays, and from the activities of the Meister-singers — bands of amateur actor-singers who were then the favorite entertainers over a considerable section of Germany — the shoemaker-poet, Hans Sachs, of Nuremberg, drew nourishment for his unique art. His is the one important name in the sixteenth century German theatre. He wrote dialogues, based on the older religious plays, in which the action is admirably simplified and made palatable to the simple audiences of the time. Escaping most of the coarseness of the transitional farces and avoiding the sensationalism, the blood and thunder and violence, which were to distinguish the adaptations of the next century, he created a type of comedy that is the only true folk-play of his period. He spent little effort in either characterization or literary embroidery; nor was his type of play carried on recognizably by successors. But he made straightforward little verse plays, contrived with simple artfulness, getting fun out of recognizable types of people without malice or great exaggeration. He is something more than a picturesque humorist, but something less than an epochal figure, in the theatre of his time. He and his fellow-amateurs staged plays in the inn-yards, in convents or in churches. They were doubtless a bit crude in their craftsmanship; but every-

Scenes from a student production on a market-place stage, 1574. [From F. R. Lachmann's *Die Studenten des Christophorus Stymmelius,* by courtesy of *Theatre Arts Monthly.*]

thing considered, play, stage, and acting, they were more notable as theatre artists than the native professional acting companies that were to carry the burden of the drama for a century and a half after them.

That phenomenon which we have noted several times since the Roman theatre faded out under the pressure of Christianity, the persistence of an active *student* theatre at the universities and schools, often affecting the professional drama, and in turn absorbing into itself such notable influences as Italian humanism and French classicism — that phenomenon we find again obscurely in the Germany of the Renaissance and Reformation periods. The universities have kept alive the interest in the classic authors, more especially Plautus and Terence. The students act in plays, sometimes as exercise in Latin, sometimes as seasonal festival. New special student-plays are written — first rewritten from old models, then more originally, finally with incidents from the lives of the students themselves and the townsmen about them.

1545 : HANS : SACHS . ALTER . 5 1 JAR.

The student productions are likely to be given with more finish, certainly with more care, and often with more elaborate settings and costumes, than the contemporary crafts or professional offerings. And certainly the large indoor assembly halls or the secluded open courts of the universities were more attractive settings than the platforms and booths often utilized by itinerant actor-troupes. At Salzburg, where the Italian influence flowed very early and very persistently (the town is one of the most interesting meeting-grounds of mediæval and rococo in all Europe), there were very elaborately staged productions; and this independent current flows throughout the time of the rule of *Hans Wurst* on the German popular stage. Occasionally one hears of a leading actor-manager of a popular troupe who has come from undergraduate university experience to the despised professional stage; Johannes Velten who managed the Electoral Saxon Comedians toward the end of the seventeenth century was such a one. But in general the universities and the regular stage are oceans apart, in aim, in tastes, in achievement.

What did serve to leaven the popular theatre, to stir into its heavy bulk some new quickening, was the example of the invading troupes of foreign players. Not that these visiting " artists " brought anything pure and different, and stuck to it. Sooner or later, they all add *Hans Wurst* to their casts of characters, even in tragedy. But they do bring new plays, and doubtless at first new methods of acting and staging. The most notable, though coming long after the Italian companies, are " the English Comedians." There is record of a *Commedia dell'Arte* company visiting Linz and Vienna in 1568, and remaining six years, and the Bavarian court had seen examples even earlier. But the English arrived in the late sixteenth and early seventeenth centuries. These troupes from across the Channel brought a repertory of English plays, but they seem to have picked up on the way into Germany some trimmings not so obvious in London; for we are told that the productions were not only full of bloody incident and exciting intrigue but horrific and violent as drama seldom has been elsewhere, and that the vogue of " grotesque " acting in Holland, where the comedians had been, influenced their presentations. Some accounts have it that the players were at least in part students from the Dutch universities. At any rate, the English drama was introduced into Germany, and if it had little lasting effect on German playwriting endeavor then, it built well toward the time when eighteenth century Germans were to challenge French rule of the theatre.

The visits continued over a long period, and in time the French companies are as much heard of as the Italian, English, and Dutch. To the remnants of drama from these countries, even adaptations, the Germans add elements that have become more or less their own, so that a later "native" play may easily be tagged as having the plot of *Hamlet* or *Romeo and Juliet* or *Tartuffe*. Soon after the classic period in France, one finds adaptations of Corneille, Racine, and Molière beside the plays out of Shakespeare and Italian comedies. Some of the troupes seem to have been well organized — they even attained to the dignity of official appointments to one petty court or another — but for the most part they were as second-rate and go-as-you-please, and as loose-living, as the cheaper *Commedia dell'Arte* companies in Italy. Some returned home soon or late, others doubtless stayed to become wholly Germanized — until no one knows how much of seventeenth century theatre activity is native, how much borrowed.

One thing is certain about the material, the story, and characters, in the plays: the level of dignity and truth was lowered for the groundling audiences. All plays apparently were presented with generous additions of acrobatic, juggling, dancing, and clown acts. Traditional comic characters, not to say buffoons, played their way through not only comedies but tragedies. These additions were quite in place when the piece was something handed down by the Italian comedians, but hardly added to the dignity of a Noah story from the Miracles, or an Iphigenia. In short, vaudeville, of a particularly cheap and coarse sort, was made out of every material, whether Italian comedy or opera, Shakespearean romance or French classic drama.

The visible symbol of the spirit and practice of these centuries is *Hans Wurst*, the "Jack Pudding," the debased Harlequin of the time. He may be, indeed, only an Italian Harlequin, brought lower by German coarseness. But there are no talented and famous actors associated with his name, as in Italy; in general, he is warred upon by those who would better the theatre, as the very impersonation of stage trickery, grossness, and obviousness. At his best he is an amusing buffoon, the typical blundering fool, sticking his nose into everything funnily, here fatter and more beery than elsewhere. The difference between him and those vigorously alive clowns of the better *Commedia dell'Arte* productions, which we admired so much if so vulgarly a few chapters back, is the difference between the intelligence behind those Italian parts and the coarseness of the German professional actor and groundling audience. The filling in of the scenarios of the Italian comedies was left to the actors, often quick-witted and inventive comedians, with the broad background of citizens of the world; the German dialogue was quite often partly improvised (because rehearsals were few, were hard work!), and the written text was as likely as not the work of a member of the company, after a foreign original — but this company was composed of near-outcasts, of half-educated show-people, acrobats, quacks, etc. Many troupes were hardly more than family groups; for one reason, if one were connected with actors, there would be little else by way of respectable occupation open.

Hans Wurst appeared, of course, in many variations, and it is impossible to disentangle his lineage entirely from that of the Dutch comic, Pickle-Herring. Not only is he mixed at times with Harlequin (or is it Pulchinello?), but there is a " female Harlequin " who borrowed some of his characteristics. For special sections he might take on the characteristic drolleries of a neighboring district: Vienna saw him for long as a caricature of the Tyrolean peasant. But he remains essentially Hans Wurst, dominating figure in the German theatre for two centuries, symbol of its unliterary clowning and of its obvious appeal.

Even when plays presumably more serious — *Hauptaktions* — are taking the place of mere interludes, farces, and turns, their titles are as likely as not to use Hans Wurst as bait to the potential audiences: *The World's Great Monster or The Life and Death of the Late Imperial General Wallenstein, Duke of Friedland, with Hans Wurst.* A typical comedy is announced as *A Schoolmaster Murdered by a Pickle-Herring, or the Bacon Thieves Nicely Taken In.*[1]

In this time the producing stage was so far divorced from literature that the few men who became imbued with the idea

[1] The titles, together with many other details in this chapter, are taken from Karl Mantzius' *A History of Theatrical Art* (London, 1909). It is unfortunate that none of the excellent histories of the German stage, in German, has been translated into English; but the material can be dug out piecemeal, and pleasantly, from the fifth and sixth volumes of Mantzius, and from W. Scherer's *A History of German Literature* (Oxford, 1906), or the shorter *A History of German Literature,* by Calvin Thomas (London, 1909).

of creating a German literary drama comparable to the Italian, English, Spanish, or French — and of course in the image of one of those types — remain merely names in history, with no known body of drama to illumine them: such are Andreas Gryphius, Jakob Ayer, Martin Opitz, and Christian Weise. A more lasting fame was achieved by Daniel Caspar von Lohenstein, but only because he stepped down somewhat, to meet the taste of the times: he wrote some of the most violent and bloodiest plays ever penned. Still, his reputation seems to have been of the library rather than of the stage.

And so we come to 1750. Acting is still ultra-exaggerated. A declamatory and bombastic delivery is considered a true sign of tragic art, of the " sublime." Movements are stiff, over-deliberate in tragedy; over-hurried and boisterous in comedy. If settings are anything more elaborate than platform-curtains, they are meagre painted stuff, probably not more than three scenes for the entire repertoire of plays (you will find them like that still in some stock theatres — particularly in French municipal playhouses: " cottage," " palace," and " wood " settings). The theatre might be an open-air booth or rough curtained platform, a town hall, or, on occasion, a ballroom in a castle. Companies by this time were wandering all over Germany and Austria, not a few with court titles; and often they carried their productions far outside of what we now know as those countries, to Scandinavia, to Russia, to Switzerland. But still there is no unity, no group purpose, no centralization.

Enter, a pretty girl. The time is 1727; the scene — badly enough painted, I daresay! — is this chaotic world of the theatre. Frederika Carolina Neuber, lovely of face, with a well-proportioned figure, comes onstage with that authority, that sense of combined capability-and-fairmindedness, which leads an audience to mark a character immediately as heroine. She is already an experienced actress; ten years ago she and the boy who was to be her husband ran away and joined a theatrical troupe — hardly any other shelter would be open to her after *two* elopements from her unhappy home. The husband is with her now, but he is rather a supernumerary in the drama of the awakening of a national spirit in the world of the theatre.

Hans Wurst (in black) on a roadside stage. Below, a theatre in a market square in Brussels, as seen by the painter F. van der Meulen. [From the original in the Liechtenstein Gallery, Vienna.]

The youthful Goethe, after the portrait by Angelica Kauffmann. The history of the German drama through two centuries might be adequately summed up in the phrase, "from Hans Wurst to Goethe."

There are two villains in the piece. One is symbolic, obviously villainous, standing for all the cheapness and coarseness that are to be driven off the German stage, our old friend Hans Wurst. The other, as so often happens, appears first as hero, and is only found out as a sinister influence several acts later: a Prussian named Johann Christoph Gottsched, who has become literary dictator of Leipzig and aspires to organize and rule literature and the theatre throughout Germany. We see Carolina Neuber make an alliance with him, pledge with him to lift the stage from chaos to the heights.

Now anyone should have been able to see through Gottsched's pretensions: he is organizer above all, an ambitious, dictatorial sort of person, not at all a poet, and without real knowledge of the stage. Worst of all, he has capitulated to French classicism, and his idea of elevating the theatre is to bring it under the rule of the unities and the other laws fixed in Paris for the guidance of the world's dramatists. Still he has written books on rhetoric and poetics, is president of the Leipzig Poetic Society, and has already succeeded in making himself a sort of centre toward which flow all the channels of information about intellectual advancement throughout Germany. Carolina Neuber has recognized two things in her dreaming about establishing a new stage in Germany: first, Hans Wurst must be overthrown and cast into outer darkness, while acting is purged of the excesses that persist even in the *Hauptaktions;* and second, there must come somehow a union between the stage people and literary, or at least "cultured," circles. The Neubers have brought their company — yes, it is theirs now — to Leipzig, the intellectual centre of an awakening Germany, in this memorable year 1727. And the first act ends with our lovely Carolina and the dictatorial Gottsched clasping hands in a pact which really is going to go far toward vitalizing theatrical life.

Years pass, and we see the Neubers with their "Royal Polish and Electoral Saxon Court Comedians" travelling over Germany in the difficult effort to lead the public from a love of *Hans-wurstiades* and old-favorite *Hauptaktions* to appreciation of translated "sublime" French tragedies or comedies-in-verse. Gottsched has been true to his bargain in one way: he has supplied trans-

lations of the approved French classics, and he and his friends
have written native plays in imitation of them.

There is something heroic about the determination with which
Carolina Neuber undertakes and persists in the task of reforming
a reluctant public; and something pathetic too, for there is no

A stage with wing settings, as seen at Strasburg in 1655.
This is probably truer to the average effect achieved
than are the usual idealized depictions, with wing edges
suppressed. [From *Wiener Szenische Kunst,* by Joseph
Gregor.]

reason why the audiences should like this pompous, lifeless fare
better than the clowneries that at least are amusing. About all
we see as gain toward her central idea, in these first years, is the
emergence of a new spirit in a group of actors — and beyond that,
a spirit among literary men and students who now have been led
to take a first-hand interest in the stage.

Out of that change in the spirit (and practice) of acting is to come Carolina Neuber's own tragedy: for beautiful and experienced as she may be, she is not one of the very great figures among actors, and after she lifts her company to a certain new standard, she is destined to see the world move on without her, to find her talents outgrown. Partly the inevitable actress' tragedy of a lost youth; partly the glorious flight of the human spirit beyond human capability. Her bravery persists for long; and perhaps it is bravery rather than common irritation that leads her to quarrel openly with her audiences in Hamburg — a thing theretofore unheard of — until the company's performances are officially cancelled. Certainly it is bravery that prompts her to refuse the dictator Gottsched's proffer of a new translation of Voltaire's *Alzire* (by his wife), because it is obviously inferior to the version already in her repertoire; though we see her antagonize the dictator thereby, see him become her enemy, an enemy discomfited but powerful enough to break her.

But first that other villain, Hans Wurst, is officially cast into outer darkness. Returning briefly to Leipzig, the Neubers put up a booth-stage — they have lost their old stage in the Butchers' Guild-hall to one of the hated Harlequin-companies — and there, with Gottsched's moral support, they put on a ceremony of the banishment of Hans Wurst (and all his Harlequin and other aliases). For a moment Carolina's star flames bright again, for the symbolic gesture stirs interest throughout Germany.

In the next act, however, Hans Wurst comes to life again. Hardly a year has passed when we see the Neubers' company itself presenting a play "with Hans Wurst." From which we know that things have gone so badly with our heroine that there is nothing to do but stoop to the old tricks. Indeed the world has ill treated the once beautiful, brave, and far-seeing Carolina. Hamburg has received her again, only to punish her spirited rebellion with a perpetual ban; she has lost the most valued members of her company; a tour in Russia has brought financial disaster. She pauses in Leipzig long enough to all-but-slay Gottsched, now her most hostile critic, by producing an act out of one of his plays *exactly* as he has clamored to have it produced, and by staging a satire she has composed portraying him as

Censor. There follows change after change, an almost frantic effort to catch hold here, there, or anywhere. Debt, dissolution of troupe after troupe, official discourtesy, public indifference, finally abject poverty.

Her death-scene, in a little farmhouse near Dresden, affects us by the proud spirit she shows to the very end, and by the devotion and tenderness of all the other characters — no longer the actor-friends but those simple country people whom she has drawn to her in the final years of retirement and poverty. Perhaps she smiles a little, toward the end, to think that Gottsched too has come down, has been deposed from his pretentious position as arbiter of literature and stage — has even been ridiculed by the younger artists, writers, and actors. We hope that she knows that she, more than any other one person, has made possible the march of this new generation directly on to one of the world flowerings of dramatic art. With the cruelty of youth, the adherents of the new stage have found her " old-fashioned "; but perhaps some glimpse of the ultimate truth comforts her. She has accomplished the union of stage and literature, and she has given a new purpose to acting.

In a scene so incidental that it escaped our notice, in next to the last act, we might have remarked a young Leipzig student named Gotthold Ephraim Lessing, one of the intellectuals who were drawn into association with the troupe of the Neubers. Indeed the boy Lessing was hanging about for some two years — a pretty soubrette in the company had something to do with it — and he gleaned first-hand knowledge of stage methods without which he never could have become the world's second notable " theatre theorist " and Germany's first great dramatist. Carolina Neuber even staged an immature play of his, about his fellow-students; and of course from that time he began to neglect his theological studies and to shape his life toward the professional theatres.

Even the most superficial student of the stage knows by name the *Hamburgische Dramaturgie,* which is really little more than a series of dramatic criticisms, such as scores of critics write today after the important " openings " in the theatres of Paris, Berlin, or New York; but there must have been more than average meat in them, because scholars still read and refer to them — and besides they were the first serious " reviews " of play performances published in Germany. But immediately the many capital cities were full of imitations, and indeed of pirated editions of the *Dramaturgy* itself. Another impetus had been added to the stream started by Carolina Neuber.

The occasion of Lessing's *Dramaturgy* was the attempt to establish in Hamburg the first German National Theatre, during the years 1767–69. The company was doubtless the best yet brought together in Germany, including both Konrad Ekhof and Friedrich Ludwig Schröder, noted ever since as the greatest two actors ever to grace the German-speaking stage; and the standard of play choice was high. There was, however, grievous mismanagement and not a little intrigue among the players; and the attempt to set up a permanent national stage proved abortive. The event may be marked as significant, however, as the first effort toward an established theatre in a country where the institutional playhouses have proved to be Europe's finest in the nineteenth and twentieth centuries. (Vienna, however, had had a " resident " theatre from 1712 on, and the famous *Burgtheater* traces its history back to 1741, although it became a " National " theatre only in 1776.) And there is that more tangible monument, the criticisms of the Hamburg theatre's " official critic " Lessing.

The publication of the *Hamburg Dramaturgy,* indeed, had not only local and national but international implications. For it was here that Lessing laid down the challenge to French Classicism. He has been called the first great critic after Aristotle — but that is perhaps crying down the Frenchmen a little. Nevertheless the German was broad enough to see world drama as a whole, he was the first outside England to set Shakespeare's name among the stage immortals; and he did more than any other to turn the attention of German dramatists away from the stiff French tragedies and toward the more human and freer English ones. He even had the audacity to prove that the Voltaire-Racine tradition wasn't " classic " at all — was, indeed, anti-Greek. He had no German masterpieces to offer as substitutes for the French which were being deposed; he kept on, however, " plugging

Shakespeare," as our theatre people of today would put it. It wasn't long until Shakespearean production became a great national pastime in Germany, until today the real home of the great Bard is in central Europe — while English-speaking nations remember him only in the reading and in very occasional and timid productions.

Among the occasional productions at the German courts, apart from any connection with the popular stage, were operas in the Italian style. This is a scene from *l'Erinto* at Munich as early as 1661, with perspective setting on a proscenium-framed stage. [From *Geschichte der Münchner Oper*, by Max Zenger.]

Lessing went farther. Even while disclaiming any serious pretensions as dramatist — he had refused the post of official poet in the Hamburg venture, preferring that of paid critic — he proceeded to write some of the *humanest* dramas ever staged up to that time. He was, doubtless, following hints out of another and somewhat apostate Frenchman, Diderot, as well as impulses gained out of his study of the Elizabethan playwrights. His prettiest play, *Minna von Barnhelm*, is still acted endlessly on the German stage. It is a tender, rather serious, prose comedy, dealing with real characters. His tragedy, *Miss Sarah Sampson* approaches the later *bourgeois* type, is a play of ordinary life that avoids the false sublimity and courtly twaddle of the transplanted French mode; and *Emilia Galotti* treats regal characters with new honesty and reticence. None of these plays by Lessing can properly be enrolled among the works by the great immortals of the stage: they are a bit too slight for such company. But they are eminently actable, and sympathy-provoking; and they mark Germany's entry into dramatic literature.

Brander Matthews, who insisted vigorously that drama should always be studied with relation to contemporary conditions of representation, notes illuminatingly that Lessing is the first dramatist to shape his plays so that changes of scene occur between acts; avoiding breaking any act into scenes demanding different settings, and thus avoiding the long waits, the disillusioning pauses, except after the act-dénouements. By this time, of course, the Italian picture scenery had come to dominate legitimate as well as opera stages, in Germany as in the rest of Europe.

Sturm und Drang. The name is usually applied to the period following Lessing, and covering the theatrical activities of a courageous and zealous group of playwrights from which emerged the immortal Goethe and Schiller. The words signify both unrest and excesses. It has seemed to me that one might carry the application farther back: the story of the German theatre has been stormy enough from the very start, and certainly this particular tempest has been brewing ever since those days when Germany was a meeting ground of the *Commedia dell'Arte* players, the English Comedians, and the correct French troupes; and the Neuber-Gottsched episode was something more than a gusty prelude. But it has seemed to many historians that just now, immediately after mid-century, Germany was quite suddenly alive with stirrings of young genius, with wild experiment, with painful travail — was caught in the storm and stress of a violent literary and dramatic rebirth.

The term *Sturm und Drang* is taken from the title of a play by a minor dramatist now all but forgotten by the rest of the world — Germany was simply teeming with playwrights intent on establishing the forms of German national drama. The storminess was evident not only in the general restless activity, not to say upheaval, but in the violence and extravagance within individual plays. There was the flood of horrors and licentiousness that often follows after a new-found freedom. But when the succeeding steadiness came, there were many solidly productive dramatists; and on the crest of the storm waters, the great Goethe and Schiller had been carried into the theatre.

In the matters beyond playwriting, in acting and staging and theatre architecture, there was similar activity and progress. Ekhof — since called "the Garrick of Germany " — had already set an example of unstilted, sincere acting, and the conventional declamatory and ranting method was losing its one-time popularity. More important, the wave of *purpose* among actors had strengthened; great numbers of them preferred the new plays and dignified company-effort, to the old *Hanswurstiades* and catch-as-catch-can trouping. Even at this time not a great deal can be claimed in regard to *thoroughly*-rehearsed productions — not a little of the old methods of careless improvisation (not the creative sort) persisted. And in more serious realms even a fairly natural and blunt tragedy would be played in stiff courtly costumes, in correctest Versailles fashion. But there are stirrings and promise of greater things. And Ekhof's successor, the young Schröder, is already on the scene.

Stage settings improve, too. That is, they tend toward operatic display: the new picture settings are well painted instead of badly painted. "Machine effects " have come in: plays are advertised " with metamorphoses, machines, and disguises." Here and there a really fine theatre is being erected. Already there are proscenium-frame stages like those of France and Italy; one of the earliest of those permanent Court Theatres, which are to become so distinctive a feature of German theatrical life, is built, at Gotha, in 1776. (It was here that Ekhof spent his last years, acting and directing.)

Out of the period — between Lessing and Goethe — a very few names of dramatists should be recorded. Friedrich Gottlieb Klopstock wrote a number of religious and patriotic plays. Christoph Martin Wieland wrote dramas that are no longer important; but his translations of Shakespeare give him a memorable position. Heinrich Wilhelm von Gerstenberg and Maximilian Klinger were more the *Sturm und Drang* culmination. But all these names, and all the works of these men, pale into insignificance in comparison with that Johann Wolfgang Goethe whose name remains even today the latest in the list of unquestioned world geniuses in the field of stage literature.

Of those six or eight " immortals " of the theatre, Goethe is least of all the typical theatre artist. He is greatest of all the writers who went into the theatre but became not of it; the mightiest literary figure who came to dominate but not to exist on the boards. Sophocles, Shakespeare, Molière had been stage people, with no other thought, life, or purpose; but Goethe, next in that noble line, walked apart, ever the lone poet.

Certainly here was one of the profoundest minds that ever came into the service of the theatre, in any capacity, and one of the noblest characters. Had Goethe given his life to writing for the stage, instead of making that one out of several interests — philosophy, politics, science, literature — he might have been accepted in all later times as on the very height with Sophocles and Shakespeare; as it is, there is always that reservation: his dramas are not shaped to actability, to exist primarily as *stage flow*. As related to the theatre, there is a sense of fragmentary grandeur about them. Dramatic conflict is interrupted by illuminating philosophic speculation and by compellingly beautiful verse; but these things are not immediately born out of an acted story.

He was for twenty-six years director of the Court Theatre in Weimar, and he thus had every opportunity to learn practical stage technique and to gauge the relationship between actors and audience. But still he remained somewhat detached, aloof. There is not the exact, the perfect rightness of the play *in the theatre,* as with Shakespeare or Molière, or even — to take lesser examples — with Lope de Vega or Lessing. The peculiar life of the stage, the " feel " of acting, the sheer stageworthiness, is not in his works. And yet, such magnificent fragments! For the first time since the Elizabethans, we feel that drama is again, in the wider implication, " of a certain magnitude."

He began, as might be expected, with a play only fumblingly dramatic, but with the marks of genius on it: originality, spirited emotion, daring freedom — and poetry. *Götz von Berlichingen* was, indeed, a final landmark in the way marked out by the *Sturm und Drang* progression. There could be no longer any doubt that the French domination was ended, that the classic rules were shattered, that the German national drama would follow a line drawn nearer to Shakespeare's practice than to that of the Corneille-Racine-Voltaire school — and with a native spirit and freshness added.

Other dramas followed, prose and poetic, similarly unequal in values; including a series of pastorals for his court. With a belated Renaissance interest in, and study of, the remains of antiquity, Goethe wrote an *Iphigenia* and a *Tasso,* but the formal limitations of his own conception of Neo-Classicism curbed what might have been the dramatic effectiveness of these plays. A minor domestic drama, *Clavigo,* is perhaps most effective of all in performance; and *Egmont* has extraordinarily dramatic scenes, but loosely held together in the play-framework. It is really only in the masterpiece *Faust* that Goethe exhibits the qualities that warrant naming him with the highest.

This tragedy was the fruit of almost a lifetime of thought and endeavor. The first conception preceded the finishing of Part II by more than a quarter-century. It is almost hopeless to attempt a summary or description of the work, for only the poetry, the profound philosophy, and the occasional intense feeling of it make up for a framework disproportioned, a tale undramatically slow. Goethe took the old legend of Faust, who sold his soul to the Devil, as a basis for the drama; and he set out to shape a tragedy that would have all of personal experience in it, his own and that of mankind.

The play (doubly inadequate word here!) begins with a "Theatre Prologue," wherein the manager, the poet, and the Merry Andrew of a booth theatre debate life, the stage, and audiences. A second Prologue, in Heaven, shows Mephistopheles wagering with the Lord that he can lead Faust astray — a portion of the drama that is sometimes considered blasphemous and unprintable. How close Goethe molded it to the simplicity and naïvety of the mediæval religious plays becomes apparent in the closing lines:

MEPHISTOPHELES *(alone)*
I like, at times, to hear the Ancient's word,
And have a care to be most civil:
It's really kind of such a noble Lord
So humanly to gossip with the Devil!

But in the first scene of the play proper, in a Gothic chamber, we find the serious motive of the drama set out, the erudite Faust pushing against all limitations in his intellectual curiosity, tempted to suicide but putting the poisoned goblet aside. From there the action moves on, never swiftly, but with the most varied embroidery: Faust out among the people, Faust in his study tempted by Mephistopheles, Faust making the pact, Faust deserting Knowledge and Theory for the pursuit of enjoyments; and so on to the story of the simple and innocent Margaret. From her first entry to her final tragic appearance in the dungeon with reason gone, her story is told in eighteen scenes or episodes, varied by minor flights and by that major one known as *Walpurgis Nacht* — seemingly interruptions to the human drama, and yet so right in a higher sense that the tragedy cannot be visualized without them.

To this Part I, Goethe added in later years a Part II which is in itself a full drama, but far more difficult to grasp, more obscure, without a primarily human story as basis. It is indeed a flight into the supernatural that has daunted all but the German theatre directors; and they as a rule have been content to overcome the very grave dramatic difficulties of Part I. It was G. H. Lewes who wrote of that, in his excellent *The Life and Works of Goethe,* as "this wondrous poem, the popularity of which is almost unexampled. It appeals to all minds with the irresistible fascination of an eternal problem. It has every element: wit, pathos, wisdom, farce, mystery, melody, reverence, doubt, magic, and irony; not a chord of the lyre is unstrung, not a fibre of the heart untouched." And, indeed, outside of the three Greek tragedy writers and Shakespeare, no dramatist has given the world a tragedy more sought out by serious readers the world over. I would like to quote here excerpts that might stand for the quality of the poem; but the design is so vast and the excursions so bewilderingly rich, that no chosen bits could be adequate —

and it is a sad fact that the translations into English are hardly more than serviceable, bringing the larger drama vividly before us, but with grievous loss of poetic values.

The poet-dramatist who wrote this *Faust* appears, in later histories, like a giant among the Lilliputians of the Weimar court. There is a tragi-comedy there — you will find yourself both amused and moved if you will read through one of the biographies. The great dramatist, so aloof from the stage in a way, is yet, professionally, the head of a special sort of theatre; intimately connected at first with amateur theatricals, he is then the active director for twenty-six years of a company of second-rate professional actors. He is even author of a very detailed code of rules for acting. And he is seen, toward the end, at the mercy of his petty master, the Duke of Weimar, and of the Duke's mistress. Together they make Goethe's life miserable over a term of years, until finally by insisting on the production of a play in which a trained poodle is chief actor, they force his resignation from the directorship of the Court Theatre. It is a pleasure to add that while in the position Goethe enjoyed ten years of collaborative producing with Schiller, before that poet's premature death.

Johann Christoph Friedrich von Schiller (1759–1805), combined a lesser poetic gift with a far better grasp of stage technique. He wrote historic dramas that continue to stir us in performance to this day: *Maria Stuart* and *Wilhelm Tell*. And the romantic *Don Carlos* and a play of intrigue, *Cabal and Love,* remain among the most effective of sheer "theatre pieces." Far from being aloof from the stage, Schiller learned every value and every trick of production, so that modern *régisseurs* find his dramas perfect media for *tours-de-force* of staging. He had a way, indeed, of dressing something very like melodrama in fine poetic clothes.

His first play, written when he was twenty-two, and entitled *The Robbers,* wobbled between melodrama and passionate tragedy, all done up with the uncertainty of immature genius. But he was immediately accepted into the theatre for it (the Mannheim National Theatre made an "event" of the production), and he set to work to master his art from the stage point of view as well as from that of the literary man. He even had some idea

Homage to Schiller as he leaves the theatre in Leipzig after the première of his *Jungfrau von Orleans,* 1801. [After a drawing by Theobald von Oer, in *Illustrirte Zeitung.*]

of becoming an actor — an ambition he did well to give up. Gradually he brought his extravagance under some sort of control, and by the time of the first verse-tragedy, *Don Carlos,* he is marked as one of the great serious dramatists. He treats history with a great deal of freedom, being less reverent toward historical accuracy and toward what earlier had been considered good play-form than toward a certain unity of human-dramatic expressiveness. He did nothing to further that compacting of the play-structure, that tightening of technique, which is to mark so distinctively the playwriting of the nineteenth century; he is rather a late flowering of the impulse that gave Calderon and the lesser Elizabethans to the theatre, the more romantic, more sentimental, far-riding poet-dramatists of extravagant eras. His *Wallenstein,* sometimes considered his most impressive work, rides a bit outside the limits of ordinary theatre production, though its serious literary values and philosophic implications cannot be denied.

There was in Germany in the time of Goethe and Schiller a spirit of idealism, of glowing personal initiative, that led directly to the choice of subjects like Joan of Arc (*Die Jungfrau von Orleans*) and William Tell. At Weimar, where Goethe and Schiller spent so much time together, there was developing a new nationalism, a devotion to liberty and humanism; there is a breath of that wind of Revolution that is so soon to fan destructive fires, overturn political institutions, and incidentally transform the theatre. One root of the new growth goes back to Rousseau, whose ideas had been subscribed to in Germany widely and passionately.

The one-time current toward naturalness and prose, on the other hand, was arrested. Times were too exciting, the storm-and-stress violence had been too great, the new idealism of young Germany was too strong, to permit immediate drifting of the theatre into that realism which will mark the nineteenth century. First there will be the so-called Romantic Period. And just preceding that is this flowering of the poetic, the high, drama under Goethe and Schiller — something far finer than mere Romanticism, and the very opposite of Realism — but again, with a freedom, vigor, and freshness unknown to the then accepted Classicism.

Among playwrights immediately after Schiller and Goethe,

however, there is a lapse to a sentimentality that is in direct line toward Romanticism. The tearful domestic drama becomes a special favorite, though most of the popular authors alternate between that and imitations of the two German masters. " The Great Schröder " — the theatre's historians still call him that — wrote many plays now forgotten except in name. Another actor-dramatist, Auguste Wilhelm Iffland, was likewise prolific, and made good his claim to a place among those who wrote plays " for acting, not reading." They attained an extraordinary popularity in the theatres of the time; but their vogue was as much based on current taste and a passing emotionalism and as little on eternal principles as are those plays of earlier and later actors, Garrick and Pinero, or David Belasco and George M. Cohan.

But while Schröder and Iffland retain a place in history for their acting and for their service in establishing institutional theatres in Germany, August von Kotzebue has been a more or less permanent victim of his fame as playwright. He was mistaken by critics of his time as a genius of first water, and his plays were pirated throughout the Western world. When the reaction came which showed up his work as thinly disguised melodrama, he became suddenly the typical bad example of playwriting, achieving a notoriety as great as his fame had once been. He is the logical culmination of the bad enthusiasms of the storm-and-stress group, as Goethe and Schiller had been of the better tendencies. He is the embodiment of the good craftsman who mistakes sensational action for essential drama.

There are those who would treat the story of the German stage before Romanticism (and aside from the two outstanding literary figures) as a chapter in the story of " the Great Actors." Mantzius in his six-volume *History of Theatrical Art* covers this whole period in the volume devoted to " Great Actors of the Eighteenth Century "; and he portions the material under the three names, Ekhof, Schröder, and Iffland. Schröder's was perhaps a strong enough and a universal enough genius to support such head-line fame; the others are hardly world figures. Ekhof brought in restraint and sincerity when those qualities were much needed; but he was quietly and humanly effective rather than commanding.

Schröder, however, was not only the best German actor of his time but the dominating figure in the most formative period of the national stage, a recognized example to all other actors; and he directed his companies with true command and insight. He carried on the fight for a national theatre from the point where the ill-fated venture in Hamburg (that had been made famous by Lessing) left it. It was in that same Hamburg that he directed a later theatre, over two periods totalling twenty years, with such success that this became the theatrical centre of Germany. He built a company ensemble as no one before him had done; he introduced Shakespeare on the stage — and thus the dramatists saw that what they had accepted in their reading as model was equally effective in the theatre; and he imparted a sort of grandeur to the acting profession. At the time of his retirement to a life of ease, at a comparatively early age, he had accomplished to the full those purposes which to the youthful Carolina Neuber had seemed like golden dreams. The stage of Germany had been " established," actors had become creative artists, and out of the union of stage and literature had flowered the works of Goethe and Schiller. This was no longer a Germany relishing *Hanswurstiades,* or grateful for a foreign company importing sometimes academically good, and more often very bad, dramatic art. It was a Germany enjoying the most prolific and most original theatre in the world, exporting plays to the rest of Europe; a Germany in which " the best minds " were excited about the stage, creating for it, finding inspiration and sustenance in it.

CHAPTER XVII

The Theatre and the Birth of Democracy

ALONG toward the end of the eighteenth century some large bonfires were lighted in Europe and America by men variously calling themselves patriots, rebels, sons of liberty, brothers, and — Democrats. As is usual in times of Revolution many good people actively disapproved, and the great mass of mankind merely looked on apathetically. But such was the burning sincerity and the intense energy of the rebel minority that soon one could see, by the light of the red glow in the sky, here a royal head popped off by a very bloody guillotine, and there the remnants of a Royalist army fleeing before a handful of lusty Republicans. And very soon democracy was an established fact, and all the kings of Europe were sitting up rubbing their eyes and wondering if that really could have happened to brother Louis of France (and more horrible, to his once beautiful Marie Antoinette), and whether those upstart American colonists had really whipped Cousin George's troops.

Since the days of the Renaissance and the birth of Humanism, when man reached out after knowledge and refused longer to let the Church do his thinking for him, there had been no overturn comparable to this one. Before the Renaissance the Catholic Church had ruled, by divine right. After the Renaissance, kings and queens ruled, also by divine right. After the American and French people threw out their kings, presumably the Democrats were going to rule, again by divine right. Whatever else had happened, clearly the spirit of man had found a new release. And since the theatre has to do first with the spirit, surely this must be a great moment for the stage, another Renaissance perhaps.

379

A revolution in ways of thinking, such as that which ushered in democracy, goes back to causes and events and abortive efforts through many generations earlier; and similarly, its full effects, and right judgment of its values, will not be evident until many generations later. Indeed, today, a century and a half after the event, we are likely to be so blinded by sheer superstition toward the institution of democracy that we hesitate to ask whether the freedom that was born and reborn in 1776 and 1789 did not bring with it disadvantages almost as great as the advantages. It would be a doughty one among us who would admit allegiance to any other political faith before democracy. There is, indeed, our common sense telling us that the spirit of man must be free, that the Divine Right of Kings is an illusion, and that only out of liberty of conscience and action can justice be born. But in the theatre particularly there is reason for dissent and wobbling. Within the year I have heard the artist whom I consider the greatest in the world theatre, protest after this fashion: " The old theatre is dead, the new theatre is not born. The stage is in the hands of tradesmen and upstarts. It all started with that damned French Revolution! "

The melancholy fact is that the birth of democracy neither ushered in a Renaissance of the arts of the stage, nor even served to carry on the impetus of the only fresh theatrical achievement of the period immediately preceding, the development of a poetic drama under the banner of Goethe and Schiller. It would be pleasant to record that immediately upon the coming of the spirit of democracy, the theatre burst into glorious activity, revived something of its old nobility, and became again the hand-maid to man's reawakened spirit. As a matter of fact it entered into a decline, or else continued a decline which in most of Europe had been under way long since. For a full hundred years there will not be a playwright of more than near-immortal fame; not until the Democrats who more or less rule Europe and America come under fire for their bourgeois morality and for their capitalistic exploitation. There will be no new giants or near-giants until Ibsen and Shaw. If the mantle of divinity was transferred from kings to the common people, it was a sort of divinity from which the Dionysian spirit was notably absent.

Immediately preceding the French Revolution the courts of France and Germany and Spain had kept up at least a tinselly show of theatrical activity; and in England and Italy there had been real flare-ups of playwriting genius, in Goldsmith and Sheridan, and in Goldoni and Gozzi. In reviewing these pre-Democratic developments, before turning to the actual years of the Revolutions, we shall do well to note certain relevant facts: that in this earlier time the theatre is still being coddled at courts, aided with patronage which it may find necessary beyond the support of popular audiences. And that drama has not yet been brought down to common life, in the analytic and fact-finding sense; it is still more theatrical, with a life of its own, than reportorial and photographic. But that there are unmistakable signs that drama, in a larger view, is marching on, if jerkily, to greater familiarity, to closer identification with life; the old aloofness and remoteness are giving way to a personal emotion growing out of nearness to ordinary events of living.

SINCE Voltaire there has not existed a dominating figure in the theatre of France. There has been the age of great acting, but now even that is more a memory than a fact. The world has moved on; but French officialdom and the French stage, with their characteristic indifference to — nay, scorn of — all art that develops outside of French territory, go on sleepily in the old worn paths. The Germans have demolished for all time the superstitious "rules of playwriting"; but officially the laws still hold in France. German and English players have put new life and humanity into acting; but you would never guess it from anything you might witness at the *Comédie Française*. Tragedy is still played "with much convulsion and contortion." France is living on the past, dying slowly.

The stage of the time does not fail to be characteristic and, as we shall see presently, picturesque. There is the elegance persisting from the great days of Louis XIV, a hollow elegance, perhaps, now that there are no truly noble forms to fill out the gorgeous clothes; and the *salles* are still the most beautifully decorated and the stages the best equipped in Europe. There is too a tradition. It is tradition, indeed, that has made the *Théâtre*

Français the stereotyped, half-alive institution that it is. Without leadership from among its own personnel, it submits tamely to capricious court rule. Courtiers, completely ignorant of stage art, but appointed by the King, regulate every detail of the running of France's official playhouse, not least of all the matter of which ladies shall be elevated into the showy parts. Their only other concern is the censoring of plays so that nothing derogatory to the old régime shall be spoken from the stage. And there are no Racines at court now.

There are individually picturesque figures crossing this strangely dead-alive stage. Here is the actor Ducis discovering Shakespeare at second-hand, falling in love with the plays of the Barbarian from across the Channel, but rewriting them in accordance with the sacred classic unities, devitalizing them by banishing all violent action to offstage, adding such conventional characters as the confidant, and beautifully decorating the texts with high poetry! Imagine *Hamlet* squeezed into one day's time and into one place; Polonius as the King's confidant, a new character inserted as confidante for Gertrude, and much of the original action deleted and the events recounted by these four; and the Hamlet-Ophelia love interest played up — all in rhymed Alexandrines!

There was, of course, a succession of vivid courtesan-actresses (an official-ruled stage makes for that); but the strangely contrasting Mlle Raucourt was a better artist than any of them. She made a sensational success with her first appearance, as Dido, at the age of sixteen, and after the *Comédie Française* discharged her a few years later, for the fault, unforgivable in stage circles, of unexplained absence on a night of performance, her unrivalled ability soon led the company to recall her as a permanent member. Still it was her flaunted masculinity, and such extra-theatre affairs as beating up her landlord, serving prison terms, and continuous scandals in the rôle of *galant* that got chronicled the more vividly for later generations. In this period there was, too, the early acting of the great Talma — but he will appear where he better belongs, up in the thick of the French Revolution, and as Napoleon's favorite.

From among the crowd of futile but popular playwrights there stands out one figure by contrast — the only dramatist to be

remembered out of the period, Beaumarchais. His pleasant and
shrewd comedies, *The Barber of Seville* and *The Marriage of
Figaro* are still played today. But their author is more famous
for his independence of thought and action, in a time when wise
people pretended blindness and authors as well as common folk
buckled neatly to authority. Beaumarchais fought firmly and
courageously against court censorship and against the powers

French stage costuming of the mid-
eighteenth century — symbolic of the
stage and theatre of the time.

that ruled in the official playhouse in Paris. He insisted upon an
author's right to have a say about casting, thus crossing no end of
favorites, as well as a number of powerful " protectors," and he
even wrote out detailed " stage directions " for the productions
of his plays, a proceeding theretofore unheard-of. In refusing to
be cheated out of his royalties by the actor-group in the *Comédie
Française,* he made a stand that ultimately led to those author-
guilds that today guard the dramatist so effectively from pirating
and exploitation.

But most apropos here, Beaumarchais contributed to the stage the only play that may be said to have forwarded, through its performances, the march toward democracy. The witty *Marriage of Figaro* is so full of references to a decadent nobility, and so patently a reflection of widely current but carefully suppressed bitterness, that Louis XVI personally ordered the play banned; and it took the tenacious dramatist five years to fight through the various censorship offices to a first performance. It was a sign of gradually changing times that he was able to win through, after an expression of royal displeasure. It was even more significant that this ironic comedy, painting boldly a feeble aristocracy in contrast with rising common folk, should be played at the official subventioned theatre of France, to crowded houses, through what was for those times a " long run." The opening at the *Théâtre Français* on April 27, 1784, was occasion for smashing in doors and near-rioting. The spirit was already abroad that would find climax in the storming of the Bastille and in considerable reflected violence within the walls of the great national playhouse.

But in general the French stage of these years was tame, undisturbed by genius, content with the old acting and routine plays, servile or at least complacent under domination by an enfeebled but still ruling court. Its staging was as artificial as the old playwriting that decreed the longest way around as the prettiest way of expressing a sentiment: its costumes as puffed and ornate as its tragic poetry; its relation to full-blooded life as insecure as that of the affected court society. Its actors were as often as not ignorant in every department except that one so admirably but so disproportionately prized in French theatres: *diction*. In Paris at this time there were five regular theatres: the specially privileged and subventioned *Comédie Française,* with a company known as *Les comediens ordinaires du Roi,* an institution with a monopoly on " tragedy and comedy "; the Opera, known as the *Académie royale de musique;* the *Théâtre de l'Ambigu-Comique* and the *Théâtre Nicolet,* given up to farce, spectacle, and pantomime; and finally the *Théâtre Italien,* at times a real rival to the official theatre, but usually forced to a policy of music-plays. For many decades the artificial limitation of legitimate theatres, the court-decreed monopoly, had militated against new stage creativeness.

A private theatre as seen from the stage. [From an engraving by LeRoy after Binet.]

Two famous actor-managers of Court theatres. At right, Queen Marie Antoinette, as painted by J. S. Duplessis. At left,

When the Revolution puts an end to the monopoly, we shall see nearly half a hundred theatres in place of these five.

In France in the half-century before 1790, the important theatres are really less interesting than the unimportant, i.e., the amateur, ones. One might have seen, in these years, real theatres in kings' palaces, miniature theatres in chateaus, stages in country houses, even in the town houses of society leaders. In Germany, the court theatres are already becoming the " standard" playhouses, fully professionalized, and there is real dramatic progress there, in the historic sense. In France they are toys, for the amusement of amateurs, and interesting only because kings and queens are concerned. Back in the days of Louis the Grand, as we have seen, the court had to do with the development of a national art. Under Louis XVI the private opera house at Versailles is used but fitfully, with productions brought out from Paris.

But in the Chateau at Versailles there is also the *Théâtre des Petites Apartements;* and out in the park, over toward the Trianons, is the private theatre which has been specially erected for Marie Antoinette. It is, indeed, a queen's plaything, *par excellence.* Today we damn quite heartily the decorators who strew our modern playhouses with faded and sterile copies of regal magnificence. But what could be more fitting in a queen's own personal theatre than this profusion of decoration, this jewel-box prettiness, this boudoir intimacy? One may note in the illustration many details and principles common to the larger theatres of the epoch: It is designed on the usual horse-shoe plan, with three floors of seats. Features not uncommon are the presence of the prompter's box, the comparative shallowness of the auditorium, and the very low orchestra floor designed to throw the best seats into the first balcony. (This balcony in Marie Antoinette's time was not so large as that shown in the drawing, and probably much more graceful in line; it was enlarged by the addition of the cross-boarded portion of the floor, with a consequent squaring of the railing, in 1836, under King Louis-Philippe, " to accommodate his large family.") The stage was equipped with every device that money could buy, and leading artists were drafted to design the settings. Marie Antoinette acted on the stage, when the whim took her, over a period of five years — though not so regularly as Mme de Pompadour in the less pretentious theatre in the Château.

The last performance under the Queen's " direction " occurred on the evening of August 19, 1785, when the shadow of revolution was already over the land. And as if it were not indiscreet enough for the court to flaunt its wasteful extravagance and its flippant pleasures in such a time, Marie Antoinette chose the comedy *The Barber of Seville* as a vehicle (playing Rosina herself), and invited Beaumarchais to the performance. The incident of the opening of *The Marriage of Figaro* at the *Comédie Française* had but just occurred, and the town was already agog over Beaumarchais' audacious criticism of the nobles and his defiance of the royal ban on the play; and yet here was the Queen inviting the author of that play to the performance of another of his comedies, at the palace where he would necessarily meet the King. One may ask whether it was bravado, or if there was, as some think, personal point in this gesture of an actress-queen conspicuously crossing her none-too-faithful King for the sake of a favored courtier. In any case, one may be sure the court theatricals had their bit of effect in stirring public hatred toward that day when the Democrats were to use the guillotine alike on this King and Queen.

But if play-acting on the part of a Queen was odious to a portion of the French people, it might be indulged in by Royal Mistresses and courtiers with impunity and as a natural part of the interminable round of fêtes, balls, and entertainments at Versailles and the other palaces. And to at least one noble courtesan, theatricals proved a godsend. To put it bluntly, Mme de Pompadour had felt herself slipping as favorite of the pleasure-surfeited Louis XV. She must devise a new means of diverting him and showing herself to the best advantage. She could act, she could sing, according to historians, and she was very beautiful; all she needed was the proper stage. In one of the smaller galleries of the palace a tiny auditorium was arranged, and a lavishly equipped stage was appended. The nobles of the court responded to the call for a company of actors, and Mme de Pompadour became the most prominent and most applauded member of one of the most distinguished amateur companies the world has

Interior of the dainty theatre of Marie Antoinette at the Trianon. [After a drawing by A. Benard in Adolphe Jullien's *La Comédie à la Cour*.]

The theatre of Madame de Pompadour in the palace at Versailles. [From the etching by Guilmet after Cochin's drawing.]

known. Her success was so great, her charm and ability so irresistible, that she not only won her King-lover completely, but established the private court theatre as a four years' attraction at Versailles.

We are fortunate in having a pretty drawing by Cochin of a production of *Acis and Galatea* in this private theatre. It shows Mme de Pompadour on the stage as Galatea, and the Vicomte de Rohan as Acis; and one may discern the King and Queen and members of the court among the spectators, as well as every detail of the seating arrangement. It is worth while to pause and note the daintiness and intimacy of the auditorium, so appropriate to a theatre which was in reality a toy of a monarch's favorite. There is in this drawing, too, a graphic illustration of the seventeenth and eighteenth century drift toward picturized setting. A theatre building is necessarily architectural, and the stage is presumably a platform for acting. But here one sees the architecture lost out of one-half of the building, and the platform absolutely disguised. The painter's ideal has wholly prevailed, and the actors are (the modernists point out) ill-fitting figures in an easel picture.

The court theatres were but one phase of the widespread amateur dramatic activity of this time. What the King and his circle did, the next stratum of society below must do, and so on down to the very fringe of the elect and near-elect. " A little theatre," wrote the Goncourts, " is set up in the city mansion, a great theatre is built in the château. All society dreams the theatre from one end of France to the other. . . The *grandes dames* cannot live without the theatre, without a stage to themselves." And yet the phenomenon has importance only socially. Occasionally amateurs are better than professionals, less stilted, more sincere, truer to the spirit — as we happily know today, when a " little " theatre movement is sweeping over two continents. But not for long does any stage but the professional demand attention when the theatre is being studied.

In England, during this period, audiences had been enjoying the late fruits of Garrick's epochal innovations, though the British theatre was already entering upon a decline. Acting, to be sure, was far advanced as compared with that to be seen in France; but when Garrick retired from management of Drury Lane in 1776, the greatest of English actors left the stage, and at the same time the London theatre lost the only director who had been able during his century to organize dramatic activity in a masterly fashion, to make the stage a dignified and worthy companion to the other arts.

Playwriting had been at a low ebb for a very long time; and what Garrick and his fellows had done to earlier texts — particularly those of Shakespeare — is enough to mark current taste as decadent and inhuman. Tediously bad plays were being written, but worse was the almost unbelievable adaptation, nay, mutilation of earlier masterpieces, to make good "acting vehicles." Still the theatre had been raised to a position of respect, of wide public interest, and of widespread critical attention among men of letters. And a group of actors had achieved a dignified standing till then unknown in English society.

Here there was no wave of interest in amateur playhouses, and the Court, least of all, felt any devotion to the stage — at least, only the masculine side of the royal family felt it, and then only toward the feminine side of the theatre. The tradition of the actress-courtesan, indeed, persisted. The public expected a reigning actress to have a noble or fashionable lover, or perhaps one after another; and many a prince and duke enters here into the annals of the stage. The vivacious and popular soubrette Dorothy Jordan even achieved a somewhat matrimonial connection (ten children) with him who later became William IV; Elizabeth Farren, described by Horace Walpole as the most perfect of actresses, cut short her stage career to marry the Earl of Derby, when the fortunate death of his less esteemed first wife made possible her elevation to ladyship; the versatile Mrs Robinson, after experience of "society," authorship, imprisonment, and acting, achieved two years of mistressing to the then Prince of Wales (later George IV) who ill rewarded her devotion. But these were not connections that in any sense wedded royalty to art. In fact, from this time on, British kings and queens were to go their separate untheatrical way (their allegiance and patronage were to be turned thenceforth to "sports"); and thus the theatre, even before the recognized birth of Democracy, had been made wholly dependent upon "the people" for its maintenance. The shrewd Garrick had actually made a fortune out of Drury Lane, even while maintaining a high standard in production and as near a standard in play choice as the artificial and skeptic taste of the time would permit. But with his relinquishment of that theatre, there begins a record of ups-and-downs, of the struggle of the stage to establish itself as an independent economic institution, a record spotted with brief flare-ups of beauty and prosperity, but without sustained importance. In all the 150 years since, England has had nothing approaching a "national" theatre.

The one burst of genius came in the three years preceding Garrick's retirement, and curiously enough, at a rival playhouse, Covent Garden Theatre. Oliver Goldsmith's *She Stoops to Conquer* was first produced in that one-time pantomime-house in March 1773, and Richard Brinsley Sheridan's *The Rivals* in January 1775. Thus appeared suddenly, in the deadest of times, England's only near-immortal dramatists of the eighteenth and nineteenth centuries.

Goldsmith is less indebted to the great comedy-writers of the past, and more a forerunner of nineteenth century dramaturgic developments, than is Sheridan. He brings a certain freshness and naturalness, comes nearer to an escape from the coldness of wit and the careful aloofness from life that had characterized the great Restoration playwrights — although one can hardly yet bring in the word "realism" when the characters act under names like Croaker, Hardcastle, and Lumpkin. And yet the homeliness of the opening lines of *She Stoops to Conquer* persists through the play, in spite of generous asides and many " Zounds! ":

MRS. HARDCASTLE

I vow, Mr. Hardcastle, you're very particular. Is there a creature in the whole country but ourselves, that does not take a trip to town now and then, to rub off the dust a little? There's the two Miss Hoggs, and our neighbor Mrs. Grigsby, go to take a month's polishing every winter.

HARDCASTLE

Ay, and bring back vanity and affectation to last them the whole year.

I wonder why London cannot keep its own fools at home! In my time, the follies of the town crept slowly among us, but now they travel faster than a stagecoach. . .

. . . I love every thing that's old: old friends, old times, old manners, old books, old wines; and I believe, Dorothy *(taking her hand)*, you'll own I have been pretty fond of an old wife. . .

A snatch of dialogue between Marlow and Kate exhibits this fresh tenderness coupled with an old artificiality:

MARLOW *(aside)*

By heaven, she weeps. This is the first mark of tenderness I ever had from a modest woman, and it touches me. *(To her.)* Excuse me, my lovely girl, you are the only part of the family I leave with reluctance. But to be plain with you, the difference of our birth, fortune and education make an honorable connection impossible; and I can never harbor a thought of seducing simplicity that trusted in my honor, of bringing ruin upon one, whose only fault was being too lovely.

MISS HARDCASTLE *(aside)*

Generous man! I now begin to admire him. *(To him.)* But I am sure my family is as good as Miss Hardcastle's, and though I'm poor, that's no great misfortune to a contented mind. . .

Goldsmith had previously written another comedy *The Good-Natured Man,* but it is less vivacious and less celebrated, and less honestly merry, than *She Stoops to Conquer.* The dramatist died the year after the première of that success — when it had hardly begun its triumphant march across the stages of two continents.

Sheridan flamed brilliantly across the theatre sky, as dramatist and producer, and then faded away in a dull haze of politics, " good living," and debt. For a brief few years he was the most spectacular figure in the British theatre, not only as playwright but as producer; but then, even though he nominally controlled Drury Lane for a score of years, he progressively sank further from serious importance in either capacity. *The Rivals* and *The School for Scandal* remain on library shelves, and in repertoire where repertory theatres still exist, to attest his phenomenal gift as comedy-writer. Even schoolboys who have forgotten the titles of his plays remember Mrs. Malaprop, and Lydia Languish, and Sir Lucius O'Trigger, and Lady Sneerwell, Charles Surface, Lady Teazle, and Sir Benjamin Backbite.

At twenty-four the gay blade Sheridan was already famous as the author of *The Rivals,* was already a sought-after wit and society man, and hero of a romantic elopement. At twenty-five he scored a second sensational success with *The Duenna,* a play written for presentation with music, which had a phenomenal run, and his fortune was so made that he was able to buy a controlling interest in Drury Lane Theatre from the retiring Garrick. At twenty-six we find him managing that historic playhouse (with the aid of half a dozen members of his family), apparently initiating a new and glorious era in the London theatre; and bringing out, as the event of the season, his own *The School for Scandal,* at a première of incomparable brilliancy. Walpole wrote, "It seemed a marvelous resurrection of the stage."

Sheridan was no mere man-of-letters stepping into the theatre with a script and some theories of staging. His father was an actor, not too able or successful, but respected, and his mother a writer. He had moved in circles where the stage was a living interest. He came equipped also with — considering his years — a rich personal experience of life. When he took over Drury Lane he fell heir to the best acting company in England, and he knew how to value that asset. He knew also the elegant world of playgoers whom his productions must please. For a few years he gave London the very best possible dramatic fare within the limits of what was then considered theatre art. If a vacancy occurred in the ranks of his players, he shrewdly went out and secured the best new talent in the country.

But it is a fact that Sheridan wrote only one additional play — *The Critic, or a Tragedy Rehearsed* — and there were no other living dramatists worthy the name. Shortly it became patent that with four plays Sheridan had burned out his playwriting genius, or ambition. Moreover, it soon developed that the theatre after all was only a secondary interest and avocation with him. Politics and the demands of social life — being a fashionable gentleman — were too exacting to leave time for the activities of authoring or producing. Management was left more and more to other hands. One night his theatre, which he had rebuilt to be the second largest in Europe, with a capacity of 3900 spectators, caught fire; but he refused to leave a debate in the House of Commons when told that the house was burning. That was in 1809, thirty-three years after he had taken over the directorship. With the conflagration ended his direct connection with the stage. His connection with it as an art had all but terminated twenty years since.

First, lack of direction had permitted disorganization and intrigue to creep into the once beautifully efficient company. Others than the director managed affairs, sometimes well, sometimes ill. As the theatre became more and more merely a " business proposition " to the now preoccupied director, his ambitions developed in the direction of greater size and display — looking only to wider popularity and increased receipts. Perhaps Sheridan's need for money and more money, to keep up his position of fashionable host and social leader, was at the root of the whole trouble. More and more he grasped at those adventitious " aids " to drama: spectacular scenery and interpolated sensational incident. The settings for some forgotten plays and an acting dog seem to have been equally talked about in the later days of his ownership of London's " first theatre." The time had passed when the retention of Sheridan could be urged on the grounds of art. It had been long since he entered the theatre except at night, and then he was able to see his actors only through an alcoholic haze; for he drank like a gentleman, as was the custom of important persons in his time.

But *The School for Scandal* is the most delightful comedy out of two whole centuries of British playwriting. It derives from Restoration models, but it brings a freshness and a later heartiness none the less. As an example of sustained " style," it is inferior to Congreve; but there are deeper qualities — without ever touching into the field of serious satire. We somehow take to ourselves these characters, feel personal sympathy with them, as we never did in Restoration days. And that is a sign that England, like Germany and France, is moving along toward the *human* comedy of a democratized theatre, a realistic time. The humor of *The School for Scandal* is so much of situation that no brief extract could convey the quality of it; and as a taste of Sheridan's

MRS. SIDDONS

The School for Scandal at Drury Lane Theatre. The famous screen scene as performed with wing setting. The bookshelves, windows, and landscape are painted on the backcloth. [From *Shakespeare's Theatre*, by Ashley H. Thorndike.]

witty characterization we may be content with these bits from the more obvious but celebrated Mrs. Malaprop in *The Rivals:*

Observe me, Sir Anthony. I would by no means wish a daughter of mine to be a progeny of learning; I don't think so much learning becomes a young woman: For instance, I would never let her meddle with Greek, or Hebrew, or Algebra, or simony, fluxions, or paradoxes, or such inflammatory branches of learning — neither would it be necessary for her to handle any of your mathematical, astronomical, diabolical instruments. — But, Sir Anthony, I would send her, at nine years old, to a boarding-school, in order to learn a little ingenuity and artifice. Then, sir, she should have a supercilious knowledge in accounts; — and as she grew up, I would have her instructed in geometry, that she might know something of the contagious countries; but above all, Sir Anthony, she should be mistress of orthodoxy, that she might not mis-spell and mis-pronounce words so shamefully as girls usually do; and likewise that she might reprehend the true meaning of what she is saying. This, Sir Anthony, is what I would have a woman know; and I don't think there is a superstitious article in it. . .
. . . There, sir, an attack upon my language! what do you think of that? an aspersion upon my parts of speech! Was ever such a brute! Sure, if I reprehend anything in this world, it is the use of my oracular tongue, and a nice derangement of epitaphs!

Sheridan and Goldsmith, then, are alone memorable for anything bequeathed to later times. But there are several minor figures, in the period, with claims to passing mention for their picturesque qualities or great contemporary fame — and in the case of one actress a lasting celebrity. Among playwrights there were the two George Colmans, father and son, Thomas Holcroft, John O'Keefe, and Frederick Reynolds, all of them characterized by prolificness — the last named is said to have written a hundred plays. There is something a trifle ludicrous and infinitely pathetic about these writers who know their theatre of an era so perfectly that they succeed sensationally, become " all the rage," and then disappear utterly. In treating the stock characters bequeathed to them from older tragedy and comedy, this group even progressed toward the future. The comic characters begin to be more than butts: a bit of sympathy is aroused for them. The gruff old father is seen to have a heart of gold. The *ingénue,* the sweet innocent girl, bewitchingly childlike, starts on her conquest of the popular comedy stage. There is here a thrust toward " modern " character-writing, toward the conception of characters as rounded-out human beings; but the execution is vitiated by a rank sentimentalism.

Among actors, for a long time, there is even less breaking away from traditional type characterization, very little dipping deeper than a stereotyped stage conception of life. The period is an "elegant" one, wherein real feelings are properly concealed, and a hard brilliant surface presented to the world. A witty skepticism covers over all evils and all good feeling. Emotion and spirituality are alike out of fashion. How then should actors get down to anything like sincerity of feeling or deep purging emotion? Up to the time of the Kembles, the eccentric characters among actors are the more interesting: that "Gentleman" Smith who was thus named because he was so different from the general run of players, in being educated, elegant, dressy, rich, and married to a nobleman's daughter — he could bring authentic dandies to the stage; and sharp-tongued and capricious Mrs Abington, who had certainly "lived a life-full" before she made such a success of Lady Teazle; and George Frederick Cooke, the typical actor who finds his inspiration in drink, occasionally rising briefly to mad heights of genius under its stimulation but wrecking his fitness for sustained acting, and wrecking many individual performances when the inspiration went to his legs rather than his creative centres. (He left for America after making London untenable for himself, and achieved a prodigious success even while wilfully insulting the provincials — and ended with the utterance of moral sentiments about the wickedness of drink.)

But Sarah Siddons was of stature beyond these, one of the truly great figures on the British stage; and her brother, John Philip Kemble, ruled nobly if less brilliantly at her side over a period of a quarter-century. As she was outside the superficially gay life of the fashionable world, being virtuous, dignified, even a bit cold, so she also rose above those difficulties, intrigues, and quarrels that honeycombed the stage realm. Only one failure marked her career: a too early début at Drury Lane Theatre after she had enjoyed great success in her father's company, as child-actor and then as leading lady (though not yet twenty). But a second Drury Lane début, in 1782, when she was twenty-seven years old, proved to be one of those occasions when a metropolitan public recognizes and hails a new and undisputed queen of the stage. From that triumphant night she reigned unrivalled and unassailed, from the eminence of first actress at Drury Lane or Covent Garden. The style of acting she brought in is described as "classic." It had little enough to do with the French classic playing then in vogue; it deviated in the direction of simplicity and restraint. It was still artificial, elevated, markedly "noble" — a reflection in part of her spirit and her outward stately appearance. But somewhere in her, too, there burned fire and imagination. And the dignified and stately impersonations, when shot through with this personal passion, aroused and thrilled audiences accustomed only to tamely or extravagantly conventional acting. She played the great Shakespearean heroines, achieving particular acclaim for her Lady Macbeth, as well as the more sentimental leading rôles in current "popular" drama.

John Philip Kemble was a perfect masculine counterpart of his sister — except that he lacked the imagination and fire. He accomplished all that is possible when noble appearance is linked with resolute devotion to lofty ideals, without great inspiration. His acting was elevated, stately, and elaborate; and he studied through to a certain sincerity — where his sister had intuitively achieved it. He had studied for the priesthood, and some critics pointed to the fact later as a reason for a certain heaviness and over-dignity in his acting. This temperamental deliberateness made him ever a reliable actor rather than a thrilling or inspired one. Still he and his sister ruled the London stage for two decades.

For fifteen years he was not only leading actor but stage manager at Drury Lane Theatre, under Sheridan's nominal directorship. It was he rather than his sister who made a point of the newness of their method of acting, who showed out Classicism as a thing of stateliness, austerity, and restraint. He staged a number of more or less Shakespearean plays in a manner that amazed and thrilled London, substituting for the old and poverty-stricken settings, or the French-Italian rococo ones, a sort supposed to be "true" — but with truth interpreted classicist-fashion, elaborated and made stately or grandiose. And from the Garrick era the tradition of "bettering" Shakespeare persisted; for Kemble and his prompter readapted *Coriolanus:* it was billed as " *Coriolanus, or The Roman Matron,* a tragedy altered from Shakespeare and Thomson."

Sarah Siddons and John Philip Kemble lived well into that next century which was to see destroyed all old standards in acting, playwriting, and staging. They are less transition figures than in themselves the summation of an era. If we count that there was here a period that can be called Classic — as different from the coming Romantic and Realistic — they are the only outstanding representatives.

But if the forces of change that gave us our chapter-heading are little apparent in England (though a *measure* of democracy had come in that country long before the American and French Revolutions), there is one incident out of the Kembles' reign that betrays an underlying drift toward popular rule in the theatre. If you had gone to Covent Garden Theatre any evening between September 18 and December 15, 1809, you would have seen an extraordinary performance in the auditorium, not on the stage. In those three months Kemble's company acted its plays, to be sure, or perhaps pantomimed them; for every time a player opened his mouth to utter a speech, the spectators would begin shouting a rhythmic refrain: "O-P, O-P, O-P." And then the whole audience would get up and perform a " dance," stamping the floor or beating canes to the rhythmical shouts of " O-P, O-P," varied by cat-calls, hisses, ringing of bells, and other approved auditorium signs of protest. Through sixty-one performances, during the three-month period, this counter-performance continued — not monotonously or uniformly, for there were interruptions in the nature of fist-fights, arrests, parades with banners bearing the " O-P " device, etc., but effectively so far as excluding the actors from attention was concerned.

" O-P " stood for " Old prices "; and the audiences of London were merely showing that they would brook no rise in admission prices at their then-favorite temple of dramatic art. Kemble and his associates had found the new methods of staging, and the immense new opera-house building, too costly to maintain at the old scale of admission, and they tacked six-pence or a shilling to the price of each seat. The house was sold out continuously for the next sixty-one performances; but from the time Kemble started to speak the Prologue on the opening night till the performance when he capitulated three months later, the actors' voices were drowned in a lasting wave of noisy protest. "Old prices! Old prices!" degenerated into the refrain "O-P, O-P, O-P." The audience became organized, the O-P dance was invented, and attendance at the riots became a social affair.

A riot at the Covent Garden Theatre in 1762. [From an old print as reproduced in *The Stage Year Book*, 1927.]

By this means the audiences of London demonstrated that when royalty has withdrawn patronage from the theatre, thus tacitly turning the art over to the care of the masses, the people may express their will no less effectively and capriciously, if less curtly, than a purse-holding and law-making monarch. They proved that in one part of the theatre democracy had come with a vengeance.

WE HAVE seen that a spirit of liberty had grown up at Weimar, where Goethe and Schiller were associated at a Court Theatre that was significant out of all proportion to the importance of the company of actors there, or the Duchy that supported it. But the flame of Democracy really did not burn more than feebly in

Germany either then or for long after; and we may think of the liberty in the air as a very vague and elusive ideal. In Goethe himself the theory and the practice clash most instructively. His devotion to liberty is unquestioned; no more sincere idealist ever lived. But there he was, serving, in his capacity as theatre director, a petty puffed-up duke, tyrant of a tiny principality, who for years allowed a frivolous and ambitious mistress to strike at the poet through humiliating " state " orders. (Just how petty this little monarch was, the famous poodle-dog incident finally proved.) And Goethe himself, despite his expressed ideas about freedom and equality, was a notable despot in his theatre. He ruled aloofly, severely; and he even extended the despotism from the stage part of the house to the auditorium. Clapping and hissing were alike prohibited.

It is recorded that hissers were arrested; and once a critic who really criticized a performance was banished from the dukedom. The rules for actors were pitilessly enforced. One actress who went away to an engagement in a Berlin theatre, in violation of the rule that the Weimar players should not appear elsewhere, was arrested upon her return and imprisoned in her own house for a week, with the further penalty of paying for the sentry who guarded her.[1] Thus did love of liberty and parade of authority go hand in hand in Germany while actual democracy was being born elsewhere. The next period in Germany is to be called Romanticism; the Democratic era is skipped.

In Italy there has been a flare-up of playwriting genius, in a country too chaotic to claim a national theatre. In tragedy there is a real spirit of liberty embalmed in the more or less political dramas of Vittorio Alfieri. These are in the grand historical style, impassioned after the eighteenth century fashion, lofty in sentiment, but more suited to stir Latin peoples (when presented

[1] This matter of Goethe's despotic ways is treated at considerable length in Vol. VI of Mantzius' *History,* whence I have drawn much of my material about this whole period. The author seldom gives any space to *drama* except in occasional relation to acting; but he presents, in Vols. V and VI, the most readable picture of stage conditions in Germany from the beginnings of Romanticism. The interested reader will find more detailed accounts in the excellent *Life of Goethe* by G. H. Lewes (most accessible, perhaps, in the *Everyman's Library* edition). True to his prejudices as a professional actor, Mantzius dismisses Marie Antoinette and the whole subject of the French amateur stages with a word; one must go to the French for information, most usefully to Adolphe Jullien's *La Comédie à la Cour* (Paris, n.d.).

with Italian virtuoso acting) than to warm the hearts of more northern audiences. Still Alfieri is considered the greatest of Italian tragedy writers. The only other name in his century is that of Scipione Maffei, who wrote the famous *Merope,* and who linked up with the Voltaire school in France.

But Carlo Goldoni is more a world figure, in comedy-writing. He is still played both in and out of Italy. He was an accom-

Interior of the Little Theatre, Haymarket, London, in 1815. Note the proscenium doorway, boxes, pit seats without backs, and gas lights.

plished technician, who wrote sixteen plays in one year, and at least one hundred and fifty during his stage career. Displeased by the buffoonery and indecencies to which the *Commedia dell'Arte* had descended, and finding no models in the national literature (he could hardly turn back to Aretino and Machiavelli, when he had made a stand against licentiousness), he struck out along independent lines, and wrote of people and things about him. He was one of the bourgeois dramatists, and humanity " in the raw " interested him. His characters were so familiarly real, the language so near to everyday speech, that again we may mark a milestone in the steady march from ancient stateliness and high aloofness toward intimacy and realism. And this is the more re-markable in a country where comedy had been concerned with traditional type characters and largely compounded of stock situations and repeated scenes.

But Goldoni gave rise in his own country to opposition rather than a following. The romantic Italian nature loves neither realistic observation nor bourgeois pathos: there must be heroics in tragedy and boisterous display in comedy, and vivid characters. A critic, named Carlo Gozzi, challenged Goldoni's supremacy, and he ultimately drove the elder author to the more congenial France; and he discomfited Goldoni most by himself becoming playwright and the most esteemed figure in the Italian theatre. It is said that the two men met in a Venetian bookshop, and Gozzi, taunted by the other with the truth that it is easy to write caustically about a play but difficult to compose a good one, answered that he would undertake to compose within a few days a comedy that would please so light-minded an audience as this of Venice. And in an incredibly short time the Venetian playgoers were laughing over the humors of *The Three Oranges,* into which Gozzi had incidentally imbedded some telling satire on Goldoni's newly-invented types of drama, and not a little personal ridicule. And the audiences straightway flopped over to Gozzi's side and ever after remembered that he and not Goldoni represented the rather florid national genius.

Whether the anecdote is true or invented, it is certain that Gozzi was more in the line of logical development in Italy, where Democracy has never been at home. He grasped much out of the *Commedia dell'Arte* (which he rightly esteemed as a real and unique flowering of theatric art); and he added exotic elements out of his love for the Orient, and rich texture and extravagant incident. His was a vivid and highly decorated art, not at all like any given to the world since. But the intense theatricalism of it promises frequent revival; in adaptation if not in direct translation. (It was an adaptation that I enjoyed immensely, for its colorfulness and the heartiness of its humor, when I saw *Turandot* within the month, as presented by a troupe out of Soviet Russia, in — of all places! — the Paris *Odéon.*) Gozzi turned back the current which had started toward "freedom" in Italy. For a century and a half that country disappears from our story.

RETURNING to the scene of the true Revolution, become now terribly real in life, if only a tame evolution in the playhouse, we find Paris mobs storming the Bastille in 1789. There already have been plays on the stage expressing, more or less guardedly, revolutionary sentiments. With the first political violence there comes a wave of "appropriate" playwriting, the first impact of the deluge inevitable at any world crisis — but out of it not one drama survives as important. War-time always stirs up deep currents of feeling, but the outward clash and fevered excitement are no congenial environment for art. Man's creative faculties, along with his spirituality and his sense of right and justice, atrophy in the red glare of continuous battle. And so we find that neither the immediate heroic contest nor the shift in world thought leads directly to theatre activity. There is participation in the revolution by playwrights and actors. The members of the *Comédie Française* are so partisan that the company is split and for a time production is paralyzed. The dramatists are so fiercely democratic that their only thought is to use the stage to further their side in the political struggle.

There is, however, a meritless political drama of 1789 that has achieved an extrinsic immortality. It was one of the earliest political pieces to come to performance, appearing on the boards of the *Théâtre Français* less than four months after the storming of the Bastille. *Charles IX,* a play by Marie-Joseph Chénier, dealing on conventional tragic lines with the massacre of St Bartholomew's Eve, was presented by a reluctant company that still leaned to the Royalist side but had to bow to "the people's will." The drama happened to touch off, with the spark of righteous heroics, the tinder of patriotism in every spectator's breast. Night after night the audiences came, surcharged with feeling, and night after night their enthusiasm flamed high with every incident of aristocratic tyranny and each answering burst of democratic sentiment. Eye-witnesses reiterate that the house at every performance went wild with approval, with frantic revolutionary ardor, with self-enthusiasm. Readers of the play are equally at one in terming the text tedious, unexciting, and dramatically tame. But here the art of the piece — poetry, depth of feeling, characterization, acting — had nothing to do with the occasion. It was merely that representing a play in which a king ordered a massacre of his subjects was like waving a flag at a political meeting at just the psychological moment. An emotion wholly outside the theatrical content of the drama was precipitated. For this was the interim between the fall of the Bastille and the Red Terror of the guillotine; and a king still held court at his country palaces. Drama or anything else that stirred popular sentiment might precipitate a demonstration.

The performance of *Charles IX* brought to prominent notice for the first time a young actor named Talma, who was to become later almost the greatest of all French players; and it happened that this Talma was the one ardent revolutionary within the ranks of the still court-subventioned company. He had the title-rôle in the production — because an older actor side-stepped it on account of his Royalist sympathies — and he it was who became the specific *casus belli* when the majority of the company tried a test with the Democratic audience. These older *Sociétaires* of the *Comédie Française,* perhaps under pressure from their King and certainly sympathizing with him, decided that with the slightest slackening of public interest in the play, it would be quietly withdrawn from the repertory. The time came when the pretext of lack of support seemed likely to cover the withdrawal. Here we know not how far patriotism entered in, and how far an author's desire to see his play and his royalties continue, and a young actor's natural desire to prolong his appearance in a first big part; but the friends of Liberty bestirred themselves to protest. Finally, one night while another play was in progress, a gentleman arose in the orchestra and insisted point-blank that *Charles IX* be restored to the stage the following evening. When the actors tried to carry on the play, the audience set up the howl " *Charles IX, Charles IX.*" A canny actor stepped out of his part to explain that to restore the play would be impossible as two players accustomed to take sizeable parts were ill; at which Talma stepped out to remark that the more important one really wasn't so ill as that, and that doubtless the public would accept an emergency substitute in the other rôle. To which the house agreed with great enthusiasm; and the very next evening Talma played *Charles IX* once more. There was a riot, but the piece was presented.

This did not, however, make for amicability and fraternity within the company. Feeling ran so high that Naudet, the actor who had put forward the sick-actors excuse, fought a duel with Talma. Then the Royalist *Sociétaires* — still the King's Comedians — read Talma out of the *Théâtre Français* organization.

It was not long before the debarred actor's loyal friends organized a "theatre party," and drowned out the lines from the stage with shouts of "Talma! Talma!" They allowed themselves to be tricked into waiting for an answer till the following evening, when they found themselves in conflict with an almost equal number of Royalist partisans. This time there was not even a pretense of acting a play. The elder actors took their stand, insisting that M. Talma would not reappear until the matter could be passed upon "by higher authority" (the theatre was still technically subject to rulings of Louis XVI's four First Gentlemen of the Bedchamber). Then Dugazon, a beloved old comedian, cast for that night's leading rôle, stepped forward, said that M. Talma was right, and that he was leaving the theatre until his young colleague should be reinstated. There was some disorder after, and breaking up of railings and benches, but the audience actually settled down to a one-sided debate about these actors and the national theatre.

When the decision from a higher authority came, it was from city officials and not the King, and it ordered the company to take back Talma and Dugazon into their ranks. There was some delay, however — perhaps the Royalists still thought the Court might venture to speak; and on the evening of September 26, 1790, "the people" smashed their way into the theatre, rioted and fought and shouted down the entrenched Conservative actors. Next day the theatre was formally closed. After two months the *Sociétaires* capitulated, at least to the extent of summoning Talma and Dugazon back.

But no truce could last now; leading actresses began to resign, alleging that the company could not maintain its dignity and integrity with "Reds" in its midst. The troubles on the stage were duplicated by others in the auditorium. The old *Comédie Française* was disrupted beyond hope of either peace or artistic production. The National Assembly passed a decree cancelling the monopoly held by the King's Comedians, opening the field to any and all playing companies alike — a step away from privilege and toward liberty indeed. So Talma and his few fellow Reds seceded from the state company and formed a rival troupe. There were eighteen additional theatres opened that year; and fifty before the century was out. Naturally the new company, in the *Théâtre de la rue de Richelieu,* and the old in the *Théâtre Français,* became respectively Revolutionary and Royalist strongholds and propaganda-bureaus, picking plays frankly for political expediency. Talma's group brought on some badly adapted Shakespeare — but this was really no time to tack up the shield of art above one's portals.

The two theatres reeled through the troublous period that followed. When the time of the end of kings came, both houses grasped at patriotic titles — one must display some outward devotion to *Liberté, Egalité, Fraternité.* For a few weeks the houses were closed — the show of the terrible guillotine kept people occupied. But immediately the Bloody Month was over, everybody wanted the theatres opened again. The mad production was resumed.

The two rival companies were no longer on an equal footing; and the old *Sociétaires,* now calling their house the *Théâtre de la Nation,* foolishly widened the existing breach by retaining indiscreet political pieces in their repertory. Talma and his group played safe. Then the *Nation* group put on a play called *l'Ami des Lois* which roundly denounced the extreme element in the Commune, counselled a moderate course, and even caricatured certain popular-radical leaders. Immediately the storm broke, inside and outside the theatre. Public sentiment was still enough divided so that it was a question of battle, not mere suppression. There were riots, even the training of cannon on the theatre; but curiously the partisans of the Commune were defeated: the house was closed but after a few days reopened. This was a last and belated stand of the King's Comedians. They

were too frankly of the old privileged regime. In September
1793 the members of the company were arrested and cast into
prison, all except one comedian who was away taking a cure,
and who died of apoplexy when he heard the news. And there
was ground for fear, for these actors were apparently fated to
follow many less genuine reactionaries to the guillotine.

Ironically the indictments setting the dates for the appearance
of the *Sociétaires* before the tribunal were signed by an actor who

A theatre at Rheims in 1785: a typical small theatre of the times. Note
that part of the pit is still reserved for standees. [From Paris' *Le Théâtre
à Reims*.]

had been so bad in his art that he had never succeeded in getting
into the *Comédie Française* or any other dignified company. But
it was the ruse of another actor within the Commune councils
that postponed the executions — until a day when the Terror was
over and the popular thirst for blood slaked.

But it was no time for art in the theatre. Decree after decree
was issued to force the drama arbitrarily into Democratic channels. Laughable prohibitions were introduced: no play containing any title of nobility could be produced — even the appellations
Monsieur and *Madame* were forbidden to be spoken, as they

implied distinctions! Many classics from the kingly age were banned, others altered; every play must breathe the new Democratic piety. There was even a movement to force every town in the country to open a theatre, in the now presumably empty church, " to educate the people, to make them forget the foolishness of the priests." Talma's company did plays quite as vapidly patriotic as those offered by rival troupes.

Standards were gone, chaos ensued. Till finally in 1799 old animosities were sufficiently forgotten for the two companies out of the old *Comédie Française* to reunite. They came together in the *rue de Richelieu* house, which has remained the *Théâtre Français* to this day. And soon Napoleon helped the re-established company to bring order out of chaos. He granted a subvention far more generous than any known under the kings, restored the monopoly on " classic " drama, signed that *Decree of Moscow* under which the *Comédie* is still administered, and showed marked personal interest in the group. He failed to turn up a tragic dramatist who would grace his court as Racine had graced that of Louis XIV, though he sought assiduously and encouraged every budding talent. But playwriting as an art was dead. The only genius of this period is Talma.

We see him go on to triumph after triumph, till he has transformed French acting and become the great ornament of the Paris theatre of the pre-Romantic era. It is somewhat by chance that he is more broadly equipped for progress than any of his fellows. His father was a valet, but, being ambitious, had crossed out of France into England to set up as a dentist. His son François Joseph was sent back to school in France for a time. Then while he worked as dentist's assistant in London the boy became a leader in the amateur stage productions of the French colony there; but more important, he developed a taste for Shakespeare and the free methods of playwriting, and an admiration for English (comparatively) restrained acting. When he gave up dentistry and went to the school of acting in Paris maintained by the *Comédie Française,* he already had a horror of French bombastics and of conventially elegant French staging. He became the exponent of classic simplicity and truth, in the Kemble sense. One of his earliest exploits was to upset his elder colleagues by

appearing as a Roman Tribune, in Voltaire's *Brutus,* in a true
Roman costume, with arms and legs bare—a startling contrast
to the beplumed, decorated, and padded costumes then in vogue.

But it was only after the passing of many years, and after the
events of the Revolution, that this strikingly handsome and spirited
actor was to accomplish anything like a reform of French acting.

MADAME TALMA

By natural right he became leader of the Paris stage. He was
constantly pushing forward to new experiments in naturalness
—though there was still a mighty gap between his sort and the
intimate personal playing of today. But he put humanity into
many an impersonation, where before the same characters had
been portrayed with a stateliness, a desire for nobility above all,
a stilted artifice that removed them effectively from the plane of
life. Talma was under the handicap, much of the time, of having

to speak Alexandrine verse, a prime hindrance to naturalness of emotion. Indeed, king that he is within his own time, we feel that had he come a little later in history he might have been the great leader of leaders on the French stage. As it is, he is a hampered king, progressing valiantly through difficulties. Had he found a dramatist with ideas akin to his own, or even a skilful translator of Shakespeare, he might have transformed, totally, French acting in his own time. Under the handicap, he stirred up bitterness and conflict, and marked out the way to the future.

In his individual acting, as exemplar of his theories of freedom and naturalness, he had recourse to gloomy, insane, and horrific rôles. He acted a long line of abnormally delirious or horrible parts; here if anywhere one might escape from the shackles of stilted verse, and indulge in real expressions of emotion. The crowd and the young Romantics found the innovation exciting and praiseworthy. The critics were less convinced. Abbé Geoffroy summed up the indictment: " His triumph lies in the portrayal of passion worked up to delirium, to insanity. He is a chief and leader of the company of lovers of gloom, like Ducis . . . The gloomy *genre* is bad in itself, because plays of horror are not suited to French audiences; they should be left to the population of London. . . Talma hits upon extraordinary intonations, that produce a shudder of fear; but these happy hits are so infrequent and their effect so transitory, that he would do well to return again within the boundaries of art."

Within that fragment of contemporary criticism there is doubtless the key to the chief fault in Talma's acting: the excess that went with the newly gained freedom, the contrast between the stressed points and the constraint imposed by the psuedo-classic playwriting. But the quotation equally illustrates the obstacles in his way; by the slur at English drama (presumably at Shakespeare most of all, since a performance of *Othello* occasioned the review), and by the smug reference to " the boundaries of art." The guardians of the traditions handed down from the older theatre were bound to resent any excursion outside the " rules," and particularly any indulged in upon the *Comédie Française* stage. Talma on his part accepted the challenge, played the rôle of reformer consciously and gaily (though he went after

this critic Geoffroy not seemingly but with a horsewhip), and
set about corrupting as many of the young writers and actors as
were not too awed by tradition to listen. He died in 1826, four
years before Romanticism — that might have been the perfect
medium for him — " came in."

WHILE democracy was thus gradually, and perhaps somewhat
blightingly, making its way into the theatres of Europe, the
United States, technically a republic since 1776, was developing

An early American "opera house" at New Orleans. A survival of aristocratic discrimination in the four boxes; otherwise the auditorium has turned
very democratic. [From *Before the Foot-Lights and behind the Scenes*,
by Olive Logan.]

a life of its own, independent of English activity. The art of the
stage in such centres as Charleston, Philadelphia, New York, and
Boston remained reflective of London's activity. There were
notable variations from the customs and the fare of the mother
country, as might be expected with so adventurous and lusty a
child, including a great deal that is interesting to the searcher
after the picturesque and the racy; but there is nothing in the
story of the American theatre up to 1820 that can be considered
of world importance.

The fight of the Puritans against all vicious pleasures had been
waged with particular energy in the North, and the South had

responded earlier to the eternal dramatic urge; but in a truly colonial way. Indeed, we may better think of the activities as being about as important as those in any other cultural dependency of England: the very vital but not greatly distinctive stage of Dublin offers a parallel. The Colonies and then the States built theatres, just rude halls at first, then in imitation of approved London models. Through most of the eighteenth century such primitive theatres as the one shown here served the travelling companies; but at the century's end several pretentious playhouses were erected, most notably, perhaps, the Park Theatre in New York, opened in 1798, and the Chestnut Street Theatre in Philadelphia, opened in 1794, which had an auditorium copied in detail from the Theatre Royal at Bath. By this time American audiences expected elaborate pictorial scenery, and an Italian educated in Paris, one Charles Ciceri, aided in bringing stage decoration into line with orthodox European practice. Plays were mostly imported from London, and the real events in the theatre were the visits of English companies or English stars. But within a quarter-century America is to have actors who will dispute supremacy with the visiting artists. Meanwhile democracy in government has had no notable effect upon playwriting, acting, or theatre design in the Western continents.

CHAPTER XVIII

Romanticism: The Theatre as Escape

ON THE long road of progress from the epic and highly
conventional drama of the Greeks of the journalistic
and familiar drama of today, there have been recurrent
efforts to gain full " freedom " for the dramatist, and to bring
the stage closer to " life." The Romantic playwrights of the
nineteenth century blazoned forth the epochal news that freedom
had been won, nature encompassed, and the art of the theatre
for the first time fully and richly realized. And indeed, some
of their manifestoes announced the millennium as convincingly
as any document in criticism. Victor Hugo's preface to *Crom-
well,* 1827, is the battle-cry of the movement, and proves stirring
even today in the reading. But their practice failed to afford
more than an episode in the march toward Realism.

If we accept a broader and better definition of Romanticism,
under which we may visualize the dramatist as far-riding in imagination, unhampered in shaping theatric action and in choice
of characters, writing with constant reference to the deeper life
of the human spirit, utilizing every resource of physical staging
and acting, choosing prose or verse or silence, drenching the work
in sensuous beauty, then we may say that this is another name for
drama ennobled, made free and splendid, and rendered human;
and Shakespeare is seen emerging as the supreme artist of Romanticism in the theatre.

But the commonly accepted understanding of Romanticism, as
applying to the dramas of the French playwrights of 1830, nar-
rows the definition until Shakespeare is squeezed outside: he is
seen to be Romantic but with a foot over in the territory sometimes called Expressionistic; there is too much intensification of

life and too much carelessness of outward nature, too much insight into human character and emotion and not enough observance of surface fact, to allow his sitting well with the French
group. For while the 1830 men went far-riding after the thing
we call " picturesque," they accepted a limitation to natural detail
and plausible surface truth that curbed imagination, prevented
character-depth, and crippled truly theatrical expressiveness. Not
one of their plays lives importantly today, either on the stage or
in the library. The secret of their failure lies in that they made
Romanticism merely the first stopping-place in the realm called
Realism.

Now I know that these terms are quite often cited as opposites.
But if we continue to call Hugo and Dumas and Bulwer-Lytton
Romantic, we *must* recognize that realistic limitations are the
cause of the failure of Romanticism; or at least a companion-
cause to sentimentalism and bombast.

In the nineteenth century, art was an activity not passionately
lived, not close to life; indeed the arts in general had receded
into retreats, museums, and precious " circles." And a belief took
shape that creating and appreciating art were not so much activities of living as *escapes* from life. The gallery of paintings,
the concert, the theatre show, were occasional refuges from the
drab business of existing. What was afforded to the eye or the
ear, there, must be unfamiliar, exotic, dazzlingly brilliant. But
the age being what it was, matter-of-fact, military-material, and
disillusioned, observed fact must be respected: the dramatist going out to capture the picturesque must not violate what might
happen on the thousandth chance, must stick to observed detail,
must not go beyond what a man might dream for himself in a
sentimental moment.

The spectator wanted to be taken out of his ordinary grey
world into a more colorful realm — but one which he could
believe in as real. Indeed, he wanted it real enough so that he
could identify himself with the hero going out to adventure, cry
with the heroine abused. So we see magnificence hampered,
noble characters dragged down, imagination cramped, to compass sentimental probability. There are no Hamlets or Othellos
or Portias here — impossibly implausible characters, intensifica-

tions of the human spirit, of the living in us that begets drama; there are, rather, a lot of figures heightened in colors but believeable to us in our softer moments. And the action is what they do in contrived circumstances, picturesque but plausible circumstances like fights, betrayals, lovers' partings, heroic sacrifice, etc.

In France this Romanticism, shallow as it was, accomplished great things negatively. It swept away the enfeebled classic drama, still bound up in rules and limitations. To that extent it ushered in Freedom. It cleared the way to Nature.

The playwrights thus freed reached out for grandeur. They planned to paint humanity on a magnificent scale, limited by no arbitrary laws of time or place, by no rules that figures must be noble or situations heroic. They would portray the weak with the strong, the high with the low, and find new drama in the contrast. The beautiful would be placed beside the ugly, the sublime by the grotesque — yes, they particularly affected the grotesque. They would add a wealth of color, a welter of incident, a pageant of life.

But when they sought characters both plausible and picturesque, Hugo and Dumas found themselves constrained to choose types like criminals, bastards, and outcasts for protagonists. Other non-classical heroes were too tame or too slight for the huge play design. To gain another sort of contrast, they pitted innocence against vice, purity against passion. Here they borrowed from the despised melodrama theatres of Paris. Beside the failing classic stages had grown up some very unclassic ones that asked nothing more than to hold unlettered audiences with unliterary " plays," contrived out of surprise, shock, machine-effects, and some characters as obvious as J-O-Jo. The action of these melodramas was, in the total absence of characterization, heightened to the last degree. Romanticism, with its freedom for all effects, would grasp this raw and exciting action in its catch-all of the colorful and picturesque.

The " language " and the verse of drama were heightened, too. The result was a gorgeous lyric investiture in the case of certain of Hugo's plays; but in general a riot of rhetoric and bombast and common speech. Nothing more truly shows out the faults of Romantic drama than its literary envelope. In that is the grandeur along with the hollowness: the magnificent reach and the empty hand.

The dramatists put in too much; even while they held back their imaginations with that new conception of what is natural. They spread their characters too far — even Shakespeare for all his flights of fancy and all his extravagant piling up of incidents and figures, had character-concentration. But unless you have read one of Hugo's or Dumas' dramas this week, you probably can't name a character in them. (When we have come to Dumas *fils,* and when Romantic melodrama has been crossed with the well-made play, you will remember *La Dame aux Camélias;* but that is post-Romantic.)

It was the shattering of the classic rules that was the greatest achievement of the French group. They showed up the barren, stilted, and insipid plays for what they were. And it was because they wrenched free from the academic limitations that they first were called Romantic. The word comes from the characteristic literature of the people who spoke the " Romance " languages, the vernacular as distinguished from Church or learned Latin; and as that literature had first taken form in tales of love and adventure, the mediæval " romances," this seemed a proper appellation for any anti-classic, closer-to-life, abundant drama. But the playwrights narrowed the term instead of widening it: made " romantic " mean something far away from life instead of a deepening of life, an escape instead of an intensified adventurous experience.

The gallery of important Romanticists is small. In connection with the earlier melodrama, the playwright Pixérécourt is usually chosen for mention. He was a skilful constructor and prolific. And those early melodramas did free the physical stage for larger effects and excursions (witness the pictures herewith).

Alfred de Vigny wrote some dramas that were in the copious new style, but weighted down with rhetoric. Victor Hugo was the giant of the movement, wrote its most telling manifestoes, produced in *Hernani* (1830) its most-fought-over play, and settled the operatic splendor of his genius over the Romantic *genre* for all time to come. As he had tremendous lyrical and theatrical gifts, so the drama rose in a blaze of glory; as his genius was

Staging in the Romantic era. Above, a scene from *Les Deux Pigeons* at the *Théâtre du Palais-Royal*, Paris, 1838 — an example of novelty-seeking in the settings of the time. Below, a scene from *Le Pacte de Famine* at the *Théâtre de la Porte St Martin*, 1839. [After a lithograph by the actor Mélingue.]

The Park Theatre in New York, as painted by John Searle in 1822 (the second house of the name). Charles Mathews and Miss Johnson on the stage; in the auditorium many of the most prominent New Yorkers of the day, of whom eighty are identifiable by means of an existing key. Note the proscenium portals as in the English theatres of the time. [By courtesy of the New York Historical Society, owners of the painting.]

corrupt, lacked sensibility and depth, so the Romantic play, when it fell back out of the spent fire of its rhetoric and pathos, was found to be thin, characterless. *Hernani, Ruy Blas,* and *Marion Delorme* are remembered today as hardly more than landmarks. After Hugo were Casimir Delavigne and Alexandre Dumas. The latter rivalled Hugo in contemporary fame, but was less the type-figure of the Romantic revolutionary — and his copious and skilful plays have lapsed into a more all-blanketing silence.

Hugo defined Romanticism as " nothing else than liberalism in literature." The French literary stage before 1825 had been sadly in need of liberation. The melodramatists had already freed that theatre which was wholly divorced from literature. Hugo and Dumas made literature liberal by uniting it with the melo-drama stage. They brought the legitimate stage down, not up, to freedom.

A LONG time before, in England, a playwright named George Lillo had written a play called *George Barnwell,* wherein " a London 'Prentice ruin'd is our theme." The event is marked as the first appearance of bourgeois domestic tragedy. Certainly a new familiarly human note was then ushered into the theatre. And some critics trace the Romanticism of Hugo back to this brief revolt against the aloofness and sublimity of earlier drama. Insofar as the Romanticists claimed freedom to set the low by the high, the 'prentice by the prince, the point is well taken. And it may serve to remind us that a form known as tragi-comedy had developed, and had had a fitful progress in both France and Germany. The French Diderot had taken Lillo as model, and had written some near-natural plays that might be considered a link, if a weak one, in the chain to the future; and Marivaux had added a similar note of tenderness in sentimental-real comedy. It was rather Lessing in Germany who made tearful comedy and bourgeois tragedy widely palatable. Hugo and Dumas, even if not in direct line, may have felt influence from all these.

In England, however, the Romantic Revival of 1830 or there-abouts was less a conscious revolt than in France; and the theatre adds the least glorious chapter to the story of a freeing impulse that flowered gorgeously in lyric poetry and at least profusely in fiction. (Unless we bolster the theatre's case by claiming Shelley on the evidence of *The Cenci,* and Byron as author of *Manfred* and a half dozen other dialogue poems; but these are only dramatic in literary form, not in stageworthiness.) The English Romantic drama, indeed, is strangely like a weak reflection of Dumas and Hugo. Barnwell has been abroad, and has come back with a magnificence mixed into his simple pathos, and with a great load of rhetoric.

Sheridan Knowles perhaps was the last of the stately tragedy-writers — the activity had been maintained even if the quality had not — rather than the first of the romantic playwrights. William Hazlitt, nevertheless, writing in the year when Knowles' first play came to the boards (1820), called the age " critical, didactic, paradoxical, romantic," and therefore not dramatic; and again he wrote of Knowles that he " has hardly read a poem or a play or seen anything of the world, but he hears the anxious beatings of his own heart, and makes others feel them by the force of sympathy." Here indeed is another step toward familiar drama. But Knowles' subjects were Virginius, William Tell, and Caius Gracchus; though *The Beggar's Daughter of Bethnal Green* and *The Hunchback* tell in their titles that the author was fulfilling some of the lowly and grotesque aims of the Romanticists.

Bulwer-Lytton gave to the theatre two plays that are sometimes brought to the boards even today, and one, *The Lady of Lyons,* is quite regularly revived in the remoter provinces — wherever, indeed, weepsy audiences without too keen a sense of the ridiculous can be gathered. In this play is the very essence of nineteenth century Romanticism of the tenderer sort. When Pauline, the great Lady, has been told that she was tricked into the union with the lowly Claude Melnotte, and he, confessing fraud, has decided to return her to her parents, this scene occurs:

PAULINE *(to her parents)*

And you would have a wife enjoy luxury while a husband toils! Claude, take me; thou canst not give me wealth, titles, station — but thou canst give me a true heart. I will work for thee, tend thee, bear with thee, and never, never shall these lips reproach thee for the past.

COLONEL DAMAS

I'll be hanged if I am not going to blubber.

MELNOTTE

This is the heaviest blow of all! What a heart I have wronged! Do not fear me, sir; I am not all hardened — I will not rob her of a holier love than mine. Pauline! — angel of love and mercy! — your memory shall lead me back to virtue! The husband of a being so beautiful in her noble and sublime tenderness may be poor — may be low-born; . . . but he should be one who can look thee in the face without a blush, and to whom thy love does not bring remorse, — who can fold thee to his heart, and say, — " Here there is no deceit! " — I am not that man!

DAMAS *(aside to Melnotte)*

Thou art a noble fellow, notwithstanding; and wouldst make an excellent soldier. Serve in my regiment. I have had a letter from the Directory — our young general takes the command of the army in Italy, — I am to join him at Marseilles, — I will depart this day if thou wilt go with me.

MELNOTTE

It is the favor I would have asked thee, if I dared. Place me wherever a foe is most dreaded, — wherever France most needs a life. . . And thou! — thou! so wildly worshipped, so guiltily betrayed, — all is not yet lost! — for thy memory, at least, must be mine till death! If I live, the name of him thou hast once loved shall not rest dishonored; if I fall amidst the carnage and the roar of battle, my soul will fly back to thee, and love shall share with death my last sigh! . . .

The next act, two and a half years later, finds Melnotte returned from a glorious career at the wars; but the very day of his arrival is that upon which Pauline, to save her father from ruin, is giving herself to the wealthy villain Beauséant. Melnotte in disguise seeks an interview with Pauline to learn the truth, and she, unknowing, pours out her heart (ay, there's a situation that brings the tears!). But of course Melnotte tears up the iniquitous papers, himself saves the father from ruin, with money honorably taken as booty from the Italians, and presses Pauline to his heart. And there is a " moral " at the end:

MELNOTTE

Ah! the same love that tempts us into sin,
If it be true love, works out its redemption;
And he who seeks repentance for the Past
Should woo the Angel Virtue in the Future.

So far toward nature and no farther, the Romantic current had carried the drama. And so far toward splendor. The French had given the form heroic outlines; and their plays were usually straight verse, where *The Lady of Lyons* is mixed verse and prose. But the melodrama influence is obvious in Hugo and Lytton alike. Nor did this point escape critics of their own time: the London *Times,* in reviewing the first performance of *The Lady of Lyons* in 1838, said: " The characters are the overdrawn characters of melodrama. Claude, who in a fit of ill-humor is persuaded to be an impostor, turns out to be a prodigy of valor; Beauséant is one of those monsters not to be found in nature, but only in the melodrama of twenty years ago; but is almost equalled by the old gentleman, who, to avoid insolvency, would sacrifice his daughter to such a ruffian." And yet Lytton's was the most " literary " drama that found its way to the stage of that era. At lower strata one found unpretending melodrama, farce, and some strange special forms such as nautical drama and equestrian drama (see the picture herewith), and plays built around animal-acts. Here, as in France, the most lusty and the most inventive theatre of the time was that of the unimportant out-and-out melodrama.

Shakespeare, of course, was occasionally revived; indeed, up to fifty years ago the finest of his plays were kept in repertoire by all the great actors, in some sort of adaptation; it is only within the new century that London wholly lost interest in them. But the Romantic Revival did not notably increase his vogue: the new definition of Romance was too limited to include him.

If we are pleased to call Edmund Kean the first great Romantic actor, then there *was* a revival; but Kean had made his phenomenal entry at Drury Lane back in 1814. In one direction he perfectly fulfilled the aims of the Romantics. Certainly he *heightened* acting in a way that shattered all traditions. Coleridge wrote that " to see Kean play is like reading Shakespeare by flashes of lightning." And he added natural effects to grandeur in the manner approved by the manifestoes; only he went deeper than the playwrights did, basing his impersonations on a conception of deep and informing character. He was brilliant, even dazzling, one of the true geniuses, beyond explanation, in the annals of acting. And yet his one fault was typically a failure of the Romantic

Above, the interior of the Sans Pareil Theatre in London, 1816. Below, an example of equestrian drama at Astley's Amphitheatre, London, 1815, wherein circus and theatre elements were combined. [From contemporary prints.]

"The lecture-room of the American Museum," New York, 1853. One of the usual disguises of the theatre in Puritanical times, so that spectators might attend with ease of conscience. Note how the proscenium doors and fore-stage of the English theatre persisted in America even in mid-century. [From *Gleason's Pictorial Drawing-Room Companion*.]

school as a whole: when he came to a place where repose and serenity were necessary, his resources failed him. He must be always up on a height, always moving fast. He lived his life off the stage in the same way, violently, madly, excessively. If we grant that this is Romantic, then he was the greatest figure of the Romantic theatre. His Shylock and Othello and Richard III are the parts by which he is remembered, not anything out of contemporary authors.

Shelley wrote more of beauty into *The Cenci* than had been put into an English tragedy since Elizabethan times. The last words of Beatrice before she is led away to execution, the final lines of the play, are:

> . . . Here, Mother, tie
> My girdle for me, and bind up this hair
> In any simple knot; aye, that does well.
> And yours I see is coming down. How often
> Have we done this for one another; now
> We shall not do it any more. My Lord,
> We are quite ready. Well, 'tis very well.

But the simplicity and quietness and nobility of this sort of writing were not joined to adequate theatrical technique in the shaping of the action and the marshalling of the players. And so the finest so-called Romantic poets came not to the stage; only Romantic novelists like Lytton, who knew how to shake the last bit of tearfulness out of a pathetic situation.

Byron himself wrote of *Manfred* as " a kind of poem in dialogue or drama . . . of a very wild, metaphysical, and inexplicable kind." And indeed, though there is the true Byronic magic in the lines, it is doubtful whether the " poem in dialogue " will ever be tamed to the stage. *Manfred, Marino Faliero, Sardanapalus,* and *Werner* were all acted at Drury Lane Theatre, and certain ones elsewhere; but they have not stood the test of time as theatre pieces. The actor William Charles Macready, next most important figure to Kean on the English stage of the early nineteenth century, was chiefly responsible for bringing Byron to the boards, and he played *Werner* over a period of twenty-one years. As late as 1887, *Werner* was acted in London, at a special matinée, with Henry Irving in the title part. But still, Byron belongs to the reading public — gloriously — and to the stage hardly at all.

The tradition of the literary drama persisted long after, in "plays" by Tennyson and Browning most notably; but stage conditions in England did not invite poetic genius to an intimate collaboration. Incidentally, in the early decades of the century, the London theatres had been too large for any but broad effects; the licensing of only three theatres for "legitimate" drama, had led the rebuilders of Drury Lane and Covent Garden to the fault of great spaces appropriate only to spectacular and violent or boisterous effects. The other theatres, of course, being denied the privilege of producing works likely to be considered competitive with those at the "patent" houses, fell back on farce and melodrama, variety and operetta. Melodramas were often produced as "musical plays" as a further disguise.

And by the way, the melodrama writers form a vivid gallery of skilled theatre craftsmen. Most of their works are permanently dead; but one still hears of the last and most famous of the line, Dion Boucicault, of his *Arrah-na-Pogue* and *The Colleen Bawn,* and of his outstanding comedy *London Assurance.* Still, comedy and "drama" alike, you may compare these with the last *great* English plays, with Sheridan or Jonson or Fletcher, and see how the coarseness and obviousness out of the debased melodramatic stage had vitiated them.

Out of the "lower" theatre, too, there came one actor whose name links the tradition of the *Commedia dell'Arte* with the story of the moving picture, the greatest name between Scaramouche and Charlie Chaplin: Joseph Grimaldi. Born of an Italian actor-father in London, Grimaldi became the supreme clown of his time. To the London pantomimes, those spectacular-sentimental shows so beloved by English audiences, so like a Harlequinade refined, prettified, and sugared for the children, he brought an authentic note of buffoonery. He invented "effects" and capitalized every outward resource and trick of the physical stage to the limit; but it was personal genius as actor and clown that made him a favorite in his time and an unforgettable tradition since. He was called "the Michelangelo of buffoonery."

In Germany so many of the ideals of the Romantic movement had earlier come to fruit in Goethe and Schiller — though without the bombastic fault — that there was no room for revolution in the Hugo-Dumas sense.

At the Court of Weimar at midnight on the eve of the new century, Goethe, Schiller, and a group of writer-friends drank a toast to the dawn of the new literature. Certainly in the plays of these two men a drama of spontaneity, of richness, of depth, was taking shape. But their work was incomparably finer than any accomplished by the French and English Romanticists: it refuses to be stuffed within the limits of the French definition of Romanticism. The work of the next group of German playwrights, however, is less significant than that of Hugo and Lytton. And so Romanticism in the German theatre hardly belongs to the chapter — just sort of fades from view.

Abstractly, we may feel that Romanticism is of the very fabric of Teutonic art. And practically we might adduce evidence in that the few significant German painters of the nineteenth century are of that persuasion, and the poets and novelists as well. But the stage bequeaths us no great names after Schiller, and not a notable one until the Realist Hauptmann.

The *theory* of a Romantic theatre, nevertheless, was discussed and analysed in Germany as nowhere else; and the activity led to one great good: Shakespeare was further acclimated to the German stage, and to this day he disputes with Goethe and Schiller the honor of being the most popular " national " dramatist. The outstanding figure in the period was not a playwright but a critic and translator, August Wilhelm von Schlegel. His book *On Dramatic Art and Literature* is still a standard reference work about the theatre. It helped to consolidate the gains of those who were freeing the stage from academicism.

Of the playwrights whom the German critics called Romantic, we may choose Heinrich von Kleist, Johann Ludwig Tieck and Zacharias Werner for mention; but these were all before Hugo, and link less with later developments in the theatre. One might almost claim that the Romantic movement, in so far as it was effective in the German theatre, brought less of good than of evil — of chaos, almost. The one most important drama surviving out of the period is von Kleist's *Das Käthchen von Heilbronn*, which is more in the Shakespearean tradition than suggestive of the new aims of the French sort. Schlegel, in translating seventeen of Shakespeare's dramas into German verse, had more to do with turning the current of literary-theatric endeavor than had any German or French playwright of the times.

In Austria Franz Grillparzer was at just this period writing the finest dramas that ever came out of that country. He was an independent spirit rather than follower of a school. He took largely historical and legendary themes and developed them with his own conception of a new freedom and a new naturalness. He was too restrained, too delicate in touch, with a sort of belated Classicist fastidiousness, to link with the Romanticists. And he put more of permanent literary enrichment into stageworthy dramas; so that you will find two or three of his plays in the repertories of the Austrian and German state theatres even today.

In Germany as in England, an actor stands out as a more spectacular figure. Ludwig Devrient had those same qualities of violent ecstasy and wild vividness that characterized Edmund Kean. Mantzius has etched this portrait of the player of the time: " The German actor of the romantic type was a strange being, with long, wild hair, black if possible, framing a pale, emaciated face; deep, melancholy eyes under dark, contracted brows, and a bitter, sorrowful smile on his quivering lips; his form shrouded in a long Roman cloak, moving among his fellow men now with ostentatious, gloomy remoteness, now with hollow, rather scornful mirth." And of all these picturesque actors of Germany — the type has not entirely disappeared yet — Devrient was most strange, most extreme, most grotesque. He strained after Romantic effect in a way that resulted in the most remarkable testimonials to his genius, and at the same time some records of failure. He touched heights never touched before, and fairly dazzled audiences; but he could not compass a quiet effect, and to sustain such brilliancy for long was impossible. Like Kean, he got a good deal of his inspiration out of a bottle — always a treacherous friend for an actor, in the end.

France, too, had one of these Romantic alcoholic actors at about the same time. Frederick Lemaitre, however, neither drank so

heavily nor rose to such giddy heights.   He gained his first success
in pantomimes and in the out-and-out melodramas of the *Boulevard du Crime* — the street of the popular theatres was called that
because of the terrible murders, seductions, fires, and poisonings
that occurred nightly on the stages there. He went on, however, to
the plays of Victor Hugo and the other Romantic dramatists, and
became the chief player of his period; though not such a revolutionary as Talma had been before him, nor so spectacular as
Rachel and Bernhardt after him.

In a more specialized field, in Lemaitre's time, Deburau put
his stamp permanently on an old character and created a tradition.   As Pierrot in the French pantomime — a form that may

LE BOULEVARD DU CRIME

be considered a bastard daughter of poetic drama by the *Commedia dell' Arte* — he charmed audiences and made over the
character with a new dignity and depth. Not too deep, mind
you, but deep enough for melancholy and a bit of wisdom. Indeed, it was Deburau who fixed Pierrot in the mold we all now
visualize at mention of the name: sad, powdery, languishing, poetic.
If you like your humor with a robustness and heartiness, you may
think that this was a debasing of the Italian comedy type, a typical
Romantic sentimentalization. Personally, I would agree with
you. Nor was the sentimental-Pierrot vogue any more lasting
than that of Hugo's and Dumas' plays. Deburau's son Charles
and another tried to carry on the tradition at the theatre made
famous by the father, the *Funambules,* but the impetus was too

slight; the vogue had been due to one actor's appeal, not to the discovery of an important new slope in dramatic art.

OPERA is always artificial and is generally Romantic in the 1830 sense. Its history after Lully belongs by right to this chapter. In Italy the form developed in the direction determined by Scarlatti in the late seventeenth and early eighteenth century: that is, it continued to grow in tunefulness, and with generous inclusion of the aria. Opera was an Italian art in origin, and always it flourished most abundantly in that country. But Lully's, as we have seen, was the next important name among composers, and he produced at the Court of France. Shortly afterward England had its creative flare-up, when Henry Purcell produced, with the aid of girls at a boarding-school, *Dido and Æneas,* thus showing that he might have been a great opera composer if the taste of the times had not forced him to write incidental music instead. Later, England had its share of Italian, German, and French opera, but never again a significant composer. An isolated and unique sub-species was created and had a vogue, to be sure, in the "ballad-opera," as instanced in the still-enjoyed *Beggar's Opera,* arranged to a libretto by Gay; and England later gave birth to the matchless musical fooling of Gilbert and Sullivan. But the English-speaking peoples are not operatic creators. (New York has long seen and heard the most brilliant grand opera in the world, but it is ninety-nine per cent imported.)

The comic operas and operettas of Gilbert and Sullivan, though a phenomenon in English stage history, were the culmination of a century and a half of endeavor to capture the lighter pleasures of music in works less sedate than "grand" opera. Indeed, *opera buffa* first appeared as relief from the tediousness of the long Italian *opera seria;* the unserious *inter-mezzi,* originally presented between the acts of the serious pieces, were in the early eighteenth century put together to form the first light or comic operas. The Italian Pergolesi was the first master, and Italy long the home of the form, but later the French took over the *genre* and made of it their *Opéra Comique.* There the term was widened to include not only humorous pieces, or satiric, but any lightly romantic music-play. *Opera buffa* was, of course, a needed corrective to

The San Carlo Opera House in Naples, as seen from the stage and from the auditorium. The horseshoe and hen-coop system persisting. [From Brogi photographs.]

Stage

Section and plan of the Bayreuth *Festspielhaus*, showing the auditorium with a single wedge-shaped bank of seats: the beginning point of the modern revolt against the Italian-French type of theatre building. Designed by the architect Semper in collaboration with Wagner. [From Sachs' *Modern Opera Houses and Theatres.*]

serious opera, and often it prospered by burlesquing the more ridiculous " effects " of the form that gave it birth.

Germany, though practically without " serious " theatres, had opera at a number of the petty capitals before 1700, together with some native composing. But Handel, the first great artist in the field, forsook Hamburg for Italy, and surpassed the Italians in their own sort of composition. The German Gluck also went South and ultimately excelled. But he became convinced that Italian opera was really only a sort of concert " for which the drama furnished the pretext "; and in Vienna and Paris he set to work consciously to " reform " it. Under patronage of Marie Antoinette, he produced a series of works that broke most of the rules for composition that the Italians had elevated into a sacred international code, laws about the number and kind of arias to be included, the number of singers, etc.; and he brought opera closer to the estate of a musical-dramatic art, by fitting the music to the interpretation of dramatic situation, to the expressive words and the pathos of incident. The Italian composers, to satisfy the vanity of singers, had arranged everything for the best display of individual voices: theirs was " show " music. Gluck asked only that his music " second poetry." He waged a merry war with the Italians, and he won to the extent of lopping off miles and miles of excessive vocal ornament.

Mozart and Beethoven both brought individual gifts to the art: the one with a grace that was closer to the Italians, but expressed with original freshness and with humor (he found *opera buffa* an inspiration as well as *opera seria*); the other with a deeper musical expressiveness, but only in one none-too-facile opera, *Fidelio*. And Weber introduced some of those motives which Wagner was to employ so notably later: musical characterization, in the *leitmotiv,* and certain orchestral innovations. All three of these composers had borrowed elements from the old German *singspiel,* instead of following blindly after the models originally introduced from Italy.

The Italians themselves changed chiefly in making their melodious works less classical and more popular — some would say, more sugary. They made little progress toward harmonizing the musical and dramatic elements: to this day Italian opera belies the word " grand " by its shallowness and showiness. But there is no doubting the fact that Rossini, Donizetti, and Verdi made operatic music more widely palatable and popular. No one ever lightened or brightened dire tragedy more prettily than did Donizetti in *Lucia di Lammermoor;* and Verdi rounded tuneful tragedy into its most plausible and decorative form in *Rigoletto* and *La Traviata;* though more might be said in praise of his *Aïda* and *Il Trovatore.*

In France, at the same time, the German Meyerbeer (he changed the Jewish Jacob Meyer Beer to Giacomo Meyerbeer after studying in Italy) had travelled in the opposite direction, forsaking what the Germans called " Italian sing-song " for a grand manner that tended to the heavy and grandiose: he was Romantic in the true French sense, with the melodramatic-vulgar fault. After him came Gounod with that *Faust* which was perhaps the best example up to his time of the music-drama composed with an eye to dramatic fitness and larger effect, and not merely as a singing display.

Such was opera before Wagner. In two hundred and fifty years since Peri's historic *Euridice,* no one had been able really to produce a drama-in-music, or to overcome a certain ridiculous convention of the solo singer stepping out of the play at intervals to show off. Wagner at least was giant enough to try. And he not only made himself the great figure in operatic composition, but initiated epochal changes in the construction of the physical playhouse. He made German opera incomparably the richest the world has known.

With a revolutionary idea that opera should have unity, continuity, and cumulative interest, Wagner wrote his own librettos and learned the technique of staging at first hand, while composing his music. In that, he foreshadowed a whole school of later thought, in and out of opera. Distrusting Classicism, but noting that the superb Greek drama grew out of Greek life and tradition, he sought out the legendary background of his own people for subject-matter, and found in Teutonic mythology the richly appropriate materials for his dramas. He apprehended that music must be fitted closer to the emotional content of the drama, must be an intensification of feeling; and he shaped a new sort of music-structure designed with primary purpose to emphasize plot and word-sense; avoided individual vocal numbers that would interrupt the action or break the emotional continuity; and freely used the *leitmotiv,* or guiding motive, which could be repeated to prepare the auditor for certain characters or incidents.

As a boy Wagner showed no such phenomenal talent as did, for instance, Mozart. Born in Leipzig in 1813, he was brought up with exceptional opportunity for absorbing the "feel" of the arts: for one thing, his stepfather was actor, playwright, and painter. The boy was a reader of fairy tales and of tragic drama, and at fifteen a devotee of music. Dresden gave first productions to his earliest operas, *Rienzi* and *The Flying Dutchman.* The latter, though not one of Wagner's greatest works, was so far ahead of its time, so different from anything then known, that it failed. But it was rather with the presentation of *Tannhäuser* in 1845, and the composition of *Lohengrin,* that the world of German music became divided over the revolutionary composer: one camp hostile to this formless, tuneless, chaotic work; the other wildly enthusiastic over the glorious freedom, emotional expressiveness, and rich harmony.

The hostile camp was the larger; the production of *Lohengrin* was delayed for years, and Wagner was made to feel the pinch of poverty and the pressure of court intrigue. He also fell afoul of the authorities for his political beliefs. In 1849 he fled to Paris, found only discouragement there, went on to Zurich, and remained an exile for twelve years. But in that time he worked on his highly national *Ring,* including *Das Rheingold, Die Walküre, Siegfried* and *Gotterdämmerung,* and wrote *Tristan und Isolde,* and a number of books. In 1861 the Paris Opera decided to risk a production of *Tannhäuser,* but the audiences refused a fair hearing, shouted down the performers, and the piece was withdrawn after the third performance. In that same year the news came that Wagner could re-enter Germany, and at the age of forty-eight he returned to his own country; but only to experience further torturing years of poverty and battle. He eventually found patronage from the King of Bavaria, however, and continued planning for not only a national music-drama but a national theatre.

In 1876 his dreams were realized, more or less ideally, in the building of the Festival Theatre at Bayreuth. The *Ring* was produced there twenty-eight years after he began work on it. And for seven years longer he lived, though still not freed from worries, composed *Parsifal* in his sixty-fifth year and died in his seventieth, in 1883. He had made a gallant fight, had lived through more of abuse, intrigue, and wilful misunderstanding than any other artist of his time; and after his death he became known as one of the greatest innovators and one of the outstanding geniuses of the world stage. Today his works are current in every world capital that claims any breadth of taste in opera.

Wagner's ideas about reform of staging did not include reform of the painted setting, and his stage at Bayreuth was designed for the equipment that had grown up around Italian-stage settings. But he did revolutionize the auditorium design. Elsewhere the houses had all been very slight variations of the horseshoe plan with tiers and tiers of boxes (see the illustration a few pages back). At Bayreuth the seats are practically all on a sharply sloping single floor, as shown in the plan. And from that one house spread the influence that in fifty years transformed the theatres of Germany and America into places so democratic that practically every spectator could see the stage — whereas the older (and alas, some newer) opera houses had hundreds of seats good enough for the poorer public but wholly unrelated to the place where the performers appeared.

The chapter opened with a reference to Shakespeare, who might have been a Romantic if the creators of that term had not narrowed its meaning by a realistic-sentimental limitation, if they had not made it inevitably suggestive of bombast and strut. The chapter ends with the achievement of this other giant, Wagner, who, in opera, did most of the revolutionary things that the Romanticists *hoped* to do. But he soared into a region too splendid, too extensive for labels. The auditor (in an opera house) experiences, to a certain degree, the true Dionysian ecstasy. It doesn't come often or sustainedly — the opera medium is still too imperfect for that — and maybe, after all, it is the music and not essentially theatre that *is* the magic. But again somehow there has been brought to the stage the beauty that immerses the spirit and stills the mind.

CHAPTER XIX

Well-Made Plays and Pretty Scenery:
Victorianism

W HEN Romanticism had won its victory at the *Théâtre Français* in 1830, there had been riots, battling, and shrill cries. *Hernani* had been the first of the "revolutionary" dramas to be accepted for presentation at France's official playhouse. The friends of Victor Hugo had aggravated the irritation felt among the entrenched Classicists, by appearing at the première in violet and scarlet waistcoats, pale green breeches and yellow shoes, under Rembrandt hats and flowing locks. They were Romantic outwardly as well as inwardly. The black-frocked conservatives bravely contested the field with these flamingly youthful and militant crusaders. Duels were fought, pamphlets were hurried through the presses, and the early performances were all but lost in the tumult of battle. But *Hernani* was a success. Classicism was thenceforward discredited, Romanticism supreme.

The next historic battle over a première at a Paris theatre was that in which *Tannhäuser* was literally howled down at the *Opéra*, in one of the most disgraceful episodes in the history of the stage. The judgment of the Parisians in both cases, in accepting Hugo and in rejecting Wagner, has been reversed by later generations.

But during all this period, from the 1830 victory to the 1861 disaster, a different sort of dramatist was working in Paris, without spectacular revolutionary notions or avowals, but in a way that moved worlds none the less. Indeed, Eugène Scribe went on to quiet success after quiet success, until his plays mounted up into hundreds, and ultimately the stages of Europe and America were " sold " to his sort of playwriting as they had never been to Hugo's. The theatres of all lands capitulated completely to a vogue.

We have come now to the mid-nineteenth century. The era takes its name not from any French development, but from that half-German British Queen who typified plainness, Protestantism, and prudery as no other mighty monarch ever did. It is a time of unimaginative art, a time when extremes of any sort are avoided, the age of drabness. The power of kings is pretty well gone; those who really rule either are too weak to give direction to the age or else care not at all about the excitements of art and learning. Democracy is left to carry on without guidance. The English creative theatre under Victorianism merely dries up. But in English civilization there are elements of shrewdness and materialism that make Scribe's type of play from France acceptable on the stages that remain.

For what Scribe was accomplishing, without spectacular manifestoes or scarlet breeches, between the years 1820 and 1850, was the creation of a play-frame so perfectly articulated, so facilely constructed, that any sort of sentimental stuff could be tacked on to it and made plausible. His was the supreme triumph of mechanics over dramatic content. Even while innocent of any of the larger virtues of the dramatist — he knew nothing of character drawing, and little of dramatic grip in the profound sense — he made hundreds of plays that pleased untold audiences. He mastered theatrical device, filled his pieces with obvious type figures, pathetic incidents, surprises, skilful ravellings and unravellings, clever sayings, happy endings, etc., etc., and developed a formula for theatrical effectiveness. He gave the Victorians what they wanted — a smooth article, a neat concoction. It was no time for genius or poetry or incisive characterization.

The French *pièce-bien-faite* is the perfect emotional tickler. Prettily fashioned, superficially brilliant, without literary or spiritual value, it came pat for an age timid about beauty, afraid of the mysterious thing called art. The emphasis on neat technique in the theatre had its parallel in the other arts, of course: in smoothed-down sculpture, highly varnished furniture, Landseer painting, the architecture of the Eclectics, etc. But nowhere else was the triumph of neat mechanics so complete as on the stage.

Not that the development had no beneficent effects in later times. It was Scribe's form on which Ibsen built his " social " drama; though Scribe would have wondered what such a term could mean. Drama was for amusement — what more? If one could take the uncertain old comedy-outlines, hammer them into a shape with just the right juxtaposition of laughter and tears, make them more intricate, put surprise and tenderness and sweetness into them — what more would a Philistine audience ask?

And so there grew up, beside the grandiloquent plays of the Romanticists, this type of smooth-gliding drama, not built with reference to any theories, or conviction of any sort — just out of the desire and intent to please. It is not surprising that no works of Eugène Scribe's have lasted. He wrote near half a thousand plays (aided by hack-assistants), he shaped the stage of an era, he is remembered as father of " the well-made-play "; but you probably never will see one of his dramas performed. There were, of course, those who guessed the shallowness of his work even in his own time, but they were no large part of the public. It is said that Heine on his deathbed, when his breath was failing, was asked if he could hiss; and his answer was, " No, not even a play of Scribe's."

Scribe died in 1861, and in that very year Victorien Sardou made his first important stage successes. The tradition of the *pièce-bien-faite* was thus carried on without break. It is said that Sardou, in order to learn perfectly the technique of play-making, would read the first act of a Scribe piece, then write the other acts himself. And the mechanics of manufacture were so perfected that he picked up the knack in no time. Such was the lack of character in Scribe's plays that another could appropriate the technique without more than an exertion of cleverness. Sardou is written down as the *cleverest* playwright the French theatre has known.

Of course Sardou added some elements of his own. He even kept an eye out to the trend of national thought and fashion, and wrote topical or appropriate pieces. But his naturalness, if I may so put it, crystallized into a convention. He discovered how natural people like you and me would act if we acted invariably according to our sentimental longings. He developed a stage logic: he made up that romantic naturalness that leads us to say today that a thing is theatrically true but not psychologically true. His situations are too skilfully devised to be credible, his *ingénue* too sweet, his generalizations too sweeping. He carried the well-made-play a little of the way from mechanical-Scribe toward that branch of realism that we may term journalistic, for its facility and lack of depth.

His sort of clever shallow play interests us, of course, like a detective story or the average novel. But there comes a time when we cry with the later critics, " Sar-doo-dle-dee-dum! " For there is nothing of sincerity or deep feeling or beauty here — and the stage cannot subsist for long without those elements.

For fifty years the European and American stages largely *did.* Where the repertory theatres were strong, the classics persisted, most notably in Germany. But as for new work, everything was now imported from Paris. In Germany there is not a memorable name out of the well-made-play period; all are adapters or imitators. Russia at this time developed a playwright who caught the knack of the Scribe thing perfectly, added a satiric slant, and turned out in *The Inspector-General* a comedy that has outlasted everything of Scribe and Sardou.

The Germans were already doing valuable experimental work as regards methods of staging, and were to evolve a new type of playhouse, as we shall see. But their chief contribution to the perfection of the mechanical play-form was theoretical. Gustav Freytag published in 1863 his treatise called *Die Technik des Drama:* in translation, *The Technique of the Drama;* and well into the present century it was being used as text-book at the universities. It purported to show that great drama almost invariably exhibited a " plan " with well-marked parts: development, climax, and return. On analysis any play could be divided into exposition, first clash, rising action or complication, climax, falling action, dénouement or catastrophe, etc., etc. The system is an eminently useful one for critical analysis, and suggestive to the theatre worker. But, like Scribe's facility, it leaves out all those matters that in the final reckoning make art art.

The trick drama was as effective in one language as another: no local color, no complex characters, no troublesome poetry to translate; just some easily understood people in a series of cleverly manipulated situations. The theatre was therefore international-zed as never before. France dominated the stages of Germany, England, the United States.

In England the adapters were legion. In farce there was John Maddison Morton, who made the perennial *Box and Cox* out of two French originals; James Robinson Planché was broader, re-fitting Scribe's material and other French pickings into comedy, burlesque, and extravaganza as well. Thomas William Robert-son began as adapter of the Scribe-Sardou sort of trifle, but either through an independent urge to observation or through the in-fluence of Augier and Dumas the Younger, he took a step for-ward, in the direction of the " social " drama. *Society* and *Caste* are even mentioned sometimes as landmarks on the way to Real-ism. Anyway, London wanted the superficial thing more than seriously observed drama, and Robertson died disappointed and worn out at forty-two. Tom Taylor's unending adaptations were more popular, and the plays of that Wilkie Collins who gave utterance to the classic formula: "Make 'em laugh; make 'em weep; make 'em wait."

Aside from adaptations from the French, the story of the well-made-play in England is told almost wholly in the dramas of two men: Henry Arthur Jones and Arthur Pinero. Both came late enough to find their inspiration in Sardou rather than in Scribe. Each added his individual variations and touches. But in perspective they are seen as providing the culmination of the glorified-technical-facility movement on the English stage. They were the great playwrights of their period, but it was a period when the stage had alienated practically every important contem-porary writer. They lifted the English drama out of the triviality and falsity of the French adaptations; but viewed today, their own plays are seen as deftly articulated stories rather than as stirring character-drama. In the argot of the stage, when performed today they creak.

Henry Arthur Jones has written voluminously about the " mod-ern " theatre, and he has insisted particularly that the man of letters must become the stage craftsman, that drama must be more than mere popular amusement, and that there must be close connection between any living drama and the larger life and society in which the theatre exists. And yet his plays are defective in precisely the elements he insists upon: they possess no notable literary values, they are effective as entertainment but leave no after-thought either through deep characterization or by profound insight or philosophy, and they miss the social significance of, say, Ibsen and Shaw. They are admirably deft, they hold the spectator or the reader from moment to moment without the slightest letdown of interest, they flow oh! so smoothly. But suddenly one wonders what it's all worth. Why couldn't there be one genuine passion, one memorable character, one disturbing thought in the whole of this row of plays?

Read *The Liars* — it will be an entertaining hour — and you will have Jones at his best. You will see that he has advanced beyond Scribe and Sardou, whose plays you might easily find annoying. But note how the masterly structure builds up to the one big speech of Sir Christopher in Act IV. The play is perfectly capped. The French had learned well the value of those climactic speeches. Their term for them is *tirades*. Our meaning for the word is a little different; but believe me, by emphasis the actor made the "splendid" speech a "tirade" too. At the *Comédie Française* you will see an actor get set for this sort of scene, treat it like a thing apart from the drama, with beginning, climax, and end of its own — and then step out bowing to the applause. And the audience is trained to watch for these purple patches; is always ready to leave the drama to enjoy a virtuoso passage by the actor. The *tirade* is really a borrowing from opera technique — an operatic intrusion. And by the way, Scribe was almost as successful in the fields of operetta and grand opera as in farce-comedy, though he failed dismally as tragedy-writer.

But not to cry down Jones too easily, in this superior time when we have a satisfying social-intellectual drama behind us, and a stirring journalistic realistic drama with us, he presented an intelligent plot with masterly technique.

Arthur Wing Pinero spanned a greater range. From trivial adaptations and inventions in the seventies and increasingly serious studies in the eighties, he arrived in the nineties at a very telling sort of emotional play that verges on the true "social" drama. As deft as Jones in technique — you may prove it by reading the so-prettily absorbing *Sweet Lavender* and *The Gay Lord Quex,* or the perfectly articulated *His House in Order* — he added a certain character-depth and an intensity of feeling. One remembers Paula Tanqueray and Iris — not with the immortals of Æschylus and Shakespeare and Molière, but nevertheless theatrically and humanly. And beyond, if the plays creak a little, there is an emotional tension that helps us to get over the obtrusive mechanics.

It was in 1893 that Pinero composed *The Second Mrs. Tanqueray,* a play so advanced as compared with previous English playwriting, that it is sometimes put down as the beginning-point of modern British drama. It followed Pinero's own formula for emotional-dramatic effectiveness. He once wrote: "Theatrical talent consists in the power of making your characters, not only tell a story by means of dialogue, but tell it in such skilfully-devised form and order as shall, within the limits of an ordinary theatrical representation, give rise to the greatest possible amount of that peculiar kind of emotional effect, the production of which is the one great function of the theatre." Here is Scribe's play-structure insisted upon, but not lightly, for amusement, to draw laughter and a tear, but for some deeper response, an "emotional effect." *The Second Mrs. Tanqueray* achieves that effect even while treating a "problem" somewhat memorably. It comes so close to being trenchant social observation, indeed, that we may leave discussion of its implications until a later chapter.

The truer Pinero may be found in *Iris.* Here is an emotional theme treated without wider social application. What is the theatre to which we go, to see *Iris* played? What is the intention of the dramatist, what the response of the spectator, what the special conditions of representation?

This is the true "emotional drama." We go to experience tragic stirrings, to be moved. The Scribe technique is reshaped to compass a story serious and pathetic. Thanks to the progress made by Sardou, Pinero is able to make his drama more compact than any since that of the Greeks. And like Greek tragedy, it

is meant to wring our souls, to purge us. But as soon as the curtain is down we know that there is a great difference between
this and the plays of Sophocles. Only in a certain directness and
intensity is there likeness. Upon analysis we find two elements
lacking: poetry and nobility of conception. Pinero has come
down to prose; and we are now so close to the triumph of Realism that it is prose laboriously like everyday speech. And the
characters are no longer lofty, the dramatic struggle no longer
between gods and men. Rather the theme is, as so often since
Pinero's time, human weakness, corruption of the spirit. The
protagonist is a woman too frail for the struggle against material
reality. Emotionally effective, yes; but tragic only if treated with
profound insight and with high poetry. In the end *Iris* remains
emotional drama, not purging tragedy " of a certain magnitude."

We see the character Iris slipping down to ruin through her
love of luxury. She finds the man she loves, but in a necessary
period of waiting for him, gives in to a suitor who provides
money for her ease and her whims; and when the true lover
comes back to claim her, she loses both men. Such is the simple
fable. It is plotted with masterly attention to cumulative effect,
and with constant continuity of interest. We find, to be sure,
the typical climactic speech in Act V, and the Scribe devices of
letters, latchkeys and such aids to the facile unravelling of the
knot. But the play *holds,* it grips the surface emotions, it clicks.

For this realistic-emotional drama there is a stage somewhat
different from that of the early years of the century. The picture-
frame proscenium remains, without the apron and the fore-doors.
The acting space has mostly gone behind the curtain-line. And
the interior settings are of the " box-set " sort — that is, with
three surrounding walls instead of wings — though the exteriors
are the same old half-painted, half-built pictures. The box-set
interior affords more concentration of attention than the wing
sort; the compact emotional drama therefore gains in a physical
economy of interest. This is, indeed, a step toward the true
naturalistic stage for the realistic plays of the Ibsenites, a step
away from falsity and " spread " toward a sort of truth and concentration. The acting, too, is more natural, less conventional.
Indeed, we may believe that in the perspective of the future the

Behind the scenes during a play. Note the method of lashing the wing-pieces to the masts rising through the floor-grooves. [From Laumann's *La Machinerie au Théâtre*.]

changes in Pinero's plays, like those in his stage, will be judged as not profoundly important, but as steps toward a later accomplishment of truth and dramatic intensity.

By way of utter contrast, to prove that the old artificial comedy goes on, revives whenever a man of genius takes it in hand, whether he has an eye to naturalness or not, we may pause a moment to consider Oscar Wilde. Within four years — exactly at the time of *The Second Mrs. Tanqueray* — Wilde wrote *Lady Windermere's Fan, A Woman of No Importance,* and *The Importance of Being Earnest.* These are distinctly " old " comedies, and not a little sentimental at times; but the sheer wit of them, the epigrammatic cleverness, disarms the audience. In production the plays go not quite so fluently today as they did in the nineties, but they are stageworthy enough for as frequent revivals as Goldsmith's and Sheridan's; and they mark Wilde as the only English comedy-writer of international importance between Sheridan and Shaw. They are ingenious — though without the obvious cleverness of the typical *pièce-bien-faite* — sparkling, and delightful. They have a permanent place in some lighter theatre than that of Pinero and his serious followers. In the field of poetic drama, Wilde was only half-successful in bringing his lyric gift into the service of the stage; though *Salomé* finds occasional production in several languages — is revived oftener, indeed, than any other English poetic play since Shakespeare's. (I find myself somewhat surprised at the statement, but can discover no evidence to the contrary. Stephen Phillips *promised* more, just after Wilde's time, but there is a literary burden on all his plays, and the first, *Paolo and Francesca,* remains his best — there is no growth toward stageworthiness. Perhaps Yeats and Dunsany will ultimately outweigh *Salomé* in popularity, in a more special way.)

In the United States the nineteenth century theatre had developed after the pattern of the English: it was a reflection of Paris through London. The first notable American playwrights appeared during the *pièce-bien-faite* era. Bronson Howard was the earliest and perhaps most original: he produced immensely popular plays with a native flavor: *Saratoga* and *Shenandoah.* Clyde Fitch was more prolific, more facile, more extravagantly successful. We read his best plays today as we read those of Pinero and Jones, with mild interest and with admiration for the craftsmanship. None the less the work of Fitch seems outmoded a quarter-century after they were written. And even Augustus Thomas, who lived to progress one step farther under the influence of the later Realists, never really freed himself from the formula of mechanical play-making. These three, Howard, Fitch, and Thomas kept the American stage supplied with " native " drama to leaven the mass of adaptations from Paris. But

The wing scene varied with oblique pieces. [From *Peintre-Décorateur de Théâtre,* by Gustave Coquiot.]

they also were America's sacrifice to the French tradition; they never escaped from the limitations of what is called throughout this chapter, somewhat damningly, the well-made-play. As a last word on the subject one may add that in the nineteenth century, Spain and Italy made their sacrifices on that altar too. Facility had become a god in all the theatres of the Western world.

BACK in the early and middle decades of the century, scenery had its " well-made " era. Despite the elaborateness, even the gorgeousness, of some of the older picture settings, there had been faults of construction, painting, and lighting that made the

" scene " unnatural from all but one viewpoint in the auditorium (the king's box), and usually too " regular." The use of back-cloth and side-wings solely, in more or less regular rows, made the picture monotonous. With improvements in machinery, however, came " leg-drops," hinged wings, and other irregular pieces.

The two sketches of scenery from behind (reproduced a few pages back and in the half-tone opposite), showing the backs of the wings, illustrate both the growing irregularity of shape in those pieces and the method of sliding them in parallel grooves; the one thing promoted variety in the edges, the other monotony in the main lines of the picture. By mid-century the tendency was strong to cut across the grooves with diagonal pieces, sup-ported from the flies and with braces, and not merely by the standard in the groove. The drawing opposite tells graphically the story of the change from the conventional regularity of the wing-and-drop set toward the freely composed picture. Not *too* natural yet — but that will come! As in playwriting the new mechanics worked in the direction of Realism, but the Romantic current toward the grandiose was so strong that the chief result was a period of well-made display-scenery without either dramatic justification or the negative values of naturalness.

How far the mid-century scenographers went toward making the stage an exhibition-hall for their own talents, you may guess from the illustrations out of French and English productions. The " amphitheatre " scene from *The Winter's Tale* is an ex-treme example of the attempt to make the stage picture rival the worst excesses of the easel painters. Real actors and painted actors, real architecture and painted architecture, real shadows and painted shadows — *there* was a task, to make all those match. But nothing daunted the designers and producers who thought that by such displays they were advancing toward greater art in the theatre. The purple patches in the play-text and in the actor's delivery were no less to be added than the purple patches of the stage " decorator." These are, indeed, the *tirades,* the long *vir-tuoso* passages, in the history of scene-painting. A little later it was thought that archæological accuracy would justify such flights; but it seems never to have occurred (except to a very few

Nineteenth century elaboration in scenery. Above, the "trial of Hermione" scene in *The Winter's Tale,* from a drawing by Louis Haghe, 1856. A classic example of the attempt — always futile — to shade real actors into painted crowds. Below, view of a wing setting from behind, in process of "building" during an entr'acte. [From *La Machinerie au Théâtre,* by E. M. Laumann.]

Two of the vast mid-century theatres. Above, the Boston Theatre in 1855 (as pictured in *Ballou's Pictorial Drawing-room Companion*); exhibiting the large forestage and the increasingly democratic seating plan. Below, Drury Lane Theatre, London, in 1842, with the elaborate picture-setting for the wrestling scene in Macready's production of *As You Like It*. [From a colored print of the time.]

Germans) that the whole structure of display scenery is out of place in connection with legitimate drama. Lately we have discovered the mischief played by showy settings on all stages except those given over frankly to spectacle or old-fashioned opera.

In Germany two or three artists — most notably Karl Immermann and Ludwig Tieck — were already experimenting in methods looking toward simplification of the scene and expediting the changes between scenes. They wanted to discover or revive stages upon which they could present Shakespeare without the wholesale cutting indulged in by most nineteenth century producers. In a vague way they foreshadowed the epochal changes to be ushered in by Gordon Craig and Adolphe Appia soon after 1900. But in their own time they were little more than voices crying in the wilderness of painted canvas and *papier-mâché* edifices.

The physical theatres remained operatic throughout the century, with a very few exceptions — most notable among them, Wagner's *Festspielhaus* at Bayreuth. Curiously, that house, built for a new conception of opera, failed to turn the current of practice so far as opera producers were concerned; but by 1890 it had convinced a few architects that Wagner was on the side of the future, and by 1900 the name of Semper was heard wherever "progressive" theatres (i.e., not on the Italian-French model) were being planned.

In the preceding chapter there is an illustration of a New York house showing how the large stage apron and the proscenium doors persisted even in mid-century. The view is dated 1853, and is of "the lecture-room of the American Museum." (Out of deference to Puritan sensitiveness a respectable theatre could not be called a theatre in those times, any more than a leg could be called a leg. But "lecture-rooms" were fitted up with luxurious seats and fully equipped stages. And the "Boston Museum" was one of the most famous of American theatres for decades.) I am adding here illustrations of Drury Lane Theatre in 1842, and of the Boston Theatre in 1855, indicating the change to smaller aprons, and illustrating the disappearance of the proscenium doorways. As to scenery, the Boston stage is quite evidently given over to the even-then old-fashioned wing setting; but on the Drury Lane stage is one of those mountainous half-built, half-painted-in-perspective scenes with which Shakespeare was habitually burdened. This is actually the wrestling scene in *As You Like It.* You can imagine how much you would have got out of Shakespeare's poetry if you had sat where the artist did when he made this picture.

A reason for the large theatres in London was the licensing system under which only two or three playhouses enjoyed "patents" for the production of legitimate drama. Thus with each rebuilding, Drury Lane and Covent Garden would be enlarged to accommodate as many additional patrons as possible. After Restoration days and the culmination of the Puritan boycott of the stage, two or three theatres sufficed for the London public that cared or dared to attend "shows." The drama had become a very special recreation, for the sophisticated and the fashionable. But by the early nineteenth century the populace had reawakened to an interest in the drama, and demanded more playhouses and more kinds of play. Theatres outside the law sprang up, and disguised their shows with music, magic acts, and trick-animal numbers, to avoid seeming competition with the licensed houses. Some of the strange things that happened in playwriting in this time might, perhaps, be explained by the desire *not* to produce drama like Shakespeare's or Sheridan's. It was in 1843 that the government passed a Theatre Regulation Act, and permitted an unlimited number of playhouses, under certain restrictions of censorship and building standards.

The large houses became all but useless when drama took its turn toward naturalness and compression in the latter half of the century. There was, of course, the corresponding change in acting. It had required grandiloquence and sweep to dominate in the vast spaces of the older theatres. Now the plays began to demand quietness, intimacy, intensity. And just at the right moment a new ally came to the actor who must make more of facial expression, of nuance of movement: electric light. As the playing-space shrank back into the box-set interior behind the curtain-line, electric lighting illuminated the player's face in a new and marvellous fashion. Given a house intimate enough, he was ready, when the playwright demanded, to interpret Realism naturally, quietly, plausibly.

Since Kean and Devrient and Lemaitre, however, the world stage had seen some great actors whom we of today would call "of the old school." In Italy playing has always been grander, more impassioned, more fiery, than elsewhere — the national temperament is volatile and operatic. In the period of Romantic drama (and the quieter well-made-play sort of thing never quite conquered Italy as it did other lands), Tommaso Salvini and Adelaide Ristori blazed vivid trails across the native stages; and then carried their spectacular art into the rest of Europe and to America. The tradition of their sort of acting has persisted even into our time, particularly in the playing of Giovanni Grasso — more rugged, but spirited and compelling. Still the one greatest modern player of Italy was Eleanora Duse, who belongs in spirit to the twentieth century: she made drama live nobly and intensely, without romantic elaboration, by the revelation of her own feeling. In her the simplicity of Realism seemed to be illumined by a clear flame of personal expressiveness.

In France the great actors after Lemaitre were women rather than men; though Coquelin and Mounet-Sully will long be remembered for carrying on the traditions of "high" acting. The three women, however, Rachel, Réjane and Bernhardt, provided some of the most sensational passages in the annals of the Paris stage. Rachel and Bernhardt successively shook the foundations of the official *Théâtre Français,* the one by remaining a member of the company but as a star, the other by leaving the company because she was too brilliant. Rachel was a tragedienne born, with that unexplainable native flair for acting that is restrained by no rules of naturalness or probability. She was perfectly the *Phèdre* of Racine's drama, and specially born to the thrilling heroine-rôles of the strained Romantic plays. Sarah Bernhardt, a generation later, added the more naturally emotional rôles to the Romantic ones, but was in direct succession from the grand old figures. Her beautifully modulated voice remains almost as famous in history as her insistence upon the right to continue openly the tradition of the courtesan-actress, in a time when people accepted such irregularities only under cover. On and off the stage, personality made her a vivid figure, and her *tours-de-force* in acting gained for her the greatest international following of any actress of the nineteenth century. In view of the recent rise of the companies devoted to ensemble playing, it may be that Bernhardt's name will stand last on the list of erratic and brilliant geniuses of the stage; but it has already been a list full of surprises.

Up to the time of Edmund Kean, the great players on the American stage were visitors from London. Kean was first seen in New York in 1820, but his unexampled and tumultuous triumph ended in hardly less riotous failure. He was literally hissed back to England after needless affronts to provincial audiences that had at first wildly acclaimed him. Only a few years later Edwin Forrest, first of the notable native-born stars, made his first success, at the famous Bowery Theatre in New York. He rose to first place in the world of the American stage, and even found in London appreciation for his Shakespearean interpretations. Unfortunately he was led into a controversy — probably his own touchiness and high spirits were to blame — with Macready, the ruling English favorite; and it was the feud between factions supporting these rival actors that caused the fatal Astor Place Riot in New York in 1849. The partisans of Forrest resented the return of Macready to New York, when he was billed to play at the Astor Place Opera House; and they not only wrecked the performance from within the auditorium but attacked the theatre from without, as if it were a fort — a fort holding " autocratic English," the leaders told the mob. They even fought the police and then the militia, until twenty-two persons had been killed. Macready escaped back to London while Forrest went on to less dubious honors.

The American theatre from this time forward was alive with acting talent, and one might pause over many glamorous names. Here were the Booths, the Hacketts, the Wallacks, the Jeffersons, the Davenports, the Drews, and other actor-families. Here, among the women, were Charlotte Cushman, the first American-born actress to become a great star, the picturesque Adah Isaacs Menken, Mary Anderson, Helena Modjeska, Clara Morris, and that Ada Rehan who was for twenty years a star in the remarkable company managed by Augustin Daly. Daly himself is re-

Increasing Realism in the Romantic scene. Above, a setting for *Tribut de Zamora* as played in Paris, by J. B. Lavastre. [From Pougin's *Dictionnaire du Théâtre*.] Below, a setting for *William Tell* at the Metropolitan Opera House, New York. [From a photograph by White Studios.]

Three scenes from Henry Irving's production of *Dead Heart* at the Lyceum Theatre, London, 1889, showing the solidly realistic settings. In the middle sketch the central figures are Ellen Terry and Gordon Craig as Catherine Duval and Arthur de St Valery. In the scene below the dominating figure is Henry Irving as Landry. [From illustrations in the souvenir programme.]

membered as ablest of American producers of the nineteenth century. In his time, too, there was that strange genius — actor, director, designer, inventor — Steele MacKaye, whose mind leaped forward to many of the "reforms" and stage inventions of a later era.

But two figures may be given more space, the one as greatest of American actors, the other as great and distinctive of an American development: Edwin Booth and Joseph Jefferson. It is typical of the broad national interest in the stage that Booth first came to prominent notice in New York (when he unexpectedly filled his father's rôle in *Richard III*), but made his initial great success in California, and was thereafter idolized throughout the country. He had little of the unaccountable fire of Kean and Forrest, but his quieter art had a nobility that has become a tradition. Intellect and spiritual insight enabled him to score triumphs as Hamlet and in other Shakespearean parts. He progressed out of Romantic acting, and yet was of the elder school: a noble and dominating transitional figure. In New York during the sixties he once played Hamlet at one hundred consecutive performances. When he built his own theatre he plunged into the sort of elaborate scenic productions then in vogue in London; and due to the magnificence of the staging he went into bankruptcy. But later starring triumphs gave him a position as representative of all that was finest in American theatre life in his time.

Joseph Jefferson — the third of that name — was a slighter figure, but equally beloved. He made himself master of a type of comedy rôle particularly palatable to American audiences. His acting was appreciated for the same reason that lay behind the success of playwrights who specialized in *The Old Homestead* sort of drama. Jefferson excelled in kindly character portraits. His greatest part was Rip Van Winkle, and he played it for decades to never-failing applause.

In England, after Kean and Macready, there was no figure of similar stature among the actors until Henry Irving's time. The Bancrofts formed a company at the Prince of Wales' Theatre, that did pioneer work in group-acting, and in the encouragement of the English playwrights who were trying to rescue the stage from French domination. But it was Irving who ushered in a new era. He is a great transitional figure, holding at once to the splendor of the past and foreshadowing great changes. His acting was less realistic, in the twentieth century sense, than personal and intellectual, and he usually played in old-fashioned Romantic pieces or in Shakespeare: he was not of a typically *new* theatre either as actor or as chooser of plays. His famous scenic productions, moreover, must be set back into perspective as the culmination of the Victorian vogue for picturizing. He pictured more intelligently than any actor-producer before had done; but here was no breath of " modernism " as the term is understood today. What Irving accomplished, that entitles him to epochal fame, was the lifting of the English stage into a new importance, into an unexampled completeness of achievement, and the raising of the actor's estate in the community above any level touched since Garrick's time. It is significant, indeed, of the long pull of the stage against Puritanic prejudice, that Irving was the first actor knighted at the English Court; and suggestive of the earnestness and sincerity of his efforts to create an institutional theatre, to bring his art to an eminence where it might justly be honored with the other arts. As actor he was richly satisfying without ever being spectacular. Perhaps most famous of his rôles were Hamlet and Shylock.

It was in 1878 that Irving took over management of the Lyceum Theatre in London; though he had already tasted popular success there as an actor. He gave distinction to the term " actor-manager " — which later came into disrepute, when lesser actors used theatre-control for the exploitation of talents not worthy of stardom. In the first year of his management Irving secured as " leading lady" the beautiful Ellen Terry, and there began one of the most famous and most successful artistic associations in the history of the stage. Ellen Terry played Ophelia and Portia within the first year — and became, deservedly, an idol of the English public. Several times the Lyceum company toured in America, where the noblest of England's actors and the loveliest of actresses found their triumphs repeated.

One is tempted to say that there is such a thing as well-made acting; a sort of acting mechanically effective but lacking in depth and sincerity. Certainly one could list a number of tricks by which "effects" are achieved, and probably these were as rife in the mid-nineteenth century theatre as ever before. Irving and Booth, with their personal gifts and their intellectual approach, helped to kill that sort of trickery. If they did not go all the way toward the Realism of Stanislavsky and Moissi and the "ensemble" companies, at least they prepared the way for it.

CHAPTER XX

Realism: Photography and Journalism on the Stage

AND SO Realism arrived in the theatre. As we sit here in the darkened auditorium, expectant, we face not an apron stage, a platform to which some actors will come forth, to strut and to recite. Instead there is a curtain before us, dropped flat against the footlights. All the acting space has gone behind it. The proscenium-frame is the only convention left.

As the curtain noiselessly rises, we see everything behind just as it might be "in nature." This curtain is like the blinder the photographer used to draw out of his camera just before taking a view. Its withdrawal permits us to see a restricted bit of actuality — none the less actual for being viewed through a hole. The theorists say the producer has withdrawn not a blinder but the fourth wall of a room. We view everything beyond, within the remaining three walls, just as it would have been had the other wall remained. We, the audience, have not been allowed to disturb people at their business of living out dramatic lives. They will go on living their hates, their loves, their miseries, just as if we were not present. Not one of these actors will step out of the frame, not one incident will violate what might actually happen, next door, or down the street, or across the railroad tracks. No romantic — or æsthetic — longing of ours will ever make them forget their reality.

The stage picture has become a photograph. This is no longer a painter's counterfeit (with the stage itself sticking through the painting at a dozen points, to give it the lie); this *is* the room.

The actors walk into it just as they do into those in their own homes. This is no pretense. It is the perfect illusion of reality.

And the actors: that one might be Mrs. Jones' own sister; and this girl reminds us of old widower Smith's red-headed daughter — we used to say she'd go wrong if somebody didn't look out for her.

It doesn't take long for us to become absorbed in their actions: the playwright has provided some incidents as holding as the stories in the evening newspaper. The dialogue is interesting — and oh, so natural! We even cry a little. This scene is touching. What a curious thing life is, all mixed up in laughter and tears! But pshaw! after all this is only a theatre. And we go out after the show, into the street, and throw off the spell of the stage as easily as we throw down the evening paper.

Once in a great while, to be sure, one of these natural plays stirs us deeply — just as a bit of news will sometimes register so that we can't dismiss it for hours or days. It is generally something horrible that makes such a lasting impression — whether in the newspaper or the journalistic play. There is a difference between the response here and that to *The Trojan Women* or to *Hamlet*. There was the *glow* of the theatre in those days; now it's a downright disturbing emotional dislocation. After the shock there is no purging element — call it what you will, poetry, spiritual depth, beauty, Dionysian experience.

What is this Realism that has come into the theatre to make the " show " as natural as what passes in your own drawing-room, as common as the stories in the papers? It is an art creed. It puts forward the assertion that imitation is the first aim in art, that illusion is the purpose of play-producing. It implies that art must have to do with the familiar, the everyday, the natural, with the observed thing instead of the imagined thing.

You will remember that for centuries there had been a trend toward "naturalness," away from convention. The Romantic group were the first to let nature cramp them badly; but they escaped some of the consequences by flying into those regions where nature is wild, to unaccustomed corners and to picturesquely exotic climates and customs — though within known limits. The Realists scorned any such escape. They would find material in nature close by, in people (and places and situations) as familiar as your rector, your butcher, and your scrub-woman.

What the Realistic playwrights usually did, to make these people interesting, was to pry down into those incidents and motives and passages in their lives that were hidden from the world. Mostly they were hidden because they had to do with weaknesses, disease, crimes, and abnormalities: and so nine-tenths of Realistic drama has criminal or pathological or sexual-physical aspects — and there is a superabundance of sensational or shocking revealment. On a hundredth chance a playwright paraded a hidden thing that somehow was tinged with nobility or heroic sacrifice or sweetness — and if he were master enough we went away with a breath of the old Dionysian ecstasy on us. But most Realism in the theatre left us excited but drab, stirred but feeling ignoble.

The fight for Realism on the stage was as protracted and as bitter as any other by which new " isms " had been brought into the theatre. And the Realists had hardly got full possession of the place before a new war was declared and they found themselves the defenders and not the attackers. A fearful lot of dust was kicked up, and so much of it is still in the air that we shall have to know pretty carefully what Realism is, what its shortcomings are, if we are not to lose our way.

In the first place, we must grant that there are many kinds or degrees of Realism. The most extreme, in which observed fact is not only prominent but is emphasized, insisted upon — like the art of the painter who depicts every hair in a man's beard — we may dismiss as mere Naturalism. The true Realist looks down on the Naturalist just as you and I do; he says that art is selective: not just any bit of nature photographed exactly, but a special bit of nature, caught unawares, then the picture touched up a bit, and some unessentials eliminated. Still, the Realist adds, the main outlines and the background must not violate actuality.

Thus on the peep-hole stage — that is what the fourth-wall theory gives us in a glorified way — you may have a whole range of selective Realism, from the plain reportorial or slice-of-life sort, over near Naturalism, to the emotionally condensed sort over near Sentimentalism and Romanticism. But almost never does observed-life drama touch into lastingly significant art unless another element is added, in what we may term *intellectual-realistic* plays.

And what the modern theatre (since 1850) has achieved, of permanent value, is almost exclusively in this field where shrewd fact-observation is crossed with trenchant thought. The Realistic drama might be dismissed as a mere passing phase, had not some men of exceptional intellect lifted the photographic-familiar play to their own uses. Whether it is the deeply purposeful drama of Ibsen or the wittily intellectual drama of Shaw, it is Realistic drama first, but *drama of thought* second and more important.

We cannot here go into the æsthetics of Realism, cannot ask whether the play of familiar life does not, by working solely to accomplish an intensification of human emotion, inevitably wreck itself on the rock of " the pathetic fallacy." But from the exterior viewpoint, looking back at a half-century of accomplishment, we can make sure that only the Realistic drama with this other thing added, with implications valuable in the fields of social thought and of intellectual stimulation, has survived notably.

The theatre that has housed the realistic-intellectual drama has been the least *theatrical* in history, a place used rather than a part of the essential means and material of the art, contributing definite values to the ensemble impression. The stage became a picture so like life that its first aim was to escape notice, glamour was suppressed for fear of disturbing the illusion of actuality, and acting became subservient. The extreme Naturalists, of course — David Belasco most conspicuously — developed stage settings with a *virtuoso* naturalness, with so exact likeness to actuality that they shouted for attention to the cleverness of the illusion. But later Realists guessed that selective imitation in the background picture was better for the play-illusion. On all counts the playwright became supreme. From 1890 to 1915, the stage belonged to the author as never before. Perhaps it was a reaction to the nineteenth century divorce between literature and theatre. More likely the age of Realism kills inevitably the true theatrical appeal, implies transfer of the stage from the hands of artists to men of intellectual rather than emotional-æsthetic attainments.

By way of keeping a better perspective on Realism, before looking into the story of its quarter-century of triumphs in detail, we should remind ourselves that the rule of the Realists ended with the World War. Practically every important dramatist of the movement was a pre-war figure: Ibsen, Strindberg, Tolstoy, Chekhov, Hauptmann, and Wedekind, of course; and Schnitzler, Brieux, Shaw, Barker, and Galsworthy substantially. And among the lesser men who wrote two or three notable plays in the *genre* — St. John Ervine, Stanley Houghton, St. John Hankin, Eugene Walter — of the ones still living none has orientated himself to the newer theatre, in which theatricalism, as crystallized in a new completeness of *production,* has become a prime consideration. Since the war the dramatist has no longer been the key figure in the theatre.

Alexandre Dumas *fils,* who was born in 1824, once wrote: " I realize that the prime requisites of a play are laughter, tears, passion, emotion, interest, curiosity; to leave life in the cloakroom; but I maintain that if, by means of all these ingredients, and without minimizing one of them, I can exercise some influence over society; if, instead of treating effects I can treat causes; if, for example, while I satirize and describe and dramatize adultery I can find means to force people to discuss the problem, and the law-maker to revise the law, I shall have done more than my part as a poet, I shall have done my duty as a man." [1] By grace of the attempt to put that theory into practice — though he and his collaborator Emile Augier failed to write " thesis-plays " that have survived — Dumas *fils* is sometimes credited with originating the realistic-social drama. Augier, to be sure, is remembered for his *Le Gendre de M. Poirier* and for other straight comedies; and Dumas for *La Dame aux Camélias,* a grand but somewhat cheap emotional play. But the consciously purposeful dramas of these two men failed to establish significantly the newly glimpsed society-conscious theatre.

And indeed, there is not one French playwright of the Realistic school who remains internationally important, of stature

---

[1] Quoted by Barrett H. Clark in his *European Theories of the Drama* (Cincinnati, 1919), an anthology of theory that will prove useful to readers who wish to trace back to contemporary statements about dramatic art, from Aristotle to Shaw. Another book by Clark covers statistically and biographically, on the " study course " plan, the Realistic theatre: *A Study of the Modern Drama* (New York and London, revised edition, 1928); from it the reader may secure the main facts about each dramatist, as well as accurate references to all the books on the subject. Thomas H. Dickinson's *The Contemporary Drama of England* (Boston, 1917), and *The Contemporary Drama of France,* by Frank Wadleigh Chandler (Boston, 1920) are excellent surveys of their respective fields.

comparable to Ibsen and Chekhov and Shaw. Henri Bernstein fell heir to the overseas popularity of Sardou, but his plays were emotional-observation without the intellectual brilliancy or the true realistic truthfulness to detail. Much earlier Emile Zola had tried to bring the grand manner of Romanticism to the low-down subject-matter that he discovered through his boasted devotion to Naturalism, but his plays are the least part of his literary achievement. Henri Becque instead is the first notable figure among the short-sighted Naturalists. After him a group of facile playwrights turned their realistic spotlights upon the old triangle situation, sometimes by way of comedy, sometimes for emotional-dramatic effect: Maurice Donnay, Georges de Porto-Riche and Henri Bataille. The term "psychologic drama" came freely into currency with the emergence of their plays. Henri Lavedan and Alfred Capus ranged more widely for subject matter but are less in the direct Realistic succession. It is rather with Paul Hervieu and François de Curel that we return fully to the type of drama foreshadowed by Dumas *fils* and Augier: both are idea-dramatists; and only with Eugene Brieux do we arrive at the thesis-play triumphant. For Brieux is the moralist and the reformer consciously using the stage to set forth an indictment of society. Here the theatre has come to its most direct service as moral weapon; at the same time it has just about ceased to exist as an art, in which theatricalism has a value of its own.

If it seems possible to omit further mention of all those other French playwrights, and of as many more who give Paris its unending stream of triangle comedies, topical satires, and Sardou-like emotion-plays, without depth or stimulus, it is not possible so easily to pass by Brieux — because he is so much a culmination of the movement toward a drama of social purpose. Not so graceful a writer as a half-dozen of the others, not a shrewd psychologist, not troubled by any canons of good taste, he still has stirred the world more by his plays. He is the journalist-realist using the stage willy-nilly to force attention to social wrongs. In *La Robe Rouge* he showed tragedy growing out of that French judicial system which led the police to arrest *someone* for every murder or else be accused of inefficiency; an innocent man is sacrificed to the system, in order that a prosecutor may be promoted, with the final result that the wife of the accused kills the prosecutor. In *Maternité* he argued for birth control, and used the unpretty device of showing up society's injustice to the illegitimate child in contrast to the old-fashioned sentimental and often tragic encouragement of over-breeding. In *Les Avariés,* played in English as *Damaged Goods,* he exhibited a man afflicted with syphilis marrying, against his physician's advice, showed him contaminating others, and — not to dwell upon the really horrible details — ended with the physician pleading for enlightenment but refusing to aid the wife to divorce her tainted husband. Thus is the stage made to do for clinic and rostrum. It is a good sign that the vogue of Brieux is fading. We all went to see these plays in their time, and I think we considered them "advanced." Fortunately the theatre has since made headway in other and less noisome directions. For essentially the stage is more concerned with beauty than with morals. The theatre is the house of emotion, of passion, of ecstasy, rather than the house of correction.

During the reign of Realism in France only one theatre stood out sharp and clear from the background of increasingly commercialized playhouses; the *Théâtre Libre.* You will remember how Napoleon restored the privilege of monopoly to the *Théâtre Français* in Talma's time, after the "free" period of the Revolution; but in 1864 the field was again thrown open to all producers. Still production tended to become stereotyped, and a few people saw clearly that French playwriting was ingrowing and was becoming provincial. One of these was André Antoine, a clerk of the Gas Company. So he founded the *Théâtre Libre* in Paris in 1887, as a home for experiment, and to stage the plays that would not be seen otherwise. Realism was in the air, and Antoine's "reforms" were limited to a Realistic programme. In the end he turned up no new playwright of permanent world importance. But he established the first of those amateur and semi-professional playhouses that have carried so much of the burden of experiment and progress toward a different theatre in forty years since; and he introduced to Paris the giants out of the North, Ibsen, Strindberg, Tolstoy. After nine years the *Théâtre Libre* failed, and France has but once since become important for either sound and original experiment or theatric achievement of interest beyond routine.

Henrik Ibsen was the greatest figure of the Realistic theatre and of the nineteenth century theatre. Today the world looks back at this little man with just the trace of a smile for his crusader's conceit and his personal pompousness and somewhat tight morality, but with sincere admiration for his achievement in lifting a limited form of stage art to its highest manifestation. He took the well-made-play structure and turned it to serious instead of trivial uses. He made the play-form taut and compact as it had never been before. He cut down the limits of the dramatic story, condensed, treated only the climactic or catastrophic action. He read a new meaning into the term "dramaturgic economy."

But most notably and most startlingly Ibsen achieved the purpose of Dumas *fils;* stimulated the spectator's mind, awakened his conscience. He made the drama social, revolutionary, topical. He diagnosed the ills of humankind, destroyed illusions, satirized conceit and provincialism and hypocrisy. His was a destructive work, in the social-intellectual view — perhaps Realism *used* can be nothing more. At any rate, he stirred the world even while affording audiences absorption in shrewd dramatic reports of contemporary living.

In his personal life economic pinch, social injustice, experience of theatre management, and long exile in broader countries than his own native Norway, helped to shape his course toward the writing of keen-edged social drama. His early plays were Romantic and poetic; of them only one, *Peer Gynt,* has survived with the later thesis-plays. It is un-Romantic, natural-as-your-hat, observed drama that is typical Ibsenesque.

A woman, from being the petted and spoiled plaything of her husband, suddenly grows up to independence, and walks out of the house on her own: *A Doll's House.* A vague idealist, self-centred and ineffective, insists upon a code and brings specific tragedy and worse, mental inconclusion: *The Wild Duck.* A man grown above the expedient morality of a prosperous provincial town tries to correct evils for the sake of the people, but finds himself an outcast: *An Enemy of the People.* A woman has been persuaded by her pastor to return to her profligate and diseased husband, out of respect to the sacredness of the marriage vow; now their child, grown up, returns, and his hereditary disease and his hereditary philandering bring about a situation unendurably horrible — for audience as well as for the characters: *Ghosts.* Such are the ideas underlying Ibsen's work. He treats them humanly, with expert character-drawing; but it is the idea, not character-conception, that determines the situations, the plots.

Ibsen's plays had enormous influence outside the Scandinavian theatre. *A Doll's House,* first of the notable social dramas, was written in 1879, and others followed, at about two-year intervals, until 1899: including, besides those above-named, *Rosmersholm, Hedda Gabler, The Master Builder,* and others. As early as 1890 these had exerted an influence in Germany and in England. The tautly-constructed, natural-dialogue, thoughtful idea-play became the ideal of all "advanced" playwrights. Realism had been raised to a new importance, socially if not theatrically.

Not to follow too tortuously the trail of "the new spirit" across the stages of Europe — always in thinking of these matters we should visualize certain less learned types of stage activity as going on endlessly, as a background, farce and melodrama and burlesque and vaudeville or "variety" — we may note these figures as giants or near-giants who walked importantly in the branchless groves of Thesis-Realism:

Björnstjerne Björnson, fellow-Norwegian to Ibsen, but less the born playwright, was characteristically a dramatist of social criticism; his best-known play, *A Gauntlet,* is a dramatic plea for the single standard in "sexual purity." August Strindberg was a greater figure, writing powerfully and often bitterly, of the foibles and miseries of mankind; *The Father,* of the longer plays, and *Creditors* and *Miss Julia* of the shorter, are perhaps the best known in translation, though all the theatres that wanted Realism in its most trenchant and distressing aspects have played Strindberg occasionally. Gerhart Hauptmann in Germany went beyond the Scandinavians in one respect: he dramatized not only individuals as type-figures out of society, but in *The Weavers* an entire social class; and beyond Realism he wrote several poetic-symbolic plays that have lived to survive many of the products

Back-yard Realism, in a setting for *The Oracle* at the Metropolitan Opera House, New York. [From a photograph by White Studios.]

The Royal Theatre at Wiesbaden, showing the French Court influence persisting in a theatre built in Germany in 1894. [From Weddiggen's *Geschichte des Königlichen Theaters in Wiesbaden.*]

of the other pre-war dramatists. Hermann Sudermann was only
a Realist of the half-convinced Sardou type; his plays lack depth
and truth, though he achieved in the nineties an international
reputation beyond Hauptmann's — chiefly by the success of
Home (Magda). Frank Wedekind caused a stir as great as
those following the early productions of Ibsen's plays and the
publication and rare showing of Brieux; he set out, sometimes
mercilessly, sometimes bitterly, many of the subjects that people
are most reticent about: most notably, perhaps, in *The Awakening of Spring,* a tragedy of adolescent awakening to love. In
Austria, where German is the language of the stage, but the
people and the art less Teutonic than Latin (with a bit of Oriental
influence thrown in), Arthur Schnitzler was the master of Realism, and he carried the medium to a gracefulness unexampled
before: his studies of transient love are superior to anything in the
French, for truth combined with light sophistication.

At the other extreme are the Russians, utterly sincere, preoccupied with the miseries of the world, seeking to throw light
into the dark spots of human characters and human haunts. They
took audiences back toward Naturalism, they cut slices out of
existence, showed out life-as-it-distressingly-is. Maxim Gorky
threw aside play structure entirely, and turned to picturing vividly
his fellow-outcasts and sufferers — his was the great protest
against dramatizing life " as they write of it in books." His
plays achieve lifelikeness that is startling, in a performance such
as the Moscow Art Theatre troupe can give, but a formlessness
and a chaotic confusion far from essential theatre. Tolstoy was
more a craftsman, but only half a one as compared with Ibsen
or Scribe. Only the palpitating violence and emotion that he
caught in his writing, the images hot from observed life, could
outweigh the looseness of structure; but *The Living Corpse* and
The Power of Darkness are still widely played. Leonid Andreyeff
went deep into the portrayal of futile and miserable living, but
rose to imaginative heights at other times. Anton Chekhov was
the most individual of the Russians, and his apparently " natural "
studies, carefully etched, come to life dramatically under understanding direction and skilful character-acting. His art is one of
delicacy, of nuances of feeling, of half-hidden spiritual values, and

he has enjoyed a belated vogue after the heavier-handed Realists have begun to slip in popularity.

The Russian theatre before the era of Realism had always followed fashions from abroad, without contributing with originality to the world's store of great plays; though often the theatres of Moscow and Petrograd were among the most brilliantly active in Europe. The ballet particularly had found patronage and encouragement there, and along with Realistic plays the country has sent "Russian dancers" out to all the rest of the world. It was the Moscow Art Theatre, however, that was first to be recognized as one of the greatest of experimental centres, and as home of a troupe unrivalled for ensemble acting. It is today the best known, the most esteemed, playing company in the world — unless we want to dispute in favor of the amateurs of Ober-Ammergau. And its position, gained by its pushing of realistic acting over into a region of spiritual revelation, is maintained even in this later era when Russian directors are exploring every phase of unreal and frankly theatric acting and production.

Berlin had its *Freie Bühne,* after the pattern of the *Théâtre Libre,* in 1889, and here Otto Brahm became the arch-realist in staging. Settings and properties, like the plays, must be as familiar, as common, as your own kitchen, the office, the brothel. Here came the beginning Hauptmann and Sudermann with their timidly or precipitately natural plays, and here Ibsen and Tolstoy were first introduced to Germany. Brahm taught Reinhardt, and the impetus ran out in the latter's famous *Deutsches Theater* in Berlin. After the Moscow Art Theatre, the *Deutsches* was the most famous playhouse of the early years of the twentieth century.

It was in 1891 that J. T. Grein established in London the Independent Theatre, in the image of the *Théâtre Libre* and the *Freie Bühne.* Ibsen (already a *casus belli* in England), Tolstoy and other of the Continental iconoclasts were exhibited, talked about, fought over. The established playwrights were influenced: two years later Pinero brought out his "thoughtful" play, *The Second Mrs. Tanqueray;* but most important, a new author turned to the stage, Bernard Shaw. His first play, *Widowers' Houses,* an exposé of respectable-shameful slum landlordism, was composed expressly for the Independent Theatre. In the following eleven years he failed to bring more than one successful play to the boards in London, although he began early to dress his obviously purposeful plots in abundantly witty dialogue. In 1904, after his dramas had gained an extraordinary success in printed form (the now-famous Prefaces are as entertaining and meaty as the acts that follow), a series of productions at the Court Theatre, under the Vedrenne-Barker management, established him as the leading figure of "the new movement" in England; and he has never relinquished his claim to that position. Indeed, his fame has grown steadily, so that today there is none to dispute with him for the title of "the world's foremost living dramatist."

It was Shaw's destiny to lift the Realistic drama to its highest potentiality — by making it primarily and enjoyably intellectual drama. He is more "natural" than the average Realist: where others have to force nature at times, sentimentally or emotionally, to gain "effects," Shaw sails by on the wings of intellectual brilliancy. He more or less swallowed the well-made-play formula in its structural aspect; but he balked at the romantic and sentimental conventions that still clung to it — very obviously in Pinero and Jones, more covertly in Ibsen and Hauptmann. In his own words, he looked on "romance as the great heresy to be swept off from art and life."

As to his social purpose in the theatre, he wrote thus in his Preface to the *Pleasant Plays*: "I can no longer be satisfied with fictitious morals and fictitious good conduct, shedding fictitious glory on robbery, starvation, disease, crime, drink, war, cruelty, cupidity, and all the other commonplaces of civilization which drive men to the theatre to make foolish pretenses that such things are progress, science, morals, religion, patriotism, imperial supremacy, national greatness and all the other names the newspapers call them. . . To me the tragedy and the comedy of life lie in the consequences, sometimes terrible, sometimes ludicrous, of our persistent attempts to found our institutions on the ideals suggested to our imaginations by our half-satisfied passions, instead of on a genuinely scientific natural history."

And so Shaw raises the curtain on characters that act so naturally, with a scientific-intellectual honesty, alongside some romantically conventional ones, that the contrast becomes vividly dramatic and the world is vastly entertained. Military glory, medical infallibility, the righteous reform spirit, the masterful man, surface respectability — these and a dozen other pretenses and fictions serve as excuse for the brilliant display of his wit, his moral passion, his ability to strike to a basic human truth.

His plays are not theatrical with the warm, glamorous, human glow that has seemed in the past so characteristic of the stage art. Perhaps he would sweep away that side of the theatre as romantic and fictitious. To escape " staginess," he casts away much that made Sophocles and Shakespeare truly theatrical. To some, who see the sensuous element as legitimate in art, and who look for a deeper spiritual-emotional evocation as the characteristic excellence of the stage play, it seems clear that Shaw has — in the final view — made the supreme success in a limited dramatic field, over toward the intellectual and away from the sensuous-theatrical. He eschews theatre, but *uses* the theatre compellingly, nay gorgeously.

Certainly in the Realistic era, he has given us more to be glad for, more to entertain us intelligently, than any other writer: *Candida, The Devil's Disciple, You Never Can Tell, Man and Superman, Getting Married, Mrs. Warren's Profession, Arms and the Man, Androcles and the Lion, Heartbreak House* — the productions of these (on our American stages) afforded many of our most memorable evenings of playgoing, over a period of twenty years. A less distinctively Shavian triumph, but equally memorable, occurred hardly five years back, in the production of *St. Joan.*

The impetus of the Ibsen battling and of the Independent Theatre spirit led to the founding of the Stage Society, that notable " tryout " organization which exists to present "uncommercial " drama, and to circumvent, for the sake of select audiences, the British official censor; and to the three-year stand of the Court Theatre in London. Under the Vedrenne-Barker management a thousand performances of "advanced " plays were given, of which seven hundred were Shaw. Other dramatists arose to the opportunity created by a broad and courageous policy. The Court

REALISM 461

Theatre brought to production plays by John Galsworthy, by
St. John Hankin, and by the director of the enterprise, Harley
Granville-Barker; and three of the Greek tragedies so beautifully
translated by Gilbert Murray. And at matinées in another house,
John Masefield's *The Tragedy of Nan* was sponsored.

After Shaw, Galsworthy has enjoyed the widest vogue. His
utterly serious and emotional thesis-plays are the best of their
kind. Like Shaw, Galsworthy believes in using the stage to set
out human follies, inconsistencies, injustice. He has done this
vividly and often movingly, most notably in *The Silver Box,
Strife, Justice, Loyalties,* and *Escape.* He gains in dramatic intensity by the consistency and sympathy of his character-drawing; but
the idea is the thing that remains with the spectator after the last
curtain.

Granville-Barker — actor and director as well as dramatist —
has written some of the most sensitively conceived and delicately
molded idea-plays in the language. He approaches Chekhov in
the fineness and the quietness of his method. But his plays are
seldom seen in production — perhaps await some less noisy
theatre than that of the Realistic era. And indeed, in the reading
of his latest work, *The Secret Life,* one feels that here is groping
at least toward a theatre where spiritual values can be set out
more truly than now seems possible. In *The Madras House*
the author earlier scored a success quite in the Shaw tradition,
satirically, brilliantly.

Masefield in *The Tragedy of Nan* added a poetic touch to
Realistic emotion-play. He almost gave promise of combining
the new intensity with the old splendor — but nothing has come
from his pen in recent years to fulfill the promise, if we read one
into that notable play. J. M. Barrie dressed Realism in other
trappings — those of sly humor, fantasy, and sentiment. His are
the most palatable plays that have come out of the English progressive theatre in the last thirty years. Lacking both the conviction and the brilliancy of Shaw's, and the burning sincerity of
Galsworthy's, they have yet other qualities that are likely to give
them as long life in the theatre. For no one can forget the ironies
of *What Every Woman Knows* or *The Twelve-Pound Look,* or
the tendernesses — sometimes over-sentimental — of the less

"thoughtful" pieces. There is more of stageworthiness here than in the starker social studies of his fellow dramatists.

It was during the later years of the Realistic era that the American theatre outgrew the estate of a dependency of the European stage, that it developed individuality and a self-sufficient life of its own. Long, long before, it had claimed outstanding genius in the figures of two or three star actors. But in playwriting for more than a century it had been dependent upon London, when it wasn't sending to Paris for its materials and models. Occasionally, to be sure, it had known triumphs in minor fields: the distinctive Indian dramas, negro minstrelsy, the Harrigan and Hart farces, homely plays of the type of *The Old Homestead* and *Shore Acres,* and local melodrama. But in the well-made-play era, the first emerging literary dramatists had faithfully reflected European practice, and the bulk of plays were then still coming from overseas.

In the first decade of the new century, however, the abounding life of the country and a new will to amusement were reflected in a commercial stage intensely alive and sustained by native playwrights. This was the time of syndicate control and the killing off of all independent experiment and direction. But in turning out endless mechanical plays to the demand of the market, the American author came to an amazing skill. He made journalistic drama his own. The plays were often sentimental, crass, shallow, without purpose beyond amusement; but the activity marked the lifting of another national theatre to independence of a vigorous if crude sort.

And against this background of efficient grinding out of entertaining drama, have occurred, in the decade since, those phenomena which have brought the American stage to the attention of the rest of the world: as that on which standards of staging are higher than in any other country, excepting only Germany; on which experimental ideas are more eagerly welcomed than in any other country, excepting Russia; as that on which the plays and acting companies from every part of the world are seen (profitably), even while native plays go out to the livest dramatic centres of Europe for production. Here incidentally the Naturalist mode in staging was given its most thorough trial — in the productions of David Belasco and his imitators — an experiment followed by the accomplishment of the best in selective-realistic mounting. But as in Paris, Berlin, Moscow, and London, the " insurgent " playhouses, the theatres revolting against the slick and shallow efficiency of the " regular " stage soon came to be more important than the professional institution.

The story of the little and non-commercial theatres belongs to a later chapter: for one thing, they were established not more from the desire for a superior Realism than out of a devotion to some vague ideal of a later Expressionistic theatre. The insurgents had read Craig as well as Ibsen and Shaw. But it is proper to mention here the several playwrights who raised the standard of sincerity and truth above the elements to be detected in the plays of Clyde Fitch and Augustus Thomas. We might linger over the names of men like William Vaughn Moody and Eugene Walter. But it is rather with a younger generation that socialized Realism came into its American own: Edward Sheldon, Susan Glaspell, Sidney Howard, Maxwell Anderson, Philip Barry, Eugene O'Neill. It is particularly difficult to draw a line between passing journalistic Realism and trenchant thesis-Realism on the American stage — the playwrights here seem to confuse their aims more than in other countries.

In the end the story of the Realistic dramatist in America comes down to O'Neill alone. He is played in several European capitals soon after his New York premières. True to the traditional manner of the making of Realistic playwrights — Chekhov, Hauptmann, Shaw, Galsworthy — he is a product of a minor insurgent stage, the Provincetown Playhouse. But from compelling Realism he has gone on to other fields — and there we shall meet him again.

A different sort of phenomenon on the American stage is to be seen in the plays of Charles Rann Kennedy, not of America originally but typical of developments there. Twenty years ago his symbolic-realistic drama *The Servant in the House,* the best of its sort but not without sentimental moments, achieved a spectacular success in the regular theatres. Other plays followed, more realistic at times, literary-symbolic at others, and with an occasional tinge of what has since become known as Expressionism. The professional theatre was not ready for works so serious and so unusual. Kennedy and his wife, the gifted actress Edith Wynne Matthison, practically withdrew from contact with the "regular" stage. Stirred by the spirit that led to the founding of a thousand "irregular" stages in the same decade, they set about creating their own theatre; a company of three actors was formed, capable of playing on any platform in church, school, or playhouse, and thus economically independent. For it Kennedy wrote plays of greater poetic loveliness than any others done in English in recent years — and highly enjoyable in performance for a " special " public. The achievement of this group, that has made itself not only independent but creatively so, is typical of much that has passed in the American theatre within the last fifteen years; the amateur phase of that advance, and the new conception of " production," will provide material for another chapter.

Realism, indeed, seems to have ended, in America, not with a gradual fading out or a return to Romanticism, but with a stimulus to exploration of every phase of anti-Realism, at the hands of widely separated, self-sufficient acting groups and of playwrights not too old to experiment and readjust their vision. At the moment the American stage, without a Shaw or a Hauptmann or a Galsworthy, is still the most promising in the world, by virtue of vigor, surge, and will-to-experiment.

Realism in art came pat to the life of the late nineteenth century and the early twentieth. In the age of scientific inquiry, in the age when social equality apparently was gained for great masses of men, in the age of the clearing away of superstition and pretense, art was brought down to the familiar, the analytical, the microscopic. This was also, we might note, the era when man went farthest toward self-destruction. It was natural that he should almost destroy the theatre.

And indeed, much as we may enjoy Ibsen and Shaw, they did go far toward destroying that theatre in which Euripides and Shakespeare and Sheridan were possible — or Scaramuccia or Grimaldi. The Realists completed the process of pushing back the theatre until it all but ceased to live as such. A picture of reality lived in a peep-show box instead. The truly theatrical elements were squeezed out. But those revolutionaries, building a thousand little theatres, out of some longing for theatrical expressiveness, and their playwrights who have timidly started out to give a different sort of play — they are a sign of Realism's weakness, its limits, and ultimately its passing.

CHAPTER XXI

The Theatre and Its Swell Relations: The Other Arts

IT IS permissible to mark the convenient date 1900 as the turning-point into a new theatre. It is true that the parallel currents of the sentimental well-made play and of journalistic naturalism flow on into the twentieth century theatre. But if one judges by the " advanced " stages of the world, one recognizes that the new century has witnessed the beginnings of a different dramatic art: not unconnected with the Greek, the Elizabethan, the Oriental, but different in a very revolutionary way from nineteenth century Realism, and perhaps with a " form " shaped truly to contemporary life, to the civilization and inventions of the Machine Age.

Now this new theatre art is as yet less a matter of performance than a world-wide formulation of a different theory, and an awakened consciousness. There is performance too, or the subject wouldn't be worth talking about; and the evidence of it will be material for the three chapters after this one. But since the change in the spirit and aim of the world theatre is more evident than the practice, and since the understanding of the entire period after Realism is dependent upon a clear conception of all that change implies, it has seemed to me wise to break into the chronological continuity of my " story," and to set in here a chapter of undisguised theory.

I have no warrant from my fellow workers in the modern theatre to formulate a statement of the æsthetics of " the theatre art " — and I am only too conscious that no one has yet put down any such guide as I shall here attempt. But I have tried to see the " new theatre movement " broadly; and I have believed that

I recognized elements in recent advance and experiment that linked stage progress with that in the other arts, in architecture, painting, and the dance particularly: in short, that " modern art " has already transformed certain stages and has engaged the minds of the most promising and most effective artists in the theatre of today. And so I shall proceed to explore the theory of " the theatre art " with constant reference to the recognized advance in " general " art.

The theatre almost invariably has been looked down upon by the practitioners of the other arts, and by theorists and critics in particular. They all have made eyes at it, to be sure. The poet has seen here the very place to set forth his pretty verses the more movingly. The painter coveted the stage because he knew he could use it to the glory of picture-making — and for some centuries he did. The musician actually kidnapped drama at one time, married the jade to his own art and thus begat that strange interloper on the theatrical platform, Opera. The dancer, too, opining truly enough that drama was born of dance, has schemed to repossess the stage. And yet each of these artists, and all their apologists, have treated the theatre art itself as an inferior — if indeed they recognized it at all as a separate, self-sufficient art, and not merely a conglomeration.

It is easy to perceive reasons when one views not only the diverse people but the wide ranges of activity that actually are " theatre " in the larger sense, the complex nature of the materials of the art, the variable human element, the scattered manifestations. There is nothing clean-cut here, no neat rules, no lasting finished work. In a time when pigeon-holing was a passion with critics and with scholars, the theatre confusion was too puzzling. One might take ten examples of painting for study, and say, " These represent sixteenth century art at its best, and therefore the characteristics of that period are, etc., etc." It could be done with sculpture, with architecture, with poetry. Even with music, where a performer comes between the composer and the public; for a musical score comes infinitely nearer to fixing the values of the performance before an audience than does the written text of a play. If you buy all the printed dramas of the Elizabethan or the Greek playwrights, and study them to your heart's content, you still won't know the theatre of the Elizabethan or the Greek age until you get a vision of the complete performance and all that went to shape it: physical form of the theatre, architecture, color, light; actors, choruses, dancing; music; costumes, properties, settings, machinery; most of all, the flow of these things together, the underlying structure of emphasis, pause, interval, rhythm — the complexity brought into focus.

Not that nineteenth century scholars didn't try to explain theatre art wholly by the evidence of the plays on the library shelf. They had stage art almost stuffed into a pigeon-hole that was merely a department under " Literature "; and they dissected play texts and taught an exact formula of playwriting. They simply ignored those manifestations of theatre in which the written text is fairly incidental: dance-drama, the Professional (improvised) Comedy, pantomime, pageantry, etc. They were willing to write down acting as a minor reproducing art, and they allowed no creative value to directing, setting, and producing. They lost the very spirit of the theatre, as anyone must who fails to visualize the *flow* of the stage art, before an audience.

If this activity couldn't be squeezed in as a department of literature, on the obvious claims of a Sophocles, a Shakespeare, or a Molière, what else was there about the institution to align it with any of the recognized, the holy arts? Then in the nineteenth century, as the visual arts became more and more divorced from ordinary living — with painting and sculpture retreating into museums, and the artists getting themselves elected into academies and hierarchies — the theatre took the other road: with its degraded product it stayed by the people, in their accustomed amusement places, in tents and casinos and market-places. Such as it was — and almost never do the last shreds of glory depart from it, however incongruous — it was popular. Wherefore the high arts, the fine arts, came to look condescendingly on it. Under democracy, anything that so many people liked must be low.

There has been one disadvantage for the student in this escape of the theatre from canonization. While some of the best intellects of the late nineteenth century sought to disentangle the threads of art theory, and wrote volumes on the nature of the fine arts in general and of painting, sculpture, architecture, poetry, and music in particular (not *all* these volumes are more muddling than useful), no one has ever attempted seriously to write an exposition or explanation of the arts of the theatre, that would clearly suggest what is the nature of the appeal that the stage performance makes to a spectator, or how the theatre artists put it into a play-production. Such a book, if not too narrowly nineteenth century in outlook, might help considerably those of us who work, very near-sightedly, in the theatre, might interest those who merely have felt the glamour of the stage, might make more intelligent the reviews by thousands of critics, the lectures before women's clubs and university classes and organized audiences. But there is neither an important learned work nor a readable popular book on the theory of the stage.

It seems to me that everyone must know something of this subject, if the twentieth century stage is to be understood as we understand, for instance, skyscraper architecture and the paintings of Cezanne; if we are to interest ourselves deeply in the noble as well as the vulgar theatre, in acting as well as drama, in those several arts that bridge over from the stage into painting and music and dancing and poetry. As I take the platform, I ask my readers not to become too alarmed: I have no intention of trying to expound the deeper principles of æsthetics. For one thing, nobody has ever really discovered them, at least not in such a simple way that they can be viewed briefly. But I would like to help my audience to look around at the chief uncovered turrets and towers of the subject, so that they won't think they are in the inner sanctums of appreciation when they are only enjoying some pretty scenery, or that they have exhausted the finer possibilities of drama when some character has " uttered a mouthful " that sums up their prejudices toward an aspect of life.

Perhaps I am only setting out to show my readers how to go *around* this subject, this edifice, picking up enough of the outstanding landmarks on the way to enable them to keep to the main road in the twentieth century theatre on the other side.

The confusion within the edifice alarms me too. Just as one puts his finger on the quality that seems the essential in art creation, on or off the stage, some new theorist, having looked from a different point of view, shows clearly that his predecessor has missed the main thing entirely, has excluded more than half the really creative work. And when you get a sight of these æstheticians fighting each other, it's a show in itself, with climax, suspense, surprise, bitterness, smart dialogue, and all!

But these few points I stand upon as guide in the pages that follow: I invite my readers to accept these fundamentals of *a* theory of art and of the stage until they can themselves set up a counter-edifice — or read Hegel and Ruskin and Croce and Freud and Bell, to say nothing of Aristotle, Voltaire, Lessing, Freytag, Meyerhold, Yevreinoff, and Young.

Art, in or out of the theatre, is an activity of human beings by which they create objects or "works" that are useful to other human beings in a special way. An artist, let us say, is interested in painting, and he sees in nature a landscape, a group of apples, or a cow that interests him in relation to painting, sees it differently from anyone else, with a special sort of painter's unity; and out of the characteristic materials of his art he creates something with a completeness of its own. This something, this picture, in which nature as seen by casual eyes or by the camera lens is distorted and has become secondary, is a new object in the world, and it is capable of satisfying a spiritual or emotional hunger in others — or if you prefer to isolate the experience, an *æsthetic* hunger. No other artist can make the same object, can create a thing with exactly the same appeal or satisfaction in it.

In these few lines one may note many of the outward characteristics of the work of art. It is "made," complete, unique, and useful in satisfying a special sort of craving. It is a product of perceptive experience on the artist's part and a source of æsthetic experience to the beholder.

Practically all investigators today isolate art from the other fields of human activity with which it has at times been supposed to have close connection: industry, the working out of moral systems, recreation, etc. Enjoy art as a special sort of experience in life, not to make you "better," or to remind you of this or that, or as a super-photograph. They also insist upon an understanding of the fundamental difference between art and nature, emphasizing the "made" character of art; for both works of art and scenes and objects out of nature may be beautiful, and a complex work like a presented play and a real court trial may alike be " moving "; the responses of the spectators at times being confusingly similar. Wherefore, say the theorists, let us get clear that the emotion felt over a view or a happening in life is different from the æsthetic experience, let us drop the word " beautiful " because it applies to both fields, let us remember that what nature supplies by way of subject matter is of only minor importance in art, what the artist creates or puts in of major importance; let us be mindful of the separate identity of the work of art, with qualities and merits of its own and a potential response for every intelligent and unspoiled spectator. Only thus, dear reader, will you be able to avoid mixing your art with other activities more personal but generally less noble.

It is particularly difficult not to use art as a tickler to your memory, or to start pleasant trains of thought, or as an inspirer of good deeds, or to divert you with anecdote, prettiness, and neat invention. We were all brought up to believe that those were its functions. We are just emerging from a period wherein art was thought of as anything except an activity valuable on its own account, a period of unexampled production of merely " diverting " works, of sentimental slush, of copying, of slick technique developed on its own account. Familiar landscapes, pretty girl heads, idealized nudes, kittens, the old homestead, the father of your country, parlor fiction, jingles, neo-classic epics, Renaissance public buildings and Neo-Gothic churches, happy-ending sentimental plays and slice-of-life drama — these are signs of art watered, sweetened, or perverted, of the timid imitative attitude, of awed transcription of natural loveliness or picturesqueness, of uncreative worship of " finish." It is a salutary call that aims to bring us back to art that is valued not for its usability or for transcribed values but on its own account, for an experience important in its own kind, a response that satisfies a separate human hunger.

Just as the artist is likely to be a different sort of fellow, careless of the conventions, wearing sombreros or corduroys in the most sacred places, and negligent of his hair, so he *sees* differently. Some critics assert that to paint or write a masterpiece, he must see things in an " ecstasy," must apprehend something, out of nature or life, in a flash. Personally I think that is hurrying the fellow more than is necessary; the important conception is as likely to come to him in a tranquillity or a travail, neither of which is necessarily ecstatic.

In any case, we may be sure that three elements enter into his creative process. He gets something out of nature, something different from what the rest of the world would observe in the same bit of actuality, with certain obtrusive details eliminated, no doubt, and possibly with the structural or characteristic essence standing forth with a fullness or completeness not clear to other eyes; then he shapes this subject, distorts it, arranges it, unifies it, to bring out the deeper thing he has apprehended, applies something out of his vision or his feeling for form or rhythm, brings its complex elements into focus; then, already having his " picture," he sets it out through the materials pertinent to his own art, paint or words or stone, in that other made picture which the world sees. He executes, within the limits of the means of his art, the work that becomes effective to other men.

Some writers minimize the later activity, the getting it into paint or the stage materials; they put more stress on the seeing, the conception, the visioning. But there is importance too in getting full expressive value out of the materials at his disposal; the richest values of the paint and color; the completest effectiveness of dialogue, movement, acting, lights, etc., in the stage art. In the theatre particularly, the creative handling of the rich and complex stage materials is imperative. Else the produced play fails of being *theatrical* and remains merely poetic, or a bit of mimicry, or reportorial.

The work of art thus created is a thing complete in itself, unified at the expense of seeming natural analysable truth, a fused production, indivisible, with a fulness of its own. And then only the smaller part has been said. For still the thing that used to be called " beauty " has escaped the definition. Recently that almost indefinable quality has been pinned down a little closer to comprehension, under the name " form." Clive Bell wrote a whole book to prove that " significant form " is the true earmark of visual art. And it is not impossible to identify, after experience, a fourth-dimensional quality in the paintings of, say

El Greco and Cezanne, in the statues of Michelangelo, in a work of Bach or Sappho or Shakespeare.

That is to say, a man, mystically inspired, if you prefer the term, or just seeing in a special way, adds to what he takes out of nature, and beyond certain elementary and understood elements of surface composition, of line, mass, color, etc., a " formal " quality, a quality born of his vision beyond the usual planes, of his feeling for perfect focus, of his realization of a world beyond the seen three-dimensional one, and of his understanding of the potentialities, the richness of his art materials. And this form in his work, this " significant form," if you accept the handle most in vogue, appeals to an emotional receptiveness that is in every man to some degree, the true æsthetic or art-appreciating sense. If the beholder doesn't let subject-matter or showy technique or personal prejudices get too obtrusively in the way, he will instinctively look for the fourth-dimensional quality, the thing that speaks to a deeper self. If he isn't too much concerned that the apples in Cezanne's painting are more bumpy than those on his own sideboard, he will discover in Cezanne's canvas a formal organization, a composition, that stirs him deeply. And Cezanne and all the other painters may be judged as of more or less account to the world according to the intensity, the richness of this one half-identifiable quality in their work.

When Hamlet speaks:

> Oh, what a rogue and peasant slave am I!

· or

> To be, or not to be, — that is the question: —
> Whether 'tis nobler in the mind to suffer
> The slings and arrows of outrageous fortune,
> Or to take arms against a sea of troubles,
> And by opposing end them? — To die, to sleep . . .

I repeat the lines to myself, speaking them first for the logic, for what they " say," and then for all the known excellencies of verse, the metre, the word sounds, the variations in measure, etc. Then I know that there is a quality beyond any of these, almost magic in its rarity and elusiveness, and this I call " form " — the significant form of dramatic poetry. But, you object: it isn't necessarily *"form."* It's — well, just what makes the stuff poetry.

There we have it: I am just trying to give a handle to the thing that is essentially the heart of painting, the thing that makes poetry poetic, or a played drama truly and richly theatric; because in a moment I think it will help us to understand certain things about the actors and the dramatists and the stage and the appeal to the audiences. In a sense, form is the sum of the unexplainable and unchartable elements that evoke æsthetic response in the beholder.

Now there has been a little comedy going on ever since Clive Bell took the centre of the stage to spread his thought about significant form being the essential thing. A lot of serious and otherwise dignified professors climbed right up on the platform and began to belabor him without mercy. "Nonsense!" and "Stuff!" they cried. And then when they were allowed to have *their* say, every one of them began to talk about some equally mysterious and equally undefinable quality in art that they called rhythmic order, or contrapuntal organization, or focus, or some other name that had no more apparent immediate meaning. When they had quite destroyed poor Mr. Bell's "form" structure, they simply went on squabbling among themselves over the shape the next structure was to take, and they ended by all but murdering each other. So the crowd is left with hardly more than the pleasant memory of Mr. Bell's try at an explanation.

But when we have rung down the curtain on the Professors' Comedy, won't we find it convenient to say simply that there is an unexplainable something about the work of art, which we can experience and almost point out, and that "form" is as good a name for it as any other? Of course, we shall slip occasionally, and speak of rhythm, of beauty, of the stage flow — but day in and day out, "form" is the handiest label.

There are those who proclaim "There is no art of the theatre until it is brought to completion before an audience." I really couldn't say as to that. It seems to me a metaphysical question; and we are agreed that it would be useless to go deeply into matters of audience psychology, and particularly into crowd response. Still we must recognize quite simply that an audience at the theatre "gives" to the production as in no other art, joins the flow, helps thus to create. Beyond that, we may profitably inquire a bit into the nature of the response of an individual to *any* sort of art. It may help us to "see" the production on the stage more intelligently and enjoyably.

What little comedy there is here concerns the efforts of one group of combatants to tag the thing the spectator experiences as *emotion* of a peculiar sort. First thing we know, somebody has sent those fellows sprawling, and is pinning an entirely new label on bewildered Spectator. This time it is *pleasure* — "emotion" is far too indefinite a word to call it by. And quick as a flash someone over in the corner has picked off those pleasure fellows: pleasure is the result of the æsthetic emotion, not the thing itself. And what is the term these new comedians set up? You can *know* a work of art, that is all; it is all a special sort of knowing, unlike any other. "Go on," pipes up a voice way upstage; "It's more a matter of *feeling*."

Well, between you and me, they are never going to finish this comedy in time for us to get on to the main show. We might just as well choose the term we like best and get on to the next platform or turret. Personally I don't believe that knowing and feeling are terms definite enough to label that very true response that we have experienced before El Greco and negro sculpture and at a Bach festival; or in that hushed, glowing time when spirit speaks to spirit in the darkened theatre. I find myself drawn to those combatants who talked about emotion, who say that the greater the art, the greater the spectator's emotional response; and that the greatest works in the theatre are those pregnant with the deepest emotional appeal. *Only* I want it understood that I see emotion as embracing a very wide range, reaching over definitely into what mankind has tried to rope off as "spiritual." We can't go too deep, toward the soul or spirit, in seeking the true seat of æsthetic response.

What probably put emotion in bad repute, as a name for the spectator's response to art, is this: In the nineteenth century most people who called themselves art-lovers repressed their true emotions, and they took out their longings in enjoyment of sentimentality. They wanted art to compensate them for the barrenness of ordinary living. They asked that it be emotionalized in that part of the field at the far corner from what we have called spiritual, in that corner where emotion becomes personal, cushion-like, sweetened, and flabby. They wanted art to be a reminder of some vague ideal of a heaven-on-earth, wanted it to fit in with their sentimental dreams; they liked to identify themselves with a hero, to dream themselves the lovers. They asked that art create a field where they could enjoy a sweetened sort of life vicariously.

And the artists mostly accommodated them. That is why, for every dramatist who remembers logic, who is true to vision, there are a hundred happy-ending playwrights, aiming to satisfy the sentimental demand. Just as these hundred purveyors of slush are the most ephemeral of artists, so the public that asks for it is exhibiting the cheapest, the most watered form of emotional response.

A different angle on this response comes to view if we say that art in the nineteenth century was considered as an *escape*. Life as lived, the people argued, is hard, unimaginative, a sort of prison. Art must provide a means for periodic escape. It must devise another world into which tired and soul-hungry men may be taken at intervals, for recreation, renewment, relief from the strain of reality, from the tyranny of the commonplace. It must be as different from everyday life as possible, without ever distorting the outward appearance of nature, without disturbing prejudices or getting down to the terrible truths. This was the attitude that led to that sort of realistic Romanticism which had a fairy-tale sweetness without fantasy, a show of great deeds without spiritual conviction, a sweet false fiction of reality, wherein riches came easy and the current sort of virtue was rewarded. Flattering identity of the beholder with characters or with subject-matter is a necessity in such art. The spectator intervenes his ego, his own case, between the artist and enjoyment. Subject-matter becomes over-exploited; a theme must be proved — that life is pleasant.

There is the more recent Realism that affords a contrast to this Victorian school of art. It clings to the earthiest and least sentimental aspects of life as surfacely lived. It embraces the morbid and glorifies the wicked. The drama has been a favorite medium with these morbidizers. It has been made to show forth in merciless detail the seamiest side of life, proving that everything has a flaw, all action has base motive, every hero has his vices. There follow sewer realism, gloom, obscenity. Sex is dragged out and brought into an absurd importance, merely because before it had been hidden. Sordid living is portrayed as the natural end of the truly honest man. Disillusion, cynicism, " what is, is true " — what else can an intelligent person believe in?

This is the very reaction to the escape-into-sweetness sort of thing, from sentimental-compensation art. But don't you see, dear reader, that these Realists are perverting art in exactly the same way that the happy-ending ones did: they simply want to make art a funnel through which spectators will peer into their cynical view of surface life, instead of a gateway to a tinsel paradise. The one sort intervenes the thesis that all life is unpleasant, while the other intervenes with " Life is all pleasant." While proving their cases, over-interested in their respective themes, they both have lost all contact with the deeper bases of human living, with the nobler planes beyond the surface one, with formal expressiveness.

I am likely to get excited just here. I want to climb up on the stage and shout: " Escape! Portrayal! Gloom! What have they to do with art? What but to prevent it? If we can't accept art as an activity important in itself, self-sufficient, with a value to the spectator in its own kind; if we don't find in it an intensification of living, not a gateway to some other sweetened or muddied fiction of life, it's not worth the powder to blow it to Limbo. It is a form of deeper living, a gathering into focus of the known and unknown finenesses of life. It is the human-divine made movingly expressive, throbbingly alive, an immersion to the spirit."

IN THE theatre — I am glad to be back in the cavernous auditorium, looking at an expectant stage — a whole troop of creators, of artists and workers, appear in place of the single sculptor or painter or poet of the simpler sister arts. And as for materials there is no end to them. Here we see dramatists, composers, designers, *régisseurs,* actors, electricians, carpenters, etc.; and they will use movement, gestures, words, music, silences, lights, platforms, screens, paintings, furnishings, costumes, etc. But beyond all these things and people contributory to the stage art, there is that quality "form." We won't explore now the dramatist's contribution or the actor's place in the conglomerate, but we must speak a little of the *régisseur,* because he is the typically twentieth century stage artist, and he has most to do with bringing the theatrical form into focus for the audience.

Looking at the stage before us — a better beginning point than the author's script or an actor's performance — let us visualize the created, unified production as a whole. What the theatre artists have "made" is this "play" that passes before our eyes, greater than a story, or the contributive poetry, or the pattern of movement, or the color and lights, or the revealing acting. Call it a procession of all these things, or rather a flow, since all the elements must be perfectly mingled, indivisably fused. Implicit in that flow, beyond the appeal of any single element, is the form or rhythm, the typically theatric quality, out of which the spectator draws the theatric sustenance, the current to the spirit, the apprehension of things beyond the literal meaning and the surface seeable elements. And as color is to painting — one cannot think of significant form in the picture without a color implication — and as mass or a certain blockiness is to sculpture, so a fulness, a glow, a rich complexity unified in action, is of the essence of the stage art, is the very feel of it.

In certain types of theatre art the sensuous elements contributing to the flow, the sense-appealing attributes of the "form," are emphasized, doubly capitalized. The movement is then more musical, colorful, lilting in rhythm. The focus is brought about with the warmer, freer flowing elements rather than by the logical word, the calculated gesture, and the measured unfolding of plot. But even the less colorful and more literary play must be staged with continuous, unbroken, theatrical form. Otherwise it drags as theatre, remains literature acted. Stage people are not likely to analyse so closely, but they have their expressive terms for these things. A certain production, they say, had no pace, no go.

Surely if there is such a thing as a primarily intellectual art, it is at the far pole from this theatric one. In those minutes of wonder, those tranquil utterly unworldly times, when the mind is disarmed and the soul immersed in drama, there is poised then the high moment of the glow, warmth, and richness of the theatre medium. It has been put down innumerable times that *action* is the essence of the dramatic art, that of the " materials " it is the one indispensable ingredient, the very *clou* of the stage production. Then the definition of action should be widened to include the sensuous flow, the unseen building toward the glowing moments. The wise director, of course, knows this; and he knows also that action in its commoner sense covers two important things in the presentation of the play: physical movement (the pattern of movement having become recently of enormous moment to the director-artist), and action in the sense of development of a story, plot movement, an unfolding of something to be understood.

Beginning with action, some people prefer to explain the whole theatre art in this way: There must be actors, obviously, to carry out the action. The actors must have a platform to lift them into visual eminence, and so there comes into the list of materials of the art the stage itself, with its shape, its lighting, its " looks "; and if the age be one that values ornament and intricate invention, a whole range of added values is created here, as " stage decoration." The dramatist then supplies an outline or scenario to serve as the backbone of the production, or perhaps he uses words as a chief means of revelation; and at times he sets these down with all the embroidered values of poetry. But now — and here we come to the chief contribution of the twentieth century to theatre theory — with all these people called in, and all these elements to be brought into unity, the playwright, the actors, the designer, the movement, the story words, the poetic values, and the decoration, we inevitably need another super-artist to get the production hatched: a new creator is necessary, to whip the others into co-operation and co-ordination, into proper subordinate and contributive places, the artist-director.

This *régisseur,* the re-creator of the whole, the man charged with making continuous and unbroken the flow, the combined evocation, is a comparatively new figure to the stage. In the past he has seldom been important enough to leave a name in history, unless he happened to be at the same time an outstanding actor; but today several artist-directors are more famous than any living actors or playwrights (excepting always that one lone figure, Bernard Shaw). In our own time, Gordon Craig and Max Reinhardt and Stanislavsky are become legendary. In a later chapter, on the rise of production as an art, the artist-director and his ways of widening the meaning of action will be fully treated. Now I want only the understanding that in some sense we have found new ways of looking at the materials of the theatre production, a new approach to the art; that at the same time there has been a shift of interest from the contributive artists of the stage to a central *régisseur*.

Let me take two examples, very different, of the way in which a director shapes a production to bring out primarily the form element. We go to a dance-drama, a production of the *Ballets Russes*. Our senses are caught up by the music, the dancing, the color, the "atmosphere," the silent story, the rhythm. The "form," become sensuous here, sweeps over us like an inundation. The director, M. Diaghileff, has vivified perhaps a threadbare fable theatrically, by co-ordinating and flowing the performance into one colorful stream.

The next evening we go to a production of a modern realistic play: let us say *John Ferguson*. It is not one of the sordid, purely journalistic things, but as bare, as limited in view, as dependent upon observed fact, as any piece from which you are likely to get a formal as well as a fictional reaction. The point is that, as directed by Augustin Duncan for the New York Theatre Guild, it emerges in a production that not only holds the audience as a novel on the same theme would, but at many points stills the literal mind and speaks directly to the spiritual consciousness, provides a true theatrical experience. The actors are so rightly chosen, are so trained into one perfectly balanced ensemble, that no "performance" stands out, the setting is forgotten or never noticed, the physical movement weaves a pattern so right that it is unseen, yet so proportioned and accented that every spectator is played upon subconsciously. In short, discounting the mere story-interest of the text, the director built a production, using every resource of the stage, which stirred us *theatrically*. The theatre *form* took possession of us as truly as in the case of the dance-drama.

RETURNING to our chapter title, the contributive arts have often enough tried to take over the stage. Literature especially has attempted periodically to capture the place. Writers who had hardly more than casually entered into the playhouse as spectators wrote literary dramas, and managers, or societies bent on "bettering" the theatre, arranged productions for them — most notably during the Renaissance and in the nineteenth century "closet drama" period in England. And when the classics had gone out of vogue, "reformers" tried reviving them, as examples of what true literature in the theatre had been. Since these last producers neglected all elements of production except securing good texts, their efforts remained in the field of literary endeavor — they showed something that might be absorbing in the library, and something that once had been gorgeous in the theatre, but a thing that remained dull in their performances because they failed to make it live *in stage terms.*

About the time when I was a youth a whole generation was more or less soured on the classics of the theatre by just such corrupt producing. We decided that *Hamlet* and *King Lear* and *Romeo and Juliet* were reading plays far finer as poetry than as drama. But the greater importance now laid upon production as such, restores Shakespeare to his theatre place. His plays not only are supreme as poetry; they are figured, contrived for the stage as only the actor Shakespeare could contrive them. They are gloriously full of fat acting parts, of action, of patterned movement, of dramatic silences, of stage flow. They lend themselves perfectly to the shaping in stage form that distinguishes theatre art from dramatic literature. Marvellous as their word-beauty is, they have inherent in them every opportunity for the larger beauty of complete theatric performance. When Othello, before he stabs himself, says,

> Speak of me as I am; nothing extenuate,
> Nor set down aught in malice: then must you speak
> Of one that loved not wisely but too well;
> Of one not easily jealous, but, being wrought,
> Perplexed in the extreme; . . .

when he speaks thus, the pause in the action, as if to allow the mind a moment's comprehensive review of the whole drama up to that point, doubles the dramatic effect of his dying a moment later. Nor is " O Romeo, Romeo! wherefor art thou Romeo! " merely a pretty play of words: the entire tragedy is foreshadowed in the line.

There have been many times when conditions in the theatre were so depressing, so commercial, so false, that the authors in those periods were alienated, and talents that might have flourished in the field of playwriting were driven to fiction and other minor fields, to the everlasting impoverishment of the stage. Even authors as important as Dickens, Browning, and Stevenson seemed to knock at the theatre's doors in vain, within recent memory. But there was probably as much fault on one side as the other. It must be repeated that this is a jealous art like any other, demanding all a man's devotion or none. The people of the theatre naturally resent any attempt to make the stage a literary man's playground. If a writer fails to give his time to learning and understanding the essential conditions of staging, to bring clear his feeling for theatrical form, he will do better to stay away entirely. Where purely artificial conditions have obtained for long periods, as in stages over-centralized and commercialized like that of the late nineteenth and early twentieth centuries in New York, so that the writers met the barriers put up by the low intelligences controlling production, there is much to be said on the other side. But in general it may be said that the artist combining literary and theatric ability is welcomed. The point to remember is that the theatre as such is greater than any of its parts; that merely poetry in the theatre or music in the theatre or dance in the theatre is not theatrical.

PAINTING could hardly capture the stage as a whole; but for nearly three centuries painting imposed itself on the theatre as a supposedly important and inseparable part of the art. From the late sixteen-hundreds up to 1890 no one ever thought of challenging the painted setting as an interloper and a nuisance. But now within hardly more than a decade, progressive stages all over the Western world have been throwing out their " scenic artists," and what had practically always been a distraction for the audience, rather than an integral part of the theatre rhythm, has been eliminated. Color is left, richly, but in the light and in fabrics rather than in painted picture backgrounds. (When the picture changed from the painter's sort to a photographic sort, about 1900, in the hands of the Naturalists, it no more belonged integrally to the produced play, except to the slice-of-life sort.)

Painting came suddenly, seduced the theatre producers completely, reigned for nearly three hundred years, and now seems in process of dying out with Victorian completeness. Today the setting is flat, perspectiveless, simplified almost to bareness; surface reality no longer is pictured, but only faintly suggested, the "atmosphere" is caught in color and light. Progress today seems all in the direction of space stages and honestly architectural stages. Painting on the stage seems to have gone into almost complete eclipse.

Music more nearly belongs. The theatre, as a combined sight and sound art, relies on color pattern (if only in the lighting) for a considerable part of its glamorous appeal, and only less directly on sound: tune in speech, a balance of emphasized and subordinated sound played against stillnesses, and the more obvious borrowed musical accompaniment. There have been arguments against the alliance; but I can see no more valid reason for eliminating music from the theatre than for eliminating poetry. They both fit perfectly into the complexity, the created flow that is theatre — as the painted *picture* by its very nature never could.

The real objections to music in dramatic art can be found not in any separateness within the whole, but in certain questionable unions with acting and drama. Music is a respectable and respected contributive element in dance-drama and in certain forms of legitimate. But among its questionable if not downright disreputable offspring are opera and musical comedy.

Opera is still the most aristocratic, the most sought-after, the most fashionable among the arts — a sort of Episcopal Church among the art temples. But, my dear, you should hear what they whisper about its origin! Indeed, many a critic has said right out that it is a bastard art. We all of us go to hear and see it, for various reasons, social and otherwise. It may be the music of Wagner, or Chaliapine, or Urban's new settings, or the new dresses and the debutantes in the boxes; but did any of us ever see a perfect opera production, or even one that held together, in that sort of unity that we experience at a play, at a symphony concert, or in reading or hearing,

> O Captain! My Captain! our fearful trip is done . . . ?

Opera is essentially a mixed, broken thing, with beautiful and compelling patches. Of musical comedy, except as it kidnaps a self-sufficient creative turn out of vaudeville, there is almost nothing to be said. It is sentimental sweet-ending comedy linked with sweet balladry, very pleasant in its picture-postcard way, but really only " theatre " for the jaded and the discouraged.

THE DANCE as an art enters creatively today into those stage productions that are primarily sensuous in appeal; but in ancient times it was an integral part in the production of tragedy. The pattern of the great Greek dramas made particular and important place for it — for relief from the emotional intensity, some say, for re-enforcement, others. At first in Greek tragedy it was the most important element, the truly Dionysian expression. Through opera it became debased, became an artificial interlude, cramped, stilted. From the more " regular " forms of play it disappeared altogether. In the current period of revaluation one dreamer after another finds it a place again in some coming form of serious drama. As a better understanding of " form " comes to dramatists, directors, dreamers, all the free rhythmic arts converge in again toward the playhouse, music, mobile color, dance. But as yet it would be mere speculation to say how the dance is to be utilized as an integral part of our day-in-and-day-out drama.

As THE Western theatre, along with the other arts, is being shaken out of its pre-occupation with realism, its artists are impelled to examine the stages of other times, and especially those of Oriental countries where realism has never been known in our all-exclusive sense. The knowledge gained from such excursions is bearing

strange fruit even in the proscenium-frame playhouse that is designed for narrowly picturing surface life. On the Miracle stages
of the fourteenth and fifteenth centuries a character might be beheaded, and then, after a decent interval, rise, pick up his head and
carry it offstage under his arm. In the Chinese theatre the property
man is continuously on the stage, in view of the audience, erecting thrones or canopies, handing swords to the hero or hairpins
to the ladies as wanted. In the one case the audience is living
the drama so completely, so naïvely, that there is no incongruity
in the dead actor walking off; in the other the spectator never
really sees the property man consciously: this is a theatre and one
gives one's self up to its story, to its flow of action. The natural
things outside simply don't intrude. If the playwright and the
actors and the scene-setter had made a pretense of truth to surface
nature in the first place (as our playwrights and producers do),
the actor with his head under his arm would have been upsetting,
the property man a continual intrusion into the picture. But
these audiences were not fooled into thinking that they were
seeing a slice of life. They were reminded by the very form of
the stage that they were in theatres, they accepted the convention,
what belonged rightly to the theatre might come before them at
any moment or all moments.

Our theatre changes. There is no reason under the sun why
anyone should think that the institution as it existed in the early
years of the twentieth century formed a final consummation of
the art. On the contrary it may best be considered as a sick survival after the barren realistic era. Restricted in serviceableness,
its stage gone into a box with a small curtained opening, given
up to picturing the intimacies of private life, with a few survivals
of the well-made-play-with-happy-ending, it exhibits all the symp-
toms of an art ready for a revolutionary overturn. The " conventions" of the mediæval and the Chinese stages may give us
a clue to the direction that revolution is taking, and at the same
time introduce our last point of theory.

The modernists say that the stage must become a medium for
presentative as against *representative* production. For an age it
has been merely representing life, in as near to natural surroundings as the scenic artists could provide. From now on the theatre

will not pretend to show an imitation of life, will not aim above all else at creating an illusion of reality. The stage will be declared as stage (the realists tried to hide the platform, raising the curtain only to show out an actual place). Conventions, unnaturalnesses will be accepted and forgotten. Creative stage art will be presented as such, with emphasis on the formal qualities, the things that arise out of the nature of the theatre's materials and out of the artist's conception of action, flow, and show, out of sheer dramatic impact. The observed thing, the photographic re-creation, will have less and less value. The spectator instead of being tricked into believing he is witness at a real series of events, will be made to feel that he is in the theatre, on a plane of imagination and spiritual emotion, above common life, theatrically exalted.

Some such statement must conclude any treatment of theories of stage art today. For we are in the confusion of the beginnings of a great overturn. Our day-by-day " commercial " theatres are still overwhelmingly realistic. But the experimenters and creators of the contemporary stage are busy with those anti-realistic and expressionistic thoughts, are trying one channel after another in the direction of a presentative stage art. They have even given us productions which we can hold to as definite examples of a glorious new theatre that is coming, at once in agreement with the great formal stages of the past and intensely expressive of the machine-age living of today. They hold the key to our future.

I DON'T like to think of my readers, with three chapters still to go, as worn out, wearied with so much of theory and discussion. But the worst is over. I wanted — this book having been conceived as an *introduction* to the theatre, and for the younger generation of theatre-goers especially — to gain a viewpoint, to have as background something other than the conception out of the past, of art as an escape; wanted something besides the too easy inference that the art of the theatre is that of picturing reality on the stage. The casual reader who has been only a casual theatre-goer is likely to read the story of the modern stage with the notion that what passes there can be judged by the closeness of its approach to actuality, by its faithful or faltering representation of existent life.

He is likely to judge all theatres by the limited realistic one which is practically the only one he has known.

Above all, then, let us go forward to the later chapters freed from that realistic limitation, knowing the theatre to be the house of a deeper created reality, of intensified emotion, of an experience instinct with the feel of life but on a plane remote from commonplace living. When the herald or messenger of classic drama acted out movingly the approach of an army to the city gates, or recounted the exciting battle, we did not ask whether it would be better if the army were shown on the stage or the battle fought before our eyes; only whether he stood there before us as the intensification of the feeling of battle, whether our souls went out to him in communion. Let us not think that Mrs. Tanqueray is an improvement over Ophelia because she speaks a prose more like our own, or because she is first disclosed to us in a room that might be in a wing of our own house. In approaching the modern stage, let us not re-erect that mental barrier, the understood fourth wall; let us not insist upon the monotonous surface plane of life. For theatre is art, and reality has precious little to do with it.

CHAPTER XXII

The Theatre of the Early Twentieth Century

THERE is a personal tragedy in the story of the Realist-playwright. He had come to a theatre obviously sick, dying of too much sentimentality, too much mechanics, too much pretty scenery. The plays, he said, are so ridiculously artificial, the settings so faked, everything so sweetened, there is nothing living or lifelike about it; we must make it natural, and moving, like the drama of real life.

The Realist fought a good fight. He spent decades dislodging the entrenched well-made-play people. He had to justify himself not only with plays but with theory. He had to fight tooth and nail to gain entrance to the theatre at all. Realism became at once his battle-cry and his religion. With almost fanatical devotion, he slashed his way through to victory; he planted his banner at the very centre of the stage — a banner that raised the one word " Reality " as a first test of art.

Then, in the very flush of success he found that the theatre he had conquered, that he had thought to save, was dying anyway. After a lifetime of struggle, having lived for this one victory, having finally taken over the stages of the Western world, suddenly he sees revealed the futility of his productions, the cheapness of Realism as an art creed. While he had been fighting this glorious fight, pausing perhaps to enjoy his conquests, the world had moved by. Visionaries and prophets opened different vistas for art. Foundations for a new world theatre were laid in territory too distant from the realistic field for any bridge to carry over from the one to the other.

We may visualize the Realist-dramatist there on his battle-field, a bewildered victor. He has, of course, one more resource. He can plumb his own grief, he can analyse the psychology of a man victorious looking at the dead ashes in his hand. That was always his forte: with a newspaperman's flair for what is dramatic in experience, he entered the clinic of life, he dissected, he analysed people down to the last bitter detail of motive, of feeling, of thought. He showed humanity the face of its own weakness, its passions, its selfishness, its follies. He still sits there holding up that mirror.

Indeed, though Realism, the play of observed fact, of clinical examination, was treated in an earlier chapter, as if it were more a nineteenth than a twentieth century phenomenon, we must recognize here, as we cross 1900, that its story continues right up to the present, even into the second quarter of the new century. The European and American stages of today are crammed with it. In practice, it is still the rule rather than the exception. Realistic plays automatically get themselves written, automatically turn up in performance. But to keep their hold, they seek yearly more and more sensational subject-matter; they are driven to imbed shock and horror in their lines, to hold their audiences; they are even digging up hidden perversions to interest the nervous spectator — and there they parade in the name of art. The psycho-analysts found a good word for the phenomenon: " exhibitionism." That is the trouble with the realistic stage: obsession with parading what is usually left buried or undisturbed, for the sake of parade.

Meanwhile, outside the theatre, following the recognition that the realistic era was the most barren in art history, a wider revolution took place. In painting and sculpture, principles that had been held sacred for three centuries have been unceremoniously scrapped, and a new seeking has, since 1900, changed completely the aspect of the galleries (not the museums); a new architecture is appearing, after centuries of the rearranging of stealings out of old buildings. And although new plays have not been written to fill a new theatre, there have been prophets of a new art of the stage, and there has been exciting progress toward it in other departments than that of the playwright: revolutionary changes in stage form and stage settings, the rise of direction as a creative contributive art, a stripping away from playhouse architecture of the elements that used to be considered "theatrical," and shifts in methods of organization, looking to a squaring with social conditions under industrial capitalism. The fruits of these changes seem likely to outlast the plays of the realistic dramatists who flourished in the same era.

THROUGH a period of twenty years the physical playhouse has been purging itself. It has sloughed off elements of operatic display, elements out of seventeenth and eighteenth century palace

The Paris Opera House. [From *Paris in Old and Present Times,* by Philip Gilbert Hamerton.]

ballrooms, elements out of general architectural-ornamental practice of the sterile nineteenth century. The architecture of that time may be likened to the putting up of old-fashioned " scenery "; the architects were largely concerned with erecting fronts, having forgotten the basic elements of architectural " form." Uncreative themselves, they became busy with stylistic ornamentation as an end in itself, based on details out of past eras.

When they came to the designing of a theatre, their impulse toward decoration ran wild. Every playhouse must be a reminder of the apotheosis of French profuse taste, the Paris Opera. In the drawing of this building herewith, the reader may see just how little chance he would have to put his hand on any part of the façade and say "this is honest, sheer, built wall." Every inch was used for display, for the showing off of sculpture, for the hanging of stone wreaths or the support of fancy columns: it was showy, regal exposition architecture perpetuated in stone, opulent, fat, shallow. It may have been the masterpiece of typically French architecture, as so often claimed; but the disrespectful younger generation suggested that it need not for that reason become model for theatres the world over or for all time.

If you will look at the National Theatre in Prague, however, or in Sofia, or in Mexico City, or São Paūlo, or in Buenos Aires, or in Madrid, or Vienna, or Oslo, or at the "leading" theatres in the dozen large French cities, you will find examples of this sort of design, overloaded, wasteful, falsely regal, dishonestly unarchitectural, without a vestige of the repose, the intimacy, and the simplicity that are appropriate to the showing of great drama — or even realistic drama.

Let us examine more closely "a little masterpiece" in this French style, as illustrated in the photograph of the theatre at Lille. It represents what the world was building for half a century before 1910. Presumably such a building should grow out of the needs of the thing it houses, or be appropriate to and suggestive of its function as a place for staging and seeing plays. Then why, the modernists asked, those urns along the roof? Why the flowering of the whole front in the pictorial-sculptural composition at the top centre — not even in cut-stone but in modelled-clay technique? Why the melodramatic sculptures in the panels below? Why the whole façade treated as a study in dead ornamentation — instead of an honest, well-proportioned wall with three doors and three windows knocked through? There is no answer except that this is usual nineteenth century theatre architecture. It happens that the building was opened in 1922, but in a country that lives, more than any other, in the nineteenth century in matters of theatre construction and staging. It remains typical, not only in this façade, but in the over-dressed foyer (more urns), in the inevitable marble staircase of honor (more urns), in the crammed-full-of-ornament auditorium (more flowing sculptured figures, more strings of sausages, lyres, cartouches, wreaths, etc.,

etc.). Grandeur, regal red and gold, swank, display, display, display.

In contradistinction to this European model that was copied round the world almost as unquestioningly as Paris modes in dress, there is a type of commercial theatre that has risen in the last ten years: better in sight-lines, less conspicuously wasteful in either space or decoration, logically theatrical in general plan, but equally nondescript and garish in ornamentation. But beyond the examples of this " practical " compromise type, a few typically machine-age playhouses have emerged, as a promise for the future; or rather here and there a feature of the new theatre has stood out, though usually in combination with old stages or bits out of the old house. As for the honest wall with the necessary openings pierced through, the exterior of the Jena State Theatre is indication of the way the modernists are working; has been, indeed, a widely discussed and widely illustrated " challenge." And all over the world the little theatres are likely to be blessed with simple, reposeful interiors.

In Germany a few moving-picture houses show a machine-like sheerness and flashing cleanliness, warmly lighted. In Germany too the half-modernists found in Max Littmann, and more recently in Oskar Kaufmann, architects who cleared out the old ornamentation, bringing a new intimacy between auditorium and stage, and finding a fairly fresh decorative idiom not wholly out of keeping with either old or new methods of production. At any rate, when a recognizable post-regal, post-realistic drama emerges, it will find a few proven architect-engineers to erect immediately the stages and auditoriums it needs. So much twentieth century theatre architecture has proved. And there are on record *visions* — but they belong not in a book that is primarily history. Some of them seem to me as right as a motor-car.

IF NINETEENTH century theatre architecture was metaphorically operatic, the stage setting of that time was literally so. Whether intended for opera, or grandly romantic play, or intimate drama, the " scenery " became, just before the realistic era, a thing of vast spaces, acres of painted canvas, spectacular vistas. The audience

A contrast in twentieth century theatre architecture. Above, the very simple State Theatre at Jena, as reconstructed by Walter Gropius and A. Meyer. Below, the Municipal Theatre at Lille, a survival of the courtly French type.

The Munich Art Theatre, designed by Max Littmann. A simple building
that helped turn the tide away from elaboration and display in theatre design.
It may be illuminating to compare this with the Wiesbaden theatre built
twenty years earlier (page 457).

looked through the proscenium-frame into the stage box at a scene made up partly of rows of " wings " and partly of " set pieces " against a backcloth closing the vista. The painting in these picture settings was simply terrible, raw in color, muddy and crude, and the construction was flimsy. But the effects were grand.

The Realists who not only insisted on the importance of reality but composed imitative examples of the observed thing, with the detailed look of outward life, swept out the artificial and muddy operatic settings from one stage after another; meticulously real scenes, photographed from life, took their places. David Belasco, arguing from " the importance of the little thing," assembled thousands of little things out of life, in settings that touched the high spot in naturalness, and left the spectator agape at telephones, real doorframes, linotype machines, bars with real liquors, living flowers, complete restaurant interiors, thousand-cushioned love-nests, etc. But the actor was now lost, not in a vast painted picture, but in a veritable museum of ordinary surroundings, a complexity of real details. This was the naturalistic era — of photographic, not selective, realism.

Then came the " decorators." They declared war on both the old artificial " scene painters " and the Naturalists. They had some vision of a cleared stage for a typical twentieth century drama — Gordon Craig had already startled the theatre world with what a leading American professor-critic termed " reckless and daring fiats," had foreshadowed the return to a stage cleared for acting. But they had only the realistic drama to practise on. And they simplified the scene so drastically, used pictorial composition so cunningly, warmed the stage so with color and controlled light, that they developed compromise settings far lovelier than the dramas played in them. They made a background that was realistic to the extent of indicating the scene described by the author; they never actually violated what the human eye might see in nature; but within that limitation they dressed the stage with all the appeal of line and mass composition, sensuous color — even style.

What is called in current theatre practice " stylization " is usually a sustained beauty of setting, a single, identifiable mode of

Three arrangements of a "unit" setting, in which certain parts remain standing throughout many scenes. One of the recent methods of expediting change of scenery. Drawings by Claude Bragdon for Walter Hampden's production of *Hamlet*. [By courtesy of *The Architectural Record*.]

design that runs through all the backgrounds of a play. The decorator sometimes imposed it as a loveliness added; sometimes he worked well within the intent of the author and the plan of the *régisseur,* creating visually a feeling that was inherent throughout the production.

In the twentieth century theatre, indeed, the playwright and the actor have been less conspicuous, less talked about, than the scene designer. He has extraordinarily widened the capabilities of the stage for a purely theatric — not painted — visual beauty. He has afforded a succession of stage scenes so glowingly pretty, and in general so appropriate, that a new sensuous overtone is added to our mental visioning of the theatre's glamour. As the drama has become more and more drab and photographic, the stage has been made simpler, more reposeful, and compensatingly rich in color and soft light.

There was a time when the chief lighting problem of the theatre was how to get enough illumination. Candles, oil lamps, gas jets — they had their turns in history. But with the coming of the electric bulb not only was a practical problem solved but a new resource for beauty was added to the list of materials of theatric art. Electricity has been harnessed so that stage lighting can be controlled from a switchboard to the extent of flooding a scene or spotting one point in it, providing any desired color, and keeping a certain constant intensity or ranging it up or down to an unbearable glare or the barest hint of light. Banks of " dimmers," adjustable lenses on individual flood or spot lamps, and a bewildering array of border, strip, foot, and portable units serve to make the advanced theatre's equipment so flexible and so expressive that changes in lighting are imperceptible to the audience while every spectator's sensibilities are being played upon — even as by perfectly adapted offstage musical accompaniment.

Lighting has proved so serviceable a medium theatrically, indeed, that it has, on many stages, taken the place of " setting " in the old sense. A whole wing of the modernists has advocated the return to an architectural stage, practically without means of showing those individual places called for by the playwrights, but only one neutral scene to stand for all scenes, with changes of mood accomplished by lighting, with possibly bare *indications*

of actual place in one or two introduced screens or pillars or
"props." Thus the current toward simplification and conventionalization, after twenty-five years, ends where the stage is no

Sketches of Max Reinhardt's revolving stage being set with a composite
scene. Note the method of building the setting plastically, not as a painted
representation of a place, and the small portion of the construction visible
in each scene, through the proscenium as indicated at lower right. On
such a stage changes of scene can be accomplished almost instantaneously,
by rolling the turn-table part way round. [From drawings by Ernst Stern
in *Reinhardt und Seine Bühne*, by Ernst Stern and Heinz Herald.]

longer a picture box but becomes an abstract architectural thing,
constantly but unnoticeably changing under projected light.

There have been other methods developed in the search for a
truly modernist mode of staging: Expressionist painting was

dragged in for awhile in an effort to provide modernist backgrounds for current plays, but proved merely an added source of amusement or distraction. Constructivism added creatively toward the achievement of an architectural stage capable of a wide range of physical action, without changes of setting: it was a method of providing a perfectly engineered scene, the "practicables" of all the called-for settings nailed together in one composition, stripped of adventitious decorative elements, and set out on a bare stage without a curtain. Another group of experimenters have pushed as far as possible toward a "space stage"; they try to achieve a black void in which the actors are picked out by light. Most of the new methods have the immense advantage of doing away with the waits between acts which are inevitable when the old-fashioned picture-settings have to be changed in the course of the play.

Before the new dependence upon lighting, and the consequent drift toward space and architectural stages, many inventions were developed to speed up the bringing of the pictures successively before the audience; most notably the revolving or turn-table stage, on which half a dozen scenes could be set at once, ready to be brought before the proscenium opening (as shown graphically in the sketches by Ernst Stern opposite); and the wagon-stages, which permitted one scene to be set up while the other was before the audience, ready to be slid into place as soon as the curtain was down. But these improvements merely made easier the manipulation of the old spectacular settings or the less ridiculous realistic ones. At the present moment it seems that both sorts, all the variations of the picture settings, are to be suppressed — unless in opera — in favor of space, architecture, and light creatively used.

With the passing of the detailed picture there is disappearing all the heavy machinery of the nineteenth century theatre, and possibly the immense scene loft that is so distinctive a feature of recent playhouse design. As an example of the heavily machined picture stage I am adding here an "opened" view of the Prince Regent Theatre in Munich. It indicates the small size of the auditorium (it seats 1106) in comparison with the vastness of the stage space. Note, please, the tininess of the human figure on the stage-floor in relation to the space above, note the scenerystorage room at the back, and the cellarful of machinery below and the two floors of machinery above the stage. The people who have been working toward a new twentieth century theatre, which will at least *begin* with simplicity, pointed out the artificial burden placed upon producing when the stage had become such a massive and complicated thing. Sweep it all out, they said.

By way of contrast I have placed under this diagrammatic view a design by Adolphe Appia, an artist who profoundly affected the course of staging and the drift of latter-day theatre theory. The stage, he said, need be little different from the end of an ordinary room; with a few architectural elements like these, and perfect lighting control, the actor and the play can be better set out, and with more true visual beauty, than in the cavernous littered stage of the other sort of theatre.

Two men, Adolphe Appia and Gordon Craig, have been at the bottom of the change of sentiment about stage setting, and both have been more or less isolated from the busy producing theatres. Sure they were right, refusing to compromise their visions of new stages, they have fought through misunderstanding, exile, loneliness; but today their names are on the lips of the thousands of young " radicals " who are the sign that a new theatre is inevitably coming (they inhabit chiefly Russia, Germany, and America). Others long ago took the ideas of these two pioneers, compromised with the realistic-minded people who controlled the market-place theatres, and dressed realism in lovely and simple stage clothes, as we have seen. These compromising artists betrayed Craig and Appia in a sense, even while making the current " show " less offensively drab, less starkly analytical or intellectual or sensational. But the " decorators " — some of them being directors as well — include among their number those artists who are most constructively thinking toward a new theatre in the American scene today. Robert Edmond Jones, Norman-Bel Geddes, Claude Bragdon, these are men with long experience of staging who have clear vision of a different theatre in a different society — they are prophets as well as practitioners. To some of us it seems likely that their names are to live on in theatre histories longer than those of any recent American playwrights. They are more truly reshaping theatre practice. Even a produc-

Above, an opened view of the Prince Regent Theatre, Munich, showing the
immensity of the stage and the elaborate machinery above and below. Here
the auditorium has been simplified into a single curved bank of seats; but
the stage is typical of the last and most extravagant phase of nineteenth century picture staging. [Max Littmann, architect.] Below, by way of
contrast, a simple design for a stage by Adolphe Appia. (From his *L'Œuvre
d'Art Vivant.*)

Two examples of the recent tendency toward a simpler scene. Above a setting by T. C. Pillartz for *Louis Ferdinand*. [From *Das Moderne Bühnenbild* by Oskar Fischel.] Below, a design by Hermann Rosse for a formal stage. [From Cheney's *Stage Decoration*.]

ing group like the New York Theatre Guild, which conscien-
tiously angles for the best written drama of current times, has been
more conspicuously successful in the mounting of its plays, under
Lee Simonson, than in any other department. And throughout
the country little theatre groups produce unrelated miracles of
lighting and staging — while awaiting the fine plays they so
much need.

THE RISE of the " little theatres " has been the most striking phenomenon in American art-life in the last twenty years; and there
has been a parallel development, though less out-standing, in
every European country, even in Japan, South America, and
other distant lands. In the United States the spirit had been at
work many years earlier, but the first burst of activity came in
1914–15. Suddenly, it seemed, little theatres sprang up everywhere. Leaders quickly appeared, exhibitions of the new stagecraft were organized, a barrage of magazine articles was laid
down, even publications devoted wholly to the " non-commercial "
stage. The youngsters immediately drew the fire of the professionals too; the " Wizard of Broadway " deigned to notice them
in an article calling them the Cubists, the degenerates, of the
theatre art. But from that day to this the insurgents have offered
the more interesting half of the stage fare served up in America,
sometimes out through the country in their unpretentious local
theatres, sometimes in direct competition in the market-place
playhouses on Broadway.

To understand the little theatres, why Maurice Browne fought
through five years of Chicago's apathy and misunderstanding, to
maintain the Chicago Little Theatre as a center of experiment,
and in many cases, of beautiful staging; why Zona Gale and her
group tried to carry the Wisconsin spirit into playwriting and
producing; why Aline Barnsdall quixotically established the Los
Angeles Little Theatre with three directors in charge (a one-
season stand that did permanent service in bringing Norman-Bel
Geddes professionally into the theatre); why the Provincetown
group began that struggle for existense that ultimately brought
America's one internationally important dramatist to the boards;
why Stuart Walker toured with his unique " Portmanteau " stage

from Broadway to the Golden Gate: to understand these things it is necessary to know the abuses that had existed in the domain of American theatre *organization*. For the little theatre movement was essentially a revolt. What the insurgents revolted against was a commercial domination of "amusements" such as no other country has known, as pretty and powerful a trust as any that ever controlled steel or oil or wool and made millions while all competition was stifled.

The story of "the syndicate war" is overlong for a brief history like ours. We can pause only a moment over the results. Between 1890 and 1910 astute business men found that by buying up a certain number of physical playhouses they could obtain, by a combined method of jockeying, intimidation, and combination, control over the entire machinery and art of theatre production. By owning the theatres in certain key cities they could make touring impossible to any but companies playing on their terms; they could undersell rivals on occasion, then later raise prices when competition had been killed; they could force an isolated house owner to play one of their inferior shows on pain of never being allowed another from the syndicate headquarters in New York. They actually strangled independent production, swallowing the smaller producing unit or driving it into bankruptcy or exile. "Stars" who had secure publics were driven into capitulation; otherwise they found themselves without stages to act on — though there is an epic chapter there in the fight for freedom waged by Francis Wilson, Mrs. Fiske, and a few other established favorites.

At any rate, the American theatre was soon prostrate under the strangle-hold of a commercial "trust." As always, some advantages accrued all round, in greater security of bookings, in centralized responsible control of circuiting, in certainty of profits; all round, that is, except to the artist and to the public. Repertory producing disappeared: there was more profit in long runs. The actor was condemned to months and years in one part, without opportunity to develop in versatility, in richness, in breadth. Welltried types of play were demanded of the playwright, or else the conventional French or English plays were adapted by professional "doctors." The dramatist with new ideas or vision found the doors of the theatre locked to him. The public saw no more classics, no more experimentally new plays; only what business-men in New York thought popularly sweet or thrilling enough to survive as "best sellers."

That is, of course, an overstatement of the case; but in general that is what the little theatres rebelled against. They wanted to put on the plays that nowhere came to the boards, the classics of other times, the Shaw and Ibsen and Strindberg that they thought were the classics of the new time. They wanted the native drama-tist with un-French vision to see his plays acted — otherwise he would keep on in-growing instead of becoming the Great Ameri-can Playwright. They wanted to try out new ideas of staging, to challenge the old painted-perspective mode of setting — they had seen those strange designs of Gordon Craig's, had been spurred by his barbed writings about the old living-dead theatre and about new artist-directors. No matter that they opened their tiny theatres to merely amateur acting; had not the famous Moscow Art Theatre started as humbly, had not the Irish Players found new virtues in an unprofessional simplicity?

The little theatres multiplied. Some fell by the wayside, but soon two or three new groups filled the single gap in the ranks. And for a dozen years the little theatres, and the larger commu-nity theatres built on the foundations they laid, have proved the most important and interesting group of producing companies in America. Immature still, no final achievement has come out of them — but what is a decade or so in the history of an art? At least they have been significant of a deep and strong current in the national art life, have been important as destroyers and innovators, have given to the country its most promising insti-tutional stages — to which we shall return in a moment — and have brought the spirit of youth to expression.

During the late nineteenth and early twentieth centuries in Europe, the national and royal theatres continued under their old administrative form, under generous patronage, until the World War; and many, after the war, simply switched over to the name State Theatre instead of Court Theatre, and the people, in place of the kings and princes, continued the subsidies. In Germany particularly the state authorities count the stage one of the important activities of national life. The State Theatres in Berlin, Munich, Dresden, Darmstadt, Stuttgart, Frankfort, are offering today the greatest body of fairly progressive production to be seen anywhere — though not so experimentally as the stages of Soviet Russia. The German theatres touch a standard of public service unknown in most other countries because, in addition to the palpitatingly alive, but shallow and ephemeral realistic plays, they maintain extensive repertories of the greatest dramas out of the past, often mounted with fullest understanding of the saner forms of modernism.

France has many playhouses that are still under state or municipal subsidy, and these maintain repertory companies. But they either live in the past, attempt to protect the old traditions against the assaults of new generations of " progressives," like the *Comédie Française,* or, like the *Odéon,* jump half-understandingly at " modernism " in staging. The history of the *Comédie Française* in the last half-century, despite honored service in preserving a great tradition, is rather a sad chronicle of over-conservatism, petty intrigue, loss of outstanding artists, and — yes — mediocrity. This company of seventy-odd actors (including thirty-two *sociétaires,* or regular members, and a complement of *pensionnaires,* recruits and less experienced members) operates under an " administrator " appointed by the Government, and a Managing Committee of the *sociétaires.* The administrator and his superior, the Minister of Fine Arts, are not wholly free from suspicion of wire-pulling, making of nephews and favorites into *sociétaires,* etc. Of late years it has been distinctly a theatre in very old age — though a younger country cannot but admire the national spirit that holds a theatre, as Napoleon III put it, " worthy of support, for it is part of the national glory."

I recently spent two successive evenings at the *Comédie Française* and the *Odéon.* At the *Comédie* I saw a pretty and spirited revival of Molière — an excellent museum piece. At the *Odéon* the resident company was presenting *The Blue Bird* in Gallicized Teutonic settings — distinctly Munichesque — with the too usual French mixture of old-fashioned declamatory and new-fashioned " natural " acting. In these two evenings I have my picture of the French official stage: interesting like an antique, but, except for that, very mixed and rather unimportant.

Other countries of Europe have subsidized playhouses, and they vary in their sorts of excellency or unimportance. The Burg Theatre in Vienna was long one of the greatest. The repertory house is almost a fixture in European capital cities, usually with subsidy, and this is sure to afford widely varied productions of a sort. Under inspired direction one or another of the theatres of the less visited States emerges into world notice occasionally, as recently the National Theatre at Prague has done. Plays from Prague and Budapest are staples on the current New York programmes.

During the thorough commercialization of the American stage, and with the rise of the actor-manager in London, the repertory system disappeared both in the United States and in Great Britain. Today there is scarcely a first rate company presenting plays in English according to the repertoire plan as known in Europe. As a consequence Germany sees seven times as much Shakespearean drama as either English-speaking country; [1] and whole generations grow up without even a taste of the world classics. The adherents of the repertory idea have pointed out the great loss to theatre-goers in the passing of that system: in no season can one be sure there will be revivals of Shakespeare or the Greeks or even of Wilde and Shaw; one is left dependent almost wholly upon what commercial producers think will be profitable in long-run competitive production. The repertory company, moreover, is the only sort in which the actor gets continual and varied training; and it is in groups playing together year after year that ensemble acting mellows as in the extraordinary performances of the seasoned Moscow Art Theatre. As long as the stage is first of all a financial venture, a speculation, expected to return the largest possible income, repertory cannot come back. Augustin Daly's famous company of the eighties and nineties marked the last glorious stand of the repertory idea in the professional American theatre. [2]

[1] Accurate figures are difficult to obtain over a series of years. From evidence of scattered seasons, the sevenfold figure seems a conservative estimate.

[2] Within three years (I am writing in early 1928) three companies have established so-called repertory production in New York, and two are working toward a full reper-

The English-American system of private ownership of "leading" theatres, and syndicate-control, has been adopted into Germany to some extent, and all over the Continent commercially managed long-run companies have increased in number and importance as compared with the permanent resident repertory houses. Max Reinhardt's name is associated with four privately owned theatres in Germany and Austria, and two or three other important directors are free lances; but in general it may be said that the very fine work in Germany is still done at the State and institutional theatres. Italy has practically no institutional theatres playing repertory. Paris sees better producing in its "outside" theatres — but has had a very unproductive quarter-century in all directions. The provinces in France are ill-served as regards anything but moving-pictures: even cities that once boasted theatrical glories of their own are now way-stations for second-rate acting companies travelling with skimpy old-fashioned scenery or have interestingly antique municipal theatres. Thirty-five years ago France seemed at the forefront in dramatic activity, with a live conservative theatre brought to attention by the challenge of the *Théâtre Libre,* the pioneer of insurgent little theatres. But the spirit of the *Théâtre Libre* passed to Germany, where the *Freie Bühne* was established in 1890, and to England; then to America, where there was really a great deal more of commercial domination and limitation to fight against — with consequent greater gains for the battling artists. (The struggle in Europe was complicated badly by the war and the following depression, a handicap hardly felt in America.) In France, the one theatre of the immediate post-war years most likely to live in history is the *Théâtre du Vieux Colombier,* directed by Jacques Copeau in Paris. There valuable pioneering was done in meth-

---

toire plan. The Neighborhood Playhouse pioneered with the idea, but is now closed; though certain activities are continued elsewhere by groups out of the original company. The Civic Repertory Theatre, under Eva Le Gallienne's management, has made a spirited start but has still to achieve the quality that I termed mellowness above. The Theatre Guild, with an extraordinarily talented group of players, has preferred to build more slowly toward the typical repertoire feature — a stock of prepared plays coming back into the programme at intervals — but has perhaps laid the most secure foundations for a permanent institutional theatre. I omit mention here of the Western community theatres, which are more genuinely repertory than any in New York, except Miss Le Gallienne's, because they are but slowly emerging from amateur into full professional acting.

ods of staging, in experimental acting, and in encouragement to playwrights.

Where state endowment has seemed out of the question — as in America, due partly to the politician's absolute innocence of any knowledge of or interest in the mysterious thing called Art — private capital sometimes has stepped in to offer subsidy. Some of the bravest chapters in the story of the revolt against commercial domination have told of an alliance of progressive artists with interested "patrons." John Masefield once asked, "What greater glory can a man have than to build that which will be the home of knowledge, beauty and mirth for centuries to come?" But the gifts to the American stage (and to the British) have been in the nature of temporary subsidy rather than permanent endowment. In New York the Theatre Guild was helped over its initial difficulties through the generosity of Otto H. Kahn — also most generous of givers to the Metropolitan Opera; but the Guild later solidified its position by building a large subscription audience, from which it borrowed money to build its new playhouse. The organization is owned, however, by its managers. It is today the most conspicuously successful institutional theatre in the English-speaking world, and the one serving the largest audiences with thoroughly satisfying productions (it has more than 20,000 subscribers to its annual programme of five plays, but serves New York casual audiences far beyond that number, and recently "the Road" as well). It is an interesting compromise between the altruistic public-service theatre and the private-initiative theatre — perhaps a typical between-Capitalism-and-Socialism manifestation.

The Neighborhood Playhouse in New York was handsomely endowed for experimental producing over ten years by Irene and Alice Lewisohn, and in that period served nobly as an experimental centre. The Provincetown Players have done epic work while enjoying driblets of contributions from widely scattered sources. From fifty or sixty "guarantors" the Actors' Theatre collected, and spent, a quarter million dollars in an effort to compete with Broadway in producing according to the usual piecemeal system.

During the attempt to re-establish experimental or repertory theatres, an ideal of an "institutional theatre" has been formulated. Those who believe in it seldom call it that; institutions are out of repute. (You remember, perhaps, the apt vaudeville jest: "Yes, my dear, marriage is a fine institution — but who wants to live in an institution anyway?") The institutional theatre is the only sort that can restore repertory, break the strangle hold of exploitation, and permanently foster experiment and vision. Out through the country a few of the little theatres have grown solidly into permanent community-owned or trustee-owned institutions, and the story of the latest advance of new ideas in this country is largely written in them: the Cleveland Playhouse, the Santa Barbara Community Theatre, the Dallas Little Theatre, the Goodman Memorial Theatre in Chicago, the Pasadena Community Playhouse. These all are housed in homes of their own, and all are producing new plays regularly and at the same time developing repertories. The standards of acting have not in many cases risen measurably above the amateur or semi-professional levels at which they started; but — well, they are on their way, and very young yet, and they are almost the only full-sized theatres in America that can't be hired by any moving-picture or sexy review or cheap stock company. They are making the history that counts.

In Germany a real "democratic" theatre was developed before the war, and today functions as a "people's theatre" of a unique sort. It is, perhaps, historically important as a step toward a theatre for a new Socialistic time. The *Volksbühne* in Berlin is owned by its audiences. Attendance at its unusually fine productions costs the owner-spectator about one-tenth what a theatre ticket costs an Englishman or an American. The plays are either classic (from all languages) or modern, ones with a socialistic tinge being specially favored; the staging is distinctly "advanced" and the acting very good. It was here that Toller's *Masse-Mensch* was presented in a stirring production that became internationally famous. The *Volksbühne* building is truly monumental. Indeed, in many particulars this is nearer to a theatre for tomorrow than any other that you can name — unless you want to insist that only he who has been in Russia has seen the true shape of the future.

Two examples of simplified realistic staging and acting at the institutional theatres. Above, a scene in Björnson's *Beyond Our Power* at the Volksbühne, Berlin. The actors include Friedrich Kayssler, kneeling, and Helene Fehdmer in the bed. [From a photograph by August Scherl.] Below, a scene in Ervine's *John Ferguson* as produced by the New York Theatre Guild. The actors are Augustin Duncan, in the title rôle, Helen Westley, Helen Freeman, Dudley Digges, and Michael Carr. [From a photograph by Francis Bruguiere.]

Realism in acting and setting at the Moscow Art Theatre. Note in the scene from *The Cherry Orchard* (above) the attempt to arrive at naturalness by showing vistas into rooms beyond that in which the action passes. [From photographs in *Theatre Arts Monthly*.]

One other aspect of theatre organization is striking, particularly as exemplified in the past ten years: the internationalism of the stage. The acting companies of Europe have again and again been brought to America. Even during the war, France sent over the most important insurgent group in Paris, the *Théâtre du Vieux Colombier,* with a director and a designer-actor who remain today the most progressive thinkers in the French theatre: Jacques Copeau and Louis Jouvet. For two seasons this company produced experimentally in New York. Since the war there has been a succession of Russian, German, French, English, Irish, Italian, Yiddish, Spanish, Argentinian, Japanese, and other companies playing in their own tongues on American stages. These have included such world-famous acting groups as the Moscow Art Theatre and Max Reinhardt's company; and such outstanding players as Eleanora Duse and Alexander Moissi. Visits of world-famous foreign companies or stars are no recent phenomena in American stage history; but since the World War they have been more numerous than before, giving evidence that the theatre is keeping up with the march of internationalism, if not helping, incidentally, to forward it.

OF INDIVIDUAL acting in the twentieth century, there is little to record that is in any sense of permanent historic importance. Despite the spread of the star system under commercial nurturing, no new stars arose in America to take places beside the meteoric Forrest, the great Booth, even Jefferson.

Graceful acting, charming acting, radiantly appealing personalities — these we have had. John Drew was a gentleman-actor of the old school who never failed to please us thoroughly, to hold us sympathetically, gaining his steady command by never trying to rise to heights. The Drew-Barrymore nobility lives in the playing of the ever-beautiful Ethel Barrymore, and in the too-occasional appearances of John Barrymore. Maude Adams, since she quit the stage a few years ago, is tenderly remembered for her irresistible personal appeal. Mrs. Fiske, E. H. Sothern, Julia Marlowe, George Arliss, Otis Skinner — these were or are leaders, but not giants and prophets. Nor are the idols of today, the most glamorous stars of Broadway — Jane Cowl, Laurette Taylor,

Walter Hampden — seated any too securely in the theatre-as-it-is. A younger generation, youthful, charming, with a new fire, seem more significant than their more experienced elders: Pauline Lord, Helen Hayes, Clare Eames, Katherine Cornell, Madge Kennedy — there is indeed a new spirit here. But on the American-speaking stage since 1900 there have been no towering figures to dominate in the old sense. The player has been too personalized, made imitative by too much realistic material, not widely trained since repertory disappeared — or perhaps he is imbued with a new ensemble ideal, has eyes on a different goal.

In London there has been less star playing: not a figure known outside England since Irving died and Ellen Terry retired. In France the Guitrys have adherents, and also a showy actress or two, but assuredly there is no successor to Sarah Bernhardt. In German theatres solo acting has long been frowned upon; but Alexander Moissi is as near to being a world-recognized star as any living today. In Russia acting reached its peak during the realistic era in the performances of the Moscow Art Theatre, and there was some talk of Kachaloff as a player without peer; but with that company the ensemble was the marvellous thing. And it may indeed be true that the new ensemble ideal, that came in with the twentieth century revolt against one-sidedness in theatre art, will end *virtuoso* acting for good and all. There is a shrewd suspicion about, among younger playgoers, that the performances of stars were often the more brilliant because the " support " was dull. At any rate there is a growing preference for complete rounded-out performance over an exhibition by one outstanding player.

The Moscow Art Theatre productions of *Hamlet* and *The Blue Bird* and in the realistic field, of Chekhov particularly; an Expressionistic play like *Masse-Mensch* as staged in vivid flashes and often headlong speed at the Berlin *Volksbühne;* Reinhardt's spirited re-creations of Schiller; some of Arthur Hopkins' extremely *quiet* productions: these have had a new *wholeness,* a theatric completeness seldom achieved where a star was exploited. Great as Moissi is, it is Reinhardt, his director, who is the better known of the two. Production as an art seems to be eclipsing acting — for reasons to be explored in the next chapter.

Charlie Chaplin, of course, is the most widely known and celebrated, and perhaps the most individually creative, actor of the new century. He carries on the tradition of the great clown-comedians, and adds his distinctive variation to what had gone before. By grace of the new moving-picture medium, through which acting is photographically transmitted to the ends of the earth, he has pleased more people than any other performer in the world's history.

One interesting development in connection with acting is the formation of the so-called " actors' union " in the United States, the Actors' Equity Association, and its rise to power in the realm of the commercial theatre. Players had banded together in the past — we met an actors' guild, the Artists of Dionysus, when we explored the Greek theatre — but only in the twentieth century has the actor been able, by group effort, to remedy the conditions under which he worked, economic, moral, and physical. The organization was enabled — partly by a " strike " that developed stirring incidents — to gain for the players fair standing before the law, decent dressing rooms and stage conditions, and a position of equality in the community. Never since Greek times has the professional actor enjoyed so much of respect and consideration as is his lot today. That he had to grasp at trades-union methods need not detract, for us, from his glamour, since thereby he gained rights needful to him as self-respecting man and creative artist.

Our picture of the early twentieth century theatre — I am adding more of detail here than in more " historic " chapters — would hardly be complete without a glimpse of such contemporary playwrights as the Irish Yeats, the Belgian Maeterlinck, the German Expressionists, and the American O'Neill (on one side of his talent). Realistic drama, forming the main stream, has been sufficiently treated in a preceding chapter, but certain minor counter-currents and streamlets have flowed in a manner to warrant at least brief mention. At times they seemed to flow so strongly that they gave promise of developing into a major new-century drama. As a very interested spectator, I am sad to report that they were mostly trickling along in blind-end courses. Still, what *was* the drama of the early twentieth century?

If anyone had the patience to assemble a list of all the plays produced in English-speaking theatres from 1908 to 1928, say, the section covering the works of that greatest of all dramatic geniuses, William Shakespeare, would be infinitesimal. For while lip-service continues, those who control the English and American theatres simply have not had conviction and interest enough to stage the great poet-dramatist's works. (One has had to travel to Germany to see any large number of Shakespearean plays presented in any one season. They are always in repertory there, and new productions at the various resident theatres are regular occurrences.) But at times a poetic current has come to the surface. The Irish School had a vogue, even in production. Just when William Butler Yeats was writing his plays, a happy combination of circumstances brought into existence the Abbey Theatre group in Dublin, now generally known as the Irish Players. They not only had a taste for the frail poetic dramas of Yeats, but added a talent for beautiful speech as such; and these virtues, combined with a natural simplicity of acting, brought a refreshing note into the larger British theatre. The Irish Players also found in J. M. Synge a dramatist who took fairly realistic material and treated it in language that extraordinarily captures the poetic values of Irish-English speech. Within their limited field the plays of Synge are as full-flavored and distinctive and poignant as any in the whole range of theatre literature. He touched Realism with fresh verbal beauty, irony, and salty satire. But the blossom that came to its fulness so quickly, in the decade 1900–1910, was too fragile to last among perhaps ranker growths. The Irish Players discovered other playwrights; but the most recent and most conspicuous of them is typical of the group's change of direction. Sean O'Casey has written realistic studies of the seamiest side of Dublin tenement life, imbedding scenes of delicious comedy and patches of starkest and genuine tragedy, but depending most upon depiction of observed detail, on naturalness and occasional shock. Yeats turned to other interests than the theatre; the players turned to Realism unadulterated.

In France the Romantic current flowed along feebly up to the time of the World War, all but submerged in the flood of triangle studies of which French audiences never tire, but calling attention to its persistence by an occasional new play of Edmond Rostand or Maurice Maeterlinck. Rostand sometimes broke through to spectacular success: *Cyrano de Bergerac,* with Constant Coquelin in the title rôle, and *l'Aiglon* with Sarah Bernhardt. But in the end he must be judged a good stage craftsman seduced by the beauties of a poetic-romantic literature that is no longer vitally alive. Maeterlinck is even more definitely of the school that makes art an escape from life. *The Blue Bird* is a symbolic, other-worldly fable-play, rather too heavily sweetened for normal consumption, and generally hung with too much tinsel in the producing. It seems to me, too, that there is a lot of false mysticism, playing with veils, in some of the less popular pieces. Indeed, only in a rare play like *Pelleas and Melisande* did Maeterlinck rise out of a rather forced romanticizing into the field of true poetic tragedy — and the contemporary theatre has hardly been in a mood to welcome anything so gentle, slow-moving, and — yes, literary.

Hauptmann, too, not the crusading Hauptmann of *The Weavers,* but a more yearning and poetic creator, wrote a memorable symbolic-romantic play in *The Sunken Bell,* and a more touchingly human "dream play" in *Hannele.* Hugo von Hofmannsthal did over some older play-legends in what at the time seemed the modern spirit; but they faintly remind us of those re-creations in the graphic arts which we know, and ultimately abhor, as examples of Munich Neo-classicism. Ferenc Molnar, departing occasionally from his gracefully sophisticated realism, brought out a semi-romantic piece that would have delighted audiences in the nineties. D'Annunzio made the highest poetic flights recorded since — since — when was the last great poetic playwright? . . . The truth is that not one of these diverted the world for more than an instant from its preoccupation with realistic drama. A single play here or there may survive into later theatres; but the romantic-poetic current has been weak, unconvincing, uncongenial to the modern world and the current theatre.

The Expressionist playwrights caused more of a stir, in the few years immediately following the war. They were far more revolutionary in aim than the Romanticists or Symbolists or any of the others who thought they were challenging Realism.

Expressionism, in the larger art sense, means expression of the artist's emotion rather than depiction of the object exciting it; means emphasis on "form" rather than on observed fact, escape from the limitation of what can be seen with the eye; means intensification, not portrayal of life; means presentative as against representative production, with consequent shift of emphasis (in the theatre) to creative use of the characteristic means of the stage art, to movement, color, lighting, acting, as well as words and their "meaning"; means usually the violation of actuality, the piling-up of emotionally effective incident.

The Expressionist (no working artist admits the name, of course) aims to get back to a place where the vast imaginative conception, the direct appeal to the soul, the gorgeously rich sensuous impression — all impossible to Realism — can be compassed on the stage; having regained that freedom, he will use it not as in Greece or in Elizabethan London, but to project in terms of the new intensity of modern life. He hopes to hold to the incisiveness, the precision of the Realistic method, while regaining the old splendor and gaining a new intensity and a new directness (jazz-age speed and machine-age sheerness are considerations here).

Several playwrights have emerged whose intentions are obviously Expressionistic, most notably the Germans Ernst Toller and Georg Kaiser, whose plays have been seen on the American stage, and the native experimenter, John Howard Lawson. But it is apropos to note that Gordon Craig — who would be the last artist in the world to bow unprotesting under the label Expressionist — has done more than all the playwrights to bring a sane Expressionism into the theatre: by his leadership in the fight against Realism, by his clearing out from the stage the old picturing paraphernalia, by his insistence upon the use of the stage itself, the actors, the movement, the lights, the color, as a creative medium, by his sweep of imagination that transcends all sense of surface actuality, by his ideal of "a noble artificiality" as against that of naturalness, by his fathering of those hundreds of artist-directors (still only children, in his view) who have made over the stage from a photographic peep-show box to a *theatrically* articulate medium.

There is no masterpiece of the Expressionist drama as yet. But most of the promising and the startling playwrights of today are committed to the mode. Italy's only outstanding dramatist, Luigi Pirandello, is allied with the group merely by the way in which he tangles up reality; he is comparable to the Cubists in painting, who shift the planes of actuality to rearrange them in a more revealing pattern. He plays with the planes of consciousness. This is anti-realistic, but it grew out of the Realism in which study of abnormal psychology played so important a part. He climbed above photographic Realism, but failed to attain to the larger freedom that must be gained before the next superlative achievement in the theatre.

America's one internationally known playwright, Eugene O'Neill, is significant for his achievement in lifting American drama out of a purely provincial or reflective activity (as viewed from Europe); and as the one English-writing dramatist who has made Expressionism a broadly successful mode. American plays, to be sure, can be seen in the theatres of Moscow, Vienna, Berlin, and Rome, and so many in London that English critics berate us almost continuously; but these are generally the cheaper pieces with obvious appeal, melodramatic crook-plays, slangy and racy comedies, journalistic but picturesque emotional dramas — which merely means that the centre of routine commercial playwriting in English has shifted from London to New York, that our vulgar theatre is the livest in the world. But O'Neill is a phenomenon because everywhere he has challenged the attention of those who are watching for the dramatist original enough and able enough to restore the theatre to its old eminence and its old freedom.

He was a Realist first, with a keen selective sense and sometimes an uncanny knack for the revealing unpleasant word, and it is not yet clear that he is to transcend Realism in any great way; but in *The Emperor Jones, The Hairy Ape,* and *Lazarus Laughs* he threw off the chains of imitativeness and widened the expressiveness of our stage. He did this with violence and speed and piled-up emotion rather than with serenity and depth; he broke over the old rigidities of well-made-play dramaturgy, without even suggesting a new play-structure with positive virtues, utilizing a form still jerky and unfinished; but he moved audiences, with a new thrill, a fresh revelation, with theatrical directness. That is about all anyone has done toward the form of playwriting that is to take the stages of the world " after Realism."

CHAPTER XXIII

The Rise of Production as an Art

WHEN the wave of revolt against domination of the stage by the playwrights broke over the theatre, when the first violent protests were made against confining theatre history to what could be discovered in printed play texts — shortly after 1900, that was — the insurgents were very vague about what figure should take the place of the dramatist in the chief position. Not the actor, surely; since the decay of the *Commèdia dell'Arte,* only an isolated creative actor had lifted his head here or there in any generation. The player of the day was uncreative, interpretative, content in a co-ordinate rôle (except the so-called actor-manager who occasionally formed a company, hired a theatre and met current competition on its own commercial grounds, exploiting himself in made-to-measure star plays).

The literary people, who had been the outstanding artists of the Realistic era, raised the cry that the dramatists were going to be butchered to afford a decorators' holiday; the scene designers were going to take over the stage for pretty moving lights, and swollen spectacle and God knows what. The alarm in that direction came about logically, because the chief of the attackers, the first prophet of the new theatre, Gordon Craig, was designer as well as actor and director; he had made some very beautiful pictures of stages and scenes so different from the 1890 product that he was considered half-mad — even a shade more than that — in spite of his being the son of that wholly lovely and universally respected idol of the nineteenth century British stage, Ellen Terry.

Here is what Gordon Craig wrote in his first book, in 1905:

The art of the theatre is neither acting nor the play, it is not scene nor dance, but it consists of all the elements of which these things are composed: action, which is the very spirit of acting; words, which are the body of the play; line and color, which are the very heart of the scene; rhythm, which is the very essence of dance . . . One is no more important than the other, no more than one color is more important to a painter than another, or one note more important than another to a musician. . .

If you were for once to see an actual piece of theatrical art, you would never again tolerate what is today being thrust upon you in place of theatrical art. The reason why you are not given a work of art on the stage is not because the public does not want it, not because there are not excellent craftsmen in the theatre who could prepare it for you, but because the theatre lacks the artist — the artist of the theatre, mind you, not the painter, poet, musician.

And later he wrote: " Let me repeat again that it is not only the writer whose work is useless in the theatre. It is the musician's work which is useless there, and it is the painter's work which is useless there. All three are utterly useless. Let them keep to their preserves, let them keep to their kingdoms, and let those of the theatre return to theirs." And then, listing the scores of workers in the theatre, and the several voices of authority, he added:

" Seven directors instead of one and nine opinions instead of one.

" *Now, then, it is impossible for a work of art ever to be produced where more than one brain is permitted to direct; and if works of art are not seen in the Theatre this one reason is a sufficient one, though there are plenty more.*"

In other words, put out the literary man, and if any other one-sided artist tries to climb into first place, put *him* back where he belongs too; unless one among these artists can prove his mastery of *all* the materials of the stage art — in which case he may be called the master of the theatre. To him only should the place be entrusted.

No master arose who was playwright, music-composer, scene-designer and director-of-actors, all rolled into one. The ideal is difficult to obtain in a world where a real genius in any single line is born once in hundreds of years, and where specialization is the rule. But Craig's insistence shifted emphasis from all other theatre figures to that of the man charged with placing the play on the stage; like as not he had been called merely stage-manager before, or he had been the theatre owner and primarily a business man. But now he got to be a specialist, a *régisseur,* with extraordinarily increased powers.

Where settings had been ordered in blindly from an unrelated scenic studio before, the new artist-director imparted his conceptions to, and worked with, a sympathetic designer, or created his own scenes. Where actors before had had broad license to develop personal idiosyncrasies, they now could do so only within the limits set by the artist-director's conception of the total production. Almost for the first time the art of the theatre was being seen as a whole, with someone experiencing a complete vision of the *performance* before rehearsals started.

In twenty years the artist-director has grown from a hireling of the manager, a slave of the leading actress, a mere assistant, to the point of being the key figure in the progressive theatre. *Production* has become the important thing, as distinct from the play values alone, or *virtuoso* acting, or spectacle. The *régisseur,* the master of the production, since 1915, has been recognized as the most creative artist in the theatre.

We don't know much about this figure in ages past, of course; he didn't sign the play script like the dramatists, and his work was so unspectacular that he wasn't remembered like the actors. We suspect that his unifying work was seldom done at all. But today there are three or four examples of him that are better known than any living actor, and better advertised than any dramatist — again, except Bernard Shaw.

The development of artist-directors stimulated interest in the search for "form" as an attribute of stage art. The revelation of form is possible only through the unified stage production, the complete use of stage materials, the bringing of all the elements into focus — and that is the work of this artist-director of artists. The flow, the continuity, the sensuous undercurrent, the spiritual overtones — these are his cares.

His methods are all but unexplainable: his ways of employing not only the tangible materials like actors, lights, dialogue, movement, and setting, but proportion, stress, pace, contrast, interval, variety, etc. But one may visualize him as he brings the work to the stage, through years of study, perhaps, and then through weeks or months of rehearsal; getting it first to come to focus in his own mind's eye, then setting out to obtain the right actors and the right stage; in the rehearsal slowing the pace here, hastening it there, struggling to bring so-and-so to the peak of his performance — and the centre of attention — at a certain moment, building up the sound sequence through one stretch, playing a silence against it at the end; flowing color over the performance, then letting the stage go grey; clearing out everything for the moment when the dramatist, suddenly turned inspired poet, has provided lines too pregnant for any assisting elements. Working thus, with seen and unseen materials, the *régisseur* develops that flow of theatricality, that continuous, unbroken appeal, that constitutes the stage "form." And it is this element that distinguishes the "new" stage from that of the past.

Max Reinhardt is the most conspicuous practitioner. He has become known over all the Western world as the most sensational of *virtuoso* directors, the great popularizer of the new stagecraft. He was once a minor actor; then a producer who believed in Realism. Timidly he took leaf after leaf from the book that was being written by Craig, Appia, and other "impractical" dreamers; he adapted some surface aspects of their designs to practical producing. He trained up a group of first-class poster-artists to provide simple, colorful, and striking settings. He took over more and more power as director, and assumed an alarming freedom in the "treatment" of plays. Sometimes he buried a finely dramatic Greek or Shakespearean text under smothering spectacle or shout-and-gesture; again he developed irresistible drive in the performance of plays that before had been unsuspected of any such effectiveness.

At times he over-dressed, over-circused, over-noised the drama; at others he created *theatre* where ordinary direction would have left only deadness on the stage. He exploited cheap stuff like *The Miracle* by genuinely theatricalizing the one or two fine scenes, and glossing the rest over with violent movement, crowds, stirring music, colored lights. In such world-known events as

Design by Gordon Craig for *Hamlet:* the Ghost scene. Craig has influenced the world theatre more than any other artist in modern times, by his insistence upon simplification of the scene, upon a return to truly theatrical expressiveness, and upon the importance of the unity to be obtained only when an artist-director is in charge. This simple but essentially theatric design, though it seemed revolutionary in 1907, is perfectly in keeping with the best practice twenty years later. [From Craig's *Towards a New Theatre.*]

Two characteristic "crowd" productions by Max Reinhardt. Above, a scene from *Danton* in the *Grosses Schauspielhaus*, Berlin, as seen by Ernst Stern. Below, a scene from *Œdipus* in a "circus," as seen by Emil Orlik. [From *Das Moderne Bühnenbild*, by Oskar Fischel.]

the Salzburg Festivals he still mixes the questionably spectacular things with those in which he shows his true genius: classics re-created, with all the elements of theatrical appeal brought into one flow, one finely dramatic evocation. He is the unchallenged master of great mass effects on the stage, the effective marshalling of armies of actors. In his best quiet works he is as near a master as there is of creative and contributive direction, of co-ordinating rather than imposing. He is the more important for having taken his work from Germany and Austria to the rest of Europe, to England, to America.

Other German artist-directors have achieved a creative theatri-cality in their productions, not quite so spectacularly but with a thoroughness that has made them world-influences. At the State Theatre in Berlin, during ten years past, Leopold Jessner has given "stylization" a new breadth of meaning. In his pro-ductions one feels the same style permeating not only the settings but the acting, the movement, all the seen and heard elements. He cleared his stage almost to bare walls, and raised platforms and steps the better to show the actor out; and he thus opened the way for realizing new values in movement as such. His de-signer, Emil Pirchan, shares praise for the achievement, for mak-ing even the barest stage seem warm, colorful, and contributive, and for playing the lights cunningly as a constant silent aid to the acting.

In Russia Vesvolod Meyerhold and Alexander Tairoff have been doing even more revolutionary work in directing — and their influence, too, is world-felt — but their aim is still so largely experimental, their contribution still so incomplete in outline, that they belong to some later history than this. But be it said, if one wishes to see history in the making today, in the theatre as in government, one should travel to Soviet Russia. New ways of organizing theatres, new relationships between audience and player, new sorts of music-drama, new acrobatic acting, Con-structivist settings, bare stages, new departures in directing — they all are being tried out in that welter of wise and unwise experiment that is Bolshevik Russia. The impact of ideas from this workshop is already being felt in Western Europe and America. And you will find that the young directors everywhere know the theories of production of Yevreinoff, Meyerhold, Tairoff.

Russia and Germany provide the names of all the internationally known directors, except Jacques Copeau, who for a time administered one of the least spectacular but one of the most fruitful of twentieth century experimental theatres, and Gordon Craig, who has become so outstandingly the inspirational figure of the modern theatre that his early practical work is all but forgotten. Gemier has given France some spectacular Reinhardtian productions, and Harley Granville-Barker long ago did some Shakespeare in England with distinctly German settings; but these were very clearly reflective of the production methods developed in Central Europe, and very little original or creative. Georg Fuchs of the Munich Art Theatre and Adolf Linnebach of the Dresden Court (now State) Theatre were really more important as creative directors, though not so broadly influential as Reinhardt and Jessner.

In England and America the value of creative directing has been fully recognized, however, and each country has developed *régisseurs* of national but not international fame. Outstanding among the Americans is Augustin Duncan, who did more than any other to make realistic plays live as unified emotional experiences for the audiences, with extraordinary character values (with a resident company and continuous opportunity for production he might have given America an acting-machine comparable to that of Stanislavsky and Nemirovitch-Dantchenko in Moscow). Arthur Hopkins, most notable artist among the Broadway producers, accepts the principle of one directing mind but deplores *virtuoso* directing, tries to discover creative actors, and leaves to them as much latitude as is consistent in unified total effect; it was he who, with Robert Edmond Jones, startled New York with an Expressionist mounting of *Macbeth;* and he achieved solid and notable productions of *The Poor Little Rich Girl, The Devil's Garden, The Jest, Redemption (The Living Dead Man), Hamlet,* with John Barrymore in the title rôle, *Richard III* and *Anna Christie.* More than any other American director he has developed an individual and valuable theory of production — by a method termed " unconscious projection." There is too a group of foreign-born directors who have become fixtures in America: Richard Boleslavsky, Rouben Mamoulian, and Iden Payne.

The principle of artist-direction was early accepted by the little theatres — indeed, many of the notable groups were organized by creative directors and touched importance only by virtue of that fact. Maurice Browne of the Chicago Little Theatre, Frederic McConnell of the Cleveland Playhouse, Oliver Hinsdell at the Dallas Little Theatre, and Sam Hume and Irving Pichel, first in the Middle West and latterly in California, literally " made " their respective theatres in the image of their own visions. Nearer the professional type, the Goodman Memorial Theatre in Chicago, from planning of the building to latest programme, has been stamped with the personality and dreaming of Thomas Wood Stevens; and the Pasadena Community Playhouse has grown out of the work and thought — *social* thought as well as theatric — of Gilmor Brown. The absolute creativeness of these artists — all designers, in the larger sense, as well as directors — has surpassed that of the playwrights or actors in the same period.

If " FORM " is the ultimate consideration, if a welding together, under visionary direction, is the matter we are studying, then we may best call to witness the so-called *dance-drama,* for in that a "flow," a complete theatrical evocation, is most identifiable. Between 1905 and 1925 this type of theatre production was carried to new heights of freedom, of " purity," of gorgeousness, particularly in the practice of the *Ballets Russes.* There are those who feel that a new art was created; but it was really the old art of the ballet, recreated under a new lavishness of painted scenery, a new freedom of the dance as revolutionized by Isadora Duncan, and the new opportunities uncovered in electric stage lighting — all directed into a fresh unity.

This art of danced drama did not endanger the spoken drama in its many forms; it involved no revolution of the whole stage art. It simply came as a well-nigh perfect thing in its own kind, filling one niche completely, satisfyingly. Or, changing the metaphor, it fills one corner of the theatre's field: that corner which is farthest from literature and psychologic and intellectual drama, the corner closest to free use of color, sound, and movement.

There was a *fin-de-siècle* theory, propounded — or revived — as a reaction against too much literary, anecdotal, and photographic activity, to the effect that the nearer any art touched toward the estate of music, the purer, the more " artistic " that art became. A distinction was drawn between the more æsthetic and the less æsthetic arts, between the less and the more logical or imitational. In the division of the stage art, the territory including dance-drama was " æsthetic drama," as against, at the other extreme, " the drama of thought." One approached the estate of music, in that it used largely abstract means; the other depended chiefly upon words, used logically. A composer wouldn't think of di-rectly imitating the sound of a waterfall, or a battle, or a groan; the artists of the new ballet would depend as little as possible on story, and not at all on spoken or sung words. They would use line and color abstractly rather than illustratively, sound tonally, and movement as pure dance — so far as possible. No logic, no tied story to be untied, no legend except as a skeleton, as an excuse for dancing: thus the intellect of the spectator would be stilled, only his senses left alert.

Picture to yourself the darkened interior of a theatre; the richly ornamented theatre, warmly colored, is particularly in keeping here. In the glamorous half-light, the music has prepared you. When the curtain is drawn a sea of color overwhelms you. Mountains of swelling scenery rise up into the very skies, hugely patterned curtains are half caught up, hang down, lie in folds along the floor; gay rugs, tapestries, bizarrely ornamented arches; vermilion, orange, madder, gold, peacock blues, sea-green, pur-ples, gold, and silver — an impossible mixture of colors, but you find yourself gratefully drowned in it. The music goes on, lost to your consciousness at first, but reasserting itself, swelling with the color in that drowning of your senses. Then a dancing figure floats in, one or more, perhaps dozens, seemingly hundreds, myriads. Dancing, movement, rhythm, ever-changing line, pat-tern — completely lost in the music and the picture. A perfect synthesis of sound, color, and movement, sheerly theatrical.

A drama is played — it doesn't much matter what: one has

been filled with a lasting pleasure, a pervading current, a glow. One only asks that the rhythm of music, lights, setting, dancing figures, continue till the curtain's fall.

One has been intoxicated; but it is an intoxication that vaguely lasts, that is pleasant in memory (there are other sorts). One's senses have been bathed. A sort of sensuous ecstasy has taken possession. This is not the response one has felt after Greek

Costume designs by Bakst for the *Ballets Russes*. [From redrawings in *Play Production in America*, by Arthur Edwin Krows.]

tragedy — there one was purged by experience, taken beyond the world, left with a deeper ecstasy that clarified. Here one is of the world, knows it as lush, sensuously soft and infinitely pleasurable. The thing that the Russian Ballet gives me, as against Greek drama, is the thing that Gauguin gives me, as against the profounder rhythms of Cezanne or El Greco. It is decorative drama — with no story to be followed or dialogue to be listened for, a sheer surface delight.

Oriental richness — perhaps the Russian contact with the East added that. And the legends are as likely as not to be Oriental. *Scheherazade* at base is an unrefined tale of Arabian Nights monarchs, harems, intrigues, passion. It is full of eroticism and violence that are hardly noticed; these elements are lost in the total sensuous design. Other legends are less turgid, less wildly passionate: they are picked, one imagines, more for their setting than for the story. The whole show may be stylized, dancing included, from feeling for a color, or a place, or a musical phrase.

It was Leon Bakst who created the most sumptuous of the *Ballets Russes* backgrounds. No modernist simplification of the setting for him! He took the old muddy painted scenery, sifted the mud out, poured in buckets of raw color, and created stage pictures of more prodigious proportions, vaster spaces, and more overwhelming colorfulness than any ever invented before. His fellow Russians, Benois, Roerich, Golovine, and Anisfeld were hardly less lavish and brilliant. Whether Bakst — and his *is* the most celebrated name out of the *Ballets Russes* history — actually became artist-director, one does not know. The most famous company was always known as Diaghileff's *Ballets Russes,* and presumably Sergei Diaghileff was *régisseur* or at least *ober-régisseur.* There were other companies — the Swedish Ballet ran away with some honors a few years ago — and the type of sensuous dance-drama can be seen on other than the so-called ballet stages.

Directors of little theatres recognized the value of the form as a variation of over-light comedy or over-serious drama; and in America the Neighborhood Playhouse dancers did truly creative work. Some progressive opera houses began to substitute rounded-out numbers for the ballet interludes, and revue producers might insert a whole dance-drama in a decorative girl-and-music show. *Petrouchka* remains with me as vividly as anything I ever saw or heard at the Metropolitan Opera House, and I have the dreamiest memories of a dance evening at the Vienna Opera.

ONE MIGHT report many other phases of the " glorified-production craze " — the literary-minded critics still call it that, fearing for the dramatist. One might describe the miracle of Isadora Duncan's dancing, the utter surrender of audiences to one woman, up there on a stage hung with simple blue curtains, dancing to music — not a story, but a dance so meaningful, so dramatic, that the spectator came away moved, purged, uplifted, as if he had experienced one of the choral dramas of Æschylus. In the dance field, too, there is the "classical" ballet, still hanging on in opera (where Lully so firmly inserted it); it has gained enormously from the artist-direction impulse, and it has its masters still, within the narrow limits imposed by its lingering artificialities. Some of its graduates have made spectacular successes: most notably Pavlowa. In a similarly limited type of production, but in the comedy and burlesque field, the Russian Nikita Balieff has occasionally scored a triumph by posing just the right theatrical feeling, the perfect balance of word, music, and seen elements — by being the all-planning artist-*régisseur*.

In the field at the very opposite extreme, however, where written drama is the basic ingredient, where not a solo performer or instrument but an orchestral production is involved, the effect of the artist-director and of the ensemble ideal has been hardly less revolutionary. There is no phenomenon to report, over toward realism, so clean-cut and so outstanding as the *Ballets Russes* achievement, or that of Duncan or Pavlowa or Balieff's comedy troupe; but none the less realistic plays are being infinitely better produced, with richer effectiveness, than they were twenty-five years ago. And in at least one case a playing company has come to a perfection of ensemble presentation that has set a new standard in the world: at the Moscow Art Theatre.

There are play texts so realistic or so thought-provoking that they defeat the artist-director before his company is assembled. The very term "thesis-play" implies predominance of an element untheatric, unglamorous, unappealing. And those slice-of-life plays that are intended to afford the audience a glimpse of living in the raw, they *cannot* be treated with other than imitative, uncreative technique. But the better part of Realism — as, say, Ibsen and Chekhov — can be brought to something approaching a separate theatrical entity at the hands of an artist-director using his materials orchestrally. I have already mentioned the memorable production of *John Ferguson* as creatively shaped by Augustin Duncan; I felt something of the same living theatrical intensity in Ibsen's *The Wild Duck* as directed for the Actors' Theatre by Dudley Digges, in O'Neill's *Anna Christie* as directed by Arthur Hopkins, in two productions by the Irish Players. But all of us have experienced the quality, the fulness, most notably in the performances of the Moscow Art Theatre company.

It has been said that the directors of this troupe "treat" a play text to so complete a realization of the author's intention that they come out at a sort of reality beyond surface life — at a *spiritualized* Realism. There is a point at which a Realism apparently true to the smaller observed facts of life sometimes plunges suddenly to planes of revealment and heartbreak; and the Art Theatre actors are adept at carrying the spectator along facilely, and suddenly bringing him to a sort of illumination, to understanding. The plays in which they do this — under Constantin Stanislavsky's masterly direction — are not the journalistic Realism of the Broadway and West-End best-seller playwrights, but the serener, constantly repressed Realism of Chekhov, or an immense canvas of contrasting characters like the dramatization of Dostoievsky's *The Brothers Karamazoff.* Perhaps this is not Realism essentially, for Realism's sake, but in the one case a realistic mask which is suddenly lowered to reveal a spiritual or a theatrical truth, and in the other a character display theatricalized far beyond naturalness.

At any rate, the point here is that the artist-*régisseur* Stanislavsky, by virtue of his ability as visionary and practical director, brought into being a playing company more notable than any other in history for the perfect ensemble impression conveyed to the audience. In plays like *The Blue Bird* and *Hamlet* it helped to crystallize the thing called Stylization, which artist-directors were working for everywhere in connection with revivals. It showed that new plays, even realistic ones, could be submitted to a creative *régisseur* and to actors with machine-precision of presentation, and gain unaccustomed values in the revealment of nuances and colorings. I say *even* realistic because it seems to me clear, after ten or fifteen years of the increasing importance of production as a craft, that such marvellous treatment of Ibsen and Chekhov is an exceptional thing, not on the main road to the future: that the rediscovery of theatrical values is turning a new generation of dramatists and directors to what is anti-realistic, Expressionistic and frankly theatrical.

impressionistic, and frankly theatrical.

CHAPTER XXIV

Machine-Age Developments

NOW HERE is a picture-map of the European-American
theatre spread wide before us, showing out at a glance
the stage activities of today. What have we come to?
In the legitimate-commercial houses, Realism is still king,
Realism journalistic, pleasantly shallow, or Realism intelligently
intensified or lifted to intellectual sparkle. Beside each legitimate
house, to be sure, is a " little " theatre, and the artists there are seen
to be busy with experiments in the unnatural, better or worse, with
excursions, sometimes with recognizable splendors; and they go
over and commandeer one of the regular houses to their uses
occasionally. Then, too, a whole group of theatres play the im-
memorial game of luring hicks, tired-business-men and holiday-
makers into their shows compounded of fooling, feats, and musical
tum-tee-tum — with more girls thrown in for decorativeness than
ever before; these are the chopped-amusement theatres that descend from the street stages and fair platforms, with their sword-
swallowers, trick bears, African dancing girls, etc. Today they
sometimes sandwich gorgeously creative " turns " into their
obvious programmes: *diseuses,* a Raquel Meller, an Al Jolson,
an Yvette Guilbert, a " Russian " ballet. There are, too, operas
and operettas in our picture.
But the great distinctive difference about this picture-map —
as compared with one glanced at back in the nineties — is that,
although the above-named theatres were *all* the world theatre
twenty-five years ago, they are actually outnumbered today by a
new sort of house purveying a new sort of dramatic entertainment. This multitudinous new theatre is strange in that it often
has no stage, in that it knows nothing of the distinction between

matinée and evening performances — plays continuously; and we note that it has opened vistas to a variant theatric art with stupendous pictorial and rhythmic potentialities. But whatever its differences from the old theatre, something has made it popular: it claims the largest (and most blatant) playhouses in the world, and those farthest-flung from the centres of dramatic enterprise. Sometimes the legend over the portal reads " picture house," sometimes " cinema " or " *lichtspiel* " — or whatever is the Chinese or Afghanistan or Bolivian equivalent. Also, on this map, there is a curious tendency of the spots denoting theatres to blend into those denoting dwelling-houses, as if a man might be sitting at his own hearthside and enjoying (or cursing) the offering of some theatre artist. Physically — and that is the only way the map can register — there is some great dislocation of old theatre values here.

WE HAVE noted, in past chapters, major developments in the world theatre in relation to major changes in human civilization: the flowering of the Greek drama in that time when the life of the spirit came to blossom most revealingly, most beautifully; the degradation of the stage, even while physically glorified, under the materialism of Rome; Church domination, and the reaction in the reflowering of theatre art during the Renaissance, when man asserted his right to think for himself, to create; the coming of democracy and the overthrow of kings, followed shortly by the spread of the scientific spirit, and the arts brought down to the familiar, the common, the photographic — to Realism which has had its minor glories, but at cost of blanketing half the characteristic expressiveness of the stage.

Today we believe that we are at the crest of another flood-tide of advancing human *spirit*. We have pulled up out of the delusion that democracy would lead us down effortless into the promised land: we know that any vision of sharing the advantages of life, material, spiritual, or artistic, is futile; that freedom and beauty in life will come only when the individual man climbs up to fineness, not when advantages are levelled down. Science is on the back-track; from believing that everything, even to the soul, could be analysed down to a final material truth, it turns eyes upward and outward, knowing now that there are spirits and forces and broader causes that were entirely lost sight of in the first rush at microscopic truth — that the artists, for instance, deal in a commodity unexplainable by any scientific formula.

We in America, to be sure, under the advantages of democracy in opportunity, scientific invention, and religious freedom or license, have advanced materially beyond all earlier human experience, so that greater numbers of people than ever anywhere before have adequate food, clothing, and shelter, together with healthful recreation, a start at education, the advantages of travel. But the greater marvel is that the will to art is widely apparent: our machines — particularly our motor-cars — are works of art more revealingly expressive and more widespread than any manifestation of beauty in ages. The crafts that go to the making of the home have never been more widely practised, with efficient simplicity, with care for æsthetic values. Over all the world, but here in our States particularly, a new style of architecture, grown organically out of modern needs and visions, has pushed up into view, the first truly new style in six centuries. The graphic arts in the Western world have seen within our lifetime a revolution that destroyed codes and standards held sacred three hundred years; a complete overturn, a final discrediting of what passed for the arts of painting and sculpture from the time when the long slope toward photographic Realism began. The world of the arts and of human thought has come to a time of ferment, of flux, more marked than any since the early Renaissance. We are part of a new flowering.

The theatre, the legitimate theatre, cumbrous, expensive to change, feels influences slowly, responds sluggishly to the stimulus of new thinking, new creative vision. So far the ferment is evident more in excited activity than in emerging achievements. But make no mistake, the theatre is alive, feverishly alive. The speed and intensity of modern living have got into its people. But have they got into its performances? Have those elements of machine-precision, sheerness, simple rhythm, expressive flow (remember the stream-lines), gone into theatre productions?

Already I have hinted briefly at something appropriate, eternally theatric while essentially modern, that a group of Expressionistic playwrights have tried to capture. I have added that the directors — particularly Gordon Craig — have contributed more toward its realization. But the complete expression comes slowly in the older, the eternal, the humanly-acted-out drama. The mighty change is bound to be gradual, over a number of decades. We are in the beginning rather than in the midst of it.

But that machinery of the theatre, which we saw progressively developed, from Roman times to our own — has that been carried to new glories in this machine-age, has it become a super-stage-machine with amazingly varied and creative powers? Well, frankly, that machine has been scrapped. The entire intricate edifice of engines, wagons, turnstiles, rockers, gridirons, etc., etc., has been discarded by the most progressive designers and producers. Not *entire,* either; but so substantially that the outstanding paradox of the machine-age theatre is that machinery has been swept out. The secret is, of course, that the machine-effects never were theatric in the deeper creative sense: they were an intrusion, with their startling " effects," or else an aid to picture-making. They belonged typically to the realistic age, to the scientific-thought age. They were used to perpetuate dying types of drama. The age of vision-and-expression will let them return to the stage but warily if at all.

But electricity for lighting has brought new and perfectly assimilated wonders into the art of staging. A craft like acting and a medium involving movement need adequate illumination — and did not have it for centuries, from the time when shows went indoors to, roughly, 1900. Now the artist-director has at his command a range of lighting expressive of every nuance of dramatic feeling, in color, intensity, design. This indeed is a matter of machine-age precision — an attribute of stage art never before possible. And in the larger view, here is an element quite truly contributing to, furthering, the glamour, the glow, of essential theatre. The average production today in the United States or in Germany — where settings are designed with a new simplicity and a painstaking adjustment to the æsthetic possibilities of the new lighting — the acted drama is unfolded to an unnoticed accompaniment of color-and-light that re-enforces the dramatic and spiritual values while warming the production with a sensuous glow, a flush.

BUT THOSE other thousands and thousands of theatres that have no stage to be bathed in light, no actors to be perfectly illumined — are not they the truer example of a machine-age drama? In some points of method, yes; in general, no. But we cannot overlook them in any case, they are so prevalent, so forward, so overwhelmingly " successful " from the box-office standpoint. They are the theatre of democracy brought *part way* up. Some people will tell you that the moving-pictures have been pulled down to the standard of the mob. It is truer to say that the people and the pictures have met half way: the producers lowering the intelligence-standard and the sincerity of the film, but audiences of medium intelligence, of art sensibility, appearing in numbers never before known to theatre activity.

Let us be conservative. Let us say that this week not more than 250,000,000 people attend moving-picture theatres. Still that is a considerable figure. A year's attendance goes a bit beyond the point where ciphers have any meaning for us. All the spectators at all the Greek dramas ever played, in the theatres of Greece, her colonies, and of the later Roman Empire, over a period of eight centuries, probably numbered fewer than the attendants at the world's 50,000 picture houses last week. The next Charlie Chaplin film will " play " to more people in its first year after release than *Hamlet* has in three hundred and twenty-seven years. No wonder the picture people are making claims about the fourth largest industry (or is it the third?) and are talking loosely about enormous social influence, etc.

In 1889, in New Jersey, workers in the laboratories of Thomas A. Edison completed a practical machine for exhibiting moving-pictures. One person could look into a box and see events pass photographically. In that " kinetoscope " many principles and inventions were involved for which individual credit might fairly be divided among a half-dozen experimenters who had worked in New York and London as well as in remote places in California and Eastern Europe. But it was Edison's inventiveness that brought into existence a machine that showed photographed action automatically — even as much as 15 seconds of it. Other mileposts on the way to the present-day super-film were passed: films fifty feet in length (as against 10,000 today); films thrown on a screen, outside the box (or was the box enlarged and the spectator taken into it?); and then a 2000-foot film " reporting " the Ober-Ammergau Passion Play.

It is generally considered that the first " screen drama " was *The Great Train Robbery* presented under the Edison trade-mark in New York in 1903. From then on " the art of the motion picture " grew steadily toward bigness, toward self-reliance, toward elaboration. What had been a photographic toy was thenceforward one of the arts of the theatre, with dramatists, actors, playhouses.

The growth of the picture-drama has been attended with stirring rise-from-obscurity incidents. The change to the contemporary " picture palaces " out of the abandoned barroom nickelodeons is of itself a considerable step-up for a single quarter-century. More than twenty thousand theatres for pictures alone, in the United States — and among them more examples of " the largest theatre in the world " than any country ever claimed before. Studios that have grown from what the word originally meant to vast plants with multiple stages and unbelievable property rooms and zoos and whatnot. And Hollywood from being a favorably known minor suburb has become the most famous stage production centre in the world, and the most cursed city. It has its marvels, its Babylons built and destroyed, its armies of beautiful girls, its monumental "turnover," its Charlie Chaplin, its collection of native and foreign leading artists. It also has furnished more thousands of miles of drivel, of fatuous, trivial, and puerile entertainment than any other amusement centre in history.

But we are concerned only with the *art* of the theatre. Has the cinema, that took to itself many actors and dramatists and directors out of the regular theatre, focused its efforts into a recognized art manifestation? Well, if we lose ourselves in the total film output — there are perhaps six hundred releases in a year in America — there seems not to be much that is important from the standpoint from which we have been considering the theatre. But if we forget everything else except the pictures that have moved us, have given us a few stirring moments, or pleased our eyes gratefully, this year, there stand out things undeniably fine, with a power of evoking that spiritual-emotional pleasure that we have thought characteristic of our response to played drama.

Unfortunately a great deal of what has been accomplished in the pictures has been a fairly close reflection (if not an imitation) of legitimate drama. The early producers, after the prize-fight-reporting stage was past, saw this only as a means of duplicating stage plays — with some additional advantages in the direction of Realism, in widened background, in character-emotion (close-ups), etc. What they couldn't copy in photographs, they presented in sub-titles. Still we had *The Birth of a Nation* (1914), *The Covered Wagon, Ben Hur,* and so on. These were stage-play and pageant materials pushed to new limits of elaboration in setting, lifelikeness, display.

It is to be remarked, however, that in the picture house no one who has felt the lure of the personally acted drama in an intimate theatre can ever be fooled for more than a few minutes at a time into forgetting that this is a *photograph* of action, not the action itself. We enjoy it as we enjoy well-taken photographs of a work of sculpture. We would infinitely rather see the sculpture itself. That disability — that it is shown always at one remove from personal acting — will always be on the motion-picture drama so long as it aims at those effects belonging peculiarly to stage drama. Ninety-nine one-hundredths of the cinema output in twenty years has been in that field. That is why, when some-one asks, " what really great photoplays have you seen? " one fumbles the answer, groping, catching at a *possible* title here or there.

But the film production has characteristic excellencies or potentialities, and year by year experimenters and a few artists learn more about them. There was real cinematographic achievement in *The Last Laugh* (without subtitles, note), and in *Metropolis* and in *Potemkin*. In the making of these films and in some minor ones by American, German, and French " modernists " there was recognized the possibility of capitalizing film values

GORDON CRAIG

Charlie Chaplin, straight and in character.
[By courtesy of United Artists.]

unknown to the speaking stage. Continuous movement is the basic element in the art (and yet the producers have persisted in stopping the flow every minute or two, for explanatory or pre-paratory or smart words). But telling a story is only one of the uses of movement, need not be the main one. The most recent film-producers have recognized that objects in visual movement have characteristic appeal as pattern or flow. Rhythmic visual design is accepted as a basic value. Selective images, combina-tions of images, superimposed images; and the world a mine of material—not merely what can be made visible on a stage in a certain playhouse.

The moving-pictures continue to develop in the two directions: reporting events, then reporting typical stage plays laid out against more extensive backgrounds than the theatre before had known; but also, breaking the bounds of Realism, of primary story-telling, of part-word art, they move toward greater accom-plishment of typical movement-of-light rhythmic art. Hokum and heart interest, in the cheap film, give way before values cap-tured out of the essential character of photographic screen-projected images.

It is, of course, the cheap duplication that has carried the form into the world more widely than any art manifestation ever known before. It is the immense "market" for the pictures that attracted business men to the control of production, too often to the exclusion of creative artists. It is said that eighty per cent of the world's films are made in America — or at least of the films that have more than local appeal. Unfortunately the industry early fell into the hands of typical salesmen — cloak-and-suit merchants seem to predominate — who were innocent of any knowledge of art except in its most obvious and sentimental as-pects. The theatre people whom they called in to help them were largely of the cheaper sort: melodrama writers, romantic actors, and Broadway directors who understood "what the public wants." The game is still pretty generally played by those same people, and with the object of grading every picture to please the greatest possible near-intelligent audience. Practically every-thing is produced for the best-seller trade; and it has been scien-tifically established that the film that never puts a strain on the intelligence of a 14-year-old child pleases the widest public. The more mature, the cultivated, the educated audience comes in for a few pictures only as an afterthought. (The first signs are apparent of a "little theatre" movement in the picture world.)

So we find Hollywood today largely concerned with infantile art. But a phenomenon like Charlie Chaplin — creative, individual, authentic — happens even in Hollywood. And a Griffiths sees some new vision, almost realizes it splendidly. German directors suddenly open fresh vistas: *The Cabinet of Dr. Caligari, Metropolis, The Last Laugh.* And the American industrial kings immediately import those directors; but so far have pretty effectively tied their hands with the obligation to do what exhibitors think is more popular stuff. Russia and Germany still turn out the few most stirring and the most beautiful films. America dominates the field in all other respects. Great artists occur even in Hollywood — and the future bursts with *promise.*

A MILLION or so people may, if they wish, any evening, sit in their parlors and "tune in" on a song by Al Jolson or a scene from *Twelfth Night.* We had no sooner begun speculating as to what this radio hook-up of theatre and home might accomplish toward the spreading of dramatic art than we were startled by other and more far-reaching visions. No one could foresee what broadcasting of plays might come to: the potentialities were staggering, even after we had got used to the idea of those 50,000 picture theatres.

But now comes the greater vision not only of millions of people *listening* to a play, but of drama brought to their homes by correlated sound *and* sight waves. For television, when it is perfected into a medium with capabilities comparable to those of radio, will remove the last obstacle to transportation of drama, or diffusion, with every word and every visual value intact. Before many years have passed, any play or opera put on anywhere may be available at second hand in the homes of all owners of radio-television receiving-sets.

The film art will then be forced to capitalize other values than those it now so generally relies upon, those borrowed from the speaking stage. The talking-film (just now creating such a furore in the cinema world) will be no novelty in a theatre — when the equivalent of it may be seen and heard in one's own parlor. Better films — though perhaps fewer — will be produced, doubtless more distinctively æsthetic and with a place of their own in a dramatic field widened beyond wildest estimates.

All this may lead back to great changes in the legitimate stage art, as played by actors on a platform before an audience. Radio alone is not likely to create a new poetry or a new drama. But the knowledge that a play is being transmitted, both sight and sound of it, outside the theatre walls to innumerable secondary theatres even thousands of miles away, may affect playwriting, acting, methods of staging.

But it will be, *in that theatre,* the old eternal art of presenting action by the medium of living players. I, for one, believe that that art will go on forever — or at least beyond any developments we now can conceive of. If the legitimate drama has been hurt or curtailed during the period of the cinema's rise, it seems to me that the cupidity of producers, wanting to make ever more money by exploiting the obvious and popular at the expense of the finely creative work, has had more to do with it than has the competition of the " movies." Other sorts of competition will come, but there will always be audiences to gather where the actor personally is, where the spectator is in the presence of the stage action.

There is talk of the " actorless " theatre and many are the guesses at new forms of machine-made drama wherein no player appears — mere moving shapes or symbolized forces or whatnot. But they hardly belong to a book that is, after all, primarily a history of what has been done in the world playhouse. The story of the wooden actor, of puppets, might more properly have a place: but it is a story so long, so different, that it would need a volume in itself. The impersonality, the obedience, of the marionette actor, the different appeal of the manipulated figures — these are matters that set the subject aside from the record of the regular theatre. Suffice it to say that through most of the centuries during which the theatre of personal acting has existed, a puppet theatre has lived also, if not always in the West then in the East; and that today the marionette, after a period of degradation, promises a revival of old glories, in Europe and America.

Dismissing these machine-age picture houses, radio plays, and wooden actors, I call to mind New York and its stages. This city of skyscrapers and jazz includes a " theatre district " where more of dramatic life is concentrated in a restricted space than in any other spot on earth: more of feverish dramatic activity, of theatre gaiety, of the outward glamour of the art. Tonight the crowds are swarming toward that bright centre, thousands of people flushed with the joy of theatre-going, with anticipation, with the old excitement. The hurrying people, the taxi jams, the half-hundred playhouses brilliantly alight, with warmly gaping portals, a whole section of the city decked and brightened with colored lights for the theatre hour: all this makes Broadway at eight-thirty one of the stirring sights of the Western world. Without thought of the movie houses, not remembering the puppets or the radio, we know that here is overwhelming evidence that the old theatre survives, that the stage of the living actor entertains more spectators than ever before, that the outward glamour of the playhouse has been intensified, that it attracts with the ancient magic. Clearly this *is,* still, the place of all places one seeks when craving emotional-spiritual adventure, this *is* the brightest and gayest of all surviving communal centres.

EPILOGUE

Yesterday, Today, and Tomorrow

LAST night we went down into the Broadway district. We drowned our senses in the glamour, the surge, the seductive flow of Broadway life. That *is* the theatre of our times, of the decade when the peoples of the world have caught hold of the wings of machine-magic: when they are dragged, feeling the speed, the exhilaration, the throb, but not yet lifted, not yet riding freely, splendidly, not yet masters of the magic. They look below, not up. The dramatists, actors, directors are puzzled by the sweep of the wings, by the vistas, by the prospect of freedom; they struggle, grow panicky, grasp at the real — still fearing what their imaginations might lead them to if they capitalized their impulse, their outlook, and the machine.

This is the morning after. Those millions of electric lights are out; the glitter and the glamour gone. In the clear morning sunshine we are given to doubts about the *depth* of last night's experience. For a time the theatre came alive, surrounding us happily with its glow. For a time it gave promise of fulfilling again its service to the spirit. It opened the way, it stimulated, spread its riches about us. We entered in. But somewhere there was failure. The presented drama fell short of spiritual illumination, of purging our emotions: the moment of revealment did not arrive.

I drift toward an old distress. I recognize that the cheapness of contemporary commercial life has crept in, has corrupted the house of beauty, of passion, of spirituality; that often intrigue and personal ambition clog the machine, that the spirit is petty, the creed limiting. I see that the photographic-analytic, peep-hole

539

method has brought the stage down to a cramped outlook and a squeezed expressiveness, that the view of living has been narrowed without being intensified, that the portion examined — as exhibited in each individual play — is too small to have much of glory or joy or vision in it. This is the theatre rationalized, sentimentalized, vulgarized.

Is this to be the end of our history — does our story fade out in distress and disbelief? In many yesterdays, as we have seen, the theatre added that deeper stirring, that diviner gift, to the glamour; today's theatre affords glamour and intense activity, sensation, shock; what, then, of tomorrow's? Shall we measure only the distance from the stages of the Greeks and of Shakespeare to the feverishly active but spiritually impotent New York stage of now, and not look forward to tomorrow? Gauge only the failure, not the hope? No; the assurance of new splendors is there for all to see — limited only by the aspiration of the human soul. If the world stage has been petty or cramped or sordid, it is because the vision, the thinking, the living of the age have been so. There is a cycle in the life of the human soul. Humanity wakes from one epoch, one horizon to another, returns to splendor. What has been, in Greece or in Elizabeth's London, can be again, will be again, in different terms, but no less nobly. In two ways we may know it: by the ferment in life, and by that still undirectioned ferment on the stage.

For we are at the breaking of a new era. If fresh world wars do not overtake us first, delaying, spiritual leaders will arise who will work a revolution in the soul of man, who will correlate the "progress" of the last hundred years — progress that has seemed as yet only to draw humanity backward, toward old terrors and old sorrows; who will at once discover new bases for living and stimulate the arts into fresh expressiveness. After every decline into the commonplace, the gross and the commercial, fineness inevitably reasserts itself. The arts may even be the barometer, forecasting the remolding of life into nobler forms.

The theatre, most human of the arts and nearest to the soul, is ready. It seems to mark time over those realistic plays, over the old grind of variety amusement, over trifles, and sensations; but perhaps even these are preparation. At any rate the theatre is ready

as never before because its artists in their great activity have regained the complete view of the art, the view of it not as a literary
exercise, or a spectator's means of escape from living, or a super-
photograph, but as an activity important in its own right, self-
sufficient. For the first time in centuries the theatre is being
imagined with at once an old unity and a new splendor. I hope
that a consideration of its history in entirety has afforded you
the faith to believe, with me, in the inevitability of its return to
health, full beauty, and creativeness; and that you may believe
as I do, that of all the arts it is the one best able to compass the
vast truths, the ritualistic splendors, the precise perfections, the
human-divine intimacy, of the age that is being born.

AUTHOR'S ACKNOWLEDGMENT

NOW that the final curtain is down on my pageant of the world's theatre history, I claim the author's privilege of appearing briefly on the stage, hoping that before too many of the audience escape, I may put on record certain acknowledgments and explanations. I know that these are more usually incorporated into a Preface, before the show proper; but we of the later theatre are particular about keeping the flow of the piece uninterrupted — so to speak, from frontispiece to epilogue — and once my curtain was up, it seemed to me wise to hold out all extraneous matter, for an appendix.

If I could bring before you the persons to whom I as author am indebted, they might indeed contribute their bits to any show — character values, mostly, not without comedy appeal — for they are librarians, scholars, publishers and artists, all of retiring and gentle types seldom seen on the boards. But I must content myself with naming them, with a " thank you! " that covers sincere gratitude for aid along the way:

To the Librarians of the American Library in Paris, the New York Public Library, the University of California Library at Berkeley, and the Library for American Studies in Italy, at Rome, and to the Keeper of Printed Books of the British Museum in London, I owe thanks for the extending of numerous courtesies. To Robert Edmond Jones and to Professor Gilbert Murray I am more particularly indebted, for quotations made in the text.

In regard to the illustrations, my debt to publishers is large. Especially I have to thank Edith J. R. Isaacs of *Theatre Arts Monthly* for unfailing encouragement and assistance; and the following firms have courteously granted permission to reproduce pictures over which they exercise copyright control: the Macmillan Company, New York, and Macmillan and Company Ltd.,

London, J. M. Dent and Sons, London, George G. Harrap and Company Ltd., London, D. C. Heath and Company, Boston, the John Day Company, New York, The Eclipse Press, London, The Century Company, New York, T. Werner Laurie Ltd., London, " The Stage," London, and Ernst Wasmuth, Berlin. The Directors of the New York Historical Society, of the Smithsonian Institution, of the Victoria and Albert Museum in London, and of the National Gallery in London, have given permission for reproduction of drawings or paintings owned by their respective institutions; and other prints have been supplied by Dr. Joseph Gregor of the National Library in Vienna, Gordon Craig, Arthur Edwin Krows, and Messrs. Wildenstein and Company of New York and Paris.

Where so many illustrations are gathered together, including many by artists long since dead, and others from books published by firms long since disappeared, it is difficult to establish a standard of procedure in regard to acknowledgments. Always I have noted the artist's name if it could in any way be traced; but as for tracking down the publishers in order to request formal permission, I have done this uniformly only in regard to books published since 1900 — that being in line, I believe, with the intent of the copyright law and with the usages of courtesy between publishers. I must add, however, that the originals of some illustrations, particularly older ones, came into my possession as fugitive prints, perhaps unduly separated from parent volumes, by purchase at the book-stalls on the quays of the Seine and other places where the niceties of literary etiquette are not uniformly observed. I shall be sorry if in publishing these I unwittingly infringe upon an artist's or publisher's privilege, and I shall welcome any notation leading to proper acknowledgment in later editions.

And so, too, as regards the text. I think I have exerted all due human caution to safeguard the accuracy of dates, spellings, etc. But the book has been written " on the road," and missed the more judicial and painstaking processes of verification that would have preceded its publication had I worked patiently in a book-lined study at home. Truly, I am the man who wore out public-library dictionaries and encyclopædias in half the capital cities of

Europe, verifying dates and names; but if, even so, errors have slipped in, I shall welcome corrections from my readers, in order that matters may be set right in editions after this one. My hope is that there may be a counter-advantage in this: that the " story " I have told of the theatre has gained a little in vividness and pictorial interest through the circumstance that I was travelling, that I was in Rome when the Roman chapter was written, in Florence for the Renaissance, and successively in London, Berlin, Paris, New York, and many another centre of past and present theatre activity. Thus, though I am indebted to many specialists and " authoritative " writers, as indicated in the bibliographical footnotes, perhaps my chief original contributions as historian are a broadened view by virtue of direct contact with old theatres and local customs, and a sense of the essential oneness of stage history in all lands. Without apology I have departed from the straight historical road at times, to talk of the theories of the theatre art, or the social and moral implications involved, etc. It simply seemed to me that these excursions were necessary to the filling out of the " picture."

Last among the debts to be acknowledged is that to my wife, for the sort of aid-in-companionship not easily to be recorded. Not only did she put the entire manuscript into final condition for the printer, but often she graciously let me go to measure the stage of an old theatre or to chase down an elusive illustration when we might better have been enjoying the celebrated view from a mountain top or visiting So-and-so's tomb. Still the book was a grand excuse for making the long tour of ancient theatres from Orange and Arles to Taormina and Syracuse, and for attending a lot of shows together. Often we came to that magic moment between the fading out of the house lights and the rise of the curtain, that moment when the burden of the conscious mind is thrown off like a garment and the outward world is stilled to the accents of the soul, and we found together the fullness of satisfaction afforded so seldom — otherwise than in the theatre. I hope, dear reader, that our book has just a little increased your essential " feel for the theatre": that now your experience of that moment may be a little fuller, richer, for contact with the stages and actors — and audiences — of the past.

And so, Dionysus be with you.

GENERAL BIBLIOGRAPHY

SUPPLEMENTARY to the bibliographical footnotes that appear with each chapter, indicating sources and suggesting further reading on the individual periods and countries, I am adding here brief descriptions of the more important *general* works on the theatre arts.

The volume entitled *Drama,* by Ashley Dukes, in the Home University Library series (London and New York, 1926) is the only work in English pretending to cover the story of the theatre arts in all phases, and is an admirable brief introduction to the subject. For the rest, existing books limit their attention either to the story of dramatic literature or to acting and staging considered apart from drama.

Of the histories of drama as such, the most readable still is Brander Matthews' *The Development of the Drama* (New York, 1906); though this is necessarily incomplete and somewhat outmoded twenty-three years after publication. Donald Clive Stuart's *The Development of Dramatic Art* (New York, 1928), while not strictly a history of drama — omitting some very important dramatists because not in the main current of changing types — is nevertheless the fullest existent treatment of the subject, and the most useful. It contains more analyses of plays and the forms of playwriting down the ages than any other book. *A Short History of the Drama,* by Martha F. Bellinger (New York, 1927), will be found useful by the less advanced student; and its pigeon-hole method fits it well for club study-circles.

Among the books devoted to the history of acting and stage activities, but silent about drama, the most accurate and the most useful summary is Glenn Hughes' *The Story of the Theatre* (New York, 1928). The so-called standard work, *A History of Theatrical Art in Ancient and Modern Times,* translated from the

Danish of Karl Mantzius (London and New York, 6 volumes, 1903–1921), has the great virtue of readability, but the fault of frequent inaccuracy. The work is monumental in some aspects, and indispensable to the student, but has been subjected to severe criticism by scholars. Since there is no encyclopædic work in English, dealing with the theatre, I may recommend the extraordinarily interesting *Dictionnaire historique et pittoresque du Théâtre et des Arts qui s'y rattachent,* by Arthur Pougin (Paris, 1885). It is generously illustrated.

On the history of the physical theatre there is the very fine — and profusely illustrated — volume by Allardyce Nicoll entitled *The Development of the Theatre* (London, 1927). There is no extensive history of stage decoration; but a brief and fully illustrated summary, incidental to a treatment of modern developments, appears in my *Stage Decoration* (New York, 1928). The subject of masks is broadly treated in *Masks and Demons,* by Kenneth Macgowan and Hermann Rosse (New York, 1924). Perhaps the best introduction to the subject of puppets in the world theatre is to be found in *A Book of Marionettes,* by Helen Haiman Joseph (New York, 1920).

The theories of the theatre are usefully summarized, and a rich collection of documents set out, in *European Theories of the Drama,* by Barrett H. Clark (Cincinnati, 1918). See also Allardyce Nicoll's *An Introduction to Dramatic Theory* (London, 1924). Two suggestive books on playwriting are *Dramatic Technique,* by George Pierce Baker (Boston, 1919), and *Playmaking, A Manual of Craftsmanship,* by William Archer (London and New York, 1913).

In the footnotes dealing with books treating individual periods and countries, I have omitted histories of the American theatre; I may therefore add here that Arthur Hornblow's *A History of the Theatre in America from Its Beginnings to the Present Time* (Philadelphia, 2 volumes, 1919) is readable and covers broadly the story of actors and producing. For American drama, see the scholarly volumes by Arthur Hobson Quinn entitled *A History of the American Drama from the Beginnings to the Civil War* and *from the Civil War to the Present Day* (New York and London, 1923 and 1927).

My chapters on the twentieth century theatre are without bibliographical notes largely because it is too early for the appearance of authoritative histories. But among the indispensable studies (though mixing speculation with report) are *The Theatre of Today,* by Hiram Kelly Moderwell (New York, revised ed., 1927), and *The Theatre of Tomorrow,* by Kenneth Macgowan (New York, 1922). In the latter volume the student will find a descriptive bibliography which will lead him on to the more specialized literature of the subject, from the source books of the " new movement " by Gordon Craig and other artists to the critical accounts.

An exceptionally meaty book on one phase of theatre activity, on organization and administration, is to be found in Arthur Edwin Krows' *Play Production in America* (New York, 1916). I am sorry to be obliged to add that there are several departments of activity which are not now covered in up-to-date works in English; there is no comprehensive book on acting, none on stagecraft in the larger sense of the word, none on the design of the playhouse.

I have a prejudice against bare bibliographical lists, believing that only descriptive bibliographies can serve the reader well. I therefore pass over the several longer lists to recommend the annotated one published by Theatre Arts, New York, under the title *Toward a Theatre Library.* The reader will find therein whatever of guidance I have failed to afford him here. I may add that the current issues of *Theatre Arts Monthly* offer the fullest and most interesting view of the arts of the stage as they are developing in the world theatre today.

INDEX

Acting: 3, 4, 337 ff; American, 444 ff; Chinese, 120, 123; *Commedia dell'Arte*, 222; Elizabethan, 263, 293, 272; English, Eighteenth Century, 349; English, late Eighteenth Century, 394; French, Eighteenth Century, 343 ff; French, Revolutionary, 402; German, Eighteenth Century, 362, 377; Greek, 61 ff; Japanese, 127; Mediæval, 137 ff, 161 ff; Mediæval Guild, 167; Nineteenth Century, 443 ff; Roman, 96, 103.

Actor, Chinese, in costume, *illus.*, 124.

Actors, Roman comic, *illus.*, 73.

Adam, early Mystery Play, description of, 145 ff.

Adams, Maude, 507.

Addison, Joseph, 305.

Æschylus, 36 ff, 50 ff, 56 ff.

Æsthetics, contemporary, 466 ff.

Agamemnon (Æschylus), 52 ff.

Alarcon, Ruiz de, 253.

Alfieri, Vittorio, 398.

American Museum, New York, 1853, lecture-room of, *illus.*, opp. 419.

Aminta (Tasso), description of, 209.

Anderson, Maxwell, 463.

Andreini, Isabella, 227.

Appia, Adolphe, 441, 498.

Architectura, De (Vitruvius), 196.

Architectural perspective setting: Elizabethan era, *illus.*, opp. 257; for *Il Granchio*, 1566, 193.

Architectural setting: by Giuseppe Galli-Bibbiena, *illus.*, opp. 217; by Giovanni Maria Galli-Bibbiena, *illus.*, opp. 217; Renaissance, designed by Baldassare Peruzzi, *illus.*, opp. 197; fixed, for comedy as prescribed by Serlio, in 1545, *illus.*, 194; for tragedy, *illus.*, 195; for satyr-plays, *illus.*, 196.

Aretino, Pietro, 185 ff.

Ariosto, Lodovico, 184, 205.

Aristophanes, 69, 71 ff, 73 ff.

Aristotle, 50 ff.

Arius, 137.

Astley's Amphitheatre, London, 1815, equestrian drama at, *illus.*, opp. 418.

As You Like It, Macready production of, *illus.*, opp. 441.

Augier, Emile, 433, 452.

Auto Sacramental, performance of, *illus.*, 246.

Autos Sacramentales, 254.

Bacchae, The (Euripides), description of, 57 ff.

Bakst, Leon, 524; costume designs for *Ballets Russes*, *illus.*, 523.

Ballet, 337 ff; costumes by Martin, *illus.*, 338; costumes, Eighteenth Century, *illus.*, 339.

Ballets, Renaissance, 191.

Ballets Russes, 480, 521 ff.

Ballroom stage in the palace of Cardinal Richelieu, *illus.*, 323.

Ballroom theatre: 323; Florentine, *illus.*, 188; Sixteenth Century, French, *illus.*, 203; In the Petit-Bourbon Palace under Louis XIII, *illus.*, opp. 341.

Barber of Seville, The (Beaumarchais), 383.

Bardi, Giovanni, 214.

Baron, Michel, 343.

Barrie, J. M., 461.

Barry, Philip, 463.

Bayreuth: 441; *Festspielhaus*, 428; *illus.*, opp. 425.

Bear Garden, The, *illus.*, 275.

Beaumarchais, 383.

Beaumont, Francis, 283.

Beethoven, 425.

Beggar's Opera (Gay), 424.

Belasco, David, 377, 451, 463, 494.

Bell, Clive, 472.

Berkeley, Greek Theatre at, 47.

Bernhardt, Sarah, 423, 443.

Betterton, Thomas, 349.

Beyond Our Power (Björnson), *illus.*, opp. 506.

Bhavabhuti, 116.

Biancolelli, Giuseppe, *illus.*, opp. 347.

Bibbiena, Ferdinando, 197; *illus.*, opp. 4; Giuseppi and Giovanni, *illus.*, opp. 217.

Björnson, Björnstjerne, 456.

Blackfriars Theatre, 296.

Boccaccio, 180.

Bodel, Jean, 159.

Booth, Barton, 349.